Selected Masterpieces of Asian Art

Museum of Fine Arts
Boston

Selected Masterpieces of Asian Art

Museum of Fine Arts
Boston

Published by the
Museum of Fine Arts, Boston
in association with the
Japan Broadcast Publishing Co., Ltd.
Tokyo Japan

Library of Congress Catalogue Card No.
91-67706
ISBN 0-87846-351-8

Cover illustration:
Scenic View of Matsushima
Attributed to Ogata Korin (1658-1716)
Edo period, ealry 18th century
Six-panel folding screen; ink, colors,
and gold on paper. 155 x 370 cm.
Fenollosa-Weld Collection. 11.44584

English text typeset in
Bitstream Charter, designed
by Matthew Carter
Typography by Carl Zahn
Book produced by
Japan Broadcast Publishing Co., Ltd.

Printed in Japan

Contents

Preface

During the first century of its existence the Department of Asiatic Art has grown from a great collection of Japanese art to one that encompasses all Asian countries. The extraordinary quality and depth of its Japanese collections are exemplified by *Ukiyo-e* prints, which number more than 50,000 and 4,000 paintings of all schools, including such unique masterpieces as the *Hokkedō Kompon Mandara,* the *Burning of Sanjo Palace* (*Heiji Monogatari Emaki*) and the *Minister Kibi's Trip to Tang China.* Among the holdings of Chinese art, from the fourth millennium B.C. to modern times, are many works that have no equal in the West, nor even in China. The collection of Indian art is the oldest and one of the most comprehensive in the United States. Because this handbook is intended primarily for a Japanese audience there are more works from Japan than from any other Asian country.

As a member of the Asiatic department for twenty years, I am proud of the continuing interaction between collectors of Asian art and the department's curatorial staff. Were it not for the exceptional generosity and farsightedness of Bostonians, the collections would not have achieved their present preeminence. Likewise the Museum could not have attracted leading specialists such as Ernest Fenollosa, Okakura Kakuzō, John Lodge, Kojiro Tomita, Robert Treat Paine, Jan Fontein, and James Watt to Boston to head the department and to guide its direction.

These scholars have in turn inspired other collectors to continue the Boston tradition of giving or bequeathing private collections for the public enjoyment. Their generosity is demonstrated by the William S. and John T. Spaulding collection of Japanese prints, the Charles Bain Hoyt collection of East Asian ceramics, Tibetan paintings from John Goelet, and Paul and Helen Bernat's Chinese Imperial porcelain. Given current high prices in the art market, the days of such collecting are close to an end.

The Department of Asiatic Art looks ahead to its second century with a new sense of mission to facilitate understanding of Asia through the wealth of the Museum's collections. As Americans increase their contacts with the countries of Asia, our encyclopedic collections of the entire region, the Far East, Southeast Asia, South Asia, and the Islamic world, should be of great service to the public as well as to specialists. Attitudes have changed perceptibly since the beginning of Western expansion into Asia but advances are still ongoing. With increased appreciation of Asian arts and cultural traditions will come improved social and political relations.

I want to thank Alan Shestack, director of the Museum of Fine Arts, and Mort Golden, deputy director, for their support of this project. In addition, Saundra Lane, Trustee-Chairman of the Visiting Committee to the department of Asiatic Art, gave us encouragement. The generosity of the JBP, Tokyo, in underwriting the publication is greatly appreciated. We are particularly grateful to Tomone Ohya, executive editor of the JBP Books Editing Division, and his staff for meticulous planning, hard work, and patience. The Museum's representative in Japan, Morihiro Ogawa, deserves many thanks for initiating this project as well as coordinating preparations both in Tokyo and in Boston. We appreciate the assistance of Carl Zahn and Judy Spear of the Publications department, and are pleased with the high quality of the photographs taken by museum photographers under the supervision of Janice Sorkow.

The entries were written or edited by the following staff members: WU tung (China), Vishakha Desai (India, Islam), Darielle Mason (India), Jan Fontein (Korea, Southeast Asia), Money L. Hickman (Japan), Anne Morse (Japan), Morihiro Ogawa (Japan), Denise Patry Leidy (China, Tibet), Shelley Drake Hawks (China), and Jennifer Noering (China), who coordinated the project. Elaine Perlov, Mitcheka Jalali, Tessa Virr, and Sara Curtis assisted with the manuscript, and Yasuhiro Iguchi and Jacki Elgar prepared the works of art for photography. Last but not least, my thanks to Chin Ying, our volunteer librarian, for her research and support. It was truly a privilege for the Asiatic staff to participate in the department's centennial celebration.

WU tung
Curator of Asiatic Art

Foreword

It is generally acknowledged that the Museum of Fine Arts, Boston, has the largest and most impressive collection of Japanese art outside of Japan as well as what is probably the most comprehensive collection of Asian art in the world. Begun one hundred years ago, in 1890, when Ernest Fenollosa was appointed as the first curator, the Boston collection has grown and improved through the years by virtue of generous donations of superb collections and through judicious purchases made by several generations of expert curators, including the distinguished scholar/curators Okakura Kakuzō, Kojiro Tomita, Robert Treat Paine and Jan Fontein.

Every year the Museum of Fine Arts welcomes tens of thousands of visitors from Asia who come to see the priceless and beautiful treasures of Japanese, Chinese, Korean, Indian and Southeast Asian art housed under our roof. We in Boston are pleased to make our collections better known and to share our treasures with the public worldwide. We are thus particularly gratified by the group of excellent reproductions produced by JBP and now made available for your enjoyment and contemplation at the time of our museum's centennial celebration of its Asiatic department.

In a collection as large as ours, it is difficult to select a small sample of masterpieces which represents the entire collection in its diversity. The illustrations in this book will have served their purpose if they whet your appetite and encourage you to come to Boston and tour the museum, making your own selection of favorite Asian works of art.

ALAN SHESTACK
Director, Museum of Fine Arts, Boston

A Brief History of the Collections

It was Okakura Kakuzō who first described the Department of Asiatic Art of the Museum of Fine Arts as "the finest collection of oriental art under one roof in the world." More than eighty years later this characterization still holds true, as long as we accept it not only as a proud, but also as a qualifying statement. While each major Asian civilization is represented by some of its finest artistic creations, none of the Museum's individual collections could be said to surpass that of the national collections in the countries where the works of art originated. Yet, considering institutions in which the arts of India, southeast Asia, Islamic world, and the Far East are represented together, there is no single museum anywhere that can match the Boston Museum's collection in size, scope and quality.

The extraordinary strength of the Museum's Asiatic collection is attributable, for the most part, to the foresight and enterprise of a small group of pioneer connoisseurs of Asian art. They were either benefactors themselves or worked in close cooperation with wise and generous donors who were determined to gather in Boston examples of the highest artistic achievements of the East. Actually, the Boston Museum is probably the only major museum in the western world that gained preeminence in the field of Japanese art while all of its European and American collections were still in the early beginnings of their formative phase.

A handbook of the Museum's Asian collections is, therefore, not complete without a brief sketch of their history and an account of the unique circumstances that resulted in their formation. There is, however, another equally significant reason for including these historical notes in this handbook. While the traditional role of the museum curator has always been that of gathering, studying, and exhibiting the collections, the first generations of curators of the Asiatic department of the Museum of Fine Arts often ventured far beyond the generally accepted scope of their profession. Especially in Japan and, at a later date, in India they exercized a great influence on the cultural history of the countries in which they gathered art treasures for the Museum. Their activities had a profound effect on the appreciation in these countries of their national artistic heritage at a time when the impact of western civilization had begun to seriously undermine many traditional cultures. Thus, these curators became not only acquisitors of Asian art but also mediators between East and West. The true historical significance of the life and works of men like Ernest Fenollosa and Ananda Coomaraswamy far transcends the most impressive tangible results of their activities—the great collections they left behind for us to study and enjoy.

It is often mistakenly assumed that Boston's great collections of Asian art are a heritage of the China Trade, and the fact that several of the pioneers to whom we are indebted for our collections were indeed born in or lived at Salem, Massachusetts, one of the chief ports of trade with Asia, would seem to bear out this supposition. Yet, upon closer scrutiny, it appears that the connections between the China Trade and the presence of such rich collections of oriental art in Boston and vicinity may not have been as immediate as has often been assumed.

Like their predecessors of the European East India companies, the American mariners of the China Trade brought back to New England only what they could find in the ports: porcelains intended for export, paintings on glass, ivory carvings, wallpaper, and some textiles. The greatest works of art of China were often created in the seclusion of the scholar's studio or in the workshops of the inaccessible Forbidden City. The fact that the many early trading contacts between the Far East and New England only rarely resulted in American collectors acquiring oriental art objects of high artistic importance can therefore be explained as a combination of limited understanding and lack of opportunity. Nevertheless, the China Trade may have contributed to the genesis of Boston's collections of oriental art in quite a different way, creating a climate in which an interest in the cultures of different countries could flourish.

To the French, who readily succumbed to the magic spell of *japonisme,* Japan always remained a group of beautiful, distant islands, far beyond the horizon, to be admired from afar. Except for a few dealers, few of the devotees of *japonisme* ever set foot in Japan, and their romantic ideas inspired mainly by woodblock prints, were never enriched by confrontation with the more profound aspects of Japanese art and culture. Moreover, we may wonder whether they were really seeking such a confrontation, for *japonisme* was, first and foremost, a reaction of artists responding to the artistic message they discovered in Japanese woodblock prints and decorative arts. Their interest was not directed toward Japanese art for its own sake and did not extend beyond those aspects that they could use or adapt to their own artistic requirements. Thus, while *japonisme* provided a lively source of inspiration for numerous great works of art and aroused among people all over the world a vivid interest in Japan, it did little of a substantial nature to stimulate real knowledge of the classical arts of that country.

Unlike the French, the inhabitants of New England, where the memory of the China Trade still lingered on, perceived Japan as a tangible geographic reality, a country that could actually be visited if one were inclined to do so. Several of the New Englanders who were to play a prominent role in the vogue of things Japanese in Boston were in Paris when their first interest in Japan was awakened. However, instead of continuing to admire Japan from afar, they considered it perfectly logical to make the voyage and see for themselves what Japan was like. Their continuous exposure to the actualities of Japanese life and culture stimulated the development of different, higher standards of collecting and this resulted, within a very brief span of time, in the growth of great collections of Japanese art.

There is yet another important difference between what happened in Paris and in Boston. Following the famous example of Edmond de Goncourt who proclaimed that the best way of sharing his collection with the public was to have it auctioned and dispersed, most of the great Parisian collectors disposed of their treasures during the first decade of this century. Although the auctions of the collections of Hayashi, Gillot, Bing, and others stimulated a brief *hausse* in Japanese art, they also marked the beginning of the end of *japonisme* and soon, even in Paris, China replaced Japan in the favor of the collectors.

In Boston, on the other hand, the collectors of Japanese art seem to have had from the very beginning of their activities in Japan the idea that they should serve the public interest, and that this could best be done by donating these collections to the newly founded Museum of Fine Arts in Boston. As a result, the most tangible and lasting product of the Japanese vogue in Boston—its great collections of Japanese art—was preserved and kept together. What would otherwise have been merely a colorful interlude in the cultural history of New England became part of the early history of this permanent collection.

The brilliant scholar who acted as the catalyst in the concatenation of fortuitous events that brought together the men who assembled the Museum's superb Japanese collection was the zoologist Edward Sylvester Morse (1830-1925). As early as 1862 he had become interested in a species of marine fauna known as brachiopods, and his studies of these marine worms had even drawn the attention of Charles Darwin, of whom Morse was an ardent admirer. Upon hearing that a large variety of brachiopods inhabit Japanese waters, he decided to go to Japan to collect specimens. And so he set out for Japan, arriving there in June of 1877. Soon after his arrival in Yokohama, Morse proceeded to Tokyo by train on railroad tracks laid in Japan for the first time only five years earlier. As the train passed through the rural neighborhood of Ōmori, not far from the shore of Tokyo Bay, he noticed that the tracks cut through low mounds, which he immediately recognized to be neolithic shell mounds. Morse was quite familiar with shell mounds as he had investigated similar remains of native American settlements in Maine. Returning to Ōmori soon afterwards, Morse conducted the first, archaeological excavation in the history of Japan. The publication of his finds, *Shell Mounds of Ōmori* (1879), was the first scientific study published by the newly founded Tokyo Imperial University, (now Tokyo University).

Altogether, Morse's three journeys to Japan did not amount to more than two and one-half years of residence in that country, but he used his time well, accomplishing much more than might have been expected from a pioneer who had ventured into totally unknown territory. The tremendous impact his inspired teachings must have had on the first generation of Japanese zoologists is difficult to overestimate. But there were other lasting and tangible fruits of his fieldwork in Japan. Morse was highly systematic as a collector of zoological material and well versed in the techniques of classifying and cataloguing. He was not by nature a man of

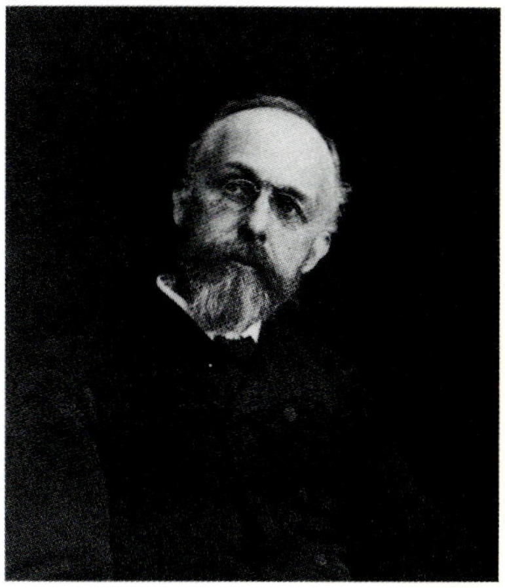

Edward Sylvester Morse (1830-1925)

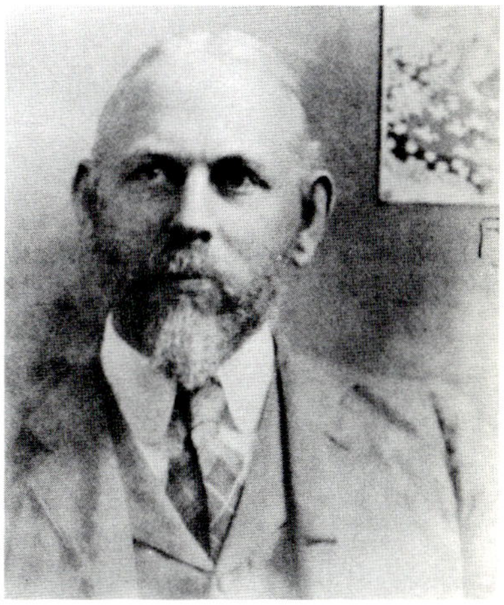

Ernest Francisco Fenollosa (1853-1908)

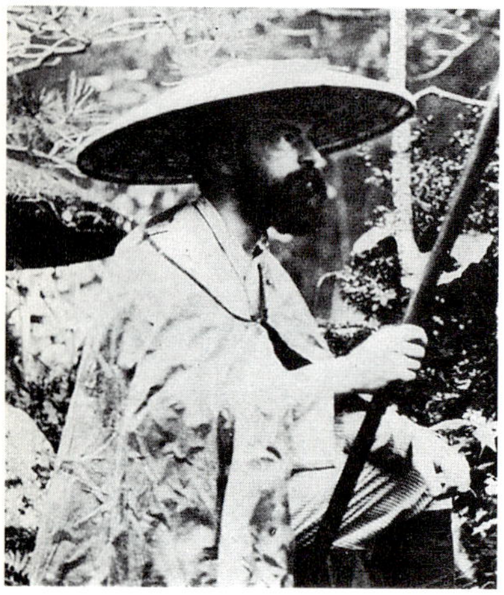

William Sturgis Bigelow (1850-1926)

great artistic perception, but when he discovered, almost by coincidence, the infinite variety of contemporary Japanese ceramics, he became fascinated by them and began to apply all of his considerable scholarly skills to assembling a collection of Japanese ceramics.

Ably assisted by the Japanese antiquarian Ninagawa Noritane, Morse succeeded in bringing together well over 5,000 pieces. Systematically arranged according to provenance and kilns, province by province, they now fill dozens of crowded cases on the third floor of the Museum. They were relegated to this secluded location at a time when the interest in nineteenth-century Japanese ceramics had declined. It is only in recent years that the importance of the Morse Collection has become apparent, here as well as in Japan.

A 1980 traveling exhibition of 200 pieces of the Morse Collection, selected by Hayashiya Seizō of the Tokyo National Museum, demonstrates clearly that the often-expressed misgivings about its artistic quality are not all justified: the collection contains a considerable number of ceramics of outstanding quality, as well as a number of well-documented, highly interesting archaeological specimens. Most important, it gives the most comprehensive view available anywhere of practically all the types of ceramics produced in Japan during the nineteenth century. Much more significant, however, than Morse's role in the formation of the permanent collection of the Museum was his influence on other Americans, who he inspired with his enthusiasm for things Japanese and whom he persuaded to come to Japan. The first of these was Ernest Francisco Fenollosa (1853-1908), the son of a Spanish-born musician of Salem, Massachusetts. It was in Salem that Morse settled when he came back from Japan, and he worked there for the rest of his long and productive career. Fenollosa had just finished his studies at Harvard when he received, in 1878, at Morse's recommendation, an appointment as Professor of Philosophy at the Tokyo Imperial University. Unlike Morse, Fenollosa was a man of great artistic sensibility; he was also an artist, although only of modest talent. It would seem that he was much more interested in art than in philosophy, and he soon found himself drawn to the study of Japanese art, a field in which he was to achieve eminence, the first foreigner to do so.

That he achieved this eminence is not just because of the virtually limitless opportunities for the acquisition of masterpieces of Japanese art during the early years of the Meiji era. His only western precursor, the British physician William Anderson (1842-1900), who is thought to have inspired Fenollosa's activities, amassed a large collection that, viewed with our advantage of hindsight, contains few, if any masterworks. Like any true pioneer, Fenollosa had to stumble before he became a successful collector and connoisseur. The recent discovery, in the library of the distinguished Japanese art historian, the late Akiyama Teruo, of one of Fenollosa's collector's notebooks, confirms the account that Kaneko Kentarō has left us of Fenollosa's first, faltering efforts at collecting:

"I visited Fenollosa on a Sunday. Surrounded by several curio dealers, Fenollosa was looking at the hanging scrolls placed on the walls of his room. On seeing me, Fenollosa told me that he found the scrolls in the curio shops in front of Daitoku-ji in Kyoto and immediately bought them. Fenollosa maintained that they were really great scrolls and that they had not before been introduced to the world. A glance at them, however, convinced me that more than half of the scrolls were fakes. When I told him what I thought, he wanted to know how to distinguish genuine articles from fakes. I told him that the best way was to see as many genuine art objects as possible and took him to the Kuroda family. As I thought that Song and Yuan paintings were still beyond him, I took out some ten Okyos, Keibuns and Tanyus, Fenollosa's eyes were instantly glued to the paintings. After some time, he took out a notebook and started recording the painter's signatures and seal impressions. He admitted that many of what he had believed genuine were false and he swore that he would never again visit the curio shops in front of Daitoku-ji."

From the very beginning Fenollosa took not only the advice of such good friends as Kaneko Kentarō, he also solicited the opinions of contemporary artists on the merits of the paintings he wished to acquire. Not surprisingly, most of the paintings mentioned in this notebook, which covers only the earliest phase of his collection activities, are not among the most important works he managed to obtain, and several of them seem to have been returned or used as trade-in later. But Fenollosa was a quick student, and many of his later acquisitions reveal a remarkable insight in and genuine appreciation of Japanese painting.

At the time of Fenolloa's arrival in Japan the prestige of traditional Japanese art had reached a low ebb. It was, in large part, the result of Fenollosa's efforts that the Japanese gradually came to realize the importance of preserving the relics of their own ancient culture. However, his many activities were not confined to teaching philosophy and propagating a revival of the traditional arts. Another of his projects can best be described in Fenollosa's own words, as he wrote them to Morse: "We have been through all the principal temples in Yamashiro and Yamato armed with government letters and orders, have ransacked godowns, and brought to light pieces of statues from the lowest stratum of debris in the top stories of pagodas 1300 years old. We may say in brief that we have made the first accurate list of the great art treasures kept in the central temples of Japan, we have overturned the traditional criticism attached to these individual specimens for ages."

The first of these excursions, undertaken in 1880, was to be followed by several more. When Morse made his third trip to Japan in 1882, he and Fenollosa were accompanied by the Boston physician William Sturgis Bigelow (1850-1926). Dr. Bigelow had worked with the famous Louis Pasteur in Paris, where he first acquired some of the Japanese *bibelots* that the wave of *japonisme* had carried to France. But after attending one of Edward Morse's lectures, instead of contenting himself with whatever he could find among the enormous quantity of Japanese bric-à-brac that reached Paris, Bigelow decided to go to the source. Once in Japan, he became so fascinated with the country, its people, its culture and religion, that he stayed on—with only one brief interruption—for more than seven years.

Bigelow was immediately drawn into Fenollosa's circle and soon started to accompany him on his trips in search of hidden temple treasures. It was during one of these early excursions in 1884 that he was able to acquire the *Hokkedō Kompon Mandara* (no. 16), the only painting of the Nara period ever to leave the country. Deeply interested in Tendai and Esoteric Buddhism, which he studied with great diligence, Bigelow also devoted much of his time to the collecting of Japanese art on a truly grand scale. He had a wide range of interests, and the great variety of important material assembled in his collection is an accurate reflection of the catholicity of his taste. In addition to painting of many different schools, the Bigelow collection contains outstanding examples of Japanese sculpture, swords, sword fittings, textiles, and lacquerwork; the collection of woodblock prints contains tens of thousands of examples.

Fenollosa lacked Bigelow's breadth of vision and appreciation, and his collection consists almost entirely of paintings. While Bigelow's spectacular success as a collector has been universally recognized, some of his other activities in Japan are less well-known. The important role that this well-connected Boston brahmin played in the development of relations, diplomatic as well as cultural, between the United States and Japan has rarely been recognized. For many prominent Japanese, letters of introduction written by Dr. Bigelow opened doors that would have remained closed to them without his quiet, behind-the-scenes diplomacy. Bigelow's support of struggling Japanese artists, such as Fenollosa's friend the painter Kano Hōgai (1828-1888) and the noted tsuba-maker Kano Natsuo (1828-1889) has remained largely unnoticed, and only visitors to the Shōrin-ji (Nara Prefecture) become aware of his deep concern and generous support for the preservation of ancient Buddhist monuments.

Fenollosa, a man of artistic temperament and vision, attracted much more attention than the quiet, often melancholy Bigelow. His inspirational speech, delivered on May 15, 1882 at the Museum of Education in Tokyo under the title "Do Japanese arts and crafts fully meet foreign requirements?" did much to restore Japanese confidence in the value of their own artistic heritage, buffetted by the massive influx of foreign ideas. In spite of their differences in background, temperament and approach, Bigelow and Fenollosa became close friends. Working from their lodgings at the Hōmyō-in of the Miidera temple at Ōtsu, they cooperated closely when an opportunity to acquire a great work of art presented itself. For example, they often divided pairs of folding screens between their two collections. Fenollosa had a deep admiration for the Kano school and he was even adopted by the Kano family, receiving the name of Kano Eitan. This profound interest is reflected in his collection, which contains fine works of most of the leading masters of the school. Bigelow shared this interest, and his collection reveals the same predilection.

Whenever Fenollosa's and Bigelow's interests ran parallel–as they often did–their combined collections are without equal. This is the case, for example, with their admiration for the ability of the "mad" painter Soga Shōhaku (1730-1781), which resulted in their acquiring more than fifty works by that master. The inevitable consequence is, however, that those schools or masters whom Fenollosa and Bigelow did not appreciate are either poorly represented or totally lacking. This is particularly true of the Nanga or Bunjinga school, the works of which Fenollosa once characterized as "hardly more than an awkward joke." By ignoring the works of this school Fenollosa and Bigelow created a significant gap in their collections, a lacuna we can now hardly hope ever to fill.

By the time Bigelow had decided that his collection should go to the Boston Museum, it consisted of thousands of pieces. But he not only sent his own collection to Boston; he also persuaded his friend Charles Goddard Weld (1857-1911) to buy, in 1886, the entire collection of Ernest Fenollosa, which was sold with the understanding that it was to remain permanently in the Museum of Fine Arts. With the arrival of the two collections in Boston in 1889, and with their exhibition in the course of the following year, it became apparent that the Museum of Fine Arts had achieved the preeminence in the field of Japanese art that was henceforth to be one of its salient characteristics.

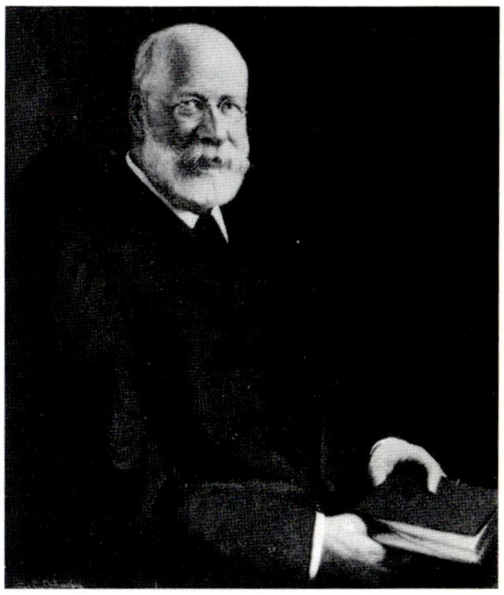

Charles Goddard Weld (1857-1911)

Ernest Fenollosa arrived in Boston soon after the collection that bore his and Dr. Weld's names. In 1890 he was appointed curator of the Japanese department of the Museum of Fine Arts. The next four years were spent cataloguing and installing the collections and in organizing a series of exhibitions of Japanese art, from Japanese as well as from the Museum's own collections, which were undoubtedly the most significant held up to that time. The last in this series was a traveling show of Lohan paintings from the Daitoku-ji in Kyoto. These paintings, dating from between 1178 and 1184–the works of two Southern Song painters, Zhou Jichang and Lin Tinggui–are among the finest Chinese Buddhist paintings in existence. Bernard Berenson gave his future wife, Mary Costelloe, an eyewitness report of the exhibition: ". . . To begin with they had composition of figures and groups as perfect and simple as the best we Europeans have ever done . . . I was prostrate. Fenollosa shivered as he looked, I thought I should die, and even Denman Ross who looked dumpy Anglo-Saxon was jumping up and down. We had to poke and pinch each other's necks and wept. No, decidedly I never had such an art experience."

It would be understandable if now, more than ninety years after the event, the objects of their highly emotional reaction failed to meet the fastidious art historical standards of our own times. However, that they were deeply moved by what are still considered creations of the highest artistic order can only increase our admiration for their early

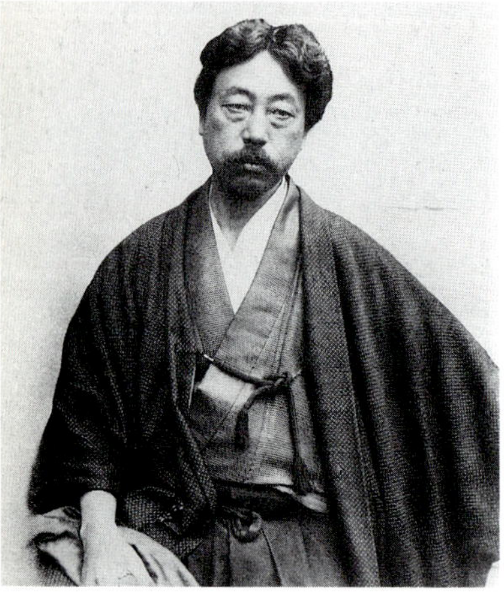

Okakura Kakuzō (1862-1913)

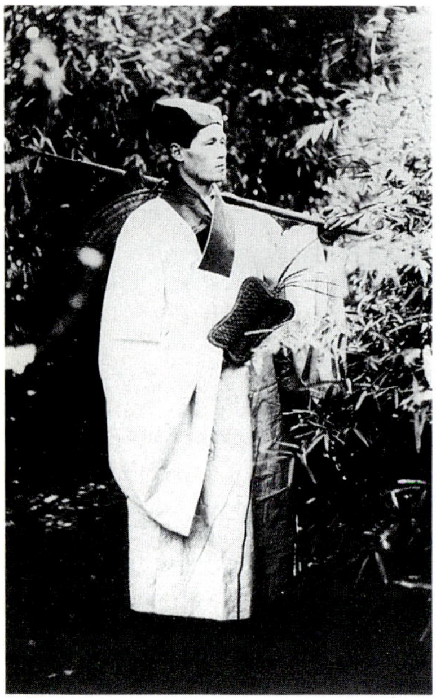

Hayasaki Kōkichi (1874-1956)

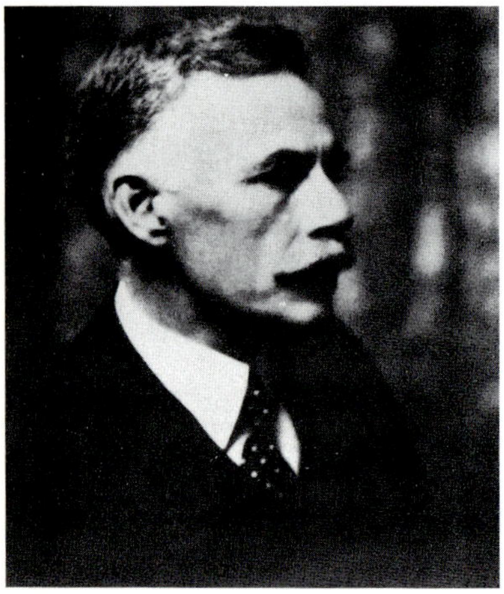

John Ellerton Lodge (1878-1942)

understanding and appreciation of oriental art.

Before the exhibition returned to Japan, the Daitoku-ji sold ten of the paintings to the Museum of Fine Arts to pay for urgently needed temple repairs (and two to Charles Freer to cover traveling expenses). This great acquisition–quite different from his first purchases across the street from this same temple–was the last service Fenollosa was to render to the Museum of Fine Arts. Shortly afterward, the circumstances connected with his divorce and remarriage led to his abrupt departure from the Museum. The incident, trivial by today's standards, unfortunately resulted in the dispersal and almost total loss of the detailed documentation on the Fenollosa-Weld collection that the collector himself had so assiduously compiled.

With the departure of Ernest Fenollosa, the rapid growth of the collections seems to have slowed down, only to increase again with the arrival on the Boston scene of one of Fenollosa's most gifted Japanese pupils, Okakura Kakuzō (1862-1913). Okakura had accompanied Fenollosa on many of his excursions in search of temple treasures, sharing with him such exciting experiences as the discovery of the Yumedono Kannon in 1884. Afterward, he headed the new Tokyo Fine Arts Academy, but in 1898 he resigned from this position, as well as from his post at the Imperial Museum in Tokyo. It was extremely fortunate for the Museum of Fine Arts that a person of such great talent was available and willing to lead the Asiatic department into what was soon to become another era of dynamic expansion.

Okakura Kakuzō was undoubtedly one of the greatest connoisseurs of Far Eastern art of this time, a man with a remarkably wide range of interests, who was equally well versed in Chinese and Japanese art. Of his numerous writings, *The Book of Tea* and *Ideals of the East* were read and admired all over the western world. But although his international fame rests upon these publications, the extraordinary talents of this versatile cosmopolitan scholar are demonstrated even more clearly by the high quality of the additions he made to the collections of the Museum.

It could be said that Okakura tried to put into practice as a museum curator his own famous dictum "Asia is one," for it was on his initiative that the collection, which consisted up to that time almost entirely of Japanese works of art, was first expanded into other fields of art. This is not to suggest that Okakura neglected the art of his native country. On the contrary, among his acquisitions for the department were such works as a superb landscape by Bunsei and a large group of wooden sculptures, of which the monumental Shō Kannon has no parallel in any collection outside Japan. As early as 1893, however, Okakura had journeyed to China, and the art of that country had become an absorbing interest to him. He was the first non-Chinese connoisseur to study ancient Chinese bronze mirrors. Later, when he came to Boston, this predilection resulted in the first ambitious efforts to assemble a collection of Chinese art.

On his first trip to China, as on all of his later expeditions to that country, Okakura was accompanied by Hayasaki Kōkichi (1874-1956), the son of his step-sister. Hayasaki, a pupil of the painter Hashimoto Gahō, was an amateur archaeologist and an excellent connoisseur of Chinese art. He was the first Japanese to carry a camera into China's interior, and many of the photographs he made show famous sites prior to the destruction and depredation that occurred during this century. For many years he lived in China, where he developed a deep interest in Taoism, associating with the priests of the Temple of the Eight Immortals at Xian and adopting for himself their traditional costume. After Okakura joined the staff of the Museum of Fine Arts, Hayasaki became the Museum's agent in China. Among many other pieces, a unique collection of dated Taoist stone statutes, a sarcophagus for the ashes of a Buddhist patriarch of the Sui period, Ma Yuan's album leaf *Bare Willows and Distant Mountains* and, above all, the handscroll *Clear Weather in the Valley,* formerly attributed to Dong Yuan, are the fruit of this collaboration.

However, for the rapid growth of the Chinese collections and the extraordinary high quality of many of their new acquisitions, the discerning eyes of Okakura and Hayasaki should not be given exclusive credit. The unconventional but enlightened policy of the Museum regarding methods of acquisition, the harmonious collaboration between Japanese and Bostonians, between gifted scholars and discerning collectors, enterprising dealers and generous benefactors–all these are factors that should be taken into account. The recent publication of Okakura's travel diaries allows us to reconstruct his peregrinations through the Chinese interior day by day. The Museum's archives, on the other hand, reveal that Okakura's communication with the Museum consisted almost entirely of cabled requests for funds. The trustees, wisely placing full confidence in what we now know to have the best connoisseur of their time, gave them full freedom of action, a policy that led, at a time of great opportunities, to spectacular results. To recapture the atmosphere in which these men all worked together, nothing would seem to be more appropriate than the text of a letter written by Okakura's successor, John Ellerton Lodge, to Hayasaki on August 18, 1916: "I am particularly anxious that, in prosecuting your labors for the Museum, you should be relieved as much as possible from any sense of constraint you may have regarding the prices you pay and the number of things you buy. To me it seems that if, for example, your last trip to China had yielded nothing more than the sarcophagus, you would be fully justified in priding yourself on your accomplishment, and the Museum would have ample grounds for satisfaction. This implies that we are interested primarily and above all in the quality of what we receive from you, and that the number of things you buy, their prices, and the ratio of those prices to your own expenses, are matters of secondary importance–provided, always that the things themselves are, as they should be, absolutely first-rate of their respective kinds."

The diligent search for excellence, of which this statement is an eloquent example, was clearly much more than the pastime of a few fastidious collectors who demanded and could afford the finest works of art. Okakura's genuine enthusiasm, and his ability to communicate this feeling, inspired in many others a unique dedication to the Department of Asiatic Art. In a world in which the appreciation of Asian art was, as yet, restricted to only a happy few, these men joined together to further the task of demonstrating that the arts of the Far East were in no way inferior to those of Egypt, Greece, Rome, and the Renaissance. They felt that this objective could be realized in a convincing manner only if the works of art they assembled were of the highest artistic quality, and in order to reach this goal they were willing to make sacrifices of the sort that still command our deep admiration.

Among the persons whom Okakura inspired were Edward Jackson Holmes, his wife Mary Stacy Beamon, whom he met on an expedition in Upper Burma, and his mother Mrs. W. Scott Fitz. Holmes gave, as he himself once wrote, his whole life and thought to the Museum, serving first as a trustee, then from 1925 to 1934, as director, and finally, from 1934 to 1950, as president. The interests of these great benefactors of the Museum ranged widely; from a collection that included many rare works from the Near East came two of the finest pieces of Far Eastern sculpture, the gilt bronze *Yaksa Yorae* from Korea and the so-called Duan Fang altar. The Museum's first attempt to acquire this last masterpiece was made by Okakura in 1911, shortly after the viceroy had been assassinated, and it was only after many years that Edward Holmes and his mother secured it for the Museum. Their determination and dedication to the cause is demonstrated by the fact that Holmes persuaded his mother to borrow money—for the first time in her life—in order to make the purchase. Holmes lived to see the day, twenty-five years later, when the five missing pieces that had been separated from the altar since it was excavated in China were finally reunited with it.

For the museum's next phase of expansion, the acquisition of Indian art, Okakura Kakuzō laid the foundations; however, it was for the next generation to accomplish the task of bringing the Indian collections to a level of excellence comparable to those of Far Eastern art. The two men who played a key role in this new expansion were Denman Waldo Ross (1853-1935) and Ananda Kentish Coomaraswamy (1877-1947). Ross, a Harvard-trained historian, became involved in the Museum at an early age. He served as a trustee from 1895 until his death, but from 1883 onward the fruits of his many-sided collecting activities began to appear among the gifts enriching the collections. In the field of oriental art—only one of his many interests—his gifts range from Japanese prints to Southeast Asian sculpture, from Persian miniatures to Islamic textiles. Just before the outbreak of the First World War, protracted negotiations skillfully initiated by Ross led to the acquisition of the entire collection of Indian and Persian miniatures of the distinguished Russian orientalist Victor Goloubew

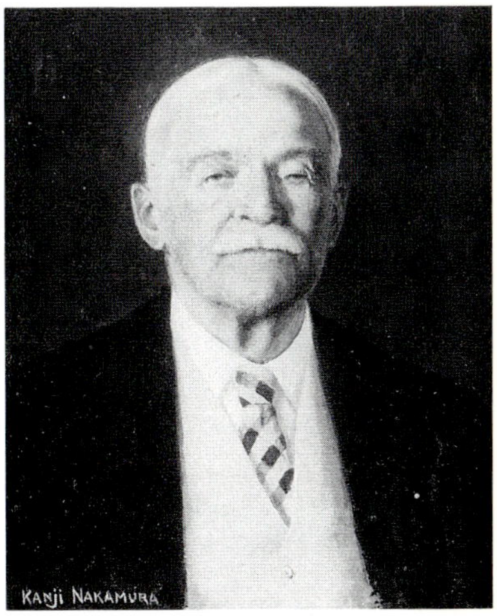

Denman Waldo Ross (1853-1935)

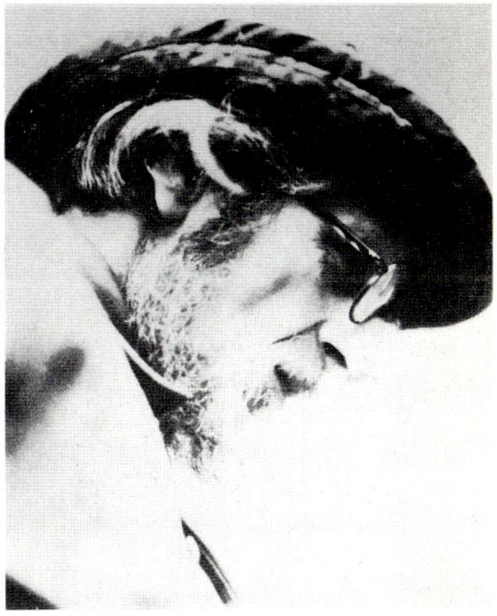
Ananda Kentish Coomaraswamy (1877-1947)

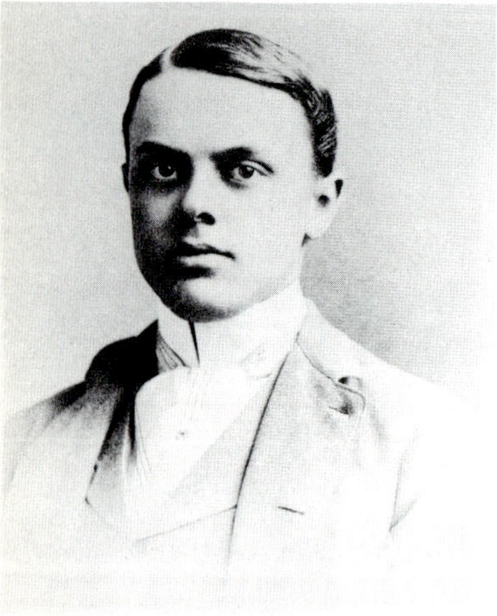

John Taylor Spaulding (1870-1948)

(1878-1945). With this collection, the Museum acquired some of the finest Mughal paintings, including the *Darbār of Jāhangīr* and the drawing of the dying ʻInayat Khan, considered by scholars as absolute gems. At about the same time, Ross discovered in Paris the large stone sculpture of a bodhisattva that Hayasaki had seen being excavated at the White Horse Monastery in Luoyang in 1903 and that Okakura had tried in vain to purchase in 1906. Though Ross did not hesitate to buy it in Paris, the news of its rediscovery unfortunately did not reach Okakura before his death. Ross donated this great sculpture to the Museum in Memory of Okakura, an eloquent and lasting memorial to their friendship.

Five years later, in 1917, Ross made what was perhaps his most important contribution to the Museum. He acquired a large collection of Indian painting and sculpture that had been assembled by the Sinhalese geologist Ananda Coomaraswamy. Here history repeated itself, for just as Ernest Fenollosa had become curator of his own collection after it had been bought for the Boston Museum by Charles Weld, so Ananda Coomaraswamy followed his own collection to Boston after it had been given to the Museum by Denman Ross.

Coomaraswamy first became interested in the art of the Indian subcontinent when he went back to Sri Lanka for geological research and became involved with the preservation of art objects there. From about 1909 on, Coomaraswamy had been thoroughly immersed in the world of Indian art both in England, where he was residing, and in India, where he mingled with the intellectual elite responsible for the resurgence of traditional Indian art. By the time Ross purchased Coomaraswamy's vast collection of Indian art in 1917 and invited him to join the Museum as the keeper of the Indian collection, the first such position in the United States, Coomaraswamy was recognized as an intellectual pioneer with a long list of publications on Indian art. He was one of the first scholars to define Rajput painting, distinguish it from Mughal painting, and bring it to the eminence that it deserved. Coomaraswamy's collection, which became the Ross-Coomaraswamy's Collection at the Museum, reflects his passion for Rajput painting. Some of the finest works of Indian art are now in the Museum's collection because of the collaboration between a great benefactor—Denman Ross—and a great connoisseur-scholar—Ananda Coomaraswamy.

Like Fenollosa and Okakura, Coomaraswamy was a man who combined a powerful intellect with an artistic temperament. Fortunately, this prolific genius came to the Museum just after John Ellerton Lodge had become curator of the department. Lodge recognized better than anyone else Coomaraswamy's extraordinary gifts, and he created the proper circumstances in which Coomaraswamy was able to function as a cultural mediator between East and West, making a unique contribution to our understanding of Indian art. The first phase of Coomaraswamy's career was devoted to the acquisition of some of the most important early Indian sculptures and to the publication of catalogues of Indian collections at the Museum—catalogues that remain to this day some of the most important reference works in the field.

Coomaraswamy's first visit to Boston took place just after Okakura had died and, consequently, the two great men never met. As products of similar environments, they had many ideas and ideals in common, but whereas Okakura remained a collector of art to the last breath, Coomaraswamy became increasingly immersed in philosophy, turning away from the brilliant art historical studies that were the product of the first decade of his activities in Boston. The next two decades of Coomaraswamy's career were filled with perceptive publications on Vedic philosophy, Hindu concepts of art, and metaphysical theories of Indian culture. Changing dramatically his notions about art and aesthetics, he turned away from collecting objects as works of art and increasingly began to see their value only in the context of the philosophical and religious concepts embodied in them. To a student and scholar of Indian art today Coomaraswamy is a seminal figure whose innumerable publications on the subject remain an inexhaustible source of inspiration.

In addition to the expansion of the Indian collection, another important accomplishment that took place during the curatorship of John Ellerton Lodge was the purchase from the heirs of Okakura of a number of works of art from the late curator's private collection, assembled in the years prior to his association with the Boston Museum. Seven years after Okakura's death, the Museum was able to acquire the painting representing Dai-itoku Myō-ō and the statue of Miroku by Kaikei, two of the greatest masterpieces of Japanese art in the collection.

It was in 1921, during Lodge's term as curator, that the Museum acquired a group of Japanese prints that, although perhaps one-tenth the size of William Sturgis Bigelow's gift, is one of the finest collections of Japanese prints in the world. From the standpoint of artistic quality, excellence of condition, and historical balance, it is of unique importance. Its donors, the Spaulding brothers, William Stuart Spaulding (1865-1937) and John Taylor Spaulding (1870-1948), began to acquire Japanese prints in 1909, and for more than a decade they worked industriously and with great discernment to assemble a large and representative collection that included all the significant categories and artists represented in the historical evolution of *Ukiyo-e.* The Spauldings approached this ambitious task from the viewpoint of the connoisseur, for they were determined to collect only works of the highest artistic quality and finest condition. Only very occasionally, when no other impression was available or when a piece was otherwise unique in its rarity, were these exacting standards relaxed. Prints came to them from a variety of dealers in America, Europe, and Japan; a significant number were acquired at auctions from the collections of distinguished earlier European print devotees. Acting as the Spauldings' representative in Japan, Frank Lloyd Wright was able to acquire many exceptional pieces for them from local sources. The result of their industry and vision is a collection of over 6,000 examples that is unique in the history of private collecting, both for the breadth and quality of its contents and for the superb state of its preservation.

The French collectors who had been the pioneer collectors of Japanese prints seem to have had a greater interest in design than in color. The fact that old French auction catalogues often add the words "agréablement bruni" (nicely browned) to their descriptions illustrates the French collector's assessment of the condition in which frequent or long-term exposure to light had left little of the fugitive colors of these prints. The Spauldings, on the other hand, were keenly aware of the importance of color in the creations of the *Ukiyo-e* woodblock artists. It was their primary concern not only to obtain works in the best possible condition but also to preserve them for the future in the best possible way. As a result, they decided to present their collection to the Museum with the stipulation that it would not be exhibited, even in the institution housing it. Their concern was, of course, to protect these superb pieces, with their delicate fugitive pigments, from the destructive effects of light of all sorts, as well as from the dangers of climatic change or extremes in humidity. It should be noted that the prints are regularly shown to interested visitors and students and scholars of Japanese prints by appointment throughout the year, as is the case with other Japanese prints in the Museum's collection. The provision attached to the Spauldings' gift has already served significantly to protect and preserve the pieces over close to six decades. While the Spauldings were probably the first persons in the Western world to request such protection from exposure to light, they were unaware of yet another danger, the acid contained in the board on which they mounted their prints and on which they made notes on the provenance of their acquistions. In recent years all of the Spaulding prints have been remounted on acid-free board, a time-consuming operation that could only be carried out with the generous financial support of the descendants of the Spauldings.

For a number of years the curator John Ellerton Lodge had divided his time equally between the Museum of Fine Arts in Boston and the Freer Gallery of Art in Washington, D.C. In 1931 Lodge decided to devote himself entirely to the directorship of the Freer Gallery. He was succeeded by Kojiro Tomita, a disciple of Okakura Kakuzō. Tomita had joined the staff of the Museum in 1907 at the age of eighteen and he retired as curator in 1962, after the longest term of service in the history of the Museum. Born and raised in Kyoto, he might have been expected to have a predilection for Japanese art. His father was a close friend of the great Nanga painter Tomioka Tessai who often took the little boy Kojiro with him on his wanderings through Kyoto. Instead of adding to the Japanese collections, however, Kojiro Tomita concentrated on the task of bringing the Chinese collections up to a level where they equaled those from Japan. The long period of his curatorship was marked by a succession of brilliant acquisitions, made possible in part by the munificence of a new generation of benefactors. He did not follow the fashionable trend in buying of the thirties, which saw the rapid growth of collections of Chinese bronzes in Japan, in Europe, and in America. While the few bronzes that were bought are of rare distinction, such as the so-called Mongolian Youth, no major effort was made to compete with other museums for the many excellent bronze vessels that were excavated in China during those years. Instead, the Museum concentrated its limited resources on a determined effort to expand the collection of early Chinese paintings. Huizong's *Five-Colored Parakeet* and Yan Liben's *Thirteen Emperors* are the crowning achievement of this farsighted policy. After the Second World War the emphasis in the department's acquisition program was shifted to Ming and Qing paintings. This successful policy was made possible chiefly by the generous bequest of Keith McLeod in 1956.

Only once during his long term as curator did Kojiro Tomita acquire a masterwork of Japanese art—and, undeservedly, it got him into conflict with his native country. The late twelfth-century handscroll *Kibi's Adventures in China* had been on the Japanese art market for some years before the Boston Museum, raising the purchase funds by deaccessioning, decided to acquire the scroll. Perhaps because of its contents, the *leitmotiv* of which seems to be how Japanese wit gets the better of Chinese hubris, the

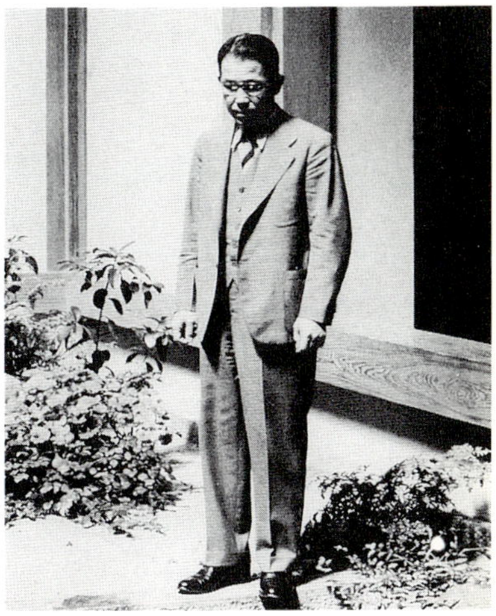

Kojiro Tomita (1890-1976)

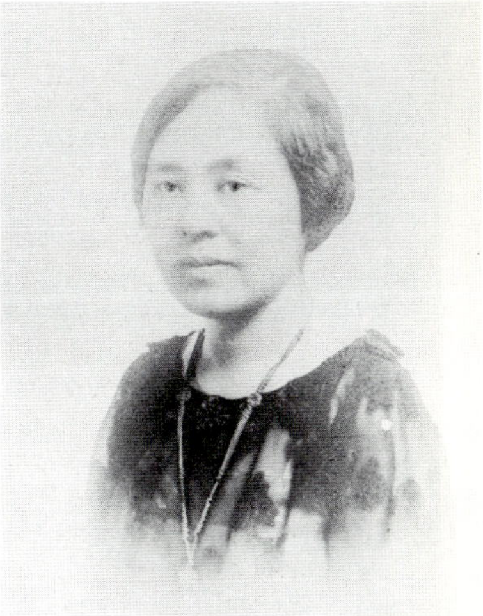

Chie Hirano (1878-1939)

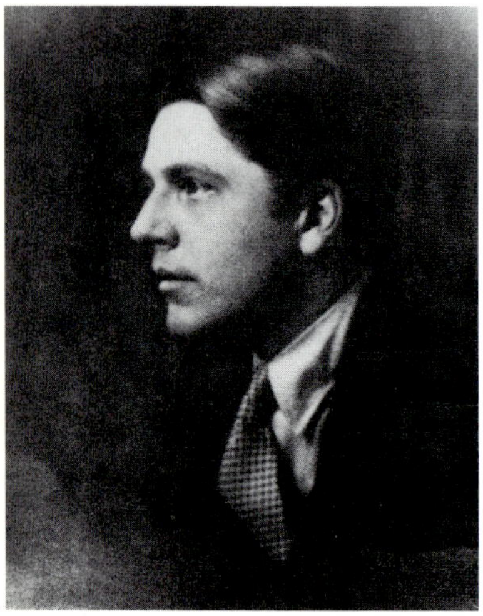

Charles Bain Hoyt (1889-1949)

departure of the scroll from Japan coinciding with the beginning of the "China Incident," caused a nationwide furor. It led, within a year, to the enactment of a law that made the export of works of art from Japan subject to permission of the Minister of Education. In the sixties the Kibi scroll returned to Japan to be remounted and to be separated, for reasons of conservation, into four more manageable sections. On that occasion it was exhibited in the Kyoto National Museum, where it aroused new controversy, this time of a scholarly nature, about its style and date, a debate that is still continuing today.

Although the aquisition of the Kibi scroll did cause a strain in the Museum's relationship with Japan, these problems appear to have been, no more than temporary. A few years later, in 1936, an important loan exhibition of art treasures from Japan was held in Boston in conjunction with the tercentenary of Harvard College. On this occasion several prominent Japanese art historians accompanied the works, and their visits resulted in important publications on works of art in our collections by such leading experts as Yukio Yashiro. A Japanese staff member working at the museum at the same time was Chie Hirano (1878-1939). One of the first Japanese women to seek a career in oriental history, she is remembered as the author of a remarkable pioneer publication, *Kiyonaga: A Study in His Life and Works* (Harvard University Press, 1939).

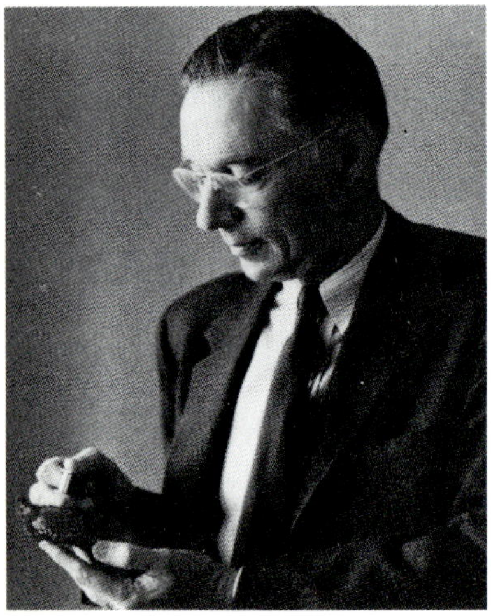

Robert Treat Paine (1900-1965)

In addition to the important scholarly contributions made by Japanese members of the curatorial staff, the Museum has profited from the services of four Japanese conservators. Motokichi Tamura worked for the museum during the years of Okakura's curatorship. He was succeeded by Yokichi Kinoshita, who returned to Japan in 1932, and Shigetaro Hayashi, who served from 1933 to 1941. After a long period in which the Asiatic Department lacked a conservator, Yasuhiro Iguchi joined the staff in 1963. A distinguished conservator to whose care National Treasures and Important Cultural Properties had frequently been entrusted in his homeland, he undertook the giant task of repairing and remounting the thousands of scrolls that had accumulated in the museum's storage area. Since the renovation of the galleries, and until his death this year, he directed these activities from the new Asiatic Conservation Laboratory, donated by Carl A. Weyerhaeuser and Charitable Trusts in honor of Kojiro and Harriet Tomita.

When the two great gilt bronze altars of the Northern Wei dynasty, now in the Metropolitan Museum of Art in New York, came on the art market, and the Boston trustees decided, quite reasonably, that the Museum, already in the possession of the slightly later, equally splendid Duan Fang altar, should not try to acquire these masterpieces, Kojiro Tomita was disappointed. But the lost opportunity made him determined to establish acquisition funds that would be restricted to the purchase of works of Asian art. The generosity of four loyal friends–John Ware Willard, Frederick L. Jack, Marshall H. Gould, and Keith McLeod–made this wish come true in the years that followed.

The scope of the collections was once more expanded in a spectacular manner when Charles Bain Hoyt (1889-1949) bequeathed to the museum his extensive collection of Chinese and Korean ceramics. Most of the other great benefactors of the department were quite well known in their time, and several–Morse, Fenollosa, Okakura, and Coomaraswamy–have already become subjects of biographical research. As little is known about Hoyt, it seems appropriate to include here a few biographical remarks about this discerning collector.

Charles Hoyt was born in Kenosha, Wisconsin, in 1889. Among his ancestors was Jonathan Edwards, founder of Princeton University. Collecting was not unknown in his family, for his cousin T. Newell had a distinguished collection of Alexandrian coins. As a child, fascinated by sea shells, he soon switched his attention to bookplates. His first ceramic piece–a Japanese teapot–he acquired in a trip around the world in 1910. When his mother died soon afterward, he inherited her share of the Bain Wagon Company, which permitted him to lead a life devoted to the study and collecting of oriental ceramics. During the First World War a large collection of fine Koryŏ celadons, brought from Korea, found no buyers in a Paris preoccupied with the battle of Marne, and so it became the nucleus of the Hoyt collection. Dividing his time between a seventeenth century chateau, the Utenberg, near Lucerne (Switzerland) and a house in Cambridge (Massachusetts), the quiet, studious connoisseur gradually assembled a collection of Song and Koryo ceramics of extraordinary quality. A close friend of Langdon Warner, Hoyt became honorary curator of the Fogg Museum, where he cheerfully spent much of his time on such humble, but extremely useful tasks as matting an entire Japanese print collection.

Hoyt was among the first to recognize the beauty of early Chinese ceramics and, with the exception of *Jun* ware (extensively represented in the Fogg Museum), his collection covers the entire spectrum from pre-history to Ming. In the later years of his collecting activity, he was often assisted by his long-time companion Rowland Burdon-Muller, a brilliant connoisseur in his own right. When Charles Bain Hoyt died he left his collection to the Museum of Fine Arts and his property in Lucerne as a public park to that city, thus becoming a benefactor in two continents. An aquisitions fund, established by his bequest, enables us to add further to this collection, already generally recognized as one of the finest of its kind.

In 1962 Robert Treat Paine succeeded Kojiro Tomita as curator of the Asiatic department. Although he became known chiefly as an expert on Japanese prints, Paine's remarkable connoisseurship of Japanese paintings is evident from the purchases he made as a young student in Japan, as well as those he made during the short period of his curatorship. A tryptic of Tōyō, which he acquired at the auction of the treasures of the Bishamondō Temple in Kyoto, and which he donated to the Museum many years later, is one of the last masterpieces of Japanese painting to enter the collection. Paine also made a determined effort to fill the major gap in the collection of Japanese painting: the Nanga school. The quality of the works by Ikeno Taiga, Yosa Buson, and Uragami Gyokudō that he added to the collection clearly demonstrates that he would have achieved this objective if his tragic, premature death had not prevented him from carrying out his long-cherished plans for the future of the department. Since his death in 1964, changes in the political climate and the proliferation of laws restricting the export of important art objects from many countries in Asia have strictly limited the possibilities for adding to the collection works of art of a quality comparable to that of those acquired in the past. In spite of these restrictions, the collection has grown in several directions.

During the period of Robert Treat Paine's curatorship the collection of Japanese prints was systematically expanded to include prints of the Taishō era, as well as contemporary works. In recent years, this expansion into the twentieth century has extended to the Chinese field by the acquisition of a large number of paintings and works of calligraphy by nineteenth and twentieth century artists. Moreover, the generous help of Paul and Helen Bernat, the ceramics collection, emphasizing earlier dynasties, has come to include superb examples of eighteenth century Chinese porcelains in the Chinese taste. During this period, too, the Indian collection, especially that of paintings, and the collection of Islamic ceramics were expanded by important donations by Museum trustee John Goelet.

In spite of the unmistakable signs that the collection, with the support of dedicated friends and benefactors, will continue to grow, it is unlikely that it will change radically from its present form and scope. After generations of trustees and curators who saw the expansion of the collection as their primary goal, we have now entered a phase in the Asiatic department's history in which the emphasis will shift to conservation, exhibition and research.

A novel element, hardly ever countenanced by a previous generation, is the possibility to share the wealth of our collection in other parts of the United States and Europe and especially in the countries from which the works of art originated. Since the beginning of the seventies, parts of the collection of the Museum have traveled to Japan on six occasions, a program that culminated in 1983 in an exhibition of Japanese paintings at the Tokyo and Kyoto National Museums.

Although many works of the Bigelow collection, especially paintings and swords, returned to Japan from time to time for conservation work during the collector's lifetime, the Trustees of the Museum of Fine Arts decided in1928, two years after Dr. Bigelow's death, not to lend his collection to other museums for exhibitions. This restriction was made at the request of Denman Waldo Ross and out of respect for Dr. Bigelow's known reluctance, expressed in a letter dating from 1902, to have his pieces travel. When Bigelow donated his collection nine years later, no restrictions were suggested or imposed. The collector's life-long commitment to Japan and Japanese culture was reaffirmed at the time of his death in 1926, when he directed that his ashes be buried at the Hōmyō-in, the temple where he and Fenollosa had spent so many happy years, and where they now lie in adjacent graves. The magnanimous support of the Government of Japan for the museum's renovation of the galleries in which the collections of William Sturgis Bigelow and Ernest Fenollosa are on display called for a reciprocal gesture. And so, in recognition of this unprecedented gesture of the Government of the Japan Board of Trustees of the Museum of Fine Arts voted on October 16,1980 to make a single exception to the restrictions, imposed in l928, and to allow parts of the collection of Dr. Bigelow to return to Japan, for the first time since 1889, to be shown at the Tokyo National Museum.

These exhibitions as well as shows from the Museum's collections of European and American paintings, have helped to renew the traditional ties of friendship between the United States and the countries of Asia. In addition to the considerable support for the renovation and installation of climate control from the Government of Japan, the Korean U.S.A. Centennial Program Committee provided funds for the renovation of a gallery for Korean art. The Nippon Television Network and the Yomiuri Shimbunsha have magnanimously provided support by establishing the Matsutarō Shōriki Curatorship. The family of the late Yura Tetsuji has generously provided a fund for the aquisition of books for the departmental research library, which was renovated with their support. This support from abroad has been matched by generous donations from the Boston community. The galleries for Chinese ceramics, bronzes and decorative arts have recently been renovated through donations by Paul and Helen Bernat and Paul and Beth Schmid.

All of these acts of generosity, which have made such an important contribution to the renovation and revitalization of the Department of Asiatic Art, demonstrate that the Museum continues to play a role in the cultural exchange between the United States and the countries of the East to the benefit of all those whose eyes have been opened to the beauty of the arts of Asia.

Jan Fontein
Matsutarō Shōriki Curator

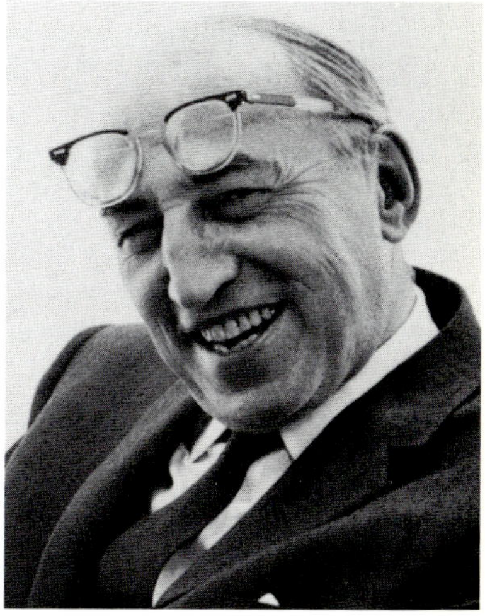

Paul Bernat (1902-1987)

Japan

The Museum's collection of Japanese art is one of the finest in existence, notable not only for its size but also for its high quality and comprehensiveness. In the area of Japanese painting, the holdings are unrivaled in the West. They include representative pieces of almost every category or school, religious as well as secular, ranging from the eighth century to modern times. The majority of these pieces were acquired in Japan well before the turn of the century, and a substantial number are of unique artistic and historical significance. Among the areas of particular strength are Buddhist painting, works in the "monochrome-ink" tradition, paintings by Kano school artists, genre and *Ukiyo-e* works, and paintings by artists from various schools that flourished during the Edo period, as well as independent painters of the period. Mention should also be made of the two early master-pieces from the *Yamato-e* school, the *Illustrated Handscroll of Minister Kibi's Trip to China* (no. 22) and the *Burning of the Sanjō Palace* (no. 23).

The collection is rich in sculpture, with many exceptional Buddhist icons. Most, like Kaikei's famous statue of the Miroku Bosatsu (no. 6), are fashioned from wood, but there are also several fine bronze pieces, such as Saichi's superb portrayal of the Shō Kannon (no. 8).

Lacquer seems to have been one of the first Japanese art forms to attract Boston collectors, as demonstrated by the small group of select pieces that came to the Museum from the bequest of Thomas Gold Appleton in 1884. As a result of the continuing generosity of many benefactors in the following decades, the collection now includes over 600 examples.

The Museum's numerous swords and sword fittings, such as *tsuba* (sword guards) and *kozuka* (miniature accessory daggers), is of remarkable balance and quality and is unmatched outside Japan.

Japanese ceramics, particularly of the Edo period, are well represented, primarily as a result of the acquisition, in 1892, of the extensive collection assembled by Edward Sylvester Morse and gifts in subsequent decades from benefactors such as Lucy T. Aldrich and Charles B. Hoyt.

Through the discerning taste and generosity of William Sturgis Bigelow and Ernest G. Stillman, the Museum has acquired many *netsuke* ("sash toggles") and other miniature personal accessories—a collection that is rich in variety and of impressive quality.

Also included are a large group of Nō robes, kimono, and other varieties of traditional clothing, as well as examples of various kinds of textiles. The metalwork represented comprises a diverse range of objects such as Buddhist ritual implements and accessories, cast mirrors, vessels, archaeological materials, and tobacco pipes.

In the area of Japanese woodblock prints, the Museum's holdings are unsurpassed anywhere. Not only is the collection, which amounts to more than 50,000 examples, one of the largest and most well-balanced; it is also one in which a significant proportion of the pieces are beautifully preserved and of the greatest historical and artistic importance. Among the many patrons who made this extraordinary collection possible are William Sturgis Bigelow, William S. and John T. Spaulding, Denman Waldo Ross, Nellie P. Carter, Lucy T. Aldrich, C. Adrian Rubel, L. Aaron Lebowich, Porter Sargent, Robert Treat Paine, Jr., Louis Black, and Mrs. Jared K. Morse.

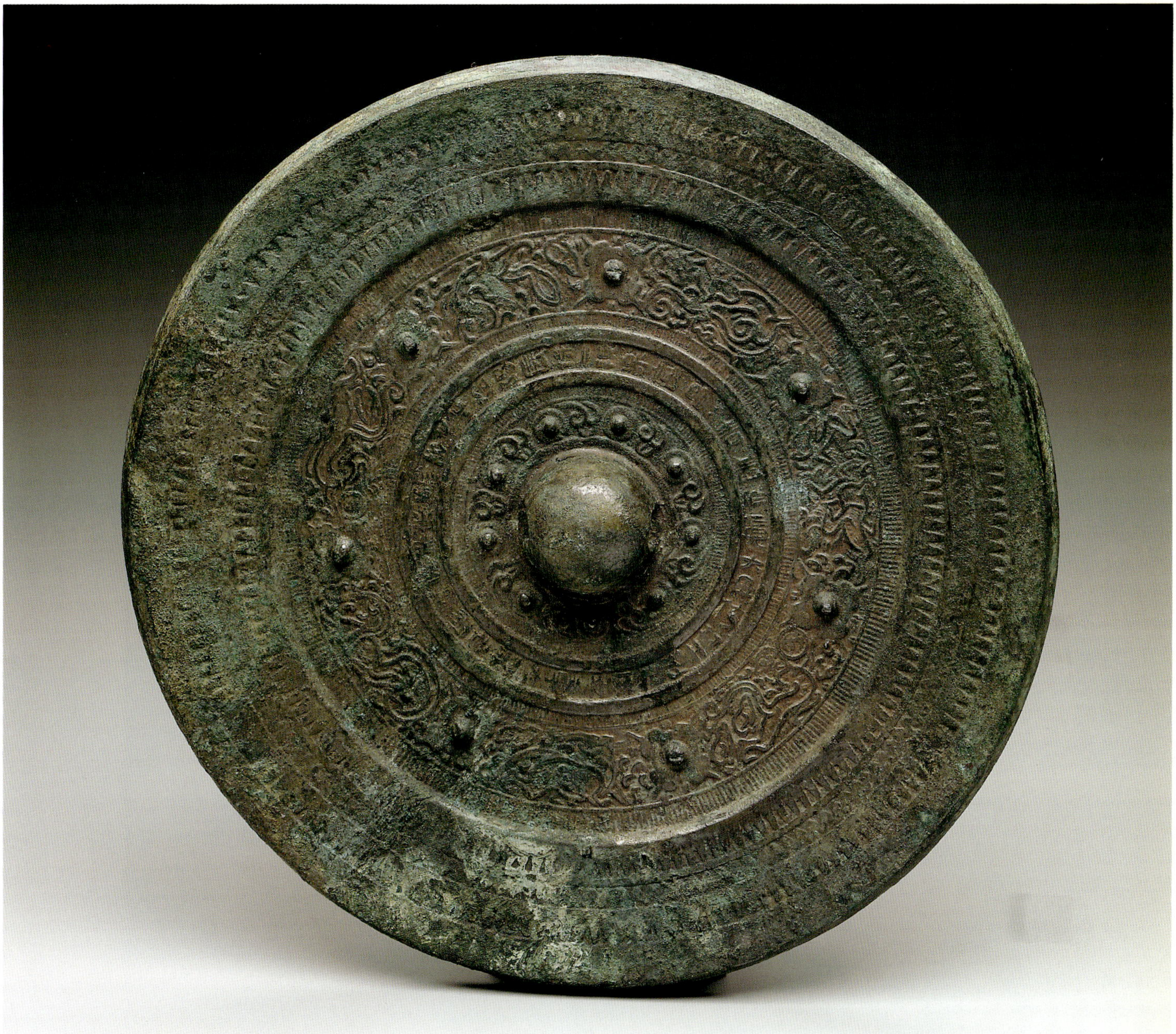

1
Mirror
Tumuli period, 5th century
Bronze. Diam: 23.5 cm.
Gift by Special Contribution. 08.160

The inner space on the back of the mirror is occupied by a hemispherical perforated knob in the center surrounded, first, by a band with nipple-like protuberances on round bases with cloud-whorls; next, a band bearing an inscription in Chinese characters; and finally a broader band in which seven nipples on quadrifoliate bases alternate with various symbolic beasts executed in fine lines, including the deities of the four quarters (the Tortoise and Snake, symbolic of the North; the Red Bird of the South; the Green Dragon of the East; and the White Tiger of the West), a three-legged crow, and a toad. The outer space is raised slightly above the inner and has two bands of saw-tooth pattern enclosing a band of wave pattern with an unembellished band on the outer edge.

This type of mirror is believed to be a product of Eastern Han China , but the lack of definition in the detail here suggests that this particular piece may be a Japanese copy made by casting a clay impression from a Chinese original. The mirror surface retains fabric impressions that are thought to be those of a three-layered silk bag in which the object was protected.

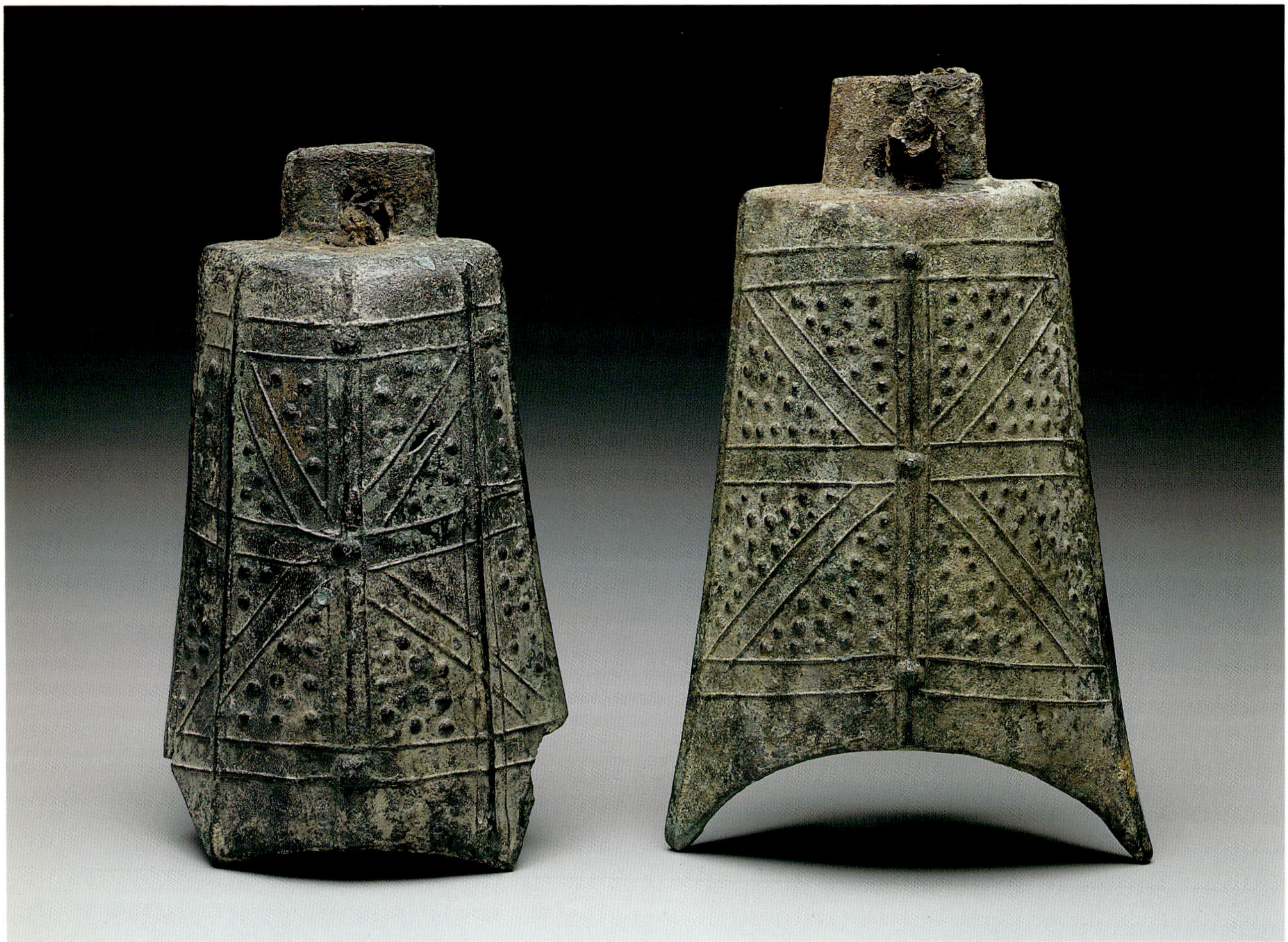

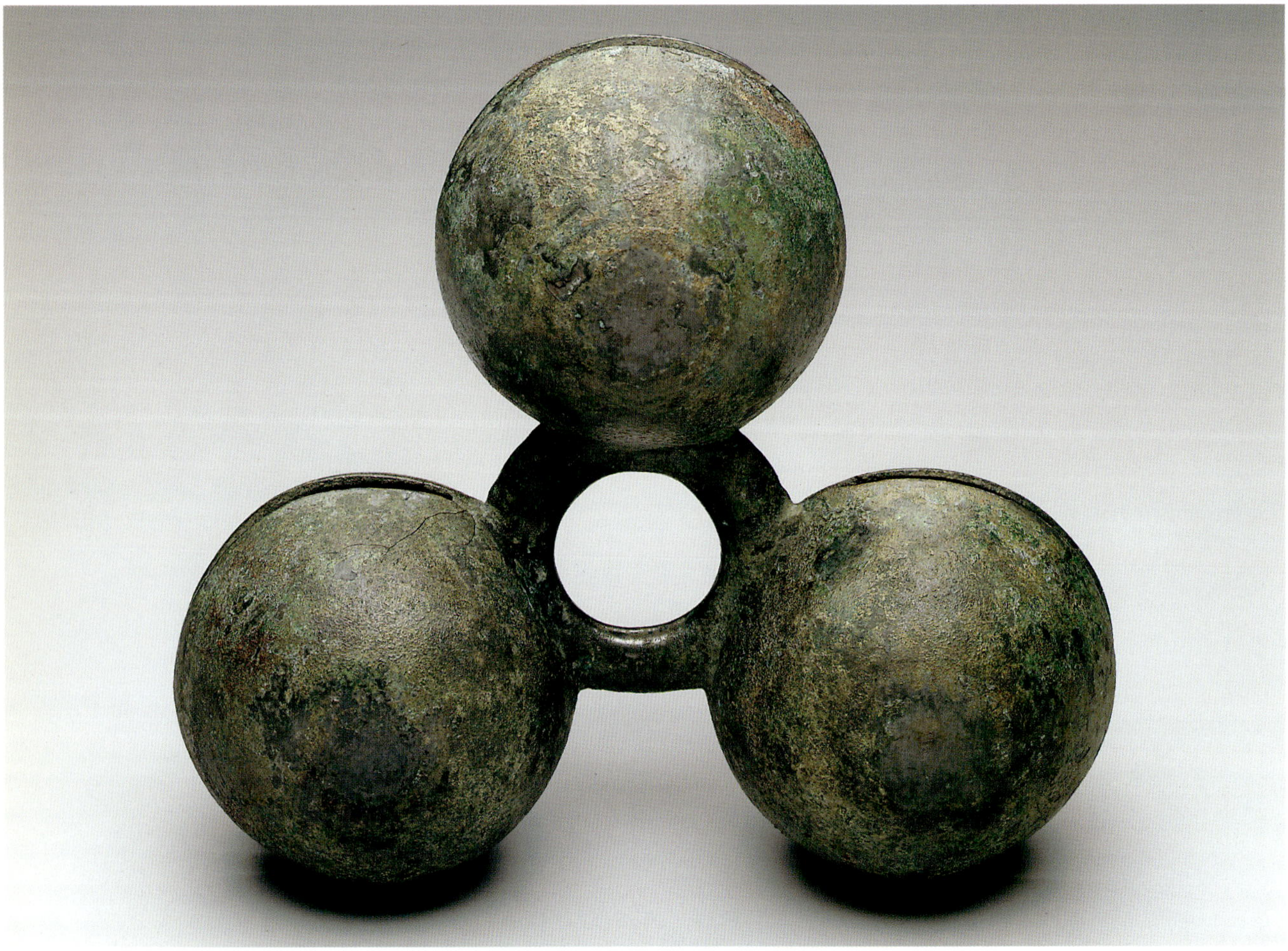

2

Horse Bells *(bataku)*

Tumuli period, 5th century
Bronze. (08.158) H: 16.8 cm. Diam: 10 cm.; (08.159) H: 18.7 cm. Diam: 11.1 cm.
Gift by Special Contribution. 08.158-9

Haniwa in the form of horses have simulated horse trappings that often include bataku *such as the ones shown here. Both of these bells consist of a smaller rectangular boss, used to attach the bell to the harness, and a hollow bell-shaped form which is almond-shaped in cross-section. A metal fitting was used to hang each bell by its handle, and a small hole was drilled at the base to suspend the clapper that struck against the body of the bell and produced the sounds as the horse moved.*

3

Ring with three bells *(sanganrei)*

Tumuli period, 5th century
Bronze. H: 6.3 cm., W: 13.0 cm.
Gift by Special Contribution. 08.157

The practice of horse-back riding is thought to have reached Japan by way of China and the Korean peninsula about the fifth century. The custom spread steadily and by the time of the latter part of the Burial Mound period equine accoutrements come to constitute one of the most important types of burial accessories found in tombs. Horses were buried with bataku, *a bell which is elliptical in cross-section, and* barei, *a spherical bell, both of which emitted a pleasing sound as the horse moved.* Sanganrei *generally have three spherical bells attached to a hollow centerpiece. Bells of this kind have also been found in Korean burial mounds of the Silla period. Such bells, which are also represented in the Museum's collection, tend to be smaller in relation to the central ring and are believed to represent an earlier form. The piece shown here, with bells that are far larger in proportion to the ring, is one of the largest surviving ones which suggests that it may be somewhat later than the Korean examples.*

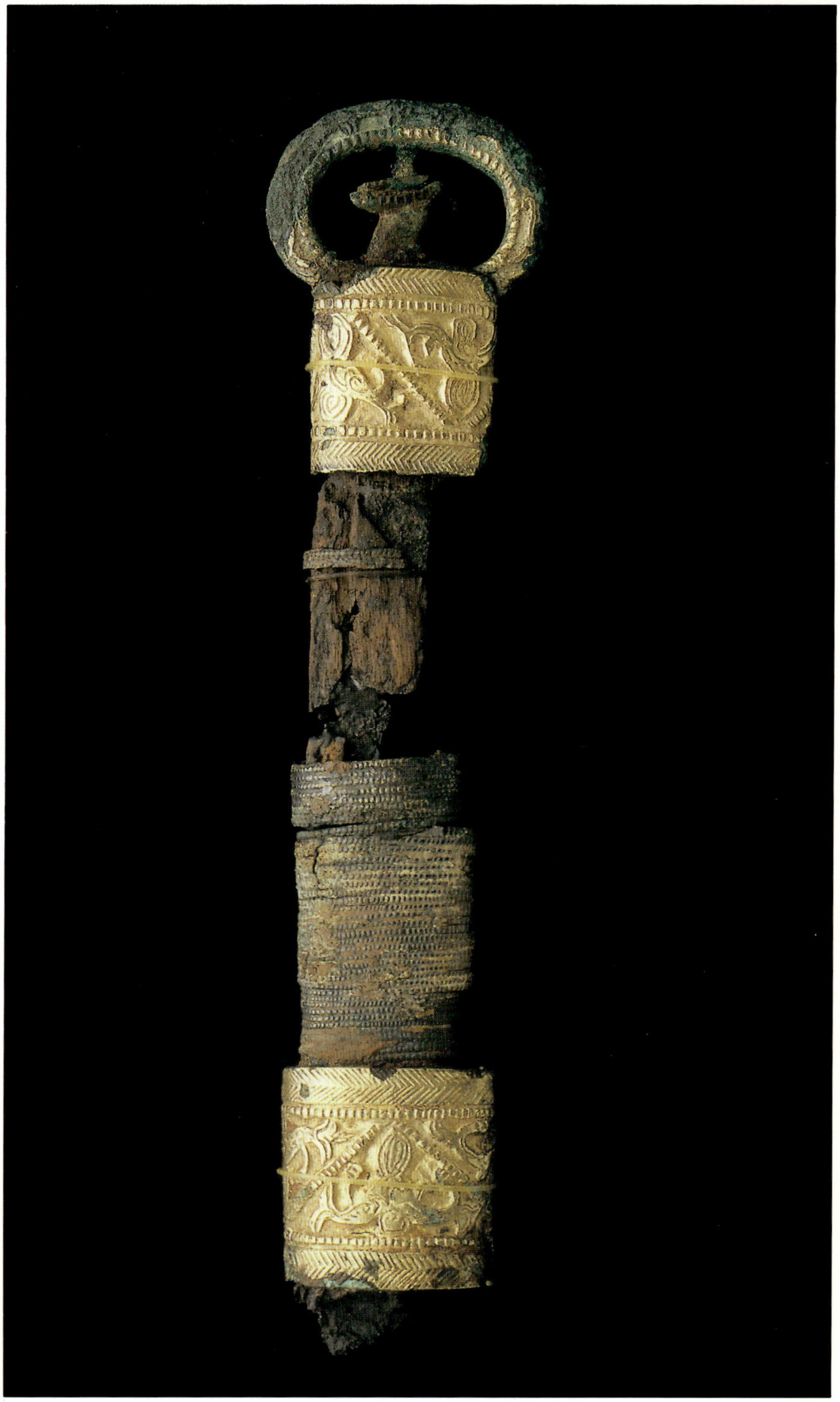

4

Sword handle and pommel

Tumuli period, 5th century
Reportedly from the mausoleum of Emperor Nintoku (r. about A.D. 395-427)
Bronze and silver; partially gilt.
1.5 x 23 cm.
Gift by Special Contribution. 08.161

This ring-pommeled hilt is now in three pieces, and a five-centimeter section of the hilt toward the base of the ring has been lost. The outer part of the oval ring is decorated with two symmetrically placed dragons confronting each other at the apex of the ring, while the inside of the ring is engraved with a ropelike pattern. In the center appears a single dragon's head in profile, which gives the impression of being carved in the round.

Conjecturing from the elaborateness of this hilt, the original mounting must have been quite sumptuous. While the exact place of its origin is not known, it was probably made in China and brought to Japan through Korea; similar pommels have been excavated from the Kongju and Kyongju regions in Korea. It is rumored that this hilt was discovered after a landslide from the tomb believed to be that of the Emperor Nintoku, along with two bronze horse bells, a bronze jingle bell, and a zodiac bronze mirror, and were acquired by Okakura Kakuzō, former curator of the Asiatic Department.

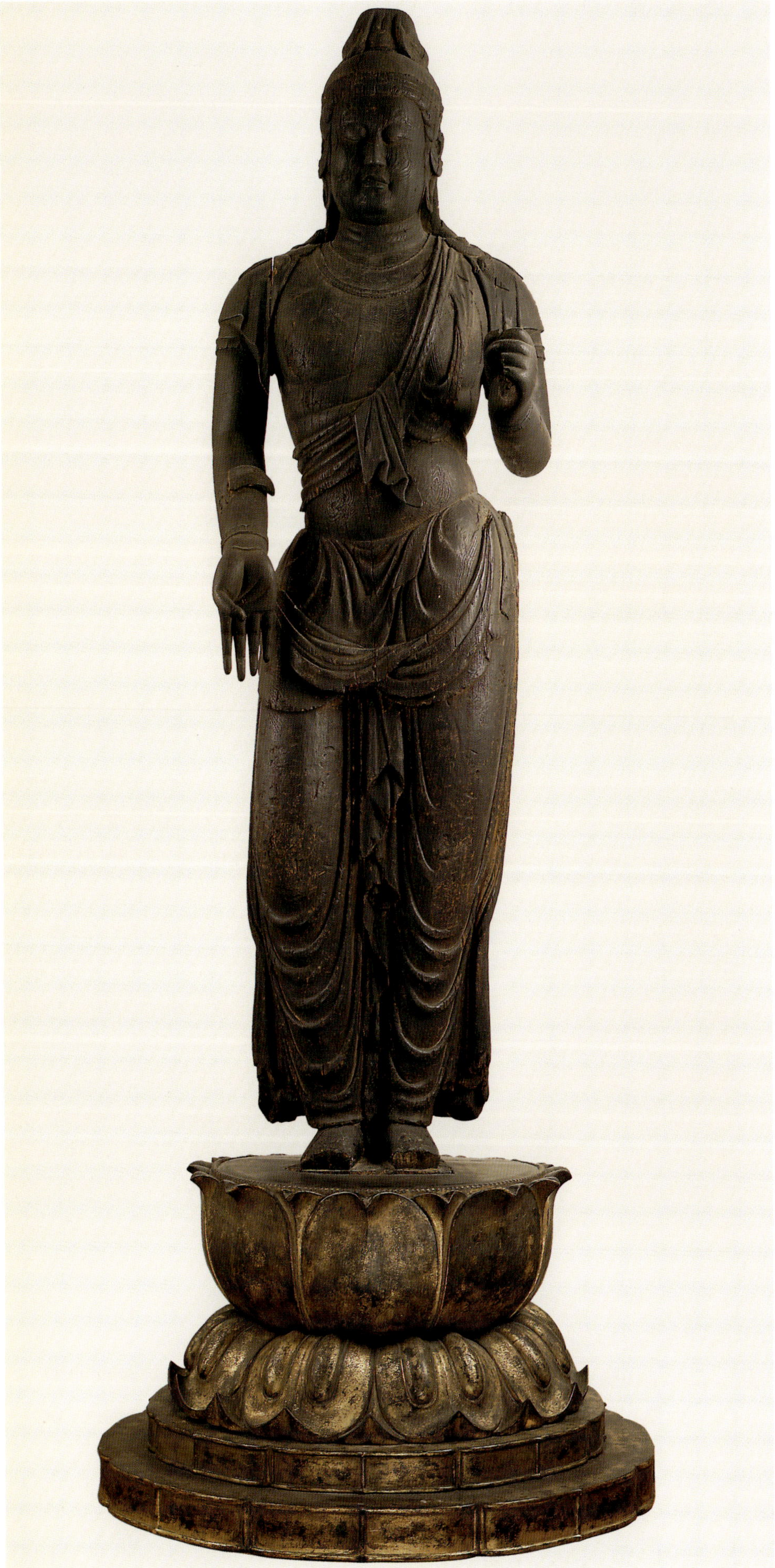

5
Bodhisattva of Compassion Bearing a Lotus (Shō Kannon)
Early Heian period, 9th century
Single woodblock construction.
H: 178 cm.
Special Japanese Fund. 12.128

Bodhisattvas *are the most beloved deities of Buddhism. While a Buddha follows the path through enlightenment to* Nirvāṇa, *a bodhisattva, the personification of mercy in the universe, chooses to forgo* Nirvāṇa *in order to assist others in their quest for salvation.*

Made from a single block of cypress wood (hinoki), *the massive bodhisattva stands on a double lotus pedestal. He has an elaborate hairdo and wears a thin scarf and full skirt, a costume that derives ultimately from the Indian* dhotī. *The full body of the bodhisattva and his slight sway, reminiscent of the Indian* tribhaṅga *(a pose common in Indian sculpture, in which the axis of the body is broken into three planes), reflect the strong cultural and economic ties between Japan and the Asian mainland during the eighth and ninth centuries. The slight rigidity in the stance of the figure and the schematized treatment of the drapery, particularly in the upper thighs, date this statue to the ninth century.*

Because the position of the left hand suggests that he once held an attribute, this figure traditionally has been identified as an image of Shō Kannon, or a manifestation of Kannon who bears the lotus.

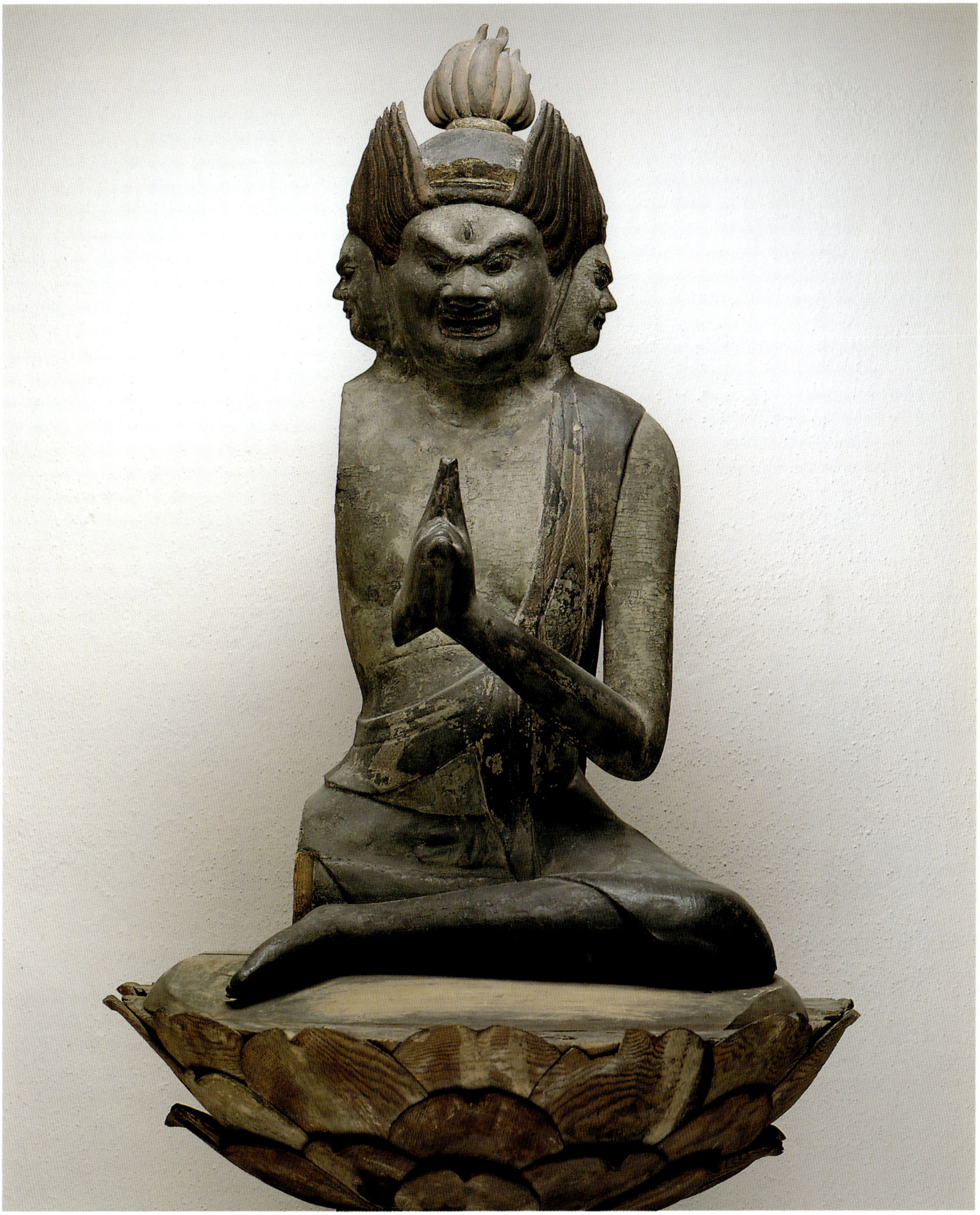

6
Dai-itoku, King of Wisdom (Dai-itoku Myō-ō)
Late Heian period, 11th century
Assembled woodblock construction; painted and gilded. H: 93 cm.
Special Japanese Fund. 05.228

Dai-itoku Myō-ō belongs to a category of deities known as wisdom kings (myō-ō), *who symbolize the awesome power of Dainichi, the Buddha of Infinite Illumination, and are worshiped collectively in Esoteric Buddhism. With his three scowling faces indicating his ferocity, he holds his hands in a gesture that signifies the power to break through ignorance and illusion, even through death, to enlightenment.*

The deity has a flaming topknot and wears a short skirt and a narrow scarf, on which remain traces of a delicate pattern painted in gold. Originally the statue rode on the back of a water buffalo, the traditional mount of Dai-itoku Myō-ō.

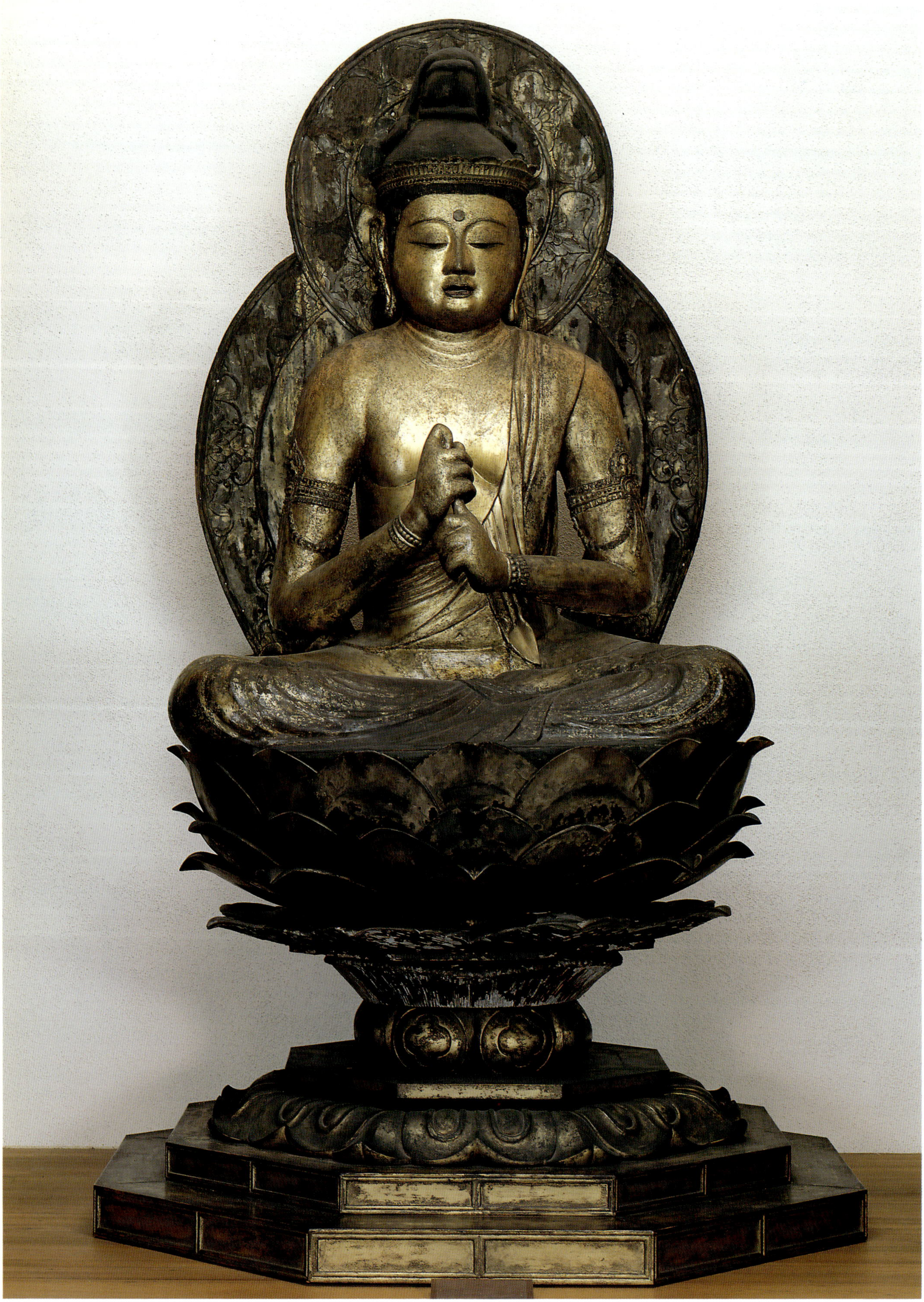

7
Buddha of Eternal Radiance (Dainichi Nyorai)
Late Heian period, 1149
Assembled woodblock construction; gilded. H: 141.6 cm.
Denman Waldo Ross Collection.
09.531

As the primary deity in Esoteric Buddhism and the generative principle of the universe, Dainichi Nyorai is intricately delineated in maṇḍala. *This image of Dainichi, wearing a full skirt and seated in a meditative posture, with hands held in the* chiken-in *gesture (symbolizing divine wisdom), is always found in the* Maṇḍala of the Diamond World, *one of two major types.*

An inscription inside the statue dates it to the year corresponding to 1149.

8
Kaikei (about 1158 - d. after 1223)
Bodhisattva of the Future (Miroku Bosatsu)
Kamakura period, 1189
Assembled woodblock construction; gilded. H: 107 cm.
Chinese and Japanese Special Fund.
20.723

A colophon added to the handwritten sūtra *found inside the figure is evidence that this statue dates to 1189 and is one of the earliest works by the Kamakura master Kaikei, who carved it possibly as an act of personal devotion. Kaikei and his colleague Unkei are credited with the creation of a style of sculpture suited to the taste of the military rulers of the Kamakura period (1185-1333).*

The fleshy quality of the figure and the free-flowing folds of the drapery in this early statue are characteristic of the increased realism of Kaikei's school of sculptors. Miroku, the Bodhisattva of the Future, holds a vase containing a lotus flower topped by a minature stūpa.

This statue, originally from Kōfuku-ji in Nara, and a painting of Dai-itoku Myō-ō (acc. no. 20.750) were once in the collection of Okakura Kakuzō, former curator of Asiatic art at the Museum of Fine Arts; they were purchased from his estate after his death.

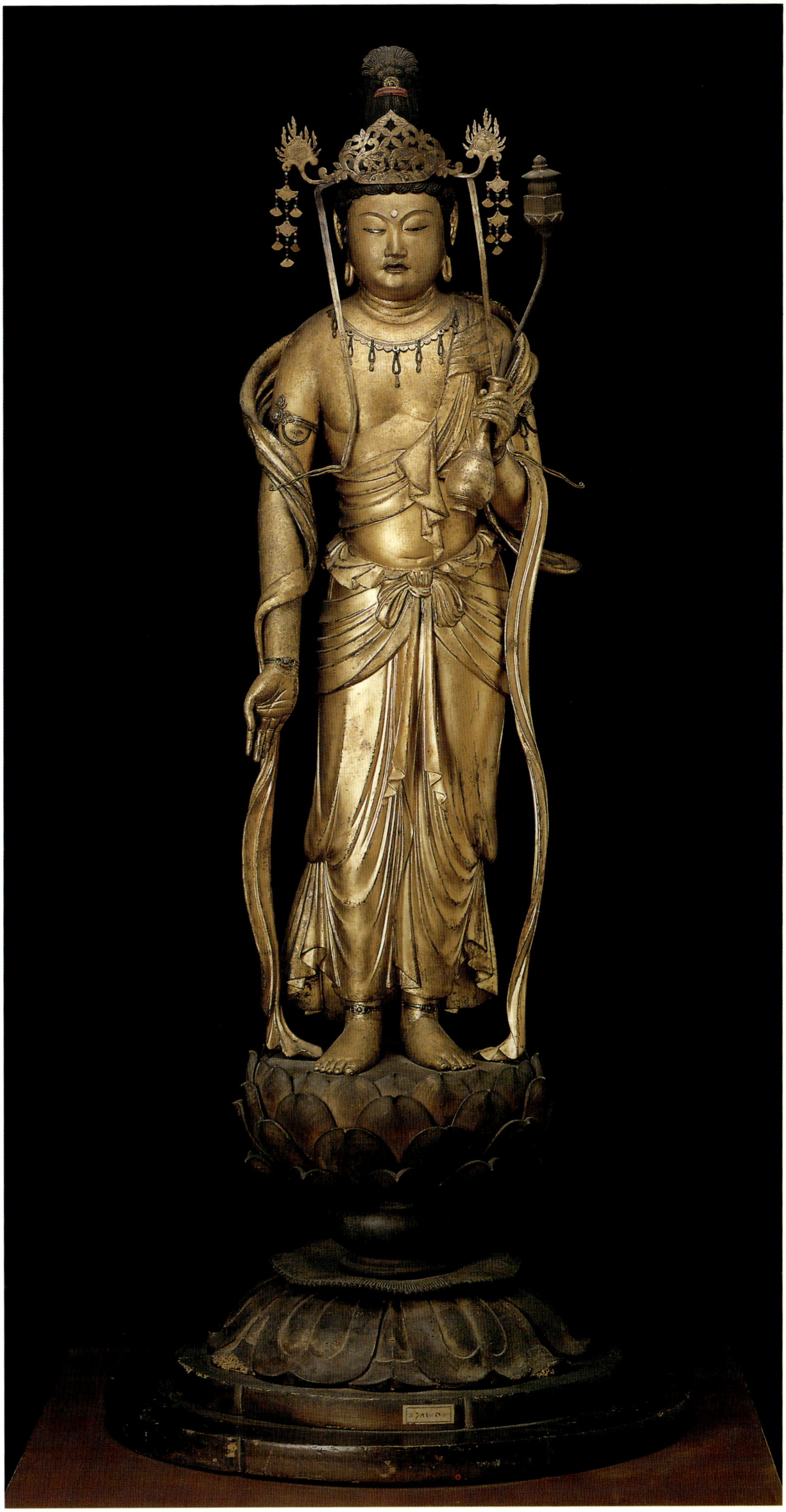

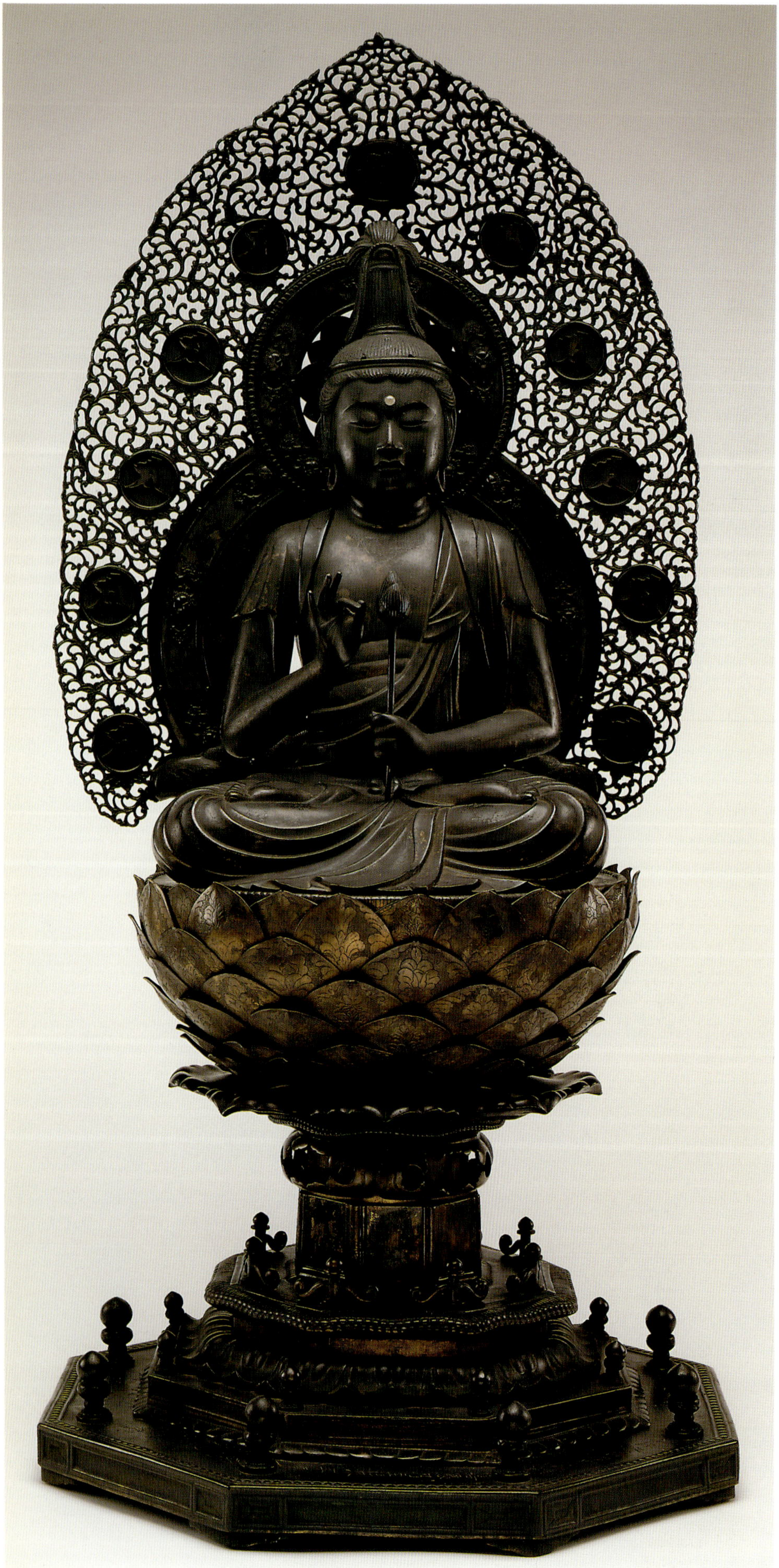

9

Saichi (active mid-13th century)

Bodhisattva of Compassion Bearing the Lotus (Shō Kannon)

Kamakura period, 1270
From Kongōrin-ji, Matsuo-dera, Shiga Prefecture
Bronze; parts gilded. H: 106.5 cm.
William Sturgis Bigelow Collection.
11.11447

This perfectly preserved masterpiece of Japanese bronze casting consists of several separately cast detachable parts. The Shō Kannon, seated in a meditative posture, holds a lotus in the left hand, while the right hand is raised in the symbolic gesture of argumentation. To the elaborate halo with its reticulated floral design are attached disks with Sanskrit letters that stand for figures of the Buddhist pantheon. The letter sa, *meaning Kannon, is repeated five times on each side. The letter* A *at the top stands for the supreme being, Dainichi Nyorai.*

On the hexagonal base of the lotus throne is an engraved dedicatory inscription, with a date corresponding to 1270 and the name of the artist Saichi. It also indicates that the statue was donated to the main hall of the Matsuo-dera (now known as the Kongōrin-ji) by a member of the Hata clan. (This prominent local family was responsible for the dedication of other Buddhist statuary in neighboring temples.) In the main hall stands a heavily decorated dais, inscribed with a date corresponding to 1288. While the date has been taken as that of the reconstruction of that part of the temple, the inscription on this statue suggests that the reconstruction may have begun at least eighteen years earlier. The Kannon was flanked originally by images of Bishamon-ten and Fudō Myō-ō, an unusual iconographic configuration that is repeated on a votive plaque from the same temple. Although it has lost its attendants, this figure remains one of the largest and finest examples of Buddhist bronze casting of the Kamakura period.

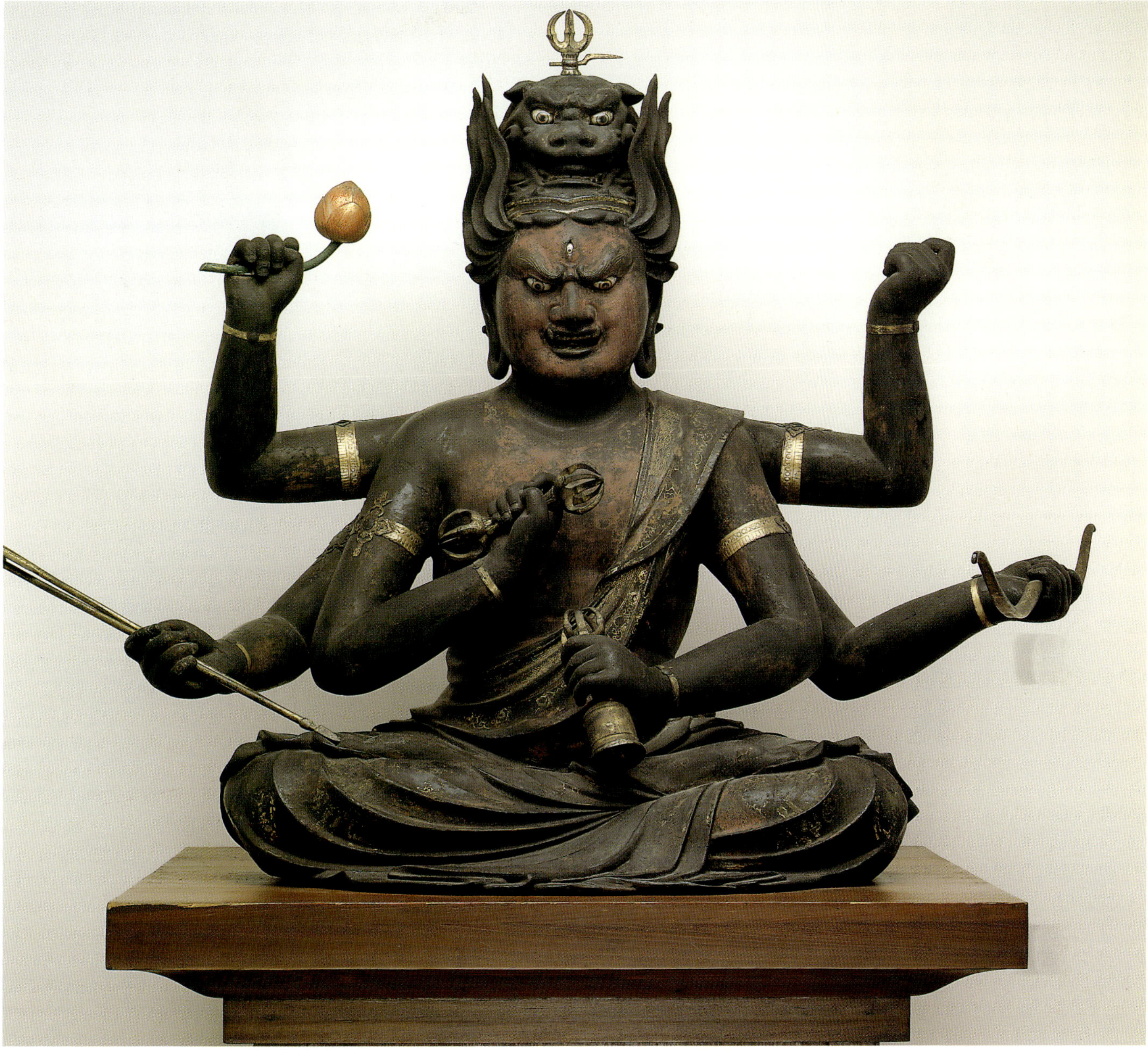

10
Aizen, King of Wisdom (Aizen Myō-ō)
Late Kamakura period, 14th century
Assembled woodblock construction; painted and gilded. H: 93 cm.
Gift of Francis G. Curtis. 09.383

Sitting in a posture of meditation, the red-bodied Aizen holds, in five of his six hands, a bow, an arrow, a lotus, a bell, and a vajra (a Buddhist implement that symbolizes the power of wisdom). His flaming hair encircles a lion's head, which is his most distinctive characteristic.

One of a group of Esoteric divinities known as wisdom kings (myō-ō), *who are worshiped as manifestations of the powers of Dainichi, Aizen symbolizes the possibility of immediate enlightenment through physical passion. His cult, which became important in the eleventh century, had been introduced to China in the early eighth century by the Indian monk Vajrabodhi and transmitted to Japan in the ninth century.*

Aizen's crystal eyes and those of the lion give this statue the immediate presence so prized in Kamakura sculpture. Because of their sanctity, such images were often installed in Esoteric temples, hidden from public view behind screens and partitions.

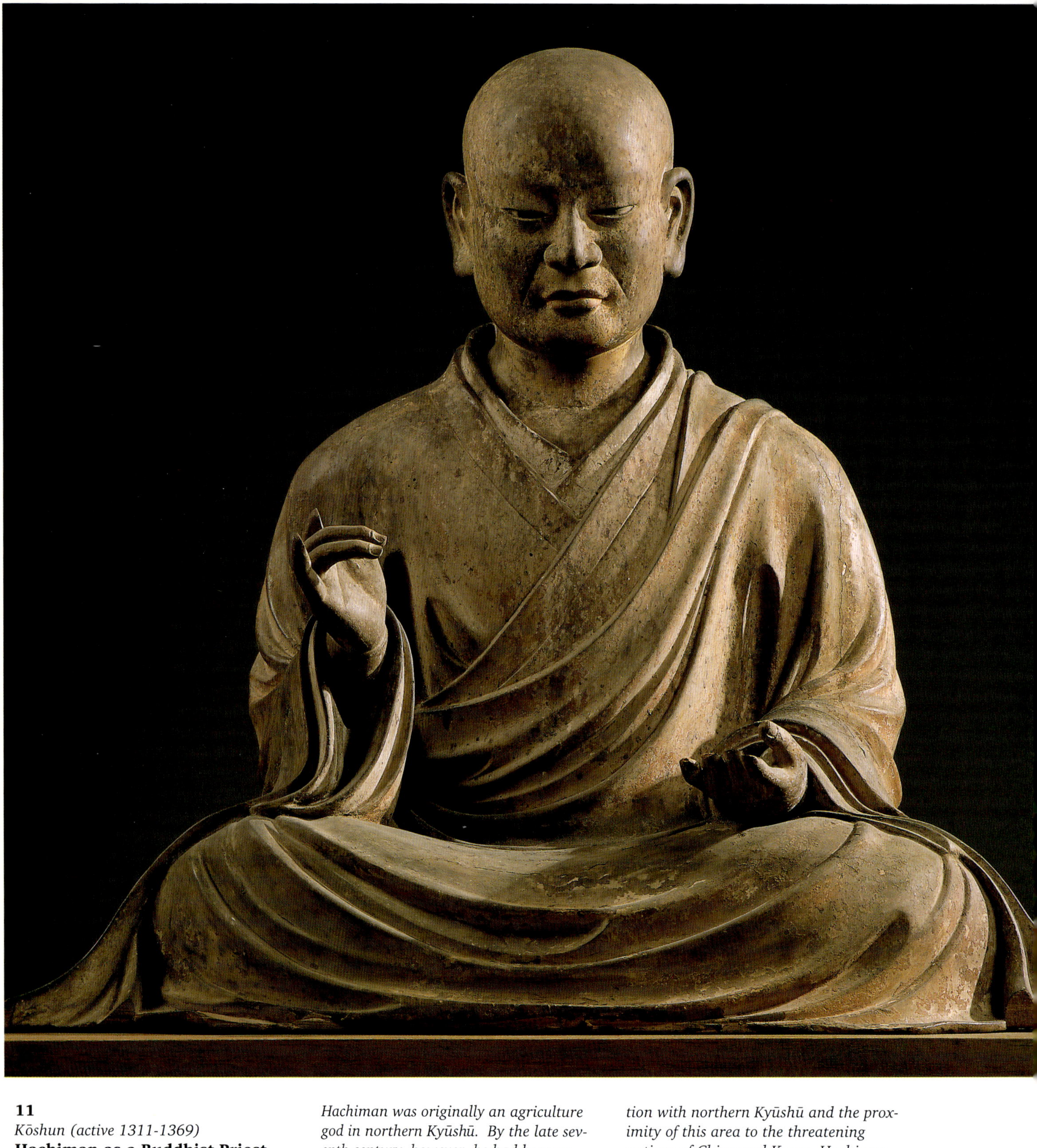

11
Kōshun (active 1311-1369)
Hachiman as a Buddhist Priest (Sōgyō Hachiman)
Kamakura period, 1328
Assembled woodblock construction; painted. H: 82 cm.
Maria Antoinette Evans Fund and Contributions. 36.413

Hachiman was originally an agriculture god in northern Kyūshū. By the late seventh century, however, he had become the tutelary god of many powerful local clans. As these clans controlled the copper mines in the area, Hachiman's protection was invoked to assist in the casting of the great Buddha of Tōdai-ji in 757. His fame spread quickly, and soon he acquired the title of a bodhisattva, thus becoming one of the first Shinto gods to be assimilated into the Buddhist pantheon. Because of his early affiliation with northern Kyūshū and the proximity of this area to the threatening nations of China and Korea, Hachiman was considered a guardian against threats from abroad and was invoked to protect the nation. He subsequently became a tutelary deity for many military families, including the powerful Minamoto (Genji) clan. Hachiman's shaved head and monk's robe are to be explained by the fact that Shinto gods must first become monks in order to seek Buddhist enlightenment.

An inscription inside the head of this statue states that it was made in 1328 at Kōfuku-ji in Nara by the sculptor Kōshun, a descendant of the famous Kamakura artist Unkei. The arresting face and sensitive hands of the figure clearly stem from Kōshun's training in the Nara branch of the Kei school.

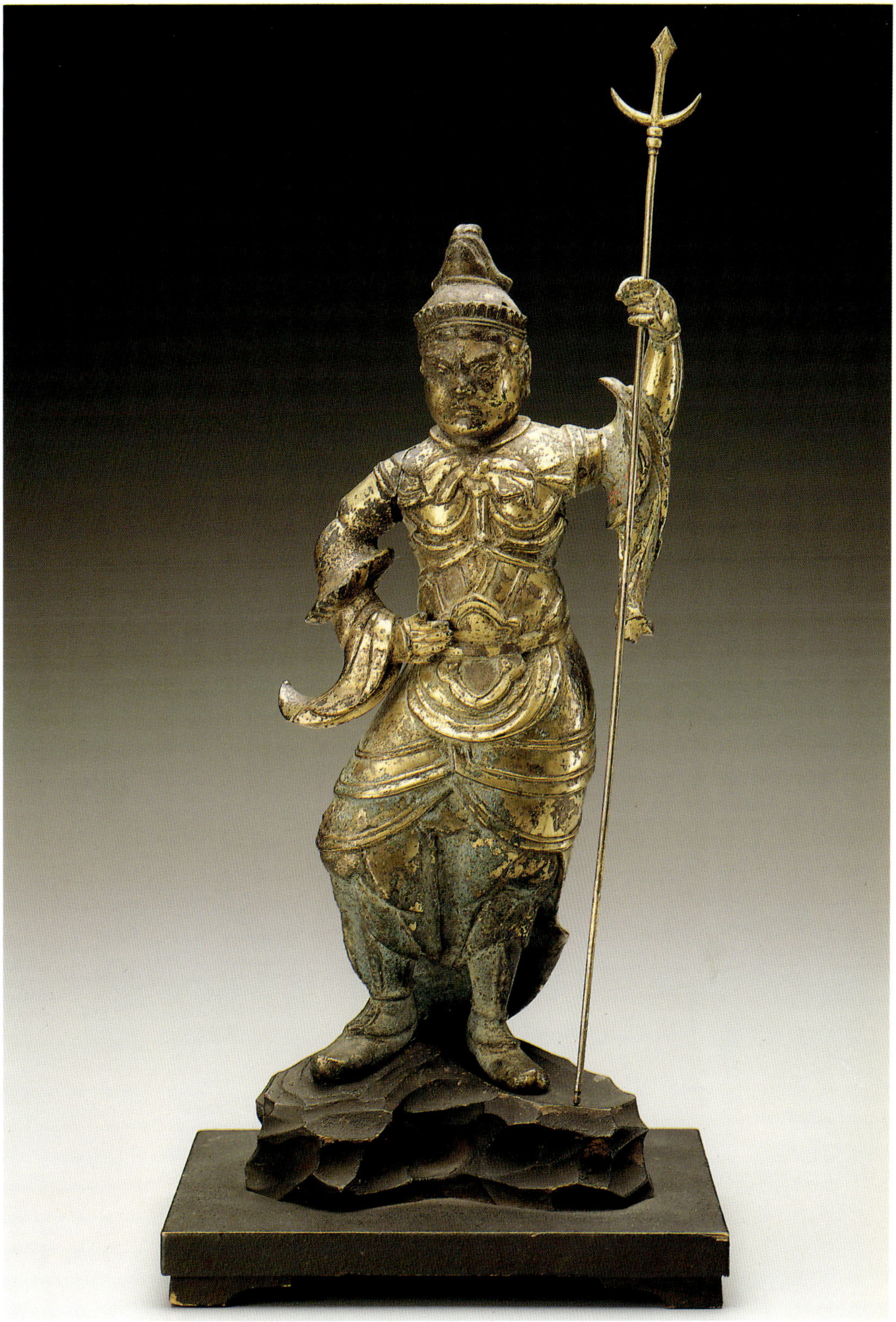

12
Guardian deity
Heian period, 12th century
Gilt bronze. H: 19.5 cm.
Gift of Ellen H. Gleason. 47.1339

Guardian deities, many derived from early Indian sources, abound in the Buddhist pantheon. Among the better-known types are the Shitennō, *or guardians of the four cardinal points, and the* Juni Shinshō, *or Twelve divine generals who accompany the Buddha of Medicine, Yakushi. In addition there are many minor guardians, all of whom wear armor, bear arms, and have glowering faces. As this small statue has no identifying attributes, it is not possible to determine which deity it represents.*

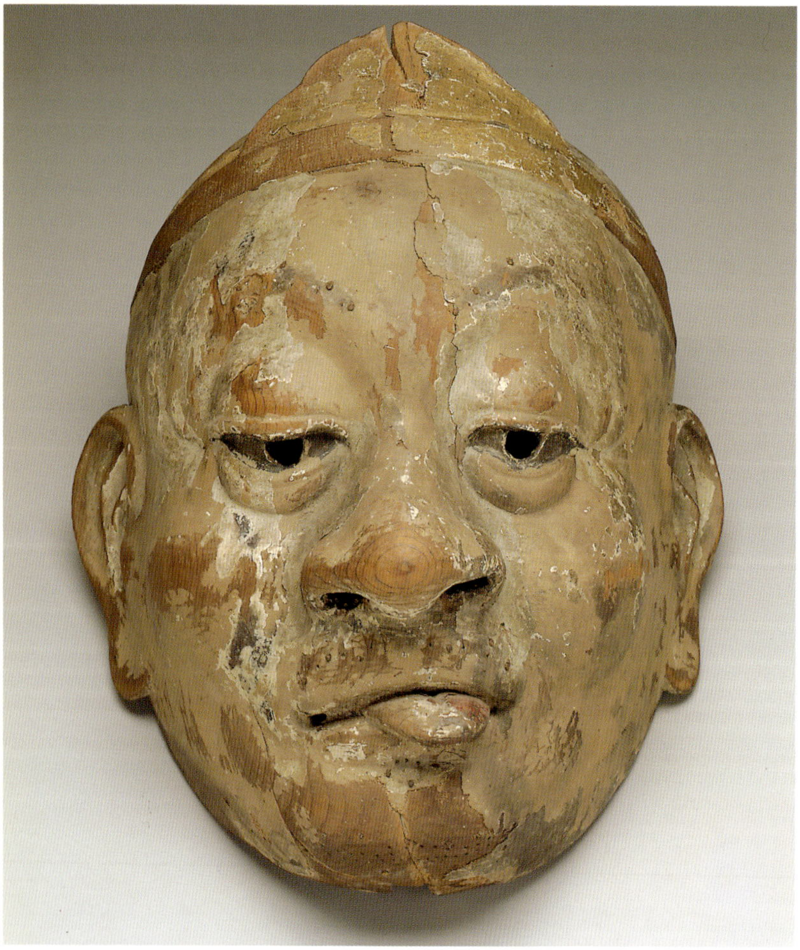

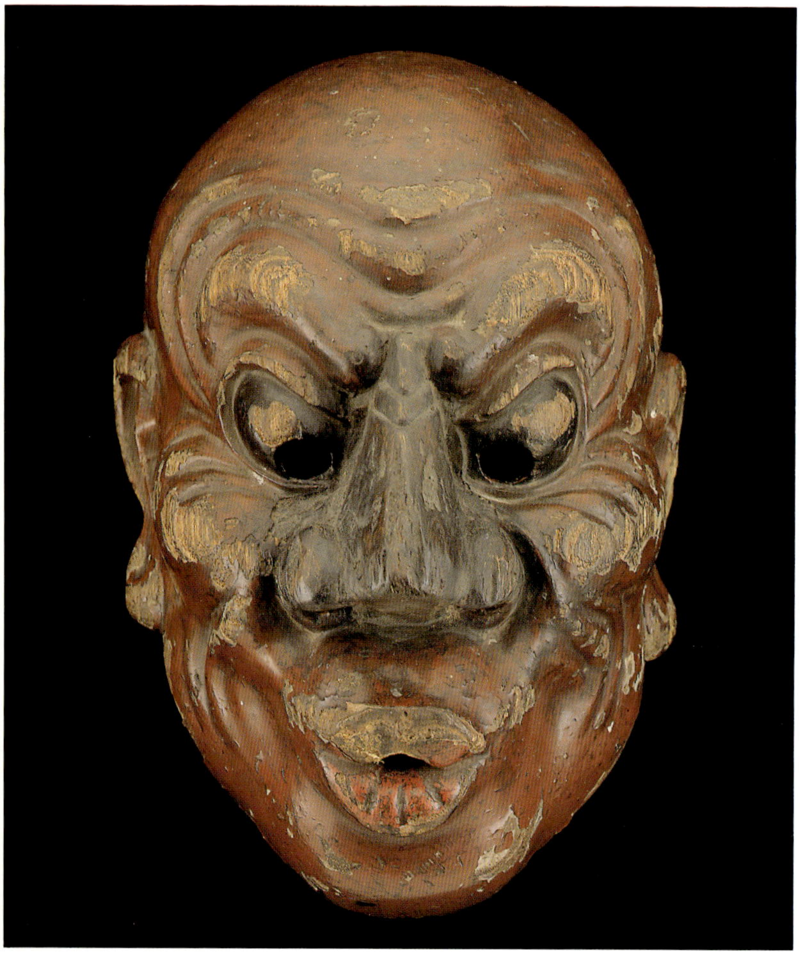

13
Bugaku mask
Heian period, ca. 11th century
Wood; painted. H: 26.4 cm.
William Sturgis Bigelow Collection.
11.5940

During the ninth century, various styles of dance, including native Japanese dances as well as those imported from China and Korea, were amalgamated into one form called bugaku. *Performed to the music of wind and percussion instruments,* bugaku *dances remain the official court dances of Japan. During the height of its popularity in the eleventh and twelfth centuries,* bugaku *was performed both by professional troupes and by aristocratic amateurs. The earliest extant* bugaku *masks date to that period of immense popularity. This mask is used by the host Kotokuraku Kempai in the dance* Kotokuraku, *in which four young foreigners, a host, and a wine bearer become intoxicated. The puffy eyes and loose tongue of this mask show clearly the effects of overindulgence.*
In the illustrated catalogue Shūko jūshū, *which appeared in 1800, Matsudaira Sadanobu (1758-1829) published drawings of thirty-eight masks in the collection of the Tōdai-ji, a temple in Nara. Of the nineteen still in the collection of the temple, one is almost identical in shape, size, and coloring to the Boston mask.*

14
Bugaku mask
Kamakura period, 12th century
Lacquered wood. H: 29 cm.
William Sturgis Bigelow Collection.
11.5912

Bugaku *dances are categorized by their content. This mask, which represents Kitoku-ō, belongs to a group of military dances in which Kitoku is variously identified as either the Chinese marquis Gui De or the Hun king Ri Zhu.*

In the oldest extant technical work on bugaku, *the* Kyōkunshō, *written in 1233, Koma Chikazane (1177-1242) divides Kitoku masks into two categories: human masks and masks with human faces and the mouth of a carp. The large, open, jutting mouth of this mask ranks it with the latter category, known as* Kitoku koi-kuchi *or Kitoku with a Carp's Mouth. When this type of mask is worn, two to six attendants accompany the main dancer.*

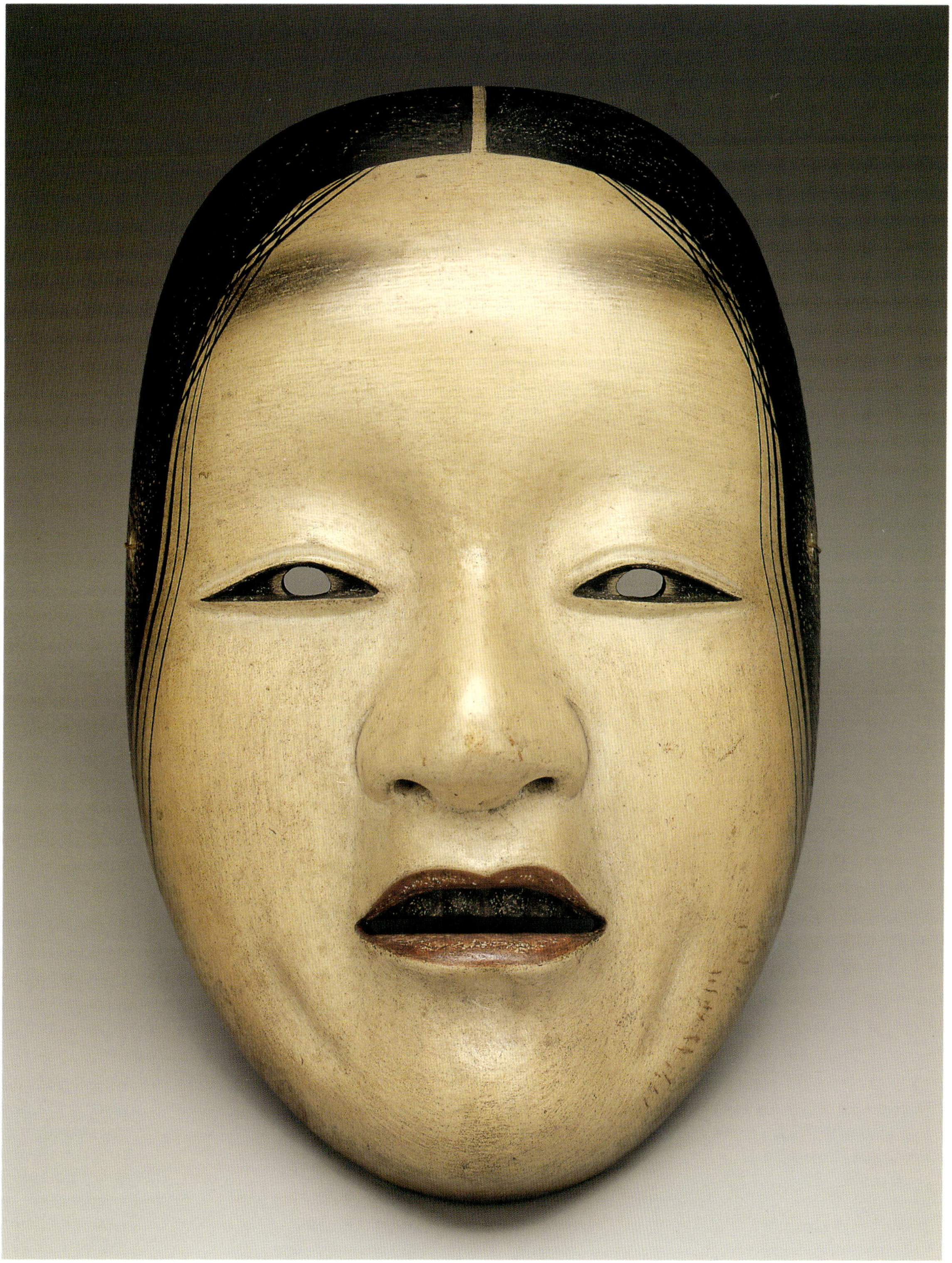

15
Deme Mitsunori (d. 1723)
Nō mask of the *shakumi* type
Edo period, 18th century
Wood with pigments on gesso.
21.2 x 14 cm.
William Sturgis Bigelow Collection.
11.5955

Unlike the highly flamboyant Kabuki, Nō is an extremely subtle theatrical form. Under the influence of Buddhist thought as well as classical literature, popular entertainments for temple and shrine festivals were transformed in the fourteenth century into performances of almost mystical beauty dealing with the tragedies of historical and legendary figures. The setting for the theater is stark, making the selection of the robes and masks crucial for evoking the proper mood of the plays.

Masks of the shakumi *type closely resemble other masks used to portray women. In some plays this mask type would be worn for the role of a mother in search of her lost child.*

Ernest Fenollosa was a devotee of the Nō theater. He studied in Japan under Umewaka Minoru, who revived the theater in the nineteenth century. Following Fenollosa's death, his widow approached Ezra Pound to complete a manuscript Fenollosa had begun on the theater and a translation of some of the plays; a preface was later provided by the Irish playwright and poet William Butler Yeats. Fenollosa's interest in Nō may have prompted his friend William Sturgis Bigelow to acquire the extensive collection of masks at the Museum.

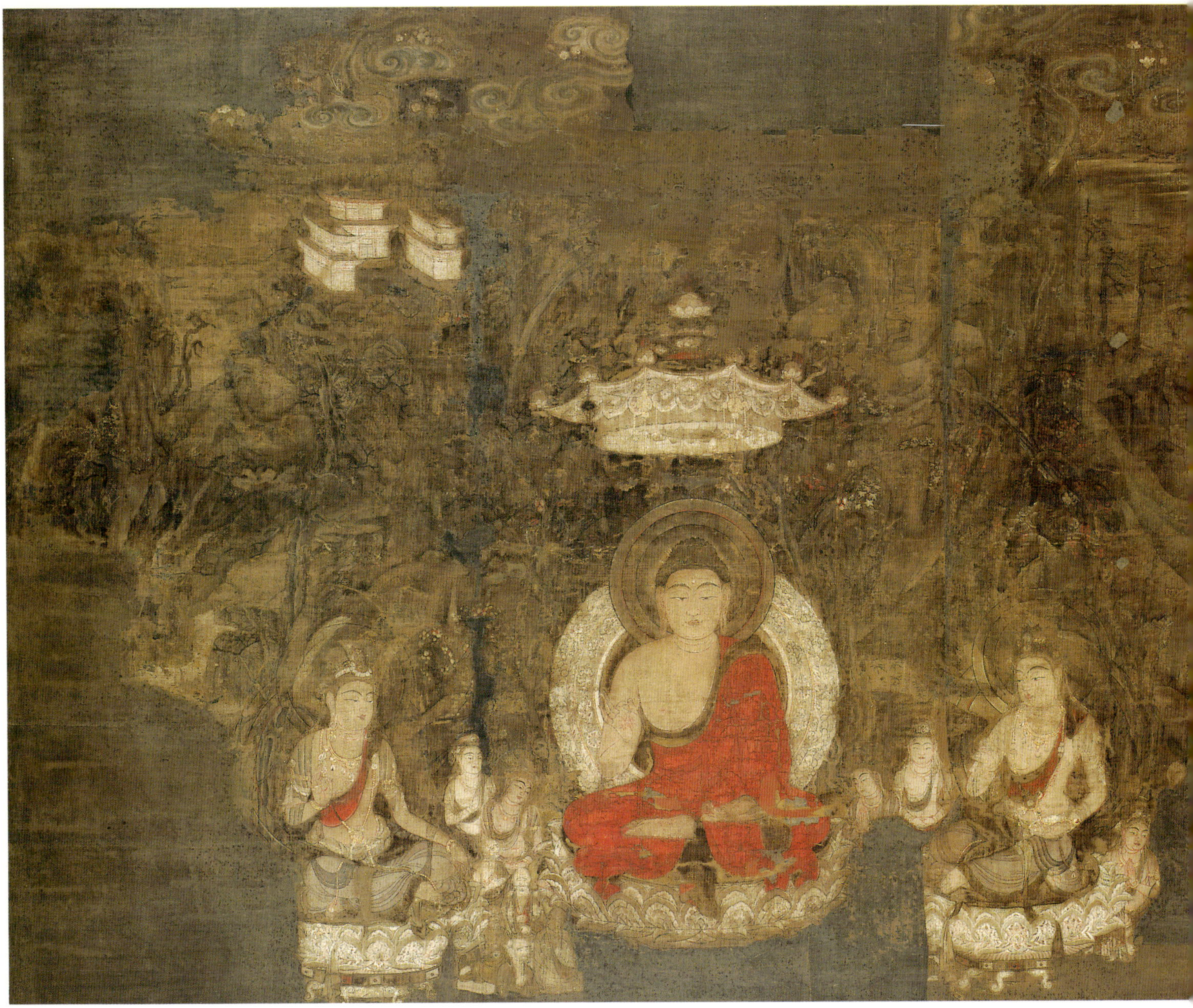

16

Historical Buddha Preaching on the Vulture Peak (Hokkedō Kompon Mandara)

Nara period, 8th century
Panel; ink, colors, and gold on hemp.
107 x 143.5 cm.
William Sturgis Bigelow Collection.
11.6120

Depicting Shaka, the founder of Buddhism, expounding the Lotus Sūtra *to a host of heavenly and human beings assembled on top of Vulture Peak, this painting was once the principal image* (Kompon Mandara) *in the Lotus Hall* (Hokkedō) *of the Tōdai-ji monastery in Nara. An inscription on the back confirms its name and records its restoration in the fourth year of Kyū-an (1148) by the monk-painter Chinkai. According to an inventory of works of art put on temporary display at the Tōdai-ji in 1726, it was among the treasures of the temple at that time. In 1884 it was acquired by William Sturgis Bigelow, the only painting of the Nara period to ever leave Japan.*

Despite Chinkai's restoration of the figures in the foreground, the Buddha's canopy, and the buildings in the background, the Hokkedō Kompon Mandara *continues to be a work of art of great interest and importance.*

17

Dai-itoku, King of Wisdom (Dai-itoku Myō-ō)

Heian period, 11th century
Panel; ink, colors, and gold on silk.
192 x 118 cm.
Gift of William Sturgis Bigelow in Memory of Okakura Kakuzō. 20.750

Dai-itoku has six heads, six arms, and six legs. His central hands are held in a gesture indicating his ability to pierce through ignorance to knowledge; additional hands hold a staff, a sword, a club, and a lasso. Because he represents the capacity of the enlightened believer to triumph over death, Dai-itoku Myō-ō sits on the back of a water buffalo, the animal traditionally associated with the Lord of Death. He is one of a group of five ferocious deities known collectively as "wisdom kings," who are worshiped in Esoteric Buddhism as manifestations of the wrath of Dainichi Buddha when confronted with ignorance and illusion. Their multiple limbs and ferocious facial expressions indicate their awesome power. This painting was originally part of the personal collection of Okakura Kakuzō (1862-1913), a former curator of Asiatic art at the Museum of Fine Arts, and was given posthumously in his honor.

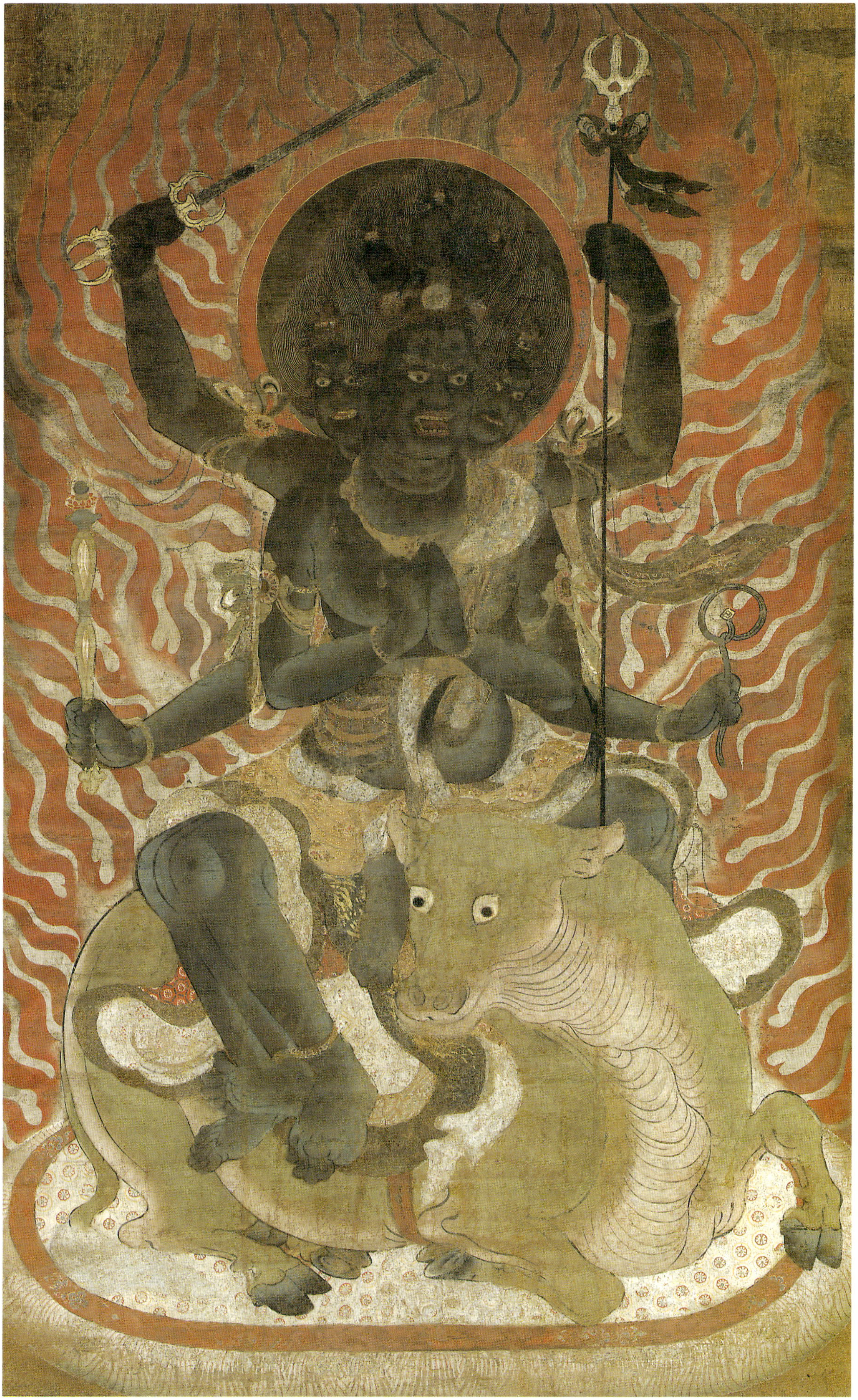

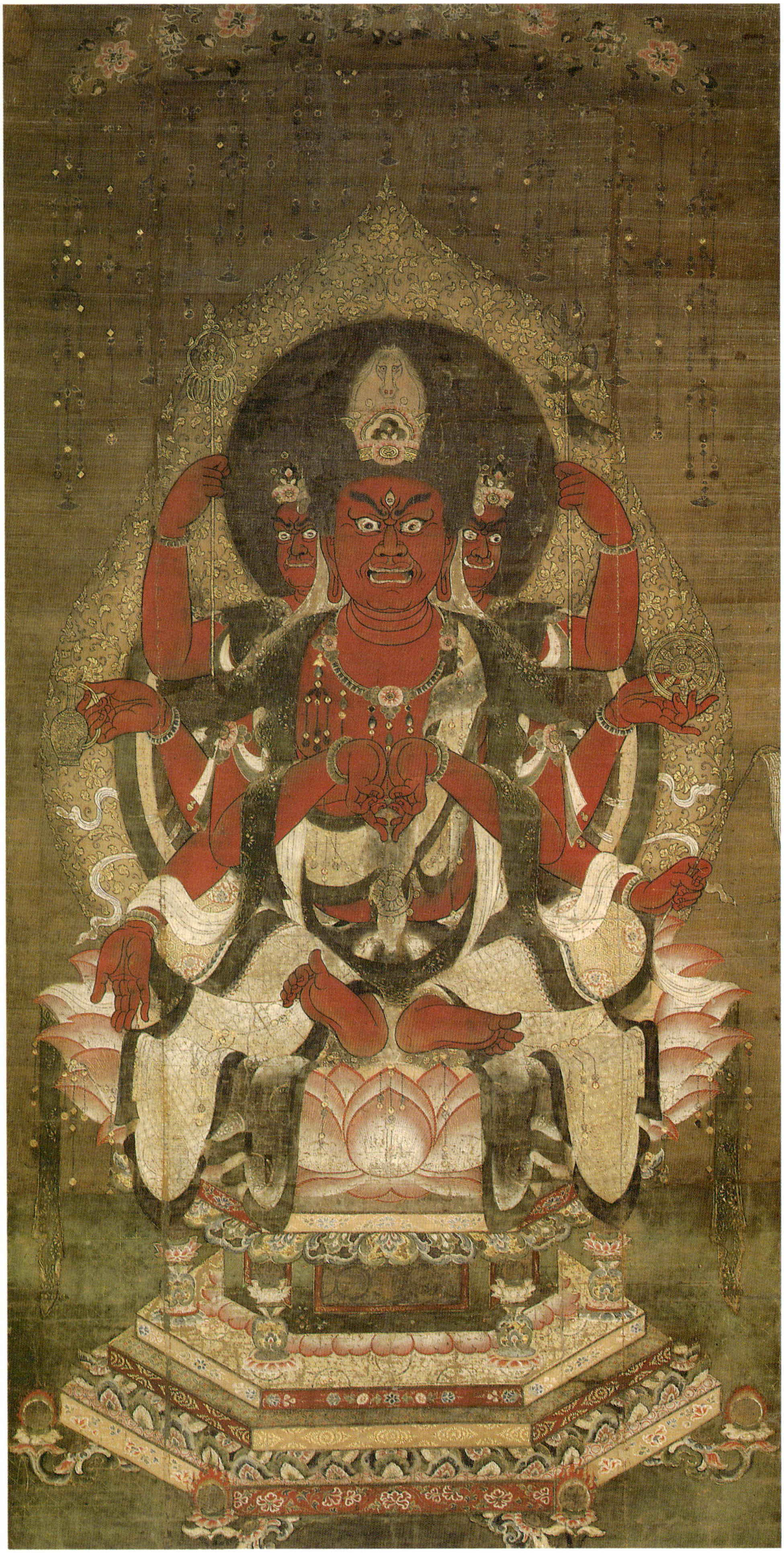

18
Horse-Headed Bodhisattva of Compassion (Batō Kannon)
Late Heian period, mid-12th century
Panel; ink, colors, gold, and silver on silk. 165 x 83 cm.
Fenollosa-Weld Collection. 11.4035

During the Heian period (794-1185), Batō Kannon was worshiped both as one of the myō-ō, *or wisdom kings, and as one of the six forms of Kannon correlating to the six realms of existence into which all sentient beings can be reborn. Popularly revered as a protector of horses, cattle, and warriors, Batō Kannon is identified by the head of a horse in his headdress.*

The red-bodied bodhisattva with eight arms and three heads is clad in lushly patterned garments, fluttering scarves, and rich jewelry. The use of gold and silver leaf to delineate the designs in his clothing and to enhance the implements he holds is typical of the mid-twelfth-century Japanese taste for elegant ornamentation. Holding an ax, a staff, a phoenix-headed jar, a fly whisk, and a çakra (wheel), Kannon folds his lower hands in a symbolic gesture known as the horse-mouth mudrā, *which promises salvation and protection.*

19
Buddha of the Golden Wheel (Ichiji Kinrin Butchō)
Late Heian period, 12th century
Panel; ink, colors, gold, and silver on silk. 125 x 79.5 cm.
Denman Waldo Ross Collection. 09.387

Dainichi Buddha is the primary deity in the pantheon of Esoteric Buddhism. Unlike earlier exoteric sects, the Esoteric branches of Buddhism stress the inherent Buddha nature of all sentient beings and the ability of each individual to achieve enlightenment instantaneously. This painting depicts Dainichi as Ichiji Kinrin Butchō, a manifestation that symbolizes his mystical strength. The name refers to the sources of this strength: Ichiji *is the single Sanskrit syllable* Bhrūm, *through which spiritual potency is verbalized;* Kinrin *is the golden wheel, a symbol of both the Buddhist law and Dainichi's role as a universal monarch;* Butchō *is the protuberance at the top of his head, a symbol of supernal wisdom.*

Dainichi sits serenely on a lotus pedestal, surrounded by a flaming mandorla. The stylized flames in his halo represent mystical emanations, while the five small Buddhas in his headdress indicate wisdom. He holds his hands in the chiken-in, *a ritual gesture symbolizing the wisdom of the Buddha.*

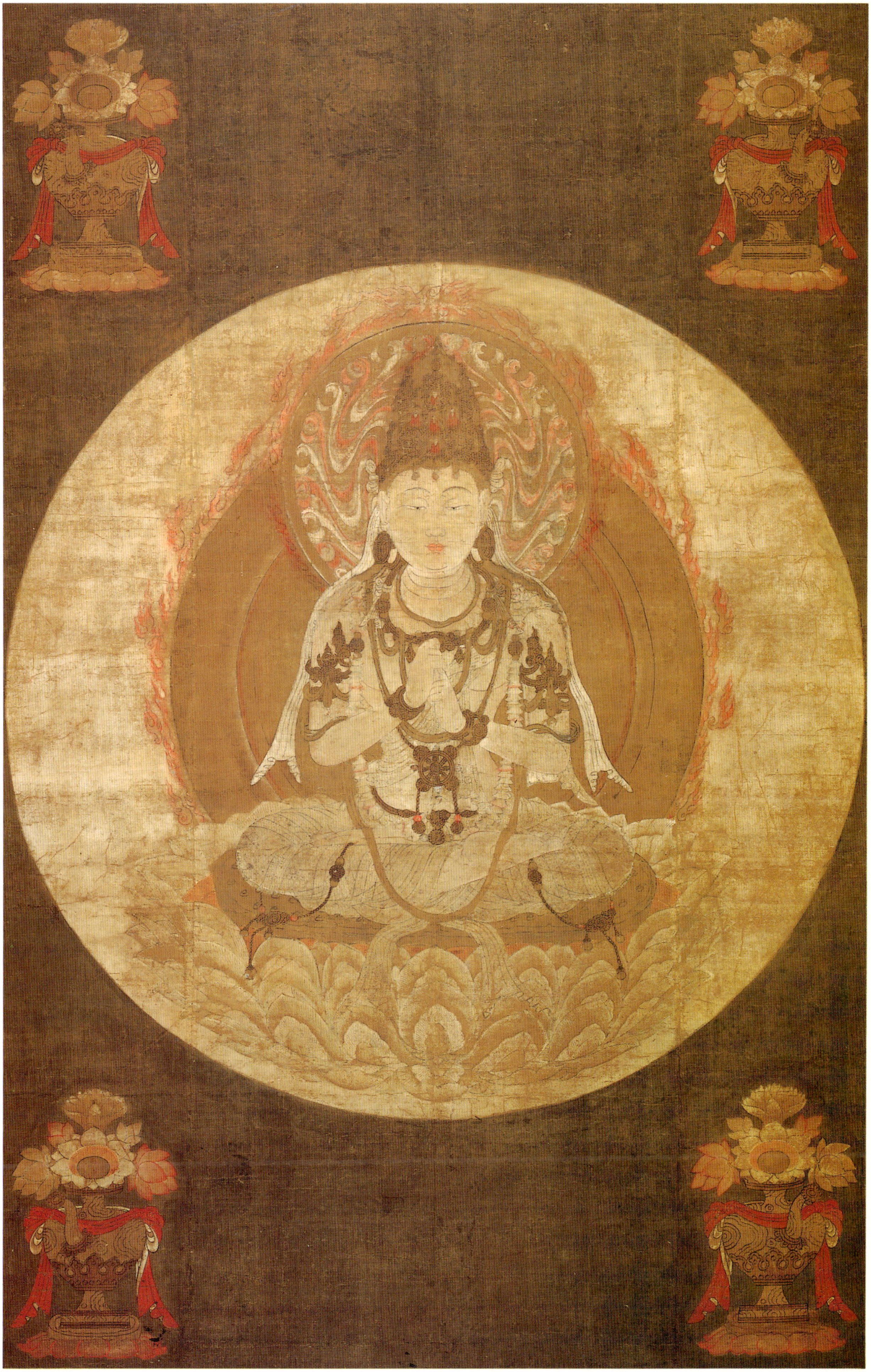

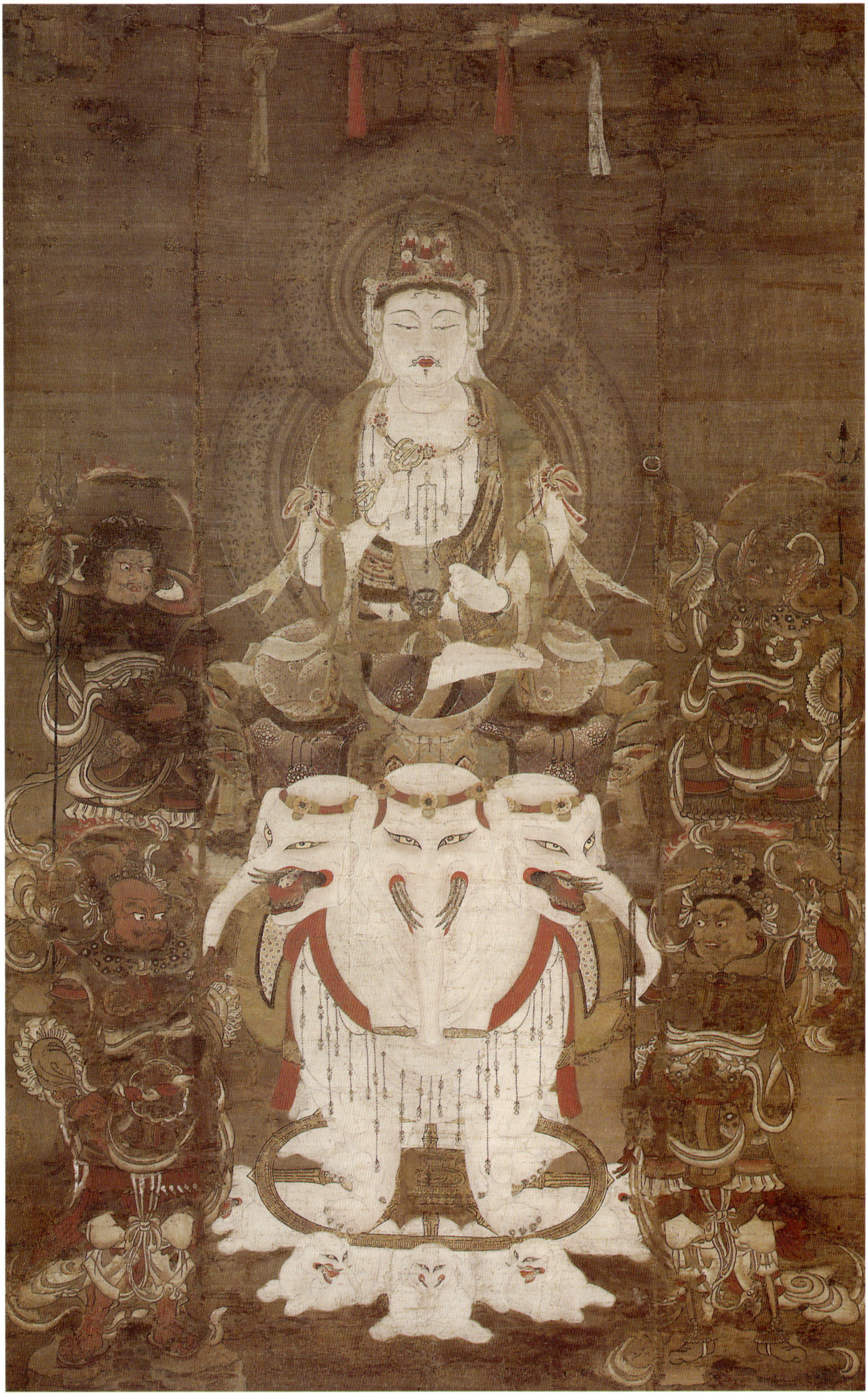

20

Bodhisattva of Universal Virtue who Prolongs Life (Fugen Enmei Bosatsu)

Late Heian period, 12th century
Panel; ink, colors, and gold on silk.
141.7 x 88.3 cm.
Fenollosa-Weld Collection. 11.4036

Seated on the back of an elegant, bejeweled three-headed elephant, Fugen Enmei, the Bodhisattva of Universal Virtue, has images of the five dhyāni, *or wisdom Buddhas, in his crown. His mount stands on a large wheel, supported by eight smaller elephants. The celestial guardians of the four cardinal points who attend him wear armor and bear arms, as befits their protective role.*

Fugen Enmei (or Fugen, the Life Preserving), is worshiped in Esoteric Buddhism for his ability to prolong life. The image of Fugen Enmei riding a six-tusked elephant and accompanied by the four celestial guardians is based on the Fugen Enmei-kyō, *a Buddhist text that describes and explains the main characteristics of the deity and cites the proper rituals for his worship.*

21

Bodhisattva of Compassion with Magic Jewel and Wheel (Nyoirin Kannon)

Late Heian period, 12th century
Panel; ink, colors, gold, and silver on silk. 98.5 x 44.5 cm.
Fenollosa-Weld Collection. 11.4032

Kannon, the Bodhisattva of Compassion, who manifests himself in thirty-three different forms to save the faithful, is the most beloved deity in East Asian Buddhism. In exoteric worship, he is often associated with the cult of Amida and consequently, as in this painting, bears a small image of this Buddha in his headdress. Like Senju Kannon and Batō Kannon, Nyoirin Kannon is one of the six forms of the deity worshiped in Esoteric Buddhism in association with a belief in the six realms of existence. He derives his name from two of the objects he holds in his hands: the nyoirin, *or wheel, and the* nyoi-hōji, *or flaming jewel. The wheel symbolizes the Buddhist law, while the flaming jewel represents the bodhisattva's ability to grant any wish.*

Behind the elegant lotus pedestal on which the six-armed god sits is a craggy mountain with a waterfall representing Mount Potalaka, Kannon's heavenly abode.

Kannon is attended by three figures: Kichijō-ten, goddess of wealth and beauty, who also carries the flaming jewel; the youthful pilgrim Zenzai Doji; and Basu Sennin, a recluse who constructed a hut at the base of Mount Potalaka in order to serve Kannon.

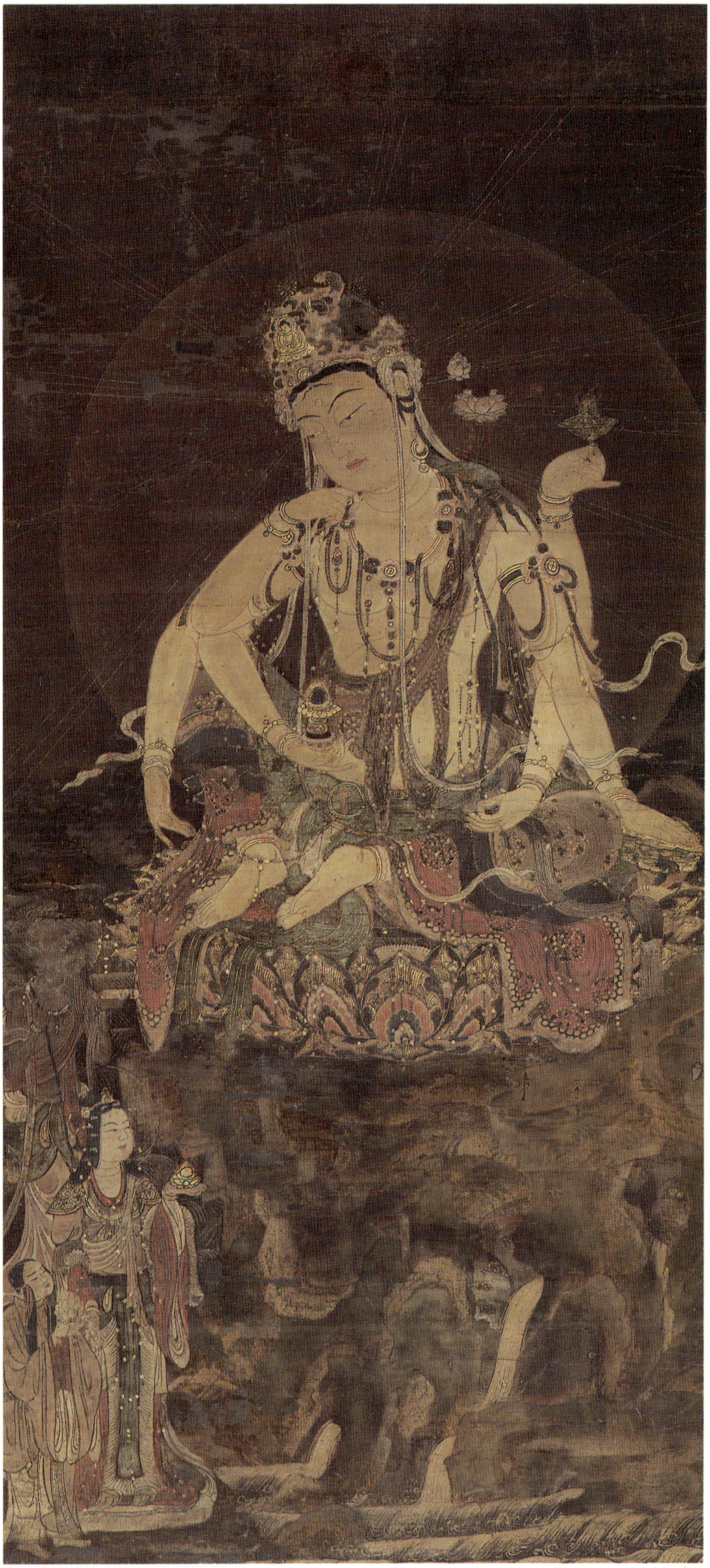

22
Divine Guardian of the North with his Retinue (Tobatsu Bishamon-ten)
Kamakura period, late 12th-early 13th century
Panel; ink, colors, and gold on silk.
119 x 68 cm.
Chinese and Japanese Special Fund.
05.202

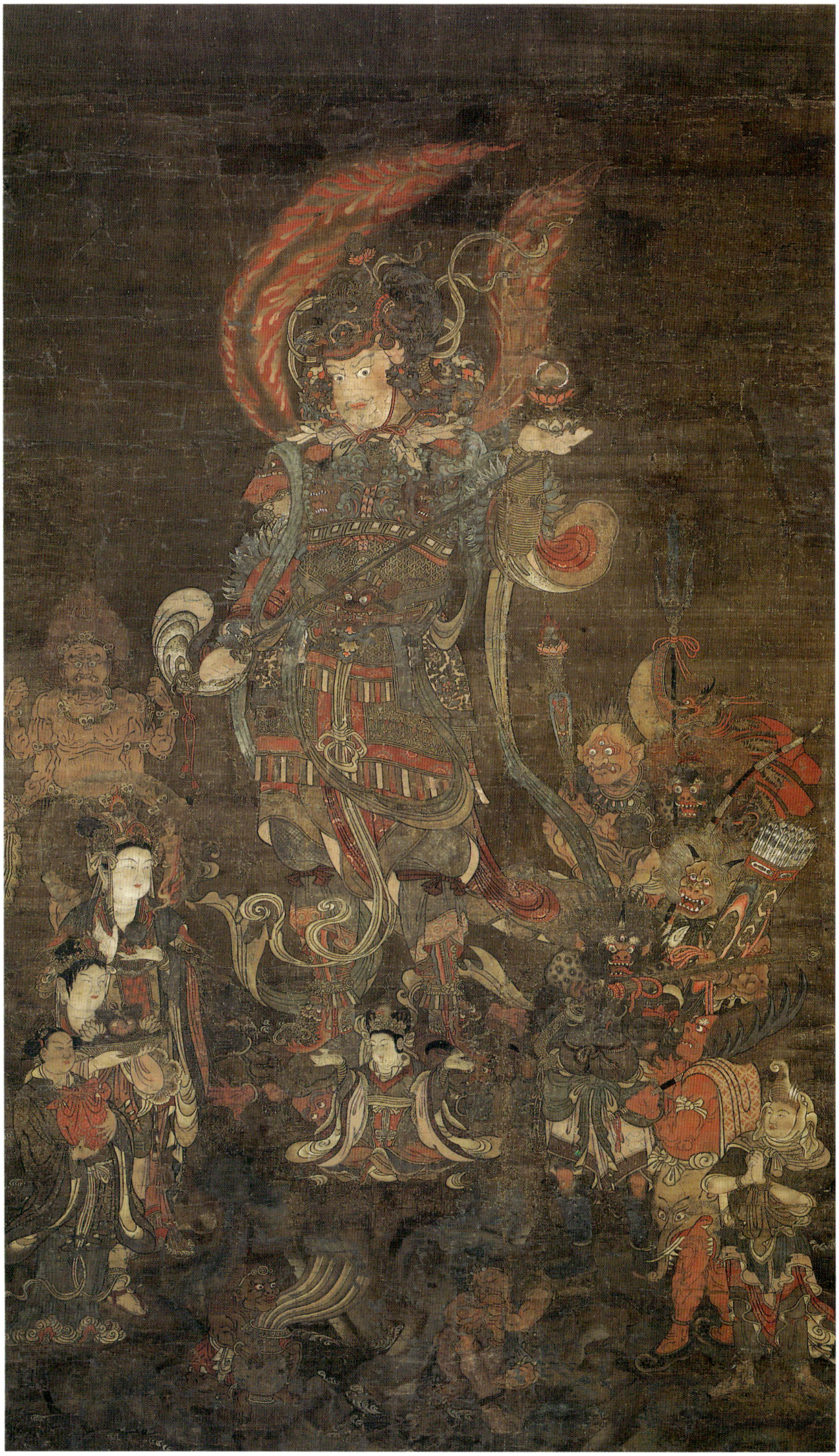

Possibly as a result of his association with the north, the traditional focus of malevolent forces in Chinese thought, Bishamon-ten is the only one of the four celestial guardians of the cardinal points who is worshiped as an independent deity. He is revered for the ability to protect his followers from illness and physical danger and to free them from fear. When Bishamon-ten is depicted individually, he is often held aloft by the earth goddess Ji-ten and is classified as Tobatsu Bishamon-ten. The term tobatsu *is believed to refer to areas of Turfan or Khotan, cities involved in the transmission of Buddhism from India to the nations of the Far East. Historical records indicate that Tobatsu Bishamon-ten was worshiped in China by the eighth century and in Japan by the ninth century.*

The painting is characterized by an abundance of detail and a lively treatment of inanimate decoration, such as the demonic faces embellishing Bishamon-ten's armor. These features and the intensity of the yakṣas' *faces probably derive from a style of Buddhist painting popular in Shanxi Province in northern China; it traveled to Japan during the late twelfth and early thirteenth centuries.*

23

Attributed to Chōmyō
(active 13th century)

Divine Guardian of the West
(Kōmoku-ten)

Kamakura period, mid-thirteenth century
Panel; ink, colors, and gold on silk.
148.3 x 72.9 cm.
Fenollosa-Weld Collection. 11.4064

Standing on the back of a squirming dwarf on a rock in the ocean, Kōmoku-ten, the celestial guardian of the western quadrant, is identified by the sheet of paper he holds in his hand. His threatening pose, glaring eyes, and bristly beard describe his role as a protective deity.

This painting is one of a set of four in the Museum of Fine Arts depicting the Shitennō, celestial guardians of the four cardinal points. Recent Japanese scholarship indicates that the four paintings may once have decorated the interior of the Shingon-dō of the now-destroyed Eikyū-ji, a subsidiary temple of Kōfuku-ji in Nara. Historical records state that in September of 1253 Chōmyō, a student of the early Kamakura painter Sonchi, was commissioned to paint sets of both the Shitennō and the Twelve Divine Generals for Eikyū-ji. The Boston Museum's Shitennō are stylistically comparable to the few known works by the elusive Chōmyō, and it is possible that this group of paintings once belonged to Eikyū-ji.

Although neither the attribution to Chōmyō nor the 1253 date for the present painting can be confirmed with certainty, Kōmoku-ten's theatrical pose and exaggerated facial features, the sense of alertness in the figure, and the concern for movement to be found in the billowing waves and swirling ribbons date the work securely to the mid-thirteenth century.

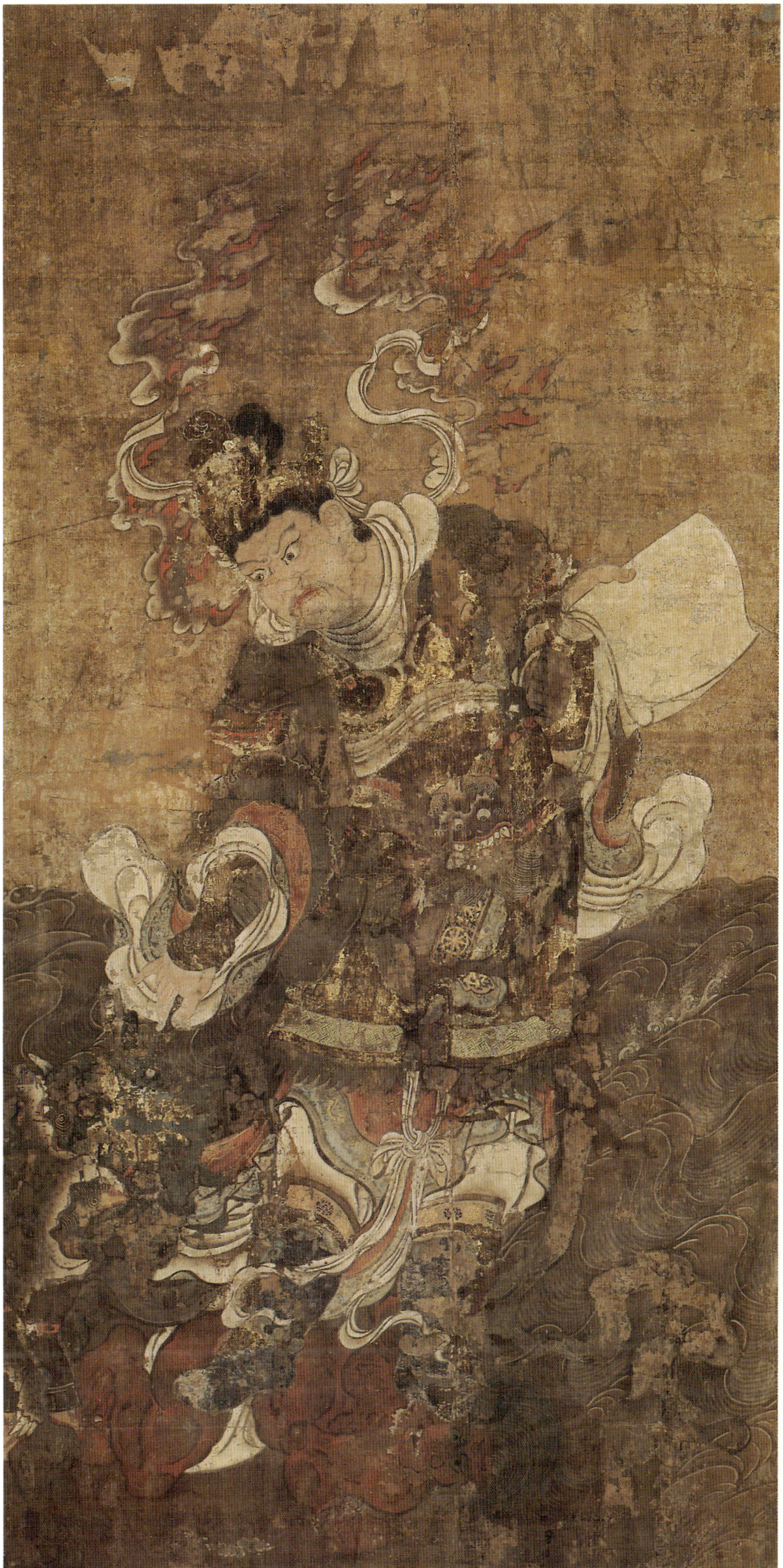

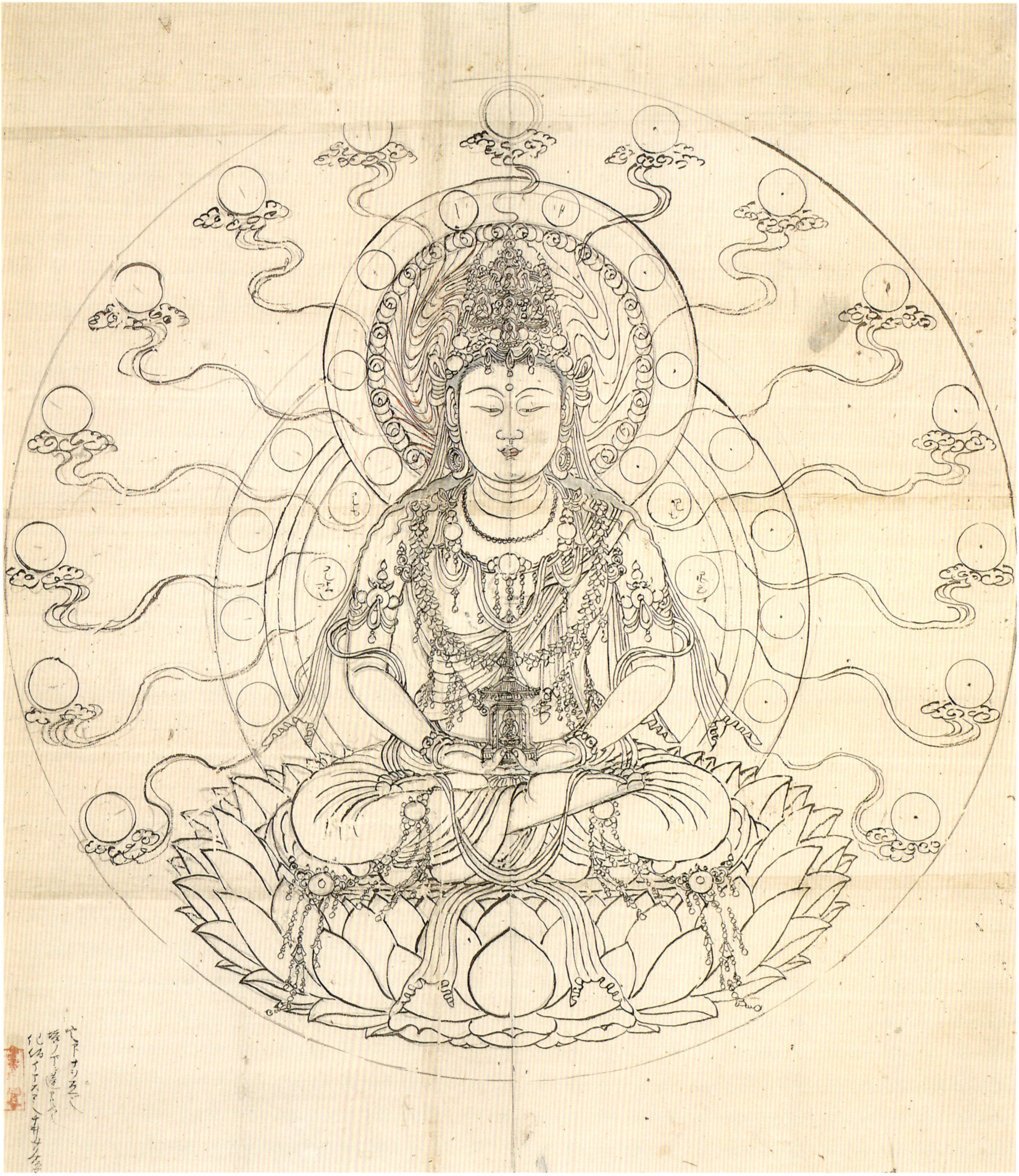

24
Bodhisattva of the Future (Miroku Bosatsu)
Kamakura period, 13th century
Panel; ink and colors on paper.
102.7 x 75.2 cm.
William Sturgis Bigelow Collection.
11.6237

This work, once in the possession of the Kōzan-ji, a temple outside of the city of Kyoto, depicts the bodhisattva Miroku (Sanskrit: Maitreya) who is destined to become the Buddha of the Future and succeed the historic Buddha, Śākyamuni. It is done in the hakubyō *technique, using fine ink lines without color. Miroku has his hands joined in front, palms upwards on his lap, and holds a miniature pagoda with a small representation of Dainichi Nyorai (Sanskrit: Mahahvairocana) inside. A jeweled crown that includes representations of the Five Buddhas adorns the deity's head and his lavishly decorated body is seated on a lotus pedestal. Small clouds, each with a disk (a symbol of enlightenment), appear around the figure while the whole is surrounded by a moon-disk. The inscription in the bottom left-hand corner reads: "The arrangement of the hands and pagoda to be corrected; there should be a lotus beneath the pagoda..." This indicates that there was a request for emendations after the picture was completed, and suggests that the work was a preliminary sketch for a full-color painting.*

25
Kasuga Maṇḍala
Kamakura period, 14th century
Panel; ink, colors, and gold on silk.
145.8 x 90.5 cm.
William Sturgis Bigelow Collection.
11.6261

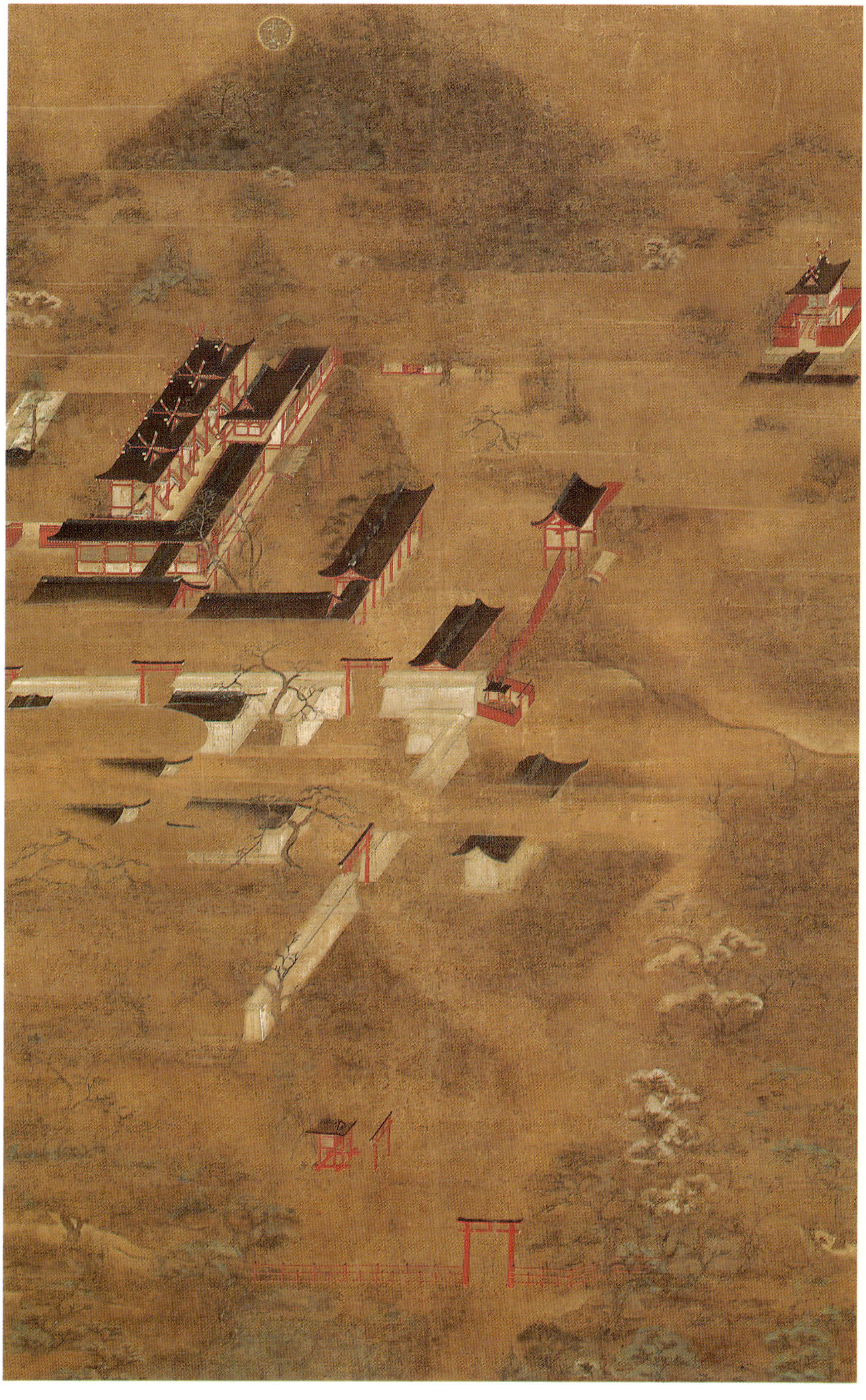

This is an example of a subject that has its genesis in the belief that Buddhism and Shintoism are alternate manifestations of a single religious system. In this belief, it was considered that Buddhas and bodhisattvas manifested themselves under the guise of various native deities. Maṇḍala are schematic pictorial icons with depictions of deities and are the most common objects of worship in Esoteric Buddhist sects. However, the term as used here has lost most of the symbolic and mystic connotations of the original Buddhist term. Three types of Kasuga maṇḍala are known: Kasuga Shrine Maṇḍala, Kasuga Divinity Maṇḍala and Kasuga Deer Maṇḍala. This work belongs to the first category; since its subject is the Kasuga shrine as such, neither the Shinto deity enshrined there nor his Buddhist counterpart is depicted, nor are the deer that are believed to be the messenger of the Kasuga deity. Mt. Mikasa, which lies behind the shrine, and the moon are shown in the upper part of the composition. Below, on the left, are the main buildings of the shrine with the Wakamiya subshrine on the right. The whole shrine complex is seen from a bird's-eye perspective. In Kasuga shrine mandalas of this type, the ichi-no-torii *(the first Shinto gateway on the approach to the shrine) and two pagodas are normally shown at the bottom of the picture. However, this work shows only the scene beyond the second gateway. Much of the deep green paint of the original has flaked off, but initially the appearance must have been far more beautiful, with the shrine surrounded in foliage and the cherry trees in full bloom.*

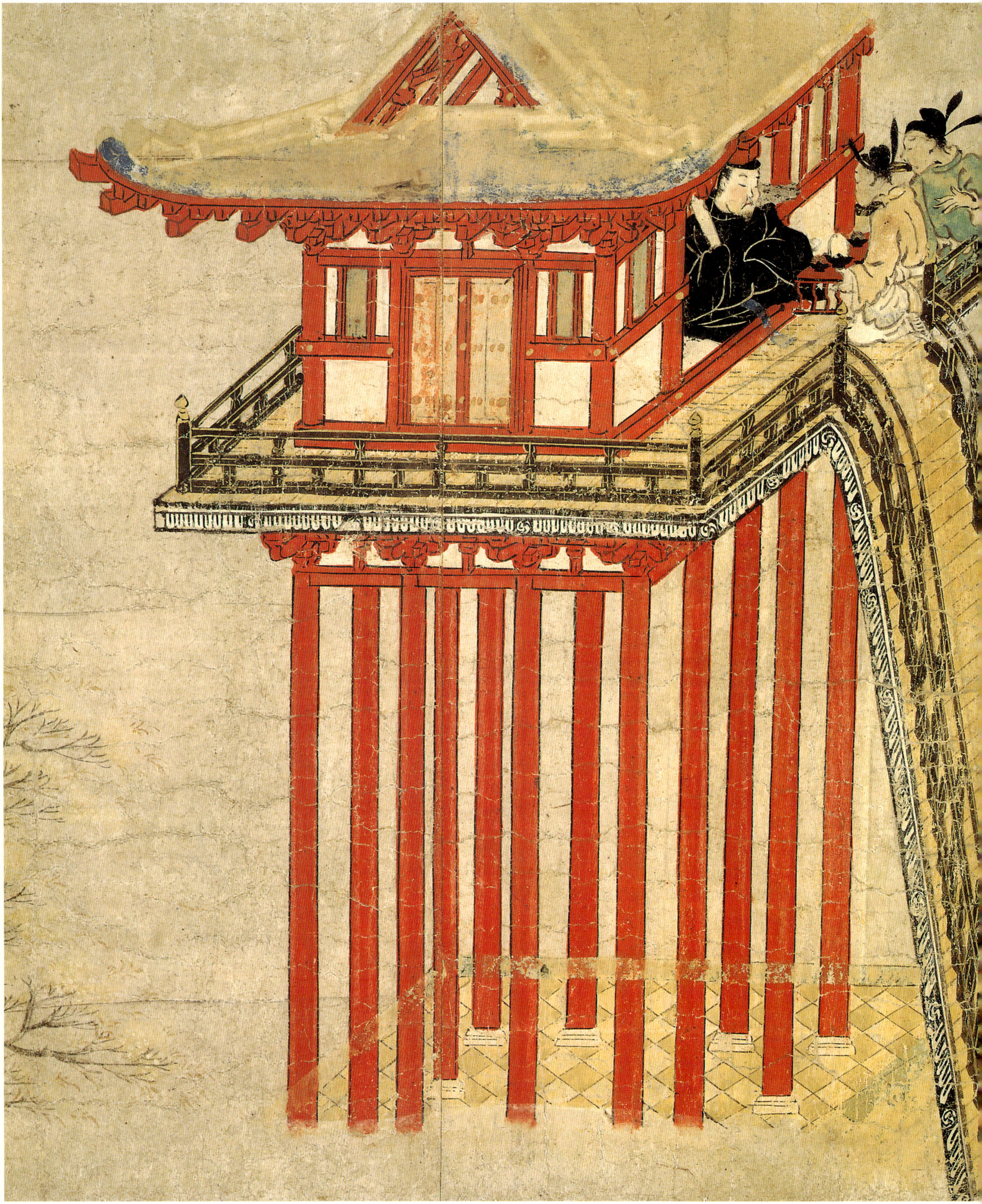

26
***Illustrated Handscroll of Minister Kibi's Trip to China* (Kibi daijin nittō emaki)**

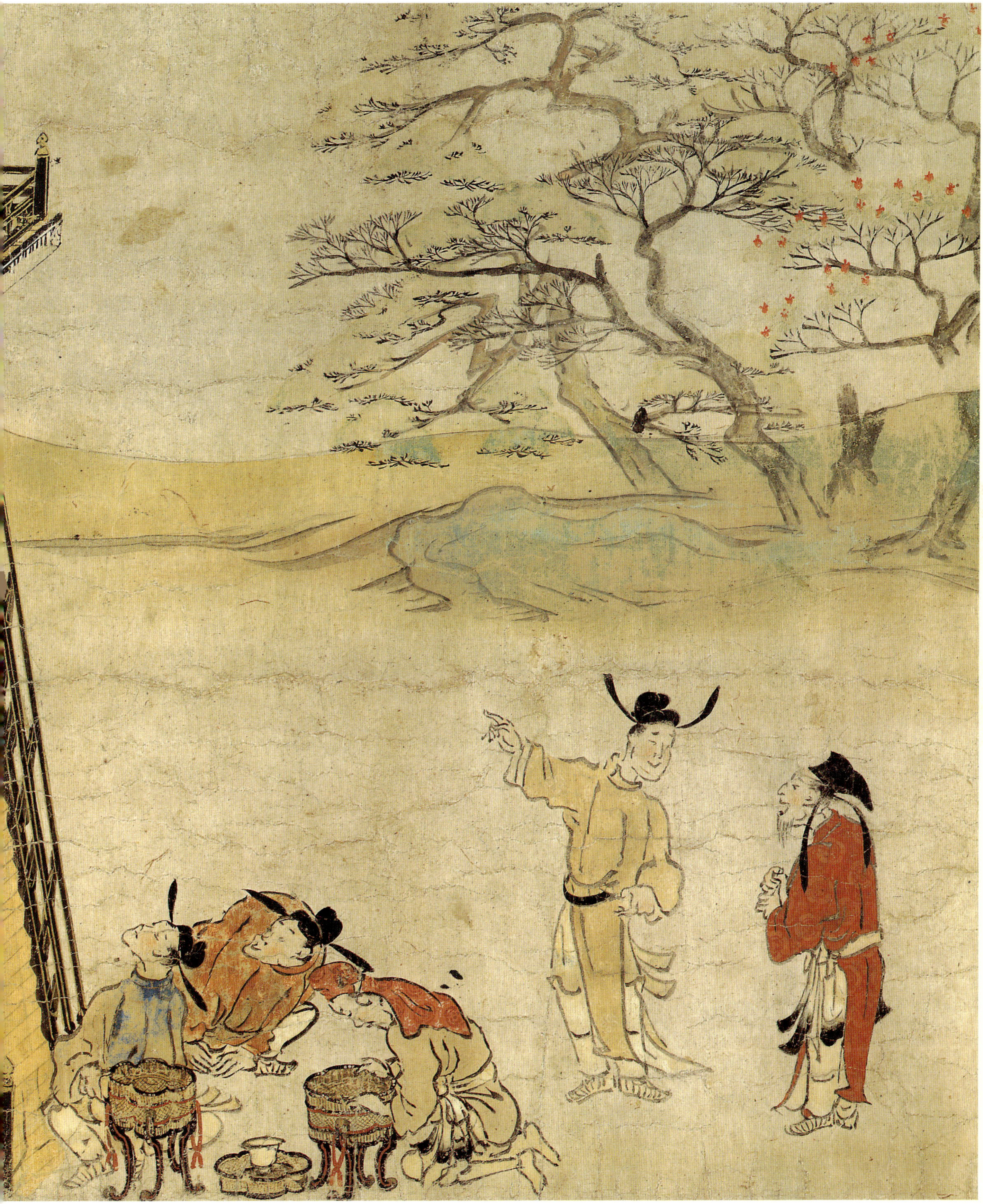

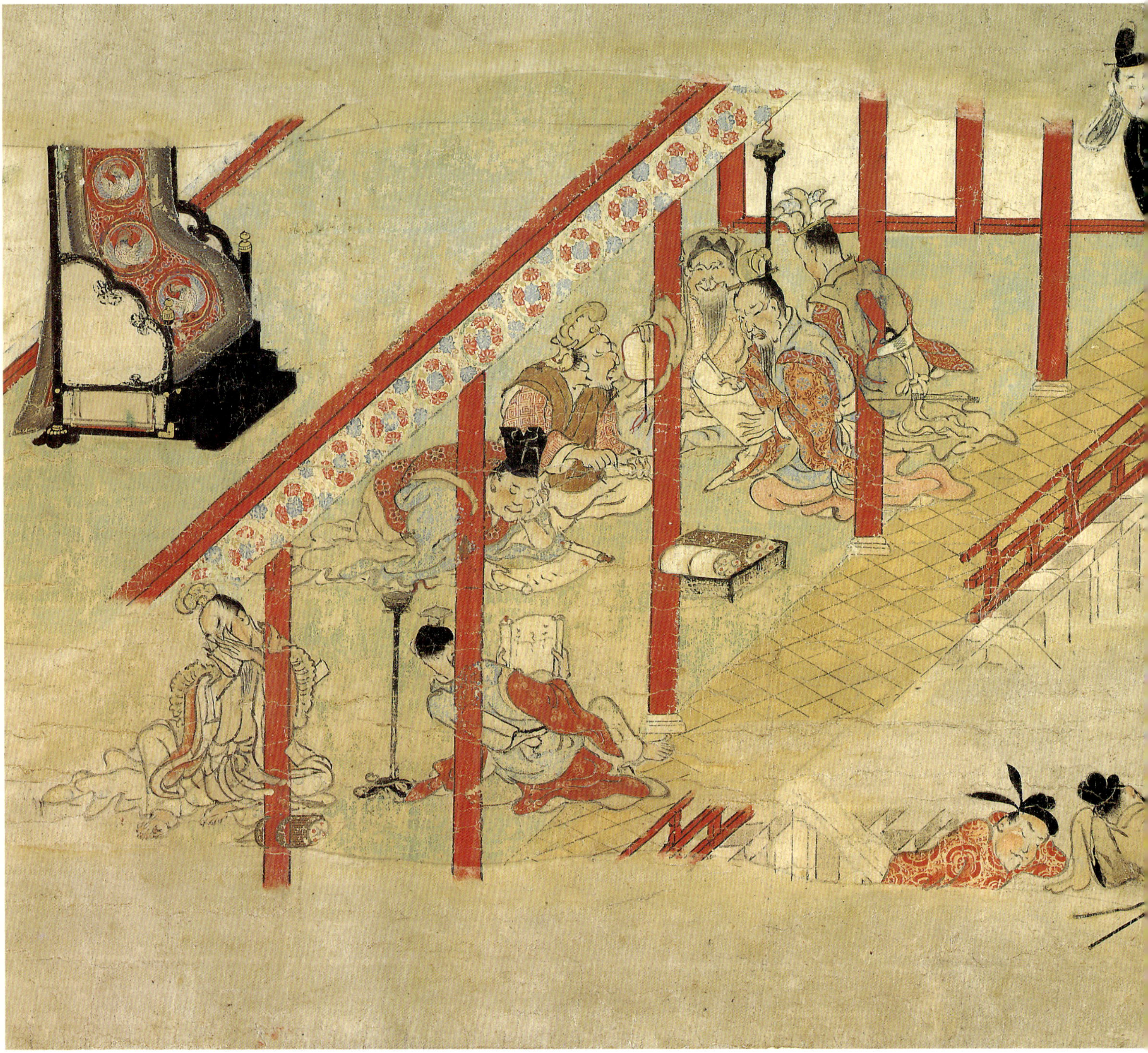

26
Illustrated Handscroll of Minister Kibi's Trip to China
(Kibi daijin nittō emaki)
Heian period, 12th century
Set of four handscrolls; ink and colors on paper.
William Sturgis Bigelow Collection by Exchange. 32.131

This famous handscroll illustrates the legendary adventures of Kibi no Makibi, the Japanese ambassador to the Chinese court, during his mission to Tang China in 753. Aided by the lively ghost of the celebrated poet Abe no Nakamaro, the resourceful Kibi successfully passes a series of tests of skill and learning to which he is subjected by his Chinese hosts. The purely fictional story — Abe no Nakamaro was still alive at the time of Kibi's mission — seems to be of the engi type, in which the origins and traditions of a historical institution or historical line are related. From the incidents depicted in this scroll, the descendants of Kibi no Makibi drew support for their claim to supremacy over the descendants of Abe no Nakamaro in the field of inyōdō, *a generic term for various magical and pseudo-scientific practices of Chinese origin. During the Heian period (794-1185), both the Abe and Kibi families competed for dominance in this arcane but influential specialty.*

Executed in bright pigments, with animated figures and a droll sense of humorous circumstance, this work is among the premier examples of early Japanese narrative scroll painting outside of Japan. Its departure from its homeland in 1932 resulted in the first Japanese legislation making the export of important art objects subject to government review and approval. Because of its great length, the scroll was divided into four sections in 1964 to facilitate handling and ensure its preservation.

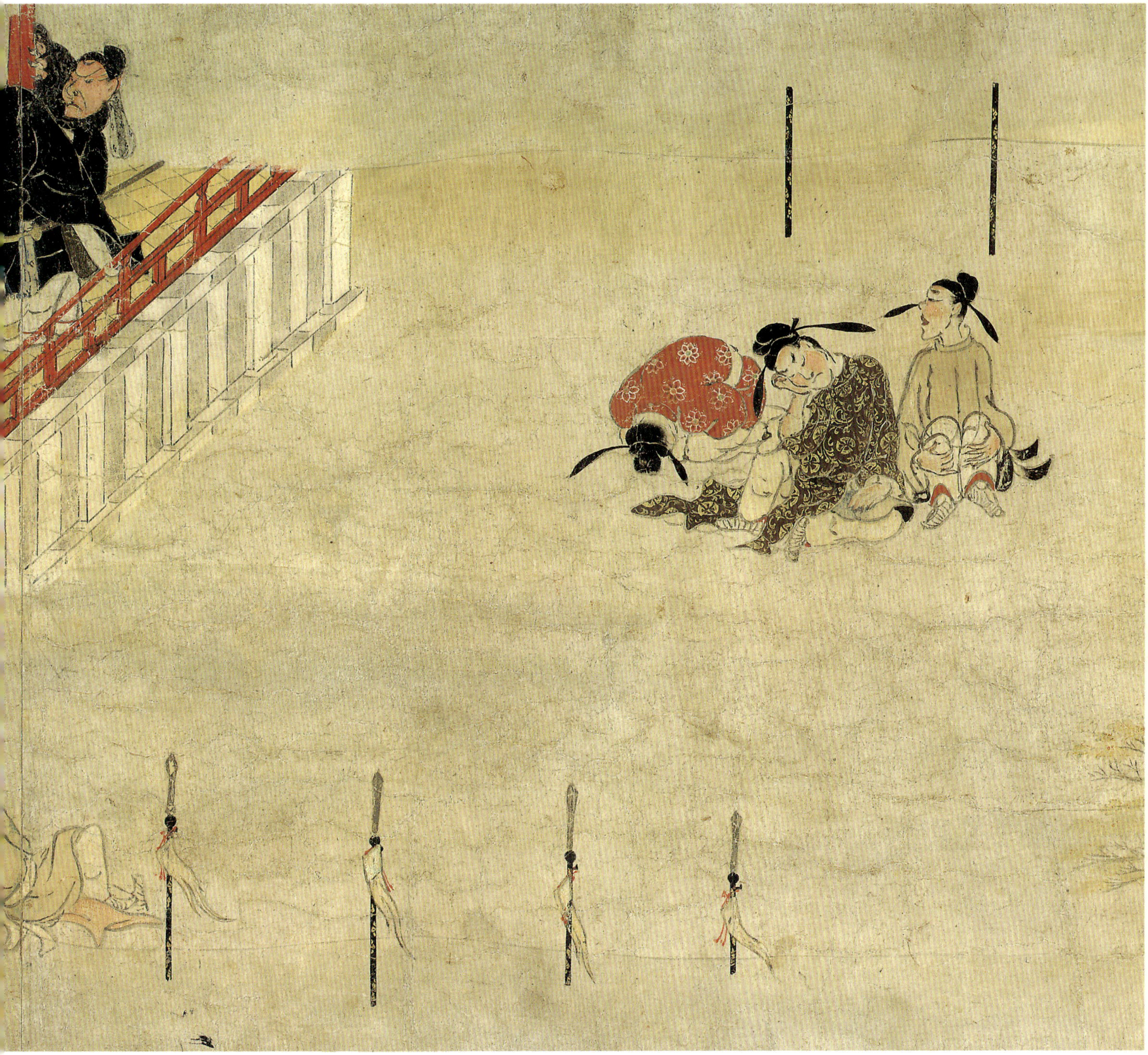

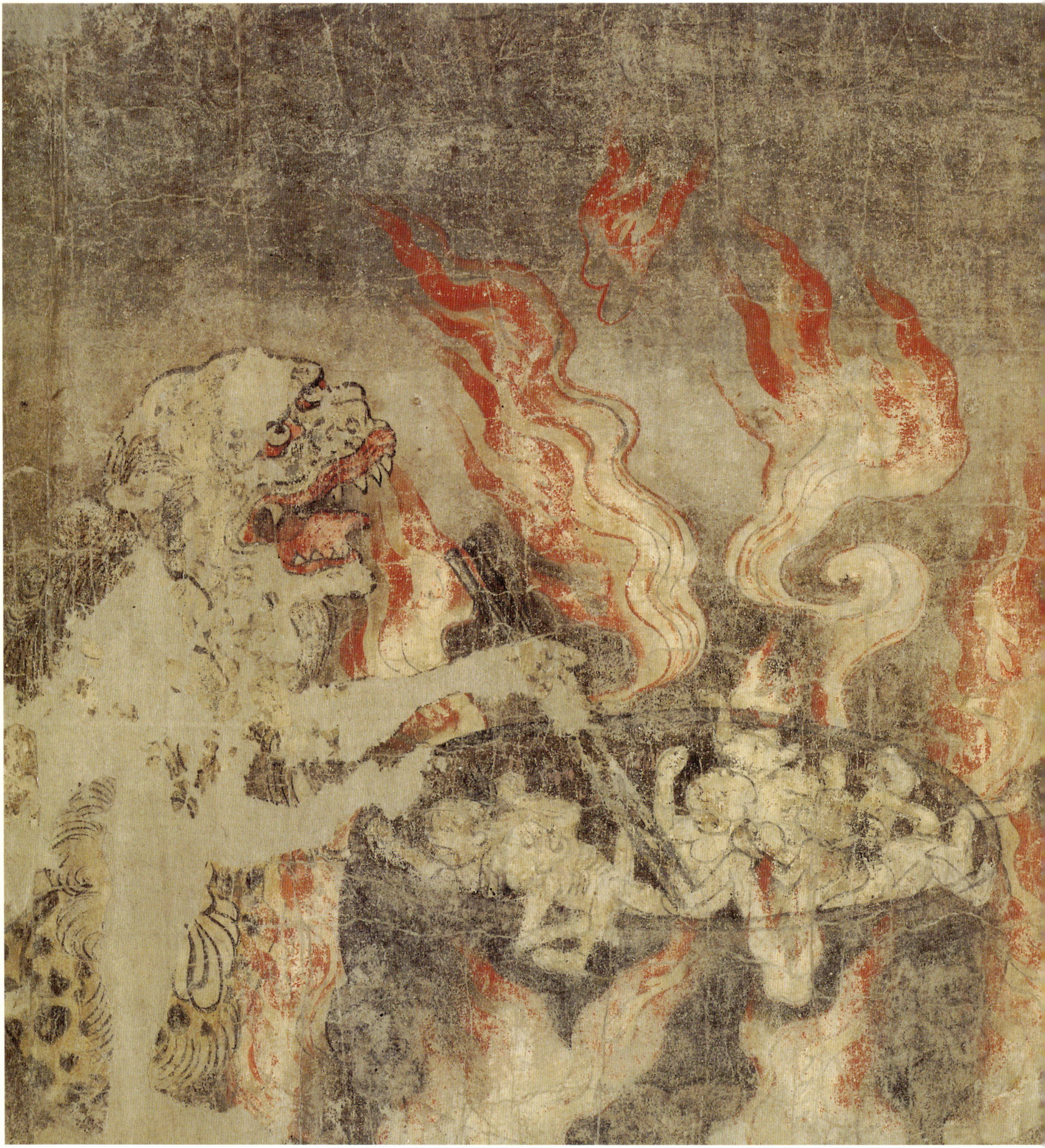

27
The Copper Cauldron Hell
(Jigoku zōshi)
Heian period, 12th century
Handscroll; ink and colors on paper.
25.6 x 51.9 cm.
William Sturgis Bigelow Collection.
11.6254

Buddhist scriptures such as the Shosei-kyō *and the* Shōbō Nenjo-kyō *give detailed accounts of the Buddhist hells. There are eight main hells, each of which is subdivided into sixteen minor hells. The scene shown here is one of the latter, the hell known as "the place of the copper cauldron." This is the hell into which people who have caused suffering to animals or to other people in their lifetime are said to fall, there to boil for their sins in a large copper cauldron. The painting makes effective use of strong color contrasts to suggest the terrors of hell — the murky darkness in black and the searing flames in red. The*

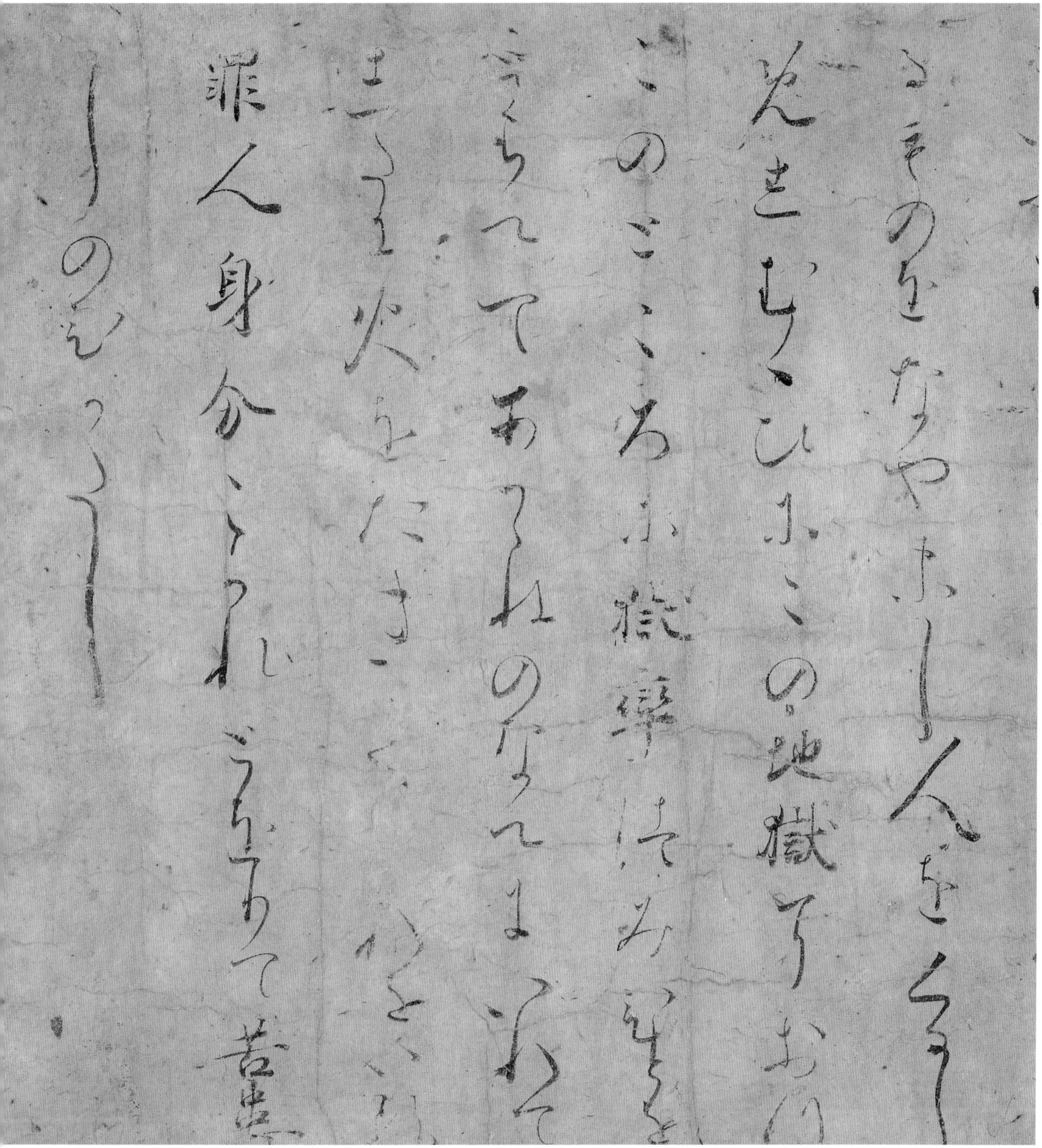

horror of the scene is compounded by the threatening mien of the demon who supervises the torture with his wierd, monster-like appearance. The damned in the cauldron, their limbs outstretched, cry out for mercy, but their voices are swallowed up in the dark and burned out by the flames.

The subject epitomizes the attitude of aversion to earthly existence and the hope for salvation in the Pure Land Paradise of the Buddha Amitābha that was widespread in medieval times. The Nara National Museum in Japan has in its possession a Hell scroll that is stylistically consistent with this fragment.

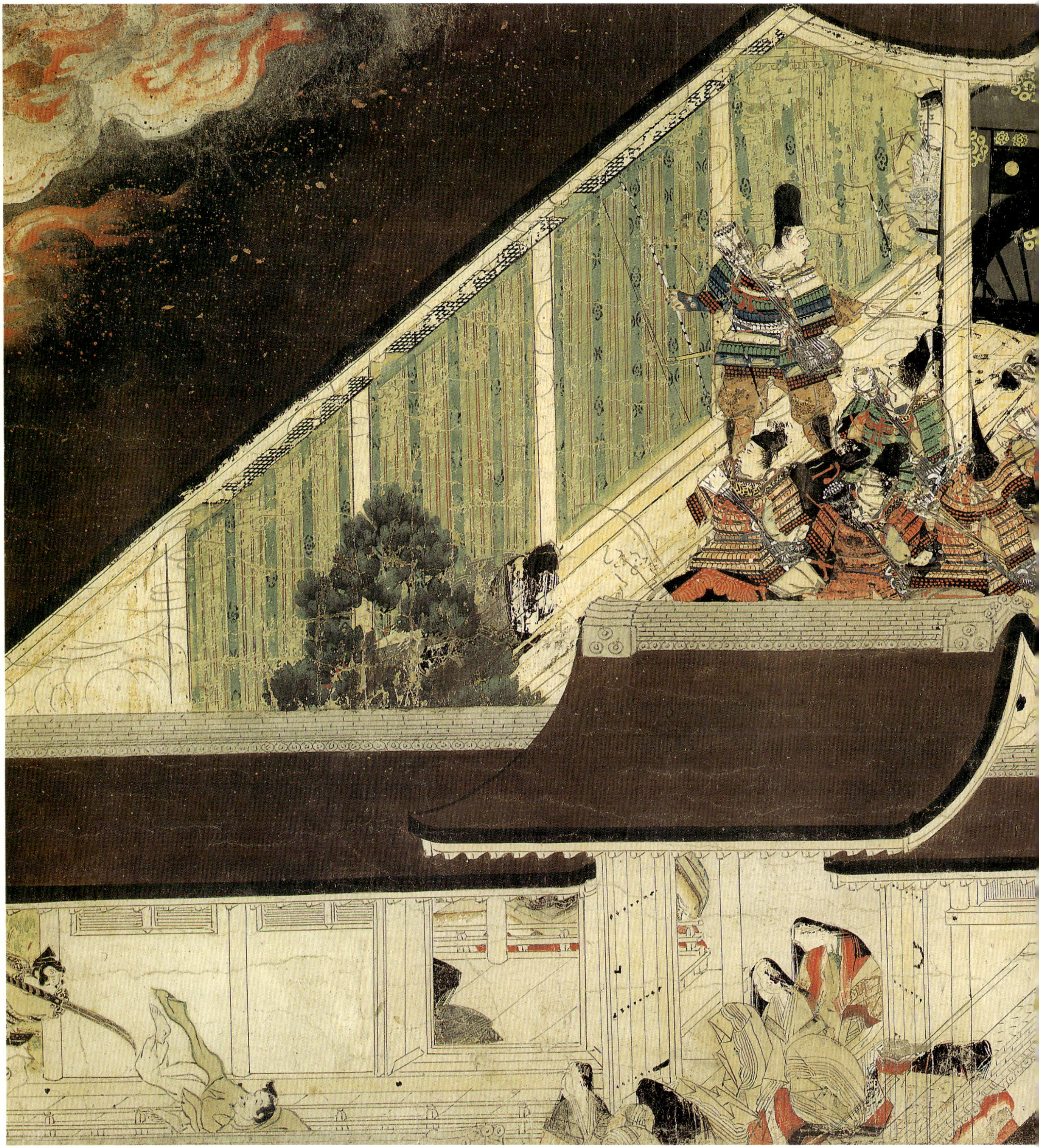

28
Night Attack on the Sanjō Palace, from the Illustrated Scrolls of the Events of the Heiji Period **(Heiji monogatari emaki)**

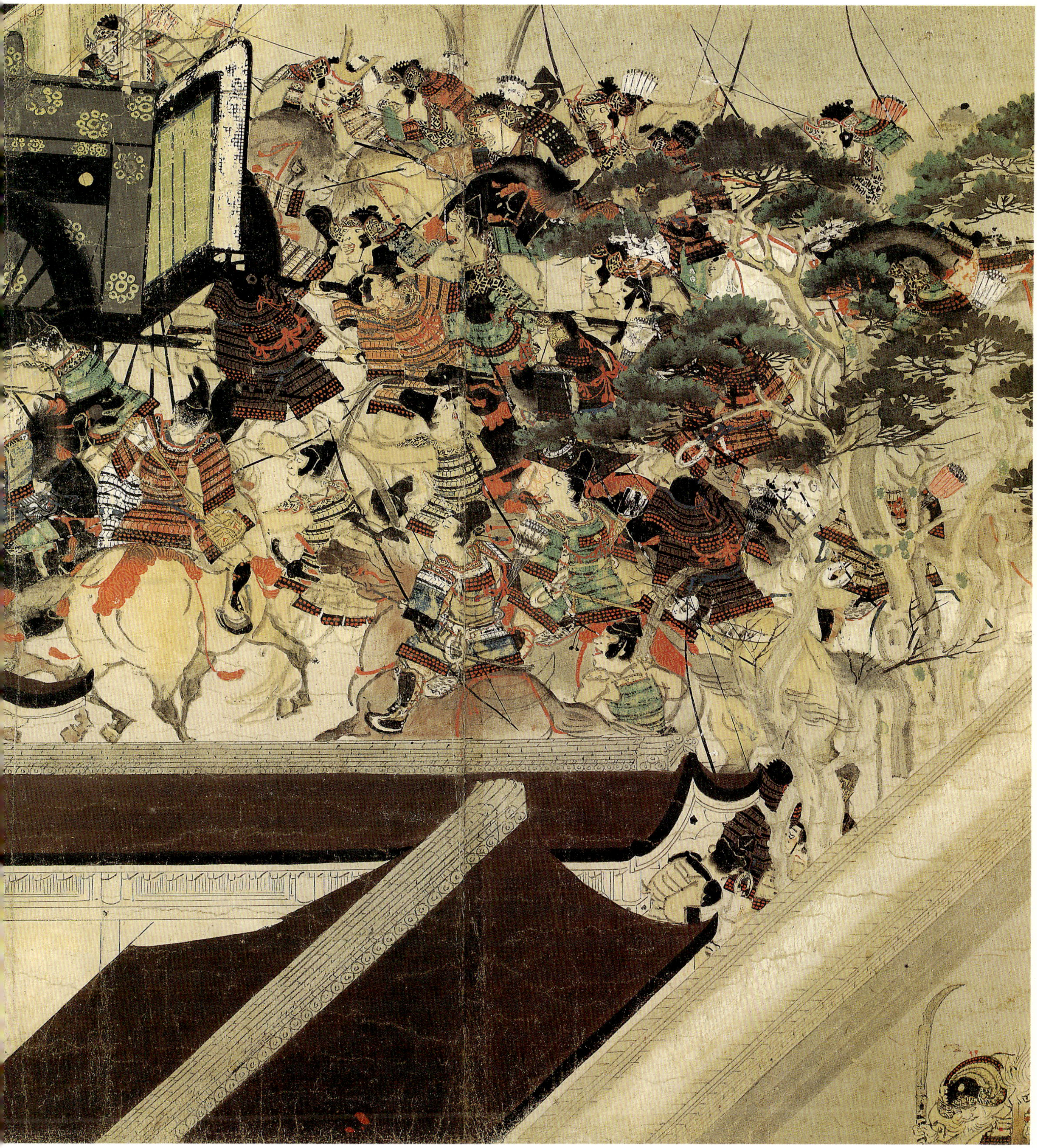

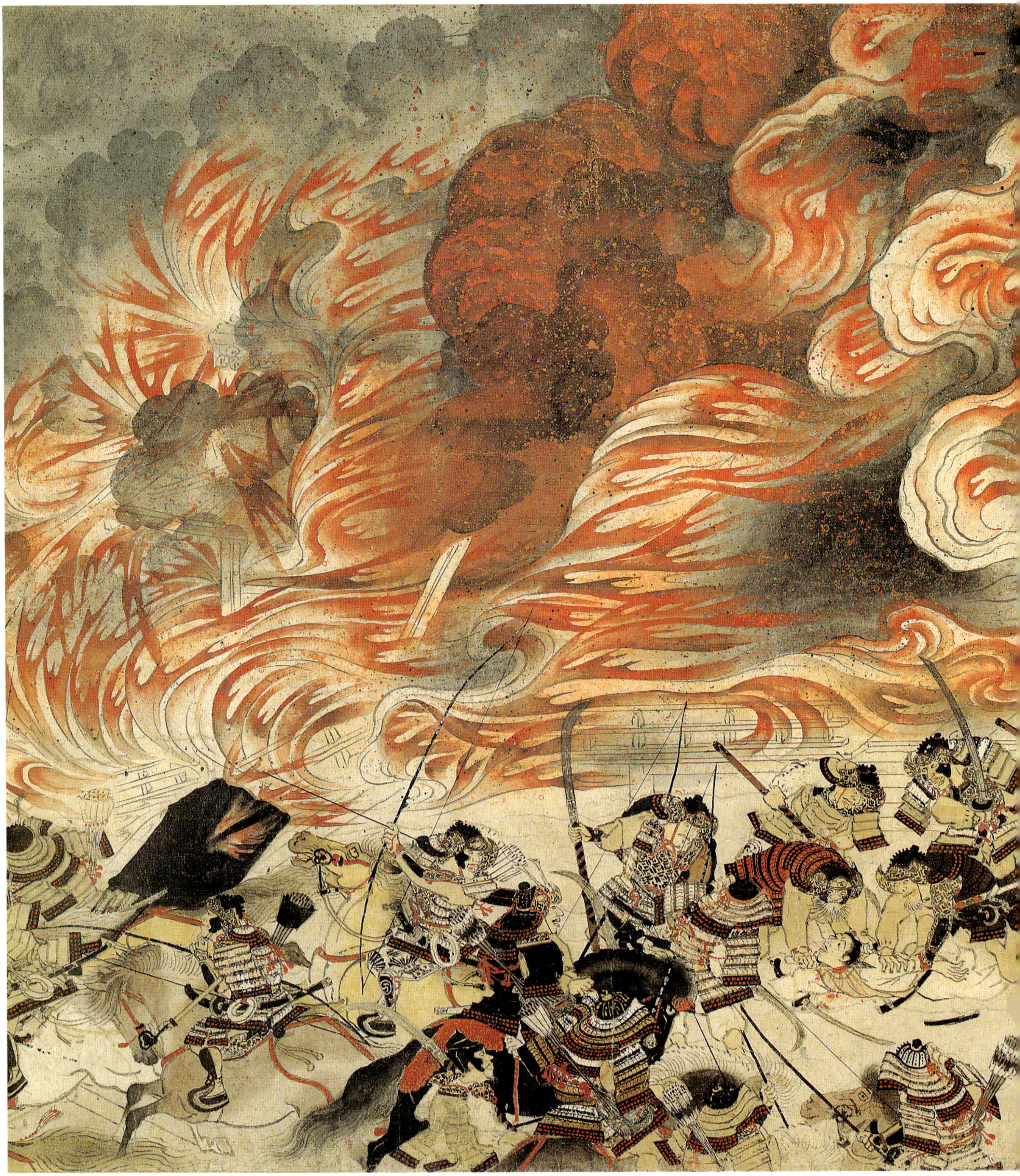

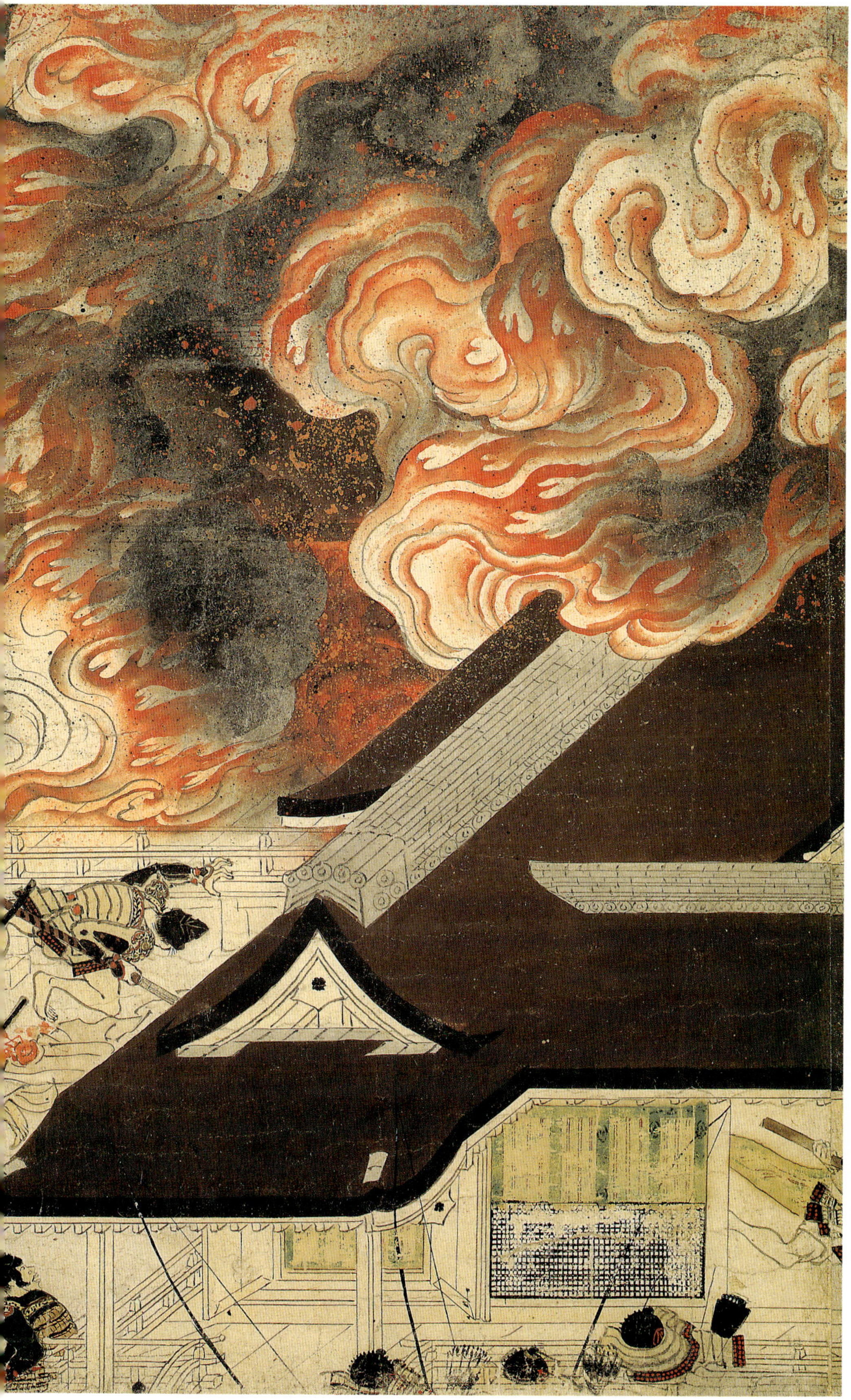

28

***Night Attack on the Sanjō Palace, from the Illustrated Scrolls of the Events of the Heiji Period* (Heiji monogatari emaki)**

Kamakura period, second half of 13th century

Handscroll; ink and colors on paper. 41.3 x 699.7 cm.

Fenollosa-Weld Collection. 11.4000

The bloody wars between the Taira and Minamoto clans during the latter half of the twelfth century served as a perennial source of inspiration for narrative reciters and artists in subsequent centuries. The earliest extant examples of pictorial narratives that relate these events are three scrolls and some isolated fragments known as the Heiji monogatari emaki, *all that is preserved of a work that consisted originally of an extensive number of handscrolls. It is presumed that several artists were involved in the production of these paintings, but none of their names is known.*

The Museum's scroll is the first in the series and the finest example still in existence. Illustrated in it is an incident of 1159 in which the combined forces of Fujiwara Nobuyori and Minamoto Yoshitomo attacked the Sanjō Palace and abducted the influential retired emperor Go-Shirakawa. The painting is an outstanding example of an artistic specialty for which Japanese narrative scroll painters were justly renowned: the skillful depiction of large crowds of people. While the artist gave each figure its own individuality, he also conveyed the nervous tension of the encounters by imbuing with an organic, vital unity the masses of citizens who move to verify the news of the impending attack and the throng of warriors who regroup afterward around the imperial carriage transporting Go-Shirakawa. Between the two crowds of figures lies the palace in flames, while the scene dissolves into scattered hand-to-hand encounters, full of the fierce brutality that characterized these civil wars. Preserved in the collection of the Honda family during the Edo period, the scroll was acquired in Japan by Ernest Fenollosa around 1884 and brought to the Museum of Fine Arts five years later.

29
Bodhidharma Crossing the Yangtze
Kamakura period, 14th century
Hanging scroll; ink, colors, and gold on silk. 68.8 x 40.8 cm.
William Sturgis Bigelow Collection. 11.6312

Apocryphal legend has it that Bodhidharma, founder of the Chan (Jap.: Zen) sect of Buddhism, engaged the Chinese Emperor Wu Di of the Liang Dynasty (618-906) in cryptic Zen discourse, but realizing that his efforts to convert the emperor were fruitless, he miraculously crossed the broad Yangtze river on a reed and traveled on to the North. This picture was inspired by this legend. The expressive brushstrokes used to portray the waves and their curling crests enliven the composition and reinforce the sense of Bodhidharma's movement across the water. This work by an anonymous painter of the early fourteenth century is one of the many depictions of Bodhidharma inspired by Zen Buddhist traditions.

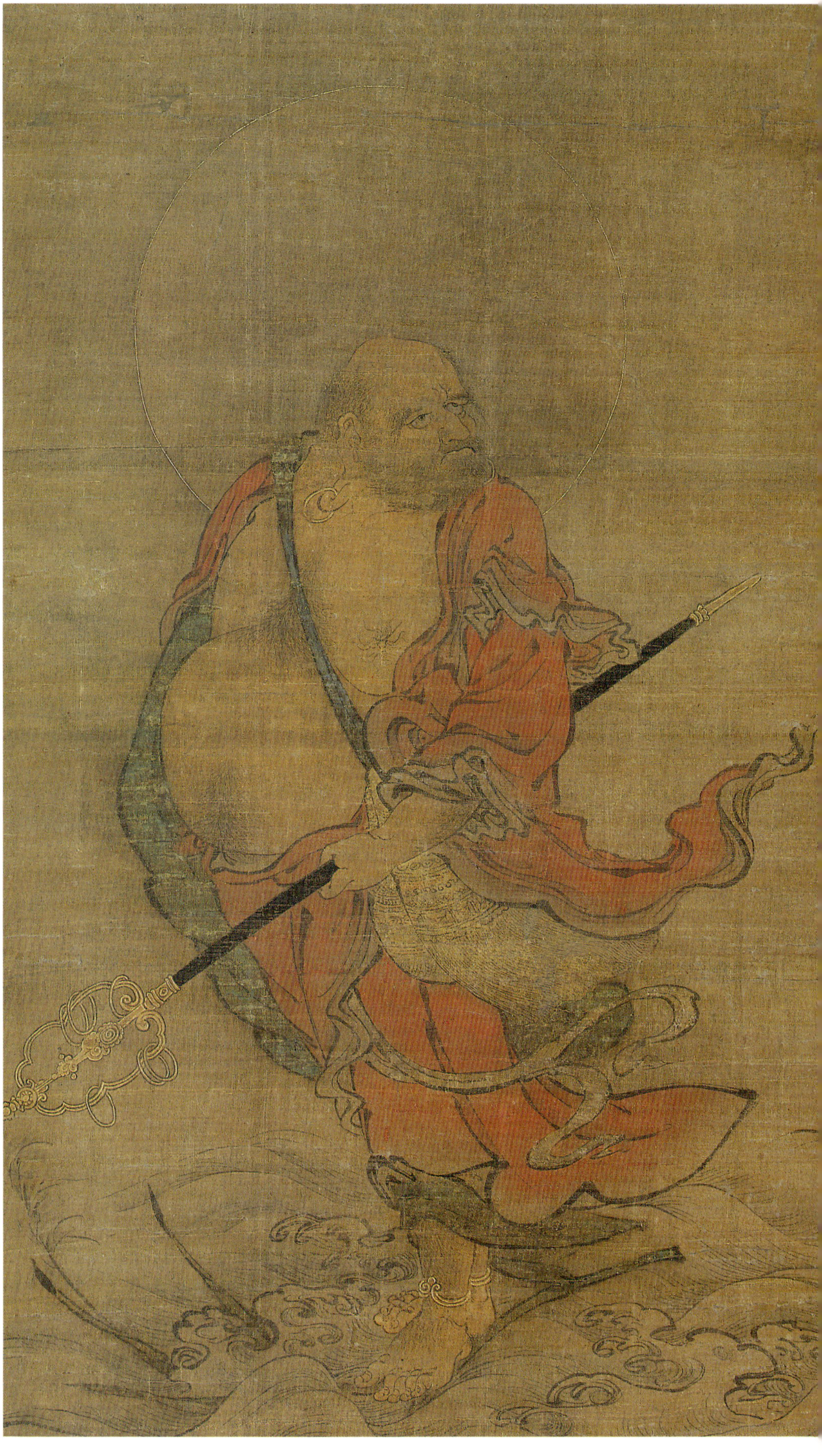

30
Bunsei (active mid-15th century)
Landscape
Muromachi period, 15th century
Hanging scroll; ink with light colors on paper. 73.2 x 33 cm.
Chinese and Japanese Special Fund.
05.203

This illustrious example of early Japanese ink painting is one of several extant works that are thought to be from the hand of a highly accomplished artist named Bunsei. He is likely to have studied under the influential priest-painter Tenshō Shūbun (fl. 1423-d. about 1460), whose atelier was located in the great Zen Buddhist monastery called the Shōkoku-ji in Kyoto.

Only two landscapes by Bunsei have been preserved — this piece and one in the Masaki Museum in Japan. Both reveal that while Bunsei was influenced by the lyrical, idealized landscape concepts of Shūbun, he was also an innovative painter in his own right, highly versatile in his use of ink techniques and original in his compositional ideas. The two landscapes show an unusual vertical arrangement of compositional components with two centralized masses set quite a distance apart, a disposition that creates an expanded spatially evocative vista.

Okakura Kakuzō, who acquired this work for the Museum, assumed it to be identical with a piece mentioned in a mid-nineteenth-century catalogue on painting, the Koga Bikō. *If so, the painting must have belonged at one time to the famous tea-master, garden designer, and connoisseur Kobori Enshū (1598 - 1647), although there is no substantial evidence of this in the existing inventory of Enshū's possessions. Enshū is known to have been associated in some capacity with the Daitoku-ji monastery in Kyoto, and the fact that two of the other authentic works from Bunsei's hand, both portraits of Zen priests, are still in the possession of the temple seems to support the thesis that Bunsei was connected with it in some manner.*

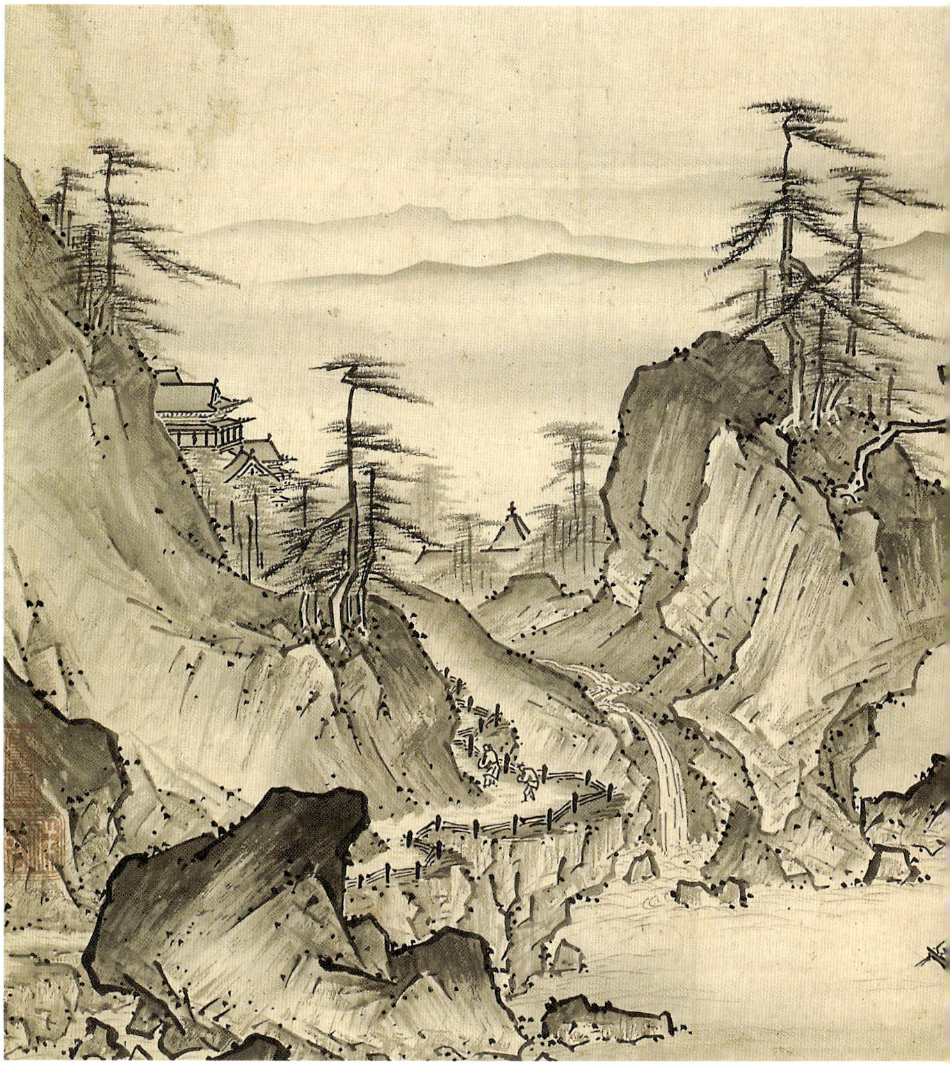

31

Landscape

Poem and calligraphy by Moku'un Ryūtaku (1422-1500)
Muromachi period, late 15th century
Hanging scroll; ink with light colors on paper. 94.2 x 22.4 cm.
William Sturgis Bigelow Collection. 11.6331

No signature or seal appears on this early example of Japanese ink painting to identify its artist, but the pictorial conception reveals indebtedness to the artistic traditions of men such as the influential master Shūbun and certain of his followers, including Bunsei (see acc. no. 05.203).

At the top of the painting is a poem written in a traditional Chinese literary format consisting of four lines, each of seven characters:

Awakening from an afternoon nap,
I open the window by the water.
Reflected back on the broad river surface
are the green hills beyond.
If heaven were to look down from above,
it would be with compassion for my solitary state.
Yet just below me, a pair of waterfowl swim happily together.

The poet, who has added the year that corresponds to 1500 and his age, 79, along with his signature and two of his personal seals, is Moku'un Ryūtaku, one of the great Zen prelates of the day, whose poems are inscribed on a number of fine paintings executed during the second half of the sixteenth century by artists such as Sesshū. Ryūtaku was a noted figure in the "Five Mountains" literary movement that flourished in Zen circles, and many of his poems have been preserved.

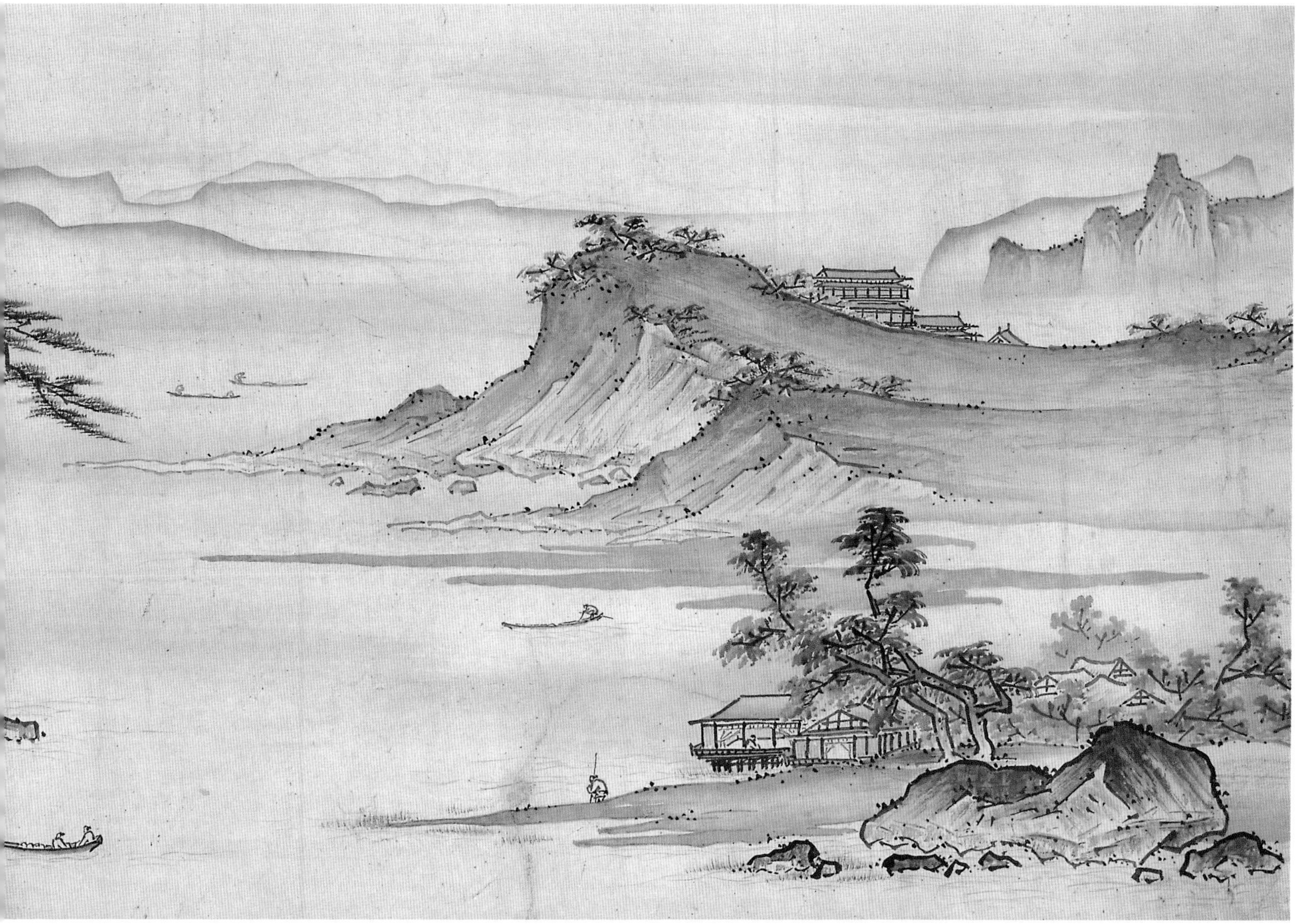

32
Kenkō Shōkei (fl. about 1478-1506)
Landscape
Muromachi period, late 15th to early 16th century
Hanging scroll; ink on paper.
39 x 91 cm.
Fenollosa-Weld Collection. 11.4127

Kenkō Shōkei is one of the accomplished artists of the branch of ink painting that flourished in the temples of the city of Kamakura and the neighboring provinces to the east. He is known to have been a monk at the Kenchō-ji, a temple in Kamakura, where his title, shoki, *indicates that his duties were of a clerical nature. In 1478 he went to Kyoto to study for three years under the noted painter, poet, and critic Geiami (1431-1485) — an experience that was influential in shaping his style. After his return to Kamakura, his atelier at the Kenchō-ji flourished, and he produced a number of followers, including Keison, Keiboku, and Senka.*

This landscape exhibits the preoccupation of Japanese ink painters of the period with idealized Chinese scenes, rendered in the incisive line and sensitive washes inherited from Chinese painters such as Xia Gui, who worked during the Southern Sung dynasty. Shōkei's brushwork here is direct, powerful, and facile, and there is a joyful momentum in the interrelated strokes that leaves a strong impression on the viewer.

The two seals in the lower corner, reading Kenkō *and* Shōkei, *are identical to those on the artist's renowned landscape in the Nezu Museum in Tokyo, a work that shares stylistic and conceptual features in common with this piece.*

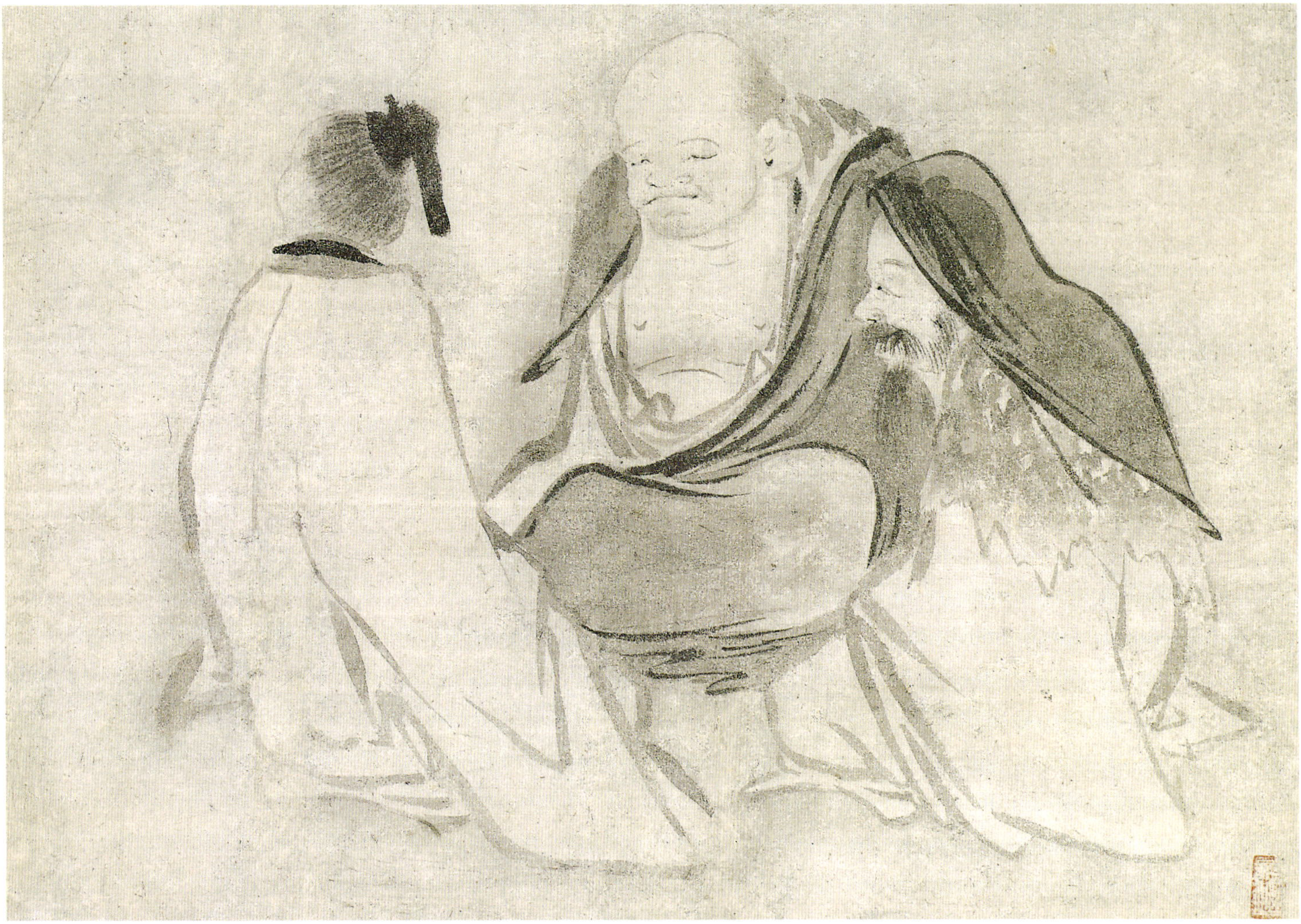

33
Sessō Tōyō (active second half of the 15th century)
The "Three Laughers of Tiger Ravine" Flanked by Lotuses
Muromachi period, 15th century
Set of three hanging scrolls; ink on paper. 33 x 46 cm. (each painting)
Gift of Robert Treat Paine, Jr.
51.2490, 52.1544, 53.509

While the three figures in the central painting were once thought to represent the founding patriarchs of the three great religious systems in China – Confucius, the Buddha, and Laozi – scholars in Japan are now inclined to reidentify them as the "Three Laughers of Tiger Ravine," a group composed of Lu Xiujing (a Confucian who died in A.D. 477), Huiyuan (a Buddhist who died in A.D. 416), and Tao Yuanming (a Taoist who died in A.D. 427). The latter subject deals with a story that has its setting in fourth-century China. Huiyuan, a reclusive priest, had renounced the world of human activities and retired to a life of seclusion on Mount Lu. For thirty years he had been successful in his vow never to cross the bridge across Tiger Ravine, which led to the world he had repudiated. On one occasion, however, his cronies Tao Yuanming and Lu Xiujing visited him. When he saw them off, they became so engrossed in conversation that Huiyuan unwittingly accompanied his friends across the bridge. Realizing what had happened, they all had a good laugh, for it struck them that the spiritual purity of a man has nothing to do with artificial boundaries. The ink lotus on either side of the central painting may be a reference to the "Lotus Society" established by the priest Huiyuan on Mt. Lu.

The identity of Sessō Tōyō, whose seal appears on each of the paintings, is unclear. While it has been suggested that the great Japanese painter Sesshū (1420-1506) may have used the name Sessō Tōyō prior to his voyage to China in 1468, most Japanese specialists are now convinced that Tōyō is a different painter of about the same or a slightly earlier period. This rare triptych, which was earlier preserved in the Bishamon-dō, a Buddhist temple in Yamashina outside Kyoto, was acquired in 1928 by Robert Treat Paine, Jr., who served as curator of Asiatic art at the Museum of Fine Arts from 1963 to 1966.

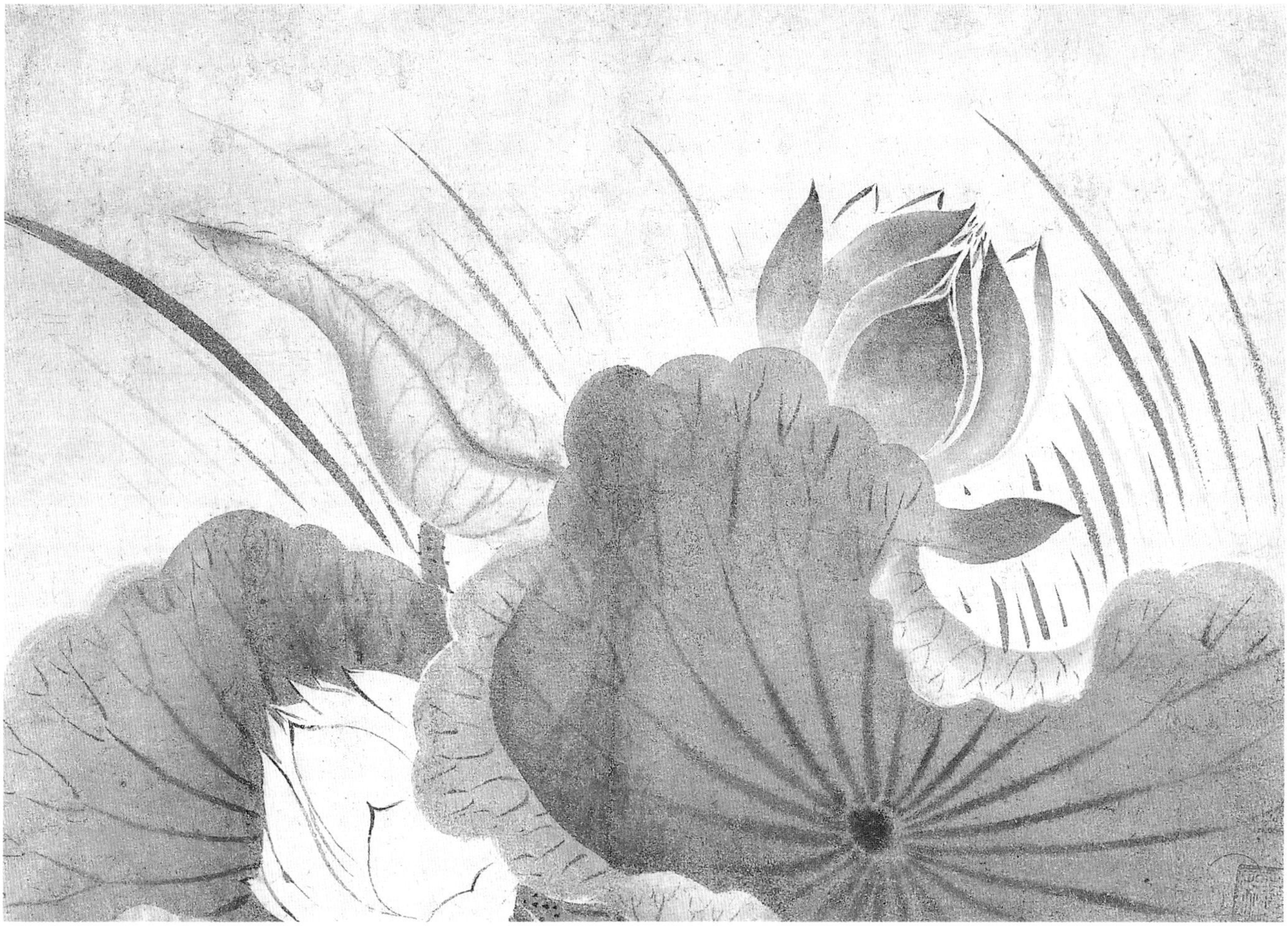

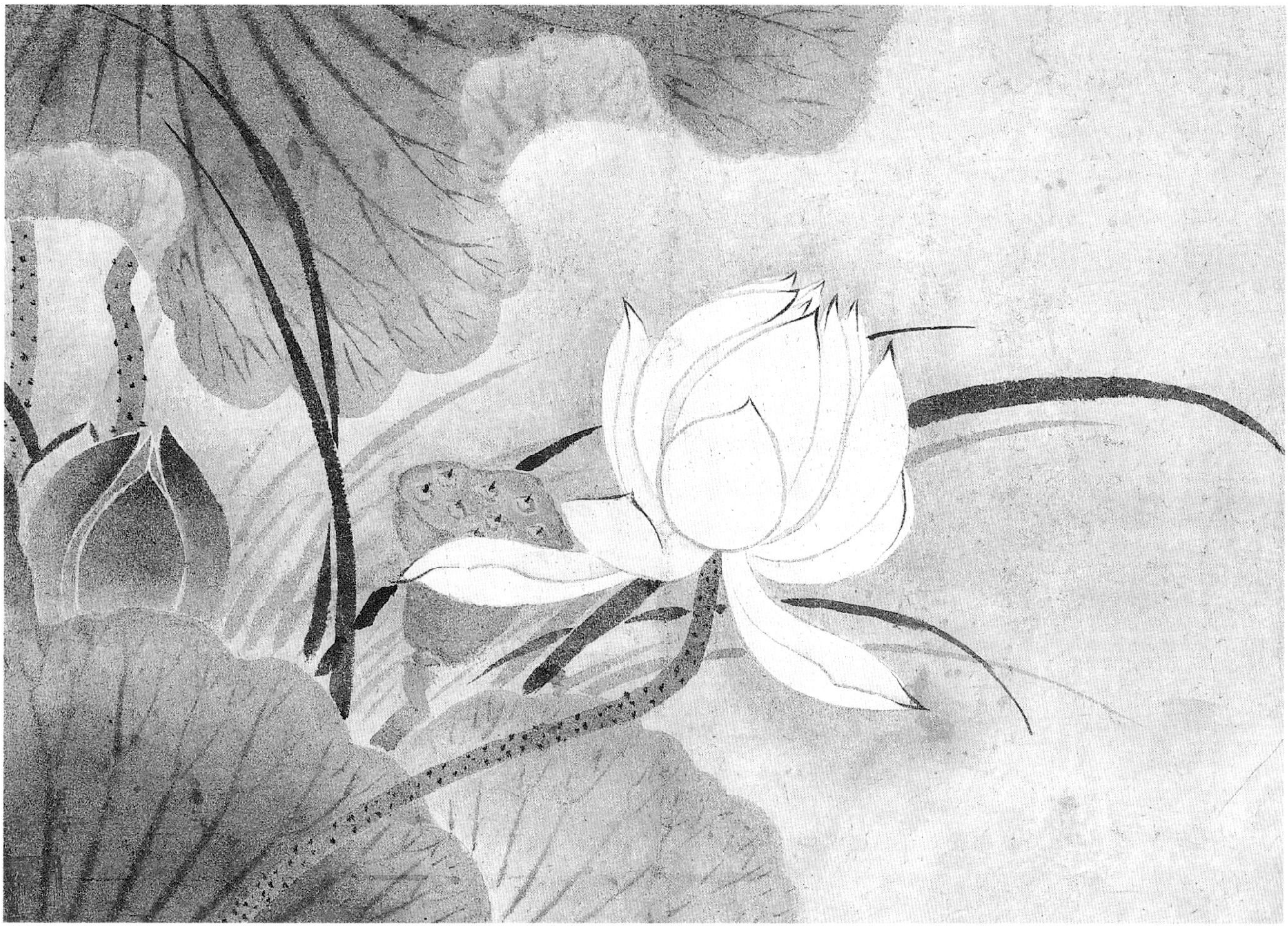

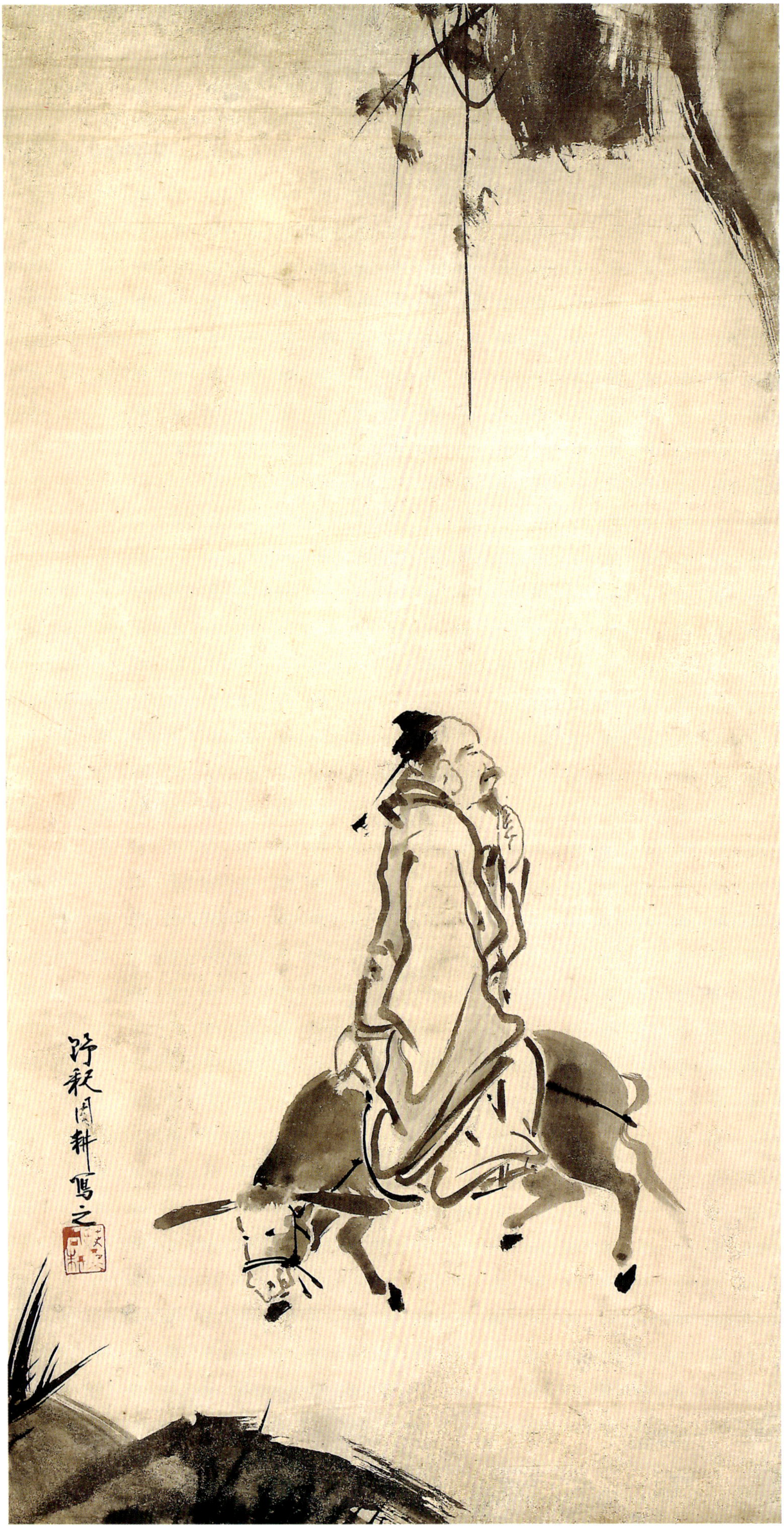

34

Shūkō (active late 15th-early 16th century)

Pan Lang

Muromachi period, 16th century
Hanging scroll; ink on paper.
87.3 x 44.4 cm.
William Sturgis Bigelow Collection.
11.6334

Shūkō, a pupil of Sesshū, lived in Tonomone in the province of Yamato (present Nara Prefecture) and is said to have traveled to China, but nothing else is known of his life or his artistic affiliations. This work is based on an ancient Chinese legend. Pan Lang, shown here riding a donkey facing backwards, was a hermit, a vassal of King Mu of the state of Zhou. On one occasion, a star fell to earth and metamorphosized into eight horses, one of which was called Hua and was in fact a donkey (the Japanese text fails to explain this clearly). Hua had a tail which was not only beautiful but also quite unusual in appearance and Pan Lang greatly admired and praised this feature. His actions aroused the wrath of the king and Pan Lang was banished to the distant mountain fastness of Huashan. Later, after some reflection, the king realized that he had been wrong and he sent the donkey to Huashan with a letter attached to its head. Pan Lang returned to the capital riding the beast, but he was so reluctant to leave the beautiful scenery of Huashan that he rode the beast facing backwards. Pan Lang, the donkey, the overhanging cliff, and the trailing vine are executed with soft, elegant brushwork. The signature says: "done by Yashaku (bumpkin priest) Shūkō," and the rectangular seal says, Fusō Shūkō" (Shūkō of Japan).

35
Tan'an Chiden (fl. late 15th - early 16th century)
Heron
Muromachi period, 16th century
Hanging scroll; ink on paper.
85.9 x 356 cm.
William Sturgis Bigelow Collection.
11.6335

Tan'an, also known as Chiden, was a painter of the Ami School active in the sixteenth century. The Tōhaku Gasetsu *(a treatise by the celebrated painter Hasegawa Tōhaku) has a brief passage on Tan'an: "Among Sōami's pupils was a man called Chiden, who was patronized by the priest Shōnyo of the Ishiyama Hongan-ji [a temple in Osaka]. He was killed at the age of 25 or 26 as a result of a quarrel over a homosexual affair. He was particularly skilled with the brush; his father painted designs on ceramics in Amagasaki, and Chiden himself also became a ceramic painter..."*

A variety of paintings by Tan'an, ranging in size from large screens to small works done on colored paper, have been preserved. Their subjects consist of both landscapes and bird-and-flower themes. The bird shown here has been identified as either a heron or a Japanese stork. Such features as the brush-stippling on the bird's body and the ink shading of the distant mountains are typical of the Ami School's style. The Tokyo National Museum also has a picture of a heron with a signature "Tan'an".

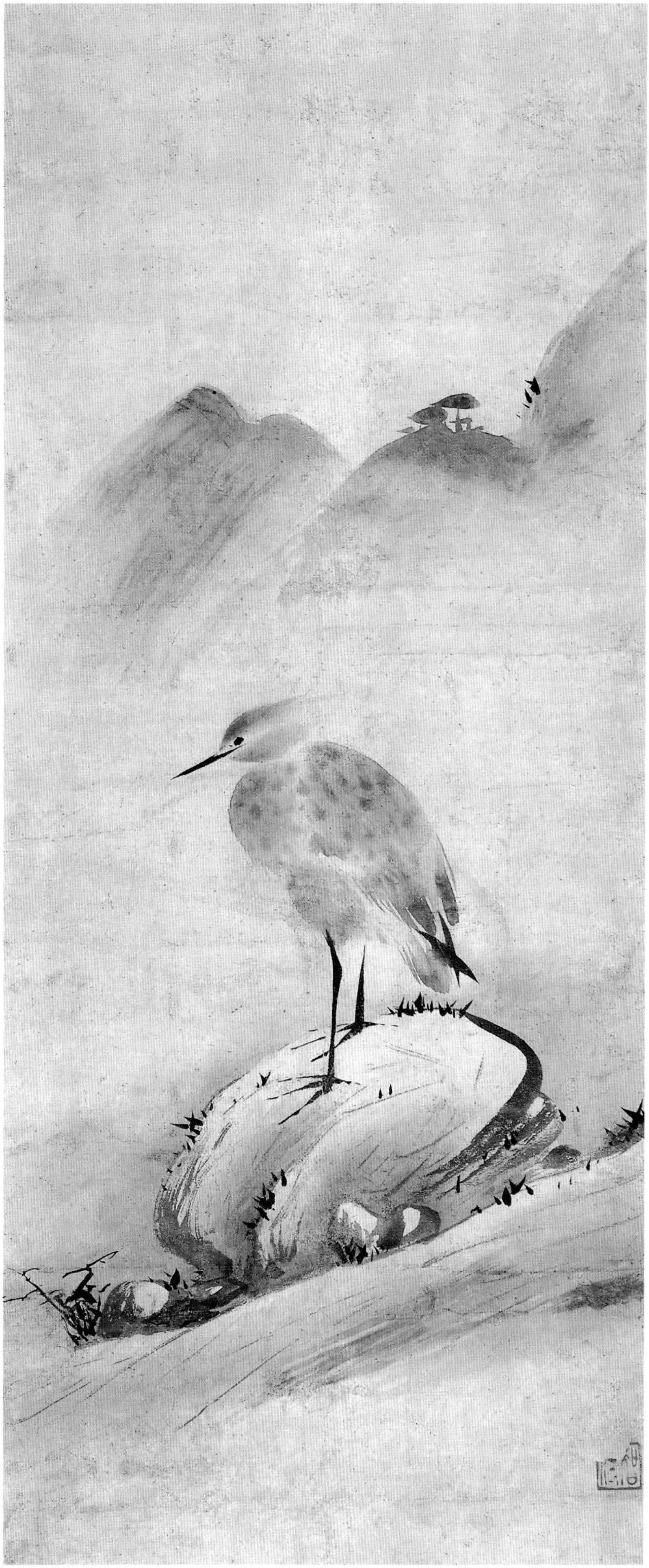

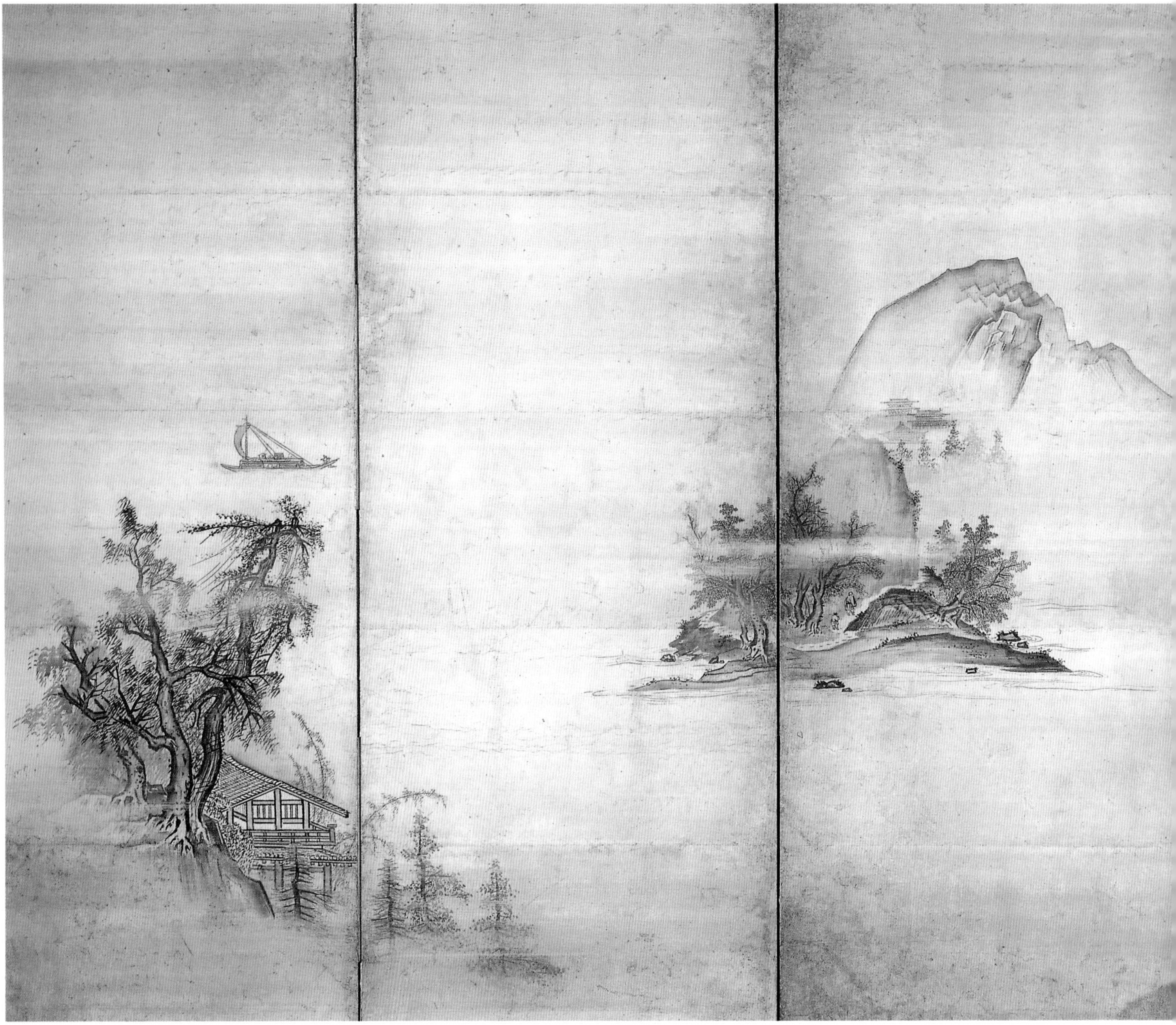

36
Zōsan (late 15th-early 16th century)
Eight Views along the Xiao and Xiang Rivers
Muromachi period, early 16th century
Pair of six-panel folding screens; ink, light touches of color, and sprinkled gold on paper. 158 x 36.6 cm. (each panel)
Fenollosa-Weld Collection. 11.4149 and 11.4150

The two screens bear the same seals, one reading Sōtan, the other Zōsan. In Kano Einō's pioneering study of Japanese painting, the Honchō Gashi, *which was published in 1678, both seals are identified as those of the painter Oguri Sōtan. The cinnabar ink impression of the Sōtan seal here appears fresher than that of the Zōsan seal, however — a fact that has led scholars to hypothesize that the former was probably added at a later time and that Zōsan was in actuality a separate artist, active at least a generation later than Sōtan.*

The handling of landscape components and compositional ideas in these screens shows a clear indebtedness to the influential pictorial precedents of Shūbun, where soaring, jagged peaks rise above pines and rustic pavilions in a strong vertical sequence; the somewhat formalized treatment and mannered brushwork indicate, however, that the screens were executed sometime toward the end of the fifteenth or the early sixteenth century. It would seem that the Boston screens are the only large pieces by the artist still preserved; other known works bearing the Zōsan seal are small hanging scrolls.

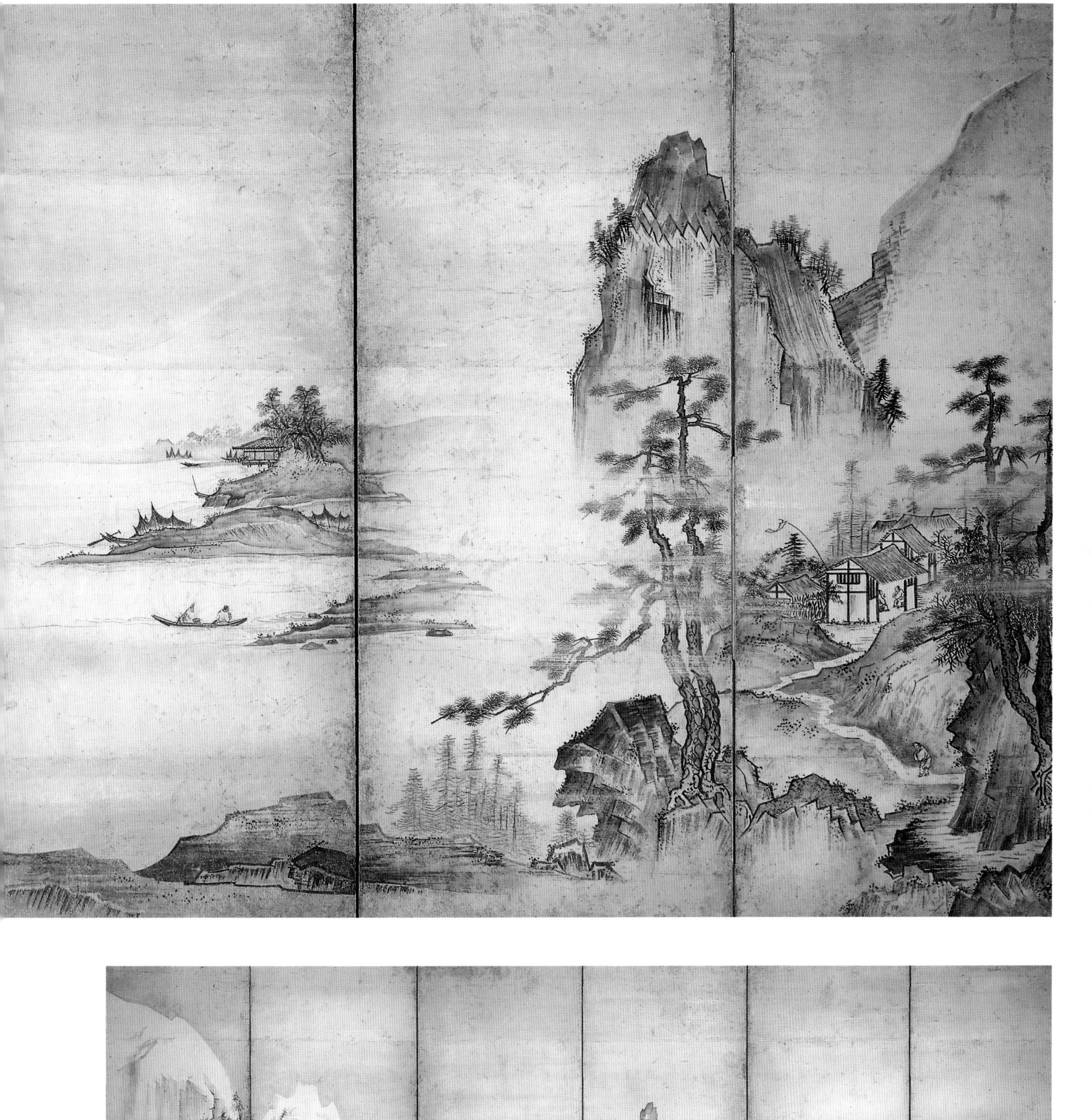

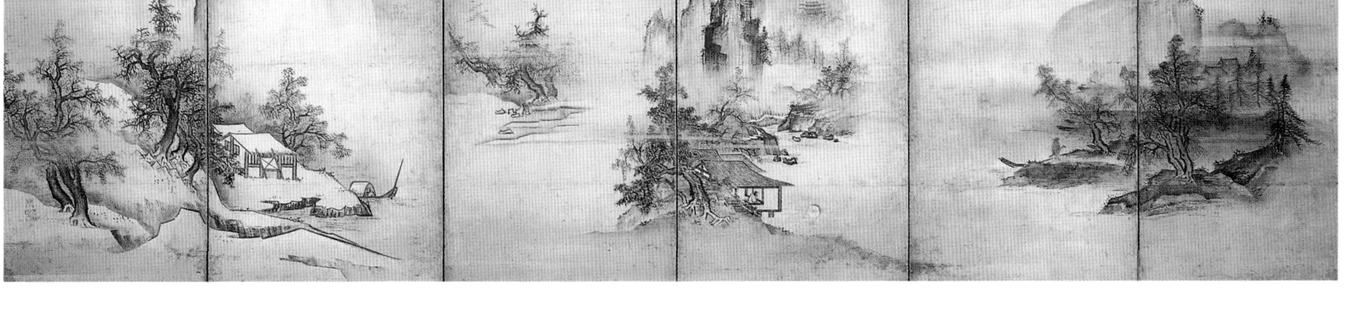

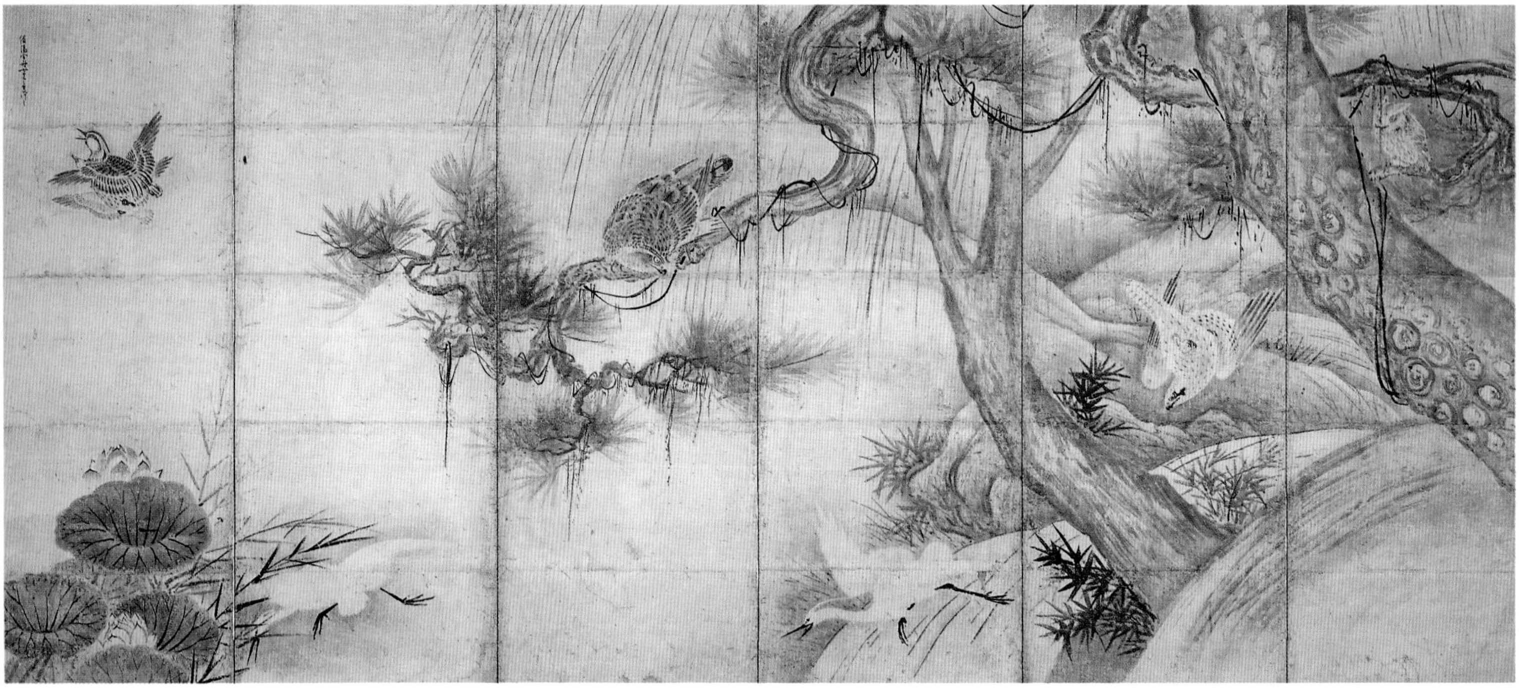

37
Attributed to Sesshū Tōyō (1420-1506)
Monkeys and Birds in Trees
Muromachi period, dated 1491
Pair of six-panel folding screens; ink on paper. 160.6 x 61 cm. (each panel)
Fenollosa-Weld Collection. 11.4140 and 11.4141

This pair of screens was acquired in Japan by Ernest Fenollosa from the collection of the Kishū Tokugawa family. The artist's inspiration for his painting of monkeys, which is extremely attractive in spite of some overpainting and repairs, was undoubtedly based on the Chinese painter Muqi's rendering of the same theme (in the Daitoku-ji, Kyoto). Although he was by no means the first master to adopt this popular subject of the Zen (Ch: Chan) school, Sesshū was certainly one of the most successful artists in the genre.

In the upper corner of each screen there is a signature that reads: "Sesshū of Southern Bitchū made this in his seventy-second summer," which would conform to the year 1491. The signature closely resembles that on other works by the master and is accepted as authentic by some authorities.

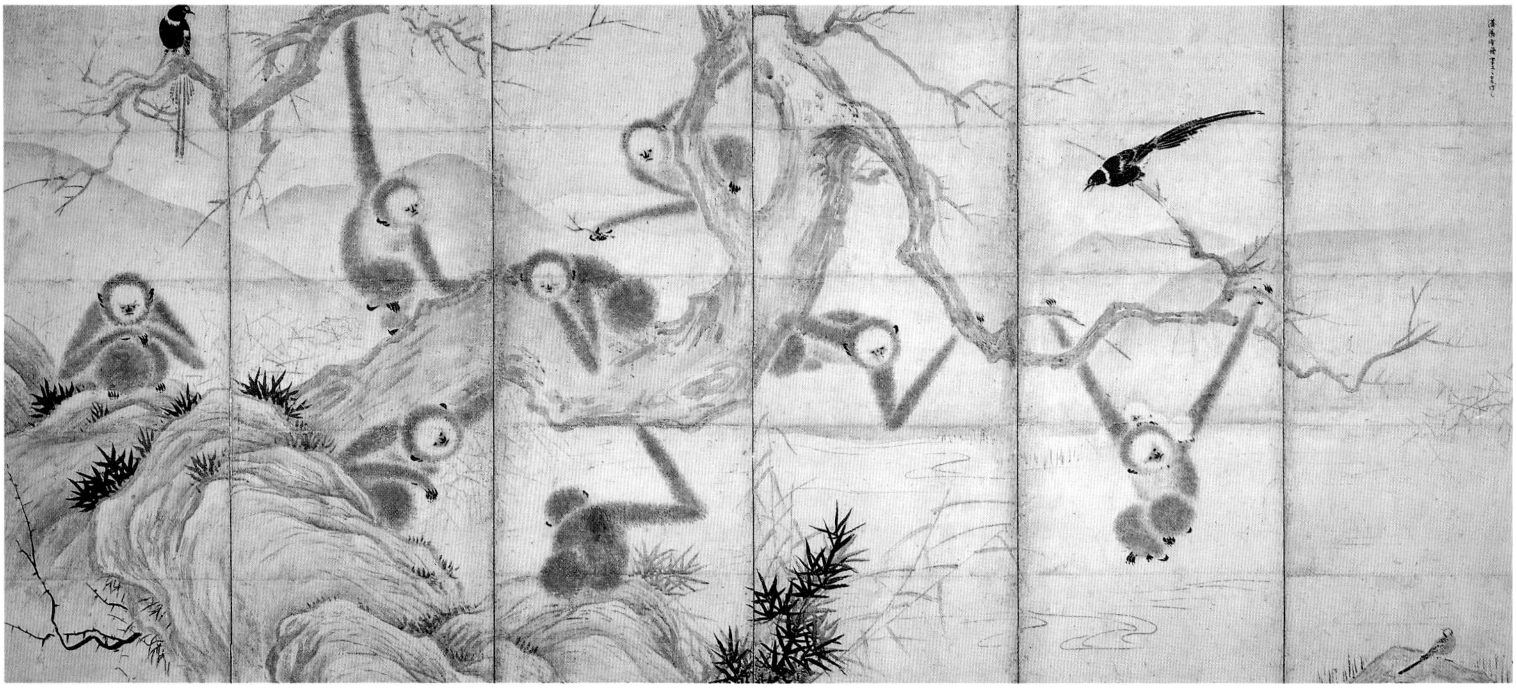

38

Attributed to Sesshū Tōyō (1420-1506)

Jurō

Muromachi period, dated 1502
Hanging scroll; ink and light colors on silk. 103.4 x 51.3 cm.
Fenollosa-Weld Collection. 11.4138

This picture shows one of the Chinese Immortals, Jurō (Ch.: Shou Lao), who was a manifestation of the South Pole star and thus, according to ancient Chinese astrology, the god of longevity. He is shown seated on a rock, with a priest's sceptre in his hand, against a background of rock and a pine tree. About him are a deer, another Immortal, Sekishoushi, (Ch.: Chi Songei) a crane and a turtle. The fine details of Jurō's face are characteristic of Sesshū's figure painting. An ink sketch of this painting appears in the Tan'yū Shukuzu, *the extensive compendium of drawings of earlier paintings compiled by Kano Tan'yū (1602-74). The painting is inscribed: "painted by Sesshū in the eighty-third year of his life", which would mean that it was painted four years before his death. A work entitled* Santō Gunsen Roku, *which describes the Immortals of China, states that Jurō is associated with the south and the color red, whereas* Tenjin, *the god of heaven, is associated with the north and the white plum. This would suggest that the picture of* Tenjin *in the Okayama Prefectural Museum forms a pair with the work shown here; both, in fact, bear red seals of identical dimensions and the same name Tōyō (i.e. Sesshū).*

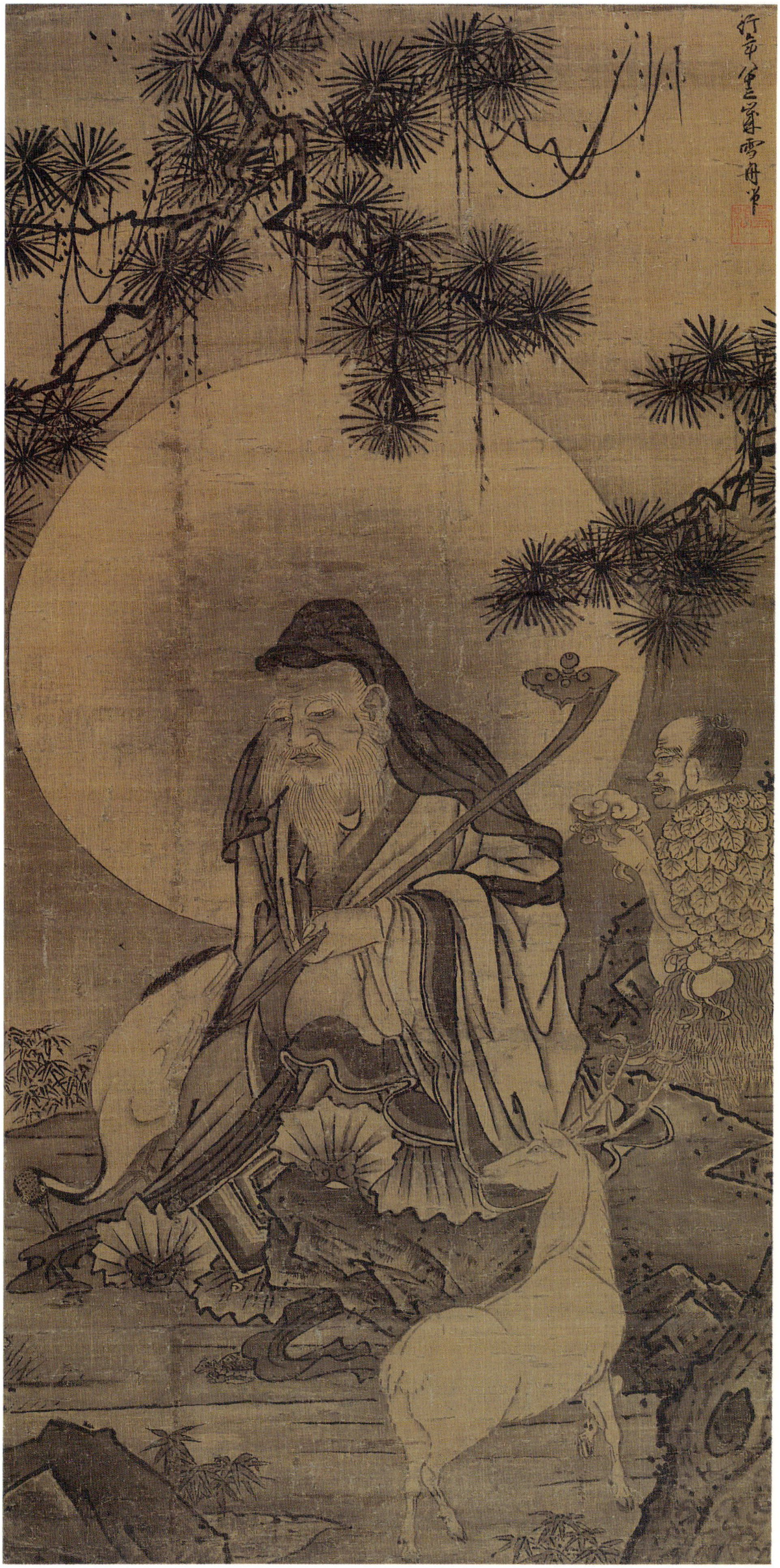

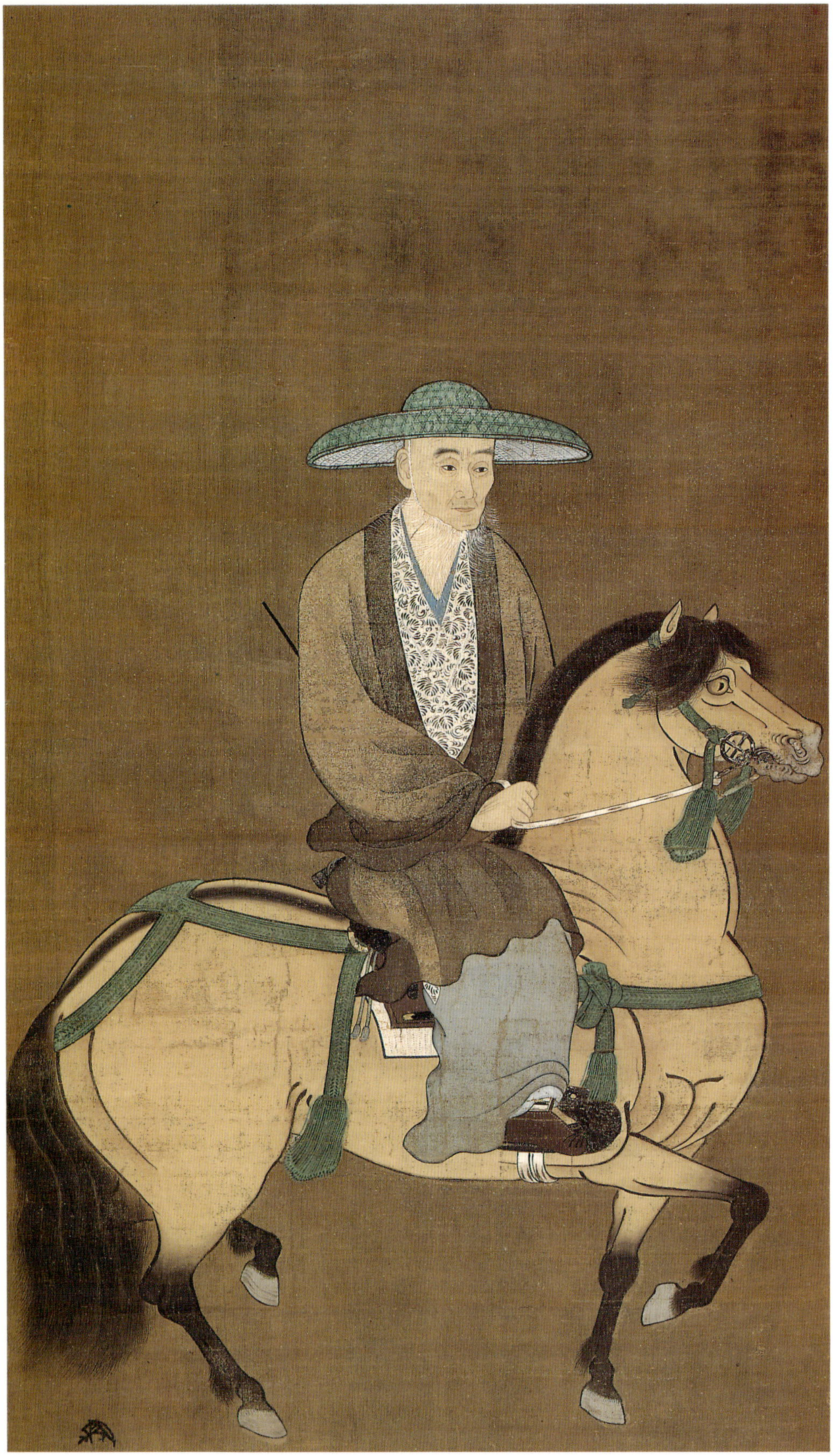

39
Attributed to Kano Motonobu (1467-1559)
Sogi on Horseback
Muromachi period, 16th century
Hanging scroll; ink and colors on silk.
97.6 x 55.4 cm.
Frederick L. Jack Fund. 58.314

This rare portrait of the noted poet Iio Sogi (1421-1501) has the kaō *(personal cipher) of Kano Motonobu, the influential early master of the Kano school, in the lower left-hand corner. The poet's face is articulated in a very sensitive manner, so highly individualized as to indicate that it is an accurate portrait. By contrast, the horse is conceived in a more mannered style, with the animal's musculature and contours rendered in hard, uninflected lines. These characteristics are consistent with the horses that appear in the pair of* ema *("votive paintings") in the Kano shrine in Hyōgo Prefecture, which were done by Motonobu before 1539 and also have the artist's* kaō *and signature. The subject in the Boston painting, which shows the poet on horseback during his itinerant travels when he refined his poetic abilities, is quite unusual.*

40
Attributed to Kano Motonobu (1467-1559)
White-Robed Kannon
Muromachi period, early 16th century
Hanging scroll; ink, colors, and gold on silk. 158 x 76.7 cm.
Fenollosa-Weld Collection. 11.4267

Ernest Fenollosa (1853-1908), the first curator of Japanese art at the Museum of Fine Arts, acquired this impressive painting from Yamanaka and Co. in Japan sometime before 1883, and his notes indicate that it had belonged formerly to the daimyō Hachisuka of Awa Province. Fenollosa's admiration for this large work is apparent in his notes: "An original work, Motonobu's best in both color and drawing. The Kanos in Tokyo have been studying and copying this design for ages without ever having seen the original or knowing where it was. Kano calls it the finest picture in my collection!"

The "White-Robed Kannon," a traditional Buddhist icon, had been a standard motif in Japanese suiboku *painting since the Kamakura period. However, the special method of using pigments in the bodhisattva's robe, with its mannered linear treatment, and certain of the background details — such as distinctive rock forms and hard contours in the cliff, as well as the decorative quality of the delicate waves — are indications of the influence of Chinese Buddhist painting of the Yuan and Ming periods. At the same time, however, the bodhisattva has a secularized quality, probably attributable to the fact that the early Kano painters were professional artists rather than priest-painters.*

There is no signature on the painting, but a small tripod-shaped seal of the sort used frequently by artists of the Kano school appears in the lower right-hand corner. As yet, the characters have not been deciphered. Although this large work traditionally has been attributed to Motonobu, it is interesting to observe the striking similarities with a famous triptych at Daitoku-ji in Kyoto, which shows the Buddha Śākyamuni flanked by the bodhisattvas Manjusri and Samantabhadra. Like the Boston piece, this work has no signature, but it has been attributed since the Edo period to Kano Masanobu (1434-1530), the father of Motonobu.

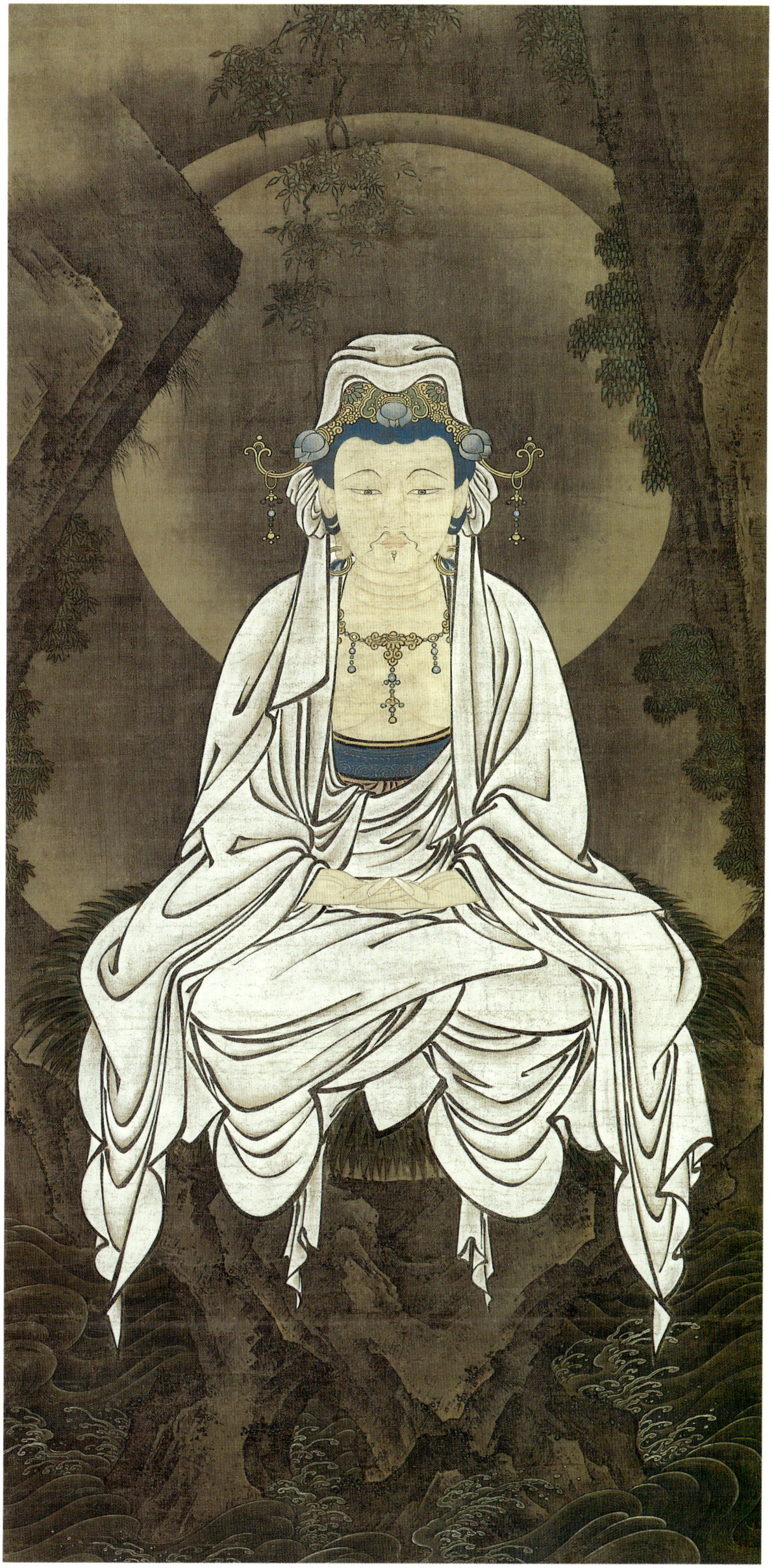

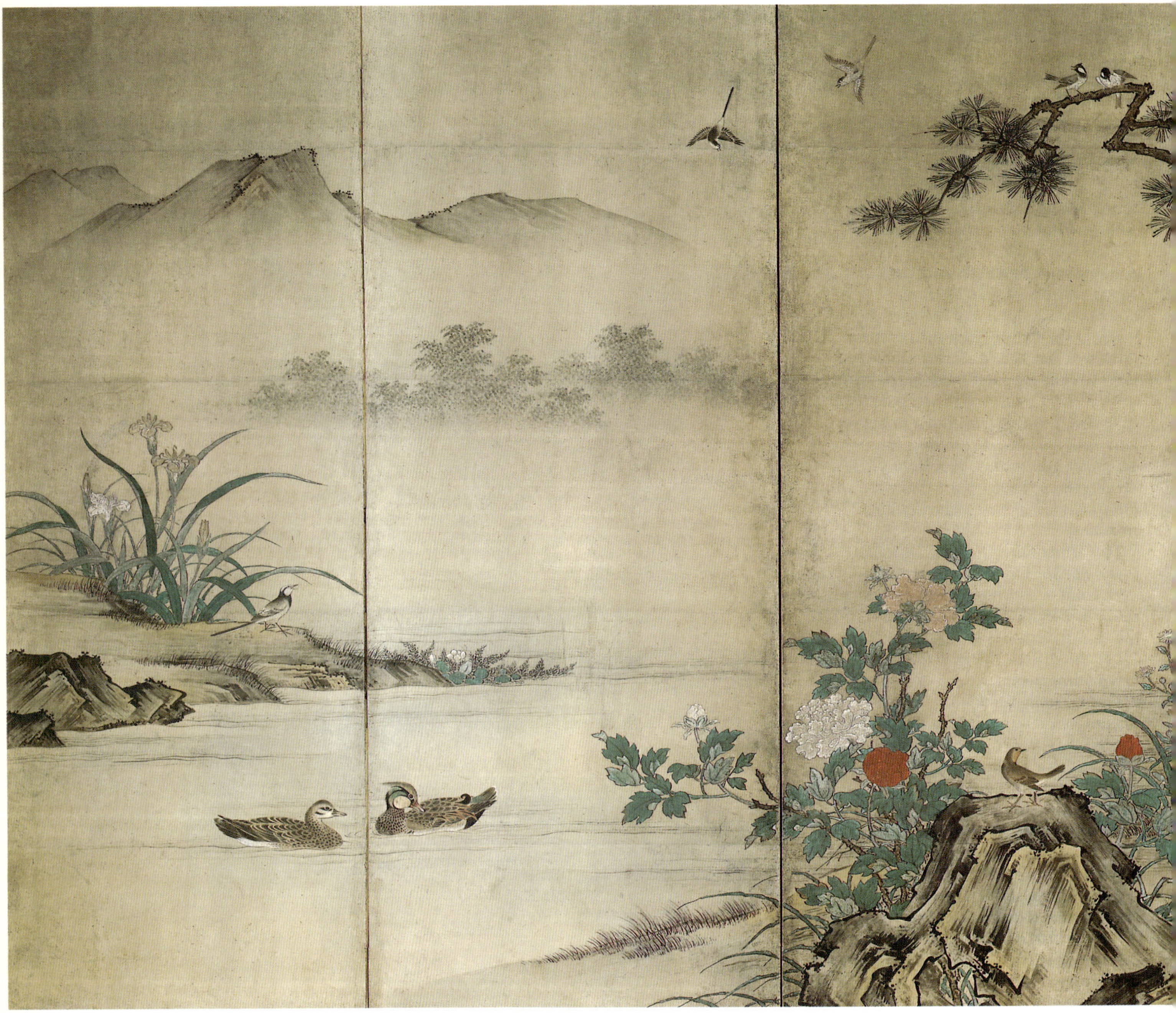

41
Kano Shōei (1519-1592)
Birds in a Landscape
Muromachi period, about 1560s
Six-panel folding screen; ink and colors on paper. 151.5 x 372 cm.
Fenollosa-Weld Collection. 11.4347

The signature in the lower right-hand corner of this rare screen is that of Kano Tan'yū (1602-1674), who attributes the work to his great-grandfather, Kano Shōei. The gifted, conservative master Shōei drew much of his inspiration from the paintings of his father, Kano Motonobu (1476-1559), the influential second-generation master of the Kano school, who established the stylistic and organizational basis for the Kano line of professional artists during the first half of the sixteenth century.

The subject matter in this work is generally representative of many large-scale Kano works of the sixteenth century, with its varied flora and birds in a sylvan landscape setting. The atmosphere is a subdued and formal one in which selective colors are utilized in a restrained manner and contrast with the skillful use of monochrome washes and incisive contour lines.

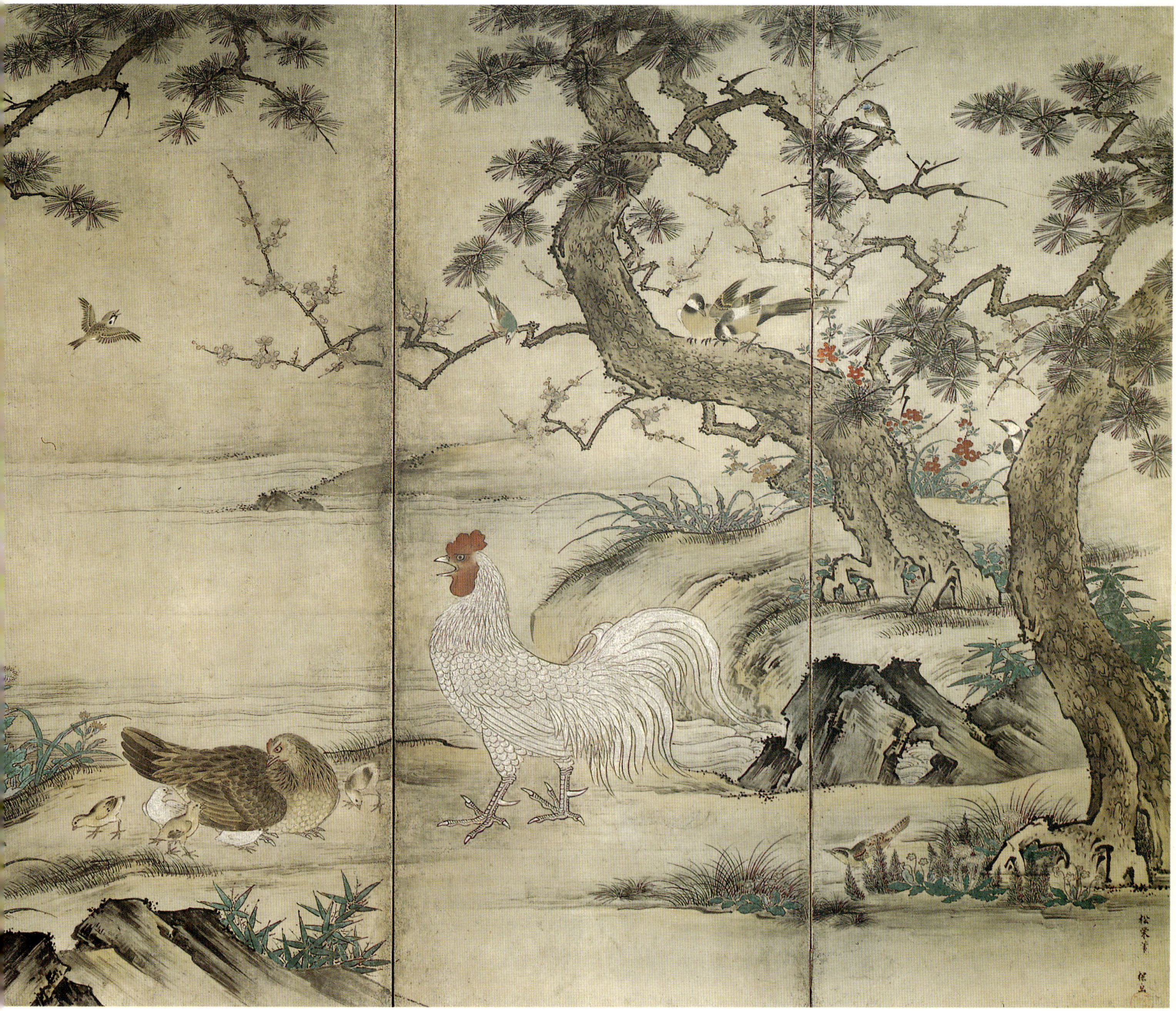

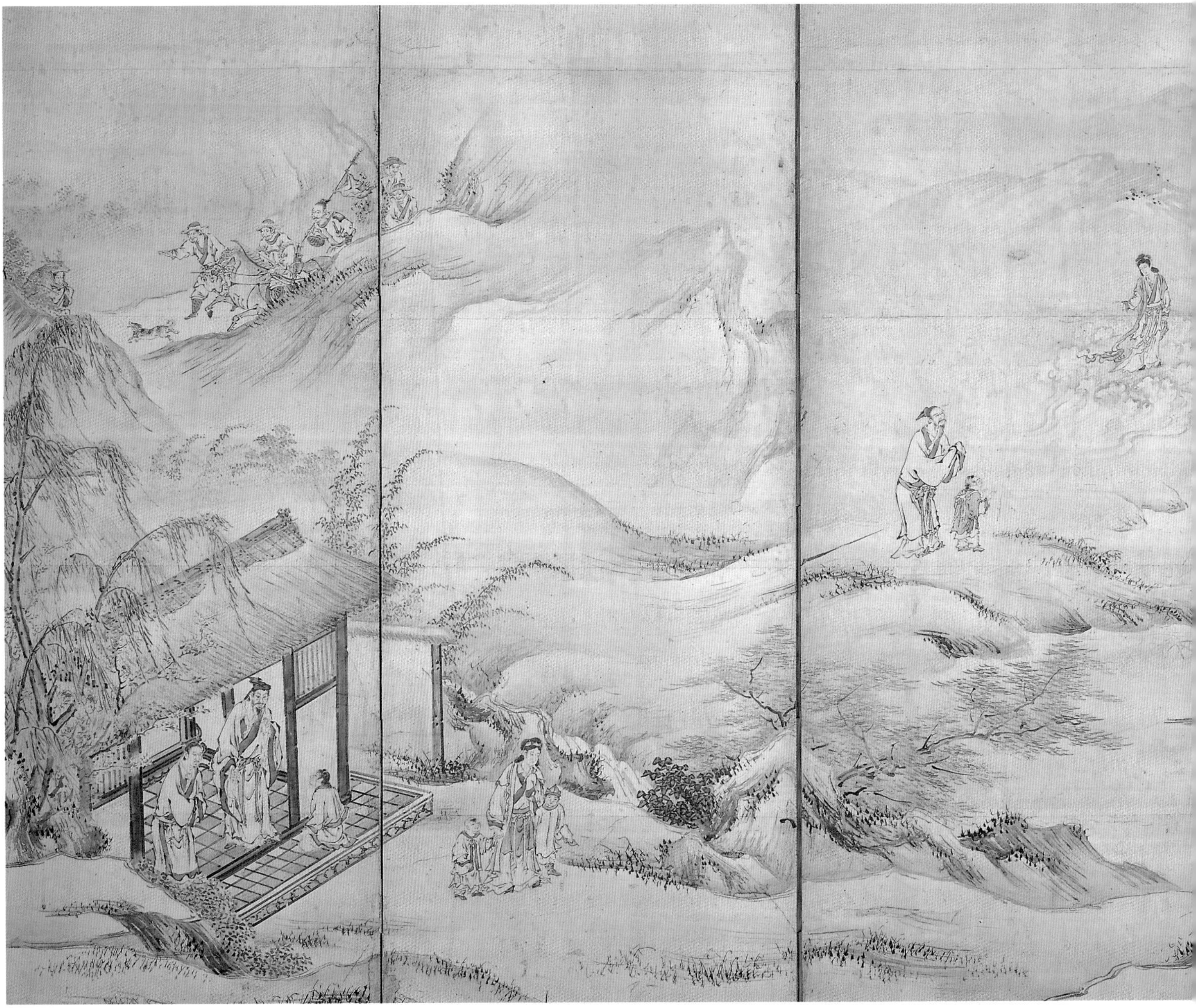

42
Kano Sanraku (1559-1635)
The Twenty-Four Paragons of Filial Piety
Momoyama period, late 16th-early 17th century
Six-panel folding screen; ink and gold wash on paper. 150.6 x 369 cm.
Fenollosa-Weld Collection. 11.4305

Although the screen is unsigned, a jar-shaped seal at the lower right-hand corner bears the name "Mitsuyori," one of the artist's names used by Kano Sanraku; the seal, which is reproduced in traditional literature, appears authentic. Other factors supporting an attribution to Sanraku are the details and style of the screen, such as the distinctive method of embellishing the rock and cliff forms with soft, dry, parallel hatching strokes; the delicate, yet incisive manner in which the robes of the figures are delineated; and the lively, individualized expressions of the paragons. Furthermore, the brushwork and particulars of the figures correspond closely to those in a series of well-known paintings by Sanraku, which have depictions of Zen incidents and Chinese personages.

Stylistic similarities may be seen as well in the ink treatment of the gnarled pine in this screen and the pine painted on a single-panel screen within a two-panel folding screen by Sanraku in the Myōshin-ji in Kyoto — a composition that depicts a meeting of the late Han dynasty emperor Guangwu and a sage.

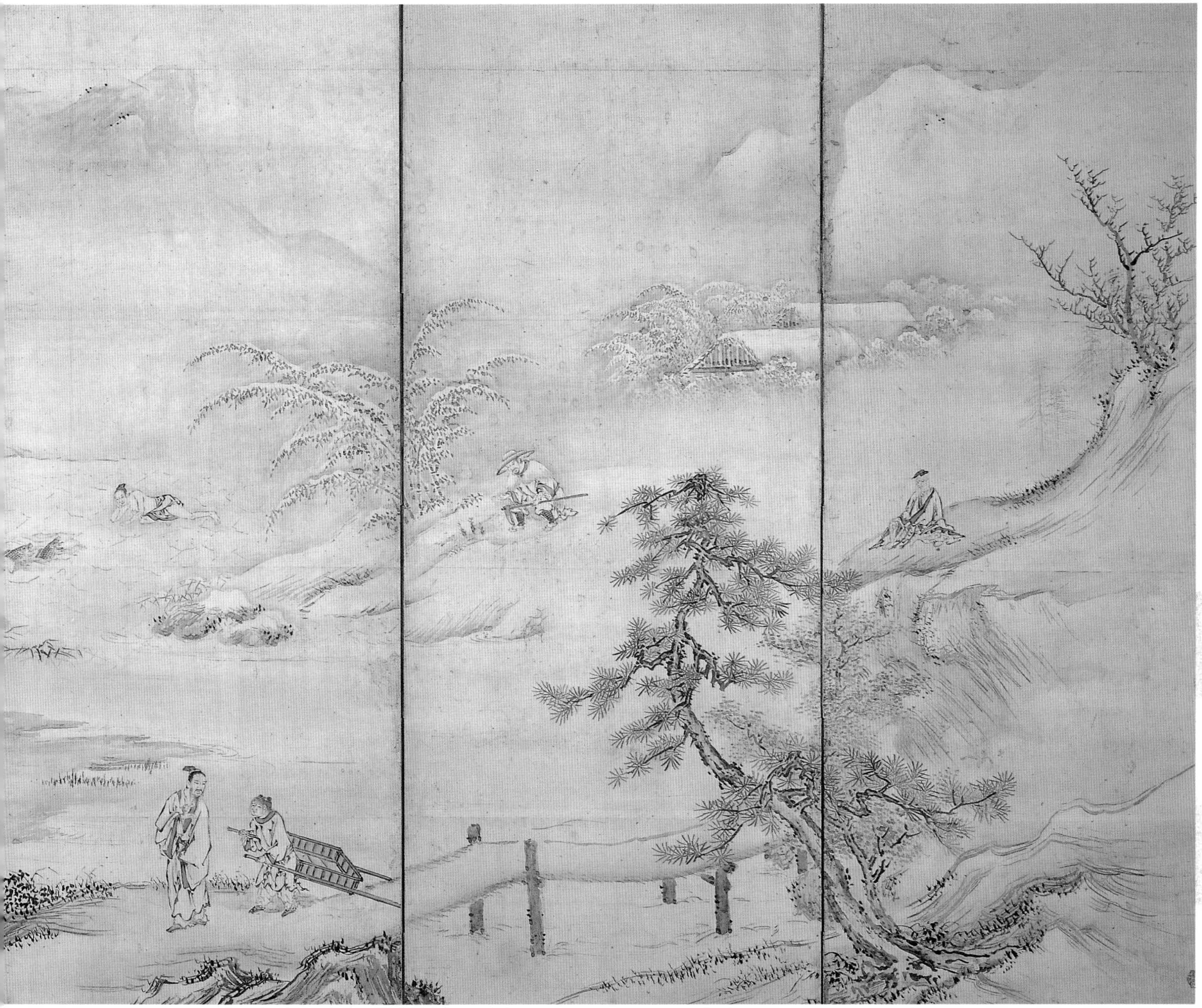

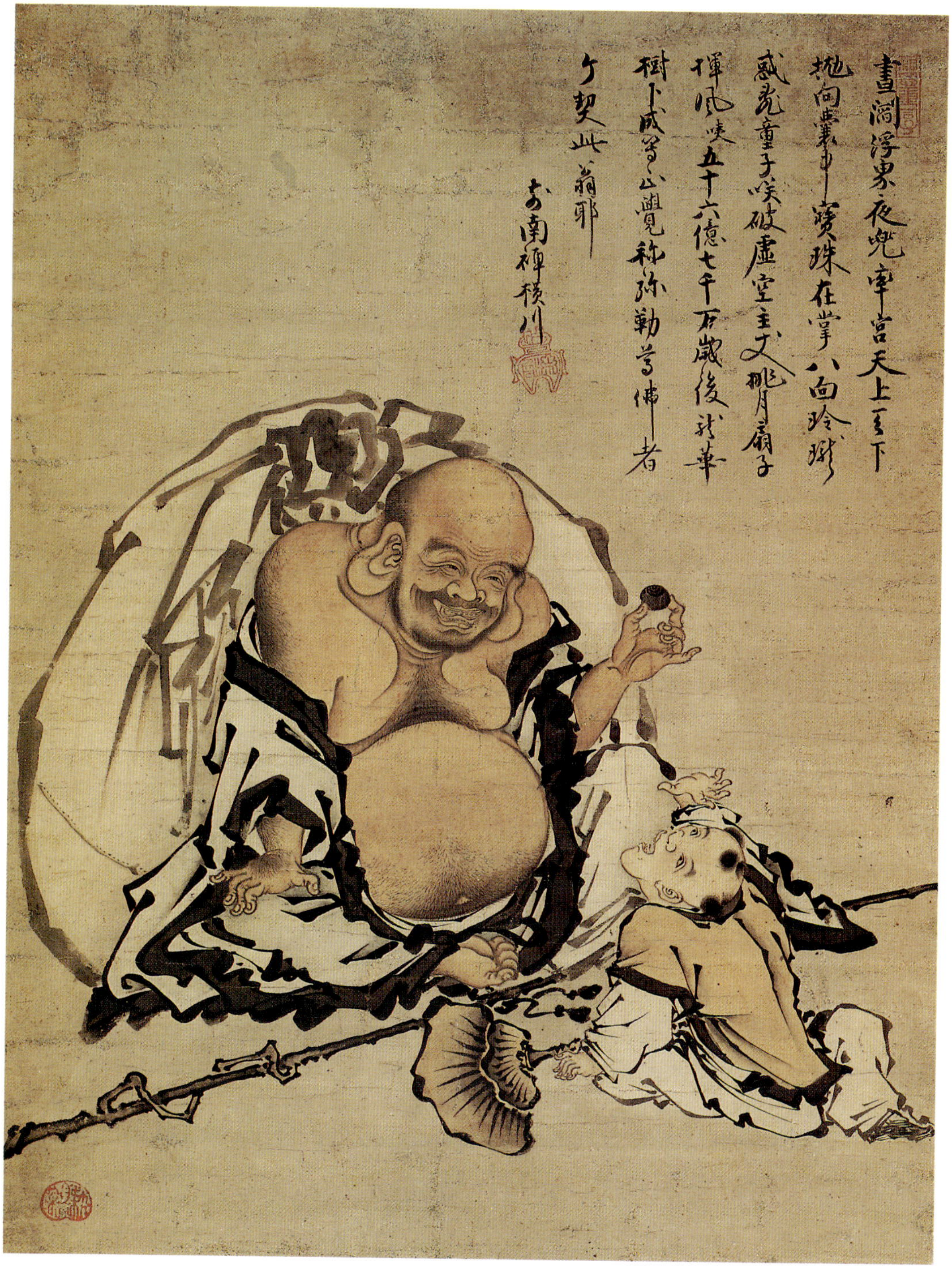

43

Hotei

Inscription by *Ōsen Keisan (1429-1493)*
Muromachi period, 15th century
Hanging scroll; ink and light colors on paper. 61.3 x 45.7 cm.
Fenollosa-Weld Collection. 11.4244

In Buddhist tradition, the eccentric, rotund deity Hotei is thought to be an alternate aspect of the bodhisattva Maitreya. The Boston painting shows the grotesque figure seated, leaning against his sack, and offering a symbolic jewel to a young boy. The work's conception and color scheme, together with the handling of anatomical details and brushwork used in the depiction of Hotei's clothing and sack, correspond so closely with comparable features in a painting of the same subject done by Kano Masanobu (preserved in a private collection in Japan) that it seems quite likely that the two paintings are from the same hand.

44

Kano Mitsunobu (1561/1565-1602/1608) and Kano Sōshū (1551-1601)

The Chinese Emperors Yangdi and Wudi

Momoyama period, late 16th century
Pair of hanging scrolls; ink, colors, and gold on paper.
115.7 x 55.1 cm. (each)
Fenollosa-Weld Collection.
11.4361-4362

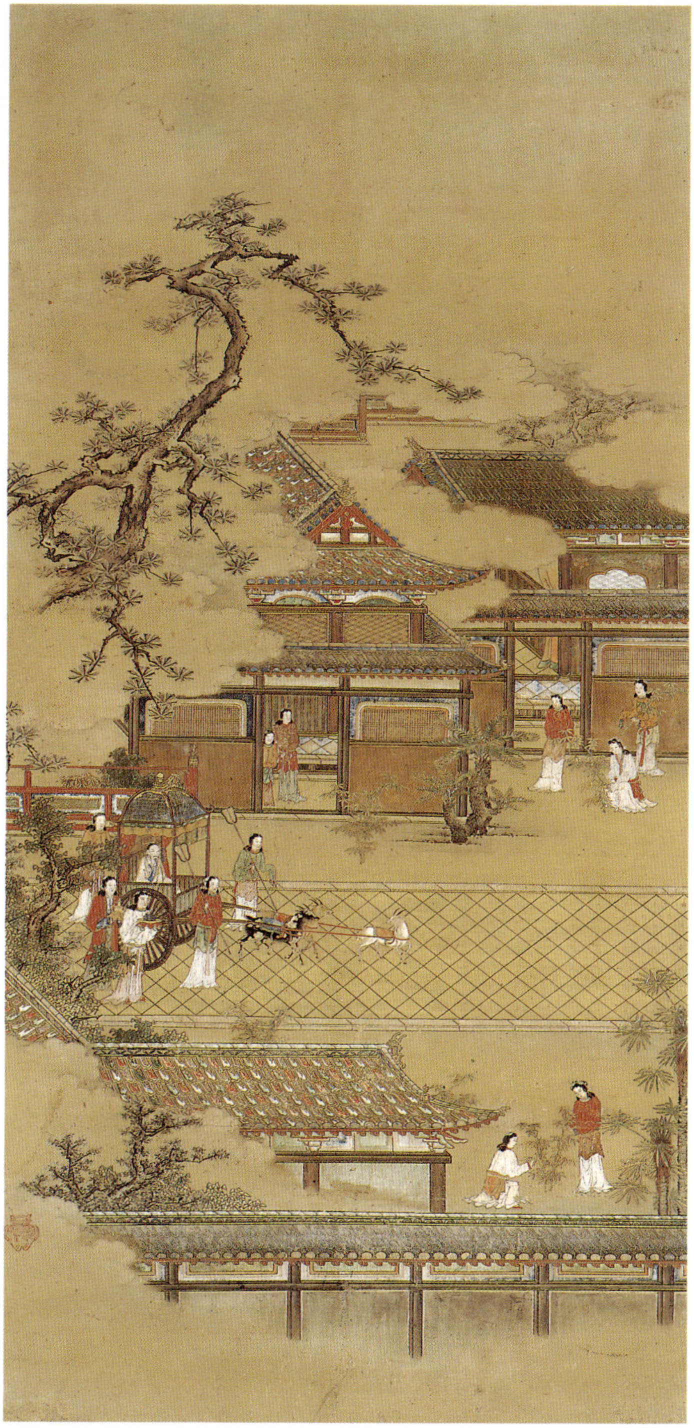

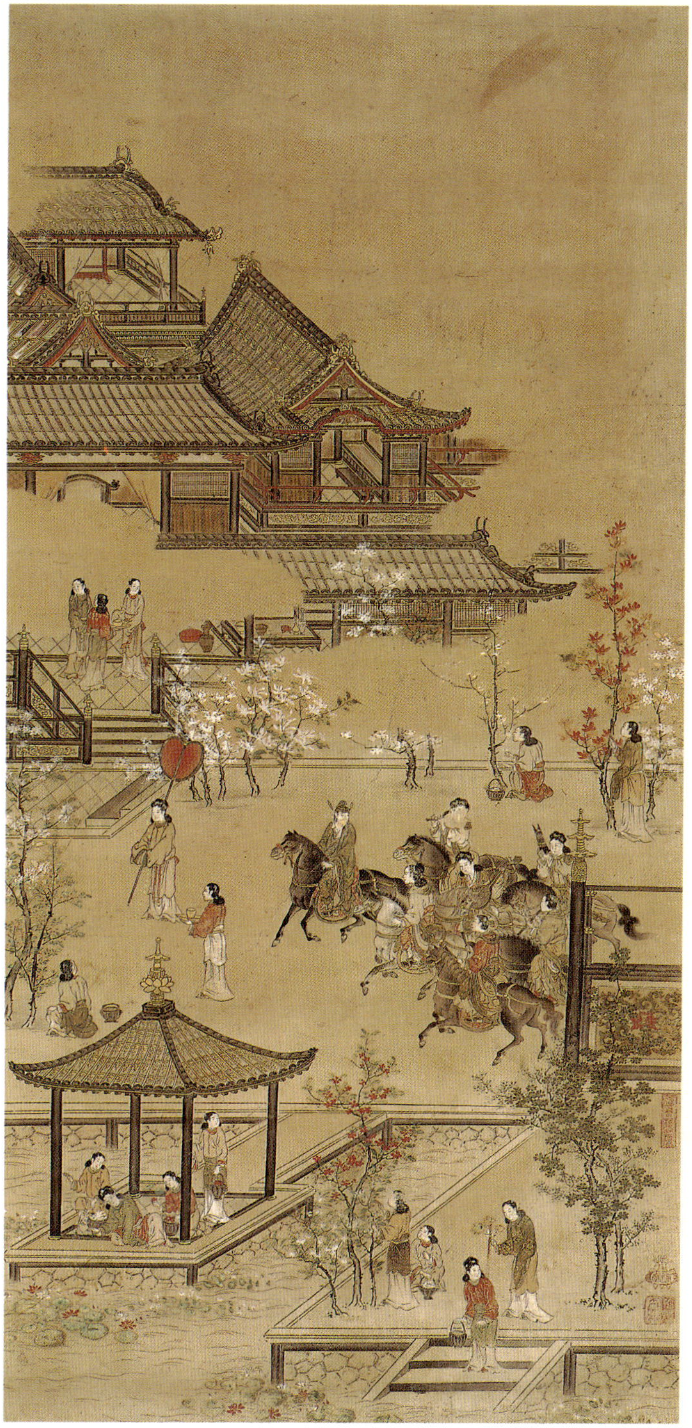

The painterly abilities of two skilled Kano-school artists of the Momoyama period — Sōshū, the second son of Shōei and younger brother of Eitoku, and his nephew Mitsunobu, the son of Eitoku — are to be seen in this pair of large hanging scrolls. Historically, artists such as these men and their contemporaries served as important artistic links between the great painting traditions of the Kano school that had flourished under men like Eitoku (1543-1590) during the earlier part of the Momoyama period and the later Kano masters who worked in Kyoto and Edo in the early decades of the Edo period. Sōshū's work, on the right, depicts the pleasure-loving Chinese emperor Yangdi of the Sui dynasty, accompanied by his female musicians, riding through the imperial garden in winter, the trees having been provided with artificial flowers and leaves made from silk in order to allay the dreary atmosphere of the cold season.

Mitsunobu's work has a depiction of the famous story about the emperor Wudi of the Western Jin dynasty, who enjoyed riding in a carriage pulled by goats. Anecdotal themes of this sort, drawn from Chinese mythology and popular historical sources, were the object of growing interest among Kano artists from the Momoyama period on, and they constitute a significant percentage of the subjects portrayed by painters of the school during the seventeenth and eighteenth centuries.

The paintings have seals identifying the respective artists. Sōshū, although mentioned routinely in traditional descriptions of the lineage of the Kano school, where it is noted that he produced works for Toyotomi Hideyoshi, remains something of a shadowy figure, and few of his paintings appear to have been preserved. Mitsunobu, who worked with Eitoku on the screen paintings for Oda Nobunaga's Azuchi castle, is better known.

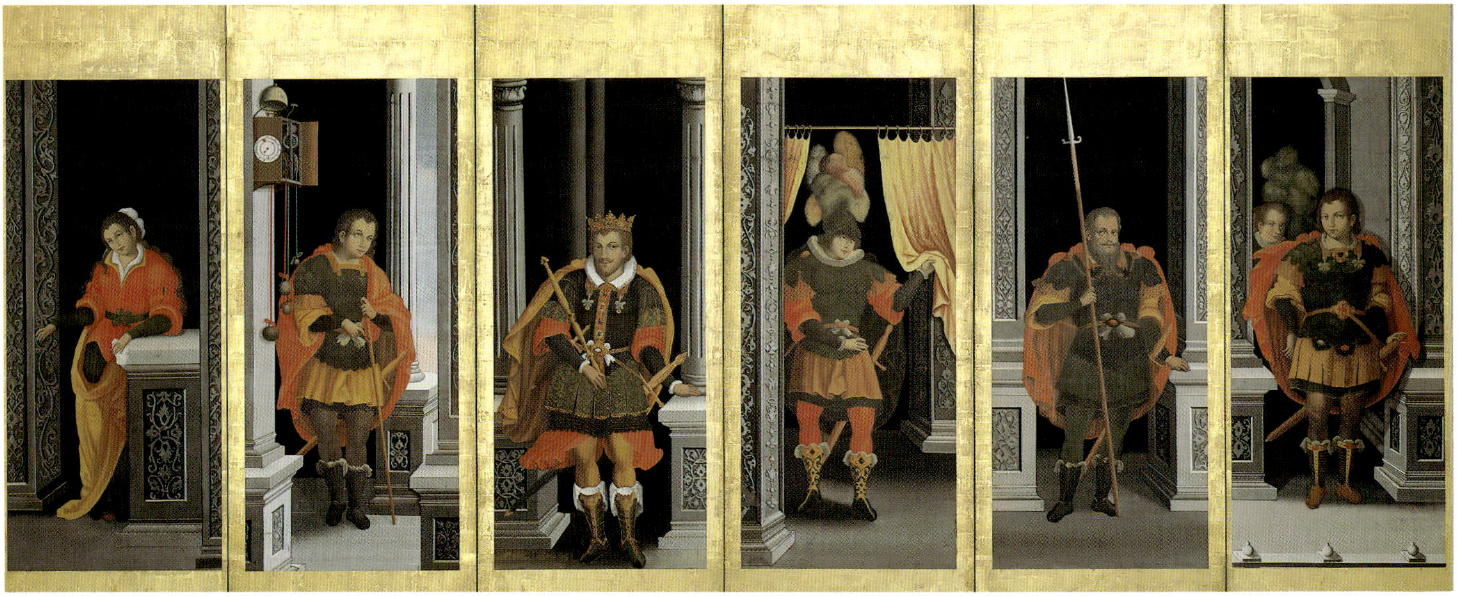

45

European King and Members of his Court

Momoyama period, about 1601-1614
Six-panel folding screen; ink, colors, and gold on paper.
127 x 333.6 cm.
Fenollosa-Weld Collection. 11.4312

This rare screen is a fine example of the small group of Japanese paintings created under the influence of European pictorial materials, such as Flemish and Dutch prints, that were brought to Japan by Jesuit representatives of the Catholic faith during the second half of the sixteenth century and the early years of the seventeenth. The Jesuit artist Giovanni Nicolao (about 1558-1626) is known to have come to Japan in the fall of 1590 and to have begun instructing Japanese converts in Western artistic concepts and techniques. His school continued until 1614, when the Tokugawa shogun Ieyasu began the suppression of Christianity.

The anonymous Japanese artist who produced this work, clearly a man of artistic ability, utilized indigenous materials skillfully to render the exotic group of foreign personalities with fidelity. In an attempt to simulate the effects of opaque oil painting, traditional water-soluble pigments were thickened with a white body and glue binder.

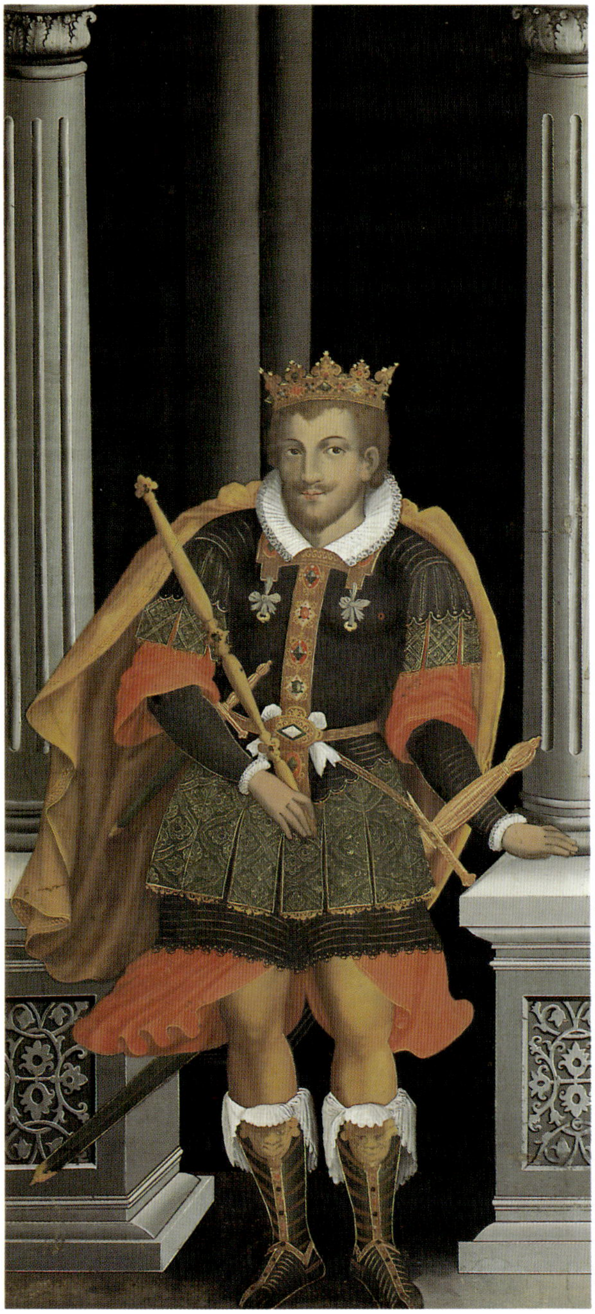

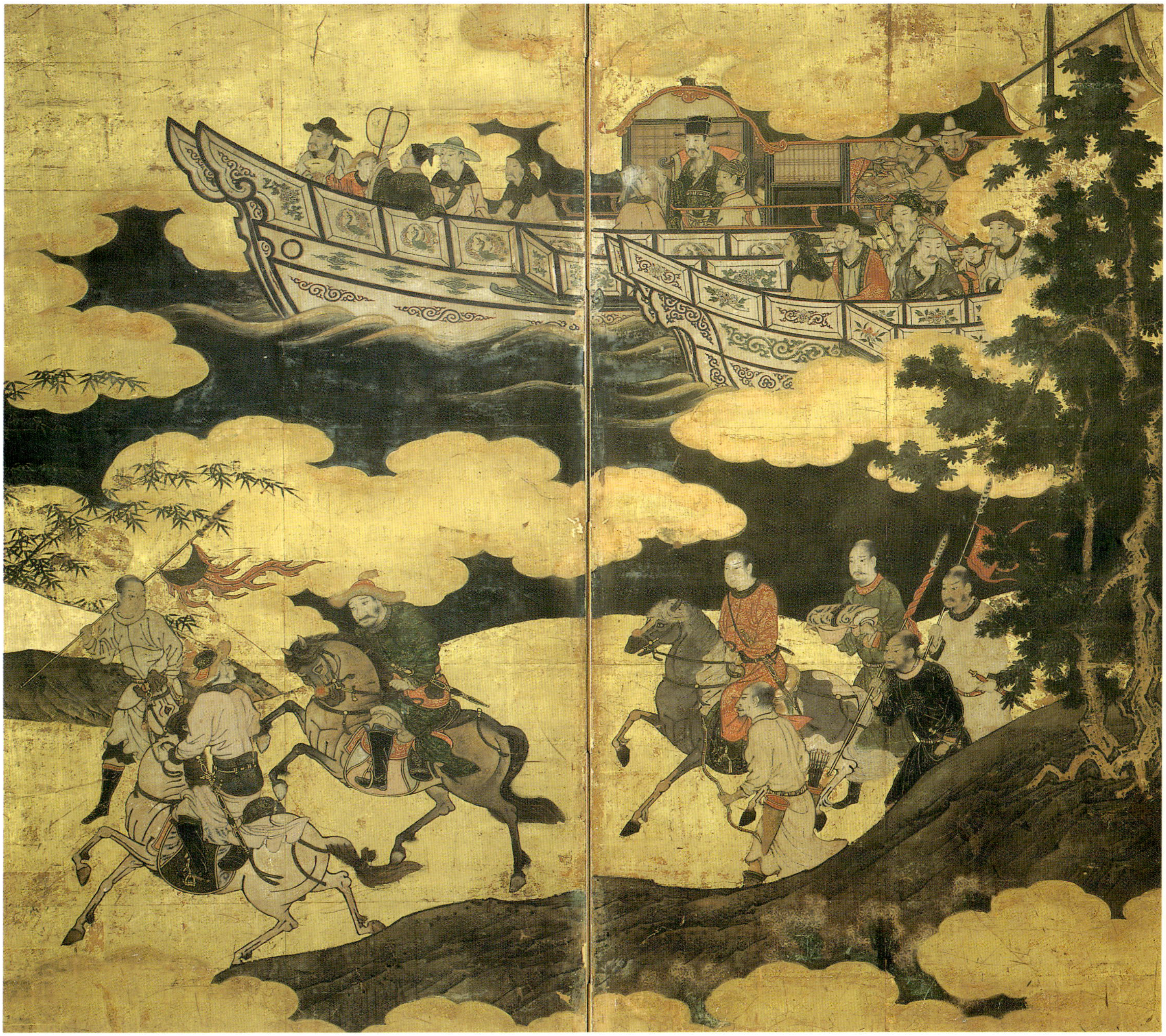

46

Tartar Envoys Arriving in Ships, Their Advance Party Ashore

Momoyama period, 17th century
Two-panel folding screen; ink, colors, and gold on paper.
153.6 x 170.4 cm.
Fenollosa-Weld Collection. 11.4450

Subjects of this sort, exotic genre scenes with depictions of strange foreigners, such as Europeans (Namban-jin) *or Chinese or Tartars — often depicted in connection with the distinctive ships that brought them from overseas — constituted a popular category of painting during the Momoyama period, when such representations were prized by members of the military aristocracy as highly appropriate for display in their residences. The general admiration for Chinese themes seems to have been a reflection of the pervasive prestige of Confucian education and values among the military class during this period, but elegant, colorful screens also served symbolically as a means for displaying the prevailing preoccupation with power and status that characterized affluent military families at this time.*

The present screen shows two ships above, in which are seated dignitaries and envoys in appropriate dress, their heightened expressions a mixture of gravity and curiosity as they approach the shore, while in the foreground, members of their advance party move briskly along a road, some on foot carrying processional banners, others mounted on spirited horses.

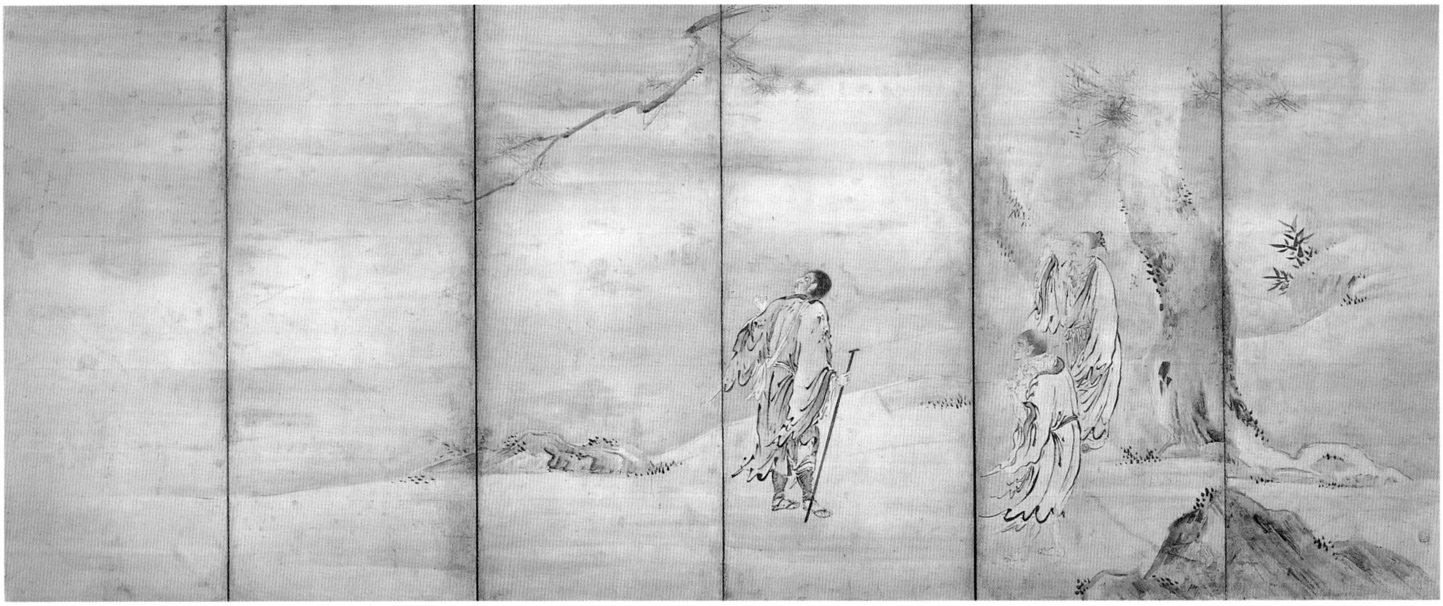

47

Kano Kōi (about 1569-1636)

Taoist Immortals and Zen Masters

Edo period, 17th century

Pair of six-panel folding screens; ink and gold on paper.

151.4 x 359.2 cm. (each)

Fenollosa-Weld Collection.

11.4233-4234

Kōi shares with Tan'yū the distinction of introducing new, lighter modes of depiction and brushwork into the Kano school — characteristics that can be seen in these screens, where the treatment of the figures and landscape components is briefer and more impressionistic than the Kano style of the later sixteenth century. The activities depicted in the screen are drawn from the traditional inventory of Zen-influenced subject matter, which first gained popularity in ink painting during the Muromachi period.

Standing in the middle of the right-hand screen is Tekkai, one of the eccentric "immortals" of Taoism, who miraculously projects his spiritual essence out of his mouth and into space. Another immortal, Gama (who is often paired with Tekkai), stands below to the right. Gama was celebrated for his occult abilities, one of which involved his constant companion, a strange, three-legged toad who followed his commands.

The left-hand screen has depictions of three Zen incidents. On the right appear two figures — one in a boat, the other in the water. De Cheng, who leans on an oar in the boat, was a revered Zen master, although he lived the simple life of a ferryman on the Huading River. One day the priest Hui came to visit the master, who asked him, "In what temple do you dwell?" Hui responded, " What has likeness has no abiding place and what has abiding place has no likeness." The master observed cryptically, " There is no likeness, yet of what is there no likeness?" and he added, "One appropriate word is like a post to which you can tie a donkey for a thousand years." Hui opened his mouth to respond, but the master took his oar and pushed him into the water. At that moment Hui experienced enlightenment.

The central scene also describes the difficulty of responding in a manner that will satisfy a Zen master. Nanquan (749-835) took up a cat and said to his disciples, "If you can state an appropriate word, this cat will be saved; if not it will be slain." No one could answer and the cat was killed. Later Nanquan met Zhaozhou (standing in front of him in the present scene), and told him about it. The latter put one sandal on his head and departed, at which Nanquan added, "If you had been present, the cat would have been saved."

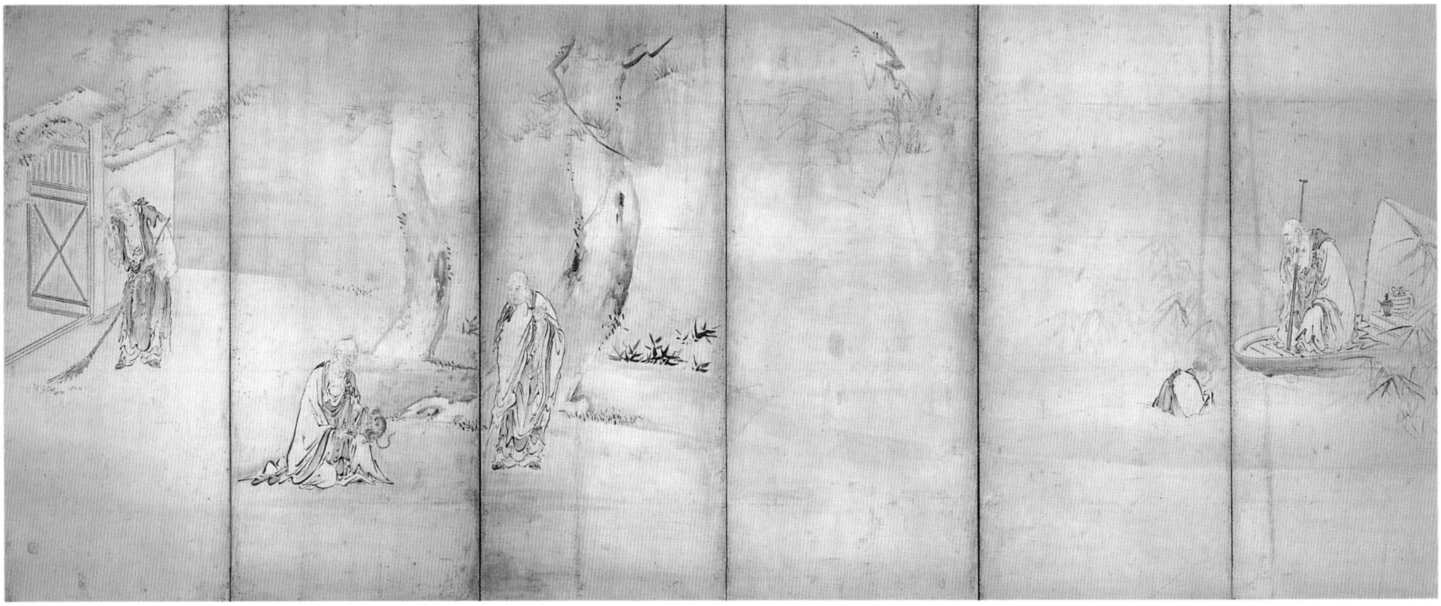

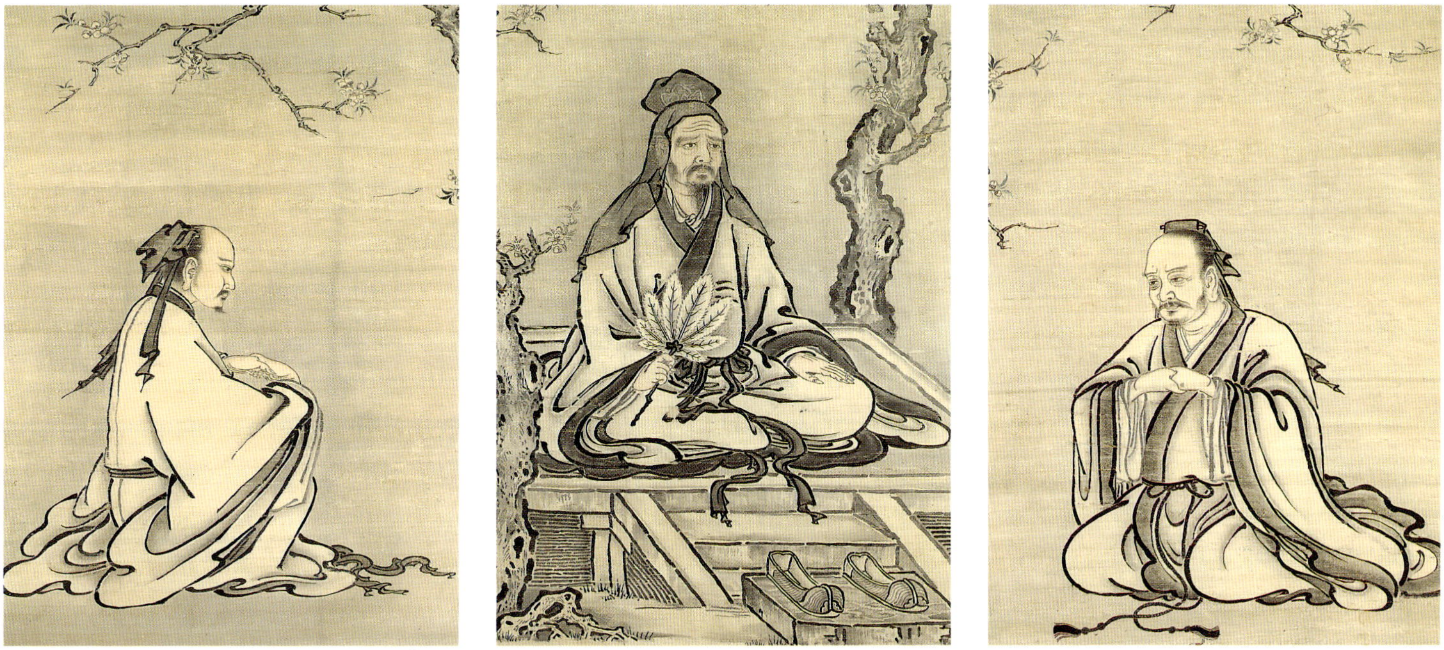

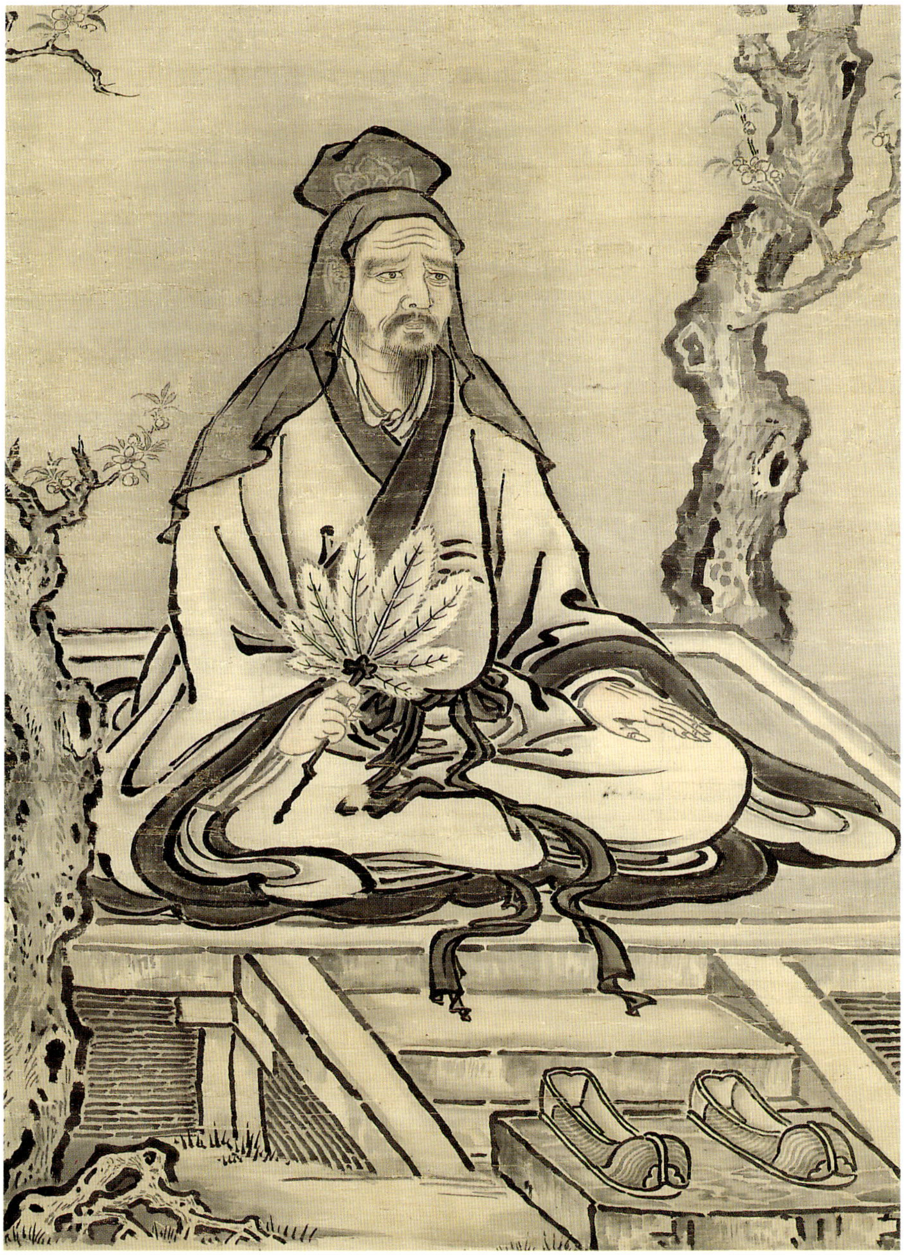

48

Traditionally attributed to Kano Tan'yū (1602-1674)

Confucius and Disciples Yan Hui and Zeng Sen at the "Apricot Altar"

Edo period, 17th century
Set of three panels; ink and colors on silk. 104.2 x 74.8 cm. (each panel)
Fenollosa-Weld Collection.
11.4399-4401

According to tradition, Confucius met with his followers at a place known as the "Apricot Altar." These unsigned paintings show the sage seated on a stone platform in the midst of apricot trees flanked by Yan Hui and Zeng Sen, his favorite students. The treatment of the subject is restrained and dignified, in keeping with the function of the triptych as the central icon in the Sekiten *ceremony, the biannual rites held at Confucian academies in Japan in honor of the sage and his followers. The earliest notice of a* Sekiten *ceremony in Japan dates to the year 701, and in the following centuries it was performed with some regularity in the imperial palace; at Confucian colleges such as the one in the city of Ashikaga established during the Ashikaga period; and with much greater frequency during the Edo period, when official sponsorship led to the founding of schools for Confucian studies and rites throughout the country.*

According to Ernest Fenollosa, who acquired the triptych in 1882 from Kano Tambi (1840-1893), the paintings are copies by Tan'yū after an earlier set by the founder of the Kano line, Masanobu (1434-1530), at one time kept in the Sage's Hall, or Seidō, *of the Ashikaga College.*

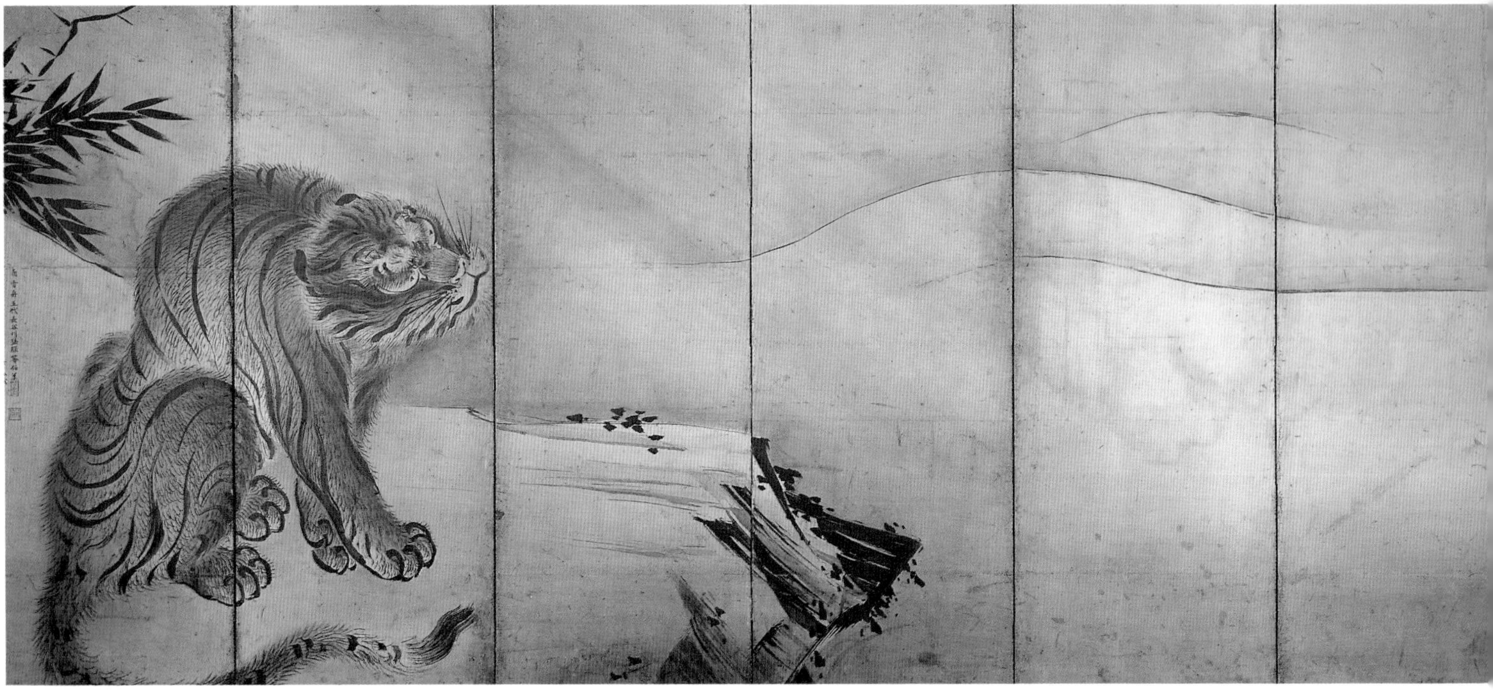

49
Hasegawa Tōhaku (1539-1610)
Dragon and Tiger
Momoyama period, dated 1606
Pair of six-panel folding screens; ink on paper. 153.1 x 335 cm. (each)
Fenollosa-Weld and Bigelow Collections. 11.4808; 11.7073

*The dynamic use of space and dramatic arrangement of compositional components in this expansive work are characteristic of the evocative paintings produced by Hasegawa Tōhaku, one of the most gifted and original artists of his time. Executed late in Tōhaku's life — in 1606, when he was sixty-eight years old — the screens reveal that he was then at the height of his creative powers. The inscriptions on each piece give his names, age, and honorary painter's rank (*Hōgen*: "Eye of the Law") and note in addition that Tōhaku considered himself the fifth lineal descendant in the artistic tradition established a century earlier by the prestigious priest-painter Sesshū (1420-1506). Tōhaku, who seems to have rebelled against the fashionable academic ideas of the Kano school, sought artistic inspiration in the great masters of earlier times — not only Japanese painters such as Sesshū and others of his day but also earlier Southern-Song ink painters such as Muqi. The Chinese master's monumental depictions of a dragon and tiger, preserved in the Daitoku-ji in Kyoto, were undoubtedly models for these screens.*

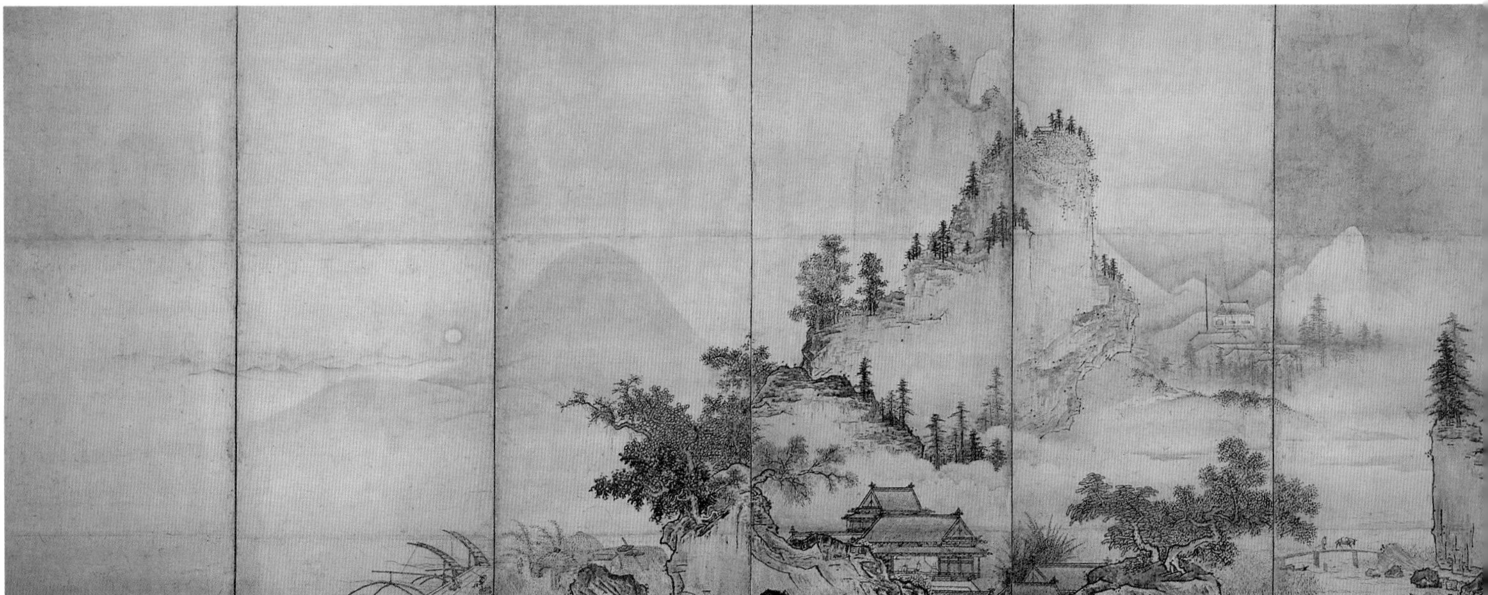

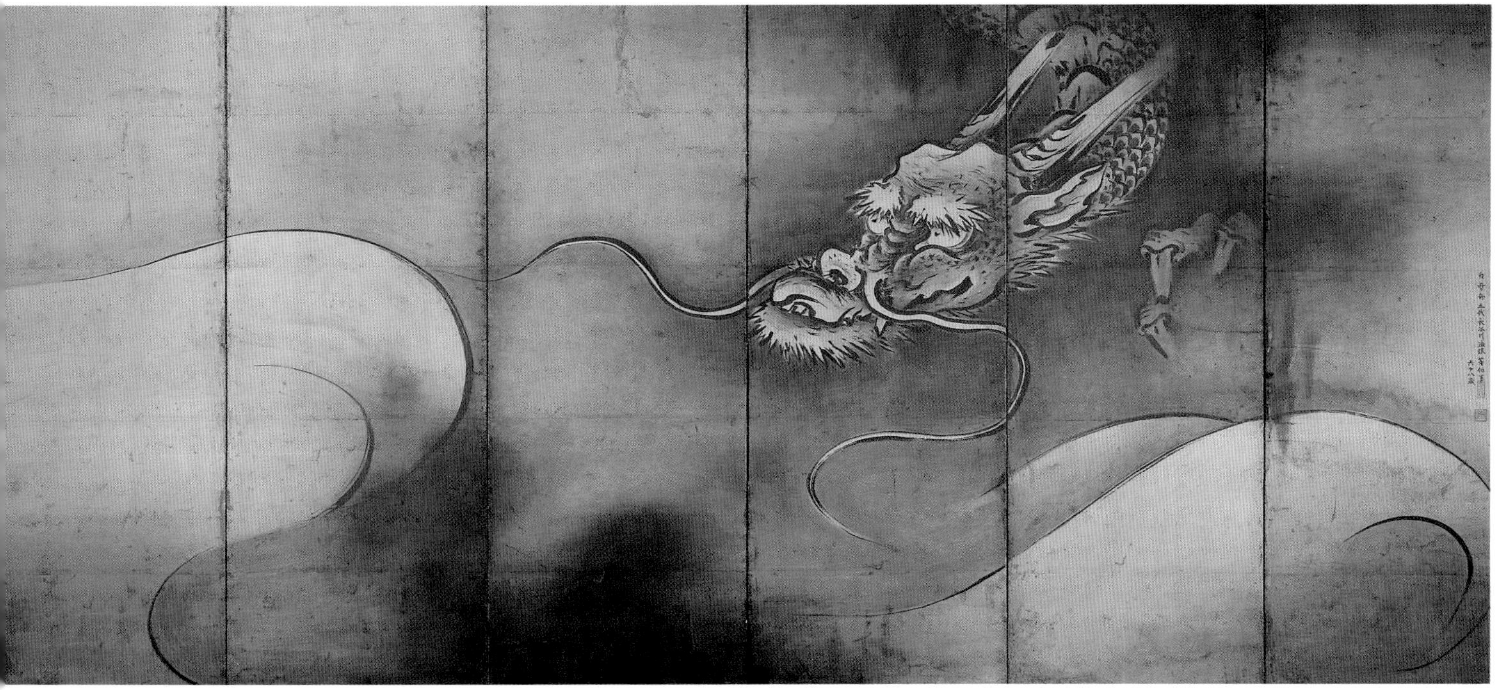

50
Unkoku Tōgan (1547-1618)
Landscapes
Momoyama period, early 17th century
Pair of six-panel folding screens; ink and light gold washes on paper.
145.7 x 348.4 cm. (each)
Fenollosa-Weld Collection.
11.4532-4533

Although Tōgan occasionally represented genre and bird-and-flower themes in color, the majority of his works are ink landscapes that draw their imaginary topographical features from Chinese pictorial traditions.

The Boston screens have neither signatures nor seals, but their firm attribution to Tōgan is supported by comparing them with one of his most famous landscapes: the set of fourteen sliding screens in the Dannanoma *chamber of the main hall of the Ōbai-in, a subtemple of the Daitoku-ji, the great Zen temple in Kyoto. These impressive works are said to have been executed about 1598, and the striking correspondences with the Boston screens in the details of brushwork, architectural and topographical particulars, and compositional conception show them to be clearly from the same hand. The treatment of the landscape components in the lower right-hand corner of the left screen reveals an obvious indebtedness to the beginning section of Sesshū's famous "long scroll," testifying to this master's influence on Tōgan.*

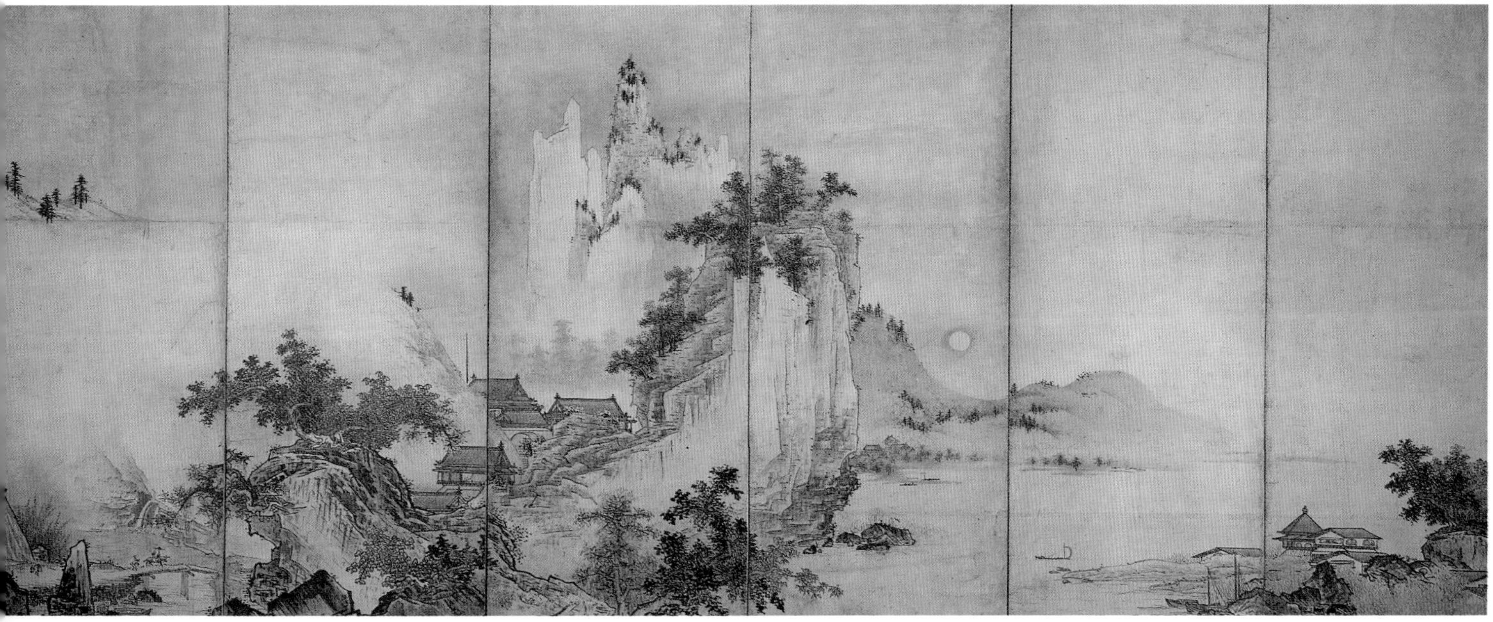

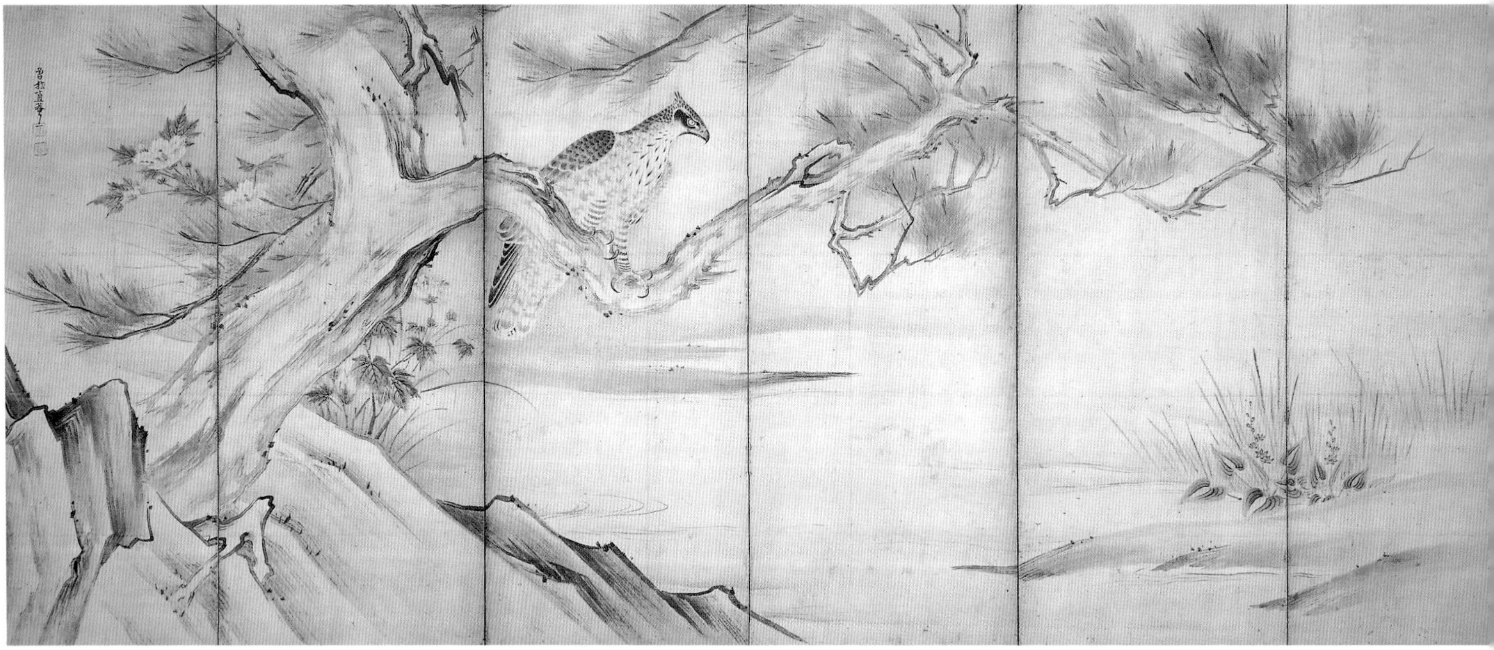

51
Sōga Nichokuan (active about 1656)
Eagle and Falcon
Edo period, 17th century
Pair of six-panel folding screens; ink on paper. 151.4 x 349 cm. (each)
Bigelow and Fenollosa-Weld Collections. 11.6912; 11.4809

The only example by Nichokuan that bears a specific date is a hanging-scroll triptych done in 1656 of hawks among pine, bamboo, and plum, which belongs to the Hōryū-ji in Nara Prefecture. As a consequence, this work constitutes the sole basis for stylistic comparison in studying other pieces from the artist's hand. In contrast to other works that have the same type of subject matter, the Boston screens appear to be influenced by the freer, more expansive style of his predecessor, Chokuan, and show less of the more arbitrary and mannered compositional ideas and brushwork ordinarily associated with Nichokuan — a circumstance that would seem to indicate that the Boston screens were executed somewhat earlier in Nichokuan's career and also perhaps earlier than the dated Hōryū-ji paintings. The two red seals that appear below the signatures on the Boston screens read "Kanetane" and "Nichokuan." The former appears also on screens in the collection of the Tokyo University of Fine Arts and Music.

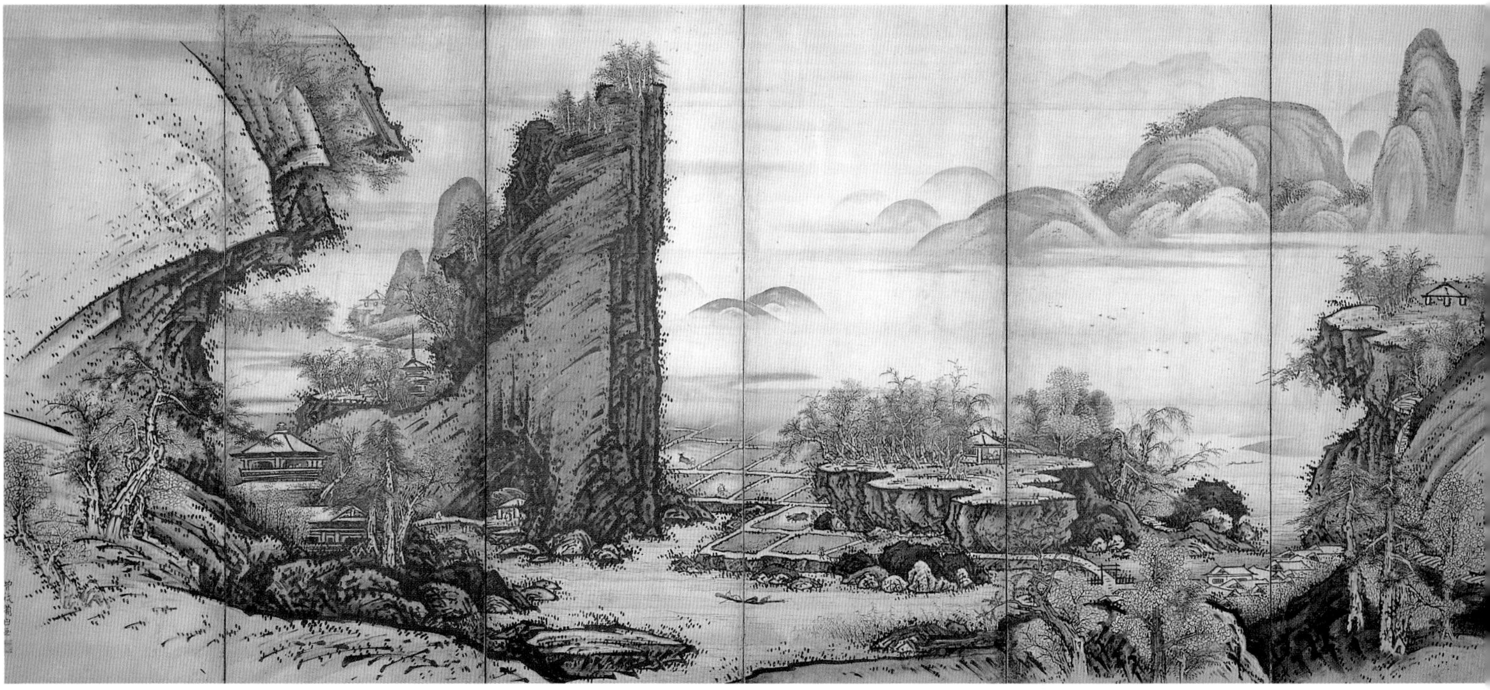

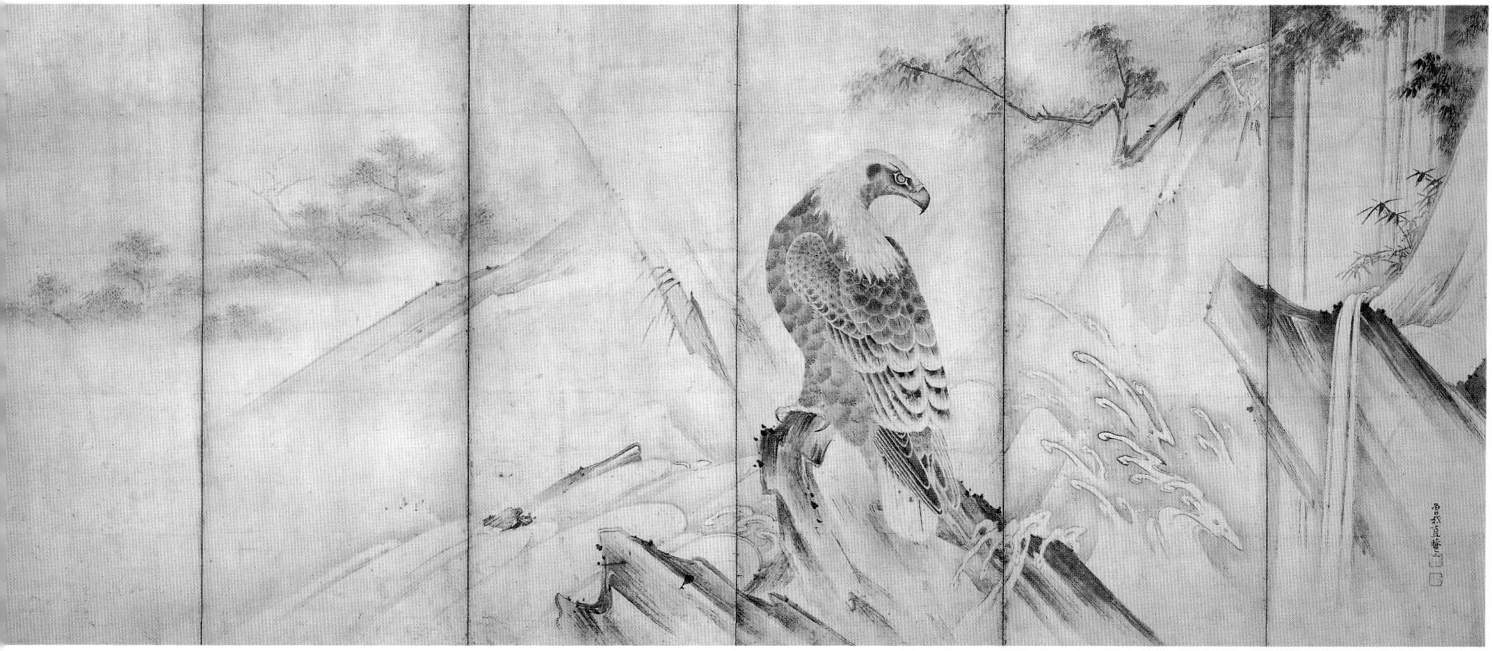

52
Sōga Shōhaku (1730-1781)
Landscapes
Edo period, about 1770
Pair of six-panel folding screens; ink on paper. 159.5 x 348.6 cm. (each)
Fenollosa-Weld Collection.
11.4507-4508

These monumental compositions rank among the artist's finest creative efforts; no other work from Shōhaku's hand demonstrates more convincingly his special affinity for landscape painting. The screens are notable for their stately rhythms balanced against contrapuntal passages of brushwork in a manner reminiscent of some grand pictorial passacaglia. Vagueness or subtle evocation is antithetical here — instead, the total impression is one of tectonic structure, with bold forms rendered emphatically. The brushwork is crisp, sinewy, and measured, but there is little sense of the calligraphic importance of the single line; rather, the brushstrokes are used primarily in a cumulative manner to build up ink passages and formulate compositional elements, and the artist's pleasure in the tactile process of manipulating the brush is apparent.

The name in the signature on the right screen provides a valuable bit of biographical information about Shōhaku. It reads "Miura Ketsumei," and this supports the assumption that the artist's family name was Miura — a claim supported both by the appearance of the name on the gravestone of Shōhaku's sister and by entries in the temple records of the Kōshō-ji, the temple in Kyoto where Shōhaku is buried.

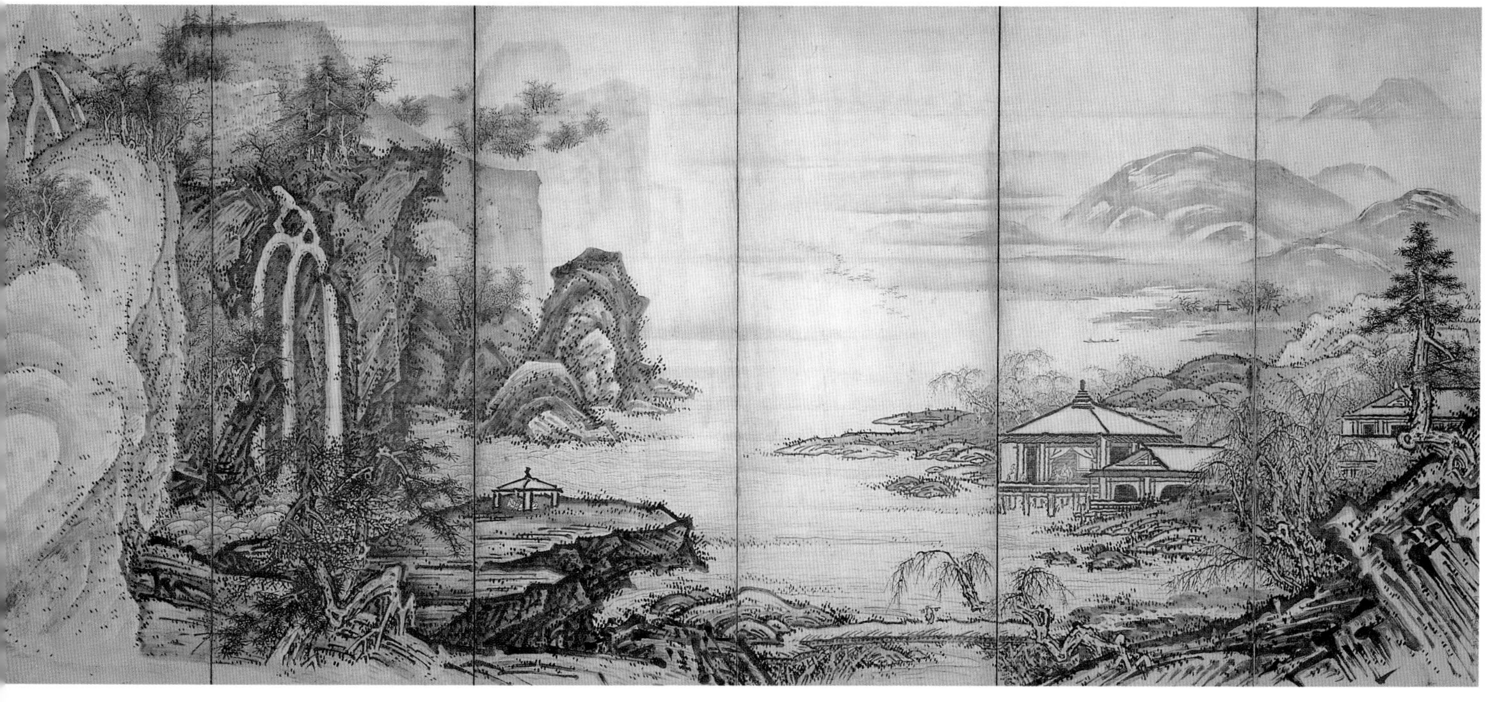

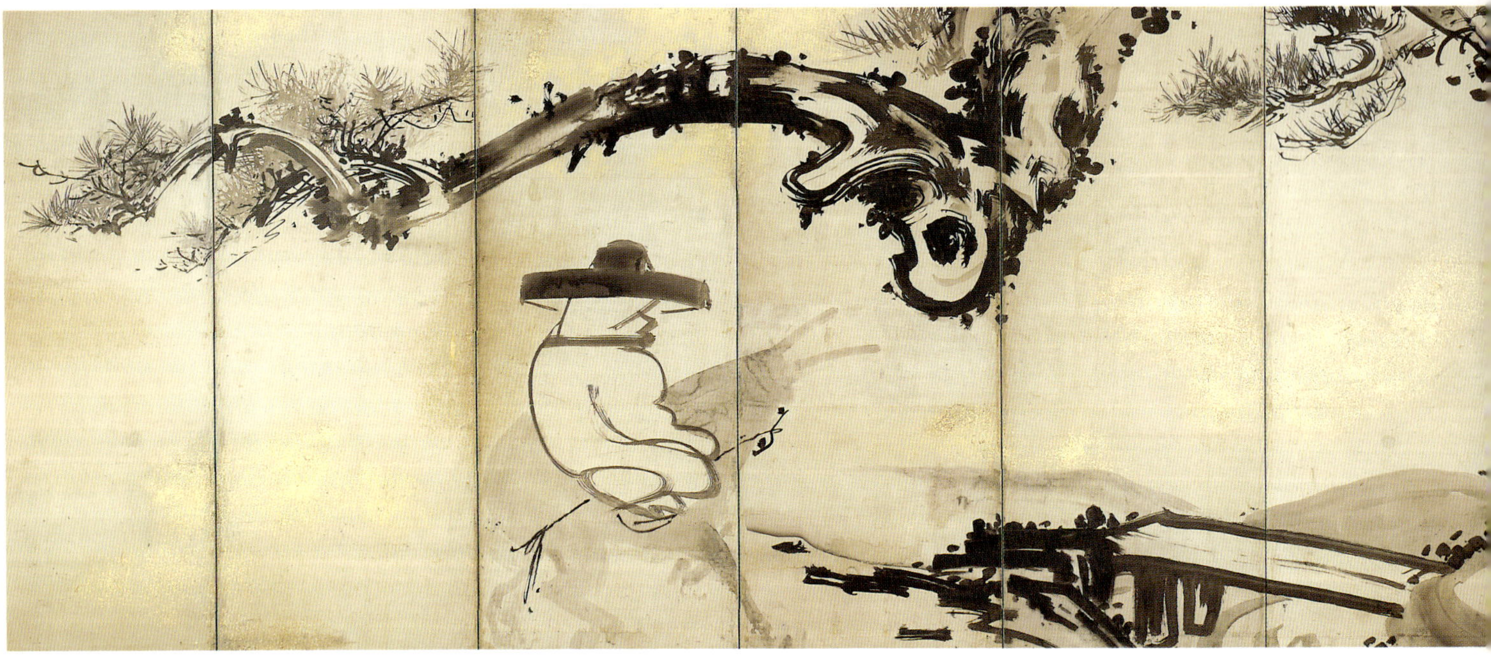

53
Sōga Shōhaku (1730-1781)
The Four Sages of Mount Shang
Edo period, 18th century
Pair of six-panel folding screens; ink and gold on paper.
156.2 x 366.6 cm. (each)
Fenollosa-Weld Collection.
11.4513-4514

These powerful screens are by the great individualist painter Sōga Shōhaku, a man whose creative vision and expressive means are so personal and idiosyncratic that his works cannot be confused with those of any other Japanese artist. It appears that he was a native of Kyoto. Although his creative activities were centered there, he also spent extended periods of time traveling in the surrounding provinces, producing paintings in one location and then moving on to another as the inclination struck him. He seems to have had a reputation for eccentric behavior and unconventional painting methods, for various of his unusual exploits are preserved in literature and popular lore.

These screens, produced rather late in Shōhaku's life, exemplify the boldness of conception and audacious, imaginative brushwork of his mature period. The subject is a traditional one, drawn from the rich inventory of Chinese legend. The Four Sages were elderly paragons of moral rectitude who retired to the remote seclusion of Mount Shang in order to isolate themselves from the political disorders that occurred at the end of the third century B.C. They remained there until they saw that virtue prevailed once again in the world of human affairs, and only then were they induced to return. Shōhaku's waggish interpretation of the subject suggests that the Four Sages spent their long isolation in a variety of pleasurable pursuits.

54
Itō Jakuchū (1716-1800)
White Cockatoo on a Pine Branch
Edo period, 18th century
Hanging scroll; ink and colors on silk.
40.1 x 55.6 cm.
Charles B. Hoyt Collection. 50.1493

Itō Jakuchū was one of the most talented of the individualist painters active during the eighteenth century. Although he seems to have studied the academic style of the Kano school during his youth, the unique qualities to be seen in his paintings demonstrate that he was essentially self-taught.

Stories mention that Jakuchū was fond of brightly colored fowl and kept birds in order to study their appearance and behavior — a tradition supported by the fact that exotic fowl, including imported varieties, constitute a central preoccupation in his oeuvre. This painting of a white cockatoo demonstrates Jakuchū's interest in realism and his acute powers of observation, for the bird is so completely represented in spirit and detail that it seems imbued with life. The rendering of the pine and its needles demonstrates the artist's ability to synthesize different techniques and contrasting natural forms into a highly personal expressive means.

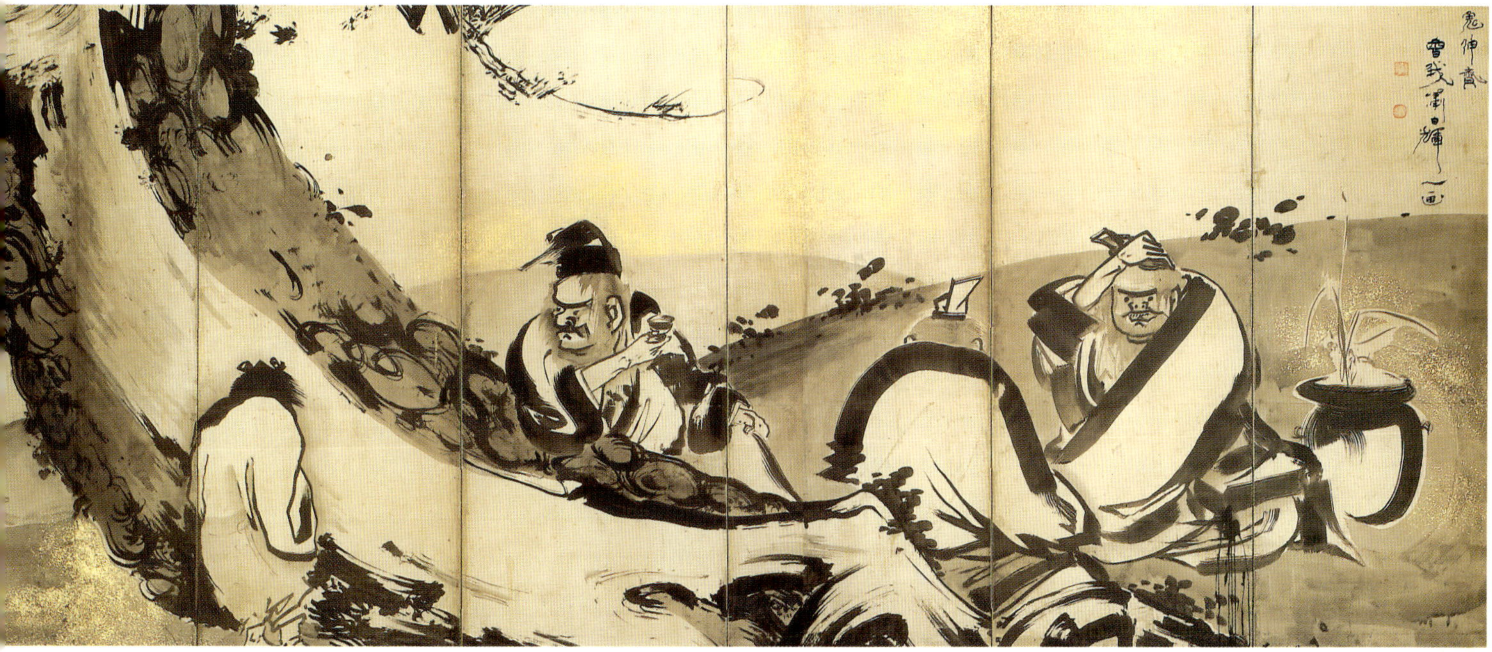

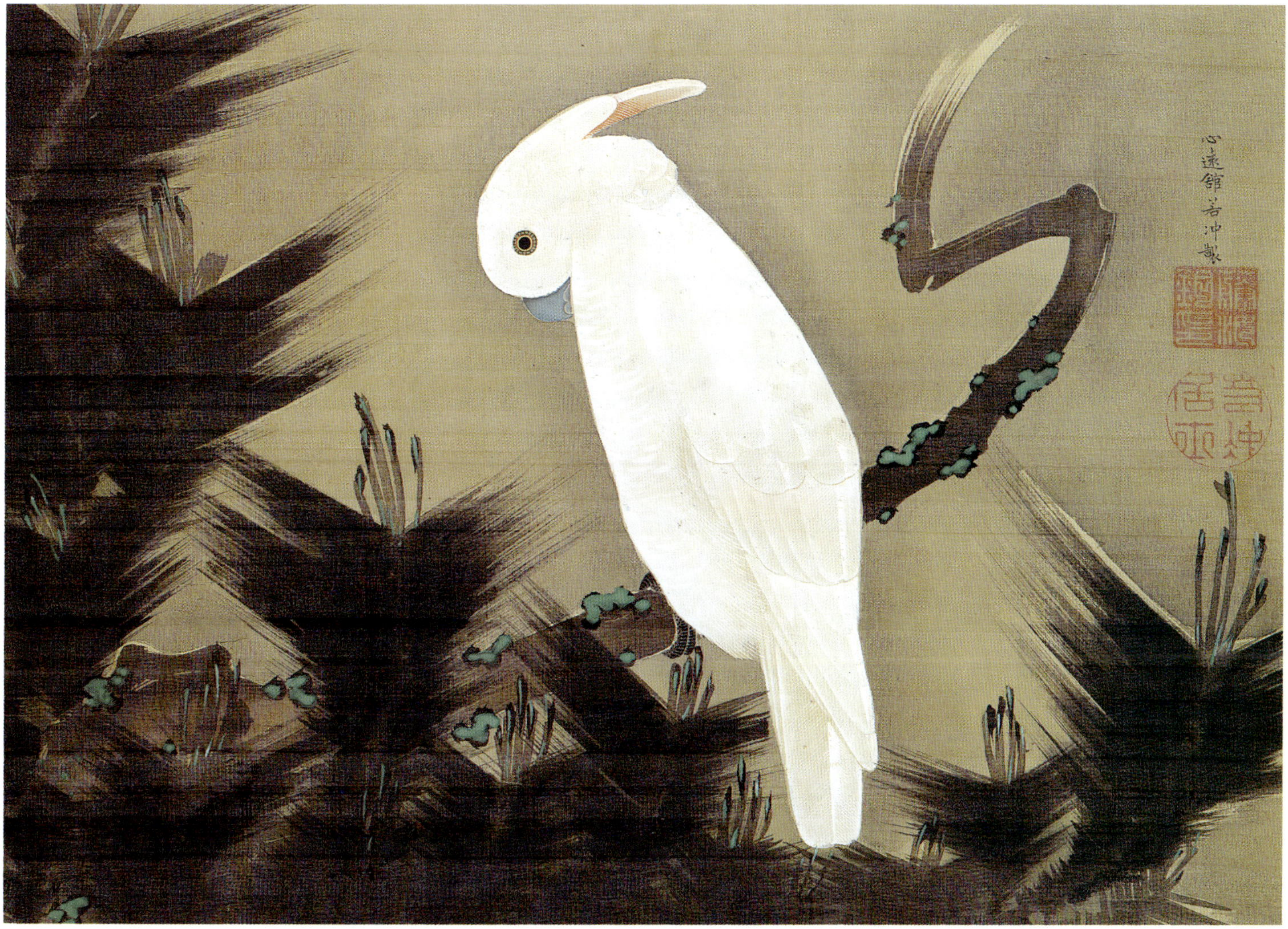
心遠館若冲製

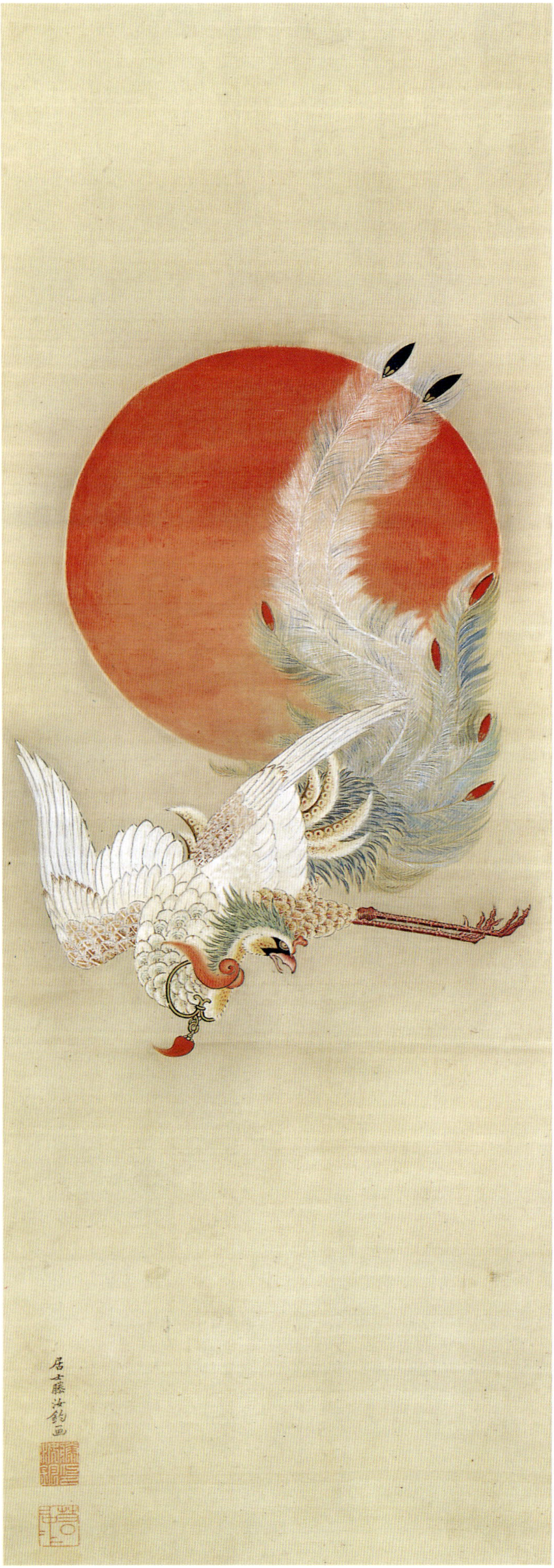

55
Itō Jakuchū (1716-1800)
Phoenix and Sun
Edo period, late 1760s-early 1770s
Hanging scroll; ink, colors, and gold on silk.
William Sturgis Bigelow Collection.
11.6940

Although a substantial number of paintings produced by the Kyoto master Itō Jakuchū during the second half of his life have been preserved, evidence of his earlier artistic activities is scarce. This rare painting, thought to have been produced during Jakuchū's early to mid-thirties, provides us with a tangible idea of his style and brushwork at this time which reflects indebtedness to techniques of the Kano school.

It is believed that Jakuchū, during his early formative years, studied under an older contemporary named Ooka Shumboku, who was trained in the methods and style of the Kano school. Moreover, the fact that the subject matter in this painting, the mythological Chinese phoenix, had already become a stock theme in the repertory of Kano school painters such as Tsunenobu (1636-1713) and Hidenobu (1640-1718) at least a generation before Jakuchū's birth, supports the contention that his inspirations came from this source. Comparison with details of Jakuchū's bird, together with its mannered execution, show the closest similarities with representations done by the two Kano painters.

56

Tosa Mitsuoki (1617-1691)

Quail and Autumn Plants

Edo period, 17th century

Hanging scroll; ink and colors on silk.

94.8 x 33.2 cm.

William Sturgis Bigelow Collection.

11.7188

Mitsuoki, the son of Tosa Mitsunori, was a painter in the Yamato-e style. Born in Sakai, he later attained a high position in the Court Bureau of Painting; this was the first time in 85 years that a member of the Tosa family had occupied such an important position in official painting circles. Mitsuoki introduced the sketching-from-life techniques of the Chinese Song academic style into the traditional Japanese Yamato-e style. This work shows autumn grasses and daisies with a quail in the foreground. The quail was Mitsuoki's favorite theme and a large number of similar works survive. The poem at the top of the picture reads: "Late autumn and deep in the grasses where the dew scatters in the cold breeze, a single quail cries". The signature reads: "Tosa Sakon no Shōgen Mitsuoki", and the square seal has "Mitsuoki no in (Seal of Mitsuoki)" in white on red.

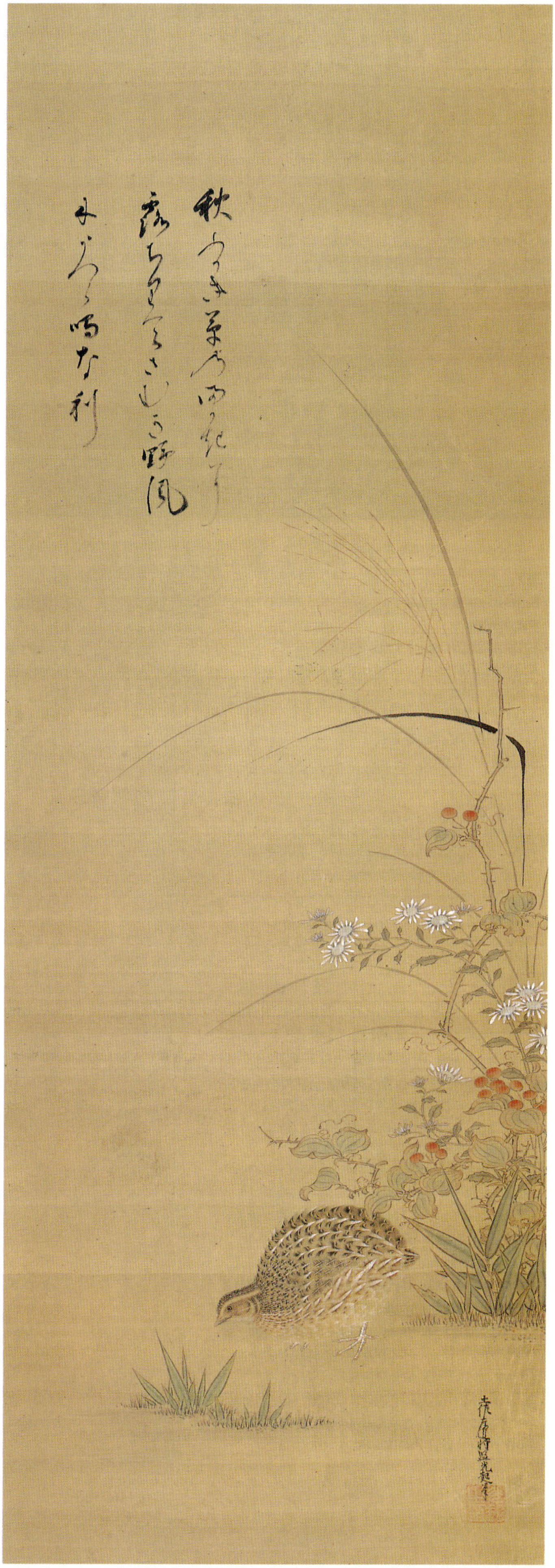

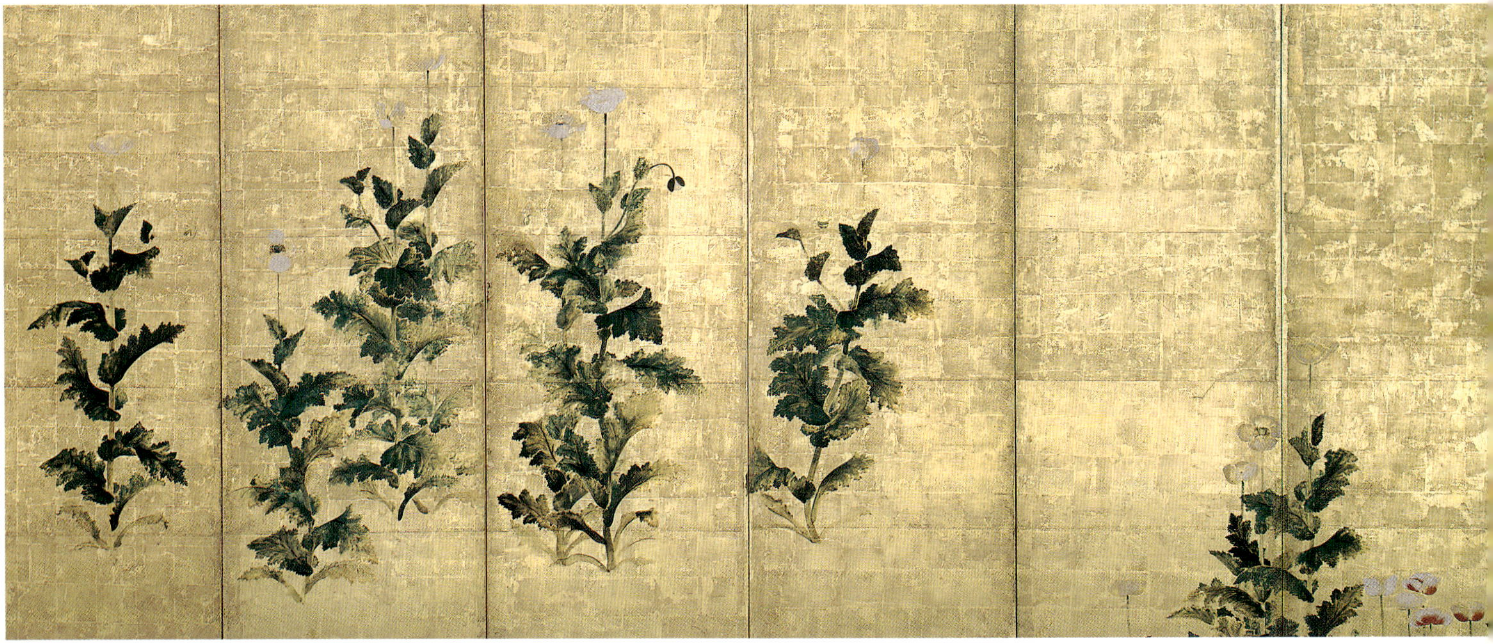

57
School of Sōtatsu
Poppies
Edo period, mid-17th century
Pair of six-panel folding screens; ink, colors, and gold on paper.
150.2 x 354.8 cm. (each)
Gift of Mrs. W. Scott Fitz.
11.1272-1273

A flowering garden of bright poppies extends boldly across the gold-leafed surfaces of both screens in a continuous composition. The plants are executed in a soft, modulated manner in thin pigments, which allows the gold ground to shine through from underneath and gives the leaves and petals an evocative quality. Each component is individually conceived and located in such an original manner that, despite the homogeneity of the subject matter, no sense of repetition or monotony is anywhere apparent.

No signature or seal appears on these screens. A label on the back of one attributes them to the renowned Rimpa master Sōtatsu and states that they were presented to the Tentoku-in, a subtemple in the monastery complex at Mt. Koya, by a certain Lord Maeda. Although there are many stylistic features in the screens that compare closely with details in paintings from Sōtatsu's hand, and their high level of artistic quality confirms that they are from the hand of a gifted painter, it is more likely that they were produced by an artist of the generation following Sōtatsu's.

58
Attributed to Tawaraya Sōtatsu (active early 17th century)
Sparrows and Bamboo
Grebes
Edo period, 17th century
Pair of hanging scrolls; ink on paper.
31.2 x 47.5 cm. (each)
William Sturgis Bigelow Collection.
11.7222 and 11.7223

Tawaraya Sōtatsu (?-1643) and his mentor and collaborator Hon'ami Kōetsu (1558-1637) are the chief figures in the new school of artists and craftsmen that evolved under Kōetsu's leadership during the cultural revival that took place in Kyoto during the late sixteenth and early seventeenth centuries. Demonstrating the renewed preoccupation with aristocratic taste in Kyoto at the time, Kōetsu and his group produced pieces that are characterized by elegant spontaneity of conception and an inspired sense of pictorial design. These artists were motivated by an interest in the courtly arts of earlier centuries, and they drew freely from Chinese as well as native traditions, which they synthesized into new expressive forms.

The monochrome ink scrolls here provide a particularly instructive example of this synthesizing process, for the subjects, although unmistakably indebted to traditional Chinese pictorial prototypes that had long been familiar in Japan, are rendered in a new and evocative manner inspired by the indigenous canons of aristocratic taste of the period. The soft, understated brushwork in the paintings, with its subtle nuances of shade and wash, is exemplary of this taste, and the use of tarashikomi *technique, in which darker ink is added to lighter, already wetted areas so that it diffuses spontaneously outward, is a distinctive characteristic of the paintings of the Kōetsu-Sōtatsu school. The* tarashikomi *brushwork in the depiction of waterfowl here compares closely with the treatment of the same species in Sōtatsu's* Water Birds in a Lotus Pond *(Kyoto National Museum), which is registered as a National Treasure.*

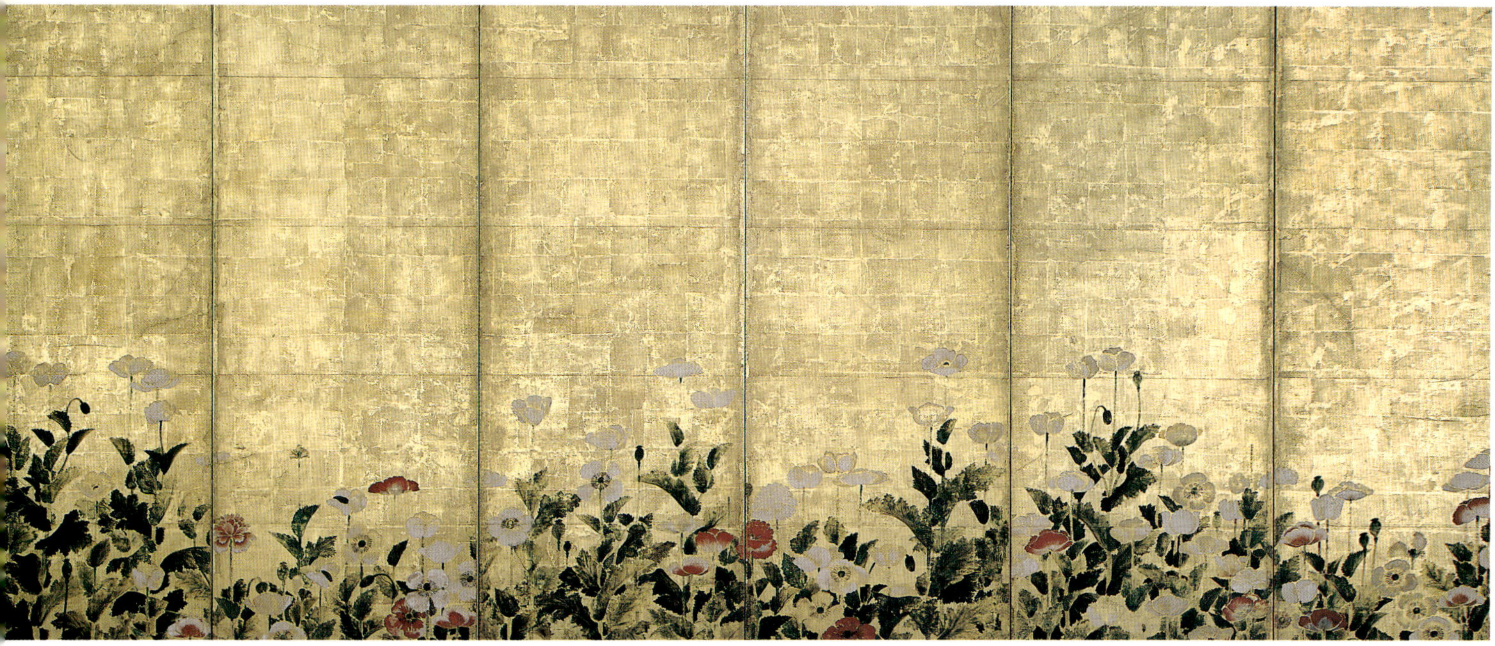

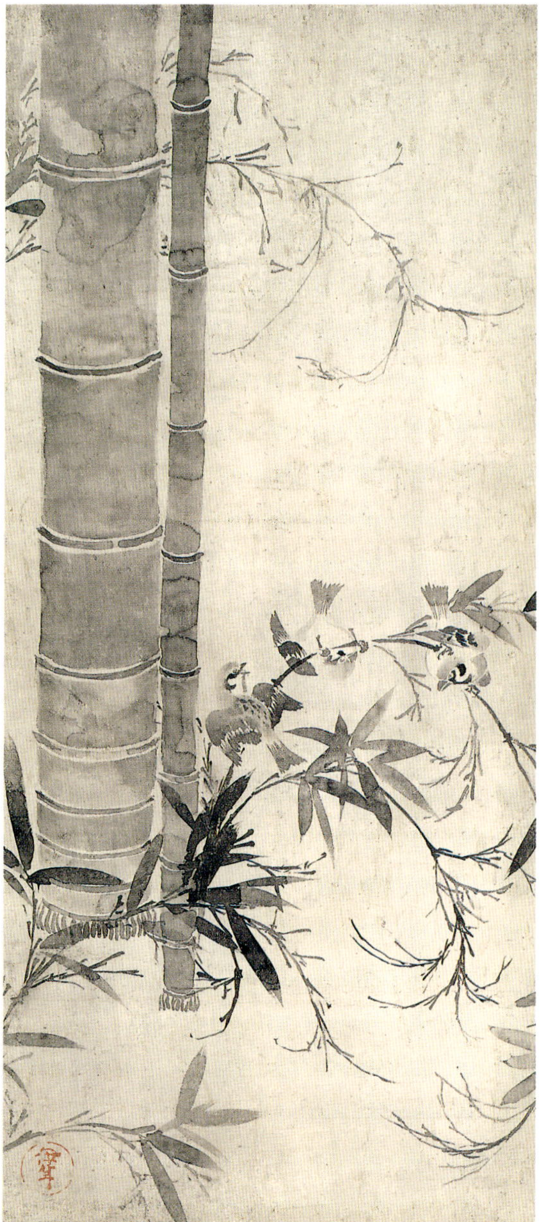

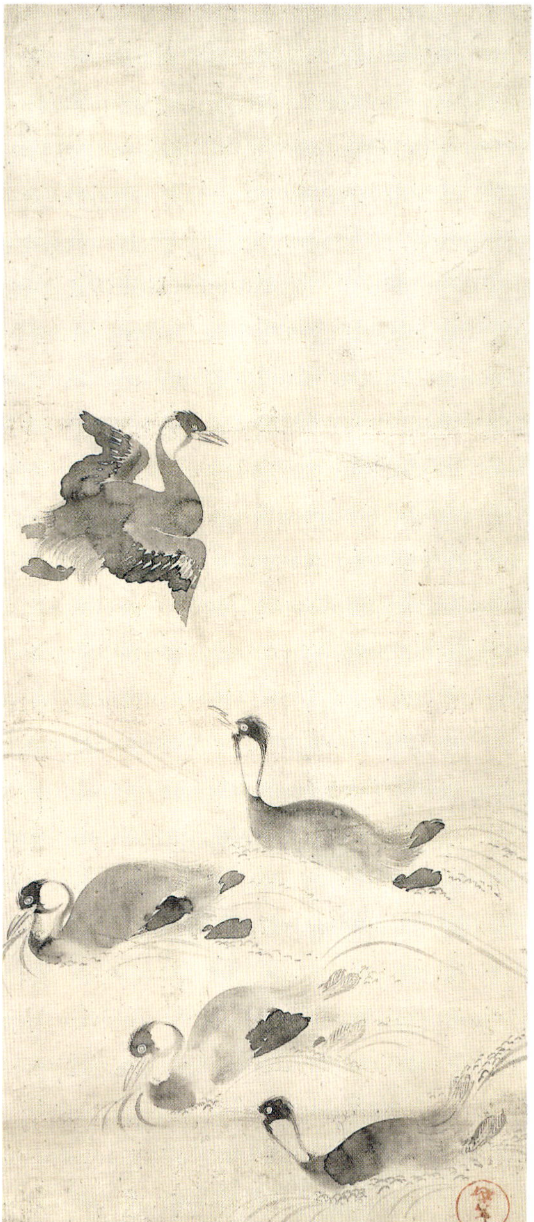

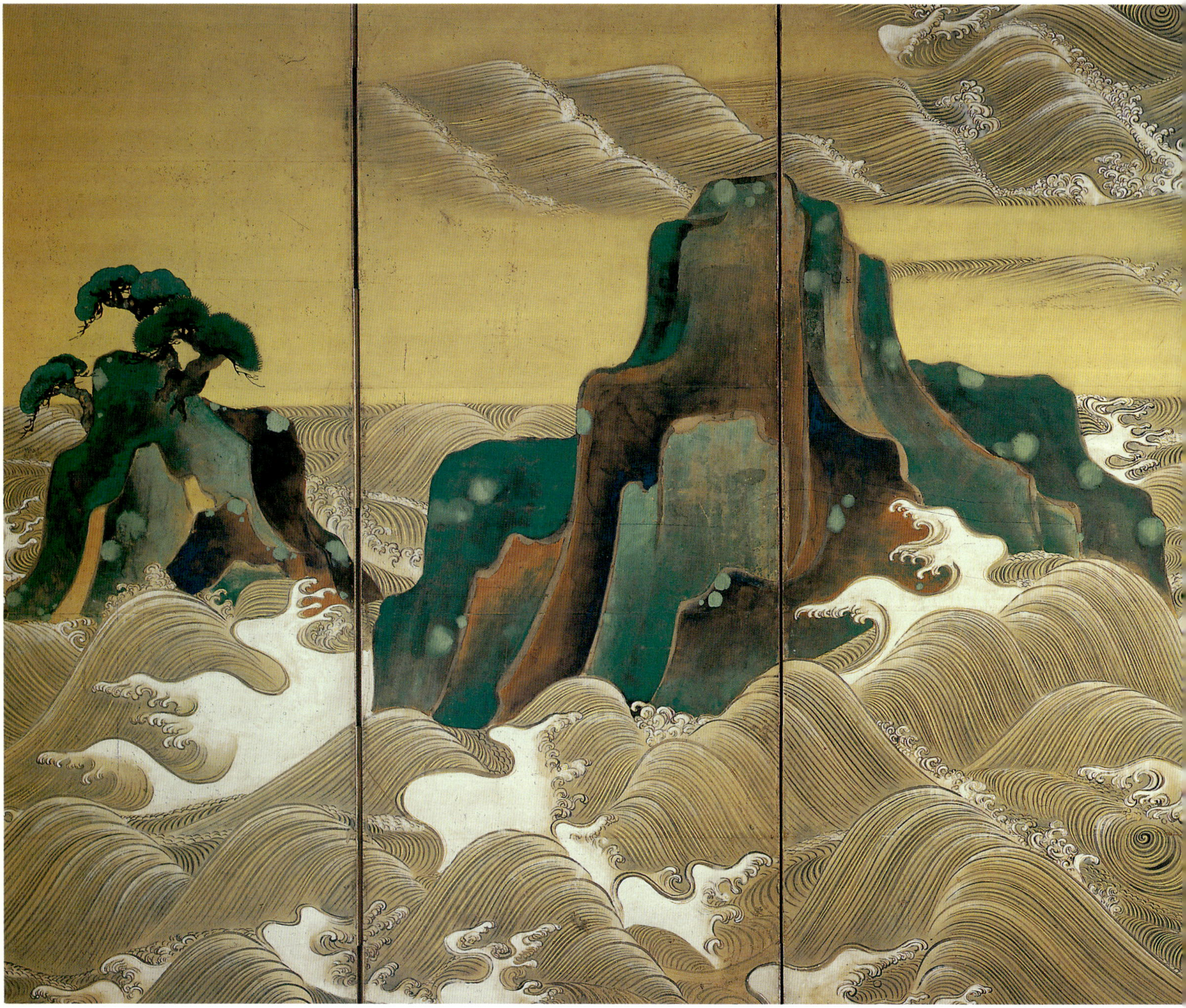

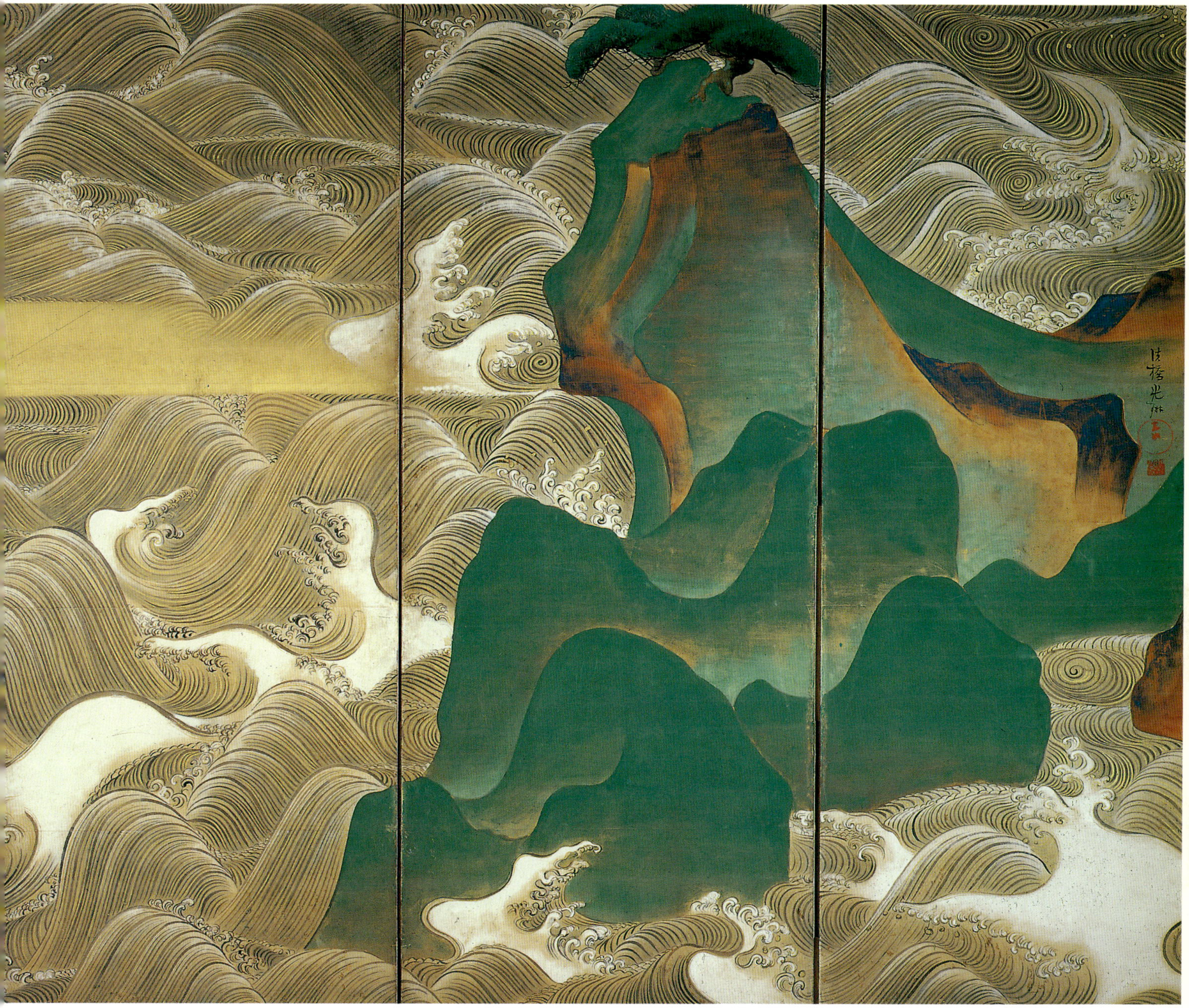

59
Attributed to Ogata Kōrin (1658-1716)
Scenic View of Matsushima
Edo period, early 18th century
Six-panel folding screen; ink, colors, and gold on paper. 155 x 370 cm.
Fenollosa-Weld Collection. 11.4584

The pine-clad islands of Matsushima, a location close to the city of Sendai in northeastern Japan, have been regarded traditionally as one of the country's three most scenic locations. The rugged beauty of this miniature archipelago, which consists of hundreds of small islands that rise precipitously from the foaming waves, has made it a popular subject in Japanese art, and painters of the Rimpa school such as Korin depicted it with some regularity. Although this interpretation of the subject was certainly inspired by the great screens created early in the seventeenth century by Tawaraya Sōtatsu (now in the Freer Gallery of Art, Washington, D.C.), Kōrin's own expressive inclinations are also clearly apparent in the assertive forms and contours of the islands and the mannered decorative patterns of the waves. The evidence of repainting in certain localized areas, which may have resulted in some slight modification in the appearance of the screen, remains to be studied.

Ernest Fenollosa happened upon this screen during his first trip to the ancient capital city of Kyoto in 1880 and it is thus one of the first major works of Japanese painting to be acquired by a foreigner.

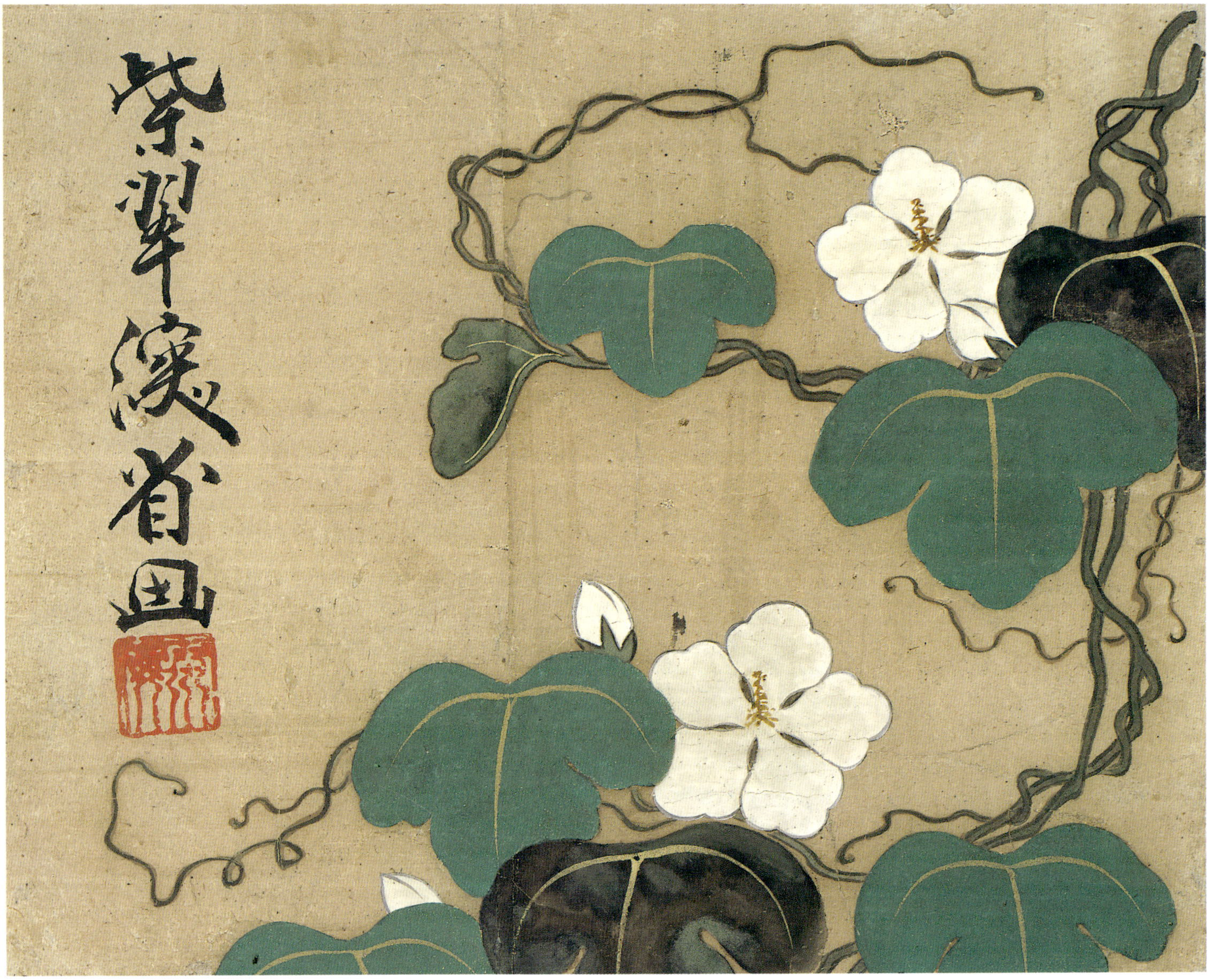

60
Ogata Kenzan (1663-1743)
Moonflower
Edo period
Hanging scroll; ink, colors, and gold on paper. 24 x 30 cm.
William Sturgis Bigelow Collection. 11.7206

Ogata Kōrin (1656-1716) and his younger brother Kenzan (1663-1743) are the leading figures among the third-generation followers of the artistic line established by Kōetsu and Sōtatsu in Kyoto during the late sixteenth and early seventeenth century. Kōrin's chief success was as a painter of screens and fans, which were often based on Sōtatsu's pictorial motifs but executed in a more forceful, conceptualized manner; while Kenzan is remembered primarily as a ceramicist who was inspired by the ideas of Kōetsu and came into possession of the master's techniques of pottery manufacture.

Kenzan's versatility was such that he was also a proficient painter and calligrapher, and a substantial number of pieces from his later years have been preserved. He seems to have been introspective and retiring by nature, and his circle of friends consisted mainly of cultivated members of the aristocracy, men of letters, and priests of the Zen sect. Basing his lifestyle on the literati ideal, Kenzan not only devoted himself to painting, calligraphy, and the tea ceremony, but also was a versatile poet.

The moonflower appears to have been a favorite subject of Kenzan's, and a number of his works with this motif have been preserved, such as the hanging scroll in the Freer Gallery, which closely resembles the Boston painting in detail and conception. The use of strong unmodulated pigments here has immediate parallels in certain of Kenzan's decorative designs for pottery.

61

Shiba Kōkan (1747-1818)

Goose

Edo period, late 18th-early 19th century

Hanging scroll; ink and colors on silk.

121.3 x 52.7 cm.

William Sturgis Bigelow Collection.

11.8121

The career of Shiba Kōkan exemplifies the restless new spirit of artistic experimentation that characterizes the evolution of Japanese painting during the eighteenth century. Kōkan received his earliest training as a pupil of the traditional Kano school, but he appears to have tired of the school's orthodox canons and tedious didactic methods and to have become a student of Sō Shiseki, an advocate of the colorful Chinese academic bird-and-flower pictorial traditions of the Ming period. Turning next to the Ukiyo-e school, Kōkan produced proficient works under the name of Harushige as well as convincing forgeries of the master Harunobu. Around 1780 he shifted his attention to yet another idiom — paintings that reflected the influence of Western pictorial subjects, ideas, and perspective, done in imitation of European etchings and oil paintings.

Kōkan's attempts at approximating the European oil medium were hampered — as were those of any contemporary Japanese artist working toward similar ends — not only by lack of instruction but also by the absence of materials such as European pigments, canvas, and brushes basic to the technique. His simulations involved the use of water-based pigments to which was added gofun, *or ground clamshell. The addition of this chalky substance facilitated the transition from one tonality to another, but the result was a murky quality that gave the medium the name* doro-e, *or "mud pictures." Although the addition of oil to this compound created a glossy surface, it could not reproduce the lustrous, translucent quality of Western oils.*

This striking depiction of a goose is typical of Kōkan's "Western" compositions in conception and execution. The artist has emulated European ideas of realistic representation and attempted to create the illusion of deep space through the use of atmospheric perspective and Western scientific principles of spatial recession. In the upper right-hand corner, Kōkan's name is written vertically in black Chinese characters, accompanied by a horizontal inscription in red in quasi-Dutch that the artist utilized often in his paintings executed in the European manner.

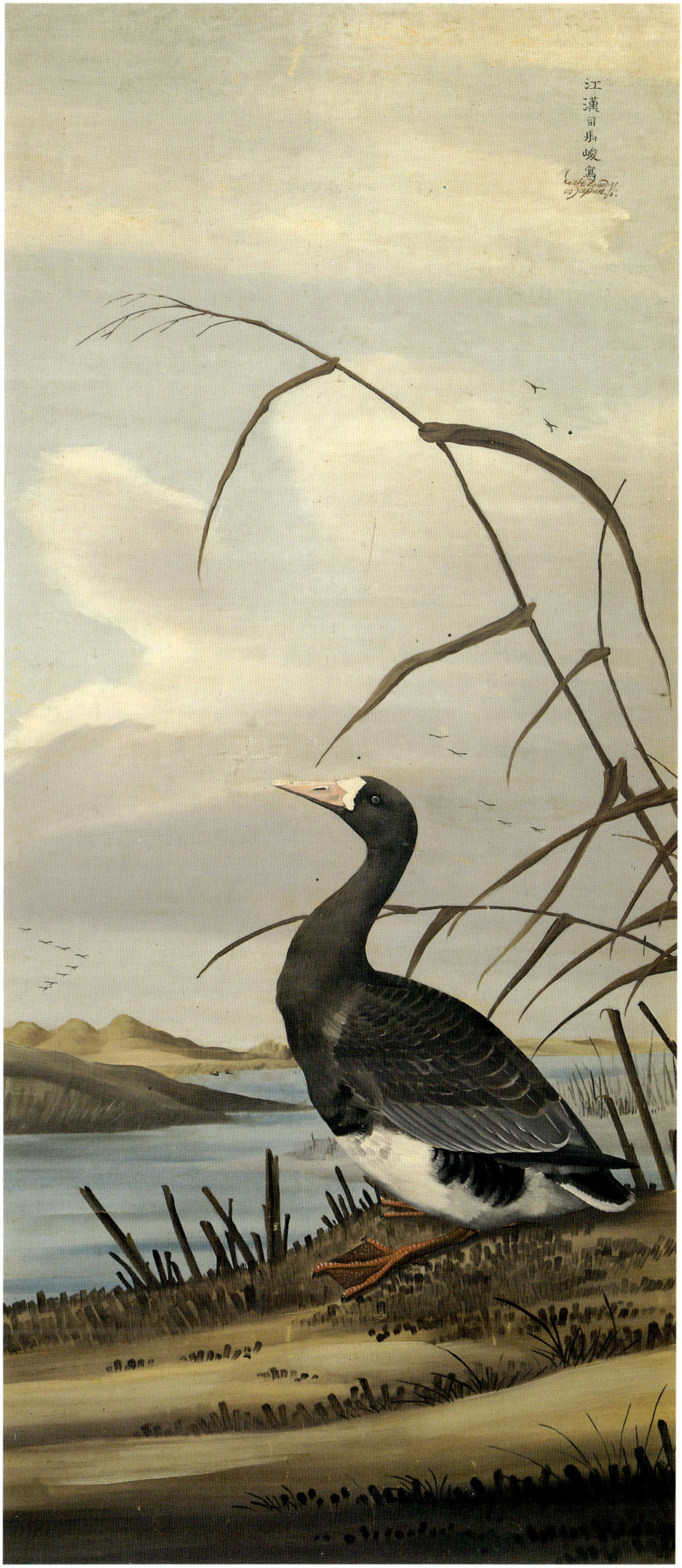

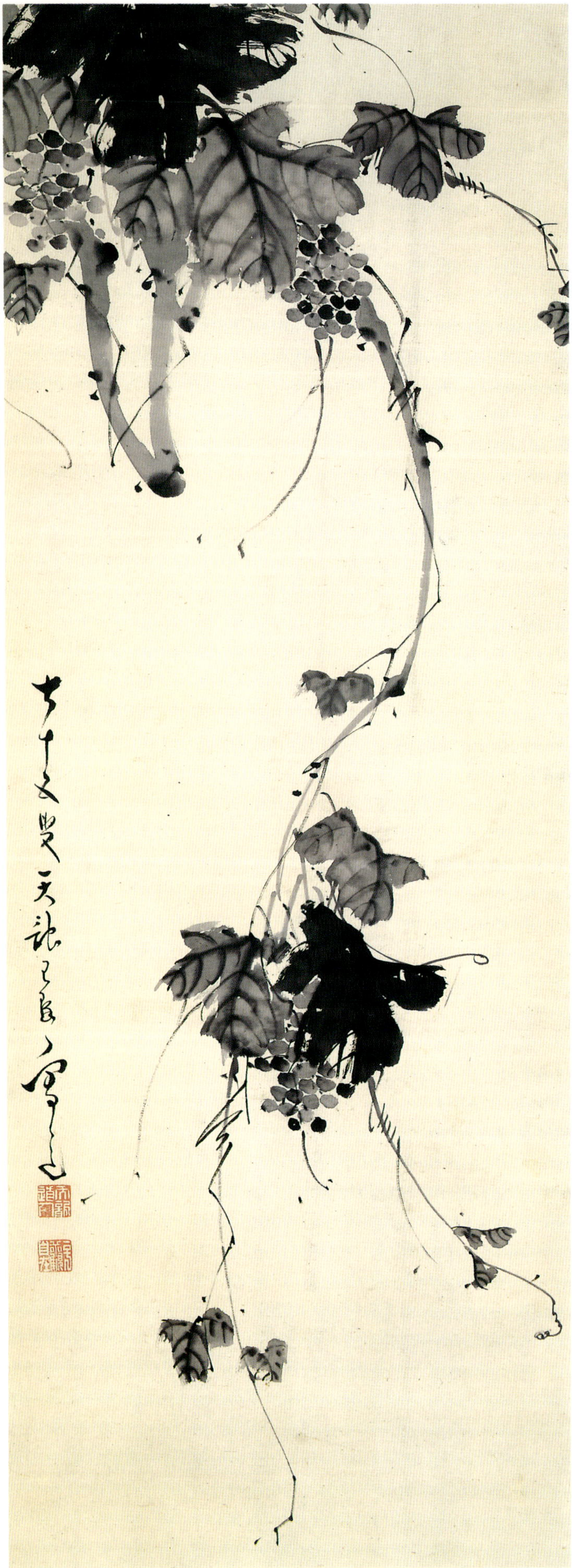

62
Tenryū Dojin (1718-1810)
Grapes Hanging from a Vine
Japan, Edo period, 1793
Hanging scroll; ink on paper.
128 x 48 cm.
Keith McLeod Fund. 1988.354

This dynamic hanging scroll of grapes suspended from a vine was painted by Tenryū Dojin, an artist well-known for his compositions of grapes. In fact, Tenryū Dojin wrote a book, Principles of Vine Painting *(Budō gafu) in 1797, four years after this painting was executed. Unfortunately very little is known of the biography of the artist except that he studied under the Nagasaki artist, Kumashira Yūhi (1693-1772).*

The subtle modeling of the grapes and veined leaves suggests their three-dimensionality, and is characteristic of paintings of the Nagasaki school, which was strongly influenced by contemporary Chinese works. The calligraphic brushwork juxtaposing the thin tendrils against the broad areas of flat ink wash convey the visual power of Tenryū Dojin's work.

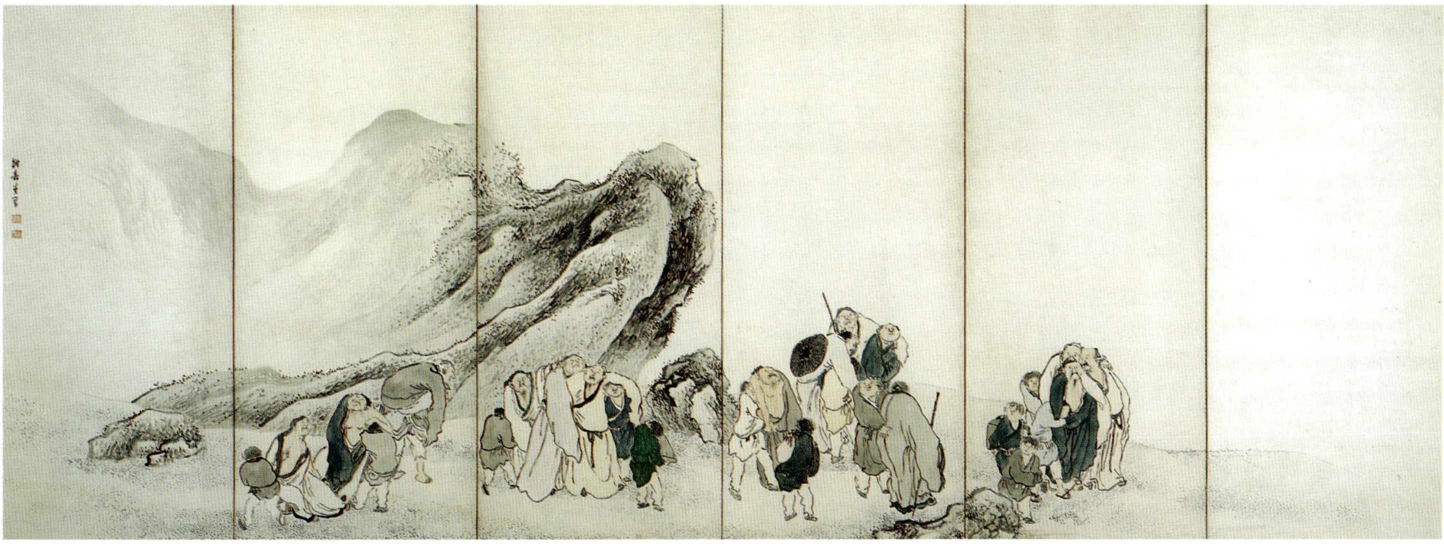

63
Yosa Buson (1716-1783)
Revelry on a Mountain Path
Boating on the River
Edo period, late 1770s
Pair of six-panel folding screens; ink and colors on paper. 136 x 361 cm. (each)
Frederick L. Jack Fund. 58.952-953

Yosa Buson is recognized as one of the most creative and original members of the second-generation Bunjin *(Literati) painters and a master Haiku poet in Japan. Buson's career as a painter evolved slowly, for he experimented with a variety of styles and concepts, inspired in the main by Chinese pictorial traditions, before he finally developed his own distinctive means of expression. As a consequence, his most accomplished works belong to the last decade of his life, and the screens shown here, which are thought to have been produced when the artist was about sixty, belong to this period.*

The screens show Buson's inspired interpretation of a typical Chinese theme, a congenial gathering of literati, intoxicated with the pleasures of nature, poetry, and wine. In the left-hand screen, a happy band of tipsy compatriots is shown moving along to the right, assisted in their erratic progress by solicitous servants and followers. Behind them, a bizarre outcropping of rock leans precariously to the right, its profile echoing the unstable postures of the figures below. On the right-hand screen, another coterie of bibulous literati is shown in a small boat, setting out on a river excursion, while several companions stand by a willow tree, watching their departure.

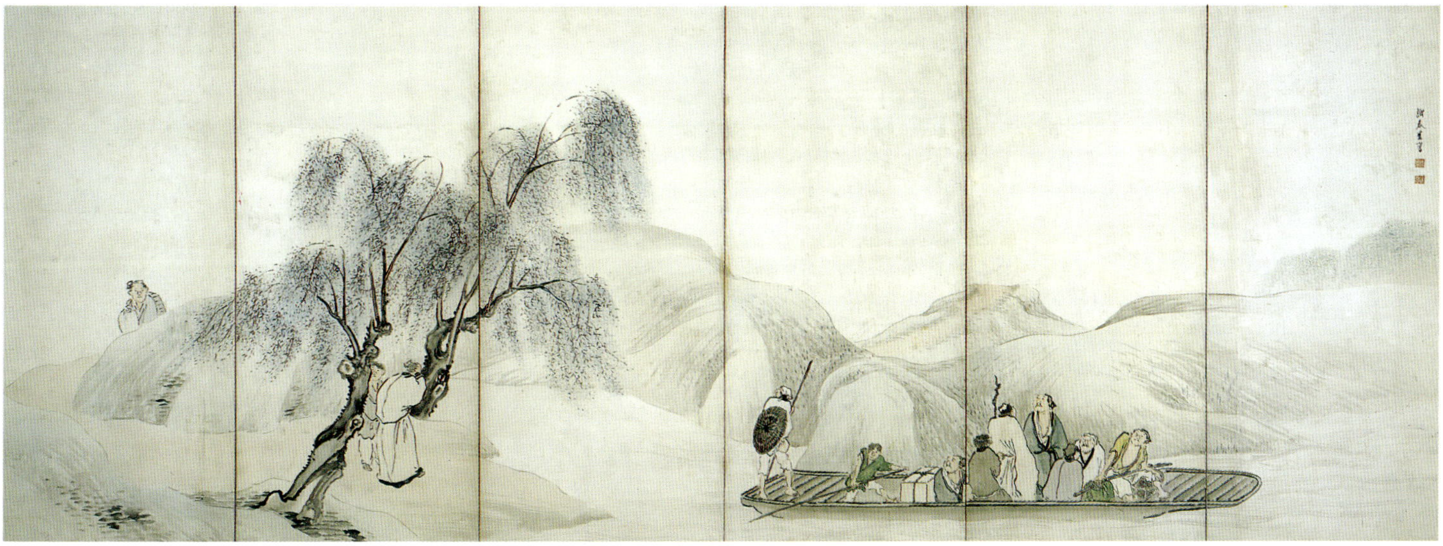

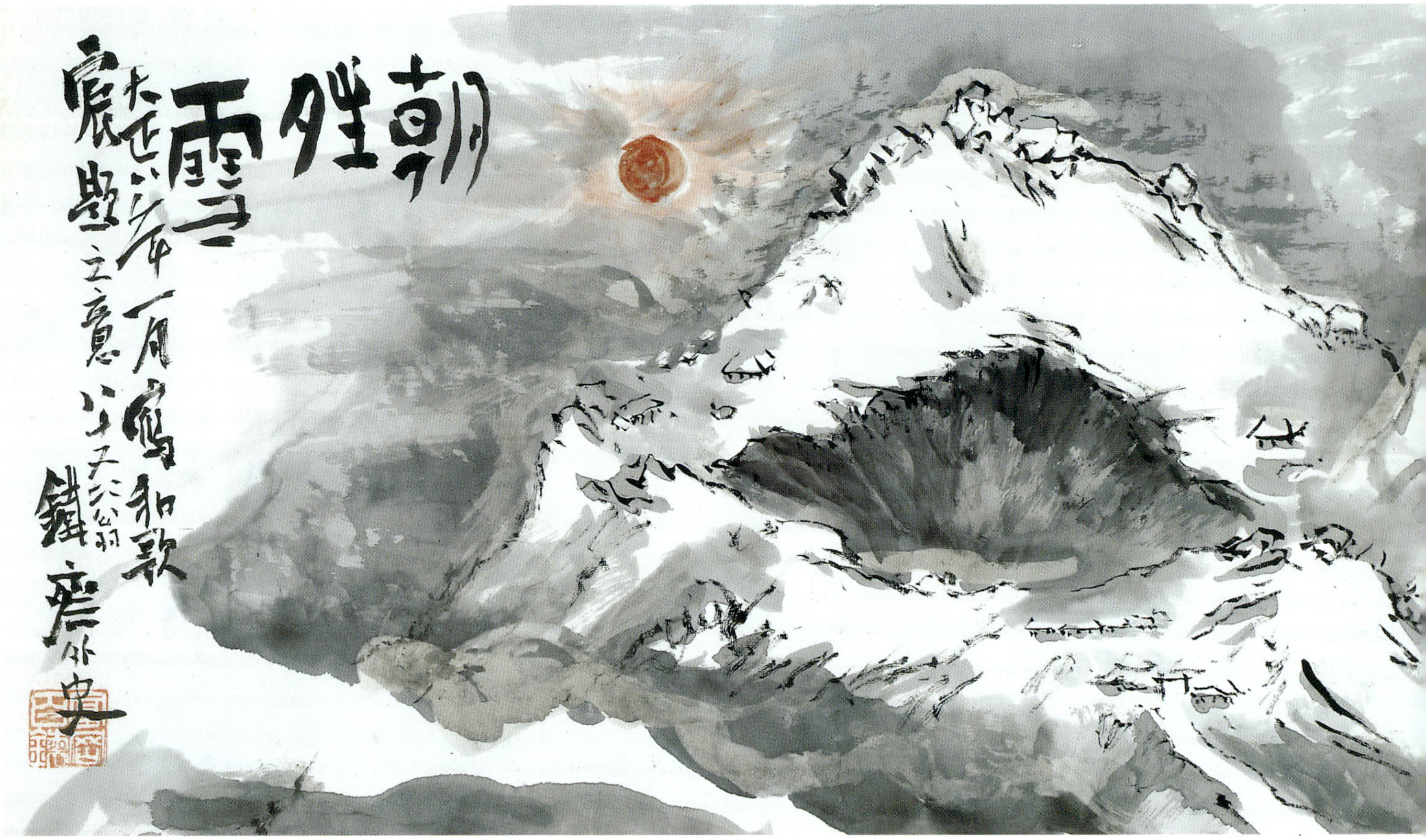

64
Tomioka Tessai (1836-1924)
Clearing Weather after Snow on Summit of Mt. Fuji
Taisho period, dated 1919
Hanging scroll; ink and colors on paper. 32 x 76.5 cm.
Gift of the Very Reverend Kojo Sakamoto. 55.492

Tomioka Tessai was one of the last and the most illustrious of the long line of Bunjinga *("Literati Painting") artists that began in the Edo period. In 1919, when he was eighty-three, he suffered a severe loss by the death of his son Kenzō and it is thought that he worked single-mindedly on his painting as a means of overcoming this grief. His work subsequently acquired a new vigorous freedom and richness. His wife Haruko regularly submitted poems in the New Year's Imperial Poetry Contest for which the theme is set by the emperor himself, and Tessai in his last years painted a picture each New Year's to illustrate that year's theme. This work is inscribed with the theme for 1919, "Snow Beneath a Clear Sky;" it depicts the snow-covered summit of Mt. Fuji in a free, eccentric manner and evokes a massive sense of scale. The brilliantly shining morning sun seen beyond the mountain suggests that the work was intended to represent the first sunrise of the year. It is one of the twelve scroll paintings presented to the Museum in 1955 by the Kiyoshi Kōjin Seichō-ji, a temple in Takarazuka.*

65
Maruyama Ōkyo (1733-1795)
Dragon and Tiger
Edo period, dated 1777
Pair of hanging scrolls; monochrome ink on paper. 134.5 x 89.1 cm. (each)
William Sturgis Bigelow Collection. 11.8498-8499

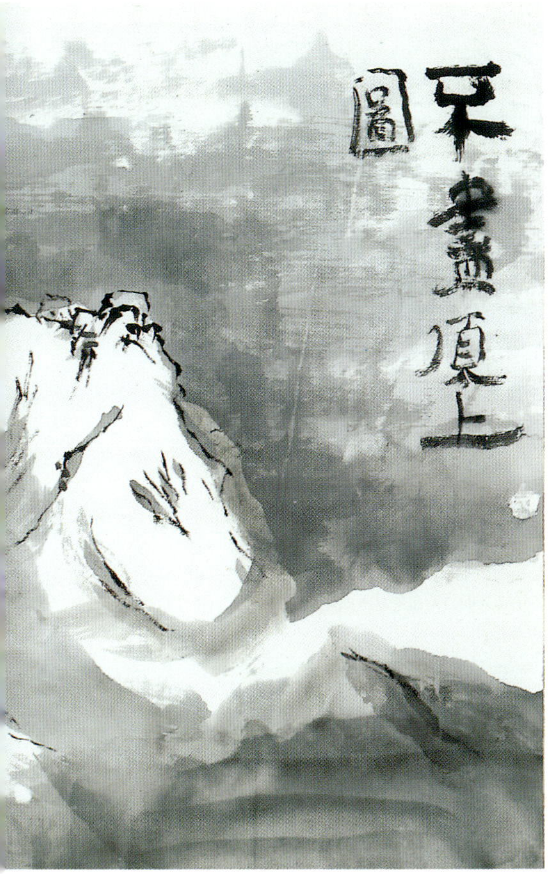

Maruyama Ōkyo, founder of the Maruyama-Shijō school of artists, was born to a peasant family, either in Kyoto or in the neighboring province of Tamba. He received his initial instruction in painting under Ishida Yūtei (1721-1786), a member of the Kano school; he studied also with Watanabe Shikō (1683-1755), a versatile master who combined Kano technique and draftsmanship with decorative elements inspired by the ideas of Kōrin and his followers. Shikō was also interested in the precise representation of flora and fauna, a feature that was to become an essential component of Ōkyo's painting. The distinctive style that subsequently evolved at Ōkyo's hands grew out of the artistic mutability of the period, synthesizing various pictorial ideas derived from native and, to some degree, Chinese sources. Among the salient aspects of Ōkyo's innovative vision was a strong sense of representational realism and a selective application of perspective and chiaroscuro *ideas from the West.*

Ōkyo's Kano-school training is revealed here both in facile brushwork and in composition, where open space is used to focus the observer's attention on the carefully conceived, rather formally arranged subject matter. Also apparent is Ōkyo's new contribution to Japanese painting: the special sense of realism in the depiction of the tiger, of nature carefully observed and studiously assessed. At the same time, the conservative handling of the subject matter is clearly influenced by the traditional nature of the theme, which had its pictorial origins in Japan in the famous monochrome Chinese paintings by Muqi in the Daitoku-ji in Kyoto, which had served as a prototypical composition for local Japanese artists for centuries. The Boston paintings were executed when Ōkyo was forty-five years of age and at the height of his creative powers. The depiction of the dragon here reveals close affinities in detail to the representation of this mythological beast in the left-hand example of a pair of six-panel screens with two dragons done by the artist four years earlier, which are registered as Important Cultural Properties in Japan.

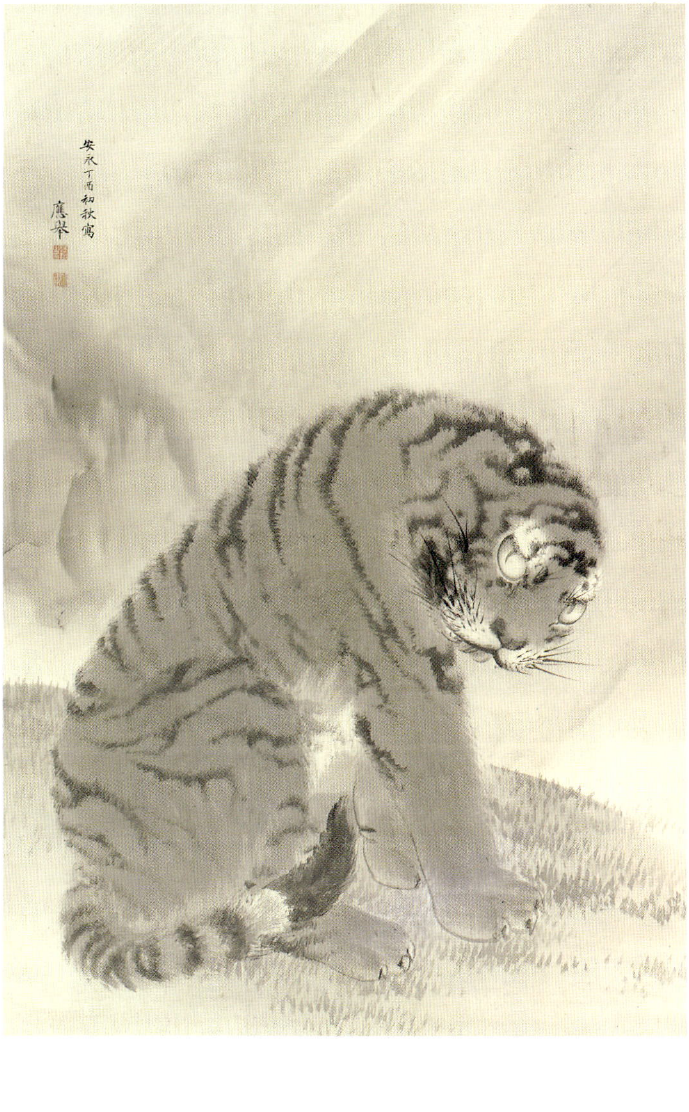

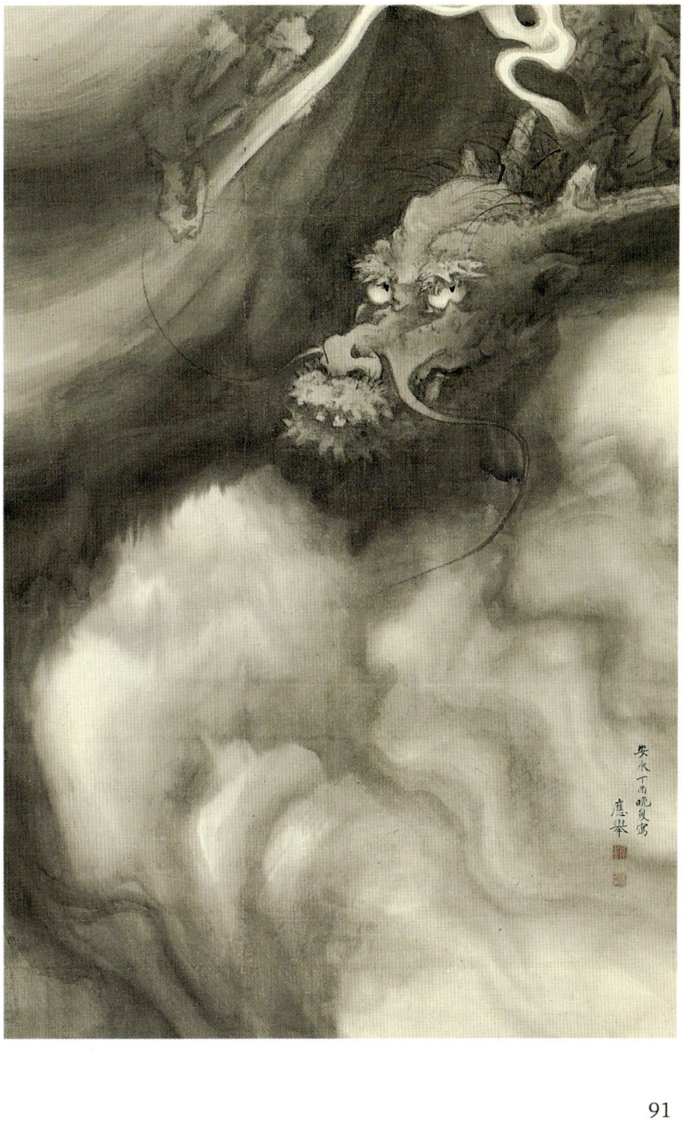

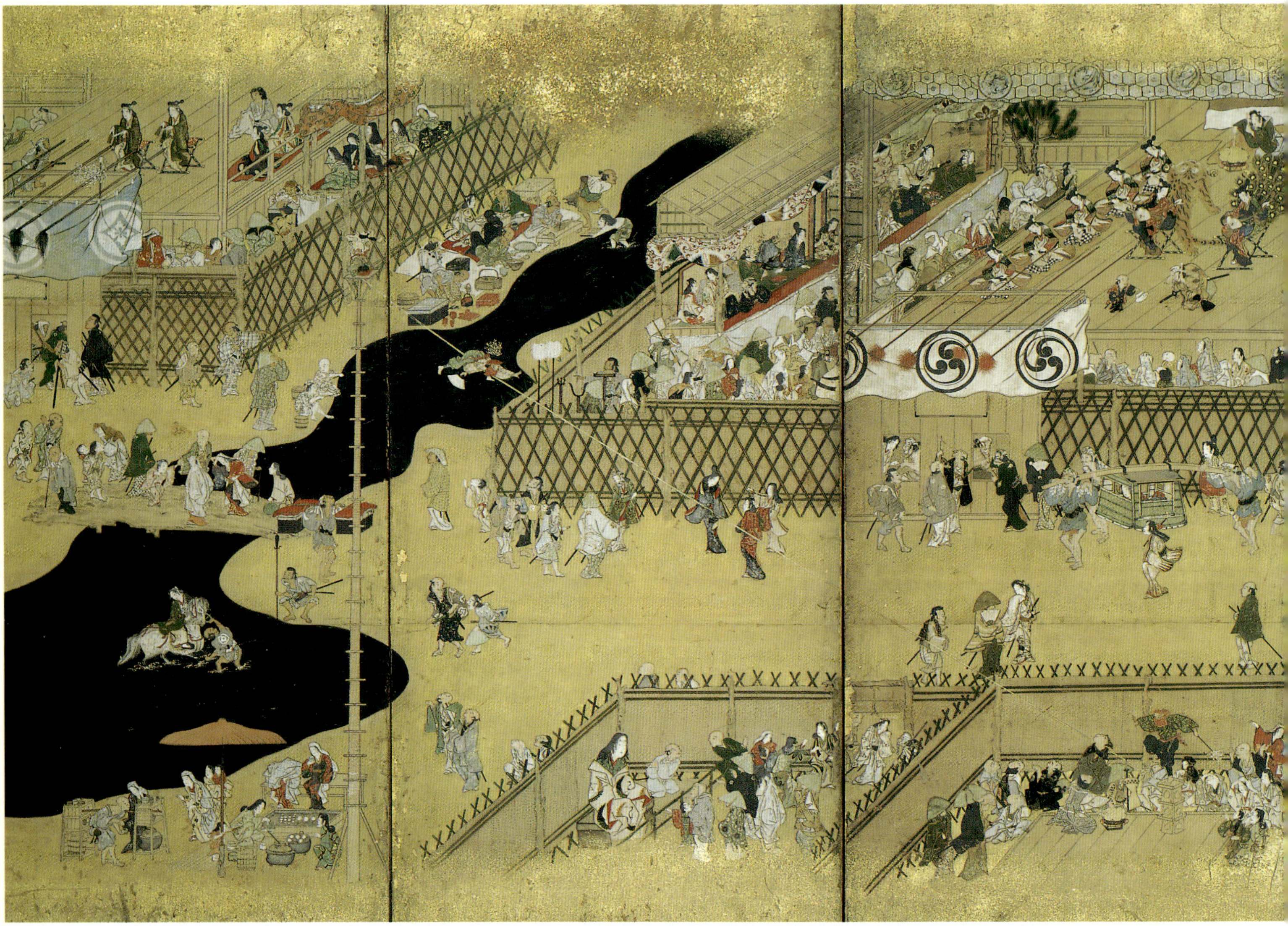

66
The Theater and Entertainment District at Shijō-kawara
Edo period, early 17th century
Pair of six-panel folding screens; ink, colors, and gold on paper.
104.1 x 290.6 cm. (each panel)
Fenollosa-Weld Collection.
11.4591-4592

The locale depicted here is the entertainment district at the intersection of Shijō Avenue and the Kamo River in the great city of Kyoto. The most complete visual inventory of this area is preserved in several precious screens, of which the Museum's pair is the most complete.

In these works Shijō Avenue runs horizontally across the screens, and the various theaters and sideshows are grouped side by side in a tight lateral sequence above and below. The stage attractions, above, include both women's and wakashū *("young men's") kabuki, puppet performances, the Nō drama (in a popular form), and a boisterous* sumō *wrestling match. Below are stalls and sideshows, with their colorful performers and exotic spectacles, including both human and animal curiosities: a woman devoid of arms, who manipulates a bow and arrow with her feet; a giantess, twice ordinary human size; two aerialists; a prancing miniature horse; a large black bull; a tiger, locked in a stout cage; an exotic quilled beast from some foreign country; and three sprightly performing dogs, one jumping through a hoop.*

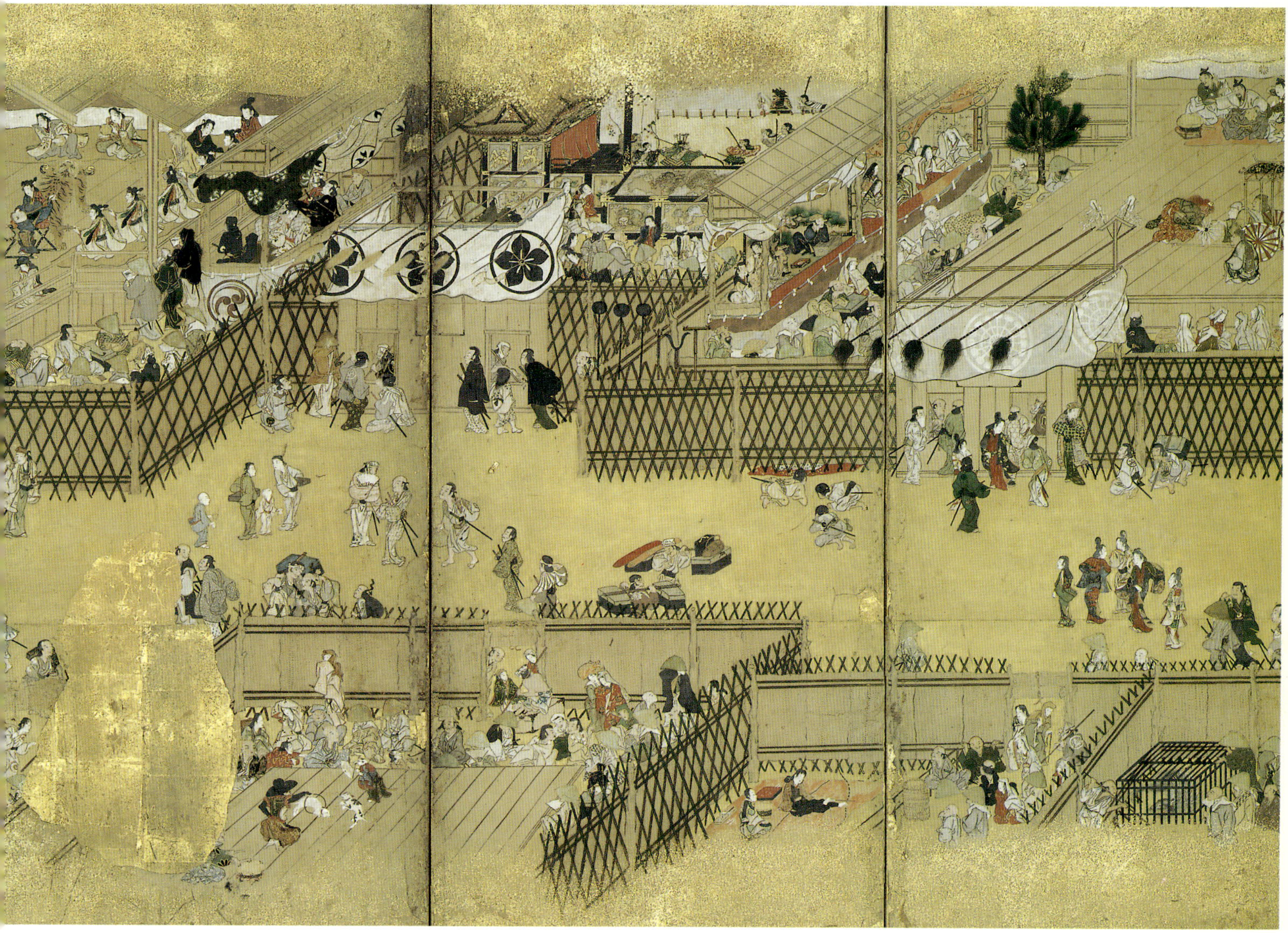

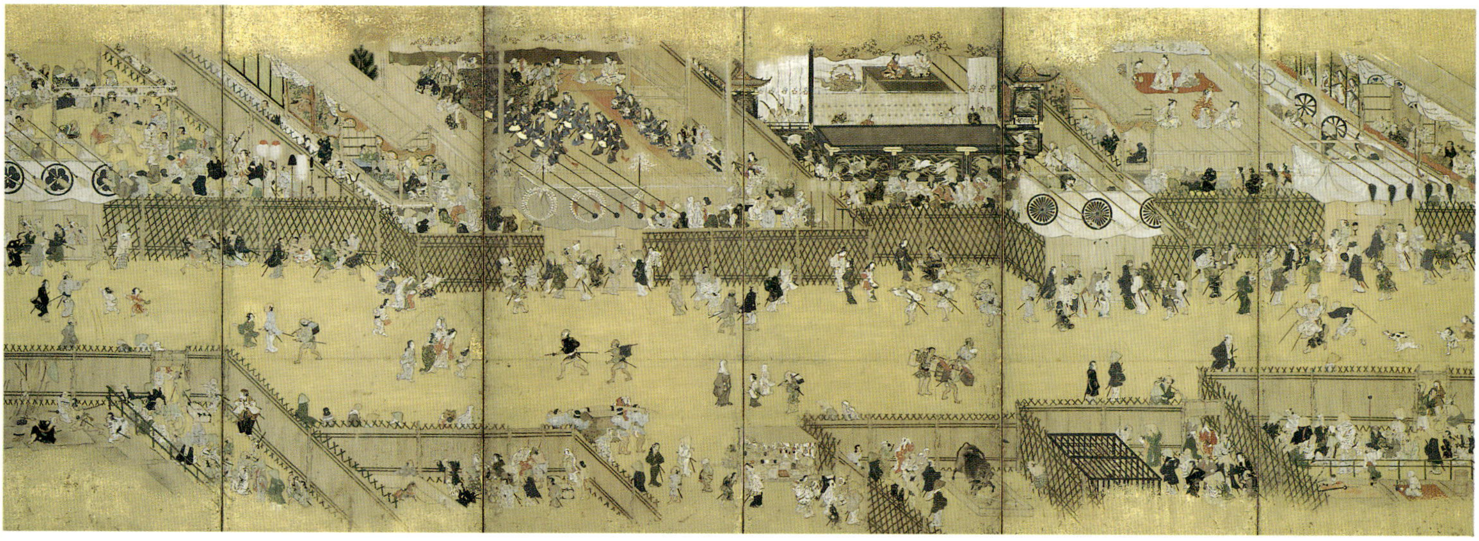

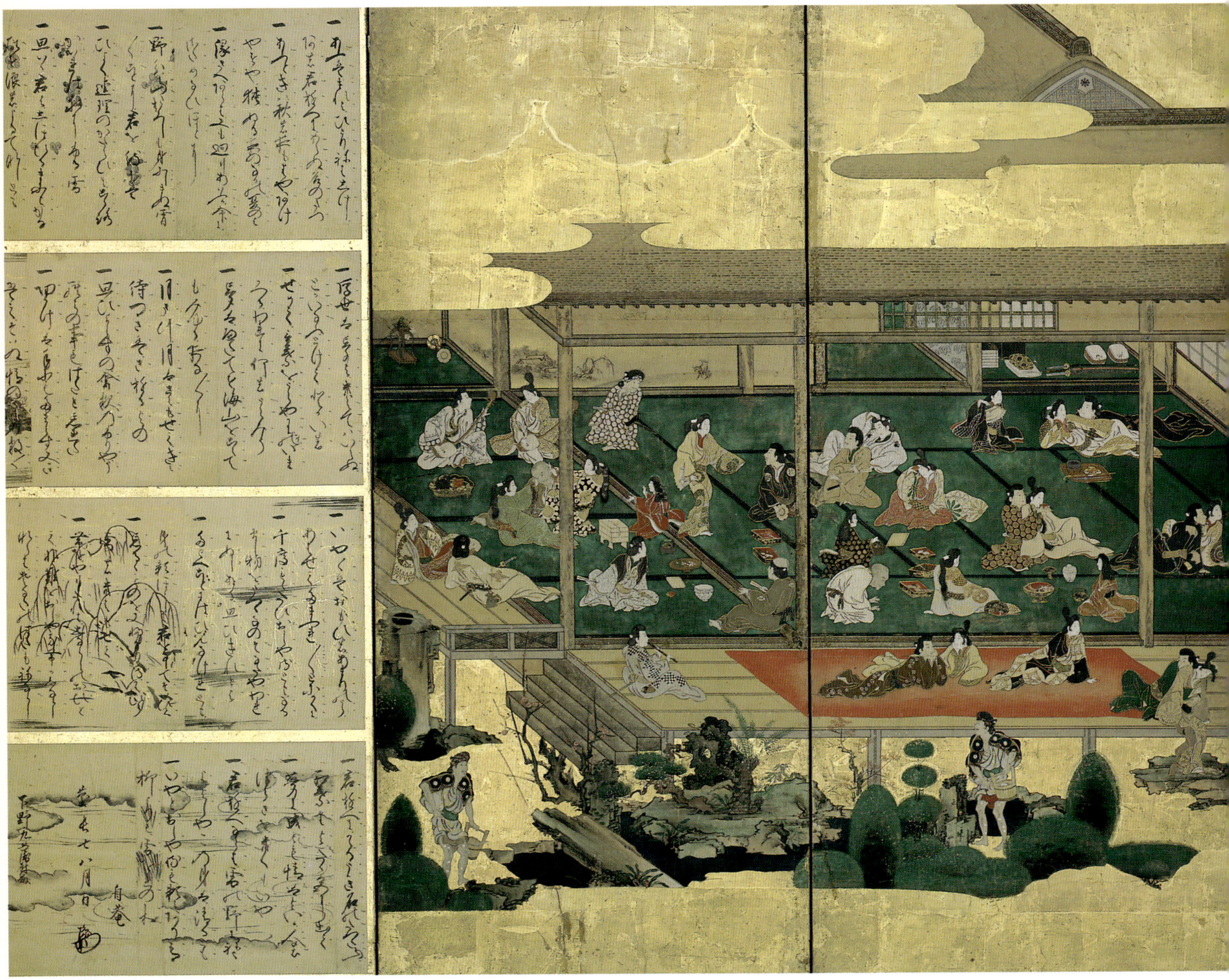

67
Scenes from the Pleasure Quarters of Kyoto
Edo period, mid-17th century
Pair of six-panel folding screens; ink, colors, and gold on paper.
104.6 x 273.6 cm. (each)
Gift of Denman Waldo Ross.
06.286-287

Paintings like these, with depictions of pleasure quarters and theater and entertainment districts, provided the basic source of inspiration for the Ukiyo-e ("Images of the Floating World") school, which evolved late in the seventeenth century and utilized the woodblock print as its chief expressive form. The two peripheral panels on the second screen were lost and have been replaced by panels with calligraphy by the priest Takasabu Ryūtatsu (d. 1611). The first of the forty-six poems from his hand, in the upper right corner, is the Kimigayo, *here written in exactly the same phrasing as that of the present national anthem of Japan. In the lower left corner the last of the eight sheets carries the signature of Ryūtatsu and the date* Keichō, *seventh year, corresponding to 1602.*

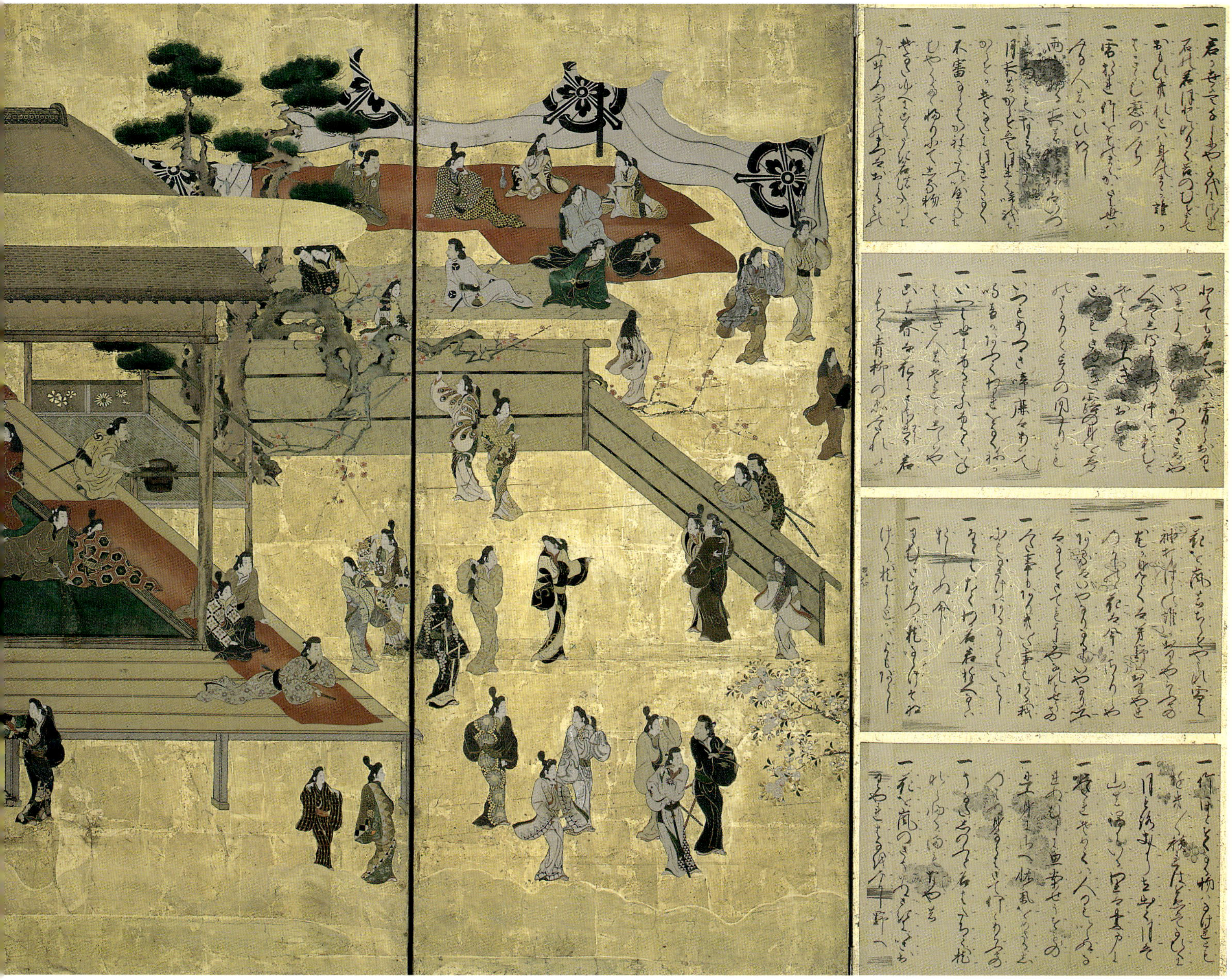

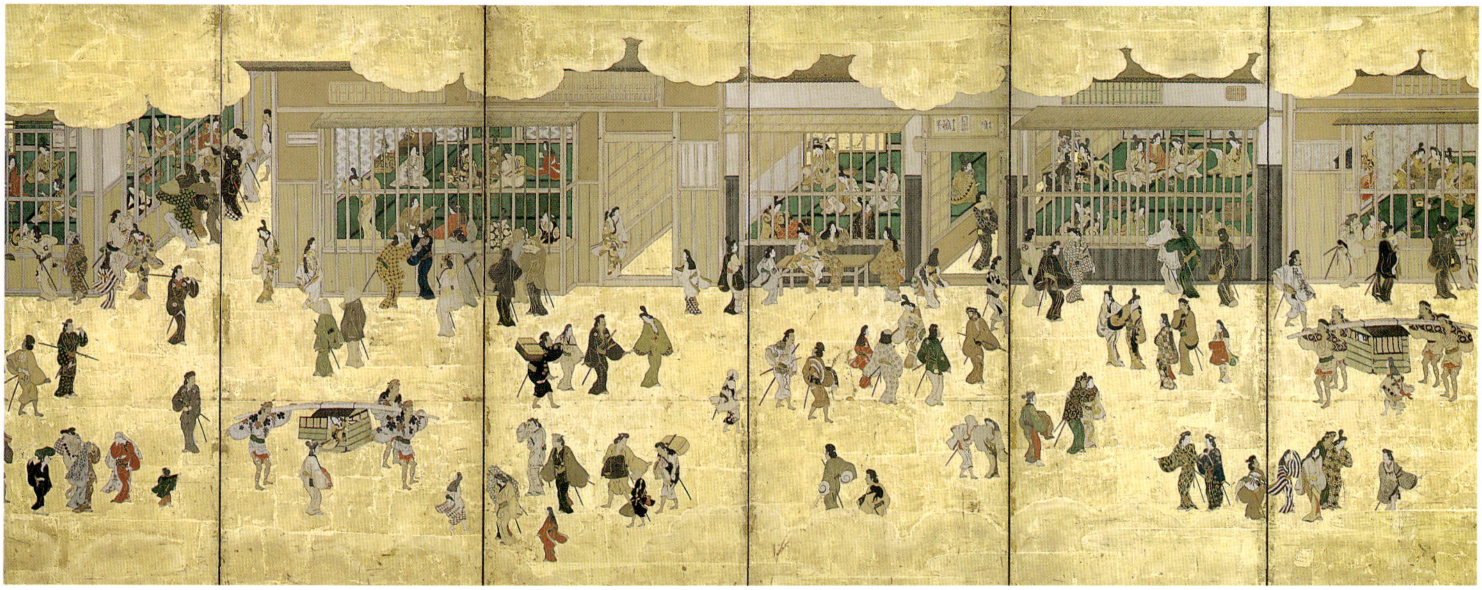

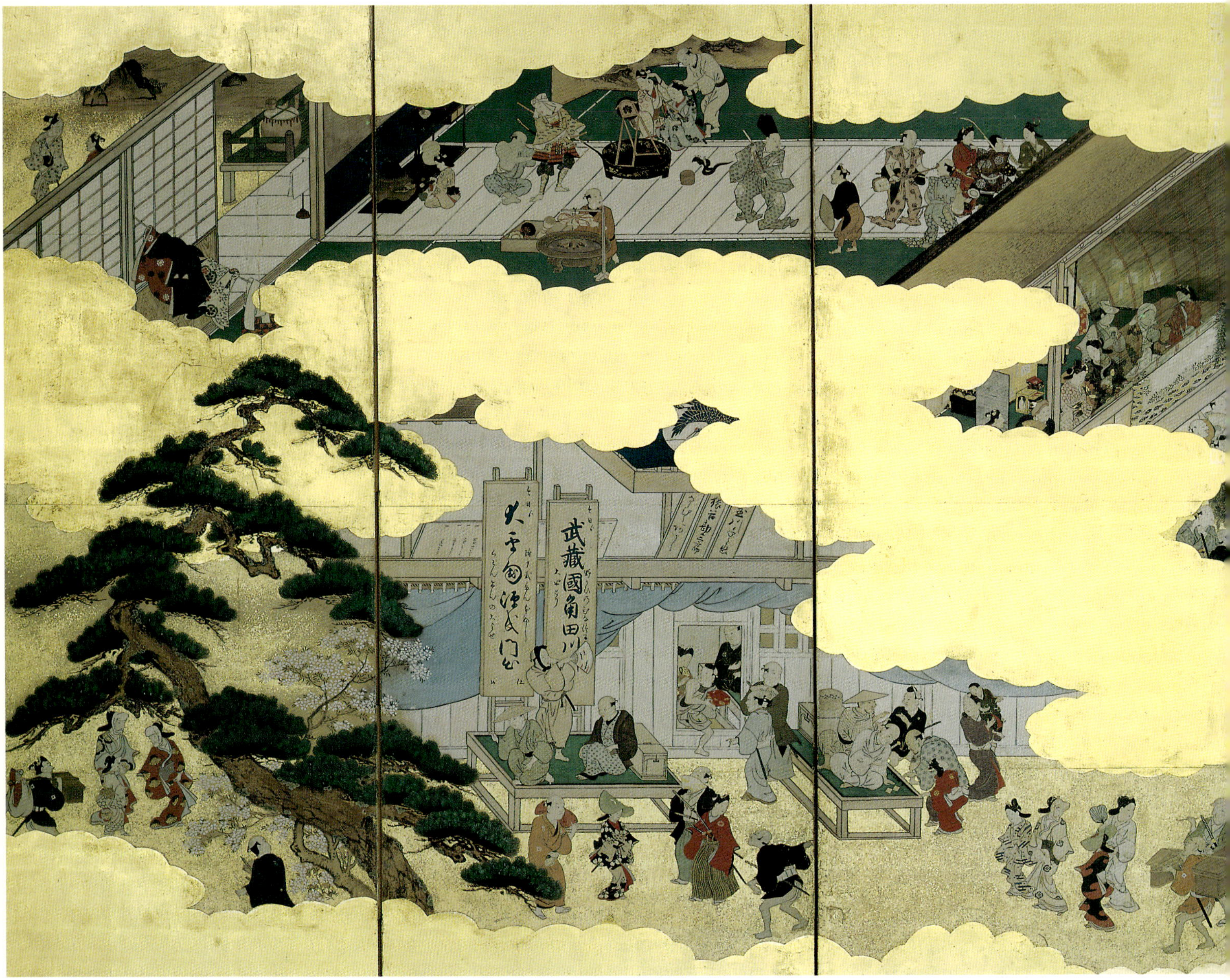

68
Hishikawa Moronobu (d. 1694)
Scenes from the Yoshiwara Pleasure Quarter and the Nakamura Kabuki Theater
Edo period, late 1670s-early 1680s
Pair of six-panel folding screens; ink, colors, and gold on paper.
140.3 x 358.2 cm. (each panel)
Gift of Oliver W. Peabody. 79.468-469

The first of these two screens shows a variety of locations in the greatest of the Edo pleasure quarters, the Yoshiwara, together with a sampling of the many kinds of people who frequented the quarter and gained their livelihood there. In the center of the composition a glamorous courtesan is admired by a group of spectators; she is attended by two young girls, an indication that her rank in the quarter is a high one. Farther on the right, a number of elegant women promenade along the street. They are viewed from the inside of two houses by several potential patrons who, wishing to remain incognito, sit behind lowered split-bamboo screens and hold fans before their faces.

The second screen shows three areas of the Nakamura-za, a famous kabuki theater. In the first (lower left) men and women of varying ages, occupations, and social levels pass along the street, among them a wily ragamuffin pickpocket who prepares to relieve a samurai *of his purse. The second area of the theater represented is a portion of the backstage (above left), where actors, musicians, and attendants are preparing for a performance. The third and largest section of the theater (right half) shows the stage itself and the area for the audience. Onstage, an animated procession of figures, colorfully attired for various male and female roles, moves across the broad platform, dancing to the lively cadences of the* samisen *and drums.*

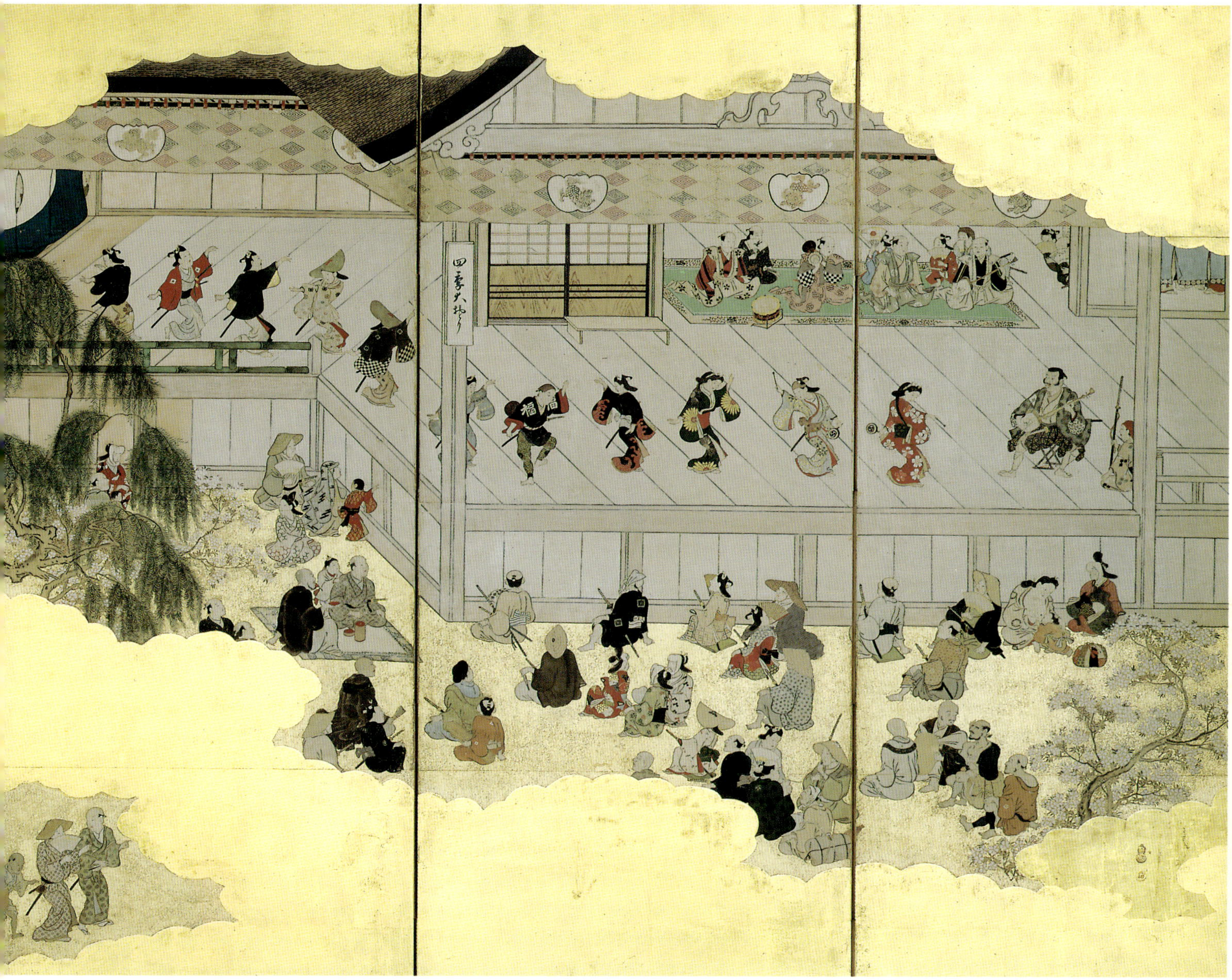

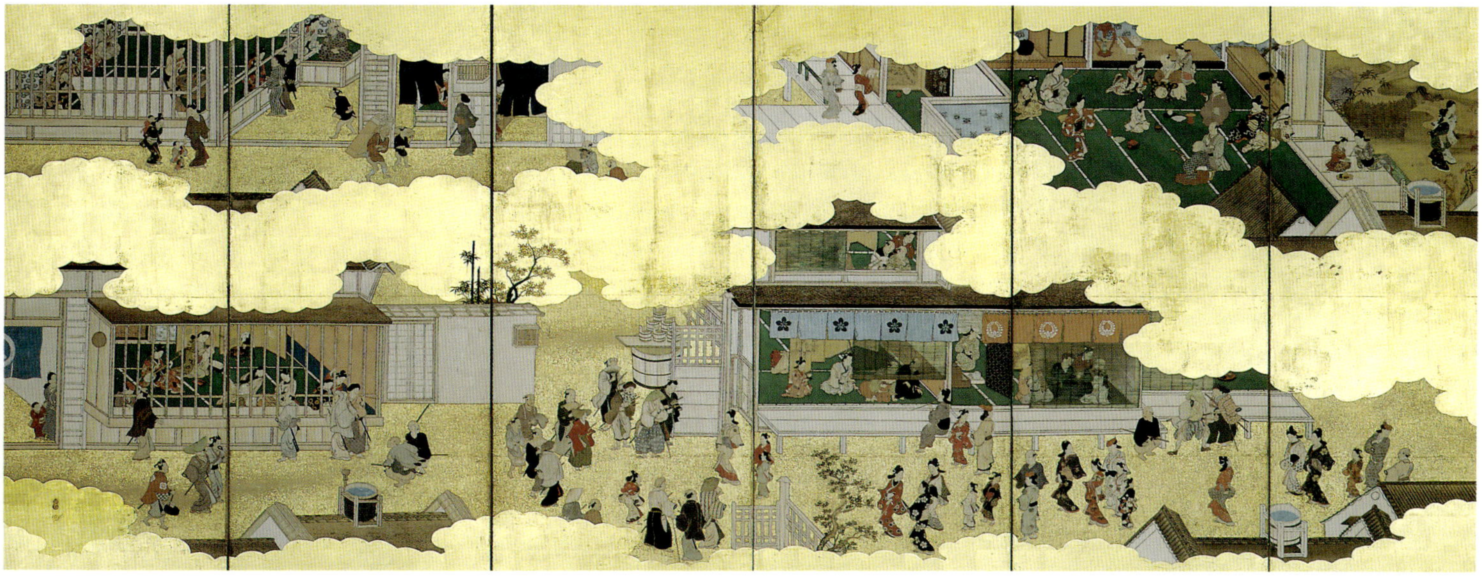

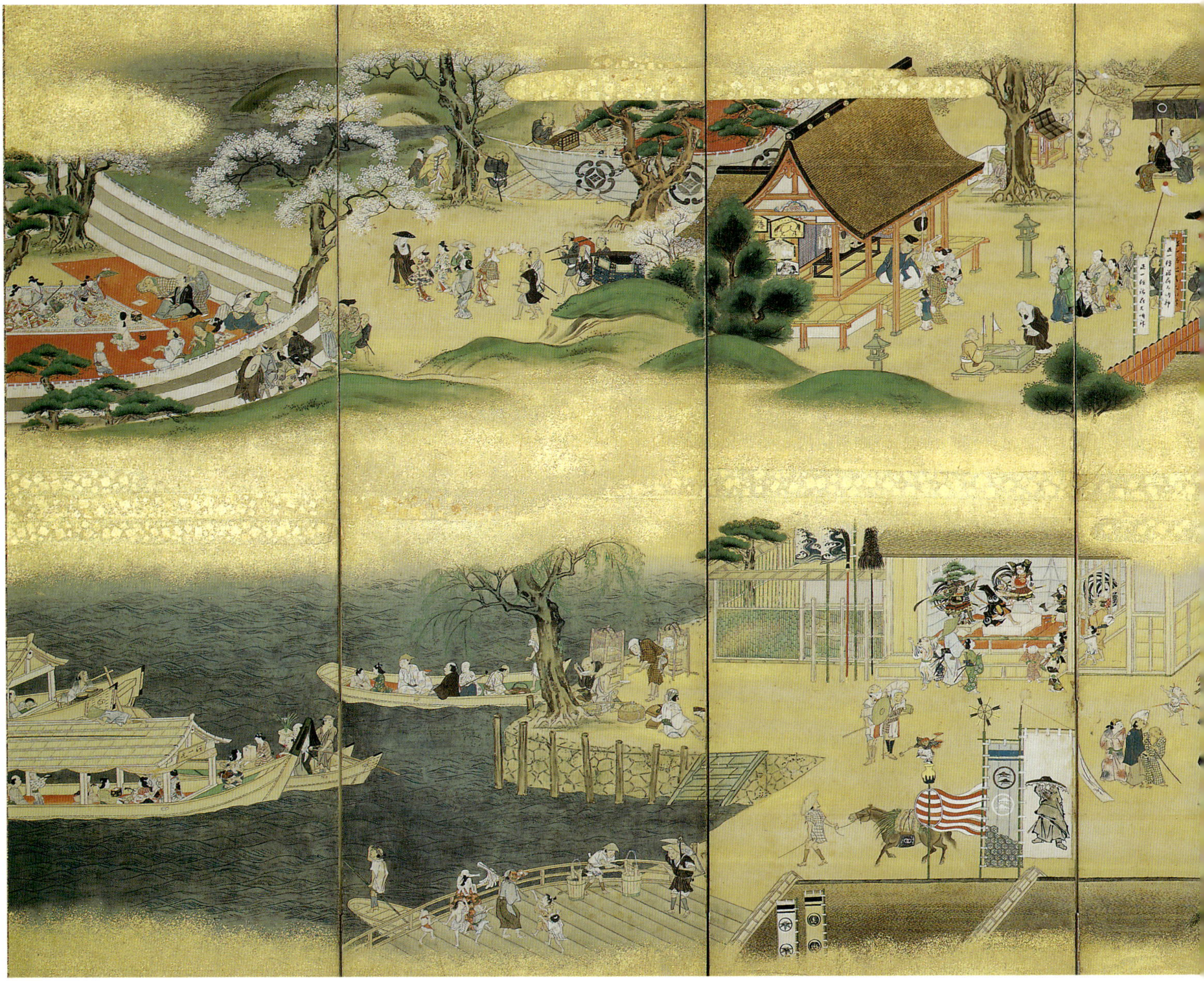

69
Hanabusa Itchō (1652-1724)
Celebrations and Festivities of the Twelve Months
Edo period, about 1709-1717
Pair of six-panel folding screens; ink, colors, and gold on paper.
162.5 x 349.2 cm. (each panel)
Fenollosa-Weld Collection.
11.4219-4220

The representation of the annual celebrations and festivities of the twelve months, established as a traditional subject in Yamato-e painting during the middle ages, typically combines genre activities and landscape components. Extending across the screens on two levels, beginning at the top right of the right-hand screen and executed in precise detail, are the characteristic themes of the respective months. First, the New Year's plum blossoms; second, "First Horse Day" festival; third, cherry-blossom viewing; fourth, Buddha's birthday celebration; fifth, boy's festival; sixth, boating excursions; (left screen, from top right) seventh, Obon festival for departed spirits; eighth, harvesting activities under the autumn moon; ninth, maple-leaf viewing; tenth, festival of the god Ebisu; eleventh, fire festival; twelfth, year-end activities.

The signature on the Boston screens, the refined quality of the brushwork, and the precise handling of detail indicate that the paintings were done between 1709 and 1717, when Itchō is said to have given up the depiction of light-hearted genre scenes and turned to more classical subjects.

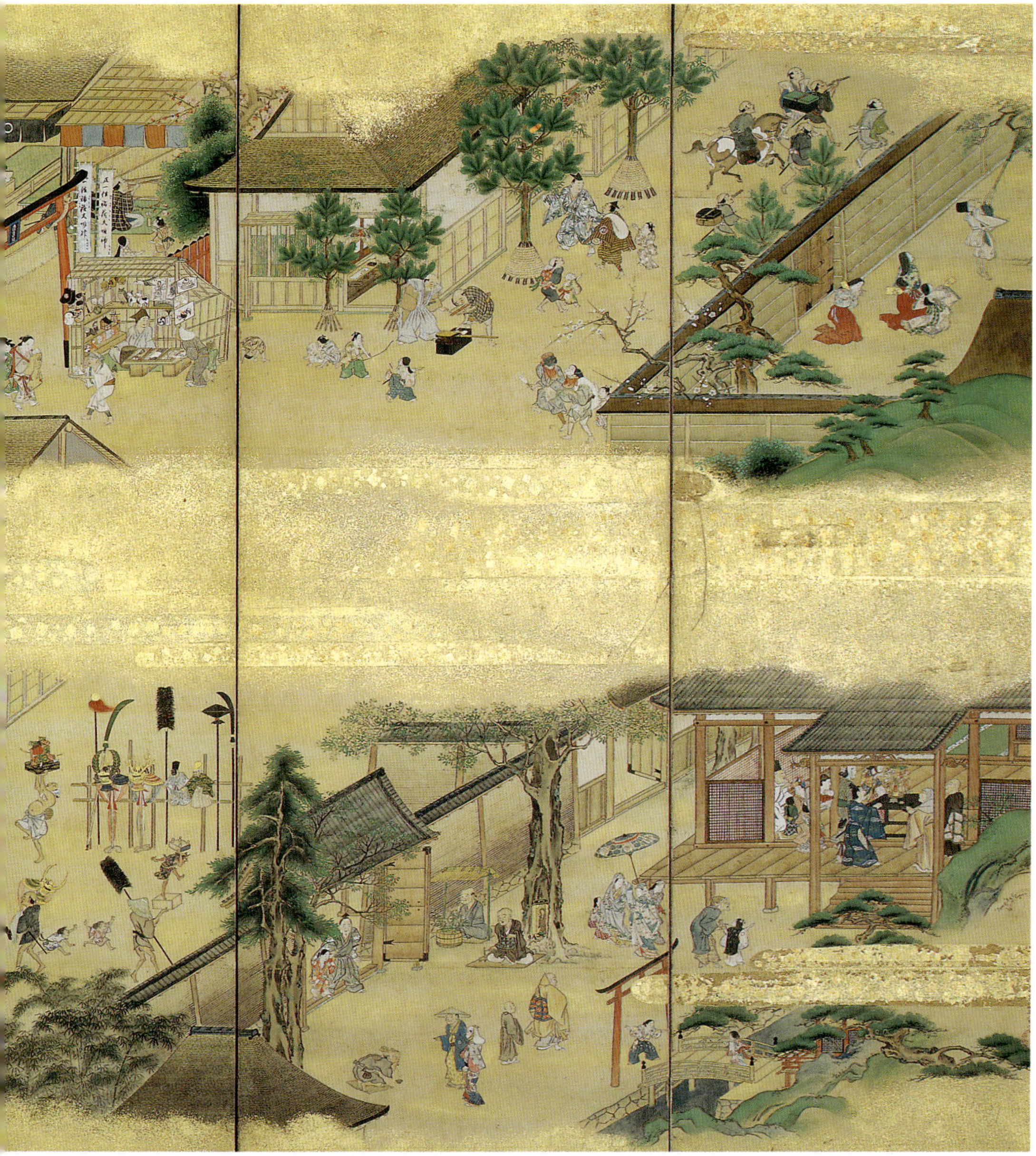

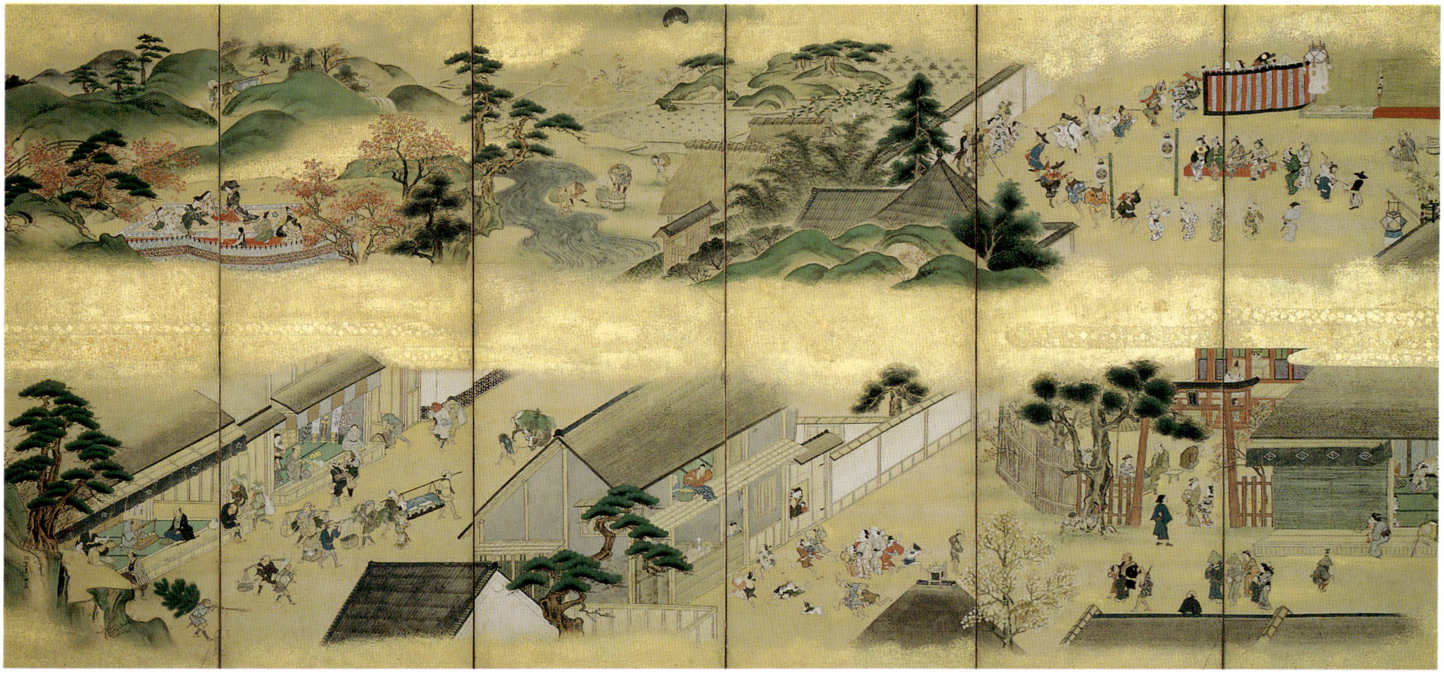

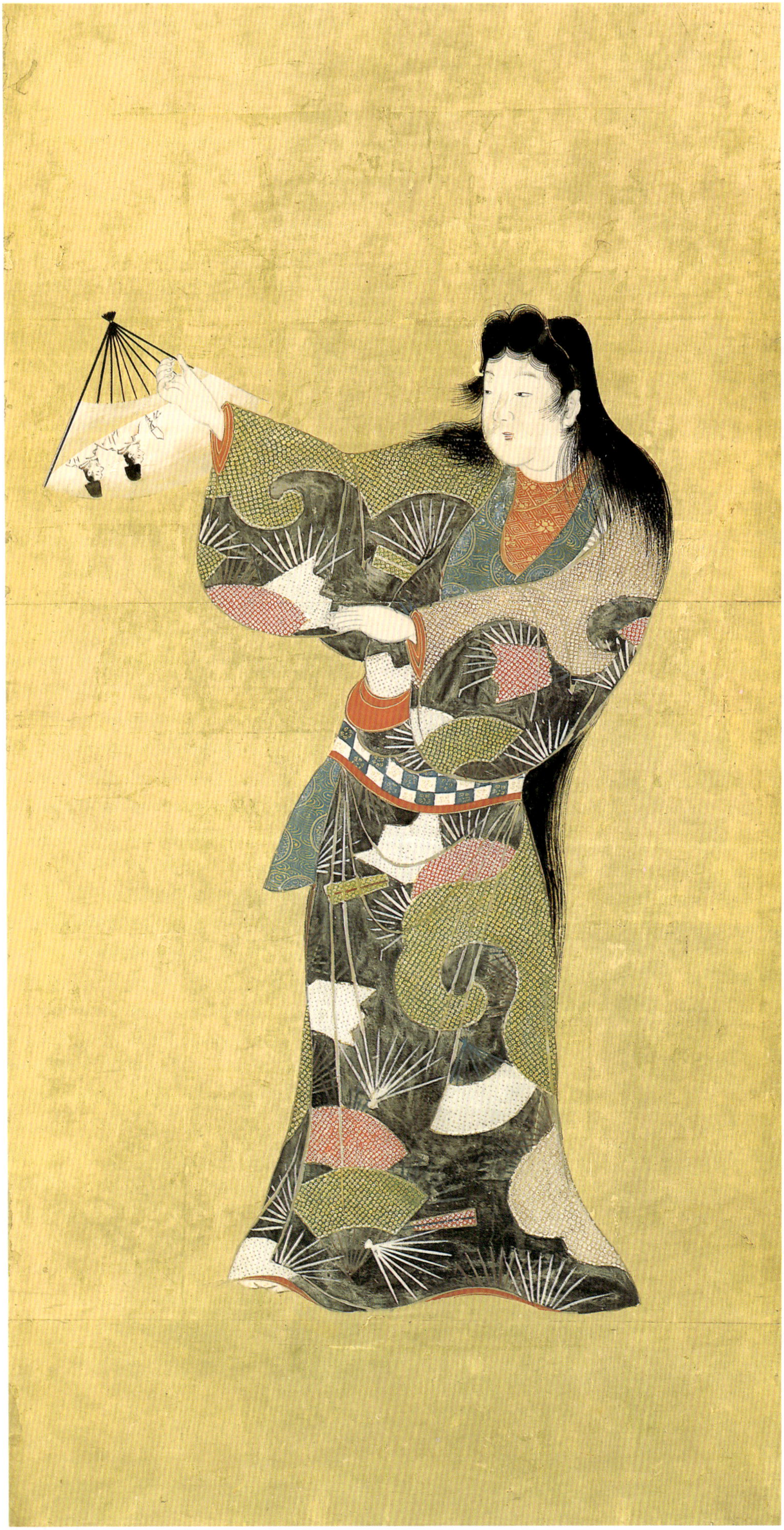

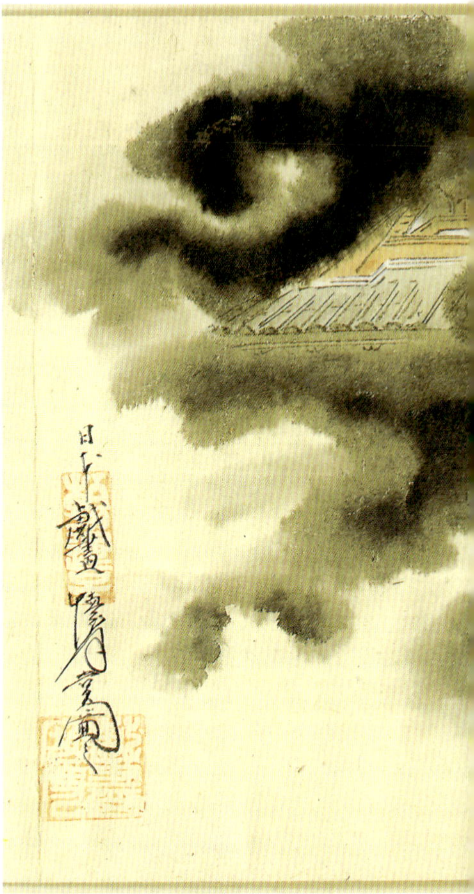

70
Dancer
Edo period, 17th century
Panel from a set of eleven; ink, colors, and gold on paper. 75.5 x 36.9 cm.
Gift of Denman Waldo Ross. 17.1091

This painting depicting a female dancer was once part of a pair of six-panel screens. Now mounted separately, this and ten similar panels were donated to the Museum by Denman Waldo Ross in 1917. Comparison with similar compositions in the Suntory Museum and Kyoto Municipal Museum collections suggests that the poses were codified, but the details of the sumptuous robes and elegant painted fans are individualized. In this composition the dancer is garbed in a short-sleeved robe patterned with fan motifs in shibori *(tie-dye). In her right hand she holds an open fan decorated with the figures of two courtiers.*

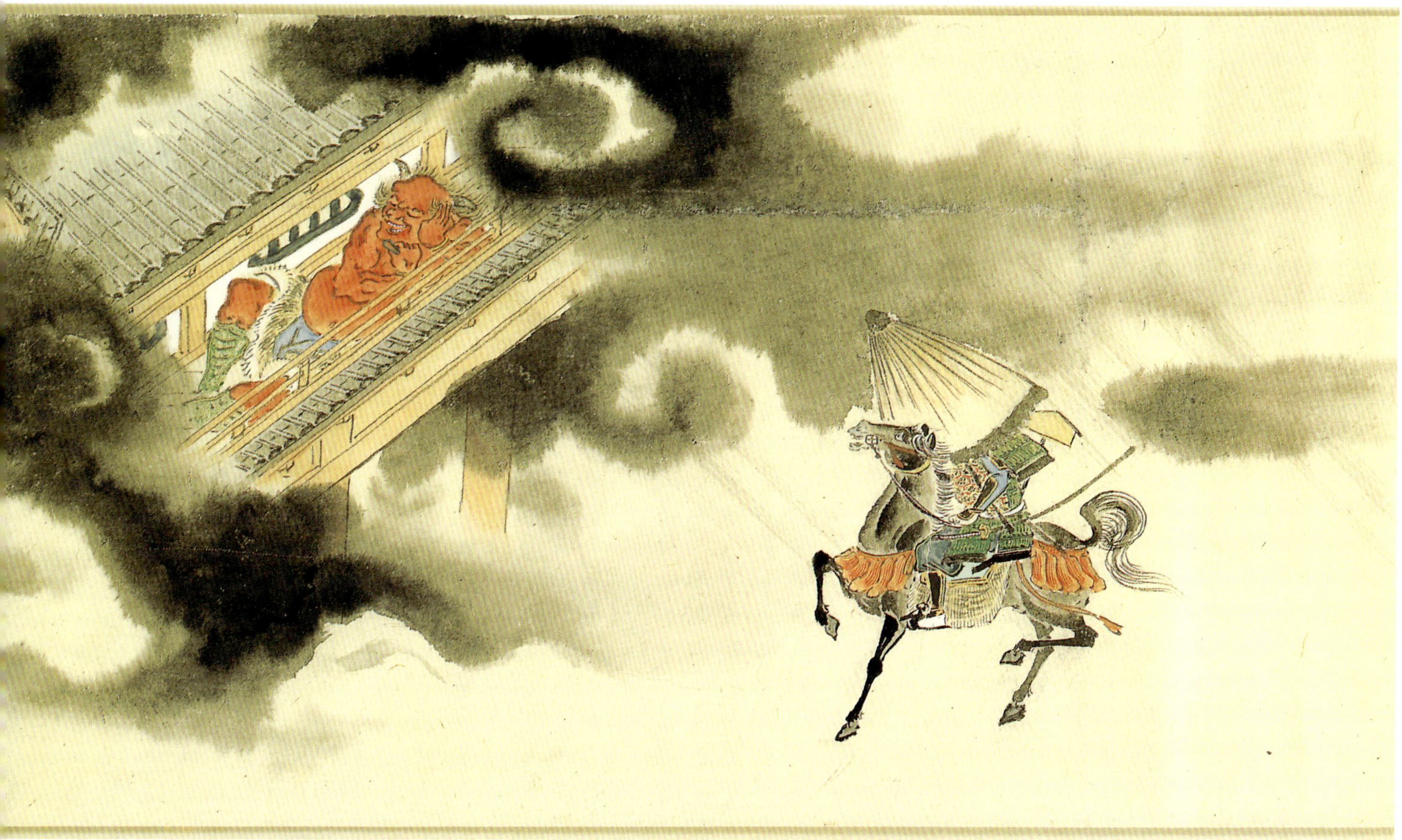

71
Kaigetsudō Ando (traditional dates: 1671-1743)
Miscellaneous genre subjects
Edo period, about 1700-1714
Handscroll; ink, colors, gold, and silver on paper. 28.3 cm.
William Sturgis Bigelow Collection. 11.7498

Kaigetsudō Ando achieved fame in the early years of the eighteenth century for his innovative depictions of the great courtesans from the Yoshiwara pleasure quarters in Edo. Although his paintings of these much-admired women evolved from the earlier pictorial tradition of Hishikawa Moronobu and also reflect the new figural canons of two contemporaries of the Torii school, Kiyonobu and Kiyomasu, Ando's representations surpass those of other masters for the elegance, grace, and proud carriage that distinguish his lovely women of the demimonde. His accomplishments in the field of courtesan painting attracted a number of followers, and he became the fountainhead of a school of pupils and imitators that flourished for half a century. Ando also seems to have served as an intermediary in the "Lady Ejima Affair", a scandal in which a lady from the shōgun's court became involved with a kabuki actor, a circumstance that resulted in those implicated being banished from Edo in 1714.

Although the extant paintings of Ando and his students consist almost entirely of representations of single courtesans, elegantly attired in rich kimono, in a vertical format, the Boston scroll demonstrates that the artist worked also in the horizontal handscroll format, and on occasion he depicted a broader range of subject matter drawn from popular tradition. Thus, although several of the ten subjects shown here relate to the world of the demimonde and its activities, there is a variety of other pictorial themes, such as the "demon-queller" Shōki, who slices a watermelon with his sword in front of his demon companions; a dramatic kusazuri-biki *depiction from the kabuki stage; a* sumō *wrestling contest; Watanabe no Tsuna and the demon of the Rashomon gate; an* eboshi *hat maker drawn from* shokunin-zukushi *pictorial traditions; and even flowers and utensils in the Chinese style and a miniature landscape showing peasants involved in agricultural activities.*

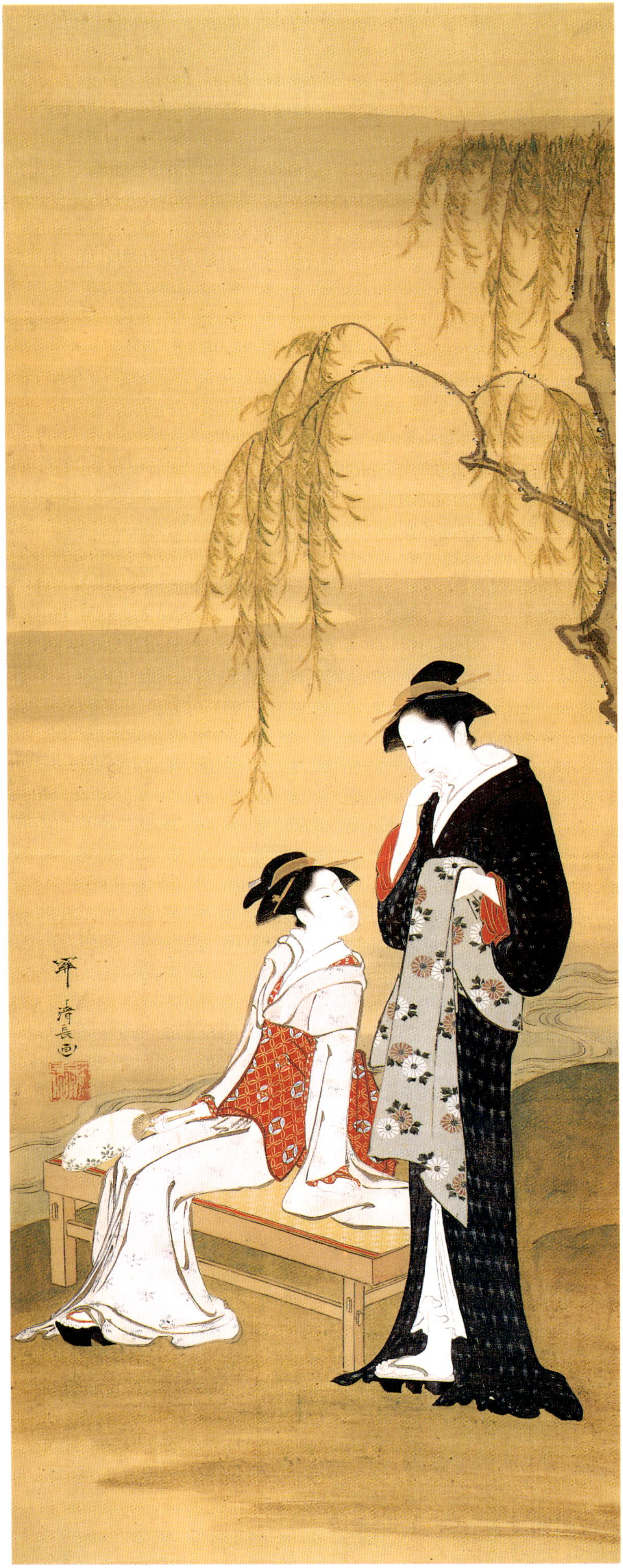

72
Torii Kiyonaga (1752-1815)
Two Women Beneath a Willow Tree
Edo period, about 1784-85
Hanging scroll; ink and colors on silk.
87.6 x 35 cm.
William Sturgis Bigelow Collection.
11.7531

Kiyonaga is thought to have been born in Edo, the son of a book dealer named Shirokoya Ichibei, whose residence was at Hon Zaimoku-chō. The family surname was Sekiguchi, which Kiyonaga later abbreviated to Seki in signing certain of his works, such as the painting reproduced here. It is said that his personal name was Chōemon, and this seems to be the origin of the "naga" (chō) component in his familiar artist's name. Kiyonaga began artistic training as an adolescent under Torii Kiyomitsu (1735-1783), and the first works that can be reliably attributed to the young artist's hand are several routine actor prints, done when he was eighteen. In the following years he worked diligently, and a growing sense of technical accomplishment and versatility can be seen in his prints. However, it is in 1781 (Temmei 1) that his most original and sustained period of creativity begins, and during the eight years of the Temmei period, he conceived, by conservative estimate, in excess of 560 print designs, more than half of his total known oeuvre, including the large majority of his masterpieces. In the depictions of beautiful women from this period, Kiyonaga alternately dazzles and enchants the viewer with distinctive, original conceptions. Their harmonious synthesis of felicitous proportion, anatomical accuracy, and idealized grace set them apart from all the other innovative bijin *figural canons conceived by Ukiyo-e masters.*

Although a very large number of Kiyonaga's woodblock print compositions has been preserved, the number of paintings extant is quite small. This example, which has been interpreted traditionally as a mother and daughter, is one of the artist's finest, done in the middle 1780s, when he was at the height of his creative powers. Kiyonaga's representations of women at this time are conceived according to an idealized physical canon, but they are also anatomically accurate and corporeally convincing. The tall, elegant figures are imbued with a distinctive sense of dignity as well as an auspicious aura of well-being, both unique in the history of Ukiyo-e.

73

Katsushika Hokusai (1760-1849)

Courtesan and Attendants

Edo period, about 1798
Hanging scroll; ink and colors on silk.
85.7 x 33 cm.
William Sturgis Bigelow Collection.
11.7445

This elegant painting of a courtesan and two kamuro *was acquired in Japan sometime in the mid-1880s. It was chosen by Ernest Fenollosa, who in 1890 became the first curator of the Department of Japanese Art (now the Asiatic Department), as the earliest example of an Ukiyo-e painting by Hokusai in his pioneering exhibition of the artist's paintings, which opened in Boston in 1892. The painting is not dated, but it is signed Sōri and thus was done during the period when Hokusai utilized this artist's name, from about 1794 to 1798.*

During the second half of the 1790s Hokusai developed a new figural conception that was no longer directly dependent on the ideas of his former mentor Katsukawa Shunshō and more closely emulated the stylistic concepts of Utamaro and his followers. It is characteristic of this new conception that beautiful women are represented as attenuated, willowy, and somewhat frail in appearance, their faces reserved and masklike — all features that are present in the Boston painting. Moreover, these features are stylistically consistent with the figures of women that appear in Hokusai's surimono *and books of the period, such as* Mists of Sandara, *published in 1798. The Boston painting is notable for the exquisite execution of the clothing, with its unusual colors and delicate detail.*

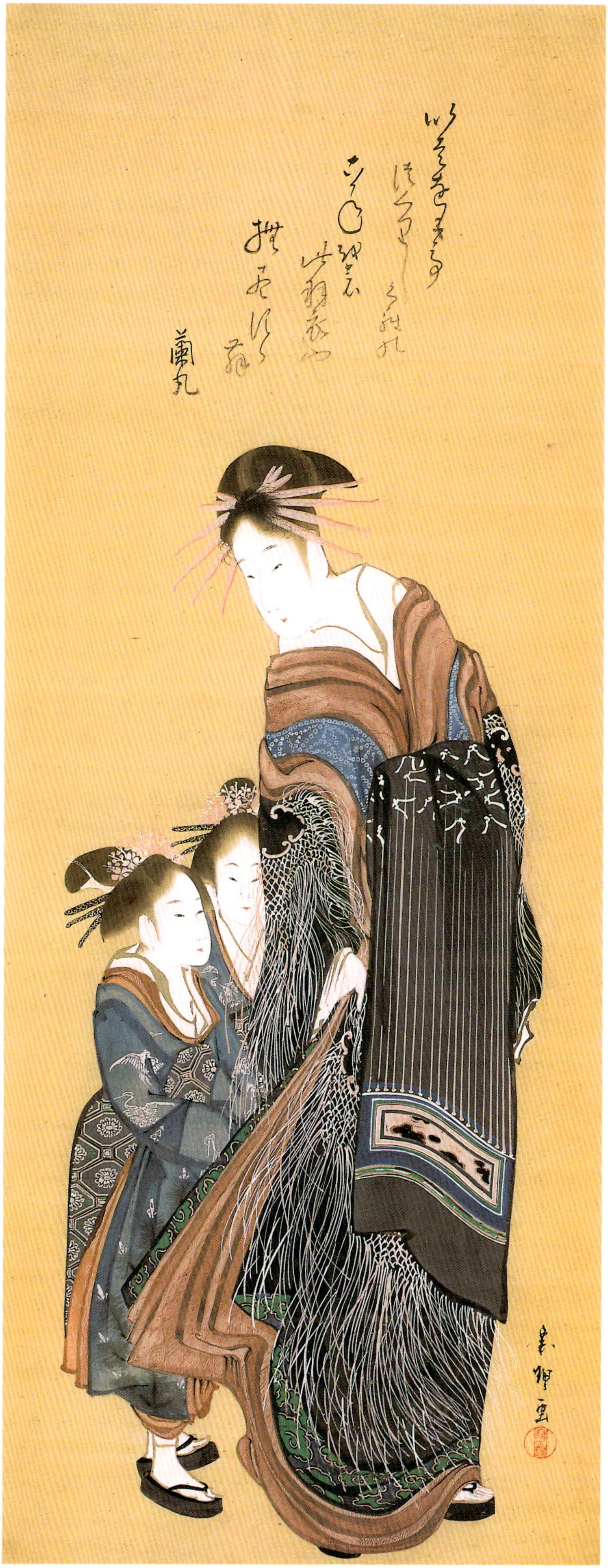

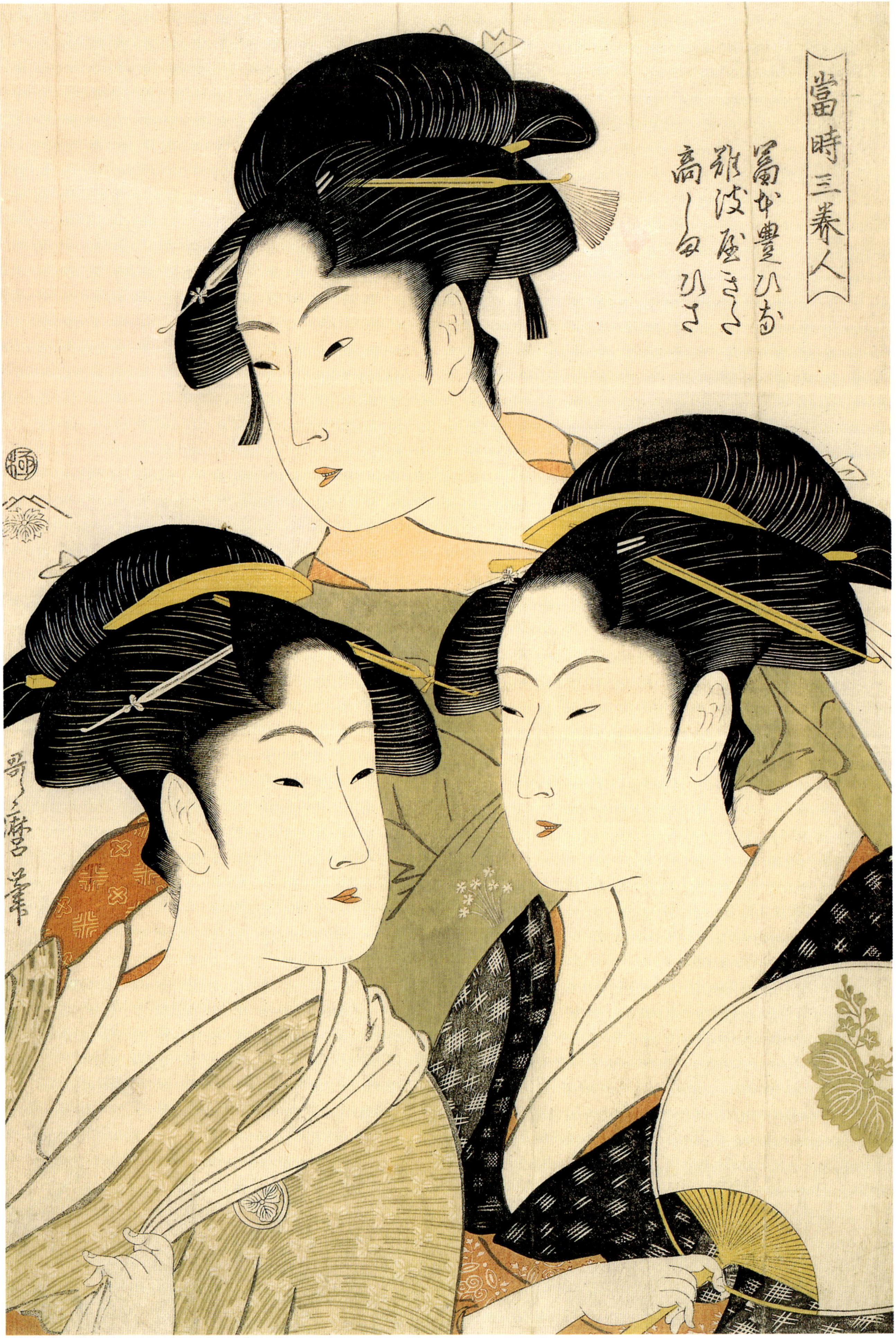
當時三美人
冨本豊ひな
難波屋きた
高しまひさ
哥麿筆

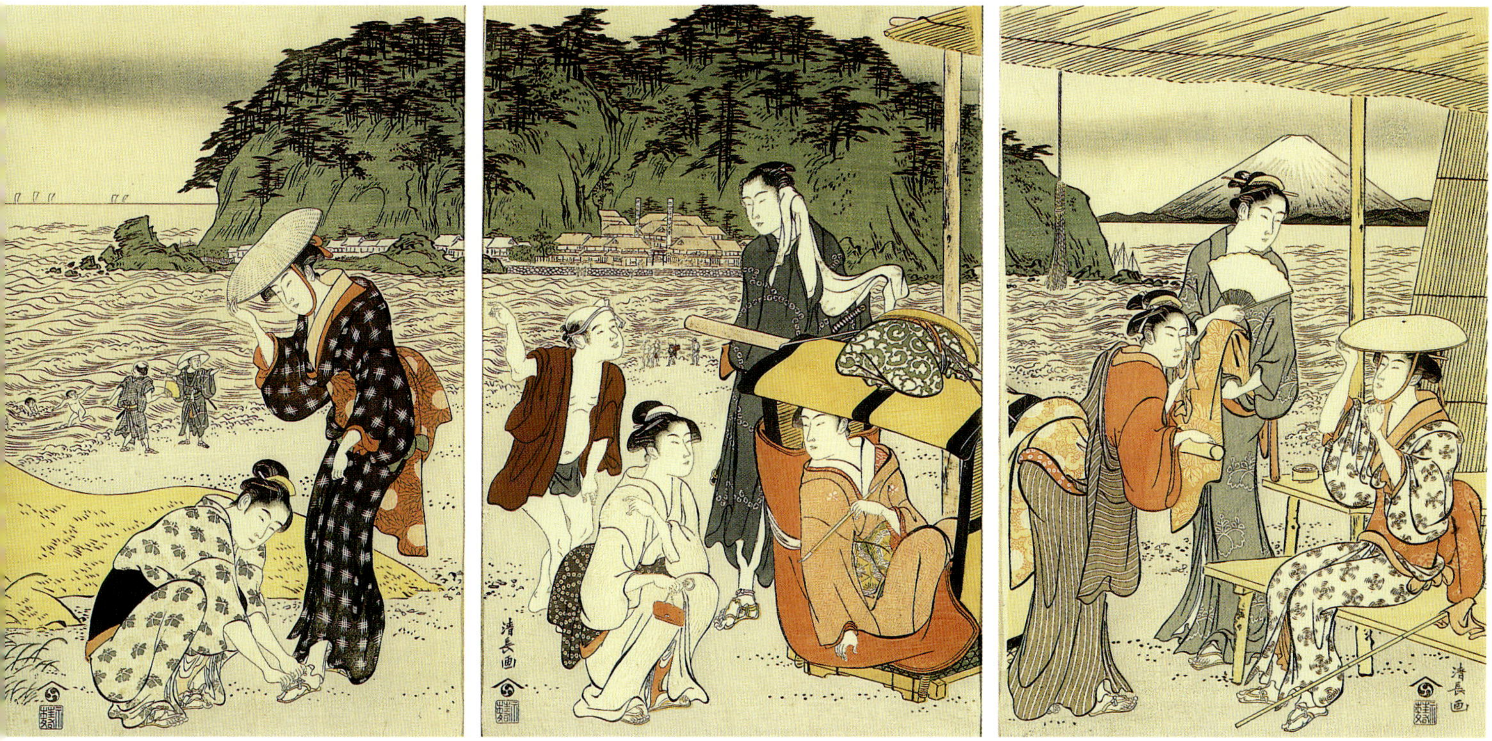

74
Kitagawa Utamaro (1753-1806)
Three Contemporary Beauties
Edo period, about 1793
Woodblock print; ink, colors, and mica on paper. 37 x 25 cm.
Spaulding Collection. 21.6382

The three women portrayed in this woodblock print were celebrated beauties in the city of Edo during the last decade of the eighteenth century. Above is Toyohina, a famous geisha *and practitioner of the Tomimoto school of musical accompaniment. On the right is Okita, a popular waitress at the Naniwaya, a teahouse adjacent to the Sensō-ji, the great Buddhist temple in the Asakusa district. To the left is Ohisa, a winsome adolescent of about seventeen, whose daily presence in her father's shop, the Takashimaya (where* sembei*, a kind of baked cracker flavored with soy sauce, were made), attracted large crowds of patrons to the establishment. The high esteem of these lovely young women among the Edo populace is attested by the fact that they appear in the works of many of the woodblock masters of the period.*

The artist, Kitagawa Utamaro, is one of the most original and influential artists in the history of the Ukiyo-e school, an ingenious designer who produced paintings as well as illustrated books and prints. His most memorable works came during the late 1780s and the decade of the 1790s, when he was the dominant influence in the creative evolution of the woodblock print.

75
Torii Kiyonaga (1752-1815)
A Pilgrimage to Enoshima
Edo period, about 1789
Woodblock prints: triptych; ink and colors on paper.
26.4 x 38.8 (r), 26.1 x 38.8 (c), 26.4 x 38.5 (l) cm.
Spaulding Collection. 21.7344-7346

Torii Kiyonaga is one of the preeminent figures in the history of the Japanese Ukiyo-e woodblock print; his best works are widely esteemed for their lyrical beauty and creative originality, and the influence of his stylistic ideas pervades the works of his contemporaries in the last two decades of the eighteenth century. During his most prolific years Kiyonaga produced one lovely group, series, or sequence of prints after another, each marked by some new stylistic innovation or pictorial metamorphosis that attests to his unique conceptual abilities.

The triptych reproduced here is one of the artist's most admired works in this format. It shows a group of visitors who have come on a pilgrimage to the revered shrine of the deity Benzai-ten, located on Enoshima, the island in the background.

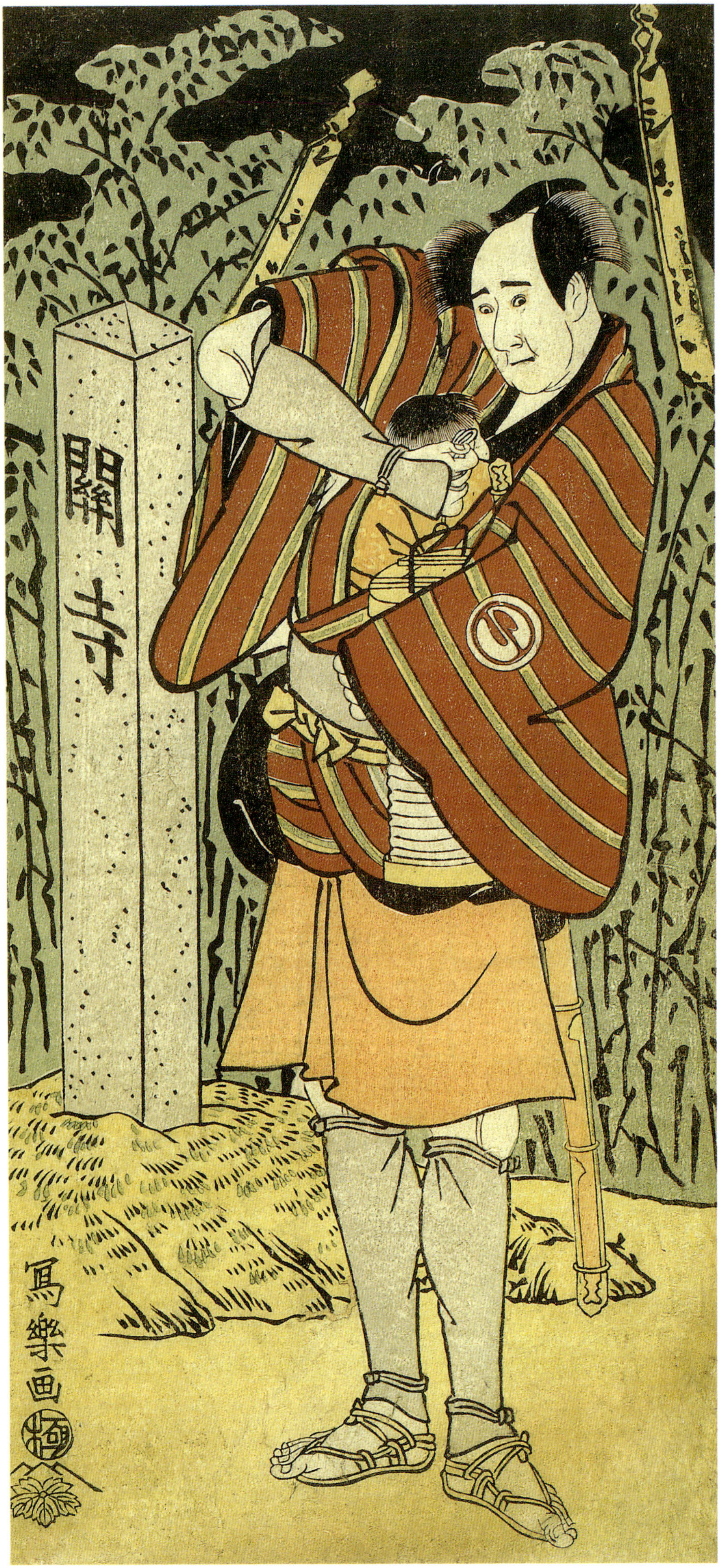

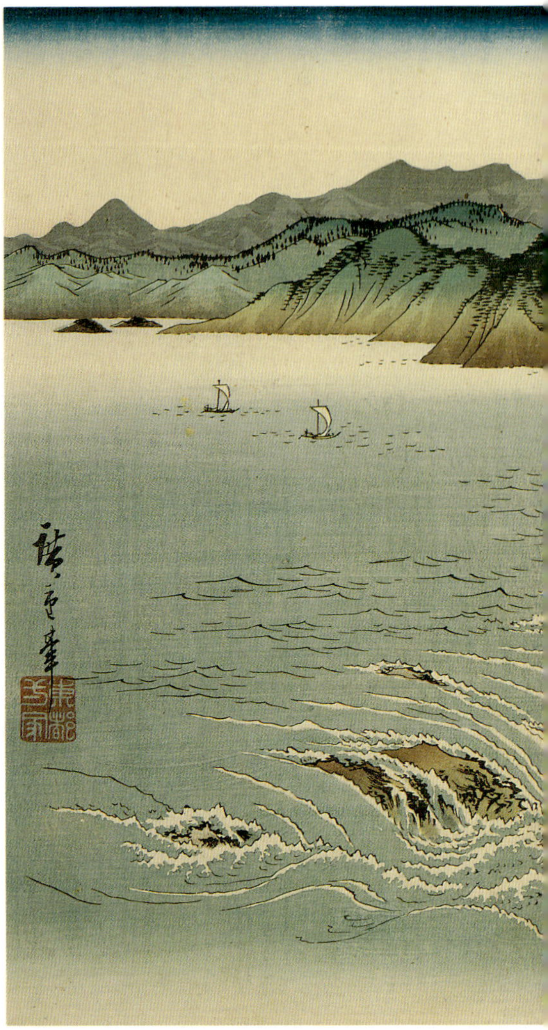

76
Tōshūsai Sharaku (fl. 1794-1795)
Kabuki Actor Sawamura Sōjurō as Kujaku Saburō
Edo period, 1794
Woodblock print: hosoban; ink and colors on paper. 31.1 x 14.4 cm.
Spaulding Collection. 21.7267

Although the identity of the artist who worked for less than a year during 1794-1795 under the name Tōshūsai Sharaku remains the greatest mystery in the study of Japanese woodblock prints, there is nothing enigmatic or obscure about the power and beauty of his conceptions, which rank among the greatest achievements in the history of Ukiyo-e. The beautifully preserved example reproduced here is among the finest from the artist's hand. It was acquired by the pioneer Boston print enthusiast William S. Spaulding and his brother, John T. Spaulding, in June of 1913. Earlier it had belonged to the collection of Baron Sumitomo. At least three additional examples are known to exist.

The print shows the celebrated tachiyaku *actor Sawamura Sōjurō III in the role of Kujaku Saburō, a loyal retainer of Prince Korehito in the play*

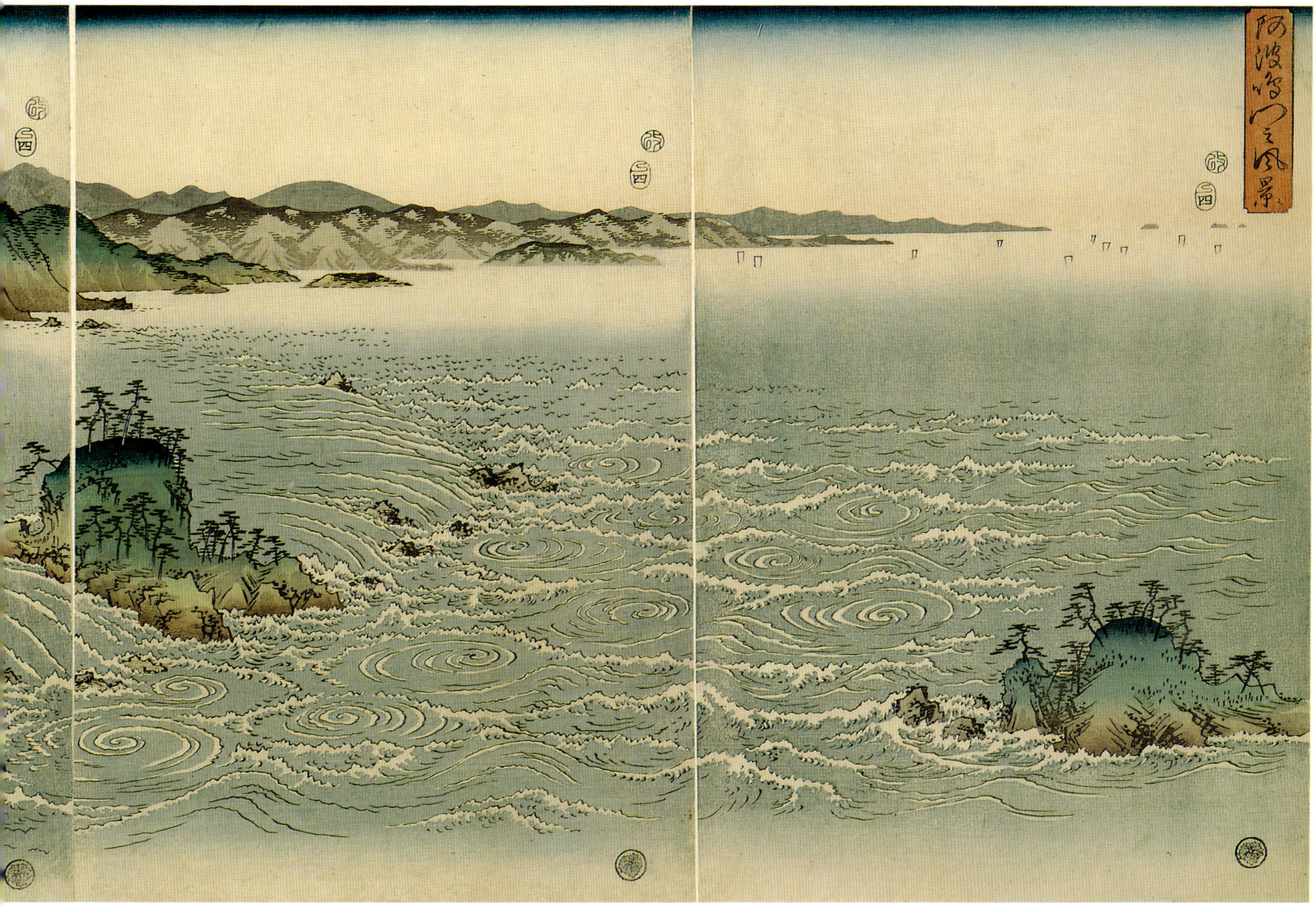

Uruou Toshi Meika no Homare, *for which unfortunately no libretto has been preserved. The play was presented at the Miyako-za in the eleventh month of Kansei 6 (1794), and there is another print produced for this program by Sharaku in* aiban *size that shows Sōjurō in the same part. Comparison of the poses, facial angles, and expressions in the two prints show them to be virtually identical — testimony not only to the artist's acute powers of observation, i.e., his ability to capture the distinctive expression of an actor in a specific role, but also to the pictorial consistency of his portrayals.*

77
Andō Hiroshige (1797-1868)
Naruto Strait
Edo period, 1857
Woodblock prints: triptych; ink and colors on paper. 37.5 x 25 cm. (each sheet)
Spaulding Collection. 21.7618-7620

This much-admired work and two other triptychs (Mountains and Rivers Along the Kiso Highway and Eight Views at Kanazawa in Musashi Province at Night) *were conceived as a set by the revered woodblock-print designer Hiroshige, an artist esteemed for his beautiful landscapes.*

The Naruto Strait, a narrow body of water at the eastern end of the Inland Sea, is famous as an inspiring scenic location because of the elemental power of the rough waves and whirlpools and the broad panorama of sea, coastline, and sky that is visible from the area. The three triptychs might be called "pure" landscapes, for there are few evidences of human activities to be seen in them, and it is obvious that Hiroshige's intention was to portray the spacious vistas and topographical variety in nature, her diverse moods and idyllic beauty.

Hiroshige was a man of advanced age when he created the designs for these prints, and it is not clear whether he drew them from the actual locations or simply recreated them according to his own artistic inclinations.

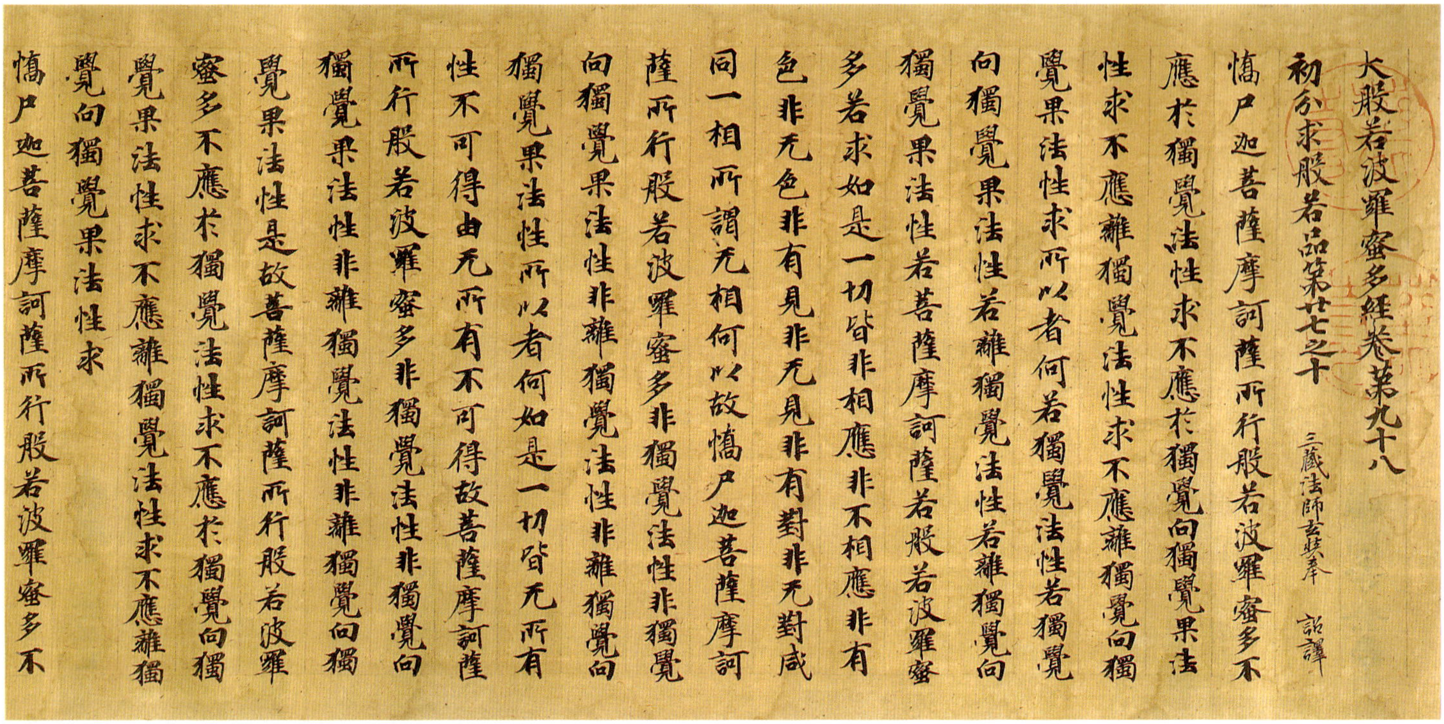
大般若波羅蜜多經卷第九十八
初分求般若品第廿七之十　三藏法師玄奘奉　詔譯
憍尸迦菩薩摩訶薩所行般若波羅蜜多不
應於獨覺法性求不應於獨覺向獨覺果法
性求不應離獨覺法性求不應離獨覺向獨
覺果法性求所以者何若獨覺法性若獨覺
向獨覺果法性若離獨覺法性若離獨覺向
獨覺果法性若菩薩摩訶薩若般若波羅蜜
多若求如是一切皆非相應非不相應非有
色非无色非有見非无見非有對非无對咸
同一相所謂无相何以故憍尸迦菩薩摩訶
薩所行般若波羅蜜多非獨覺法性非獨覺
向獨覺果法性非離獨覺法性非離獨覺向
獨覺果法性所以者何如是一切皆无所有
性不可得由无所有不可得故菩薩摩訶薩
所行般若波羅蜜多非獨覺法性非獨覺向
獨覺果法性非離獨覺法性非離獨覺向獨
覺果法性是故菩薩摩訶薩所行般若波羅
蜜多不應於獨覺法性求不應於獨覺向獨
覺果法性求不應離獨覺法性求不應離獨
覺向獨覺果法性求
憍尸迦菩薩摩訶薩所行般若波羅蜜多不

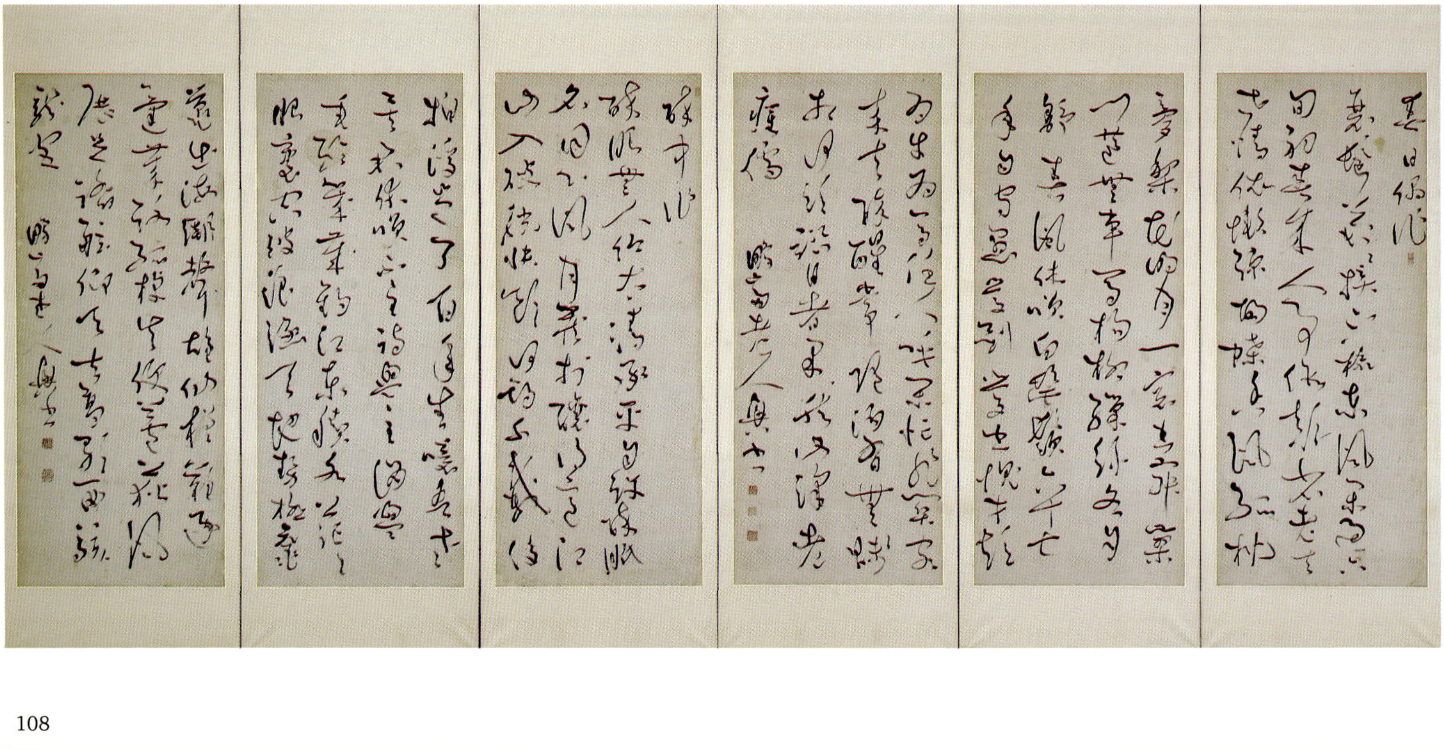

78

Greater Sutra of the Perfection of Wisdom (Daihannaya-kyō), 98th section, Yakushi-ji version

Nara period, 8th century
Handscroll; ink on paper. 27.5 x 97 cm.
Harvey E. Wetzel Collection. 19.681

The Daihannya-kyō, *first translated from Sanskrit by the famous Chinese Buddhist monk Xuanzang (600-664), is one of the great religious texts of Mahayana Buddhism. This scroll is from a six-hundred-scroll set that is thought to have been copied about 765-770 and was preserved for centuries in the Jūrin-in, a subtemple of the Gangō-ji in Nara, before being transferred to the Yakushi-ji in recent times. There the scrolls were impressed with a temple seal that reads:* Yakushi-ji-in. *The thirty-three examples that remain in the Yakushi-ji today are registered as Important Cultural Properties by the Japanese government.*

The entire set of scrolls has been ascribed traditionally to Asano Nanakai, a government official, a leading calligrapher of the second half of the eighth century, and who is said to have been the founder of the Jūrin-in. Since the writing varies in character and quality, however, it is surmised that a number of individuals were involved in the project.

This style of writing, with each character executed precisely and elegantly in the kaishō *(regular) mode, marks the culmination of early Japanese calligraphy based on Tang Chinese prototypes. The distinctive yellow tint of the mulberry paper on which the texts are written comes from the bark of the medicinal* kihada *tree (philodendron amurense), which was used in a dye to ward off insects and strengthen the fibers.*

79

Kameda Bōsai (1752-1826)

Poems written in Chinese style, calligraphy in cursive style

Edo period, dated 1816
Pair of six-panel folding screens; ink on paper; each panel 128 x 52 cm.
Charles B. Hoyt Fund and Helen S. Coolidge Fund. 1989.193-194

Bōsai is said to have begun his study of calligraphy when he was five or six under Mitsui Shinna (1700-1782), the leader in Edo of a style of writing that drew its inspiration chiefly from examples that had been introduced to Japan by Chinese immigrant monks of the Ōbaku sect in the seventeenth century. By the age of twenty, Bōsai was already established as an accomplished calligrapher, adept at three forms of writing — regular, running, and cursive ("grass") scripts. Anecdotal accounts describe Bōsai's dedication to calligraphy as a youth, and how the prodigious number of ink sticks he ground with water to practice his writing so eroded his favorite inkstone that it had to be discarded for a new one.

In his later years Bōsai became one of the most admired figures in the cultural and intellectual life of the period, a man of substantial creative accomplishments who exemplified the highest ideals. In addition to his literary talents as a writer and poet, he was also a proficient painter in the literati style. His chief contribution to Japanese art, however, was his idiosyncratic calligraphy, particularly in the cursive manner, which combined vitality and freedom with disciplined control of composition and brushwork.

Bōsai's cursive script, like that of his contemporary Daigu Ryōkan (1757-1831), was derived closely from the One Thousand Character Essay, *as written by the "mad" monk of the Tang period Huaisu (725-785) — a calligraphic style that was highly admired in Bōsai's time. The screens reproduced here were created when Bōsai was about sixty-five (by Japanese traditional reckoning), and the style of the calligraphy is representative of the cursive manner he developed in his later years. The text, which consists of poems extolling the beauty of the four seasons and the pleasures of drinking sake, is written in Bōsai's distinctive manner, fluent and curvilinear, with light, rhythmic inflections, without artifice or conceit, a direct manifestation of his intelligence, discernment, and inner spirit. Scholar-calligraphers like Bōsai were invariably interested in the history of Chinese epigraphy, and their works were usually embellished by seals that they had designed (and often carved), typically containing their noms-de-plume, elegant studio names, or brief phrases that revealed their aesthetics and learning. Six of Bōsai's seals appear on these screens, enlivening the compositions and identifying the man.*

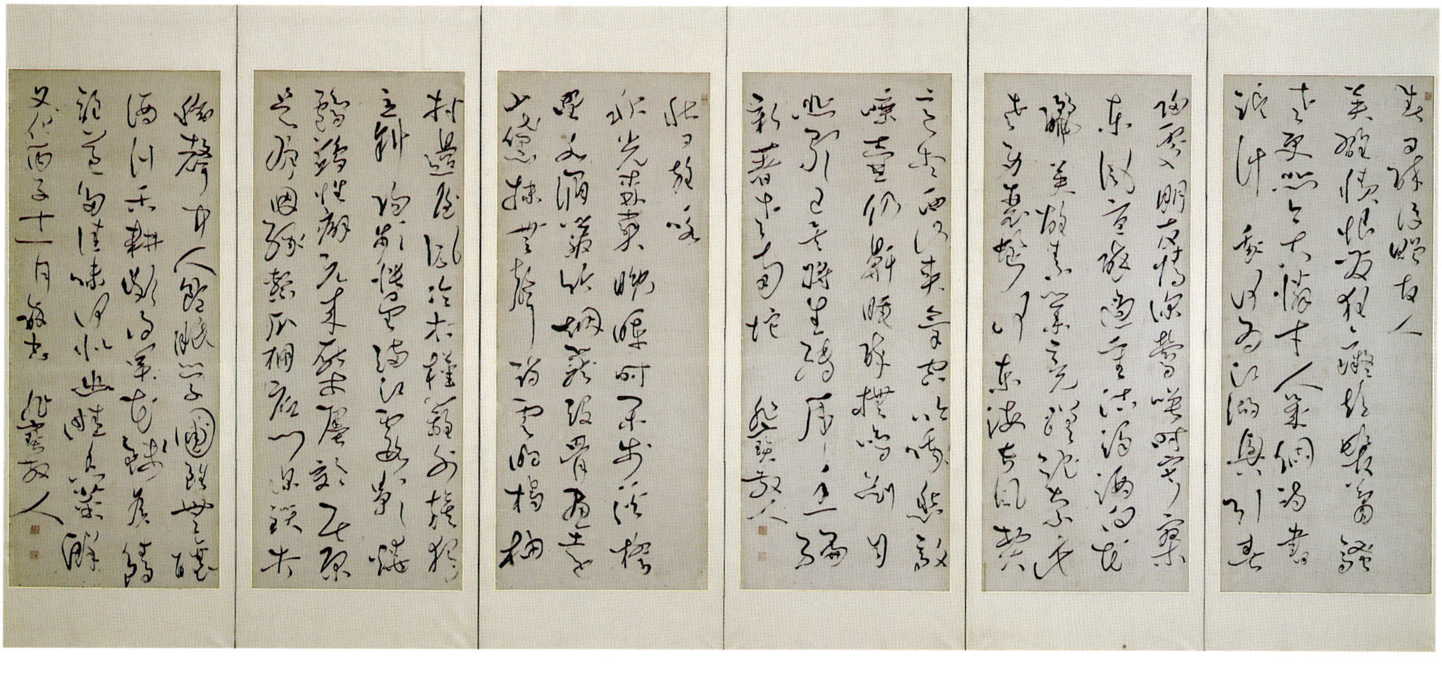

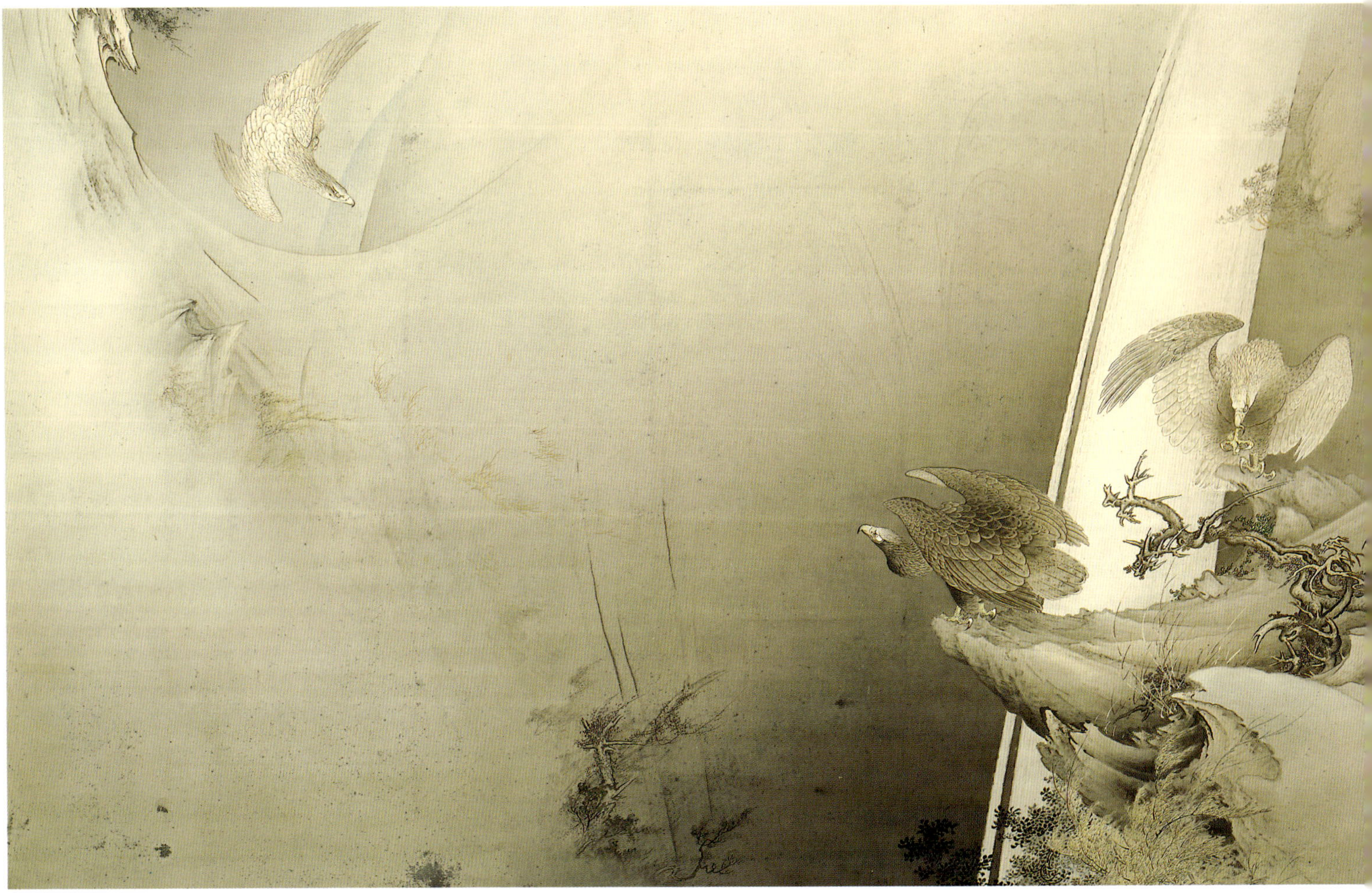

80
Kano Hōgai (1828-1888)
Eagles in a Ravine
Meiji period, 19th century
Hanging scroll; ink and colors on paper. 92.8 x 165.5 cm.
William Sturgis Bigelow Collection.
11.8740

Hōgai, the son of an official painter to the Chōfu clan in what is now Yamaguchi prefecture, went to Edo where he became a pupil of Kano Masanobu and gained recognition as a painter before returning to his native district. By the time he came to Edo again, the Meiji Restoration had occured and Japanese-style academic painting was being rejected. Despite this adversity, Hōgai in his own works preserved and continued to pursue the traditions of the Kano school. At the second of a series of competitive exhibitions for painters in Japan held in 1884, his talent captured the attention of Ernest Fenollosa. Hōgai integrated into his paintings some of the more attractive elements of Western-style painting, thus establishing the foundations for the modern school of Japanese painting known as Nihon-ga. His well-known work the "Merciful Maternal Kannon", painted at the very end of his life, is a masterpiece. The work shown here focuses on a powerful waterfall cascade, reminiscent of the earlier depiction by Sesshū (unfortunately destroyed during the Great Kantō Earthquake of 1923), and is animated by the presence of two eagles to the right and another in the distance to the left. Everything in the scene — the branches, the grasses straining in the wind, and the rushing water — creates an impression of space filled with movement and tension that forms a fitting background to the flight of the eagles. Another work very similar in feeling exists in Japan.

81
Hashimoto Gahō (1835-1908)
Landscape with Autumn Moon
Meiji period, 1880s
Hanging scroll; ink on paper.
86.8 x 47.2 cm.
11.34893

In 1884 Gahō was discovered by Ernest Fenollosa, who encouraged his work and procured financial assistance for the struggling artist. With the backing of Okakura Kakuzō, Gahō was soon appointed the primary professor of painting at the institution today known as the Tokyo University of Arts and Music. In 1898, when Okakura divorced himself from the university and founded the Japan Fine Arts Academy (Nihon Bijutsu-in), Gahō followed him.

The Nihon Bijutsu-in, as described by Okakura, "endeavored to preserve the characteristics of Japanese art while at the same time adapting itself to modern needs and notions." In this painting the composition of the landscape is indebted to the Kano school; the highlights suggesting moonlight on the trees and middle-ground slope, however, owe much to Western painting concepts.

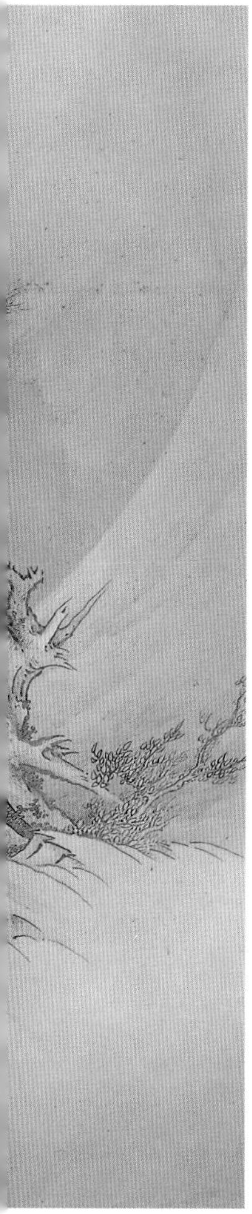

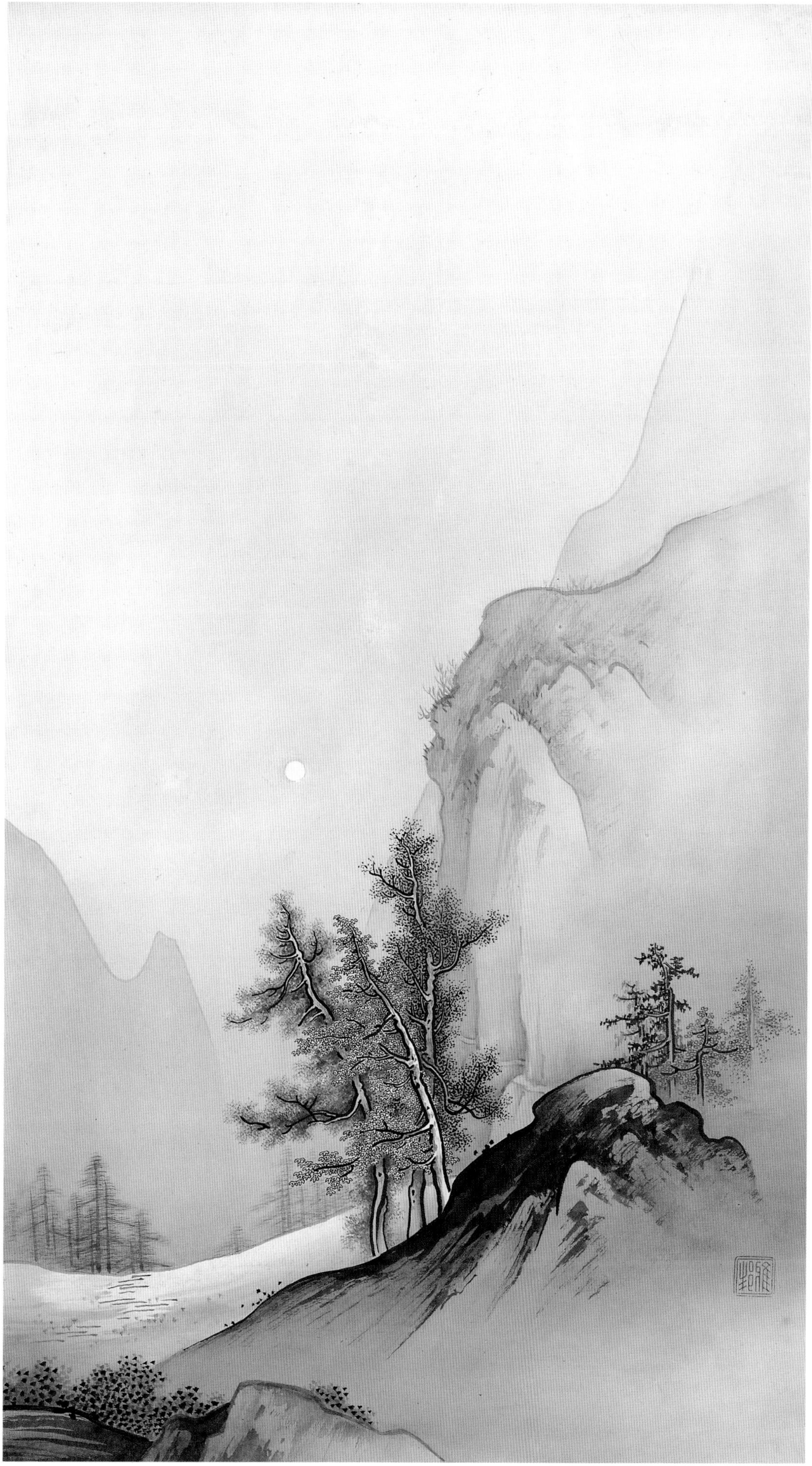

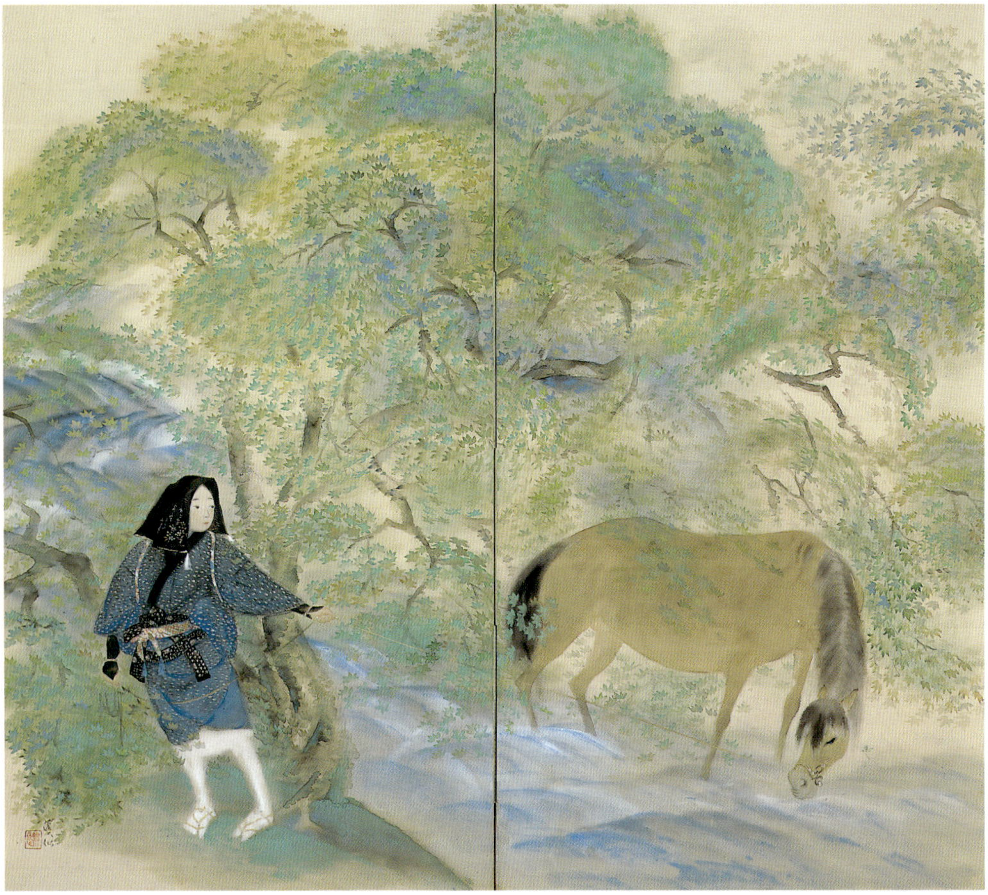

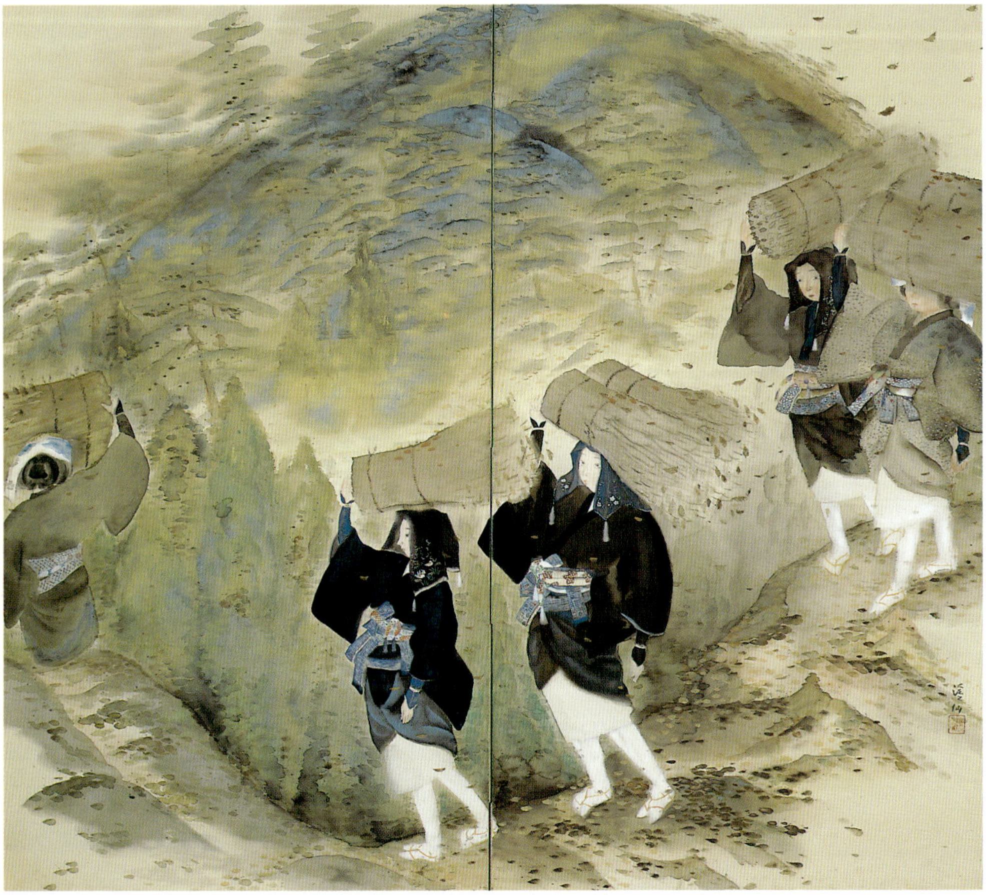

82
Tomita Keisen (1879-1936)
Spring in Yase and Autumn in Ohara
Taishō period, 1921
Pair of two-panel folding screens; ink and colors on silk.
166.9 x 92.4 cm.(each)
Marshall H. Gould Fund. 64.277-278

This pair of screens depicts two well-known scenic spots to the north of Kyoto. Painted by Tomita Keisen, a Kyoto Nihon-ga artist, they were included in the eighth exhibition of the Japan Fine Arts Academy (Nihon Bijutsu-in) in 1921. Although Keisen received instruction from the Shijō-school painter Tsuji Kakō, he was influenced by diverse styles. He often copied Nara and Heian period Buddhist paintings and studied the scrolls of the Zenga artist Sengai Gibon. His eclecticism is readily apparent in these screens in their brushwork and use of brilliant color, inspired by the paintings of the contemporary literati artist Tomioka Tessai.

83
Yokoyama Taikan (1868-1958)
Moonlight in the Woods
Meiji period, 20th century
Unmounted scroll; ink, colors, and mica on silk. 75.6 x 51.0 cm.
Gift of the Estate of Mrs. James F. Curtis. 27.806

A student of Hashimoto Gahō at the institution later known as Tokyo University of Arts and Music, Yokoyama Taikan became one of the founders of the Nihon Bijutsu-in in 1898. With the death of Okakura Kakuzō in 1913, he assumed the leadership of this group, dedicated to the preservation of traditional values in Japanese painting.

In 1904 Taikan visited Boston with Hishida Shunsō, another member of the Bijutsu-in, and the two artists held an exhibition of their work in a Cambridge studio. Boston critics wrote at the time, "We find the rare qualities which animate the best of ancient Japanese art — the probity and purity of design...the utmost beauty of tone and atmosphere, and finally, best of all, the imaginative impulse, which lifts naturalism above the commonplace plane of brutal realism and ennobles it." The interest in atmosphere is evident in this painting in which Taikan has abandoned crisp descriptive lines for a landscape executed almost completely in ink wash; the egrets provide the only spots of color.

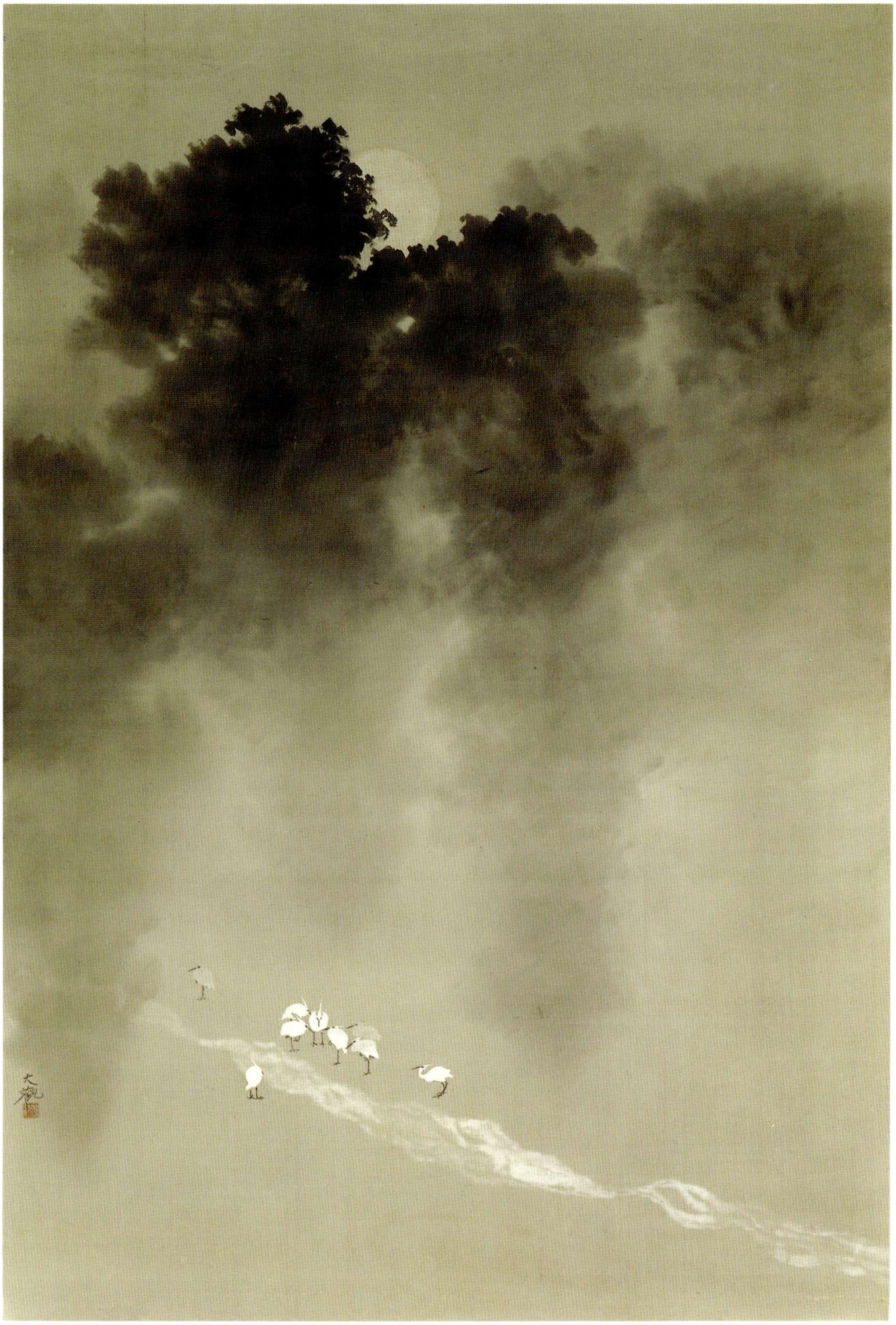

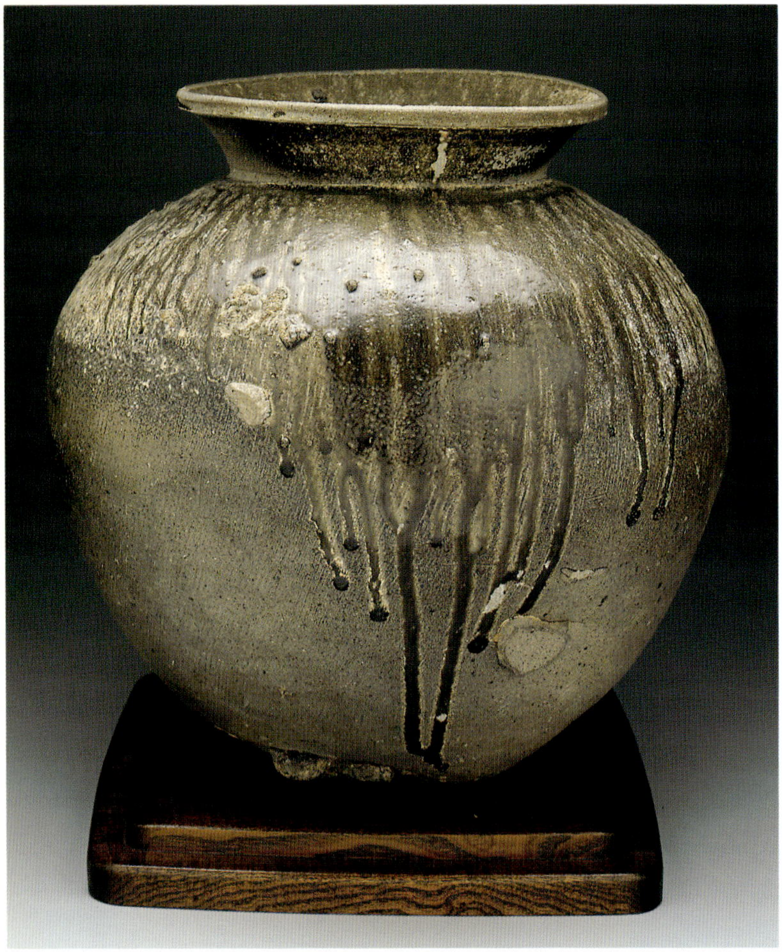

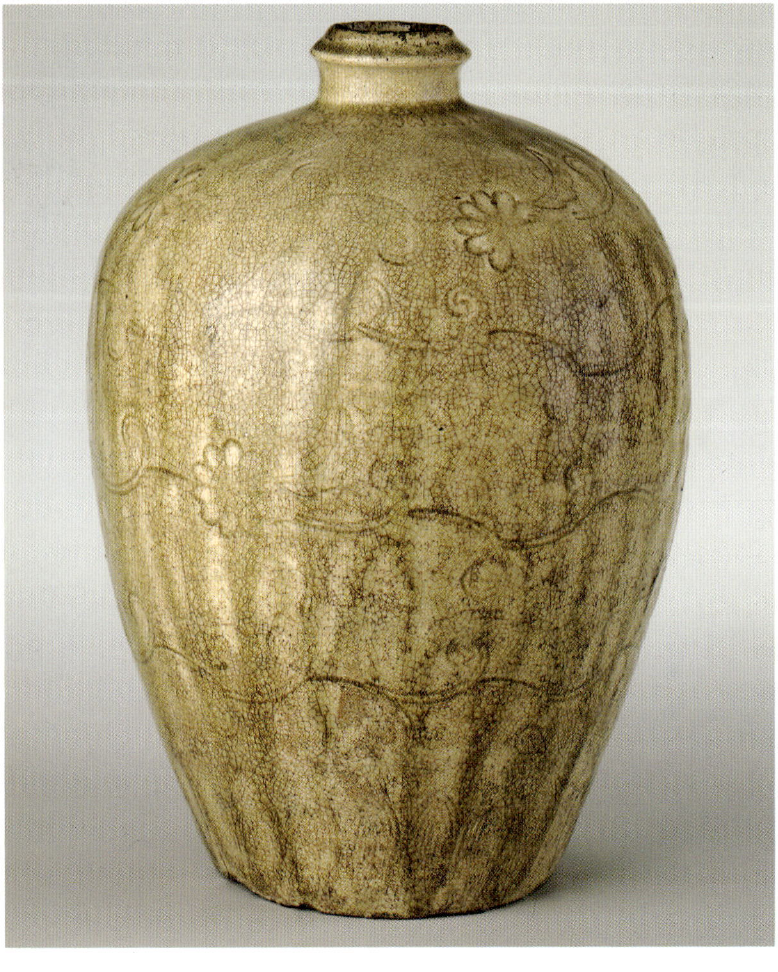

84
Jar
Asuka period, late 6th century
Sue ware; stoneware with ash glaze, hatched design, and round base.
H: 40 cm.
Gift of Mr. and Mrs. Morihiro Ogawa in Memory of Paul Bernat. 1989.241

The introduction of advanced techniques by Korean craftsmen to the Japanese ceramic industry in the late fourth and early fifth century A.D. fostered the development of Sue wares and other early high-fired ceramics. These advancements included the building of kilns capable of producing heat over 1,000 degrees Celcius, the introduction of the potter's wheel, and the ability to select clays that could stand up to the high-firing process. Unlike contemporaneous Haji pottery, Sue wares, which reflect the exotic taste and technical abilities of China and Korea, were produced originally for the court and members of the Japanese aristocracy. However, the excavation of over 1,000 Sue kiln sites indicates that by the twelfth century Sue ceramics were being produced far more extensively and for a much broader market.

The glaze of this jar is a result of fuel ash landing on the body of the vessel during firing, then fusing with the body to create a green colored glaze. Its large size suggests that it may have been used as either a storage jar or a vat for brewing wine.

85
Vase
Kamakura period, 14th century
Ko-Seto ware; glazed stoneware with carved decoration. H: 25 cm.
Gift of Theodora Lyman. 19.880

This vase, obviously inspired by Chinese Song-dynasty celadon wares of the mei-ping *type, is a product of one of the earliest kilns in the Seto area. While its shape is of continental origin, the impressed design of chrysanthemum scrolls is typically Japanese. It is covered with a thin yellowish-green glaze.*

Since the discovery of an elaborate scheme to produce forgeries of early Seto vases, the authenticity of many similar pieces has come into question in recent years. The Boston vase, donated to the Museum in 1919, was made long before the forgeries began.

86
Jar
Edo period, 17th century
Kakiemon type ware; porcelain with overglaze enamels. H: 20.2 cm.
Edward Sylvester Morse Memorial Fund. 57.383

This porcelain jar with flat shoulder, short neck, and wide mouth is decorated with chrysanthemums and rocks in red, yellow, blue, and green enamels. The vertical zig-zag design on the neck and the petal rays around the shoulder are often found on wares of the early Kakiemon potters. Several other pieces of this type have the same dull, cream-colored, crackled ground. The jar is generally attributed to one of the first three Kakiemon masters, but the identification of their wares is still a matter of speculation.

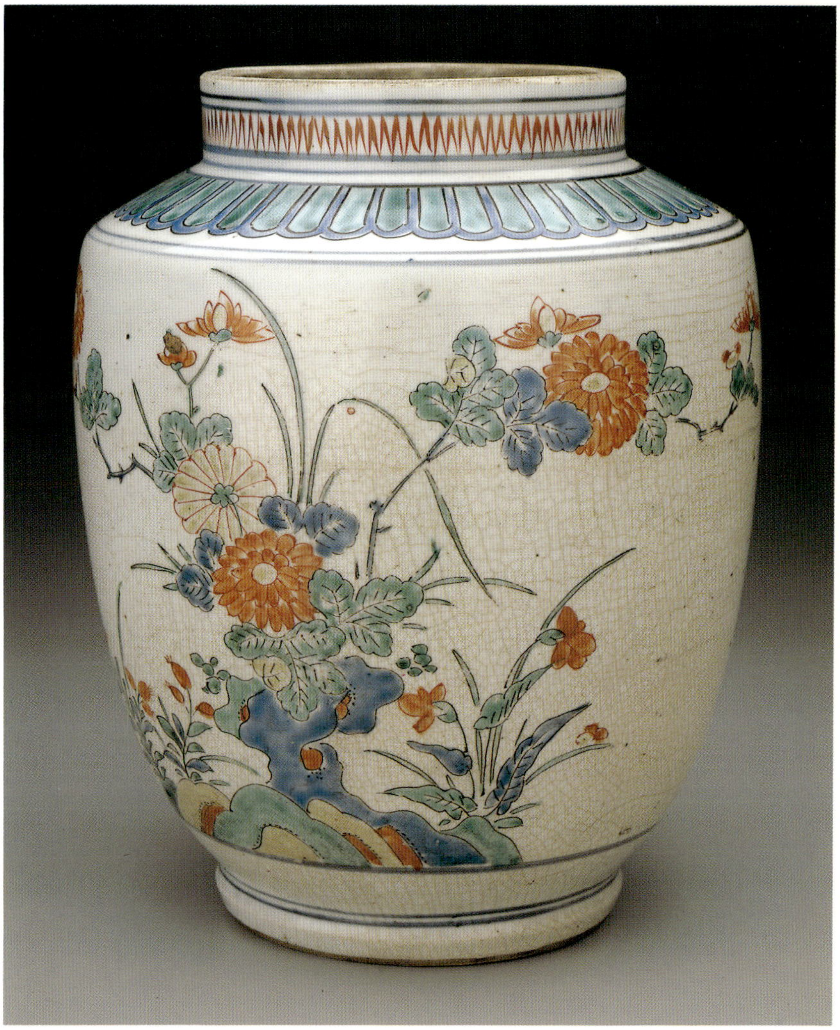

87
Dish
Edo period, early 17th century
Shino ware; stoneware with inlaid decoration. H: 7 cm.
Charles B. Hoyt Collection. 50.1698

Both Edward Sylvester Morse and Charles Hoyt had a special interest in a type of Japanese ceramics popularly known as Nezumi Shino, *or "mouse-gray Shino ware." It was made by covering the body with an iron-rich slip through which the design was then cut. Afterward the entire piece was covered with a feldspathic glaze. During firing the slip turns mouse-gray, while the cutout design appears in white.*

This deep dish is the most elegant of several pieces of Nezumi Shino *in the Museum's collection. The simple design around the rim, which frames the delicately drawn plants in the center of the plate, is typical for Shino ware. The design bears a strong resemblance to that of fragments excavated from a kiln site near Kujiri, Mino, one of the principal centers of production of this ware during the late sixteenth and early seventeenth century.*

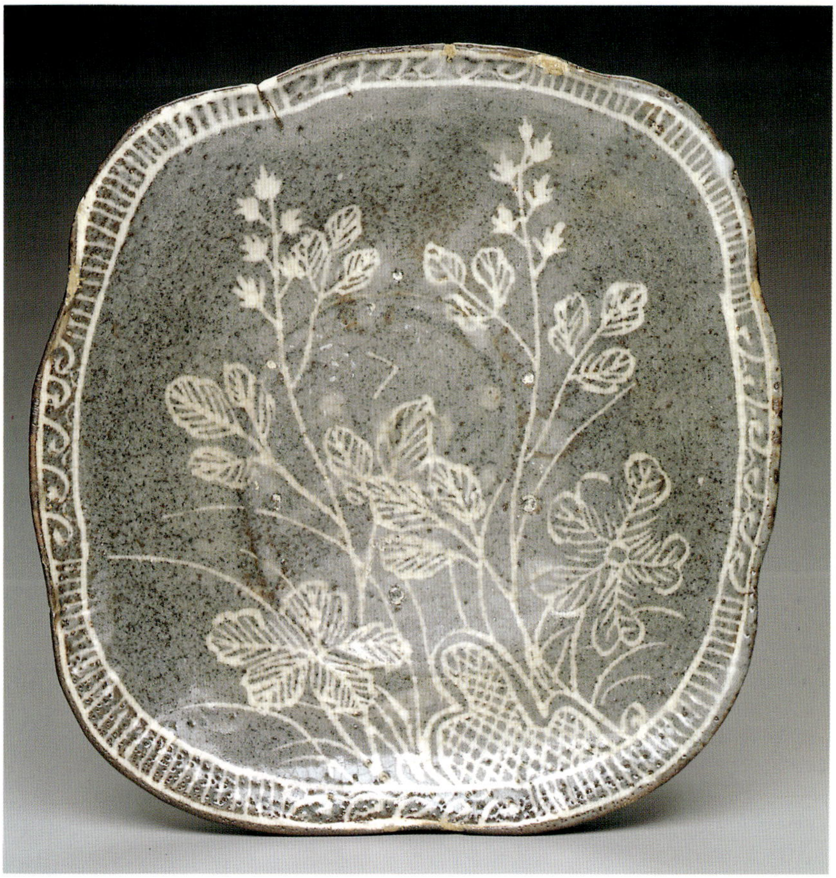

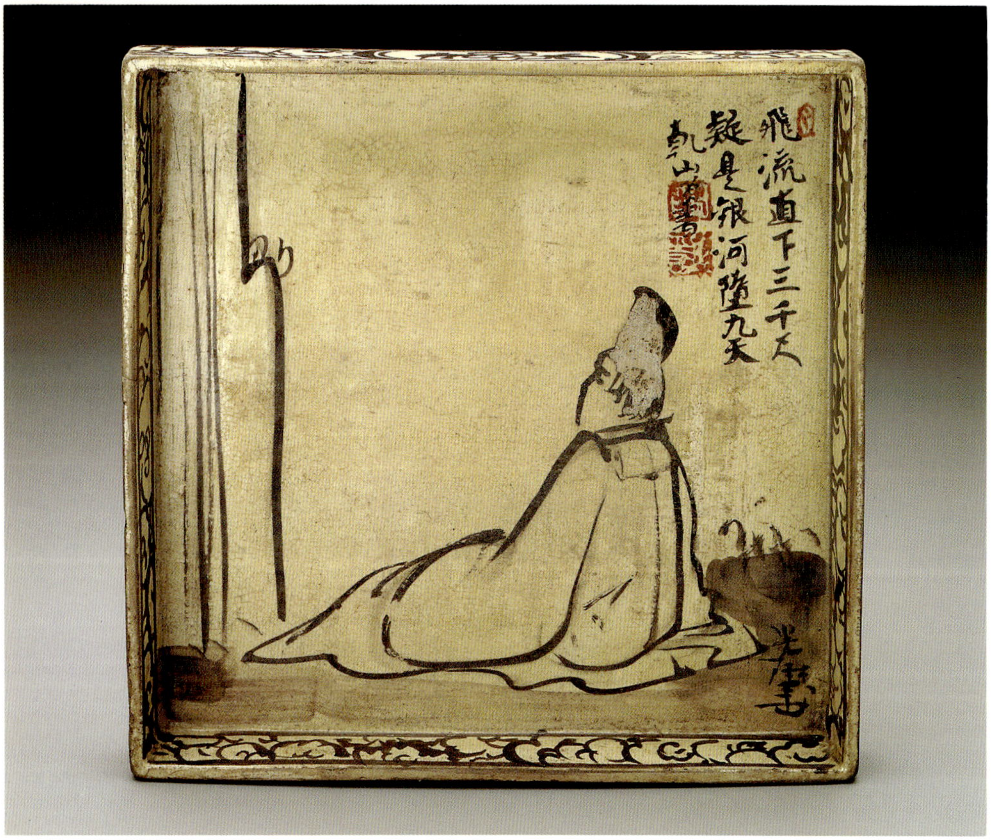

88

Ogata Kenzan (1663-1743) and Ogata Kōrin (1658-1716)

Square dish

Edo period, early 18th century
Stoneware with underglaze and enamel decoration. W: 21.8 cm.
Edward Sylvester Morse Collection.
92.6736

In 1699 the great Kyoto potter Ogata Kenzan established a kiln at Narutaki in Kyoto. His elder brother, the celebrated painter Kōrin, collaborated with him in this new venture by painting designs on the first sets of dishes that Kenzan produced there. Production of their ware seems to have been discontinued in 1712, when Kenzan moved his kiln to Chōjiyamachi in Kyoto.

Edward Sylvester Morse was the first Westerner to discover the genius of Kenzan and to make a serious study of the chronology of his work. The square plate that he acquired in the course of his search for the great artist's oeuvre shows, at the left, a scholar looking at a waterfall. Two lines of verse explain the theme: "A waterfall streaming straight down three thousand jō, */It is as if the milky way is falling from the highest heaven." The verse is signed by Kenzan, the painting by Kōrin. Three seals in red enhance the resemblance to a painted album leaf.*

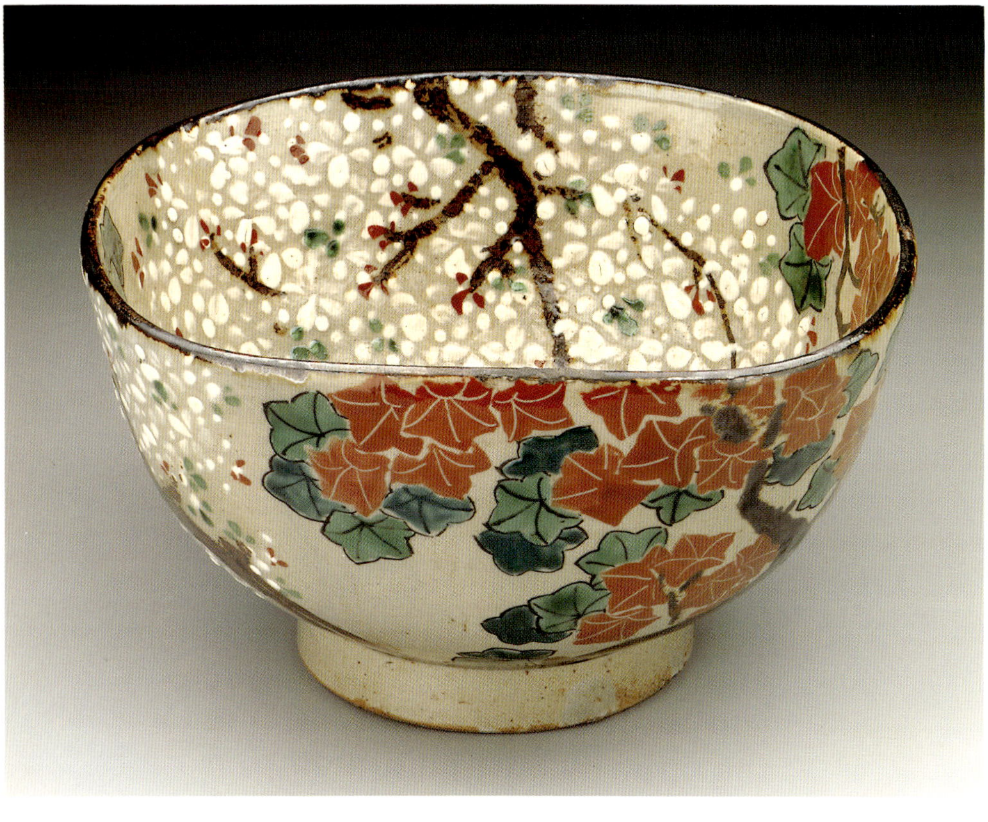

89

Nin'ami Dōhachi (1783-1855)

Large bowl

Edo period, 19th century
Stoneware with overglazed enamel decoration of cherry blossoms and maple leaves. H: 10.7 cm.
Edward Sylvester Morse Collection.
92.7651

Nin'ami Dōhachi was one of the most creative and talented ceramic artists active in Kyoto in the early nineteenth century. In the same way as his master Okuda Eisen (1753-1811), Dōhachi was deeply influenced by Chinese porcelain of the late Ming Dynasty, particularly by what is known as "Swatow ware". He is also known for porcelain modelled after the decorative works of Ogata Kenzan. The fine piece shown here demonstrates Dōhachi's Chinese taste. It is a large bowl covered with a dynamic design in which bright vermillion and green predominate, showing cherry blossoms in full bloom and maple leaves that have turned partly red. Dōhachi was fond of this design which appears on a number of surviving works. This bowl has Dōhachi's signature together with a date corresponding to 1825.

90
Box *(tebako)*
Kamakura period, 14th century
Lacquer with gold.
15.5 x 23.5 x 31 cm.
Martha Silsbee Fund. 31.1

The box, which has pewter rims and is fitted with two brass ornaments in the shape of butterflies, is decorated with a variety of floral designs. On the cover there is a weeping willow and a flowering plum tree with flying birds around it. The sides enclose a design of autumn flowers, executed in togidashi *(polished lacquer) and* taka-makie *(raised gold lacquer).*

Three rocks in the foreground of the scene on the cover are inlaid with characters reading Chō sei den, *meaning the Hall of Longevity, a palace hall built for the Tang emperor Xuanzong. Here, the term refers to a poem in the* Wakan Roeishū, *written by the Japanese poet Yoshishige no Yasutane in the late tenth century. The spring and autumn scenes on the box are also part of this poem: "In the Hall of Longevity, springs and autumns are abundant; in front of the Gate of Never-aging, the sun and moon move slowly." The motif of the* Chō sei den *occurs on several lacquer boxes of the late Kamakura period.*

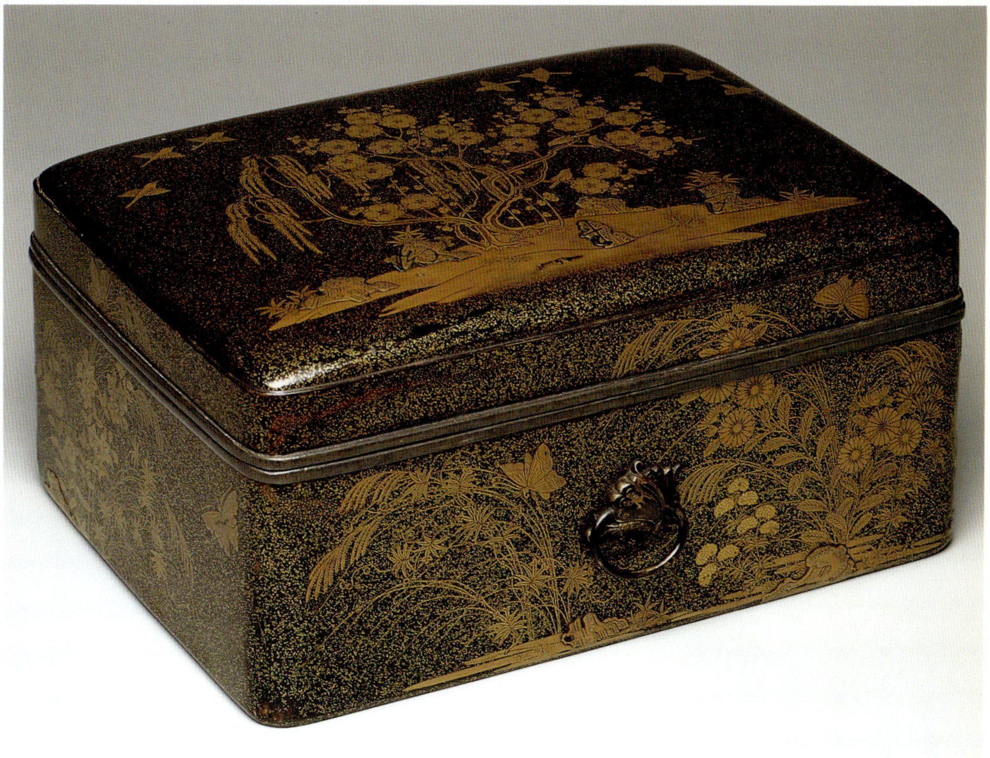

91
Inkstone box *(suzuribako)*
Edo period, 17th - 18th century
Lacquered wood with gold and mother-of-pearl. L: 22.1 cm.
William Sturgis Bigelow Collection. 11.10161

In a design evoking the thought of autumn, flowers over a garden fence are executed in lacquer relief (taka-makie) *and mother-of-pearl on a black ground decorated with gold* (hirame). *The box has been attributed traditionally to Igarashi Dōho (1643-1678), a distinguished lacquerworker from Kaga Province (Ishikawa Prefecture). The combination of gold lacquer and mother-of-pearl in the decoration is typical of the work of this master and his family.*

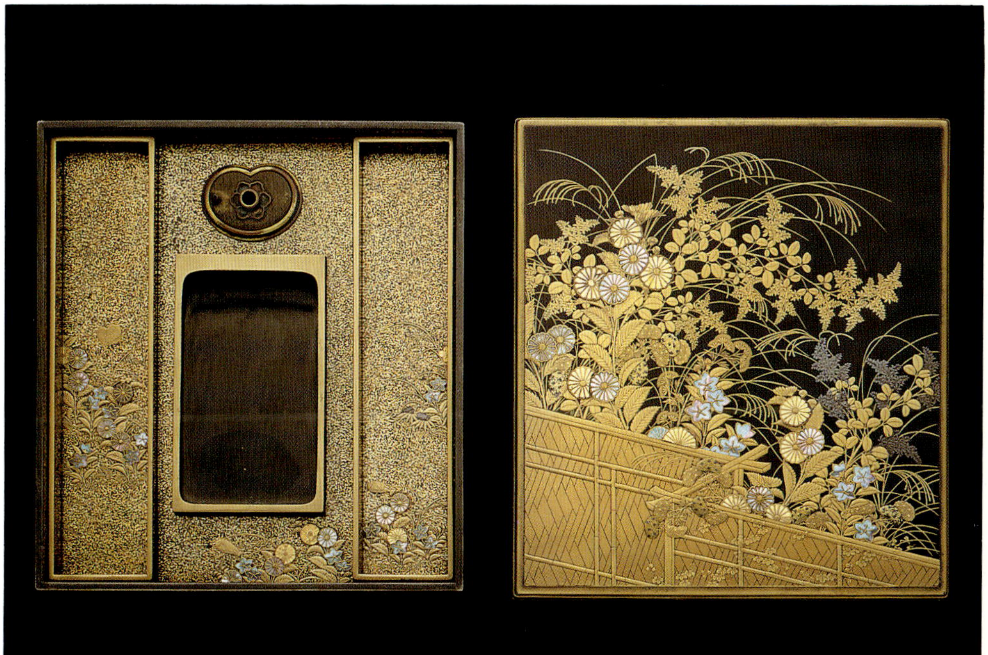

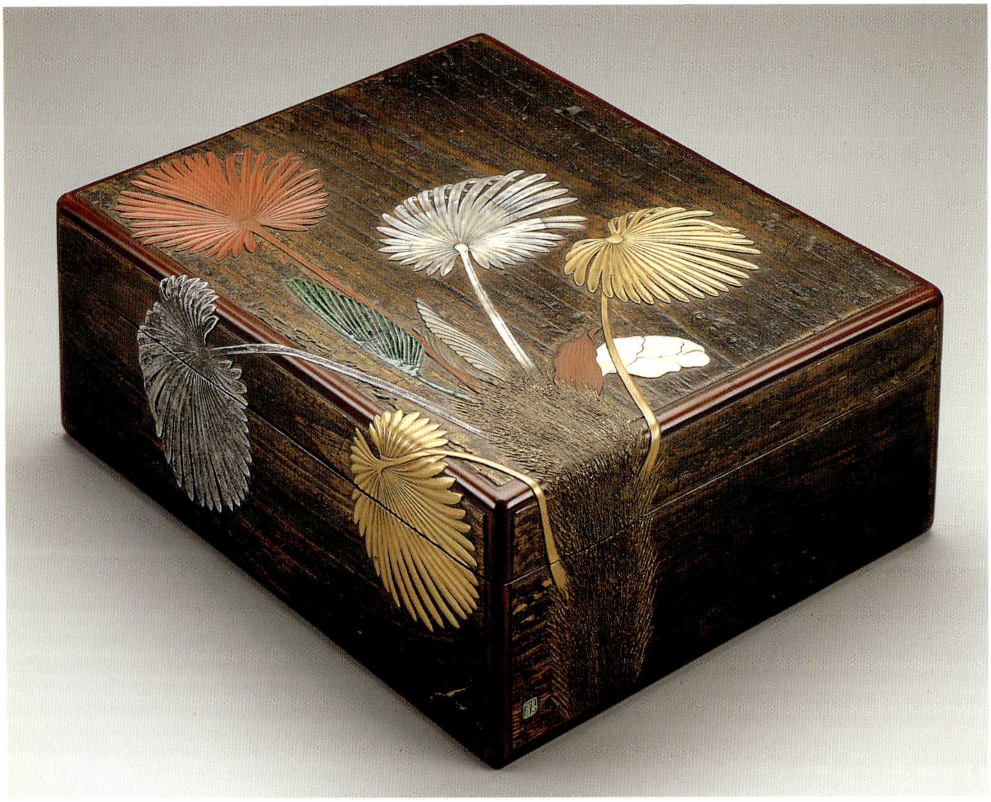

92
Ogawa Haritsu (1663-1747)
Box for writing paper
Edo period, 17th or 18th century
Paulownia with inlaid decoration.
11.2 x 28.5 x 23.8 cm.
Gift by Special Contribution. 08.170

The paulownia wood surface is inlaid with a multicolored design of palmetto leaves in gold lacquer, mother-of-pearl, ceramic, and lead; it is covered with a thin layer of transparent lacquer.

Ogawa Haritsu, better known by the name Ritsu-ō, was one of the first Japanese lacquermasters to exploit fully the decorative possibilities of inlaid designs executed in different materials of contrasting color.

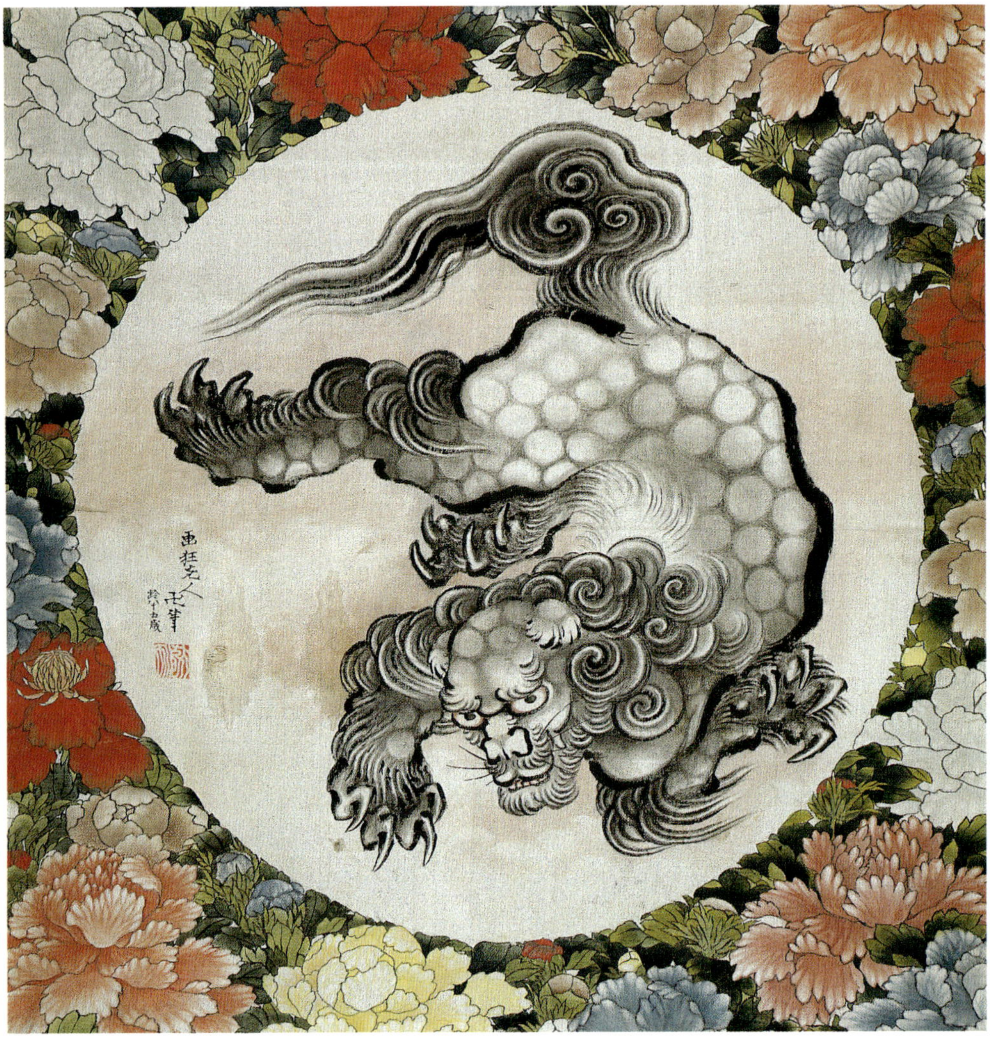

93
Katsushika Hokusai (1760-1849)
Karashishi Surrounded by Peonies
Edo period, 19th century
Silk gift wrapper (fukusa).
71.6 x 66.6 cm.
William Sturgis Bigelow Collection.
22.398

Ornate silk textiles that were used to cover gifts offered on felicitous occasions during the Edo period are known as fukusa. *By the eighteenth century the practice of placing these decorative square cloths over important objects when they were presented seems to have become common in cultured circles in the cities of Kyoto and Edo. The most prevalent manner of embellishing* fukusa *involved the use of colorful embroidery and textile applique, but some examples, like the present one, were done with artist's pigments and ink, painted directly on the surface of the silk. Depicted on the example shown here is the familiar* karashishi, *an imaginary Chinese beast, which is organized in a roundel, surrounded by the flower commonly associated with this eccentric animal, the tree peony.*

The composition is the conception of Katsushika Hokusai, who called himself the "Old Man Mad with Painting", and the waggish beast and the details of its anatomy are characteristic of the artist's many depictions of the subject. The signature gives Hokusai's age as eighty-five, and it is interesting to note that during the later years of his life, he turned away from designing woodblock prints and worked primarily on paintings that show the influence of Chinese pictorial ideas, such as the karashishi *here.*

94
Robe for the Nō theater
(karaori)
Edo period, late 18th-early 19th century
Silk and gilt paper; twill weave with pattern-dyed warps and supplementary pattern wefts. 147 x 137.3 cm.
William Sturgis Bigelow Collection.
15.1148

Karaori, *robes with sumptuous floral motifs, are worn by actors in the Nō theater, the understated dramatic form patronized in the Edo period by the Japanese military elite. Performing on a spare wooden stage with only minimal props, actors depend upon their selections of masks and robes, which are generally decorated with flowers, birds, and trees. When red is included in the intricate color scheme, it denotes a young woman.*

Although these costumes would have been viewed only from a distance during performances, they were woven with sophisticated craftsmanship. The warp threads were first dyed in sections forming the background blue and now-faded red. The motifs of wisteria and wild pinks in polychrome threads and the bands of clouds in gold were created by the pattern of wefts woven across them.

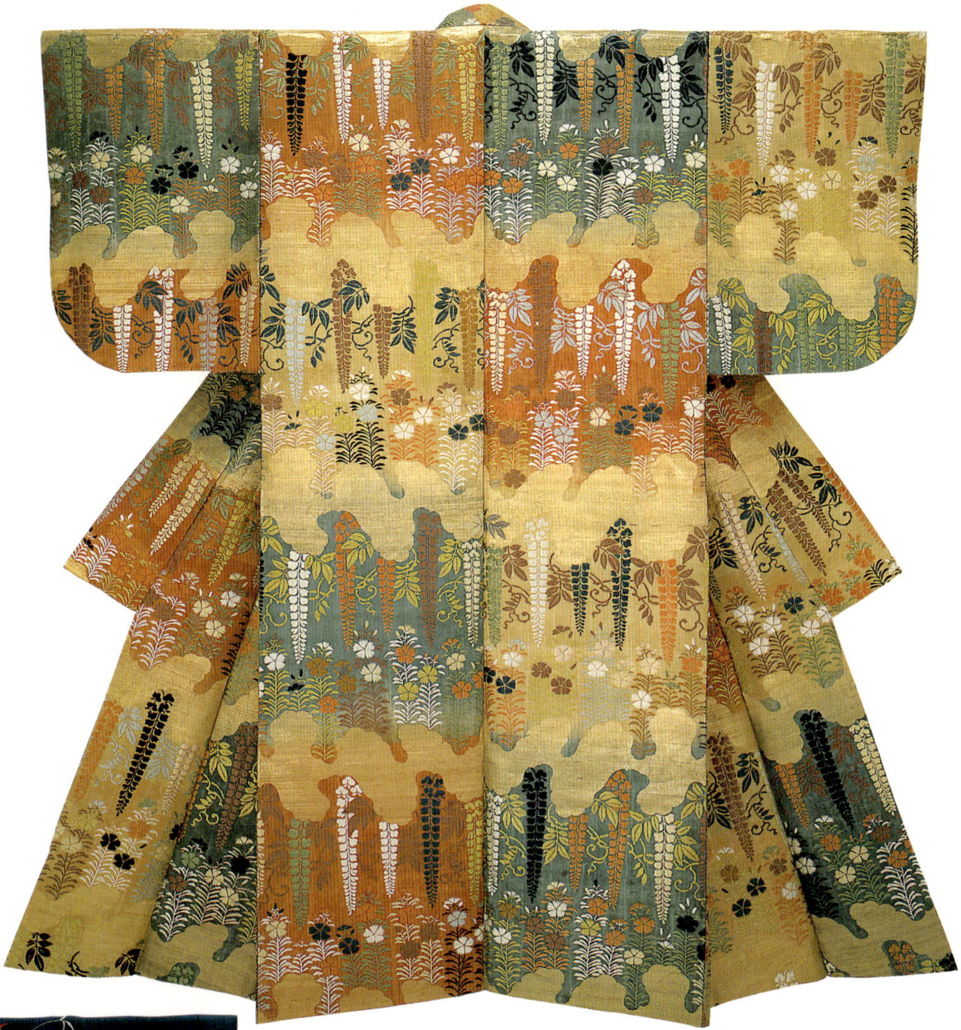

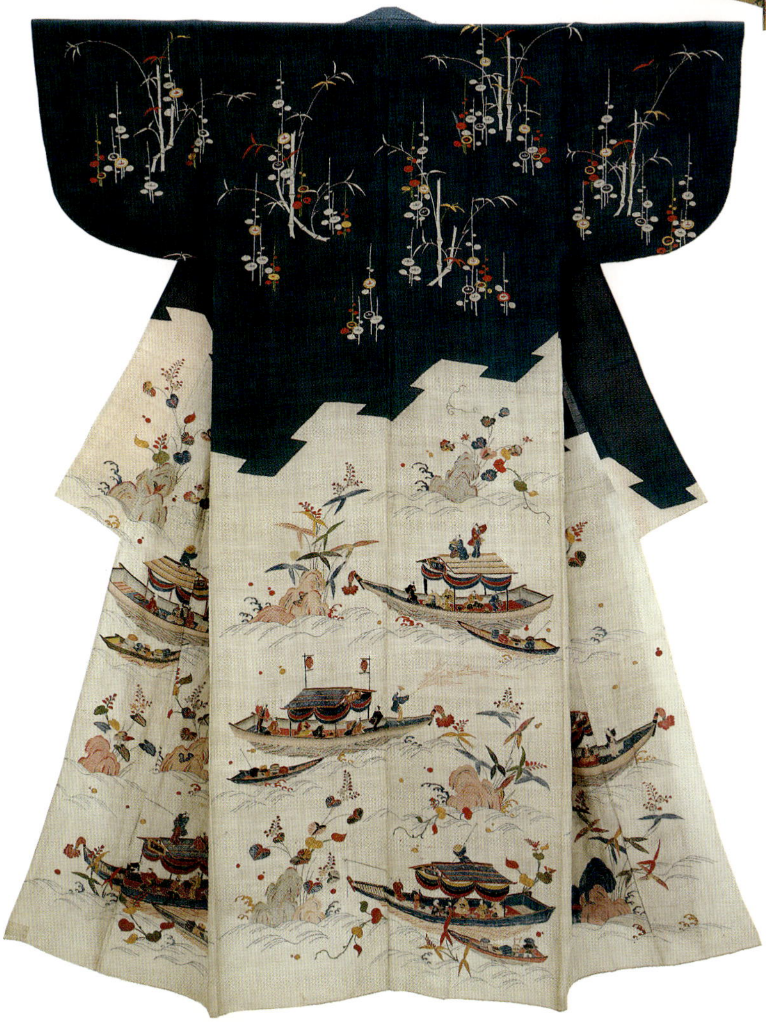

95
Summer robe *(katabira)*
Edo period, 18th century
Ramie, silk, and gilt paper; plain weave with resist and stencil dyeing, hand-painting, and embroidery.
162.4 x 118.4 cm.
William Sturgis Bigelow Collection.
21.1134

Katabira, *unlined robes fabricated from hemp or ramie, were worn during the summer months by women of the elite military class. These luxury garments usually bear designs with a water theme, which suggests coolness much appreciated during times of oppressive heat. The lower section of this robe, decorated with scenes of aristocrats enjoying themselves on pleasure boats, was executed in the paste-resist technique* (yūzen). *Plum blossoms and bamboo in the upper section were outlined using the same method and were embellished further with embroidery in polychrome threads and couched gold paper. The division of the robe into two distinct zones can be attributed to the increased width of* obi *during the preceding Genroku era (1688-1704).*

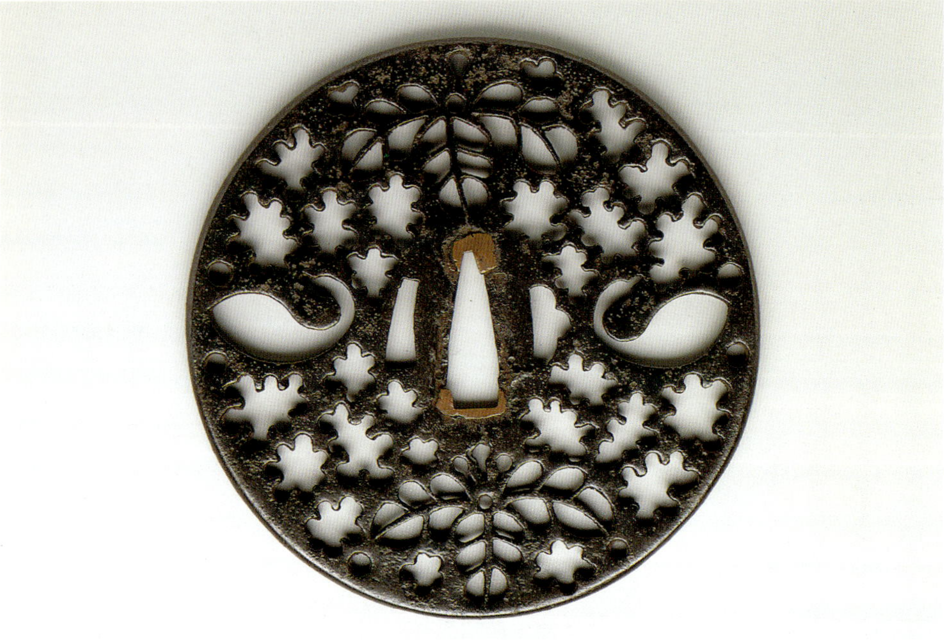

96
Sword guard *(tsuba)*
Early Muromachi period, 15th century
Iron; openwork design. Diam: 11 cm.
Denman Waldo Ross Collection.
06.233

The design of this rare, large tsuba *consists of openwork with motifs of paulownia flowers at the top and bottom, bottle gourds to the left and right, and snowflakes scattered over the surface. The pierced patterns, resembling openwork on the headgear of Japanese armor, are distinctive of what began in the Meiji period to be called* katchushi *("armorer")* tsuba. *They probably were produced from the Namboku-cho period through the Edo period. Almost all are uninscribed, and the majority were most likely made to be attached to the* uchigatana *mountings that were popular from the Muromachi to the Momoyama period.*

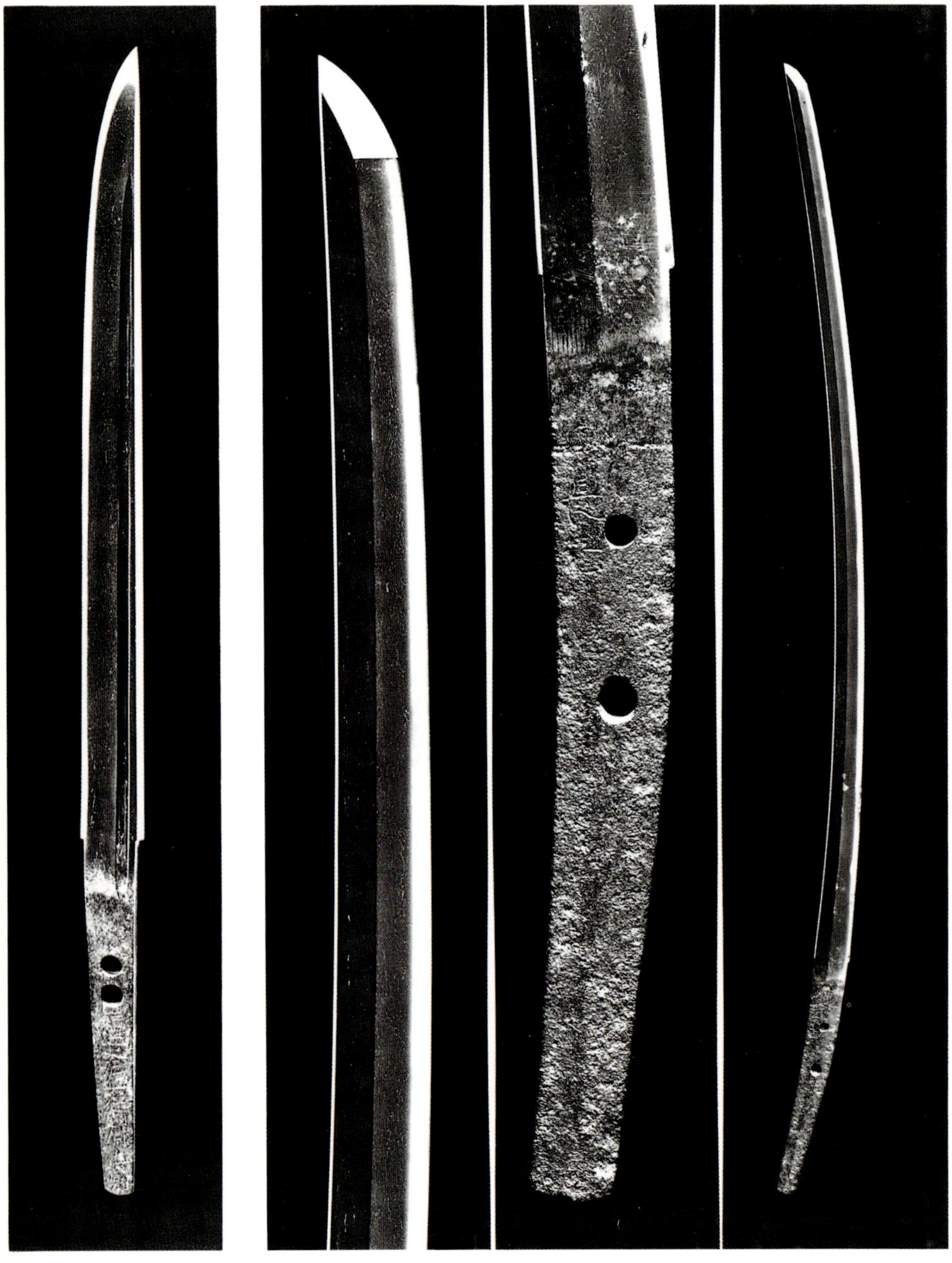

97
Naganori
Dagger *(tantō),* [complete mounting by Toshiyoshi, mid-19th century]
Late Kamakura period, early 14th century
Tempered steel. L: 26.1 cm.
William Sturgis Bigelow Collection.
11.11252

According to the engraved inscription, this dagger is by Naganori of the Fukuoka Ichimonji school. It is of the so-called yoroi-dōshi *(armor-piercing) type, with a thick blade and no curvature. There are two other* tantō *inscribed with the same reign period as this one, and they are made in exactly the same way and executed in the same style; one has been handed down in the Kuroda family and the other has been designated as an Important Art Object by the Japanese government. These three blades were probably made at the same time for a special occasion. On the steel surface one can see wood and burl grain textures. The straight line of the tempered edge is characteristic of Naganori's style.*

The sheath is finished with gold aventurine lacquer, and the design of autumn grasses is executed in makie *relief. The gold fittings are made by Toshiyoshi, Tanaka Kiyotoshi's successor.*

98
Nagamitsu
Sword *(tachi)*
Kamakura period, second half of 13th century
Tempered steel. 80.3 x 2.95 cm.
Charles G. Weld Collection. 13.1171

first millennium A.D. Although their meaning remains unclear, it is likely that beads fashioned in this unusual shape were originally believed to have protective powers and later became purely decorative designs.

101
Buddha of Healing (Yaksa Yorae)
Unified Silla dynasty, about
9th century A.D.
Gilt bronze. H: 36 cm.
Gift of Edward J. Holmes in Memory of his Mother, Mrs. W. Scott Fitz.
32.436

In this masterpiece of Korean Buddhist sculpture the style of the Chinese Tang dynasty has blended harmoniously with stylistic elements of the different Korean kingdoms that Silla unified in the course of the seventh century. The fine details of the octagonal base and the double lotus pedestal, as well as the balanced proportions of the figure, exemplify the most classic form of Silla sculpture.

The statue is closely related to a group of fifty-three gilt bronzes once placed on the branches of an ancient elm tree in the main hall of the Yuchŏmsa Temple in the Diamond Mountains of North Korea; this group was the principal focus of worship for many centuries until most of the statues were dispersed in 1916. The temple itself was destroyed during the Korean War in the early fifties. If this Buddha of Medicine ever came from Yuchŏmsa, it must have left the temple at a much earlier date, for it was for many years part of the collection of Okakura Kakuzō (1862-1913), curator of the Asiatic department from 1906 until his death.

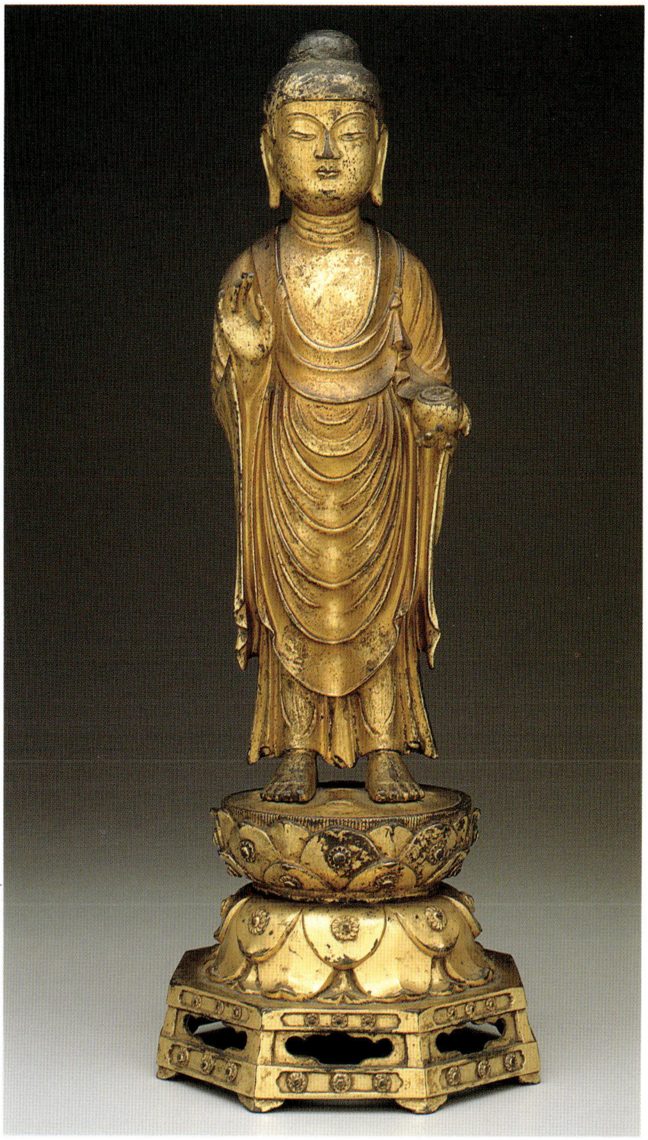

102
Figurine representing a kneeling man
Koryŏ dynasty, 13th century
Stoneware with celadon glaze.
H: 18.1 cm.
Charles B. Hoyt Collection. 50.1004

A greenish-gray glaze covers this hollow figure on both the outside and the inside. The oval face of almost caricatural expression is modeled with a large flat nose, long ears (damaged), and a small mouth. Such details as the eyebrows, the pupils of the eyes, the beard, and the border of the robe are painted in an underglaze brownish black color. Although several figurines in Koryŏ celadon exist, almost all are used as water sprinklers. The only other piece of this type—apparently some sort of tomb figurine—is in the collection of the Metropolitan Museum of Art.

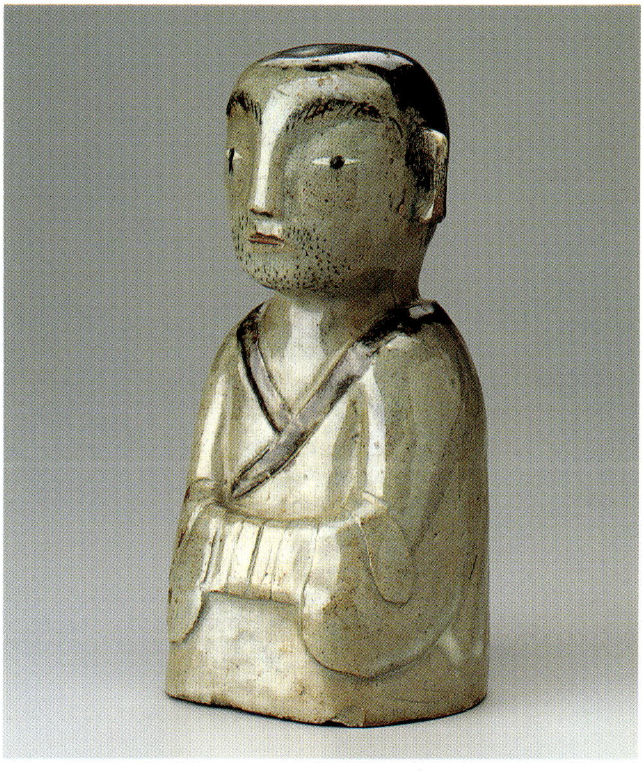

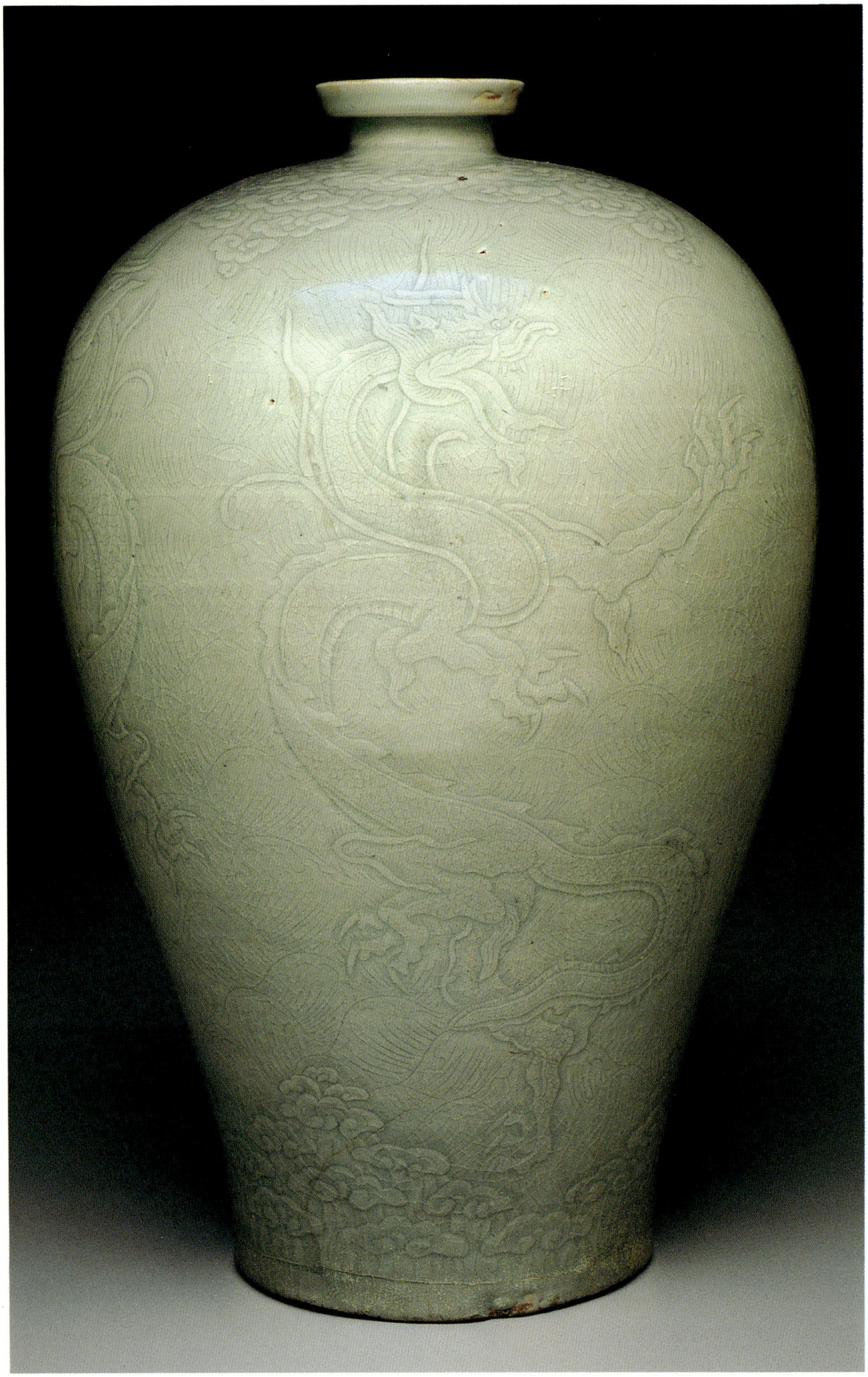

103
Vase *(maebyŏng)*
Koryŏ dynasty, 11th-12th century
Glazed stoneware; incised decoration of dragons. H: 36 cm.
Special Korean Pottery Fund. 11.1821

The body of this superb vase is decorated with a finely carved design of dragons rising up from among clouds and waves. Carved designs of stylized foliage surround the lower part of the neck. The thin, even celadon glaze and the delicate carving characterize this vase as one of the finest examples of its type that has been preserved. It was bought for the Museum of Fine Arts by Langdon Warner during one of his trips to Japan at the time when he was associated with Okakura Kakuzō and the Museum of Fine Arts.

104
Vase *(maebyŏng)*
Koryo dynasty, late 12th century
Glazed stoneware; inlaid decoration of cranes and birds in bamboo bushes. H: 31.1 cm.
Charles B. Hoyt Collection. 50.989

A smooth and translucent grayish-green glaze covers this gray stoneware vase with inlaid decoration consisting of cranes and birds in bamboo bushes executed in white and black slip. The simplicity of the design, carefully executed in every detail, suggests that the vase is one of the relatively early examples of inlaid celadon, made not long after this technique was first developed and perfected in the course of the twelfth century A.D. No other maebyŏng *of the same design is known to exist, and this elegant piece is considered to be one of the finest specimens of the type.*

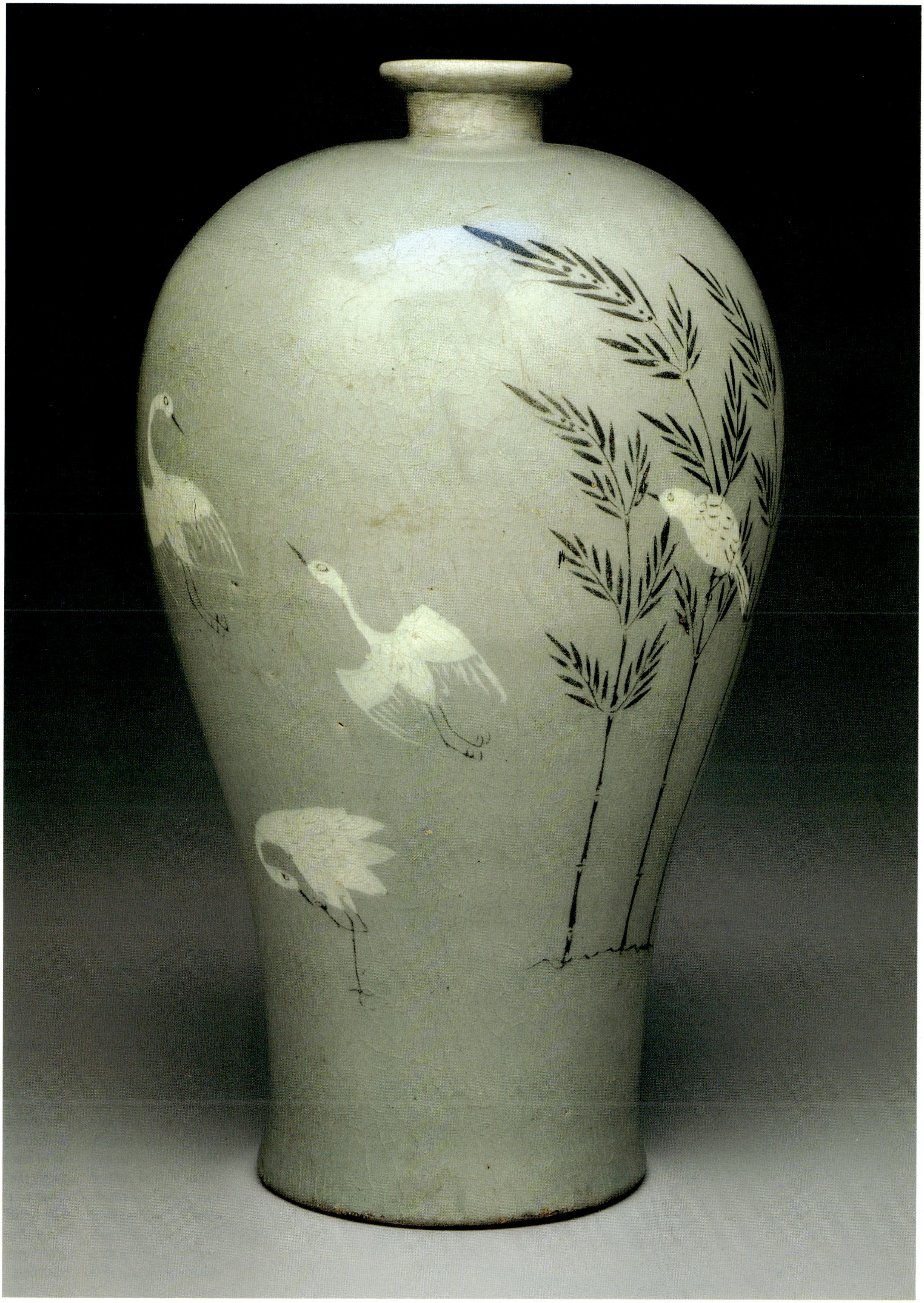

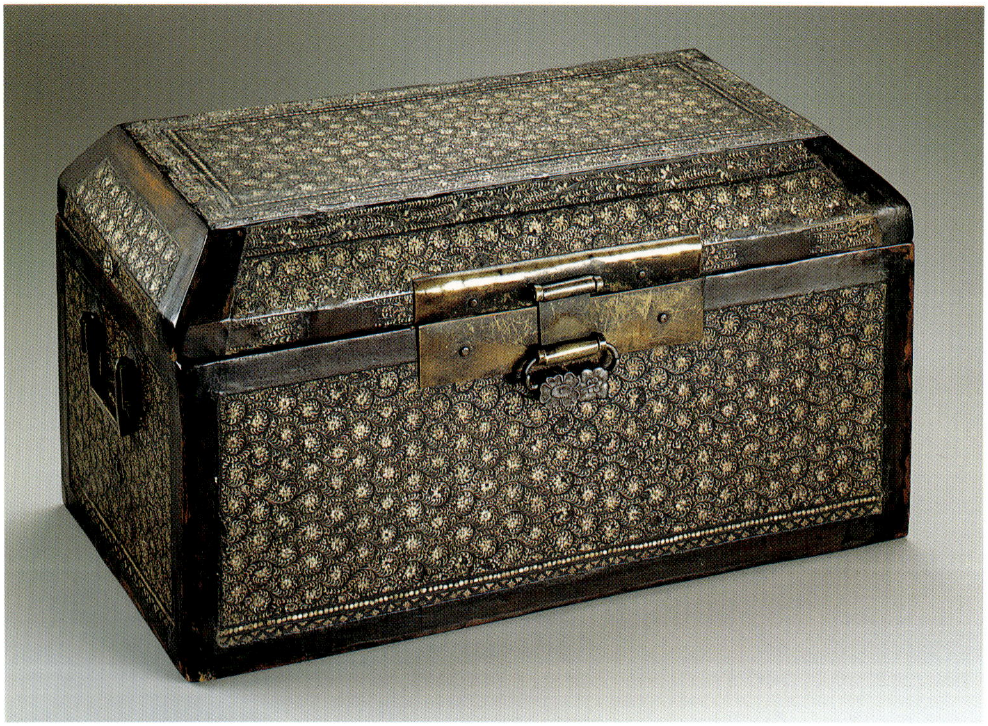

105
Sūtra box
Koryŏ dynasty, 14th century
Lacquer; inlaid with mother of pearl and silver wire (brass mountings).
47.5 x 25.5 x 25.7 cm.
William Sturgis Bigelow Collection.
11.1055

The Korean predilection for inlaid decoration may have found its expression in metalwork long before the famous inlaid celadons were first created. Early specimens of inlaid lacquer such as this are characterized by a delicate and dense decoration of scrollwork, quite distinct from the much bolder style of later centuries.

Used to store Buddhist scriptures, several boxes of this type have been preserved outside of Korea. As they are all of Japanese provenance, they could have come from a Buddhist library that was looted by the soldiers of Toyotomi Hideyoshi, who invaded Korea during the decade of the sixteenth century. It is equally possible that they were gifts brought to Japan by visiting Korean embassies. Following a practice also used in Chinese monastic libraries, the boxes were not numbered but were marked with characters (inlaid on the right side of the lid) taken from the text of the so-called Thousand Character Classic, *a Chinese school book that all educated Koreans knew by heart.*

The Koreans were famous for the textual accuracy of their printed editions of the Buddhist canon. When the printing blocks of an early edition were lost during the Mongol invasion of 1231, the king made a solemn vow to reprint this "Great Treasure of the State." A new edition in 1,340 volumes was produced between 1236 and 1251, the woodblocks of which (numbering 31,258 in total) are still preserved at the Haeinsa Temple on Mount Kaya near Taegu (South Korea).

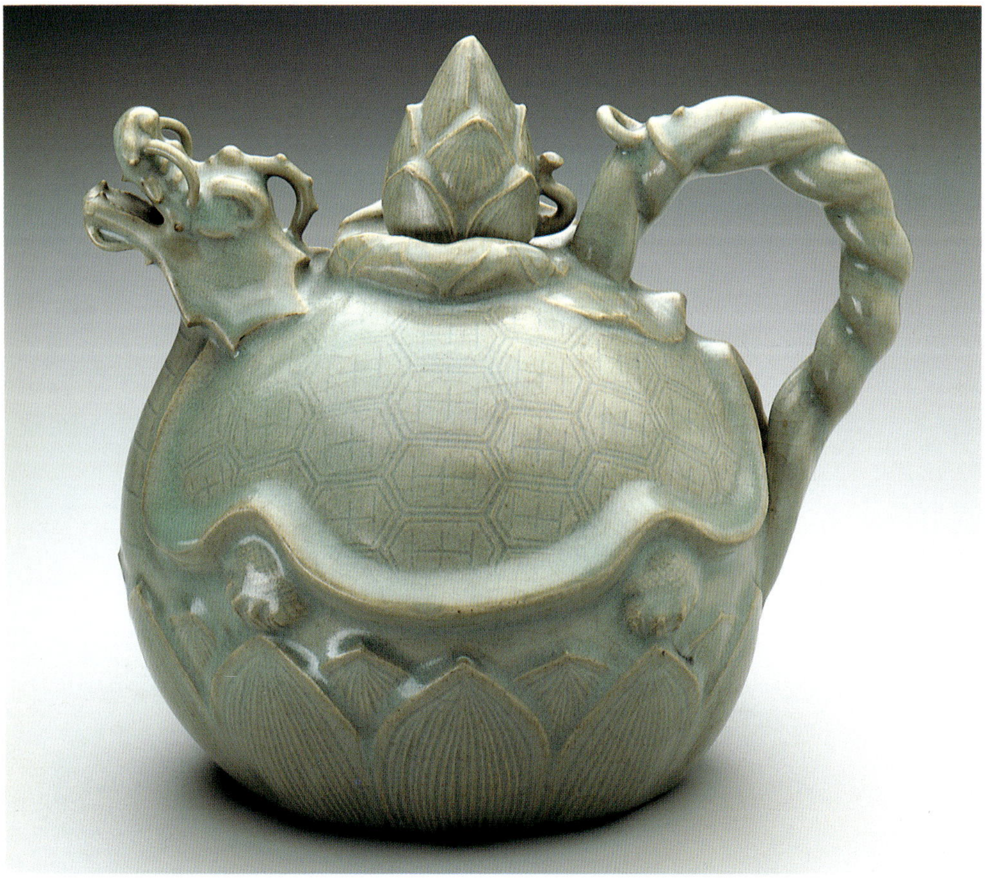

106
Wine pot and stopper
Koryŏ dynasty, 12th century
Celadon-glazed stoneware with incised decoration. H: 17 cm.
Seth K. Sweetser Fund. 38.680

The wine pot takes the shape of a fantastic animal, combining the head of a dragon with the body of a tortoise, seated on a lotus blossom. The head of the dragon serves as the spout of the vessel, which can be refilled through the aperture covered with the stopper in the shape of a lotus flower. The handle is shaped like intertwined vines. Inside the hexagons of the tortoise's carapace, the character wang *(king) has been inscribed.*

107
Incense burner in the form of the Buddhist Holy Flower *(posanghwa)*
Koryŏ dynasty, 12th century
Glazed stoneware; molded and inlaid decoration. H: 19 cm.
Keith McLeod Fund. 69.1044

The hollow body of this incense burner takes the shape of a posanghwa, *or Holy Image Flower, distinctive for its five rows of petals with serrated edges. The flower rests on six downturned leaves placed on a six-lobed platform, supported by three feet modeled as boars' heads. The ball-shaped cover is reticulated in order to allow the incense fumes to escape. Of this type of incense burner, in all probability once used in Buddhist ceremonies, only two examples survive. The slightly earlier example in the National Museum of Korea has feet in the shape of rabbits.*

Both pieces attest to the consummate modeling skill of the Korean potter, who used a brush to add simple scrollwork in white slip on the edge of the lobate base.

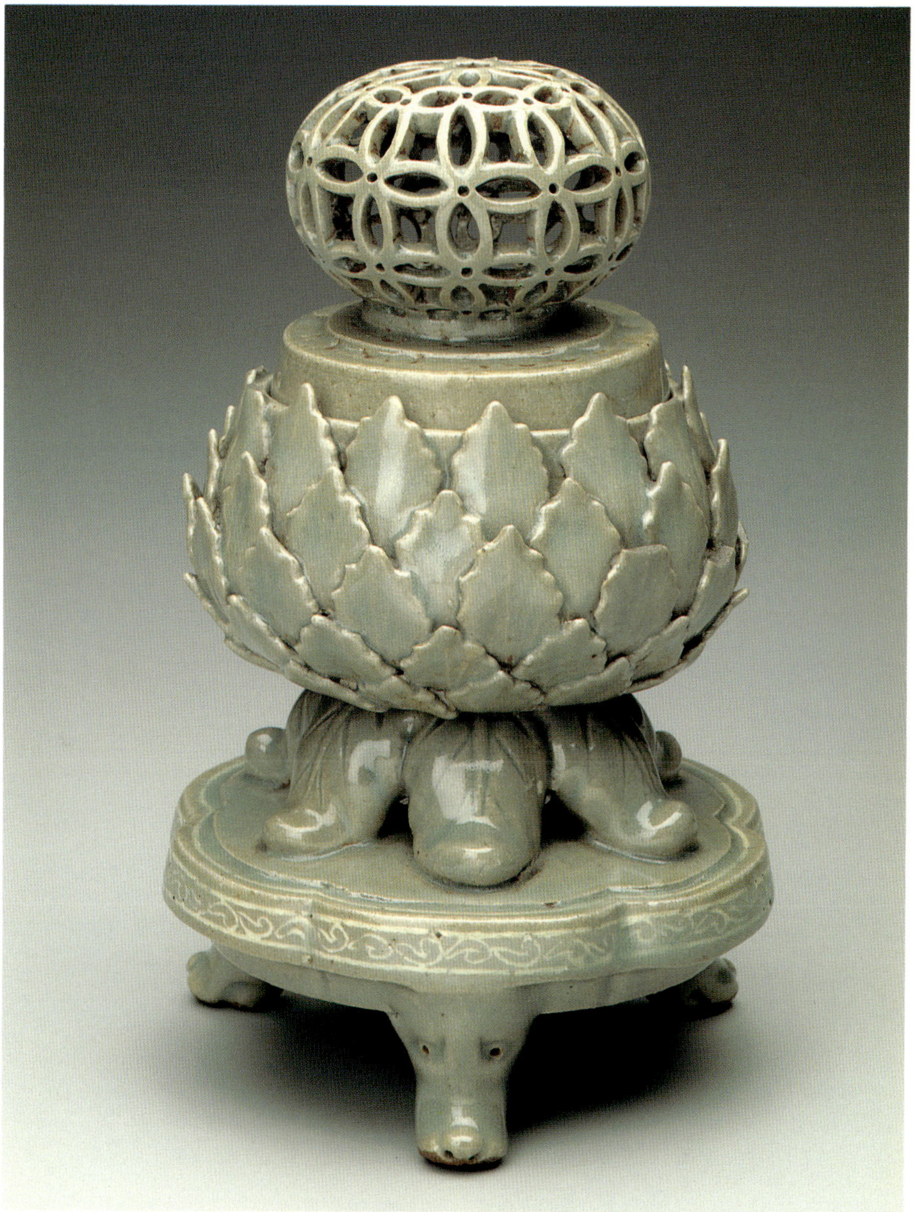

108
Six-lobed box
Koryŏ period, 13th century
Lacquer; inlaid design with silver wire, mother-of-pearl, and colored tortoise shell. H: 4 cm.
Charles B. Hoyt Collection. 34.69

This elegant inlaid lacquer box, the only one of its type that has been preserved, was originally part of a set in which it was surrounded by three or four smaller boxes of a lobed and curved shape. In all probability such boxes, as well as boxes of identical shape made of inlaid celadon, served as containers for cosmetics. A similar effect has been achieved in ceramics through the use of underglaze red to imitate the contrast of the red-colored tortoise shell with the silvery color of the mother-of-pearl.

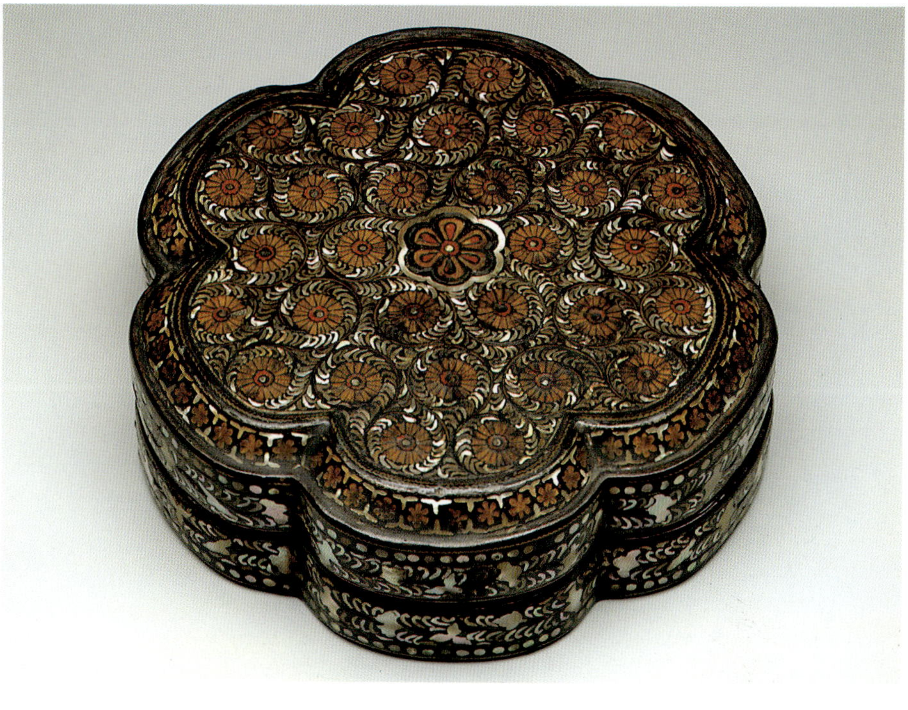

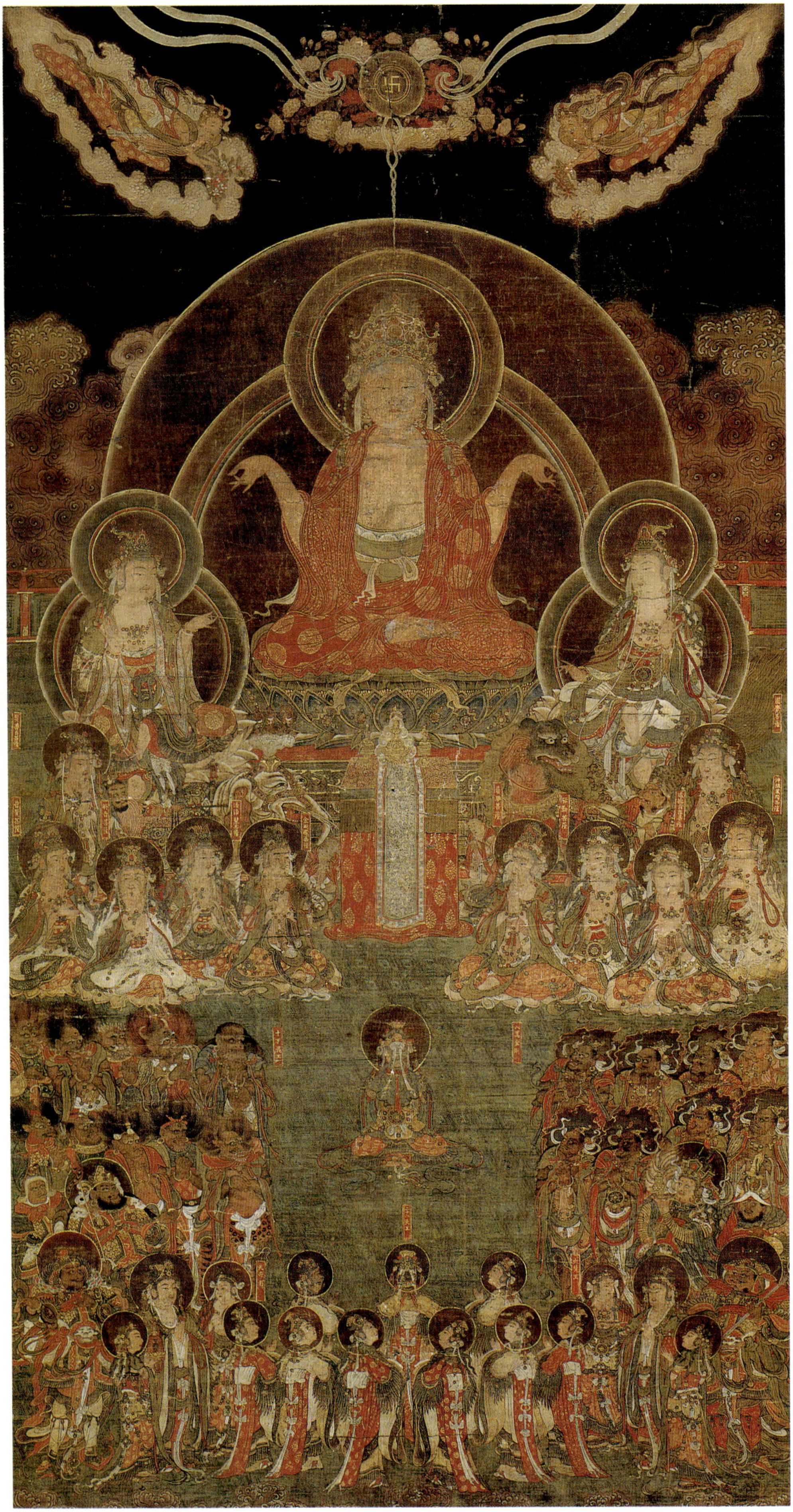

109
Śākyamuni Buddha Expounding the Law
Koryŏ dynasty, 13th or 14th century
Colors on hemp. 165 x 85 cm.
William Sturgis Bigelow Collection.
11.6142

This painting represents the Buddha Śākyamuni with an assembly of bodhisattvas and lesser divinities, as described in a Buddhist sūtra that was translated from Sanskrit into Chinese by the monk Buddhatrāta in A.D. 693. In this sūtra *the Buddha expounds the doctrine of* Perfect Enlightenment (Yuanjiao) *in response to queries raised by the Ten Bodhisattvas and the gods.*

Here the Buddha is seated on a lotus throne with his two hands raised in the gesture of exposition. On his left is Mañjuśrī on a lion and to his right Samantabhadra on an elephant. Below this trinity are the Ten Bodhisattvas, all seated and labeled with their respective names, as are the gods represented on the lower level.

This work, with the monumental quality of a wall painting, is a characteristic example of the Korean Buddhist style of painting that developed toward the end of the Koryŏ period under the influence of Chinese prototypes. Like most other paintings of the type, it was long considered to be Chinese.

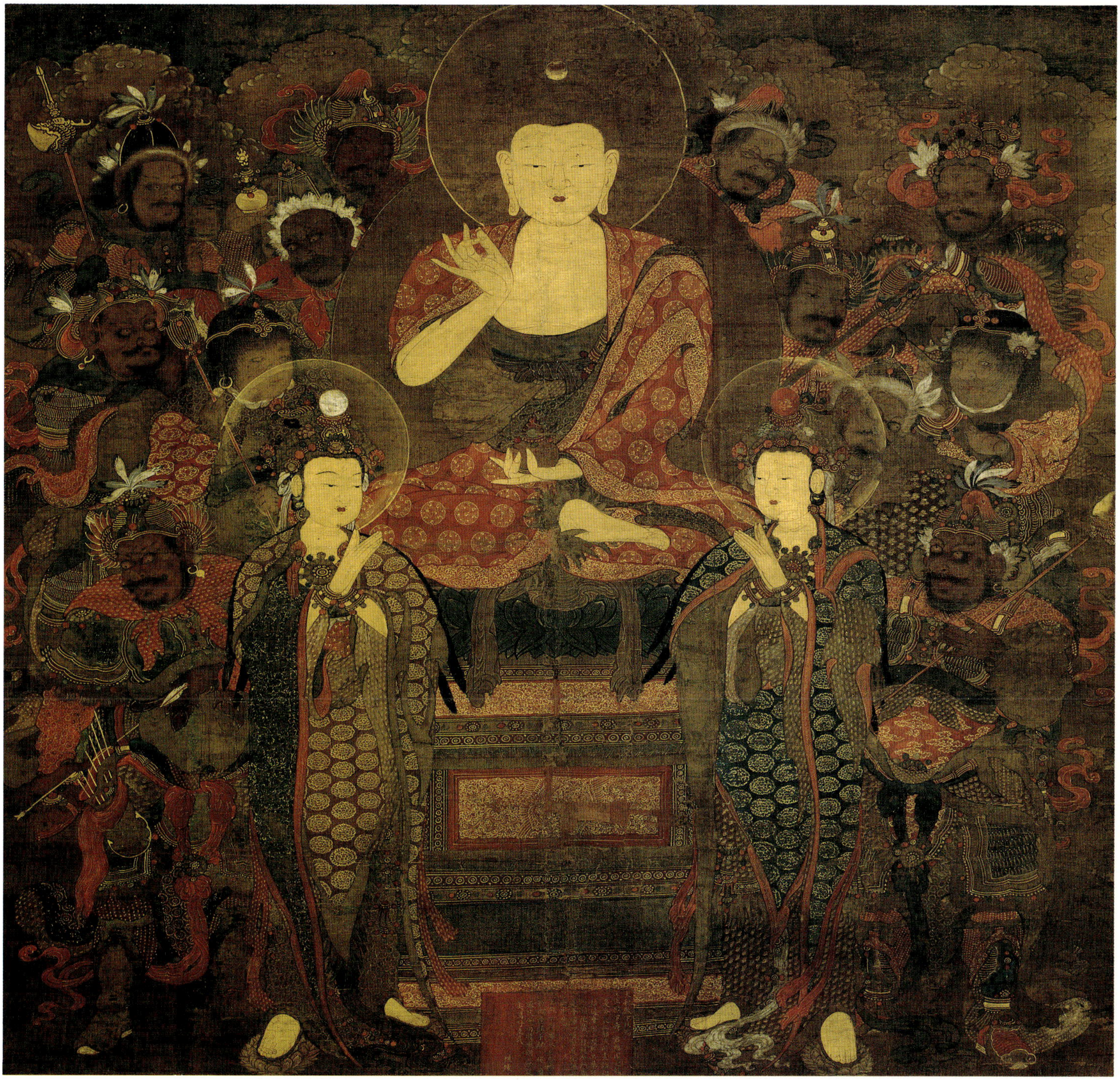

110
The Buddha of Healing (Yaksa Yorae) and Attendants
Chosŏn dynasty, 15th-16th century
Colors on silk. H: 200 cm.
Gift of the Heirs of Henry Adams.
19.265

The Buddha of Healing is seated on an elaborate throne, flanked by the sun and moon bodhisattvas and surrounded by the Twelve Guardians, who symbolize his twelve vows to cure the physical and mental diseases of all sentient beings. Meticulously painted in rich colors and gold, this assembly displays a wealth of decorative detail. From the inscription in the cartouche at the bottom center, it is evident that the icon was commissioned by a princess of the royal family as part of a set of five paintings representing different Buddhist assemblies. The elevated status of the donors may account for the distinguished quality of the icon.

While derived from Song prototypes, the Korean style of painting developed its own characteristics, retaining a freshness and vitality through the sixteenth century, much longer than Chinese Buddhist painting. With the advent of the Chosŏn dynasty and the end of royal patronage, the arts inspired by the Buddhist faith declined and painting iconography became more and more stereotyped.

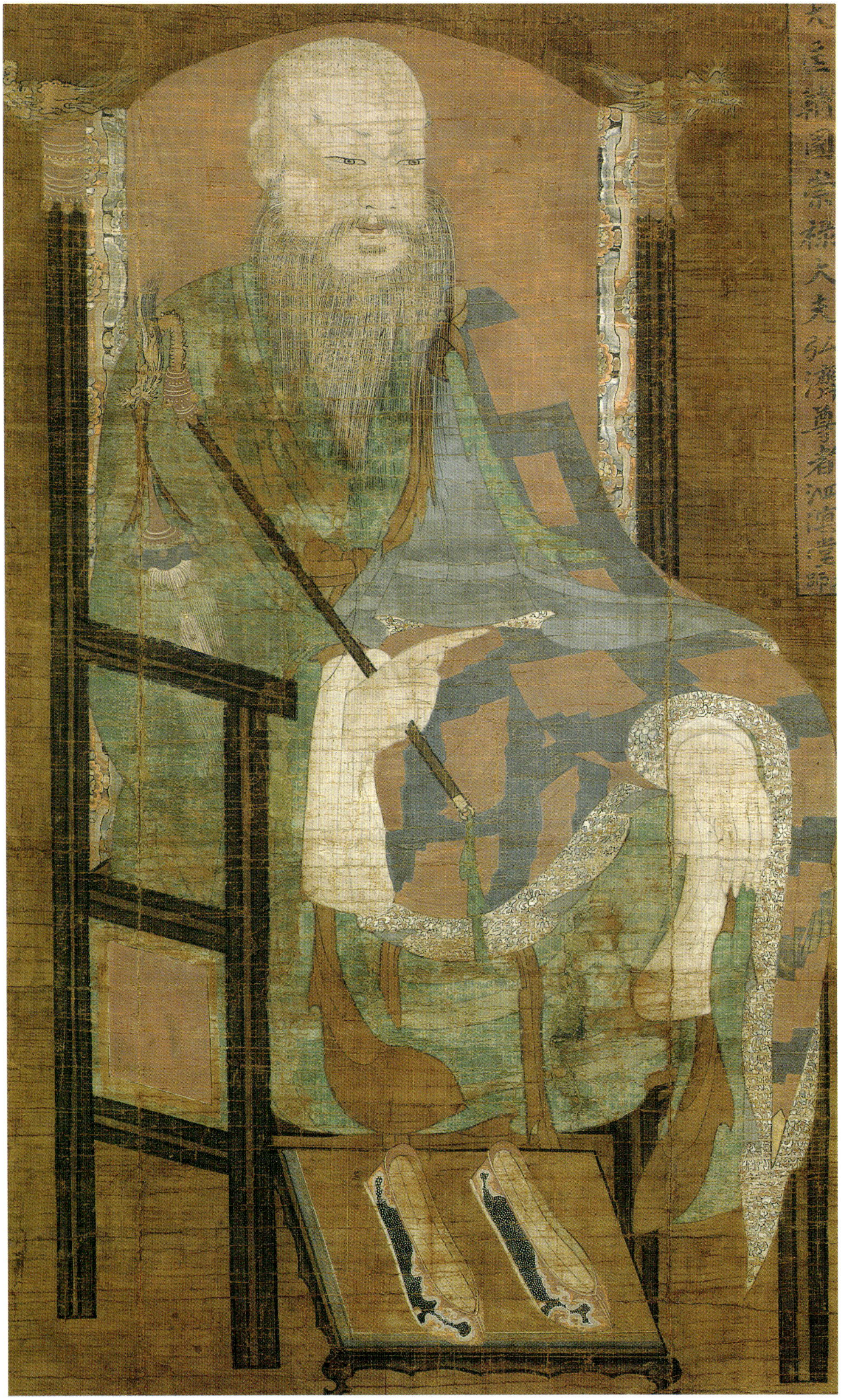

111

Portrait of the Monk Sa-myong Taesa

Chosŏn dynasty, 17th century
Hanging scroll mounted as panel; ink and colors on silk. 105 x 63 cm.
Denman Waldo Ross Collection.
25.188

Sa-myŏng Taesa (1544-1610) was a Buddhist monk who distinguished himself during the period of the Japanese invasions of the late sixteenth century. He organized an army of monks who helped to defeat the Japanese and afterward negotiated a peace treaty for the Chosŏn dynasty.

While Chinese and Japanese painters emphasized calligraphic lines that give a sense of volume to hanging fabric, the Korean artist relied on rich colors and fanciful details to enhance the flat two-dimensionality of a composition. Here the monk's highly patterned robes blend into the ornate, decorative details of the chair. His facial expression is idealized, emphasizing his spirituality.

112
Reliquary in the shape of a *stūpa*
Early Chosŏn dynasty, about 1464
Silver; parcel gilt and repoussé decoration. H: 22.5 cm.
Charles Goddard Weld Collection.
39.591

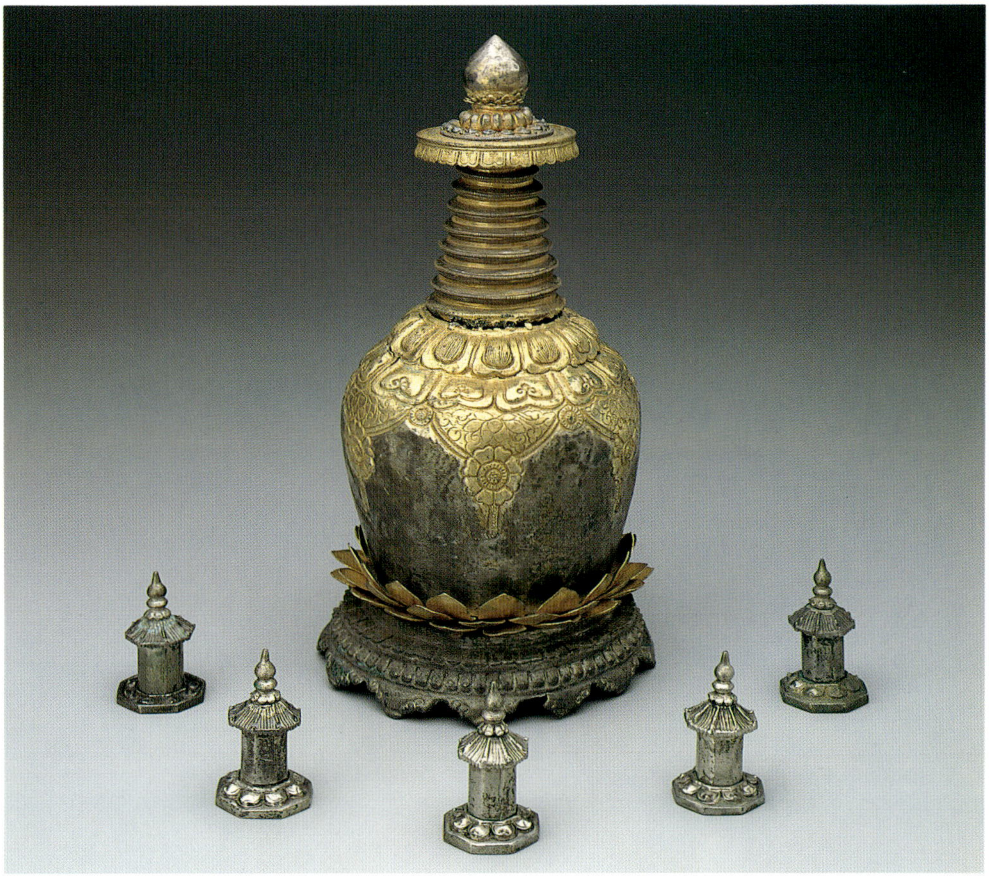

The hollow, bulbous body of the reliquary has the shape of a Lamaist stūpa *(Buddhist mortuary monument), an architectural form introduced into the Korean kingdom during the period of the Mongol invasions. It contains five silver miniature shrines, which, according to their inscriptions, held minute relics of the historical Buddha Śākyamuni, two other Buddhas, and two eminent priests. One of these is the last Indian Buddhist missionary to the Far East, the monk Śūnyādisya (Jigong in Korean), who died in China in 1363; the other is his pupil, the Korean patriarch Naong, who died in 1376. Jigong was the founder of the Hoeamsa Temple near present-day Seoul, where Naong lived and worked. The ashes of both men are enshrined in stone* stūpas *on a hill next to the site of the Hoeamsa, now almost completely in ruins.*

There is an ancient record of an apparition of the Buddha Śākyamuni at Hoeamsa in 1463, at which time a distribution of sacred relics took place. This reliquary, a fine example of the Korean silversmith's craft, may have been made on that occasion, two thousand years after the Buddha Śākyamuni first appeared in the world.

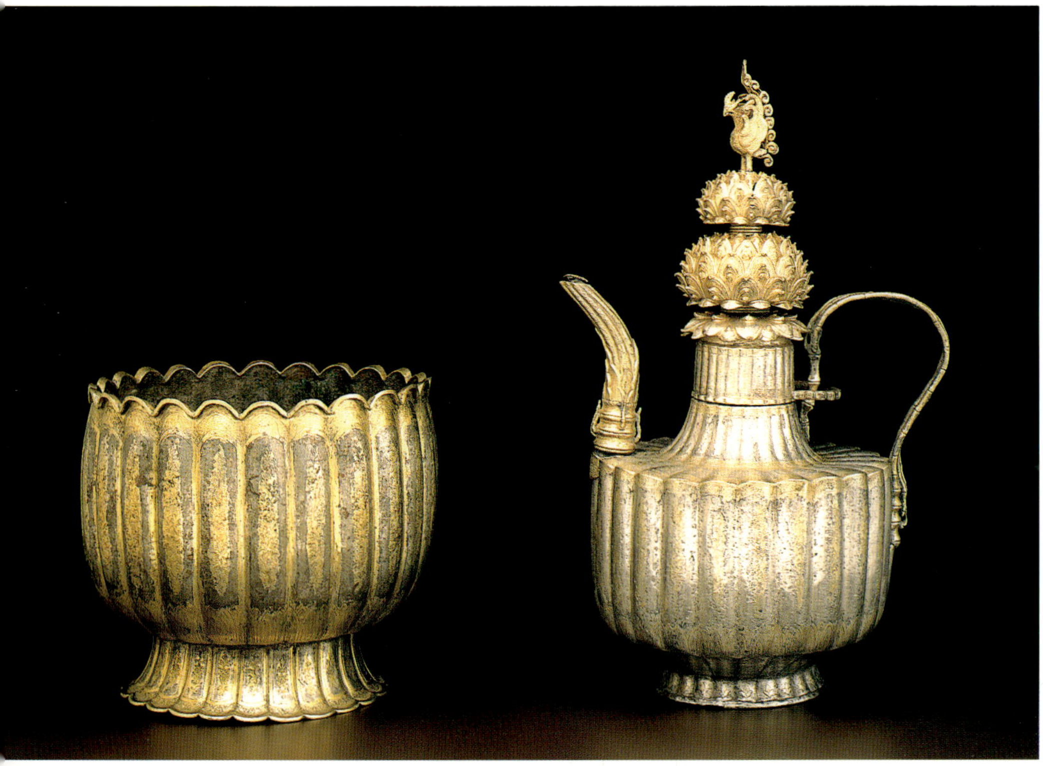

113
Ewer and basin
Koryŏ dynasty, 11th-12th century
Silver; parcel gilt and engraved decoration. H: 38 cm.
George Nixon Black Fund. 35.646

The shapes and decorative motifs of Korean metalwork, lacquer, ceramics, and woodwork are closely interrelated. While the scalloped body, the spout, and the handle of this ewer have shapes inspired by bamboo work, the cover consists of conventionalized lotuses, surmounted by a phoenix—a combination that has an almost exact counterpart in celadon ewers.

When first acquired by the Museum, the ewer and basin were thought to have been made of bronze. Only when thick layers of corrosion were removed in the course of restoration in the research laboratory did it become evident that both pieces are made of silver. Made to be used in daily life, they probably followed their wealthy owners into their grave in the vicinity of Kaesong in North Korea.

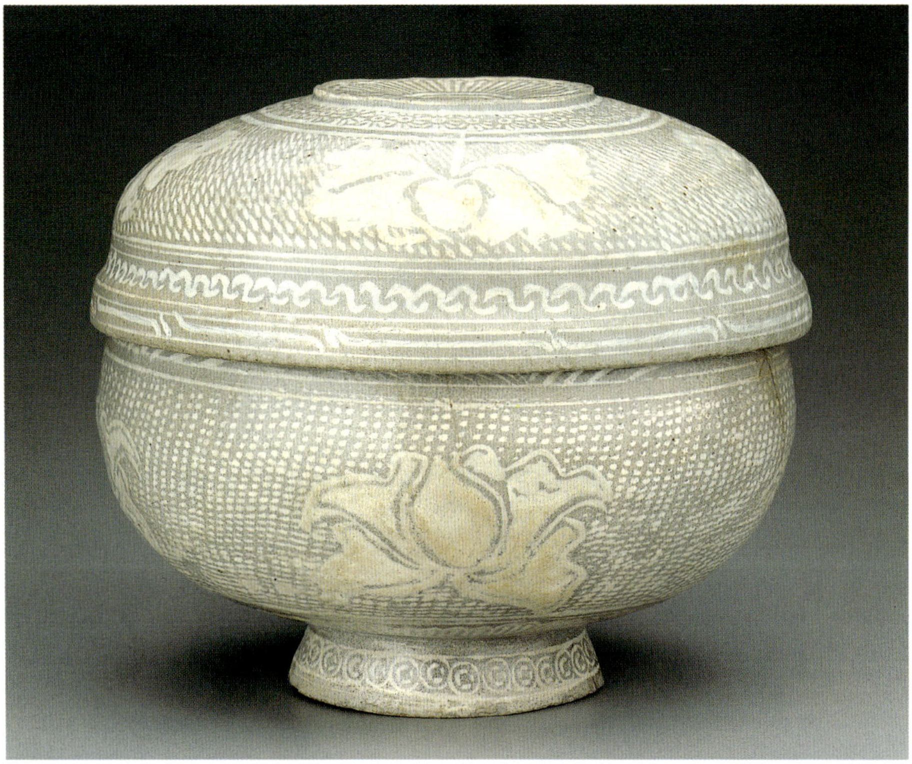

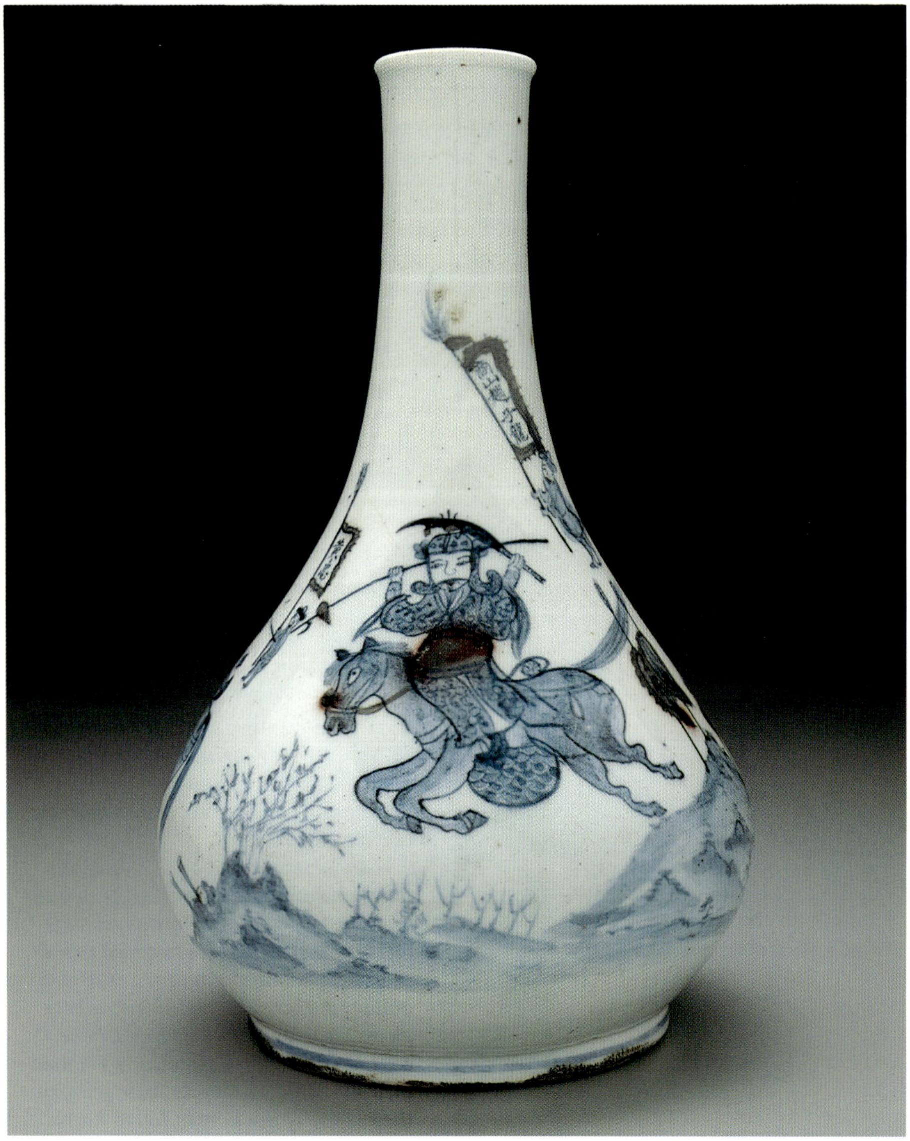

114
Covered bowl
Chosŏn dynasty, 15th century
Punch'ŏng glazed stoneware; inlaid decoration. H: 14.7 cm.
Charles B. Hoyt Collection. 50.1025

The technique of incising and stamping designs into clay and filling them with white slip is a Korean specialty known as punch'ŏng. *Covered bowls with similar decoration are inscribed with place names and the name of a government office called* Changhungu. *This office ceased to regulate the supply of ceramics in 1468, confirming a date for the present wares in the first half of the fifteenth century.*

115
Bottle
Late Chosŏn dynasty, 18th or 19th century
Porcelain decorated with figures in underglaze blue with touches of underglaze red.
H: 27 cm.
Charles B. Hoyt Collection. 50.1041

The enduring appeal of ancient Chinese tales is illustrated by this vase, whose low, ovoid body is decorated with a battle scene including the heroes Huang Zhong and Zhao Yun on horseback. Their names are inscribed on banners held by their attendants. The exploits of these warriors of the Three Kingdoms were recast by playwrights, and as early as the fourteenth century scenes from the plays were illustrated on Chinese blue-and-white vases.

China

The strength of the Chinese collections lies in the areas of painting and ceramics, while sculptures, bronzes and the decorative arts are all well represented.

The Museum's Chinese paintings, mostly collected in the early decade of this century, include some of the earliest works in scroll form that have survived to this day. Particularly well known are those attributed to the seventh-century artist Yan Liben and the Song emperor Huizong (1082-1135). The Song treasures include a group of Buddhist paintings acquired from the Daitoku-ji in Kyoto; among the later paintings, works of the Suzhou masters of the middle to late Ming period are especially well represented. Notable in the collection are a group of Taoist paintings and stone images, most of the latter carrying dated inscriptions.

In the ceramics section, the Hoyt Collection contains many fine pieces dating from the Six Dynasties to the Song period. With great taste and discernment, Charles B. Hoyt acquired a number of important pieces of early ceramics, the correct identification of which has become possible only in the last two decades as a result of recent advances in archaeological work in China. One of the salient features of the Hoyt Collection is the large number of "marbled wares" of the Tang and Song periods, reflecting a predilection of the collector. Similarly, among the many Chinese ceramics given to the Museum by Helen and Paul Bernat, eighteenth-century imperial porcelains demonstrate the special taste of the donors.

The stone sculptures include a number of important Buddhist pieces, as well as secular piece of the Six Dynasties and Tang periods. Especially impressive are those of the early eighth century, most pieces forming part of elaborate tomb structures.

The collection of early bronzes is noted for the relatively large number of Western Zhou ritual vessels and a number of Han pieces with painted decoration. The figure of a youth (no. 119) said to come from Jin Cun, near Luoyang, is perhaps the most famous in the entire bronze collection.

The Bigelow bequest to the Asiatic department includes a sizable group of Chinese lacquer pieces, most of which are decorated with inlaid mother-of-pearl. (There is also in the Bigelow Collection, decorated in a similar technique, a group of fine lacquerware from the Ryukyu Islands.)

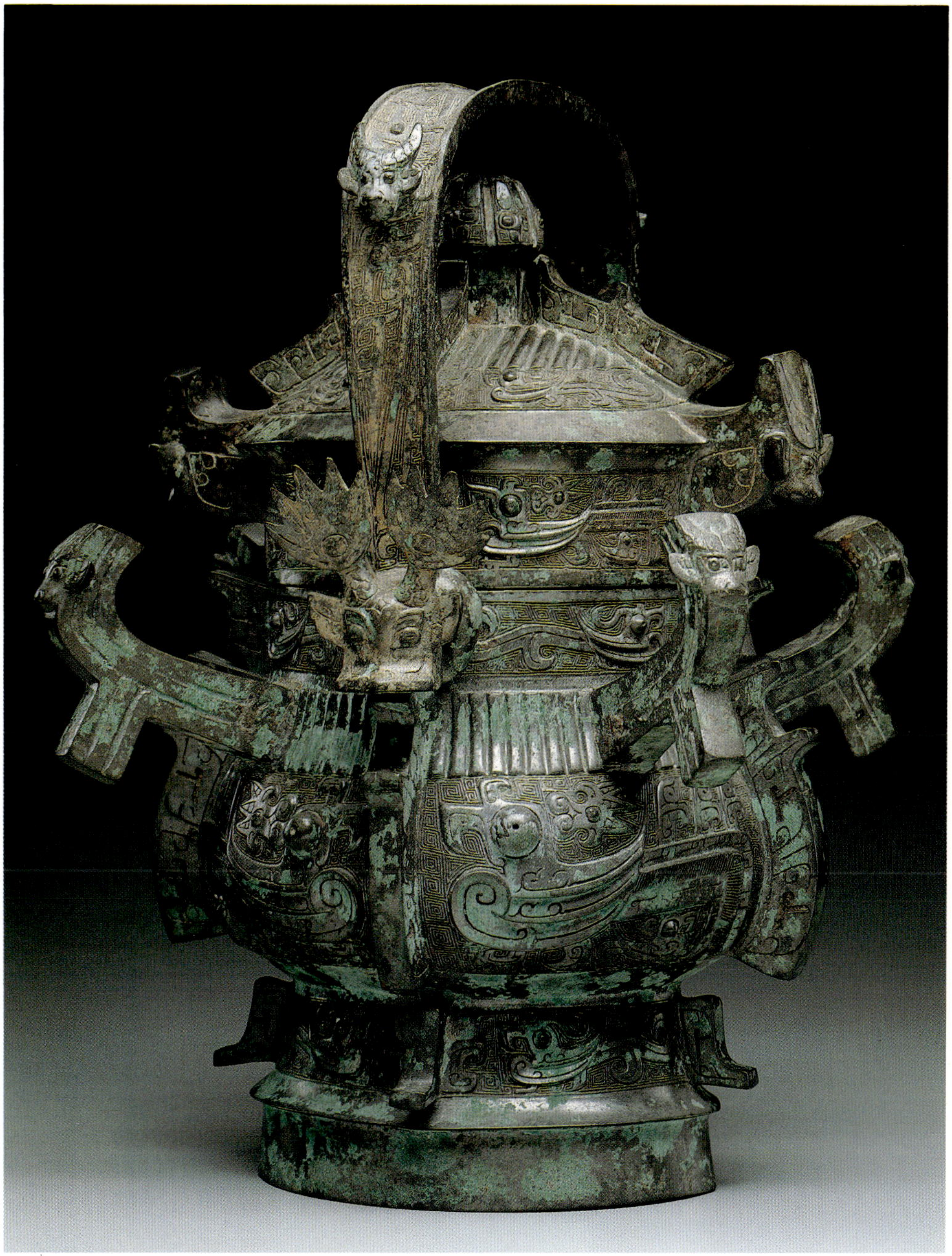

Both the Bigelow and Hoyt Collections include a number of Chinese glass vessels of the Qing period. Also represented are other branches of Chinese decorative arts such as furniture and carvings in jade and other stones, rhinoceros horn, and bamboo.

116
Covered wine vessel *(you)*
Shang dynasty, Anyang period, 12th century B.C.
Bronze. H: 36 cm.
Anna Mitchell Richards Fund. 34.66

Bronze vessels such as this you *are associated with a complex of rituals practiced by ruling clans in Shang-dynasty China. Manifesting the nobility's political and economic control, and serving as a tangible symbol of communication with deities and ancestors, they played a key role in sacrificial ceremonies in which food and libation were offered to various spirits. The vessels are often inscribed with texts referring to ancestors, confirming their use in ancestral rites.*

The form of this you, *with its projections terminating in animal masks, is not known among vessels of the same type excavated at Anyang, the classic site of the late Shang period. It is possible that the unusual style is associated with the site in which the piece is reported to have been found, once an important Shang vassal state and now within Shaanxi province.*

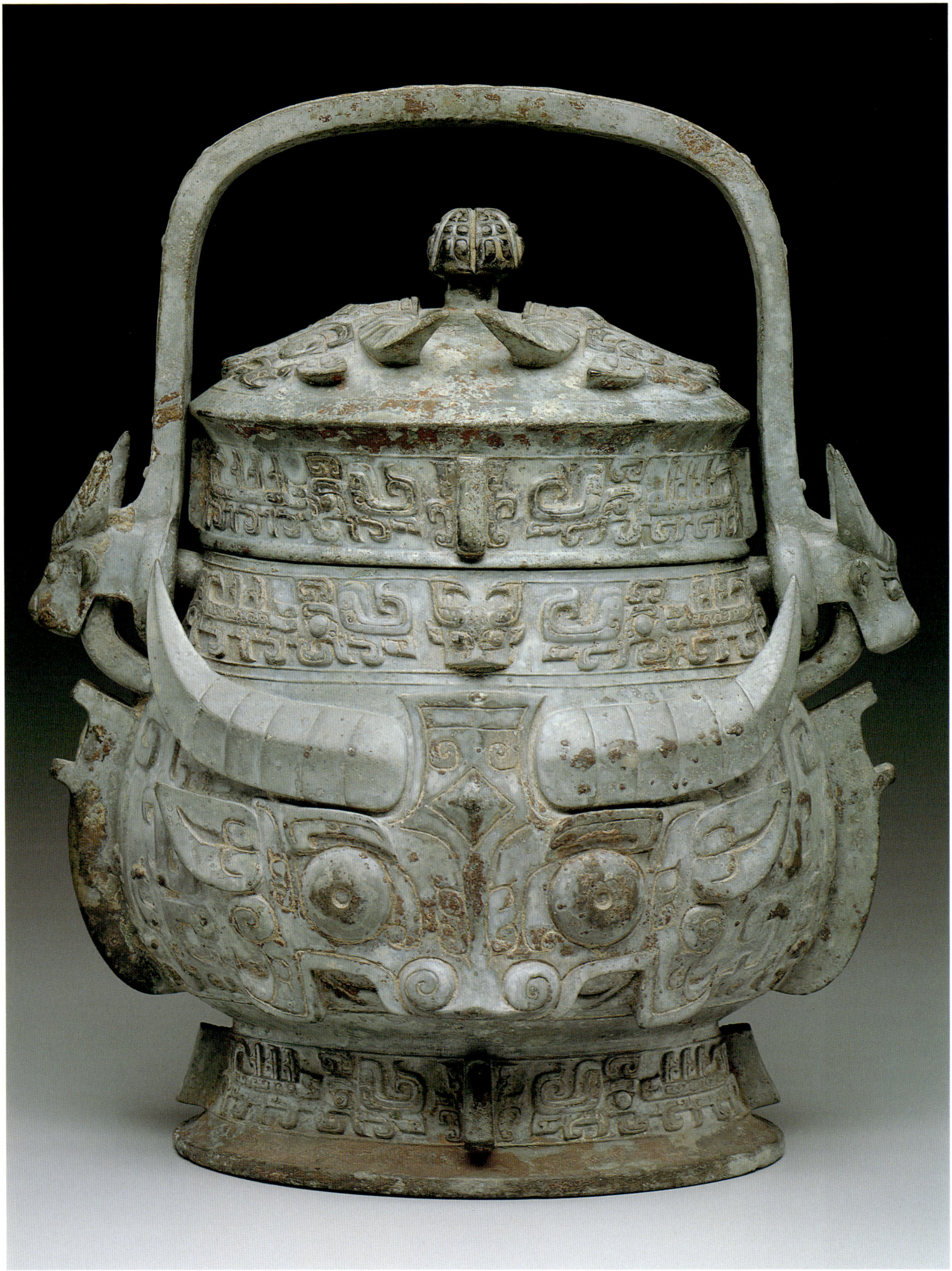

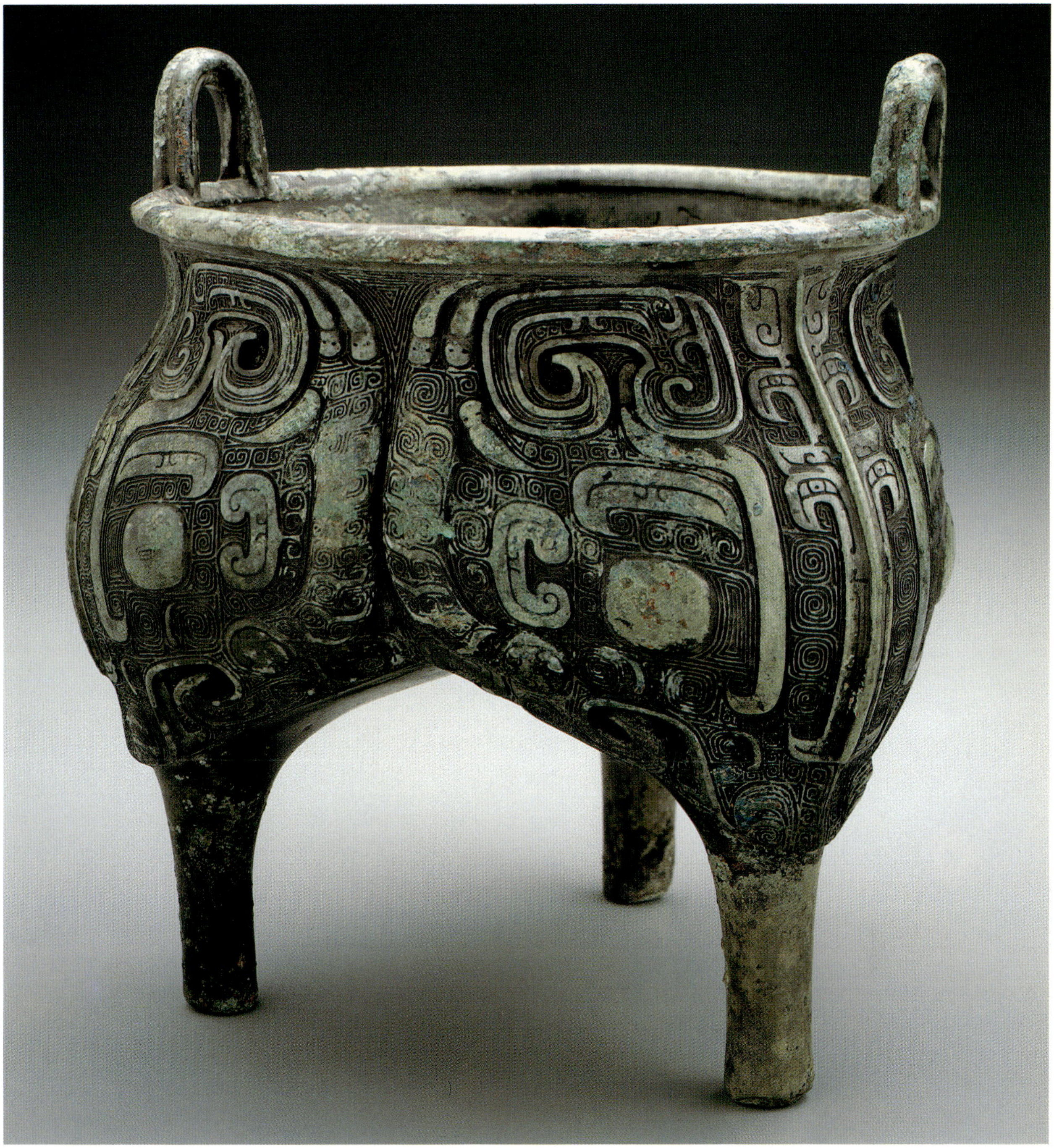

117
Covered wine vessel *(you)*
Western Zhou dynasty, 11th-10th century B.C.
Bronze with eight-character inscription.
H: 25 cm.
Anna Mitchell Richards Fund. 34.63

The horned creatures (possibly water buffalo) that dominate the design of both the body and the lid of this object derive from earlier examples executed in flatter relief. Here, the extreme plasticity of the frontal images creates a somewhat sinister effect.

118
Ritual vessel of Duke Xi of the state of Lu *(li ding)*
Western Zhou dynasty,
9th century B.C.
Bronze. H: 17 cm.
Grace M. Edwards Fund. 47.230

The inscription on the inside of the vessel translates as "Xi, Lord of Lu, had this vessel made to be used when presenting sacrificial offerings to his revered late father, the Duke of Lu." Literary evidence suggests that the vessel was cast during the first decade of the tenth century B.C. after Xi succeeded his brother as the Duke of Lu (a state situated in modern Shandong province).

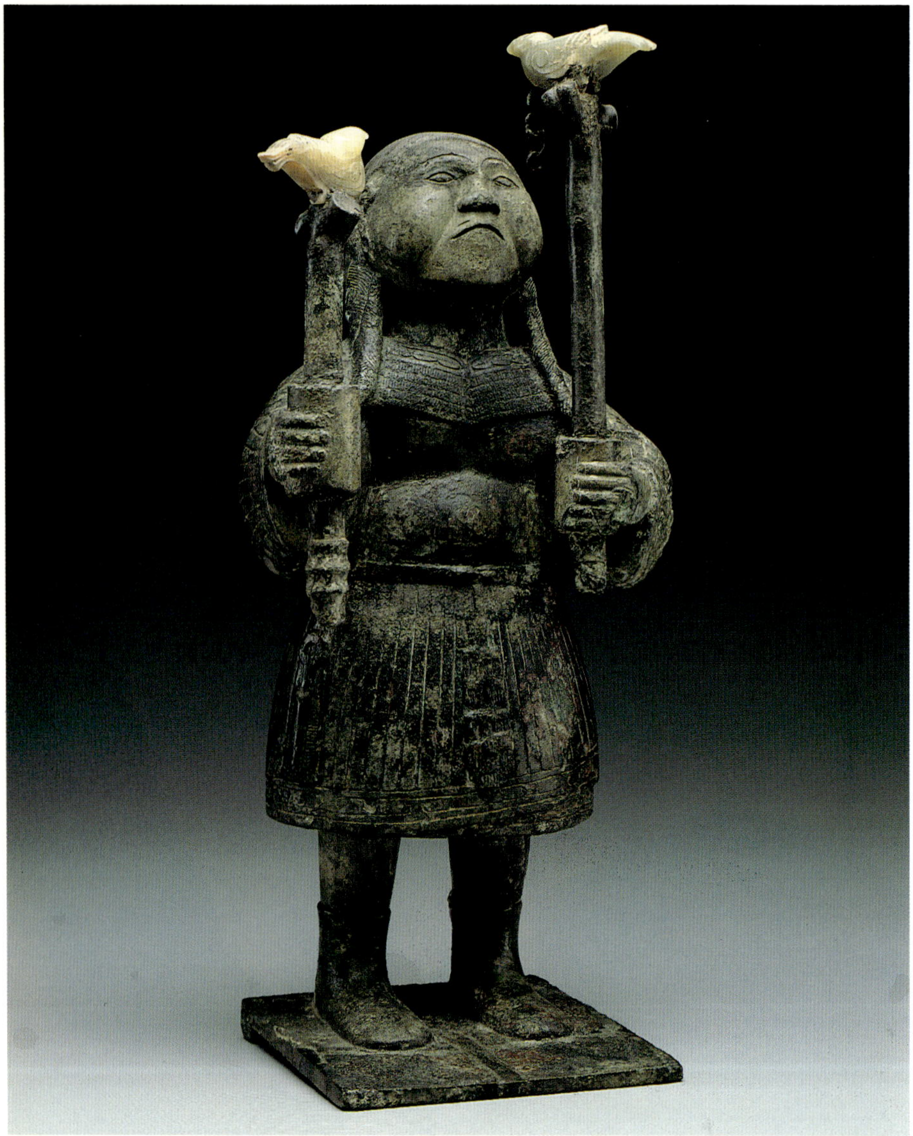

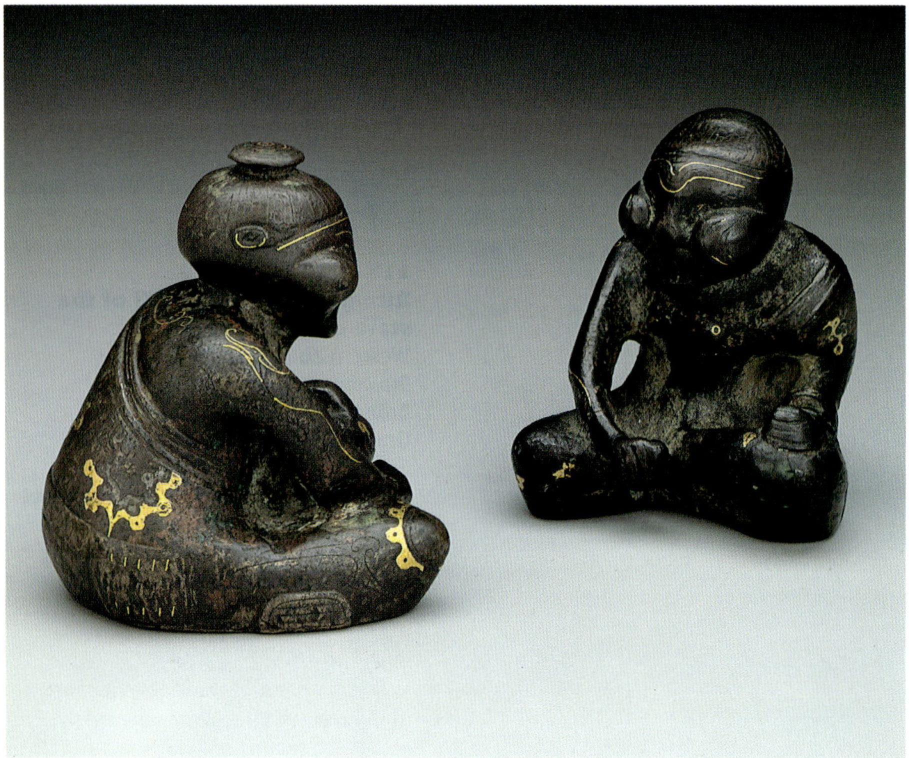

119

Figure of a standing youth

Eastern Zhou dynasty, Warring States period, late 5th-early 4th century B.C.
Bronze and jade. H: 30 cm.
Maria Antoinette Evans Fund. 31.976

Until the recent excavation of the life-size terra-cotta soldiers from the tomb site of China's first emperor, Qinshi Huangdi (d. 210 B.C.), the advanced level of figural sculpture toward the end of the Bronze Age was not recognized. One important result of the discovery is that we now have a meaningful context in which to place figures such as this powerful bronze, an isolated example of early Chinese interest in the accurate portrayal of human features.

This unusually large bronze sculpture, reportedly from Jin Cun, near Luoyang, represents a young man intently watching two birds (rendered in jade) perched atop a pair of sticks he is holding up in his hands. Archaeological evidence relates the figure to a group of images portraying attendants, animal trainers, and performing artists. Often such statues reveal facial features or dress styles native to the nomads active in China's northern border regions. In this case, the sculptor may have intended to portray a member of the Xiongnu minority (Huns) of the Warring States period.

120

Pair of mat weights in human form

Western Han dynasty, 1st century B.C.
Cast bronze inlaid with gold and silver.
H: 7 cm.
Anonymous Gift and Charles Bain Hoyt Fund. 1987.91-92

Commonly misunderstood in the West as "sleeve-weights," these striking and grotesque figures were in fact part of a set of four weights used to secure the corners of a floor mat, the traditional way of seating in China prior to the adoption of Western-style furniture. They are seated with hunched shoulders and crossed legs, and the soles of their sandals are visible beneath their thighs. Their facial structure, lighthearted expressions, exotic clothing, and tightly curled hair suggest that these figures represent a non-Chinese race.

A fascination with the people and customs of other lands prevailed throughout the Han empire in a period of internal stability, when commerce and trade encouraged the development of China's relationship with the outside world.

121
Altarpiece with Amitābha and attendants
Sui dynasty, dated A.D. 593
Bronze. H: 76.5 cm.
Gift of Mrs. W. Scott Fitz. 22.407; Gift of Edward Jackson Holmes in Memory of his Mother, Mrs. W. Scott Fitz. 47.1407-1412

Until the recent excavation of a smaller gilt-bronze altar group dating from 584, this altar (dedicated in the year corresponding to 593 by a group of eight women of the Fan clan) was the only known complete Buddhist altarpiece of the Sui dynasty of its size and importance.

Excavated around the turn of this century, it was named the Duan Fang altar after the viceroy and famous collector of bronzes who was its first secular owner. The place where it was found is in the immediate vicinity of the Zhaozhou Bridge, the oldest single-span bridge and one of the greatest engineering feats of the Sui dynasty. Only a few miles from there are two villages inhabited by members of the Fan clan; it is possible, therefore, that this easily transportable altarpiece never traveled more than a few miles before it left China after the assassination of Duan Fang in 1911 on the eve of the Chinese revolution.

The separately cast figures, all detachable and tenoned into the four-legged base, are arranged around the central seated figure of the Amitābha Buddha, the Lord of the Western Paradise, in whom the faithful who invoke his name are believed to be reborn. Among the host of attendants are two bodhisattvas, Avalokiteśvara and Mahāsthāmaprāpta (with folded hands), distinguishable by their size, as well as two lohans (Buddhist saints). Above them all towers a tree in full bloom in which the Seven Buddhas of the Past make their appearance.

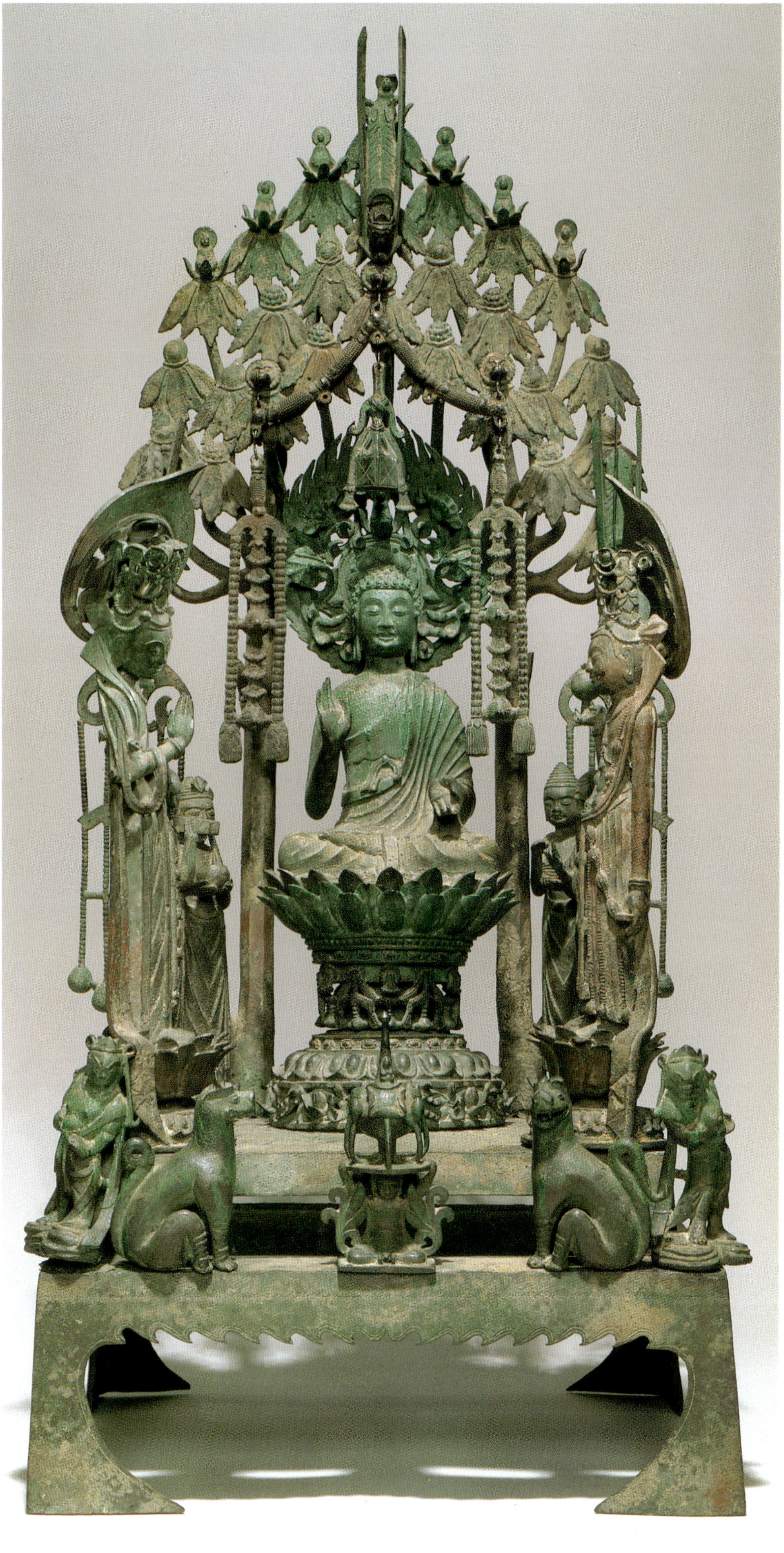

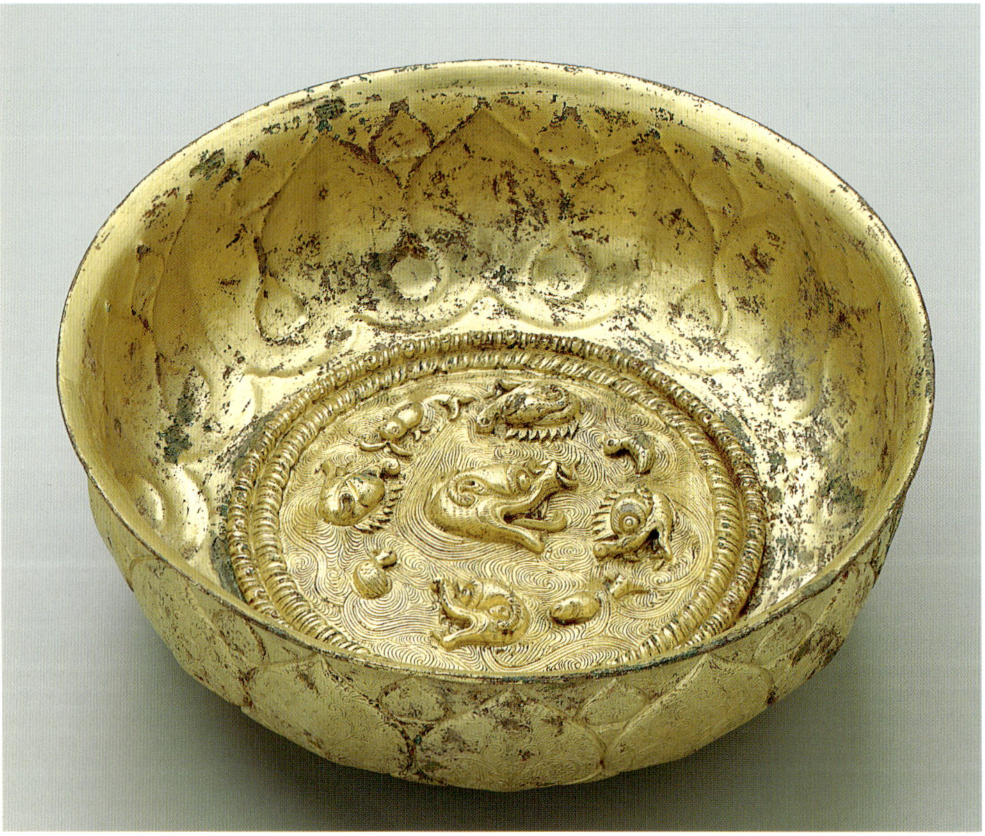

122
Bowl with mythical beasts, animals, and floral designs
Tang dynasty, about A.D. 700
Gilt bronze with cast, appliquéd, and engraved decorations.
Diam. of mouth: 17.3 cm.
Charles Bain Hoyt Fund. 1986.235

The delicate design and superb casting of this unusual gilt-bronze bowl reflect the cosmopolitan nature of China during the Tang dynasty (618-906), when China was the dominant economic, political, and cultural center in eastern Asia. Tang-dynasty China was the nucleus of an international network extending from the western Mediterranean and Persia through Central and southern Asia to Korea and Japan. The fall of the Sassanian empire in the mid-seventh century and the subsequent flight of the Persian court to China had a lasting impact on Chinese culture and art. Reflecting the synthesis of Chinese and foreign motifs and techniques that was characteristic of the art of this period is the hieratic treatment of the incised palmettes on the bowl's outside wall and on the base, as well as the use of high relief in the depiction of the interior design.

The bowl can be dated stylistically to the late seventh or early eighth century, when Empress Wu (r. 684-704) ruled Tang China. Bowls of this type were most likely commissioned by the court for use primarily by members of the imperial family and high-ranking aristocrats.

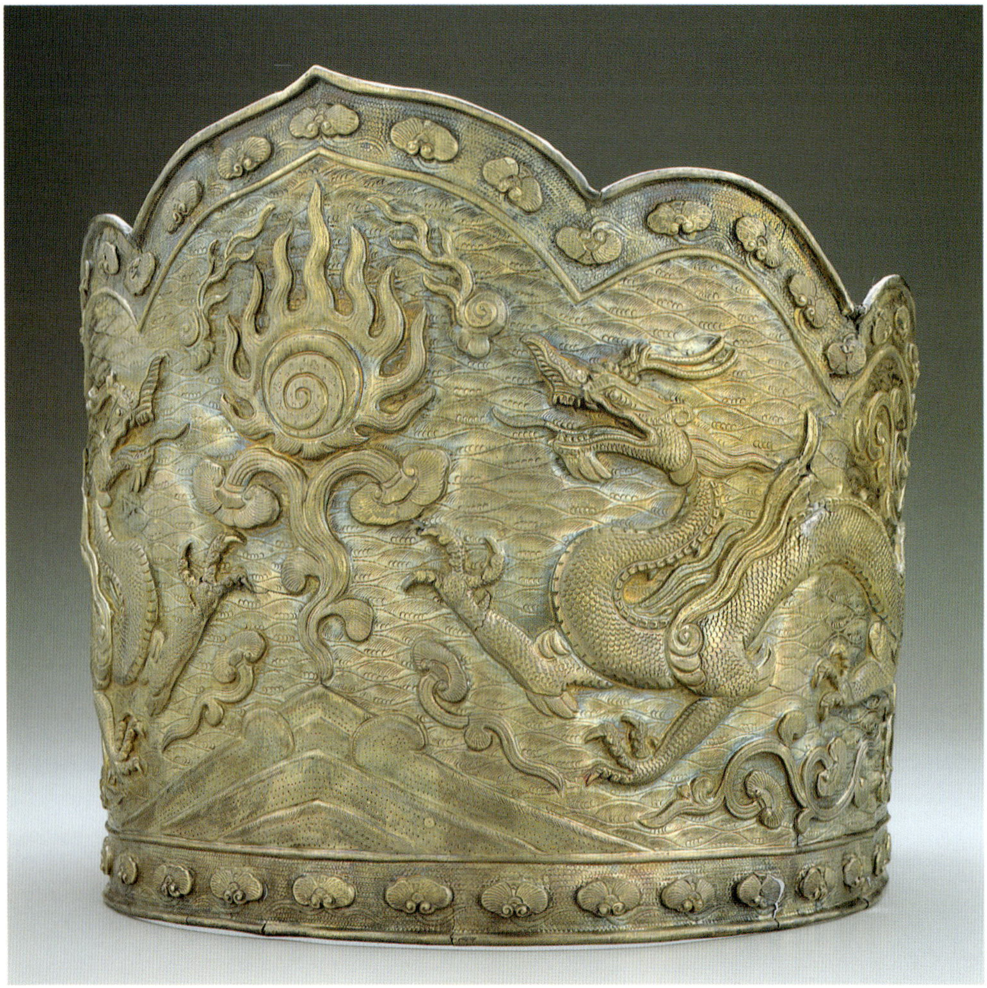

123
Headgear
Northern Song dynasty, early 11th century
Silver; gilt and repoussé decoration.
H: 20.6 cm.
William Sturgis Bigelow Collection, by exchange. 40.749

This object entered the Museum's collection in 1940 as a flat plaque, thought to be of Korean origin. Sixteen years later, the excavation, in China's northwestern Liaoning province, of a similar piece bent into a circular shape prompted the restoration of the MFA "plaque" to its original contour. The archaeological context of the excavated piece suggests that it served as a headdress, the vertical slits at each end holding a ribbon or broad band to join the two ends together. While the decoration of two dragons chasing flaming jewels is typically Chinese, the unusual shape of the piece does not seem to occur elsewhere in Chinese art, an anomaly that can be explained by the fact that these precious objects were made on order for the

Chinese court to be presented to Khitan envoys.

After the conclusion of the peace treaty between the Khitan tribes of the North and the Song Chinese in 1005, the "barbarian" invaders ceded some recently taken territory in exchange for official diplomatic recognition and an annual payment by the Chinese. Documents of the period include lists of gifts exchanged by the diplomatic missions that traveled between the two courts several times each year. Among the gifts presented to the Khitan ambassadors are pieces described as "headgear made of gilt silver." Made with the consummate skill of the Chinese court artists, this splendid headgear was carried with the tribesmen to their graves.

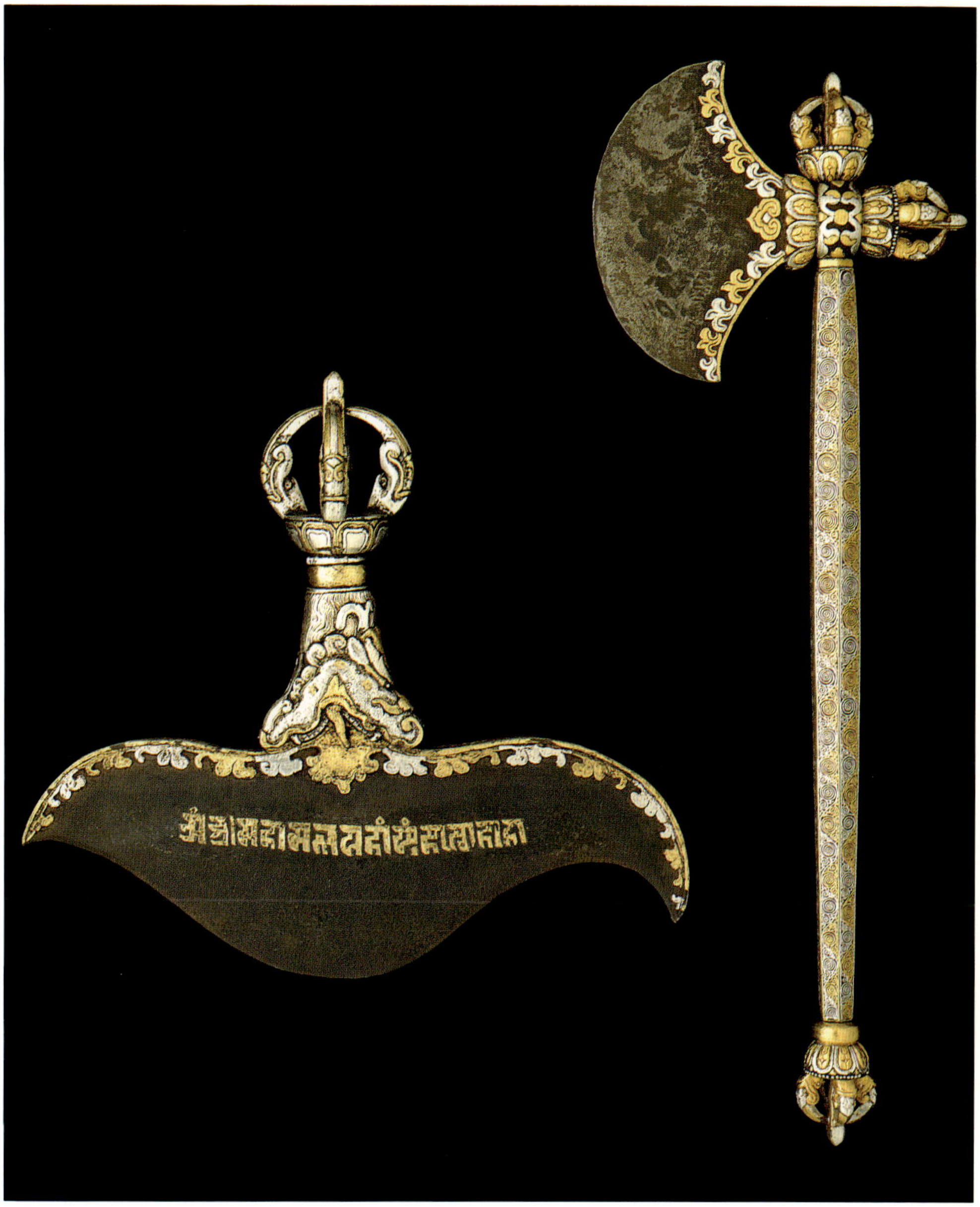

124
Ritual chopper *(vajra-kartari)*
China, Ming dynasty, late 14th century
Iron overlaid with gold and silver designs. H: 23.2 cm.
Charles Bain Hoyt Fund. 1987.256

Tibetan Buddhism has played an important role in China since it was introduced during the Yuan dynasty (1279-1367). Once part of a complete set of ritual implements used in religious ceremonies, this rare chopper, which combines Chinese workmanship and Tibetan imagery, was probably made at an imperial workshop in Beijing either for use at court or as a gift from the Ming emperor to a high-ranking Tibetan lama.

An inscription on the blade of this chopper, written in an ornate form of Sanskrit, is a mantra, *or sacred formula dedicated to Mahākāla, one of the protective deities of Nepal, Tibet, and Mongolia. Mahākāla is often represented holding a chopper such as this one in one hand, and a skull cup, a companion object in religious ceremonies, in another.*

125
Ritual ax *(paraśu)*
China, Ming dynasty, Hongwu period (1368-1398)
Iron overlaid with gold and silver; four-character mark overlaid in gold.
L: 43 cm.
Anonymous Gift and Charles Bain Hoyt Fund. 1987.93

An intricate design of scrolls overlaid alternately in gold and silver decorates the handle of this ritual ax. The three vajra *(or thunderbolt) motifs, issuing from the mouth of mythical animals called* makaras, *also on the handle, are characteristic of the Buddhist art of the Himalayas. The imperial mark at the top of the handle, which reads* Hongwu nianzhi, *indicates that this piece was made in China during the reign of the Emperor Hongwu, the early years of the Ming dynasty. This ax, a chopper (no. 124), a skull cup, and a scepter made up a complete set of ritual implements.*

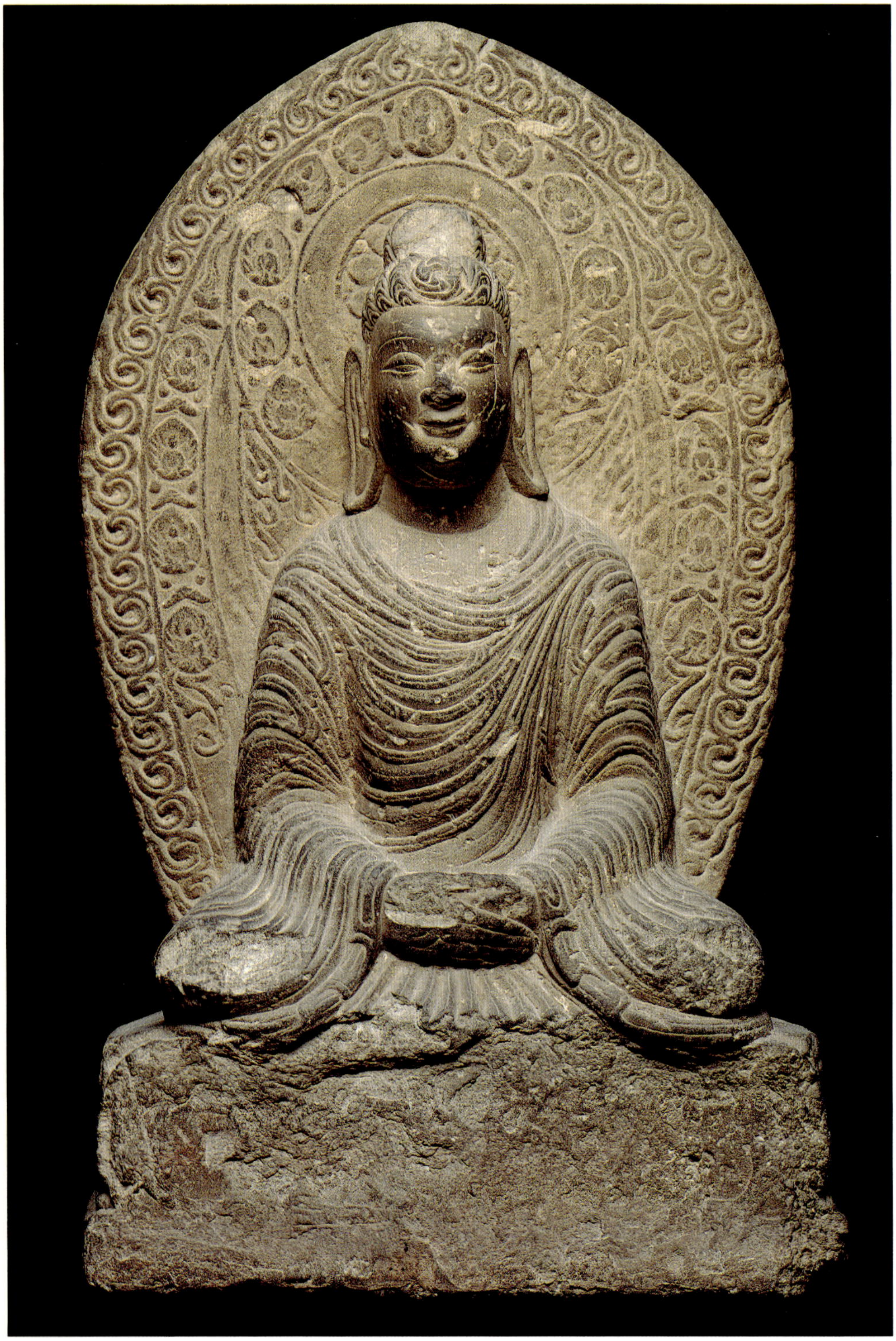

126
Seated Buddha
China, Northern Wei dynasty, about A.D. 476
Limestone. H: 73 cm.
Chinese and Japanese Special Fund. 07.750

The Buddha sits in cross-legged position on a rectangular pedestal against an elaborately carved nimbus with a border of stylized flames and two halos filled with representations of Transformation Buddhas. His hands are folded in the gesture of meditation, while his monk's garb, draped over both shoulders, falls down in evenly flowing, narrowly spaced folds across the body, arms, and legs. On the back side of the sculpture, there is a nearly effaced inscription engraved below a relief representing the Seven Buddhas of the Past. Chinese Buddhist sculpture of this early type and high quality is extremely rare; only a few examples datable to this period, through either inscription or style, are known to have been preserved in China, Japan, and the West.

127
Seated bodhisattva
Eastern Wei dynasty, about A.D. 530
Limestone. H: 196.5 cm.
Gift of Denman Waldo Ross in Memory of Okakura Kakuzō. 13.2804

Early Chinese Buddhist art relied heavily on prototypes from India and Central Asia. During the late fifth and early sixth century, however, Chinese influence began to predominate. This figure is comparable stylistically to the images carved in Cave XXIV at Longmen, datable by inscription to A.D 527.

Excavated from the site of the famous White Horse Monastery (Baimasi) near Luoyang, this bodhisattva wears a robe cinched at the chest and covered with a short stole, the ends of which are looped together through a round jade disk. The flowing lines of the robe serve to elongate the underlying figure and contrast strongly with the calmness of the face. Since the sculpture is partially carved in the back, it could not have been part of a cave temple.

The identity of the figure is difficult to determine. If his legs are crossed, however, as they appear to be under the heavy folds of his robe, it is possible that this statue represents the Buddha of the Future, Maitreya, who is frequently depicted in such a pose.

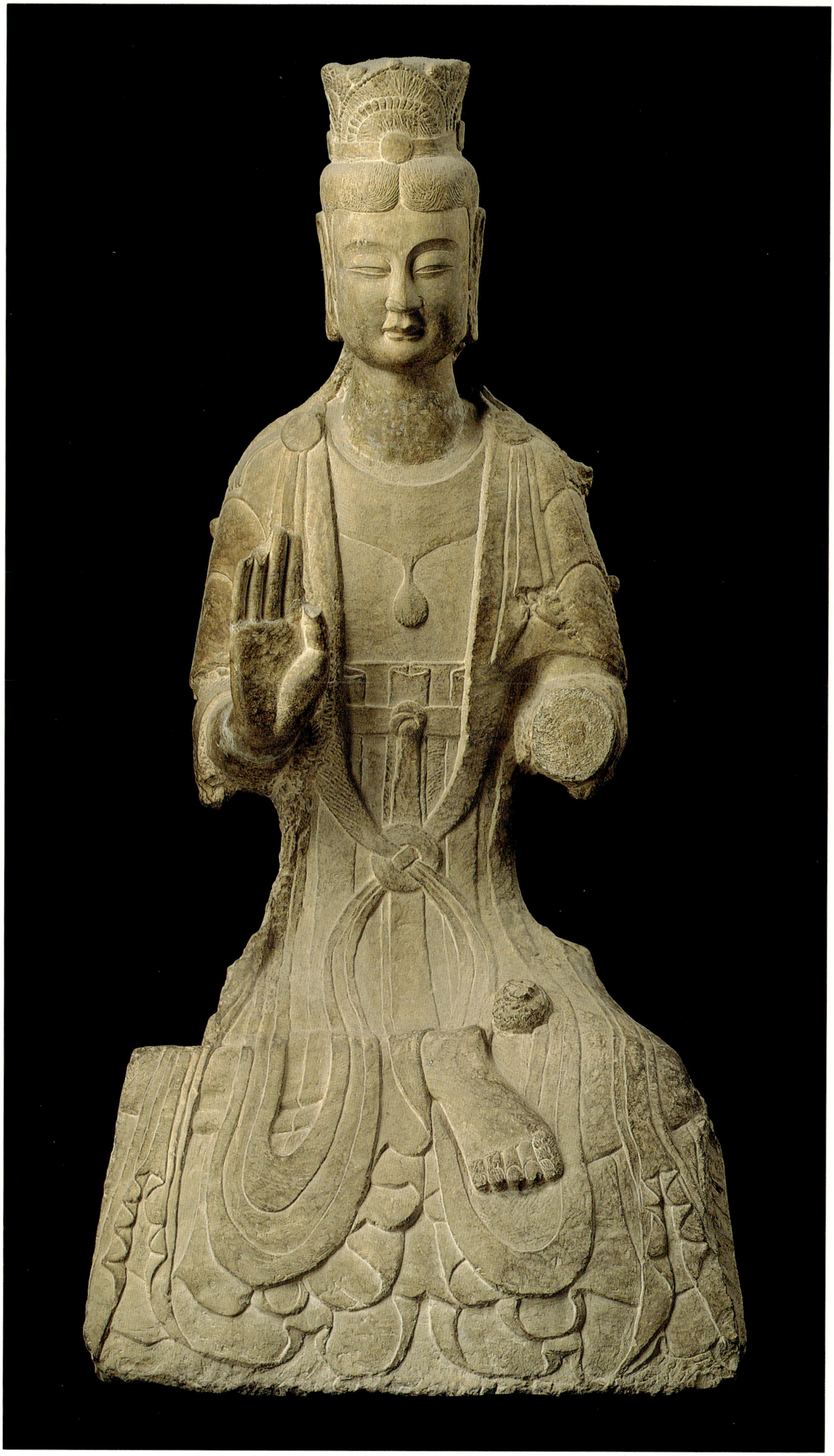

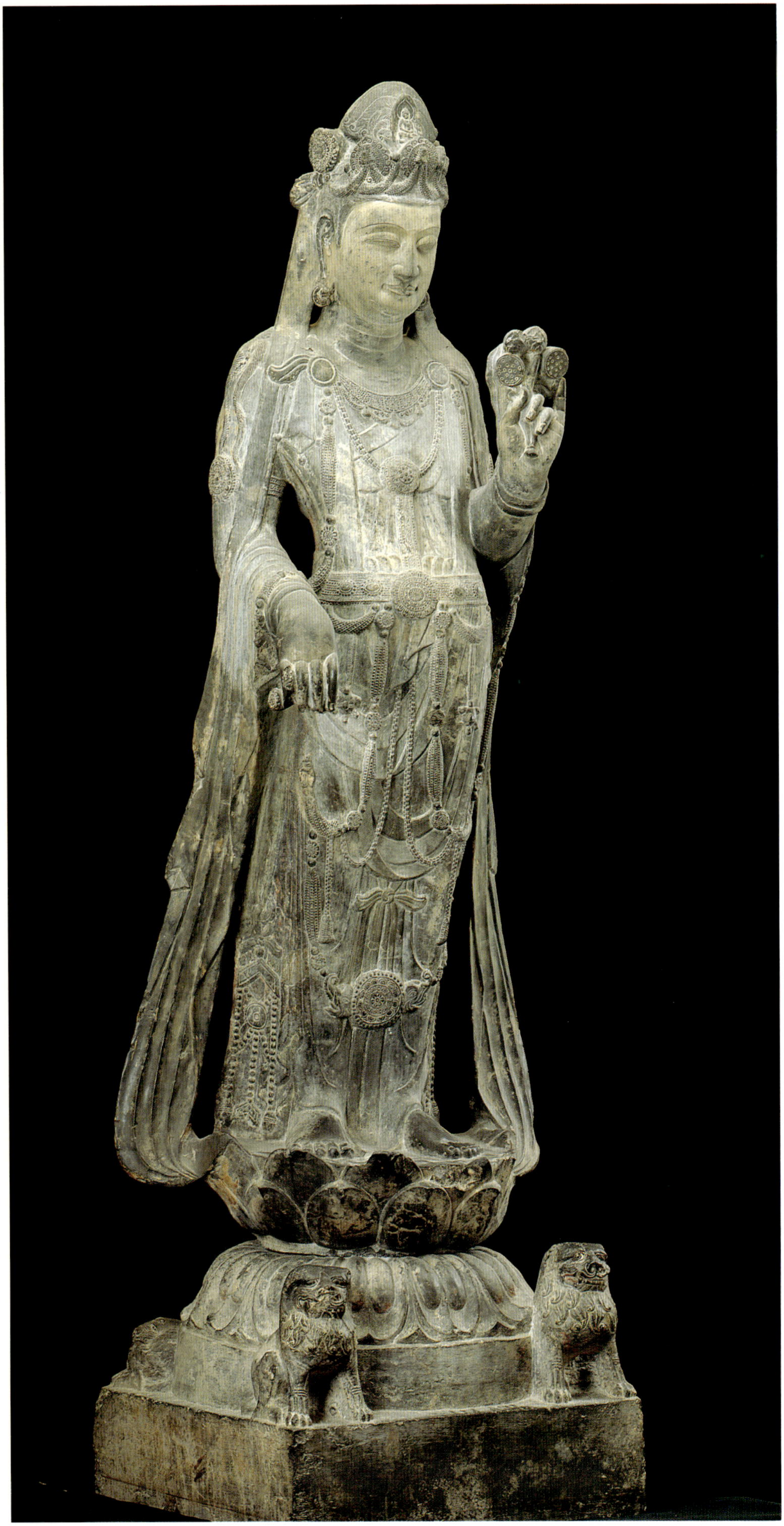

128
Guanyin
Northern Zhou or Sui dynasty, about A.D. 580
Limestone with traces of paint and gold. H: 249 cm.
Francis Bartlett Fund. 15.254

A small statue of Amitābha in the elaborate headdress confirms the identification of this figure as Guanyin (in Sanskrit, Avalokiteśvara). He stands on a double lotus pedestal placed on top of a square base, which is decorated with lions at the four corners. In his raised left hand Guanyin holds a cluster of lotus pods instead of the usual lotus flower. The gently flowing garments are richly adorned in the manner typical of sculpture of the late Northern Zhou and Sui periods. A long scarf falls from the shoulders and touches the pedestal, giving additional emphasis to the tall, monumental figure.

129
Seated bodhisattva
Tang dynasty, 2nd quarter of the 8th century A.D.
Marble, originally polychromed and gilt. H: 77.5 cm.
Chinese and Japanese Special Fund.
12.63

The bodhisattva is seated on a lotus throne of overlapping petals, decorated with beads, placed on a pedestal consisting of deeply carved, scrolling leaves and petals in high relief. The round base has inset panels with wavy borders. Wearing a robe that leaves bare the right shoulder and breast, the bodhisattva is missing the right arm, originally doweled to the shoulder, and the left hand is broken; it must have held the stem of a lotus, part of which still clings to the left of the elaborately dressed hair, which is held together by a jeweled band.

This rare statue of a bodhisattva of the esoteric Buddhist pantheon represents the last flourishing of Buddhist sculpture in the capital of the Tang empire. It would have been created just prior to a marked decline in the arts of the metropolitan area, precipitated first by an uprising led by An Lushan in 756 and then, almost a hundred years later, by the anti-Buddhist persecution of the Huichang era (A.D. 841-846).

The statue was acquired in China by Okakura Kakuzō in 1912, and the Museum's records indicate Shaanxi as its provenance. In several other cases in which Shaanxi is stated to be the provenance of a piece, it turns out that the acquisition was made in Xian, where Okakura and his nephew Hayasaki Kōkichi had their best contacts.

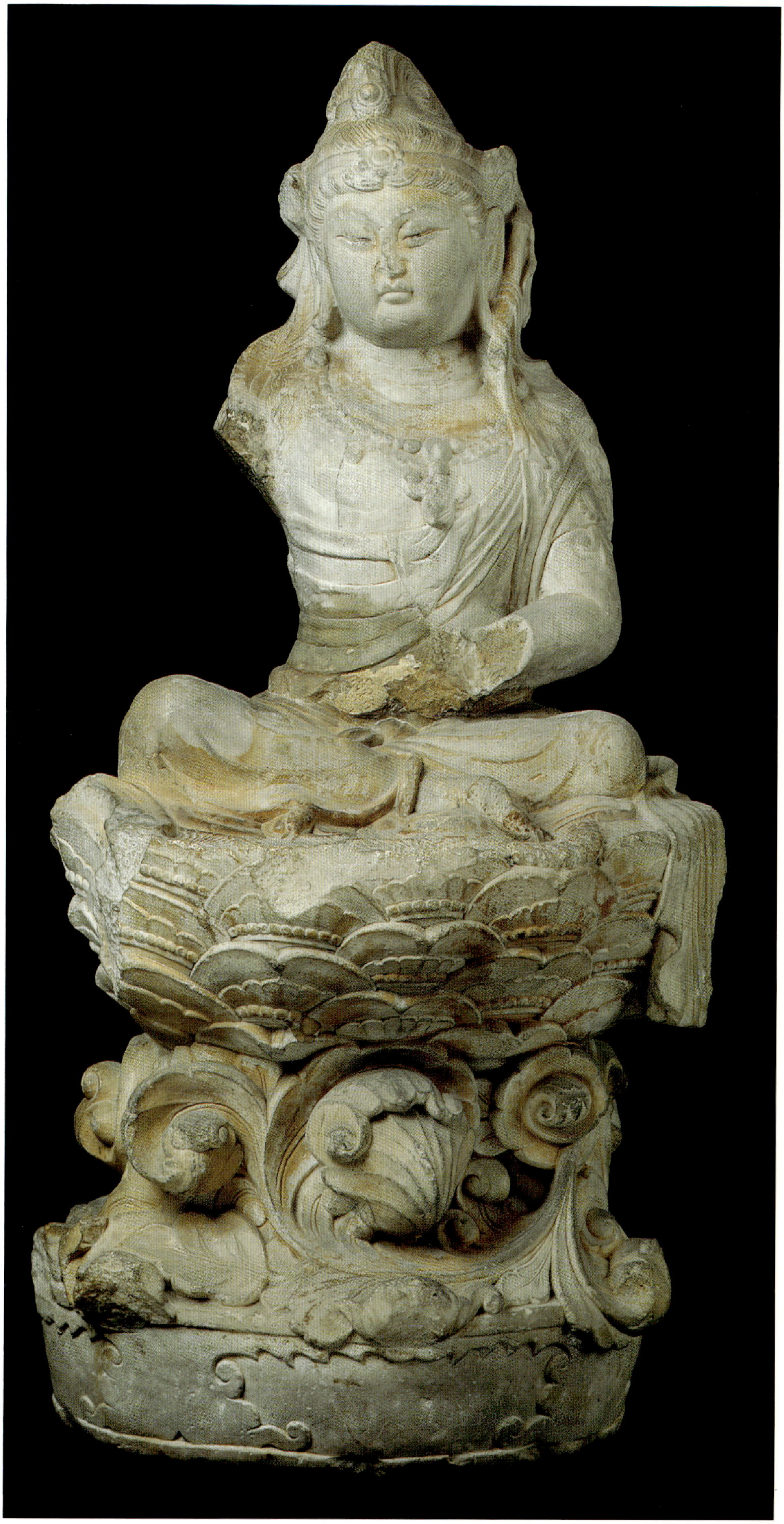

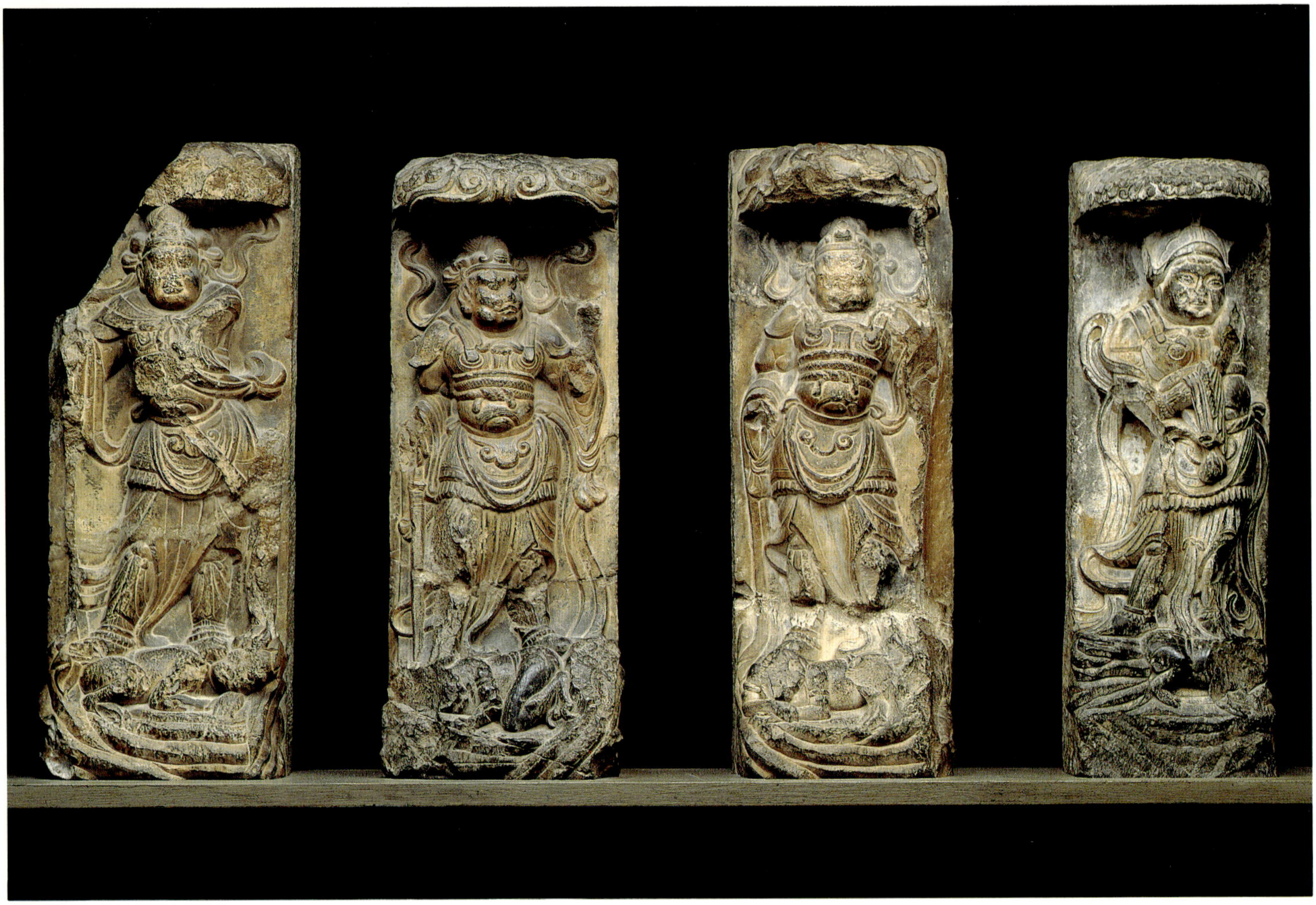

130
Four divine guardians
Tang dynasty, early 8th century A.D.
Limestone; from a pagoda of the Xiangjisi, Xian, Shaanxi province.
Guardian 1 and 3: 42 x 19 cm.; 2 and 4: 40 x 19 cm.
Gift by Subscription. 10.301-302; Chinese and Japanese Special Fund. 20.720-721

A photograph taken by the Japanese archaeologist Sekino Tadashi shows that two of these four guardian figures were originally set into the wall of a brick pagoda at Xiangjisi, a Buddhist monastery built in A.D. 706 near present-day Xian. The photograph does not show the back of the pagoda, but in all probability two sculptures that entered the Museum's collection in 1910, and are of the same size and style, came from the same site.

Despite damage to their faces and limbs, the guardian figures retain a sense of monumentality and gracefulness characteristic of early-eighth-century Tang sculpture. The fluttering sashes and taut ropes of their armature convey a vital martial spirit.

A poem by the celebrated poet Wang Wei (A.D. 701-761) describes a pilgrimage to the Xiangji monastery:

I don't know where to find the Xiangji Monastery.
Several miles away, among the cloudy peaks,
Under the ancient trees, no human tracks appear.
Among the deep mountains I hear its temple bells—from where?
The sound of streams is swallowed by steep cliffs.
The sunlight cooled by green pines
As dusk empties the pools and winding streams,
Seated in meditation, we tame the poisonous dragons (in our minds).

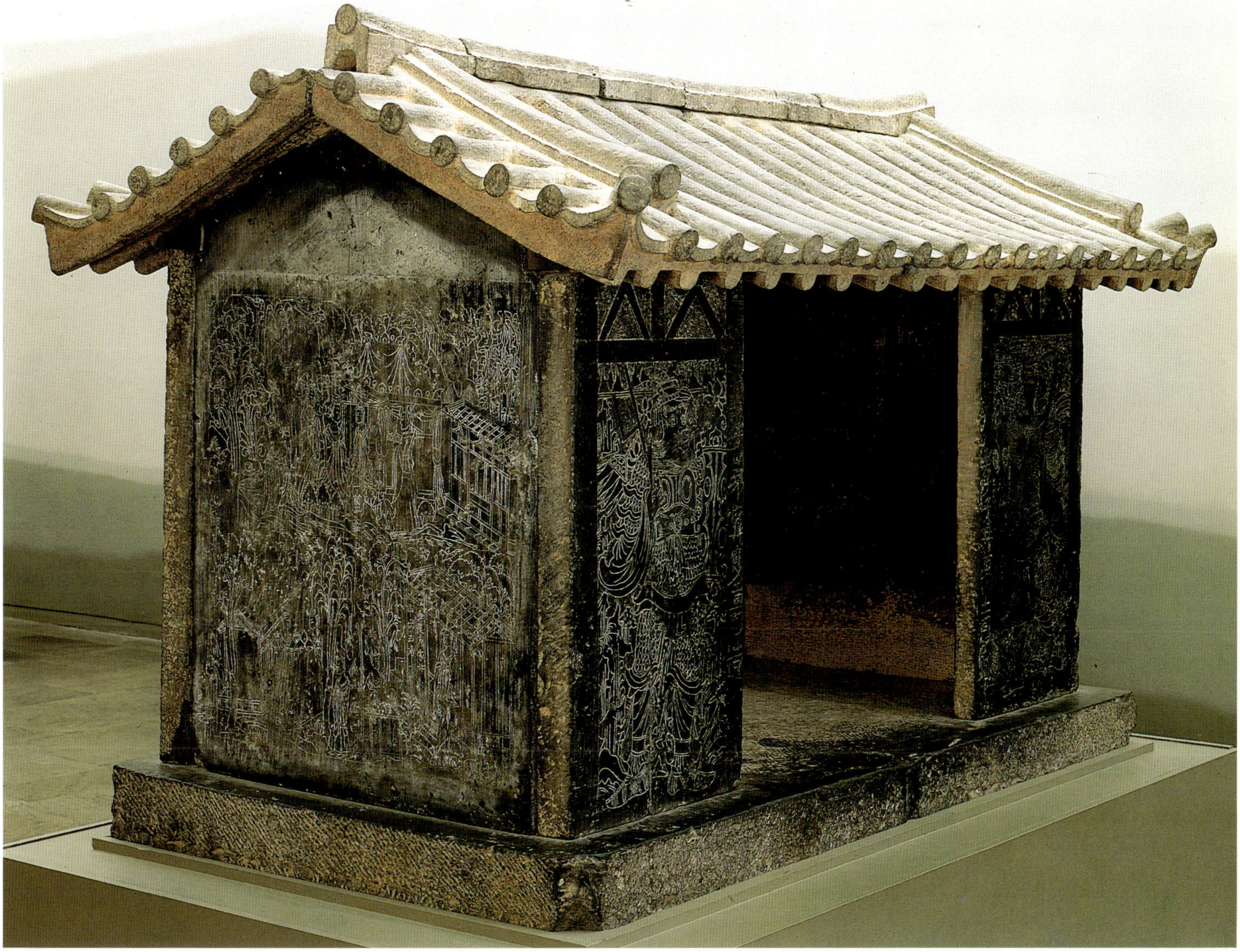

131
Offering shrine
Northern Wei dynasty, early 6th century A.D.
Limestone with engraved pictorial scenes.
H: 138 cm. W: 200 cm. D: 97 cm.
Anna Mitchell Richards and Martha Silsbee Funds. 37.340

This structure consists of five limestone slabs placed on a stone base and held together by mortise-and-tenon joints. It is covered by elaborate carving imitating a tiled roof. Slabs, posts, and trusses are indicated in incised lines. The front wall — two slabs with an opening in between — is engraved with figures of armed guards clad in armor. On the other walls of the interior and exterior are engraved representations of such paragons of filial piety as Ding Lan, Dong Yong, Dong Yan, and various dignitaries.

Inscriptions on the two front slabs next to the guardian figures have been thought by some to be connected with a mortuary inscription, reportedly found with it on a tombstone recording the life of an official named Ning Mao, who died in A.D. 527. However, the style of the script of the facade inscriptions is rather rough and could be a later addition.

The original use of this object is uncertain. Some believe it to be a citang, or offering shrine placed near a tumulus or grave. House models in stone also served as sarcophagi, but the opening in the facade, corresponding with a plain section of the interior back wall, makes it unlikely that the present house was used for such a purpose.

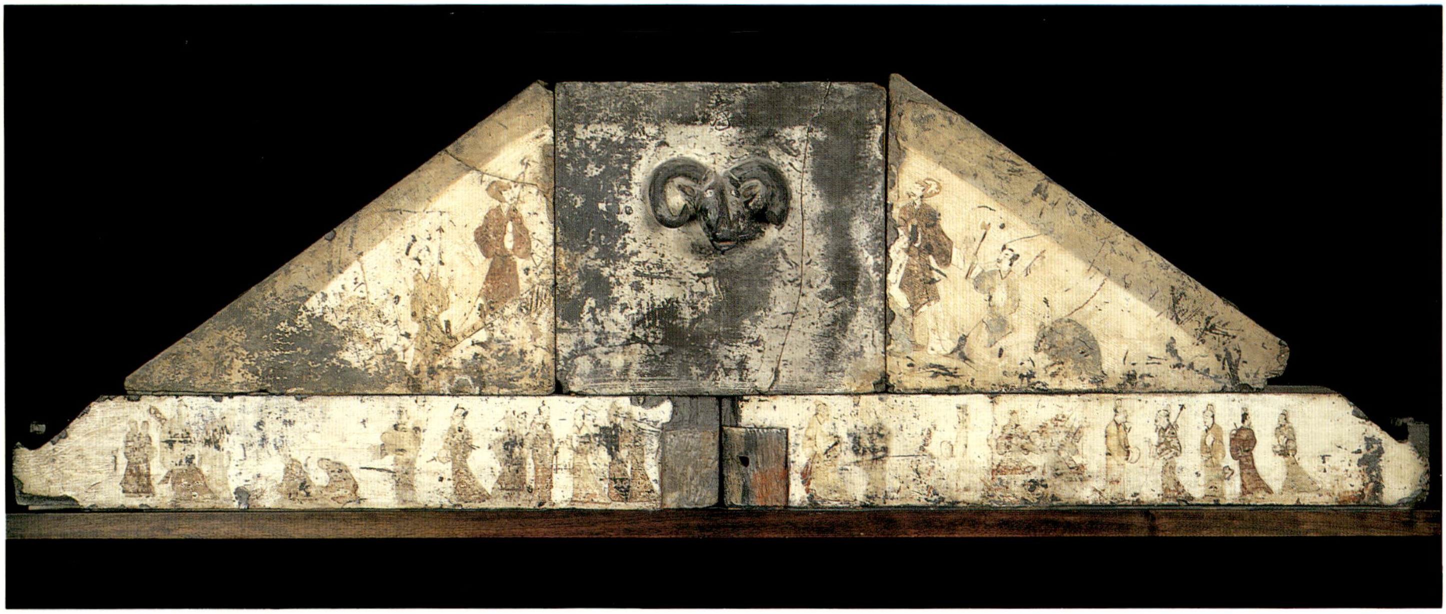

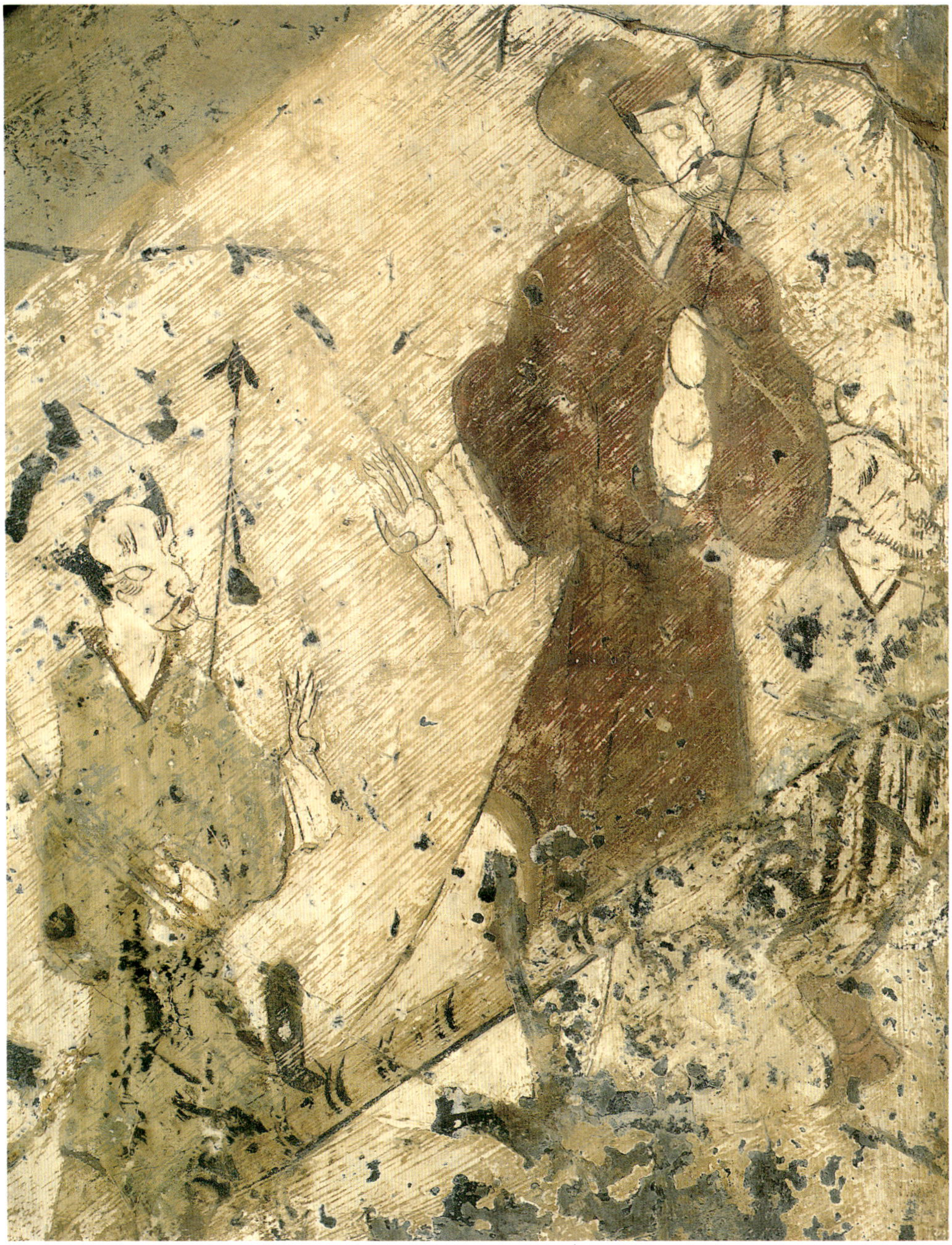

132
Lintel and pediment of a tomb
Western Han dynasty, 1st century B.C.
Gray earthenware; hollow tiles painted in ink and colors on a whitewashed ground. 73.8 x 204.7 cm.
Denman Waldo Ross Collection.
25.10-13
Gift of C.T. Loo. 25.190

This lintel and pediment served as a roof support in the center of the main chamber of a tomb. It was excavated sometime around 1915 from a tomb in the village of Balitai, to the south of Luoyang, one of the two capitals of the Han empire. Recent excavations in the vicinity of Luoyang have brought to light several tombs built of hollow tiles and decorated with paintings. Two of them contain a lintel and pediment of similar shape, providing clear evidence of the original function of the Boston examples.

For some years the central slab, decorated with a ram's head in high relief, was separated from the other pieces and lost all of its painted decoration, which is visible on a photograph taken shortly after its excavation. The two triangular tiles and the central slab bore a scene depicting a fight between a bear and a tiger. On one side of the two oblong lintels are depicted tales of loyalty to an emperor or feudal lord; the other side illustrates stories of virtuous women who served as examples for later generations. Although damage has rendered many details indistinct, at least four of the stories can be identified with a reasonable degree of certainty.

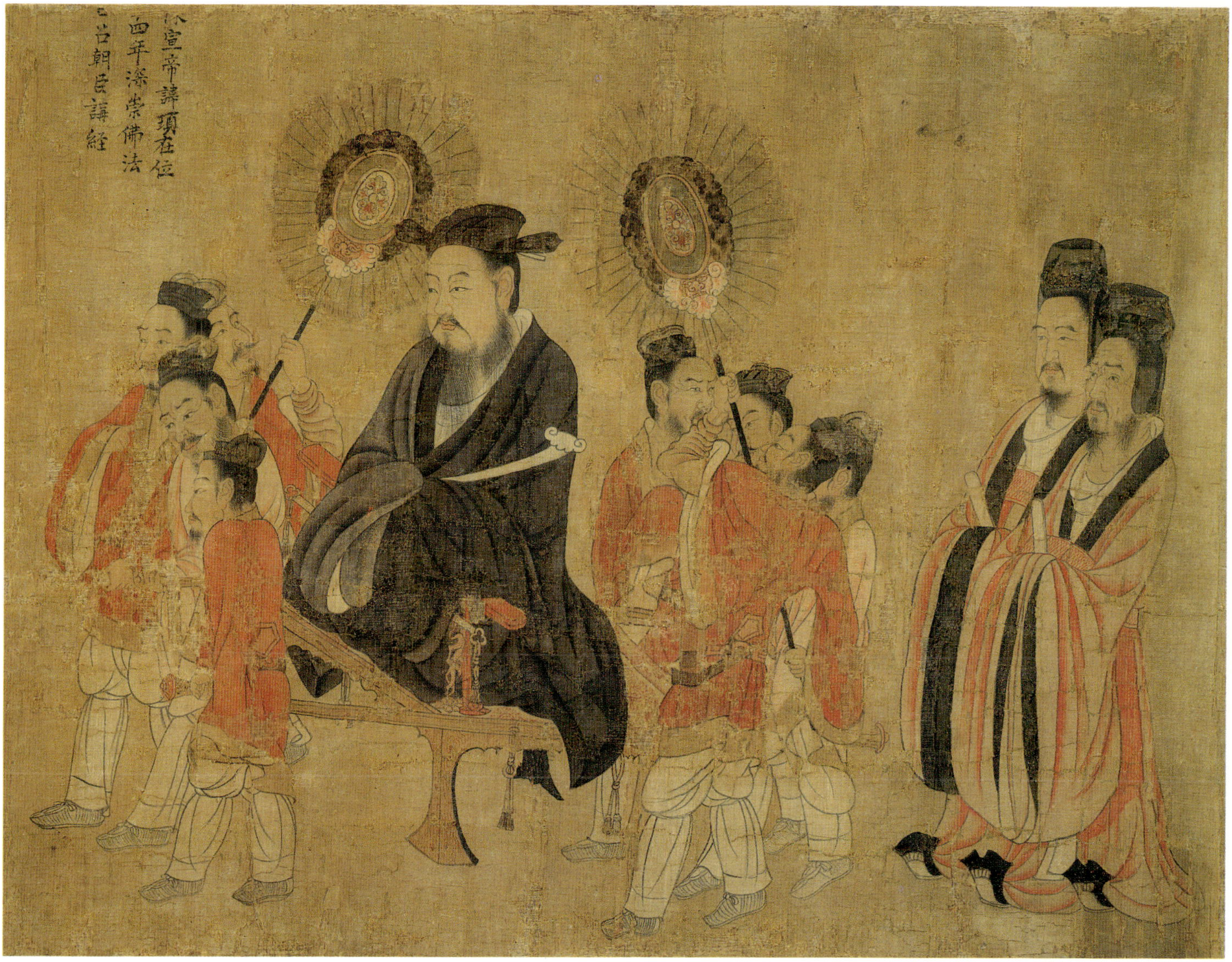

133
Attributed to Yan Liben (d. A.D. 673)
The Thirteen Emperors
Tang dynasty; 7th century
Handscroll; ink, colors, and gold on silk. 51.3 x 531 cm.
Denman Waldo Ross Collection.
31.643

The handscroll depicts thirteen emperors who reigned from the second century B.C. to the early seventh century A.D. The first six portraits are probably eleventh-century copies, but the last seven are all part of the original painting.

Attribution to the great painter and official Yan Liben is based on recent archaeological excavations that have produced a considerable amount of precisely datable tomb figurines and paintings and have brought to light wall paintings that enable us to distinguish between the style of the seventh century (i.e., the lifetime of Yan Liben), and that of the first half of the eighth century. As only a few scrolls associated with Yan Liben's name have been preserved, it is not possible to make the attribution with absolute certainty, but the archaeological material makes it clear that the left part of The Thirteen Emperors *either dates from the seventh century or goes back to a prototype created during that century.*

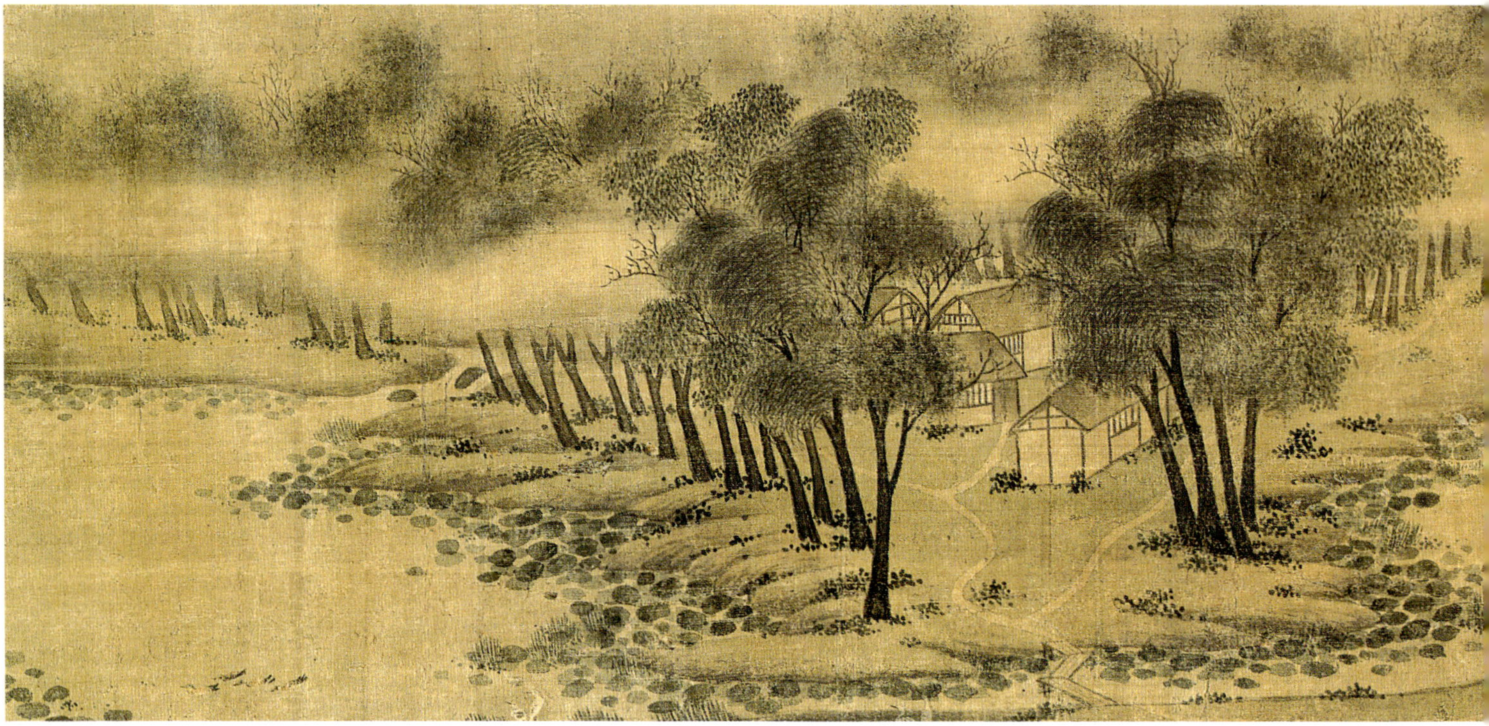

134
Zhao Lingrang (active 1070-1100)
Summer Mist along the Lake Shore
Northern Song dynasty, dated 1100
Handscroll; ink and colors on silk. 19.1 x 161.3 cm.
Keith McLeod Fund. 57.724

Toward the end of the eleventh century the monumental mountain-landscape style had run its course, to be replaced by a new type of horizontal landscape composition with "low-distance" perspective. The painter Zhao Lingrang played an important role in this new development.

As a member of the imperial family, Zhao Lingrang's movements were severely restricted; he could paint only within the northern Chinese plain between the capital of Kaifeng and the old Han and Tang capital of Luoyang. Lacking the soaring, craggy mountains of earlier masters, his studio paintings are made up of bucolic landscape elements: marshy rivers and flatlands dotted with cottages among misty groves of trees. Through the placidly flowing landscape of Summer Mist along the Lake Shore, *the spectator's eye is guided down a winding path, skirting the embankments and leading back and forth between the weeping willows in the foreground and fog-enshrouded clusters of trees in the background. An air of pleasant repose and simple charm pervades the scene, in which waterfowl are the only living beings. Once part of the Qing Imperial Collection, this handscroll is one of the very few works by Zhao Lingrang accepted by most experts.*

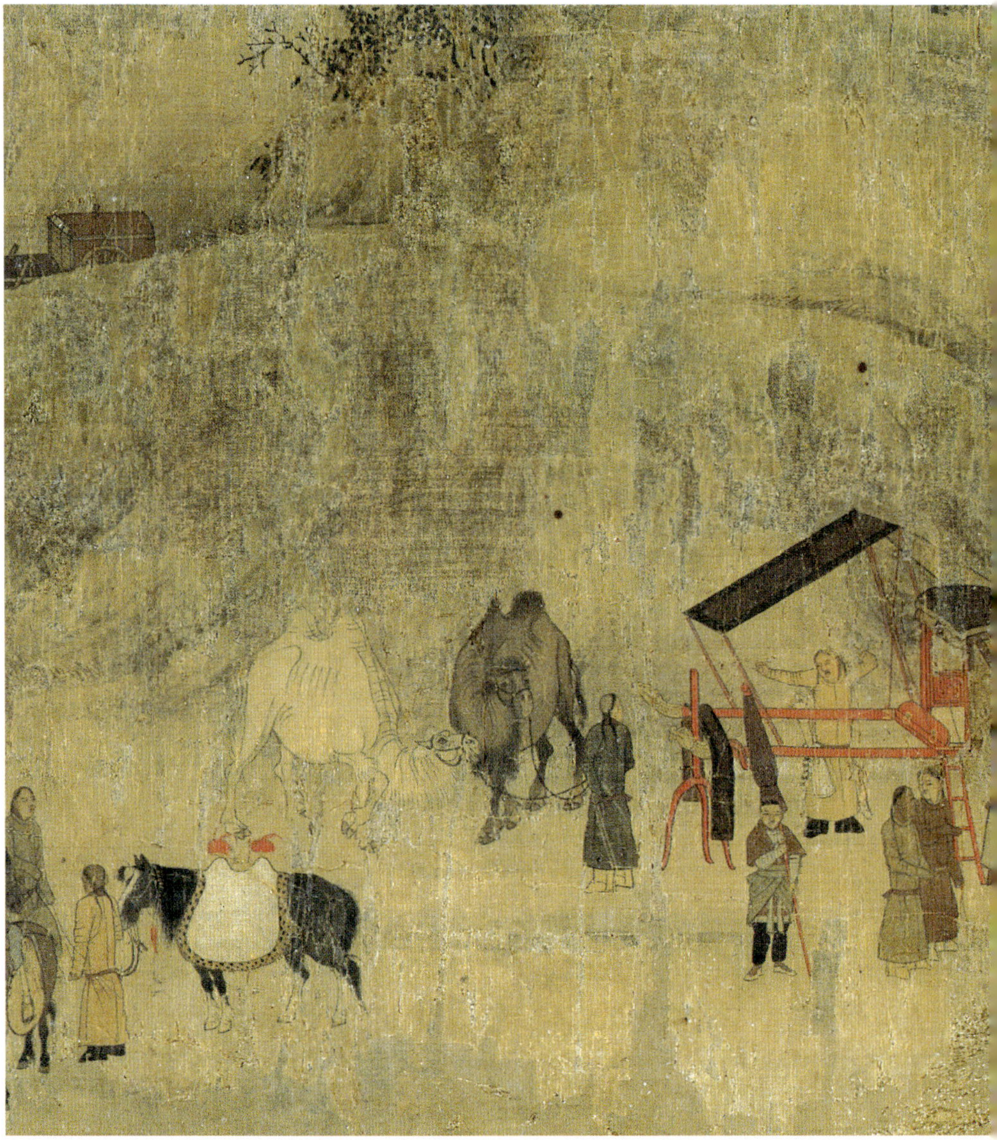

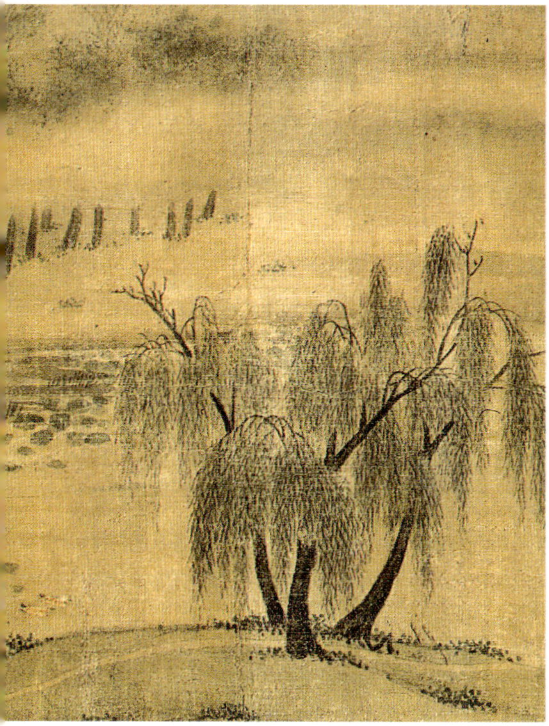

135
Lady Wenji's Return to China
Northern Song dynasty, early 12th century
One of four sections of a handscroll, now mounted as an album leaf; ink, colors, and gold on silk. 25 x 55.8 cm.
Denman Waldo Ross Collection. 28.65

Just as America has its tales of the West, China has its epics of the North. During the Han period (second century B.C. - second century A.D.) the Chinese came in contact with the nomadic Xiongnu (Huns), who lived along their northern borders. The heroes and heroines who played a role in the vicissitudes of cultural exchange and confrontation of that time inspired poets and writers throughout Chinese history.

By far the most popular heroine was Lady Cai Wenji, who was abducted by the Huns, spent twelve years in captivity, and returned to China after being ransomed, leaving behind her Xiongnu husband and two sons. The eighteen poems she is said to have written describing her tragic life were illustrated in several handscrolls with a corresponding number of scenes. Of the oldest known version, now in the Museum of Fine Arts, only four scenes have been preserved. They represent the conclusion of Wenji's captivity: her departure from Mongolia and her return to the Chinese capital.

In contrasting the Huns' and Chinese ways of life, the artist chose an imaginative device. Living in a new era of confrontation between China and the Khitans, another northern nomadic tribe, he represented the Huns in Khitan costume and with Khitan accoutrements, such as yurts, camel-drawn carts, gathered drums, etc. How accurately the nomadic lifestyle is depicted becomes evident when we compare the album leaves with wall paintings and stone reliefs found in recently excavated tombs of the Khitan nobility.

These anonymous leaves, full of fascinating detail, represent one of the last successful efforts to illustrate Chinese classical poetry.

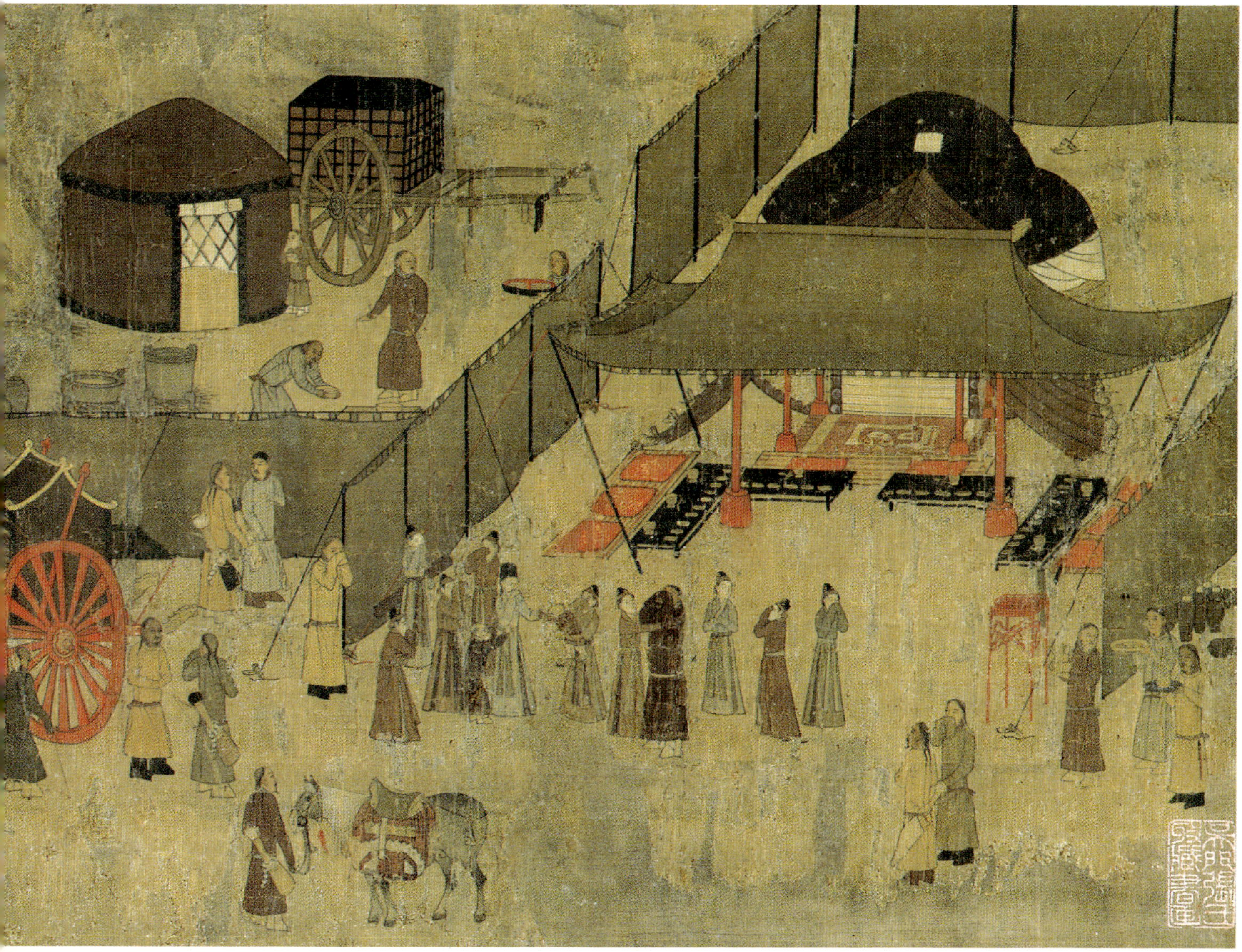

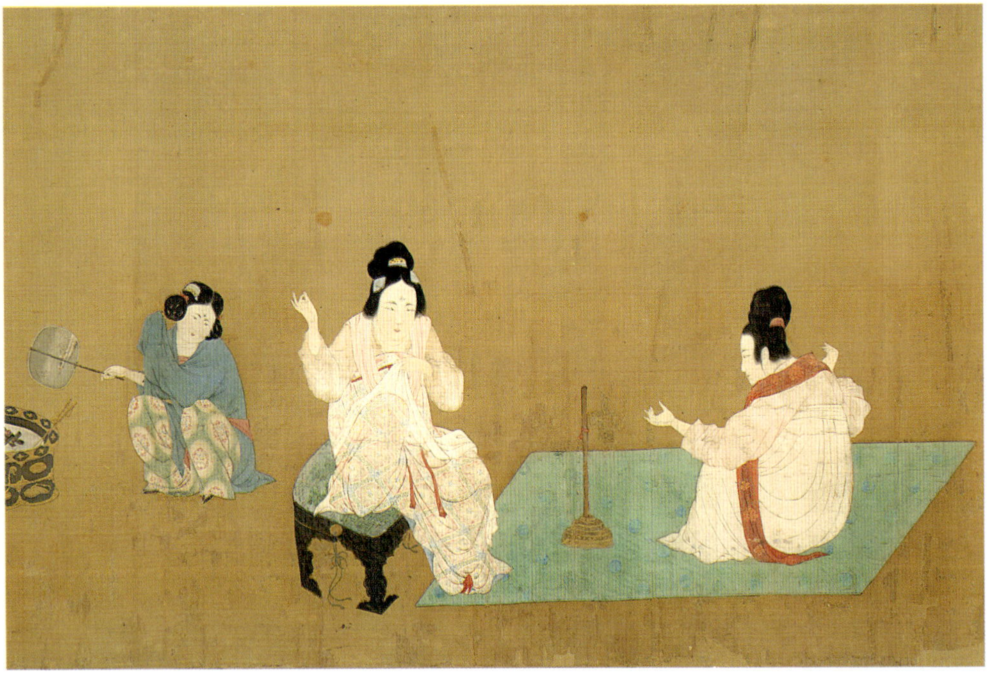

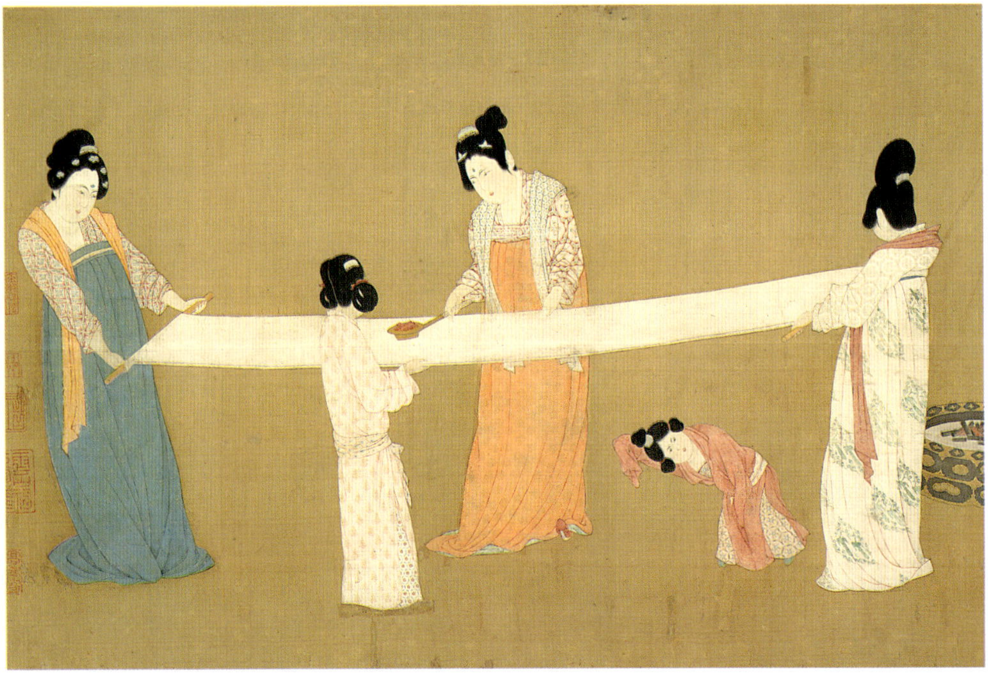

136
Attributed to Emperor Huizong (1082-1135)
Court Ladies Preparing Newly Woven Silk
Northern Song dynasty, early 12th century
Handscroll; ink, colors, and gold on silk. 37 x 145.3 cm.
Chinese and Japanese Special Fund. 12.886

Emperor Huizong was a gifted painter as well as a discerning collector. Reflecting both pursuits, this handscroll is a copy he is believed to have made of a scroll by the Tang artist Zhang Xuan (first half of the eighth century), recorded in the inventory Xuanhe Huapu as having been part of Huizong's famous collection. The imperial attribution was inscribed in the right margin by the Jurchen emperor Zhangzong (r. 1189-1208), a collector and calligrapher of repute, who inherited many of the works taken from the palace in 1126. As no less than six of Huizong's daughters married into the victorious Jurchen imperial clan, there is a good possibility that the attribution is based on inside information.

The composition – three groups of court ladies and their maids pounding silk, spinning, sewing, and ironing – is painted in light, sensitive brushstrokes of subtly varying thickness and delicate colors. A careful comparison of hair styles, textile patterns, and costumes with those appearing in Tang and Song wall paintings reveals anachronistic details that do not accurately reflect the Tang tradition. The various patterns in the silk of the garments are rendered in meticulous detail. The scene on the painted fan held by the servant fanning the charcoal fire – ducks among the reeds on a snowy river bank – represents a typical Northern Song landscape style.

Whether the painting is actually by the emperor's own hand or, as some experts believe, the work of one or two palace artists cannot be established with certainty. Nevertheless, it is one of the finest and earliest remaining examples of the ancient Chinese tradition of copying the works of great artists of the past.

Another version of virtually the same figure composition, attributed to Zhang Xuan, was described by the Yuan poet Yuan Haowen (1190-1257). It differed from Huizong's painting in that the figures were placed in an autumnal garden setting with rocks and wutong trees.

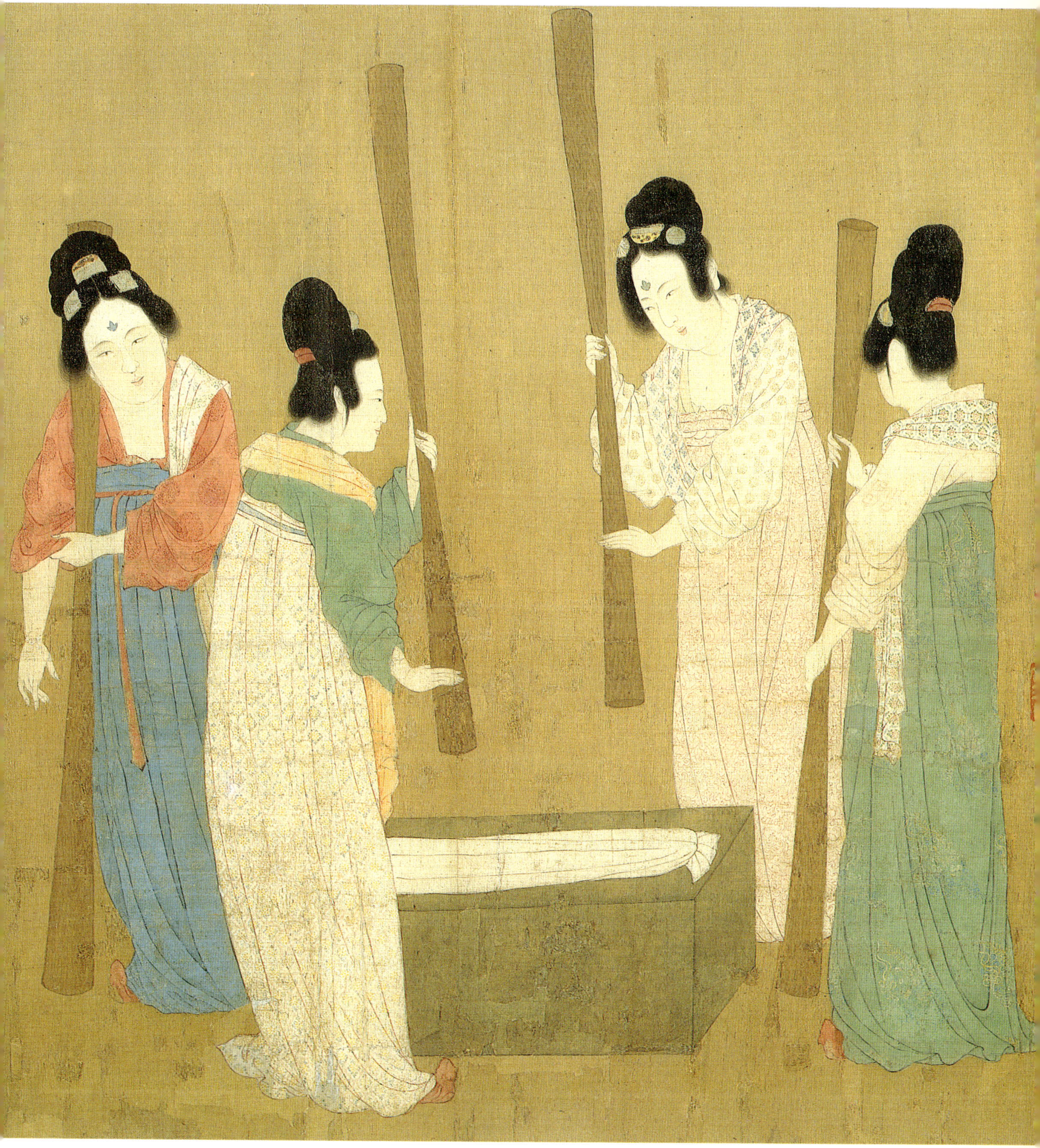

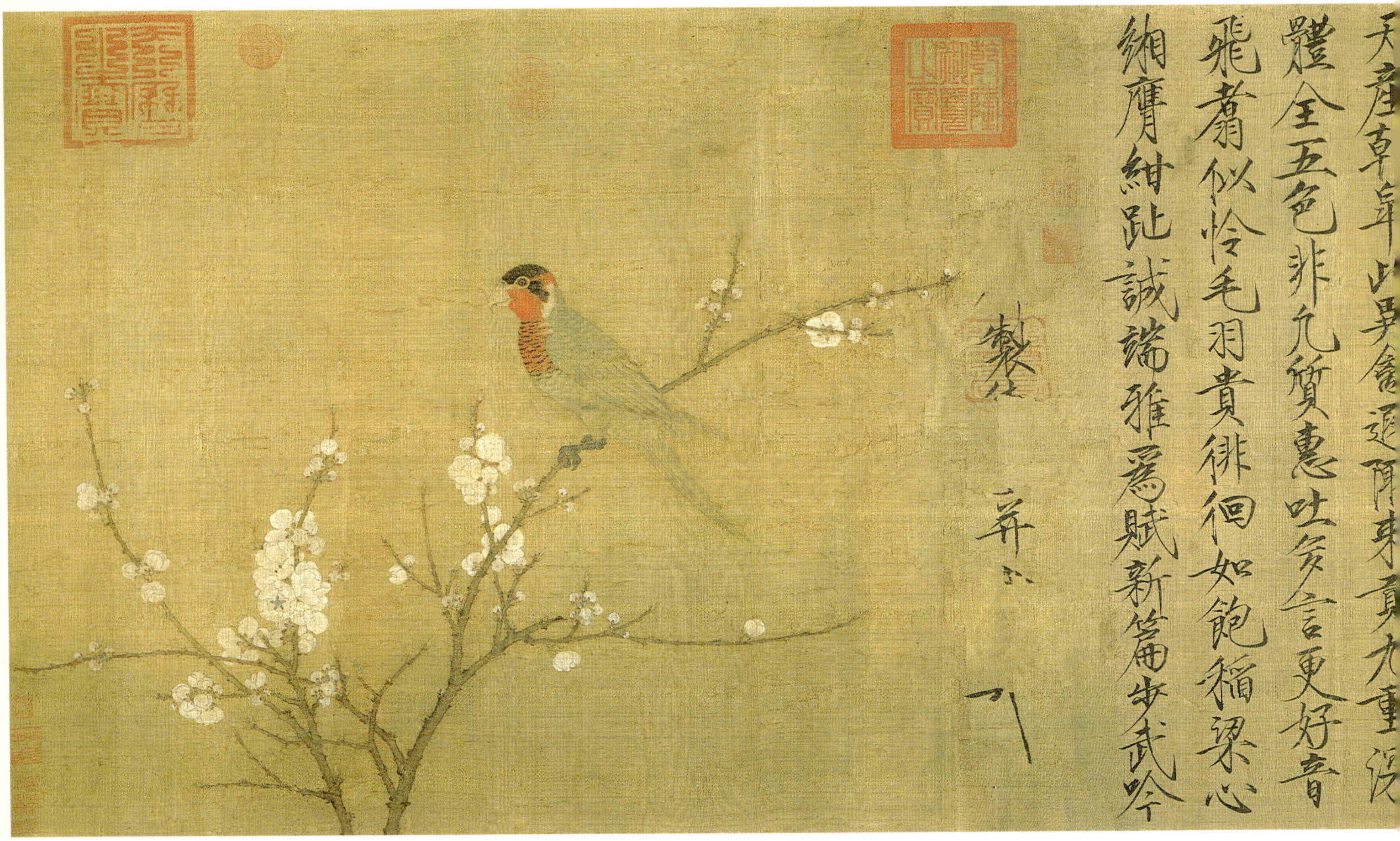

137
Emperor Huizong (1082-1135)
The Five-Colored Parakeet
Northern Song Dynasty,
early 12th century
Handscroll; ink and colors on silk.
53.3 x 125.1 cm.
Maria Antoinette Evans Fund. 33.364

The Department of Asiatic Art is fortunate to have two works associated with the most famous of all Chinese imperial artists, the Song emperor Huizong (r. 1101-1126). While his reputation as a ruler has suffered from hindsight criticism by Chinese historians because he lost his throne to the invading Jurchen, his talent as an artist has never been doubted. Yet it is difficult to separate the few surviving masterworks by his own hand from those created by court painters for his signature.

Among the works most likely to have been painted and inscribed by the emperor himself is The Five-Colored Parakeet. *In the colophon and poem added to the painting in his elegant handwriting, the emperor described the parakeet that he saw in his palace garden, perched on the branch of a blossoming apricot tree. The accurate likeness of this exotic bird is painted in sensitive brushstrokes and delicate colors on the silk - all typical features of the style of painting adopted by the members of the Imperial Academy of Painting of this time. The scroll bears a strong resemblance, in both the painting and the writing, to the handscroll* Auspicious Cranes *in the Liaoning Provincial Museum.*

138
Taoist Deity of Earth Reviewing his Realm
Southern Song dynasty, 12th century
One of three hanging scrolls, mounted on panel; ink, colors, and gold on silk.
125.5 x 55.9 cm.
Chinese and Japanese Special Fund.
12.880

Paintings depicting deities of the Taoist pantheon are seen far less frequently than Buddhist paintings, and early scrolls of this superb quality are almost nonexistent. Unlike Buddhist trinities, in which the figures of the two flanking paintings turn toward the central piece, all three of the principal deities here face in the same direction. The three figures are of the same size and are treated as equals, each one placed in the center, seated on a throne in the clouds (heaven), on a horse crossing a bridge (earth), or riding a dragon over a vast expanse of waves (water). All three deities are encircled by a host of attendant figures, depicted in different ways to express their intrinsic natures. In the painting illustrated here attendants of the god of earth are running toward the bridge, while the god himself looks down upon the demons, led by the Queller of Demons (Zhong Kui) in the foreground. The landscape setting of this painting,

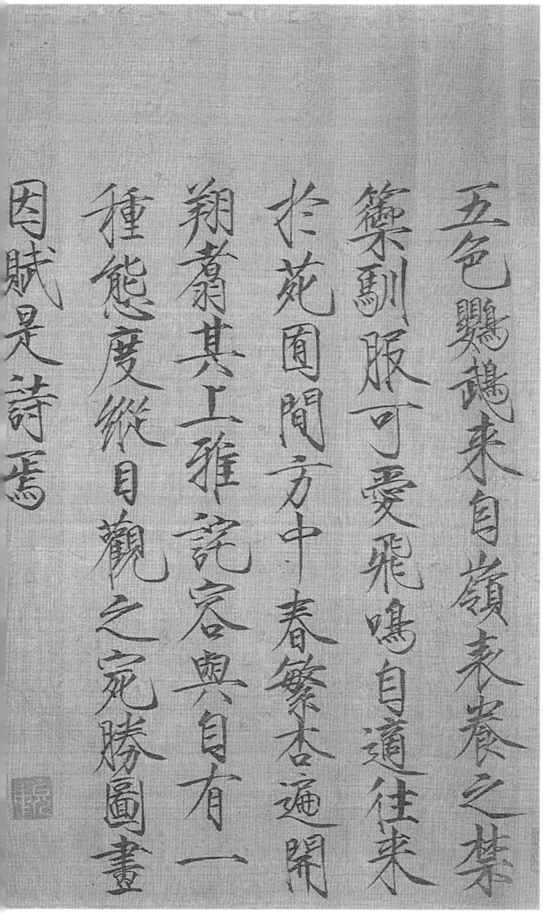

with its tree overhanging a cliff, is reminiscent of the landscape tradition developed by the early Song master Guo Xi, while the figures are of the style related to Wu Daozi of the High Tang period.

A twelfth-century date is assigned to the scroll on the basis of a wall painting recently discovered in the Buddhist temple Yenshangsi in Shanxi province. It is datable to 1158 and is remarkably close to the present Taoist trinity. The two works were presumably the creations of professional artists from the North specializing in religious painting.

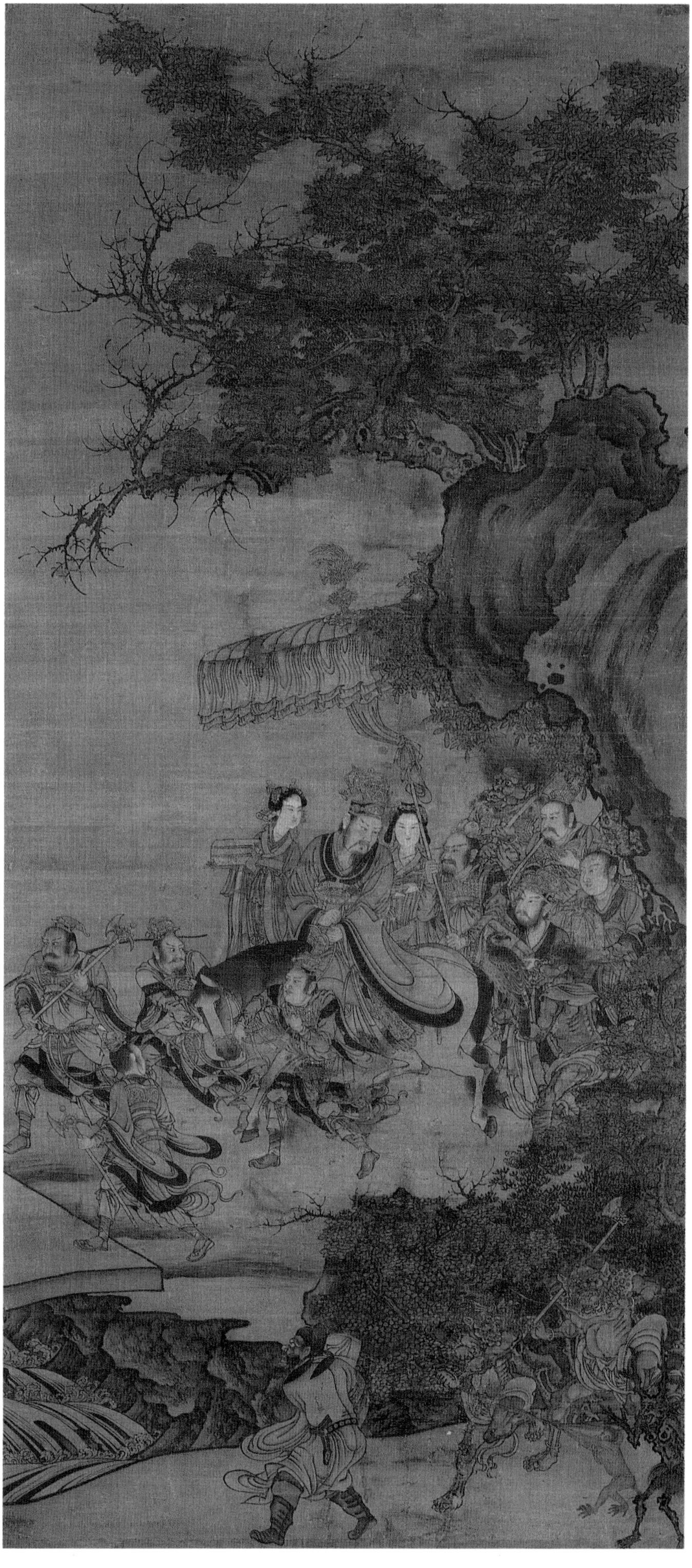

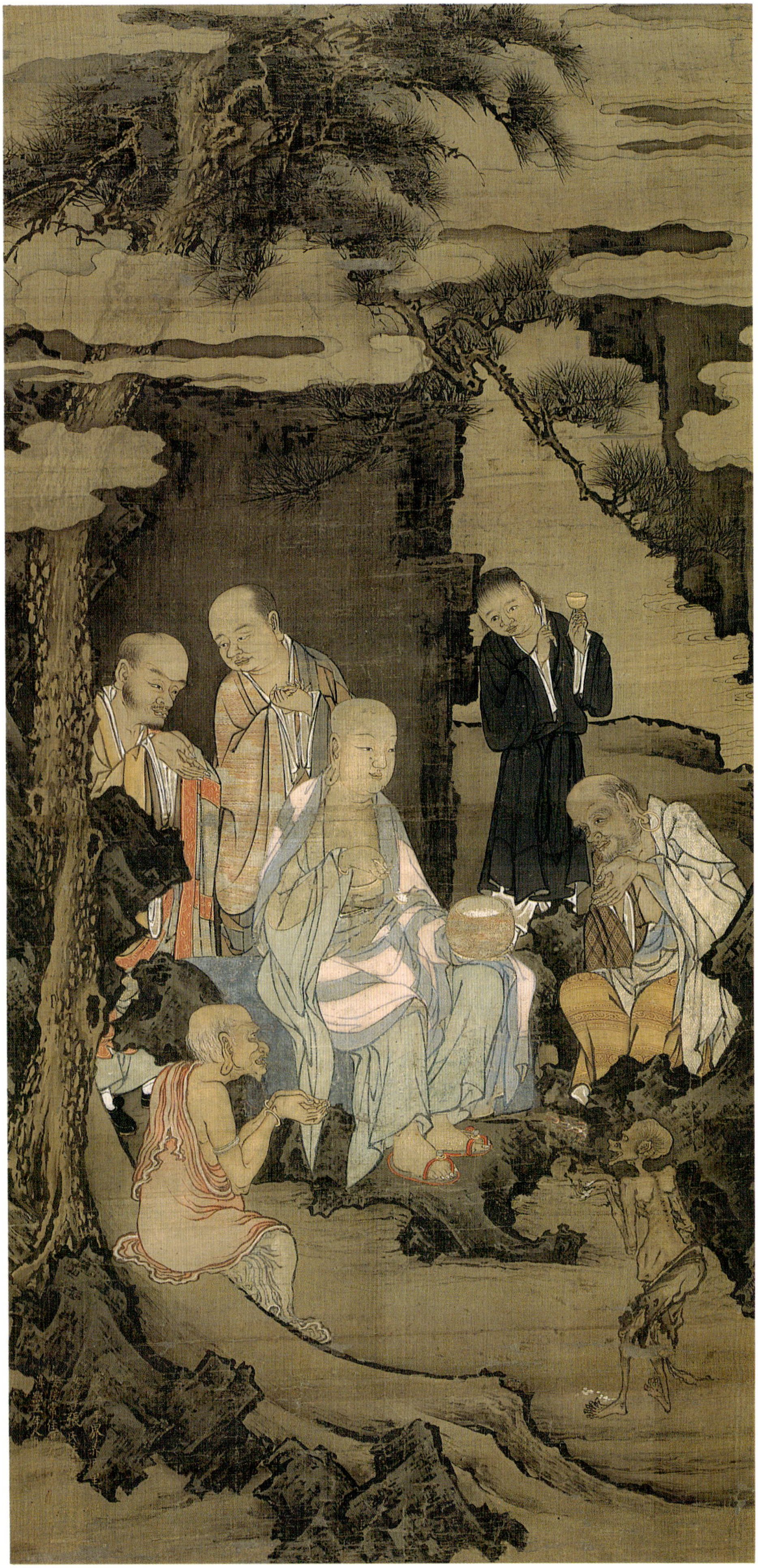

139
Lin Tinggui (active second half of 12th century)
Lohans *Feeding a Hungry Spirit*
Southern Song dynasty, dated 1178
Hanging scroll mounted on panel; ink, colors, and gold on silk.
111.5 x 53.1 cm.
Denman Waldo Ross Collection.
06.292

This painting, together with nine others in the collection, was originally part of a set of one hundred showing the Five Hundred Lohans. *The set belongs to the Daitoku-ji in Kyoto. Forty-four of them were exhibited in the United States in 1894 in a traveling exhibition organized by Ernest Fenollosa. At the close of the exhibition the Museum of Fine Arts acquired ten of the paintings, while two additional scrolls, not included in that exhibition, were sold to Charles L. Freer and are now at the Freer Gallery of Art in Washington, D.C.*

Some of the paintings bear dedicatory inscriptions in gold indicating that the set was made between 1178 and 1184 for the Huianyuan temple near Ningbo (Zhejiang province). Some of them are signed by Zhou Qichang and others by Lin Tinggui. All were taken to Japan during the thirteenth century and came to play an important role in the iconographical evolution of Japanese paintings representing lohans. *The entire set was copied by the famous monk-painter Minchō (1532-1431) in 1385; this set is now preserved at the Tōfuku-ji in Kyoto.*

140

Zhou Jichang (active late 12th century)

Lohan *Manifesting Himself as Eleven-Headed Guanyin*

Southern Song dynasty,
about A.D. 1178
Hanging scroll mounted on panel; ink and colors on silk.
111.5 x 53.1 cm.
Gift of Denman Waldo Ross. 06.289

The scene depicted in this painting, also one of the ten paintings in the museum's collection that was part of a set of a hundred paintings (see no. 139), shows an enthroned lohan *wearing a mask with eleven heads and forming symbolic gestures with his hands. He is surrounded by four other* lohans, *making up the group of five usually represented in one painting. In the foreground are portraits of the painter (with a brush in hand) and the donor (holding a sketch). Behind them, with folded hands, stands a monk who is most likely Yishao, the priest named in the dedicatory inscription as the abbot of the Huianyuan temple. The portraits of the painter, the donor, and the priest in this work make it unique in the entire series of five-hundred* lohans.

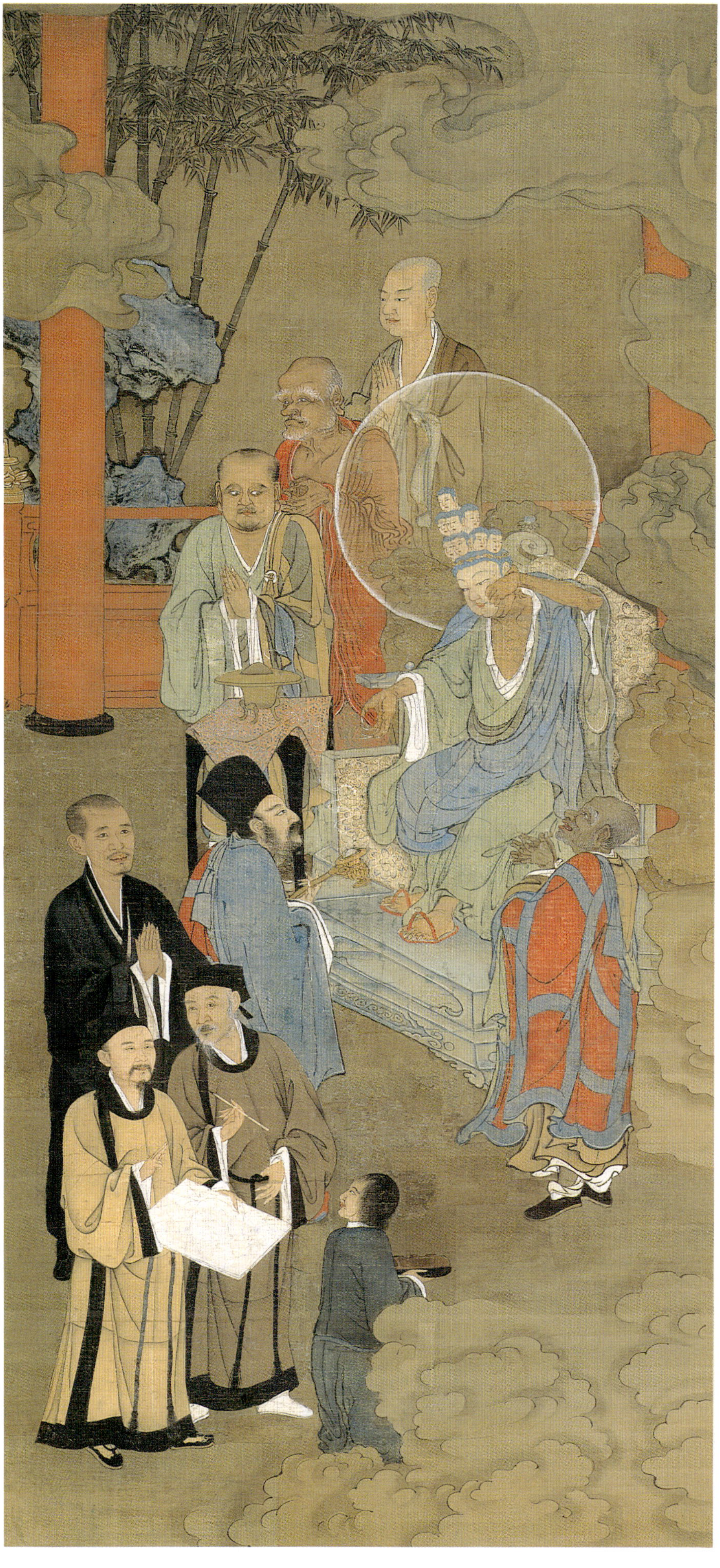

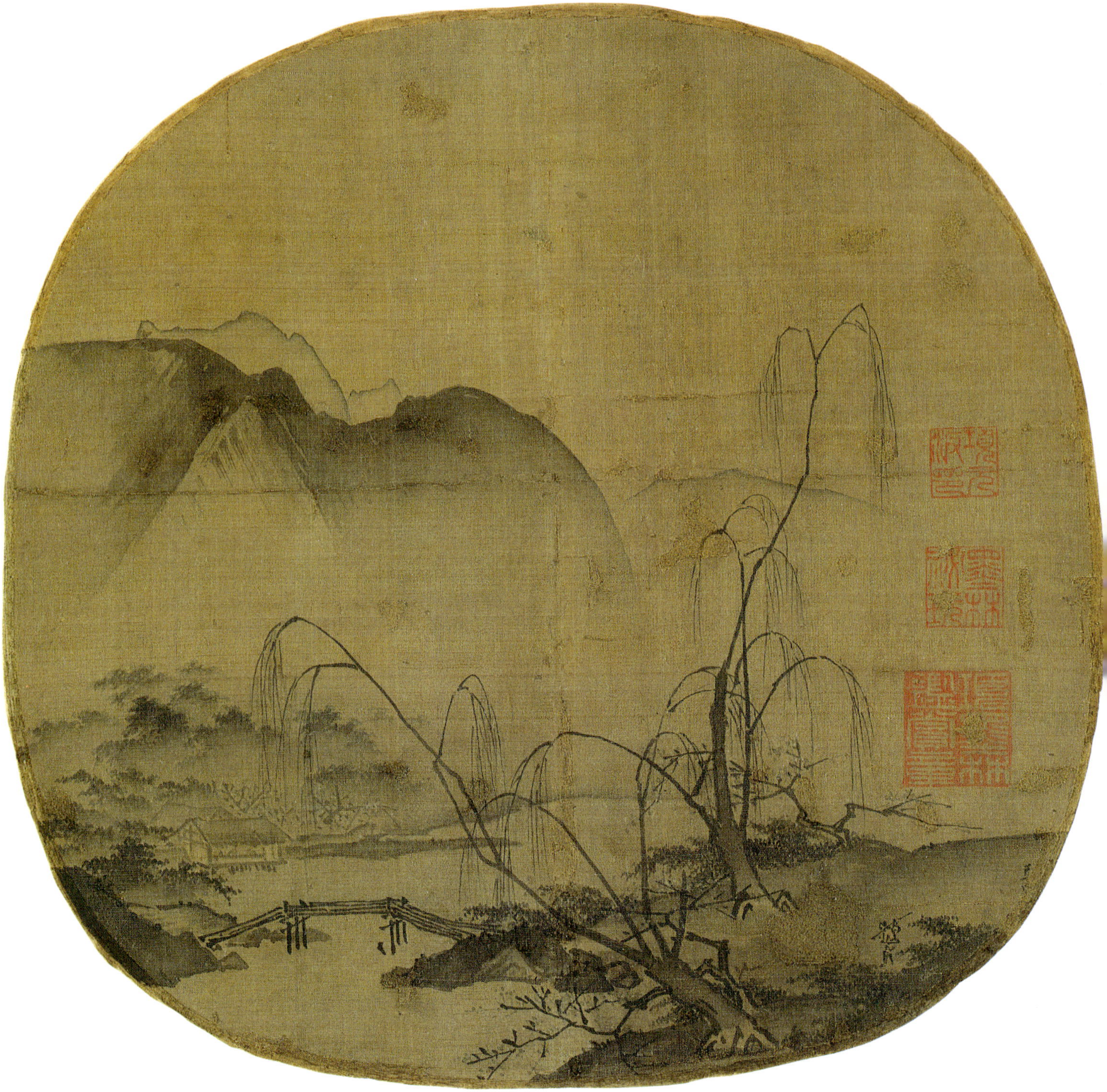

141
Ma Yuan (active late 12th-early 13th century)
Bare Willows and Distant Mountains
Southern Song dynasty, early 13th century
Round album leaf; ink and light colors on silk. 23.8 x 21.2 cm.
Chinese and Japanese Special Fund. 14.61

As early as the fourteenth century, Ma Yuan was considered by an art critic as one of the Ten Great Masters of the Imperial Academy of Painting of the Southern Song dynasty, and this album leaf confirms his fame. One of a family of painters who had fled from the North, Ma Yuan was trained in the Li Tang tradition, which had played a dominant role in Hangzhou earlier in the twelfth century and had been assimilated within the previous generation.

Ma Yuan has been referred to as "one-corner Ma" because of his deliberately lopsided compositions. But Bare Willows and Distant Mountains, *with a sophisticated arrangement of spatial elements, is exceptional for its more balanced composition and delicate style.*

Damage at the bottom right of the painting, possibly caused by application of a bright mineral pigment on the back of the silk, has resulted in the disappearance of a figure on horseback, which was originally depicted to the left of the remaining figure. The artist's signature was trimmed and damaged in the past, so that only the character "Ma" is still complete.

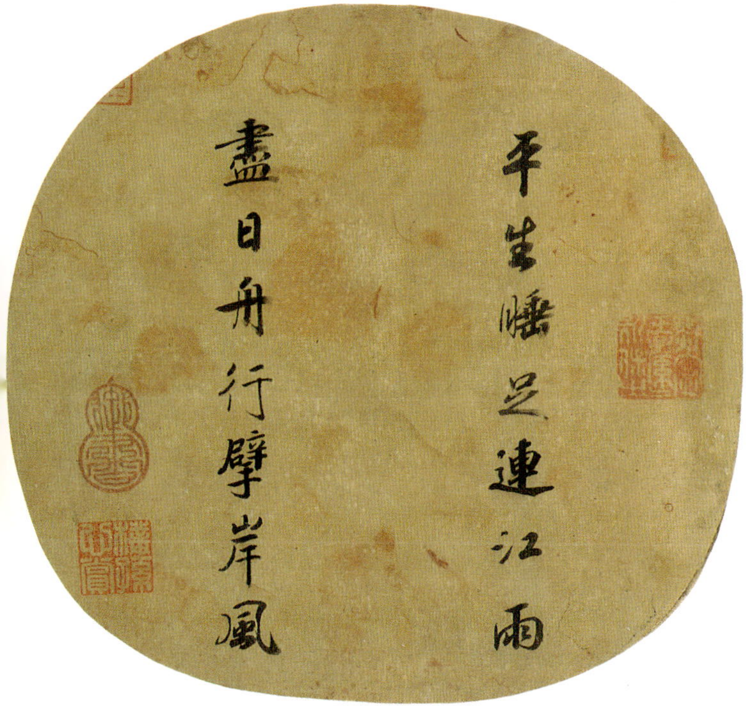

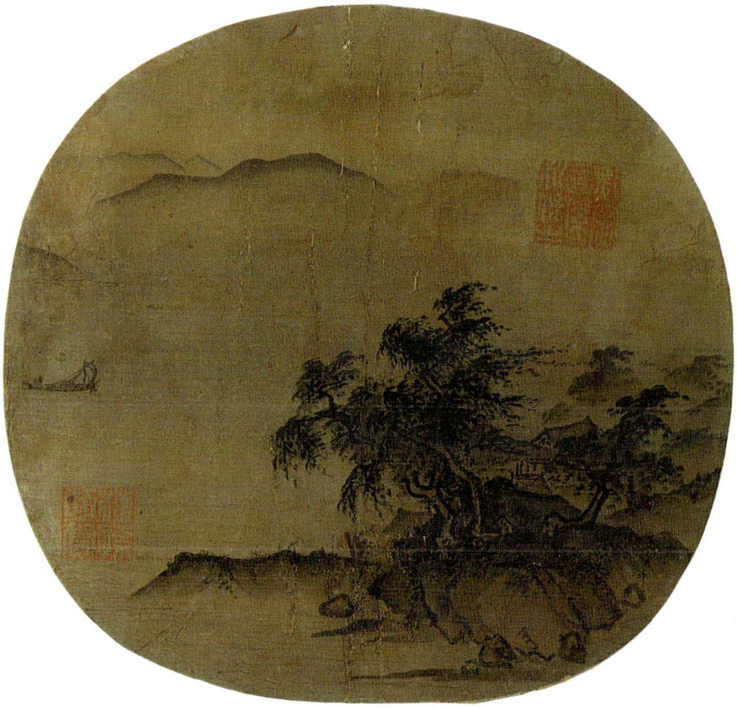

142
Xia Gui (active first half of 13th century)
Sailboat in the Rain
Southern Song dynasty
Round album leaf; ink and light colors on silk. 23.9 x 25.1 cm.
Chinese and Japanese Special Fund.
12.891

The exodus from the North in the twelfth century brought to Hangzhou, the temporary capital in the South, painters who kept alive the memory of their lost northern homeland. One of the first generation of artists with roots in the South, Xia Gui was influenced by his older contemporary Ma Yuan, who was the descendant of a northern family of painters; thus, elements from the artistic tradition of Li Tang came to be incorporated into Xia Gui's works.

Whereas Ma Yuan's style emphasized line, Xia Gui concentrated on the effects of ink tonalities, achieving greater atmospheric qualities and a more liberal spatial arrangement. Using a modified northern technique of draftsmanship, he perfected a lyrical manner of the so-called Jiangnan (south of the Yangze River) style of the tenth century. The windblown trees in the foreground of this painting are effectively balanced by the ship sailing across the water in a rainstorm and by the misty outline of the distant hills, recalling vividly the scenery of Hangzhou. Xia Gui's unobtrusive signature in the Song tradition appears at the right under a tree.

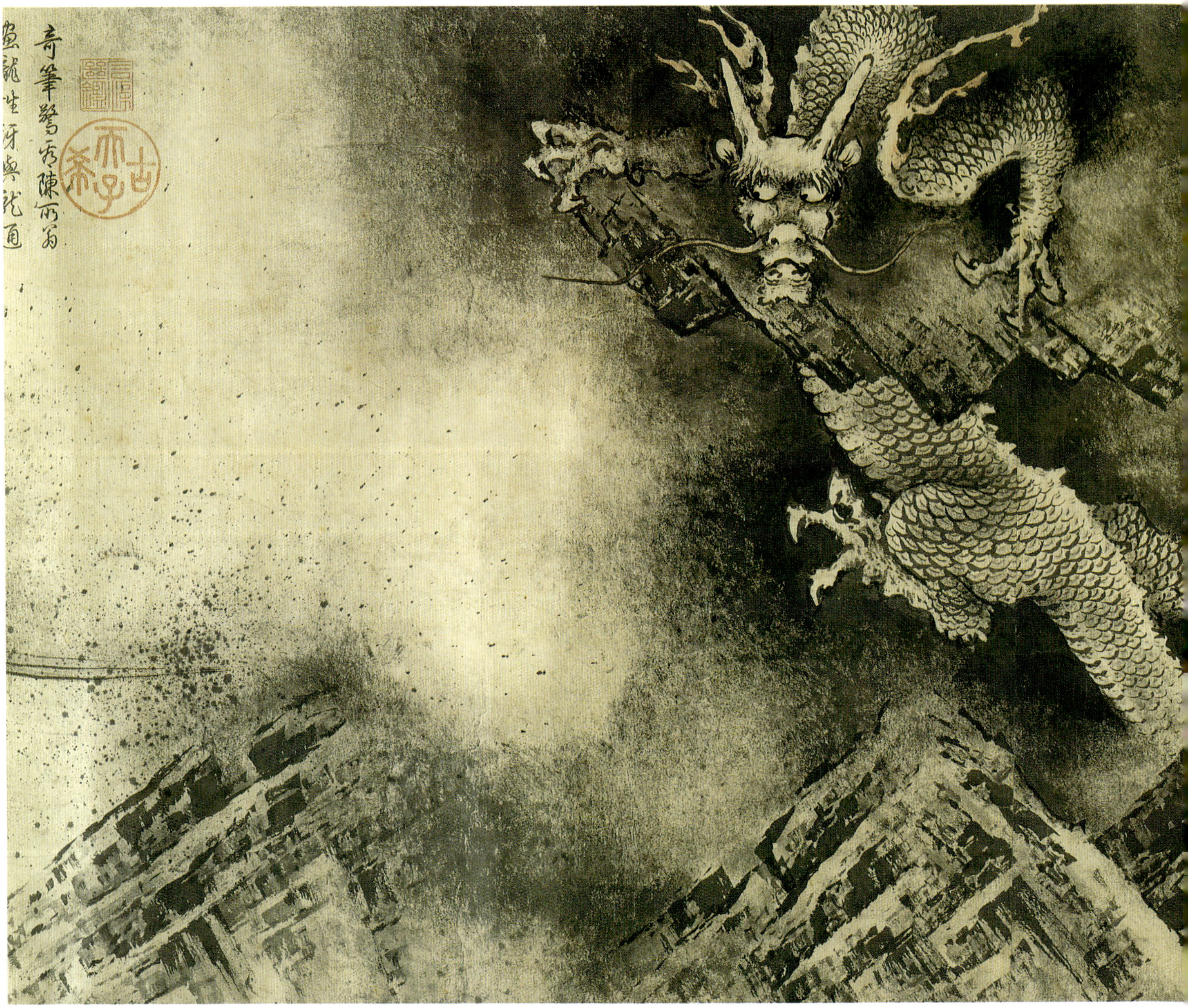

143
Chen Rong (active second to third quarter of 13th century)
Nine Dragons
Southern Song dynasty, dated 1244
Handscroll; ink with touches of red on paper. 46.3 x 1,096.4 cm.
Francis Gardner Curtis Fund. 17.1697

Of the many dragon works attributed to Chen Rong of the Southern Song period, the present scroll is by far the best and most representative one. Even more significant, it is probably the most outstanding example of all dragon paintings by Chinese artists in collections around the world.

Chen Rong was a native of the coastal province of Fujian, during the Song period the home of scholars rather than painters. He obtained the prestigious jinshi *degree in 1235 and was also known as a calligrapher and a poet in his time, as can be seen from the powerful running-style script of a long poem he composed and placed at the end of this painting. Displaying all of his abundant technical talents here, Chen Rong also expressed the fervor of Chinese Taoism. The spiritual quality is conveyed not through the Taoist deities or demons but through abstract, symbolic motifs, e.g., the mysterious dragons, the contrasting elements of waves and rocks, and the ever-changing clouds and mists. Colophons were added to the painting by prominent Taoist priests such as Zhang Sizheng and Wu Quanjie during the fourteenth century.*

An eighteenth-century copy, in a much reduced scale, is also in the Museum's collection (acc. no. 1971.324).

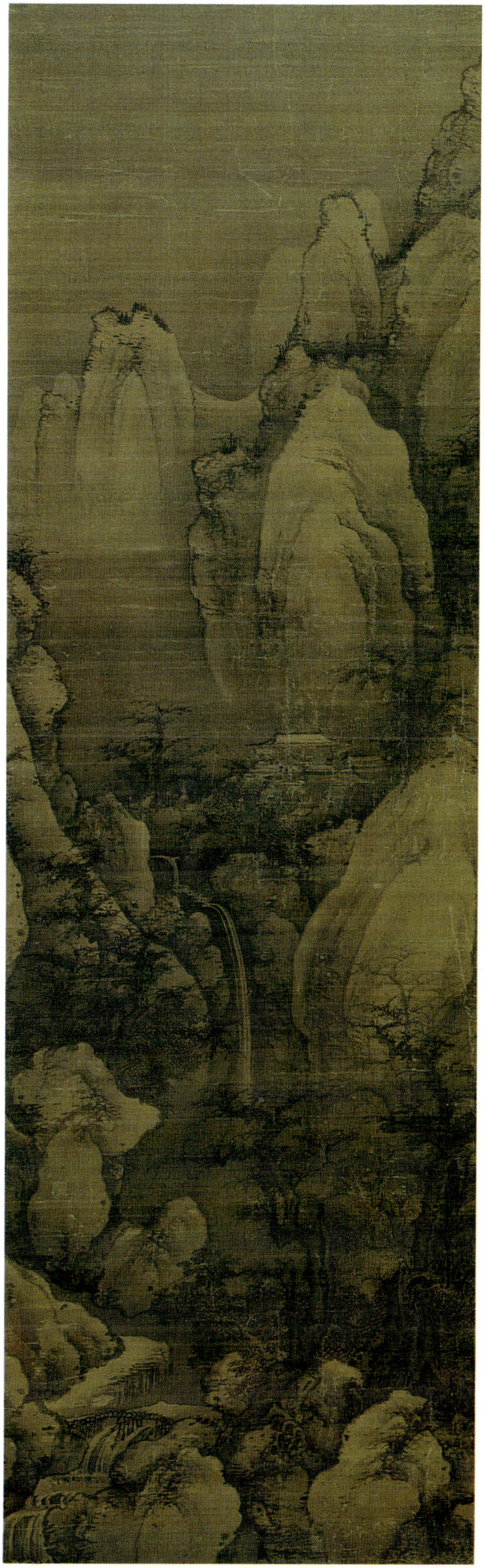

144
Yao Yanqing (active early 14th century)
Winter Landscape
Yuan dynasty, about 1340
Ink and light colors on silk.
159.2 x 48.2 cm.
Chinese and Japanese Special Fund.
15.902

Biographical information about the early-fourteenth-century painter Yao Yanqing is scarce. If Yao Yanqing is synonymous with Yao Tingmei, as some scholars believe, there are at least three known works by him, but only this example has both the seal and the signature of the artist. Although he was a southerner from Wuxing, Yao painted the barren, austere mountains of northern China. Winter Landscape *recalls the grand manner of Northern Song painting, particularly works like Guo Xi's* Early Spring, *which inspired Yao's atmospheric effects that create the illusion of space and distance. His spirited brushwork and his choice of a tall, narrow format anticipate the striking innovation made by* literati (wenren) *painters later in the fourteenth century.*

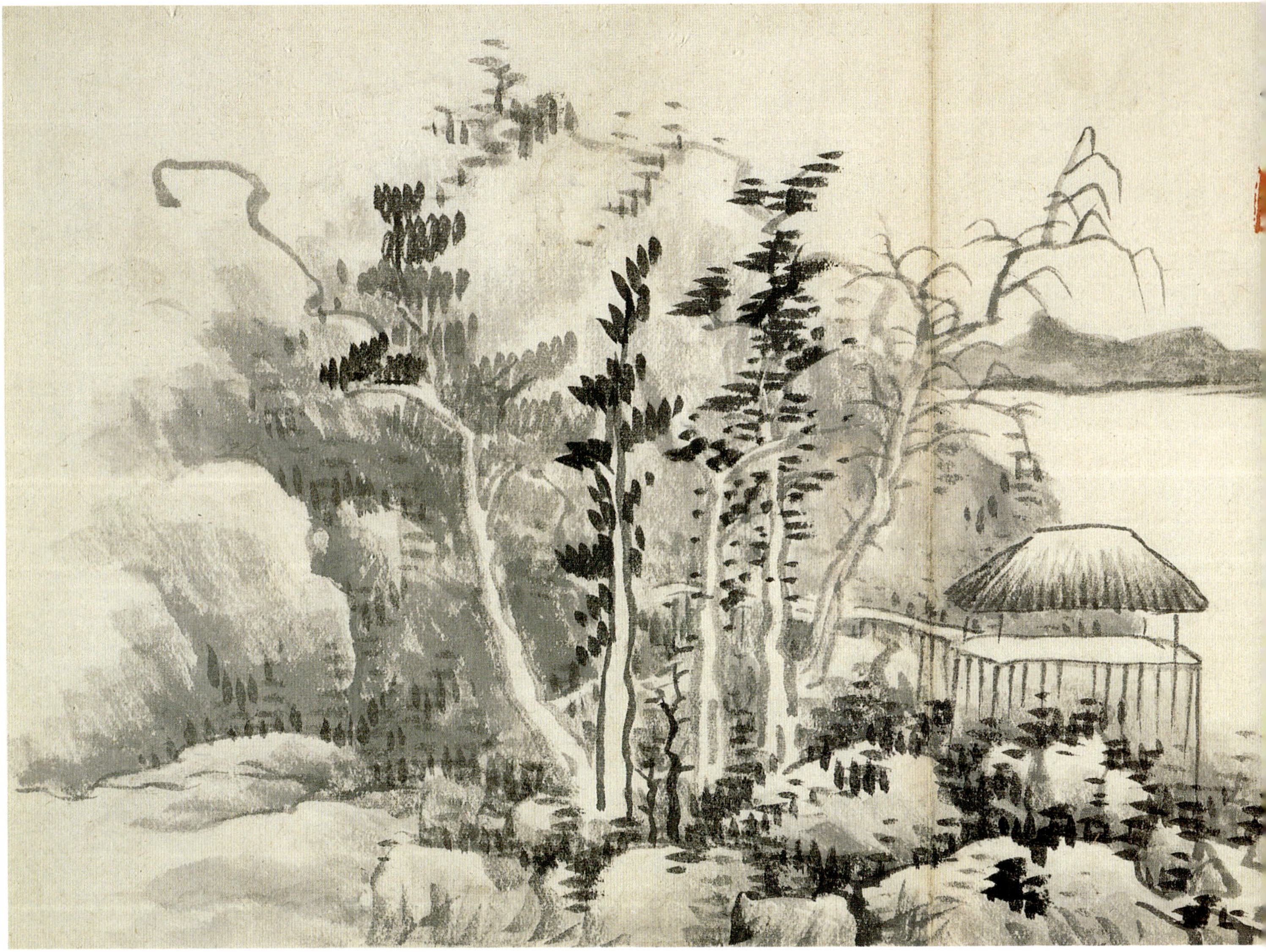

145
Gong Xian (about 1619-1689)
Landscape with Pavilion
Qing dynasty, about 1680s
One of six album leaves; ink on paper.
22.3 x 43 cm.
Annie Louise Richards Fund, Marianne Brimmer Fund,
Frederick L. Jack Fund, Otis Norcross Fund, Harriet Otis Cruft Fund,
and Gift of Reverend Z. Charles Beals, by exchange. 1986.578a

Gong Xian is remembered as one of the great individualist painters. He began painting at a young age and became acquainted with Dong Qichang (high official, art theoretician, and painter of the Ming period), whose views influenced his life as a literati painter. Gong Xian had nostalgic feelings for the fallen Ming dynasty and, therefore, associated himself only with scholars, poets, and artists who had similar political convictions.

These album leaves embody Gong Xian's personal style of the 1680s. Although Gong Xian admits to some dependence on past masters, he had by this stage of his life developed a distinct manner. He is recorded as having said in 1667: "There has been no one before me, and there will be no one after me." This declaration of individualism in art can be seen clearly in the present album leaves. Gong Xian kept brushstrokes simple by using repeated strokes of similar size and shape. He described forms by using dots of ink either clustered, forming a tree in the foreground, or scattered, to represent a mountain or clouds in the distance. The only sign of humanity in his landscapes is an occasional hut or pavilion. That Gong Xian's paintings are not inviting to the viewer is probably a reflection of his eccentric personality, fearing the intrusion of the outside world.

146
Attributed to Zhao Yong (b. 1289)
Chan Priest Gaofeng Yuanmiao
Yuan dynasty, early 14th century
Hanging scroll; ink and colors on silk.
114.7 x 46.7 cm.
Denman Waldo Ross Collection.
28.355

Of the few existing portraits of Chan priests, this is one of the rare examples in a Western collection. It has been attributed to the calligrapher of the colophon inscribed at the top of the portrait, Zhao Yong (the second son of a great painter and calligrapher of the early Mongol period, Zhao Mengfu). There is no substantial evidence for this attribution, however, as Zhao Yong is not recorded as having been a painter of portraits. Moreover, portraits of Chan priests were chiefly the work of professional painters, sometimes Buddhist monks themselves.

This is a penetrating spiritual rendering of Gaofeng Yuanmiao, one of the greatest teachers of the Meditative

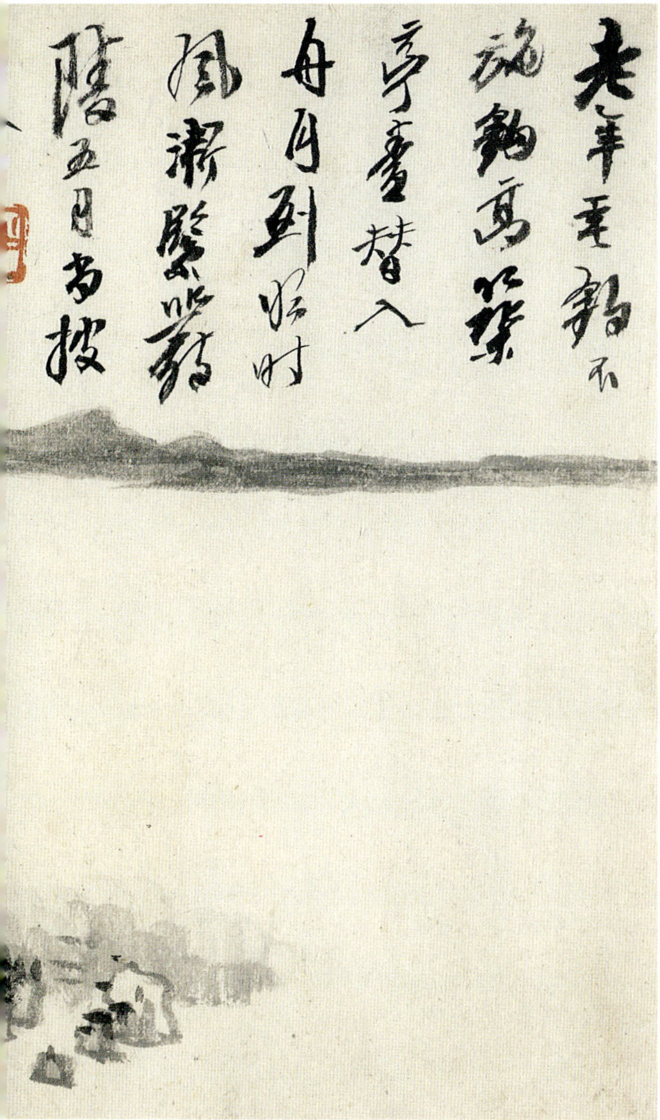

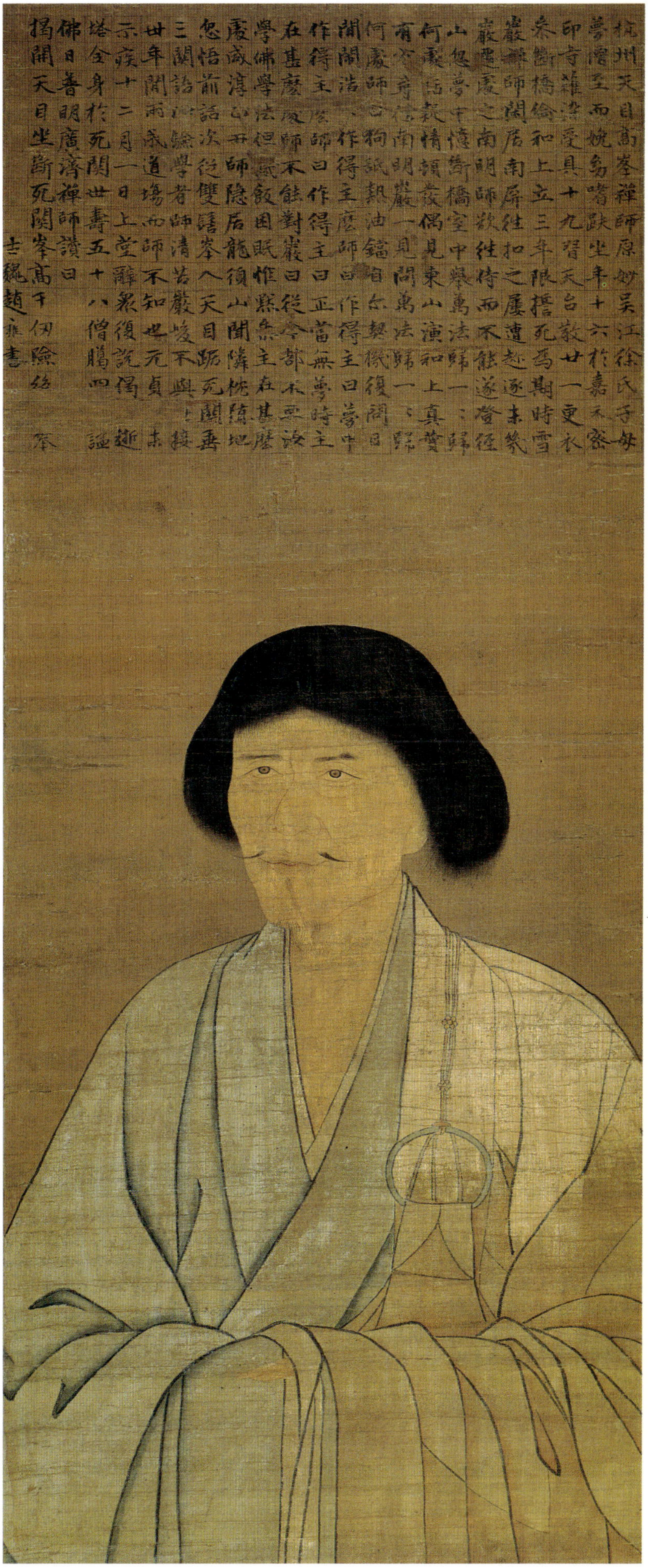

School, whose biography is inscribed in standard script above. The powerful expressiveness of his personality is undiminished by the flatness of the facial structure, defined by thin lines, or by the meticulous rendering of the monk's garb, arranged in orderly folds.

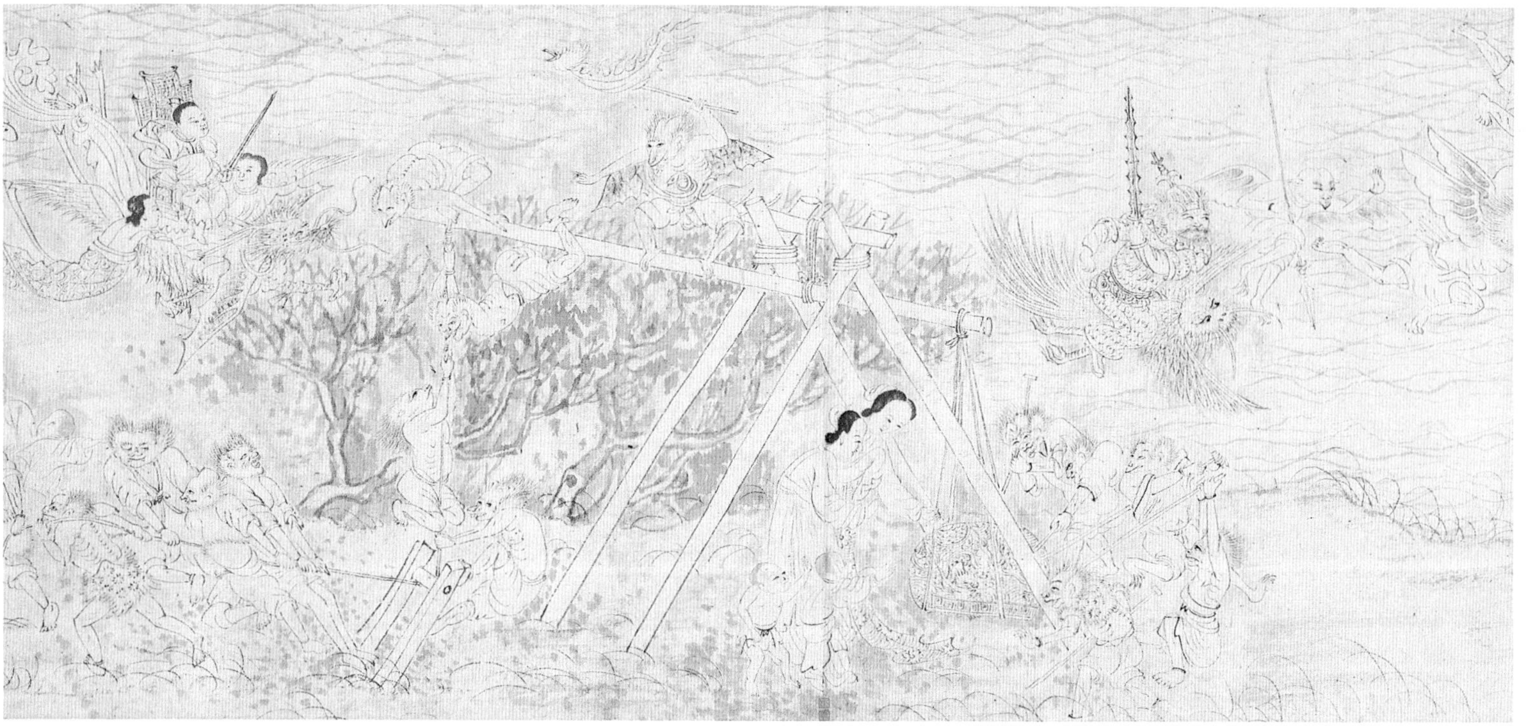

147
Shitao Yuanji (1641-1707)
The Conversion of Hariti to Buddhism
Qing dynasty, about l683
Handscroll; ink on paper.
27.2 x 353.3 cm.
Marshall H. Gould Fund. 56.1151

Shitao Yuanji, often mistakenly called Daoji, was a priest of the Linji branch of Chan *Buddhism. Perhaps the most influential painter and theoretician in the history of later Chinese painting, he left behind a corpus of work characterized by an inexhaustible variety of styles and themes. Of his figure paintings, all of which seem to date from the earlier period of his artistic career, this and a scroll representing the sixteen* lohans, *in the collection of New York's Metropolitan Museum, are the two best-known examples.*

According to the artist's inscription, the present handscroll was painted in Nanjing around the year 1683. It depicts in whimsical detail the conversion to Buddhism of the ogress Hariti, who devoured little children until the Buddha hid her own child, Pingala. Filled with remorse, she became a disciple of the Buddha.

The figures are drawn in the outline (bai miao) technique developed during the Northern Song dynasty by the great figure painter Li Gonglin (referred to in one of Shitao's seals). The landscape setting, on the other hand, is closely related to the expressive brushwork depicting the scenery around Mount Huang in an album in the Sumitomo collection.

148
Zhu Da (1626-1705)
Lotus: Homage to Xu Wei
Qing dynasty, 1689-90
Hanging scroll; ink on paper.
185 x 89.8 cm.
Keith McLeod Fund. 56.495

In this work the artist Zhu Da, better known by the sobriquet Bada Shanren, follows the style of the Ming dynasty master Xu Wei (1521-1593). One of the great eccentrics of the early Qing period, Zhu Da was renowned for his highly individualized calligraphy and ink paintings depicting a great variety of subject matters, in particular, pine trees, lotus, rocks, fish, and birds. The poem inscribed on this painting is the work of Xu Wei, except for a slight change in the wording by Zhu Da.

As a distant relative of the Ming imperial house Zhu Da often made symbolic reference in his work to the fall of the dynasty, which constituted a tragic turning point in his life. He entered monkhood to escape political persecution but became disillusioned with Buddhism after more than thirty years as a Chan *master. Zhu Da then burned his monk robes, and returned to his birthplace where he remained, disguised as a mad painter, until his death in the winter of 1705. It was during this period of his life that he painted this lotus, symbolizing Buddhism through its capacity to grow out of the mud and rise above the water, displaying its purity, beauty, and strength. In this case, however, the deteriorating lotus may represent the artist's disillusionment with the Buddhist faith as well as grief over the loss of his country, now in the hands of the Manchu conquerers.*

The spontaneity and forcefulness of the brushwork that forms the leaves and stems of the lotus is clearly derived from decades of study of Chan *Buddhism. The free and rhythmic strokes of the lotus stems attest to Zhu Da's affinity for combining word and image.*

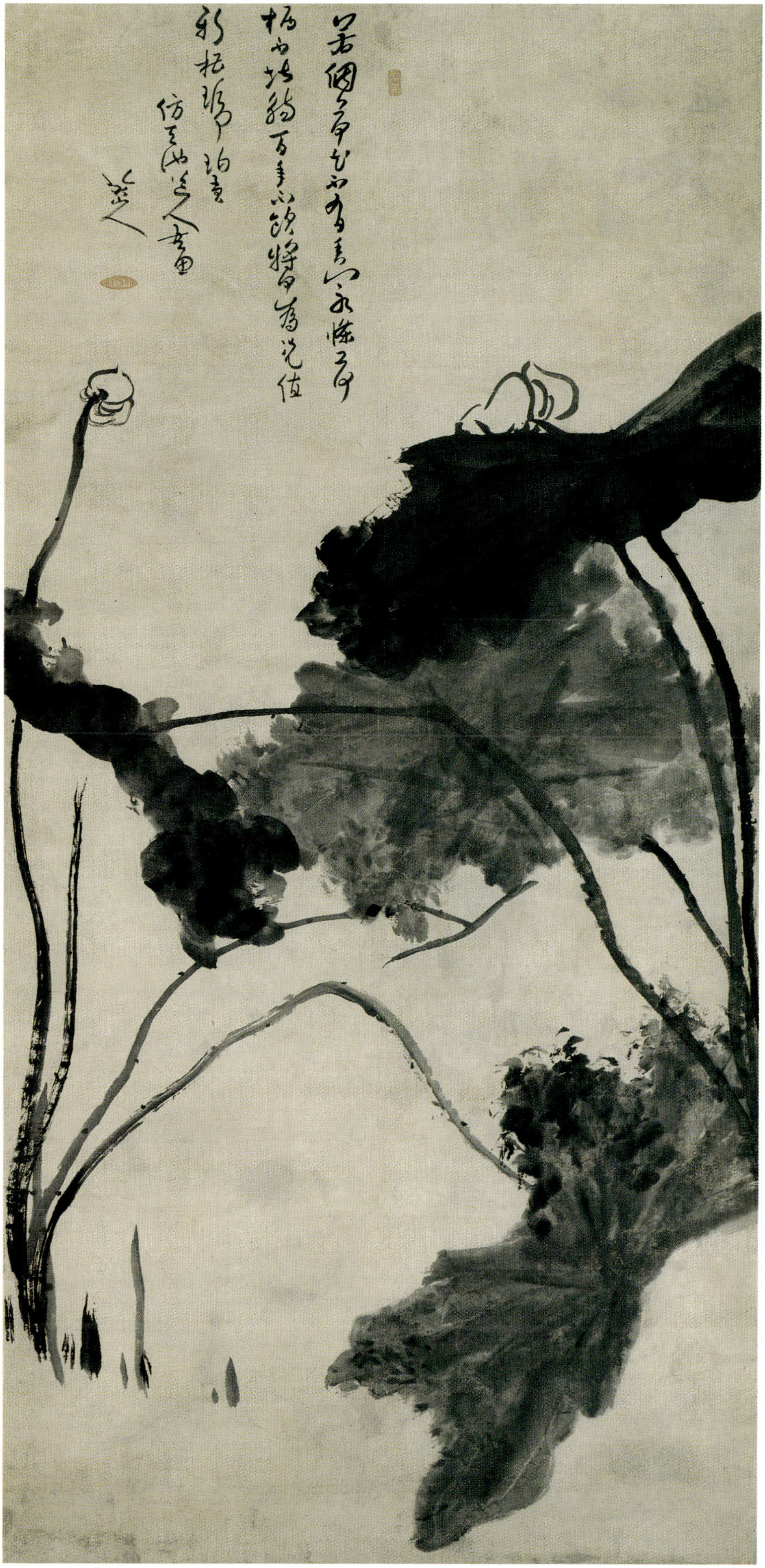

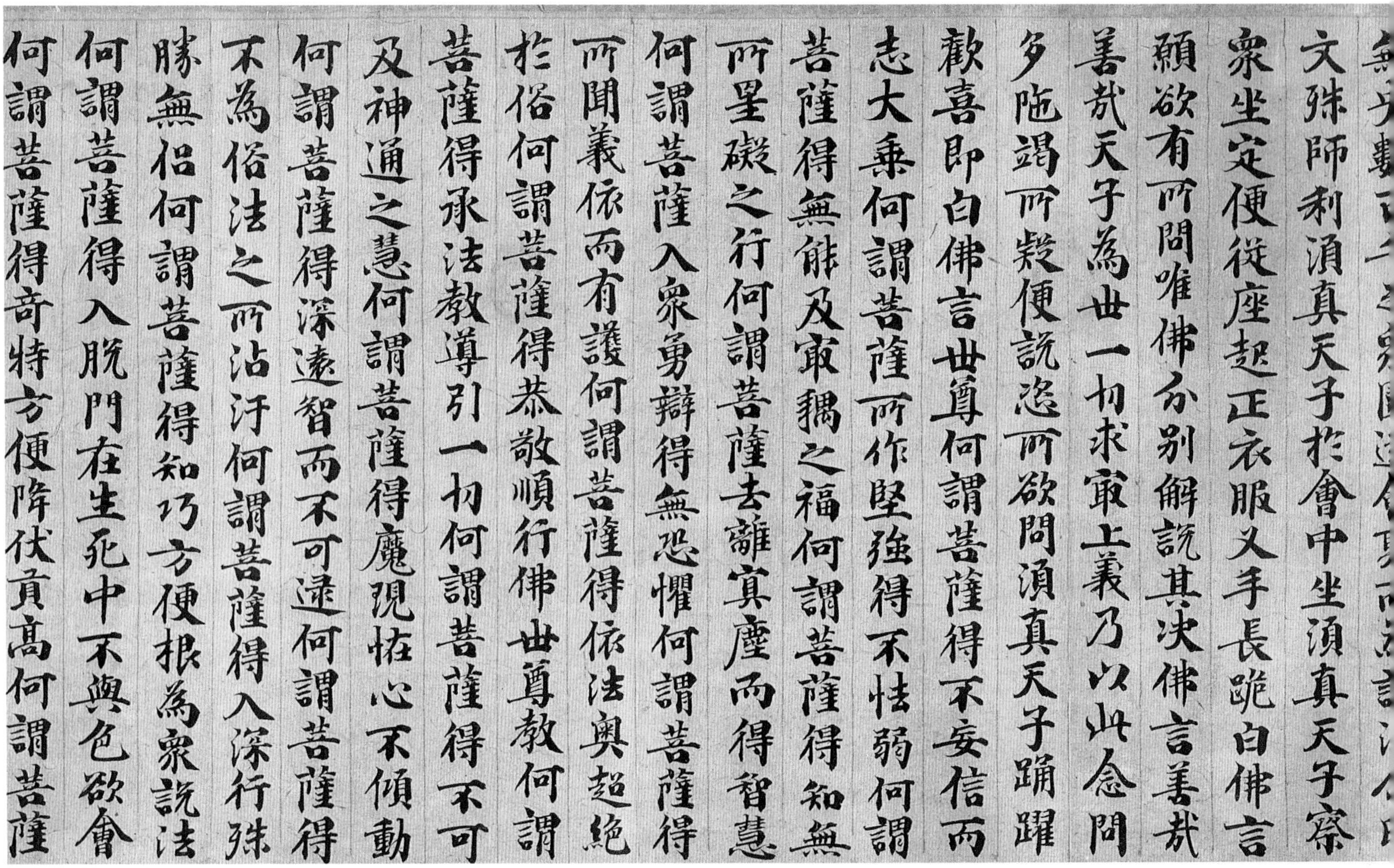

149
Shen Li (active mid-11th century)
Calligraphy in standard script:
Xu zhen tian zi jing
(Suvikranta Cintadevi Sutra)
Northern Song dynasty, dated 1069
Handscroll; ink on sutra paper.
24 cm. x 1,328 cm.
Keith McLeod Fund. 1977.176

Most early Chinese Buddhist scrolls of holy scriptures (sūtras) in Western collections come from the monastic library discovered eighty years ago in the cave-temple complex of Dunhuang in western China. This signed and dated sūtra scroll, on the other hand, once belonged to the collection of Emperor Qianlong (r. 1736-1795) and was probably made for a monastery in eastern China. The calligrapher Shen Li lived there, near the present Nanjing, and a number of similar scrolls have been excavated recently from sacred deposits in Buddhist pagodas in Jiangsu and Zhejiang.

The art of sūtra writing has always been considered a special branch of the art of calligraphy. It flourished especially during the Tang dynasty, when the great masters of calligraphy, often scholar-officials, joined professional sūtra calligraphers in producing copies of the holy scriptures. The Tang style had a lasting influence on later periods; even in this scroll, written more than a hundred years after the end of the dynasty, Tang characters are still very much in evidence. Details such as the red lines and the seventeen-word-per-column arrangement are standard Tang practice.

Because of the religious function of sūtras, the execution and structure of the characters and the relationship between them tend to emphasize clarity and precision more than do other types of calligraphy. The influence of a new aesthetics in calligraphy, developed by the Song scholar-official Cai Xiang, is almost absent in this scroll. In comparison with Tang examples, however, the work has less compositional symmetry and is less precise in its brushwork — qualities the Song emperor Huizong would have applauded, for he is known to have criticized the Tang sūtra style for rigidity, orderliness, and lack of spontaneity.

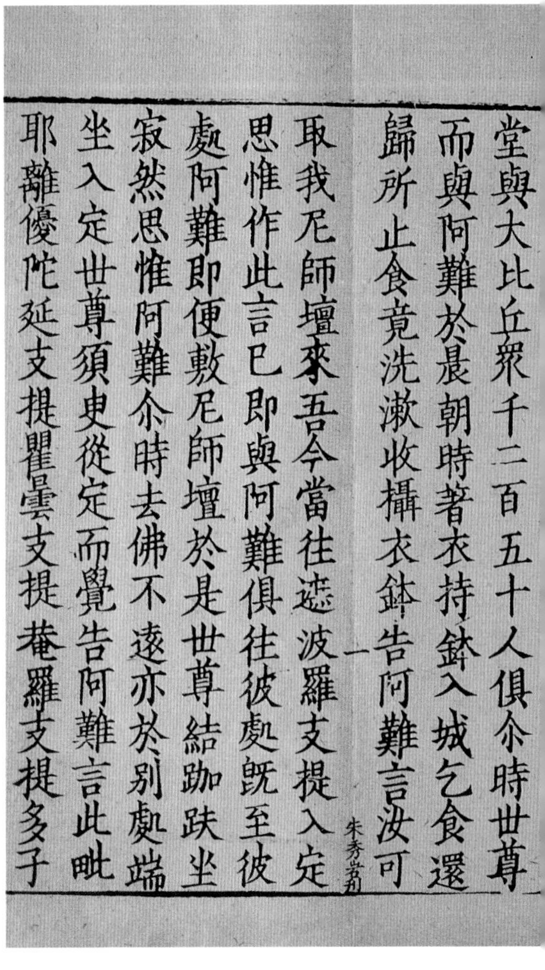

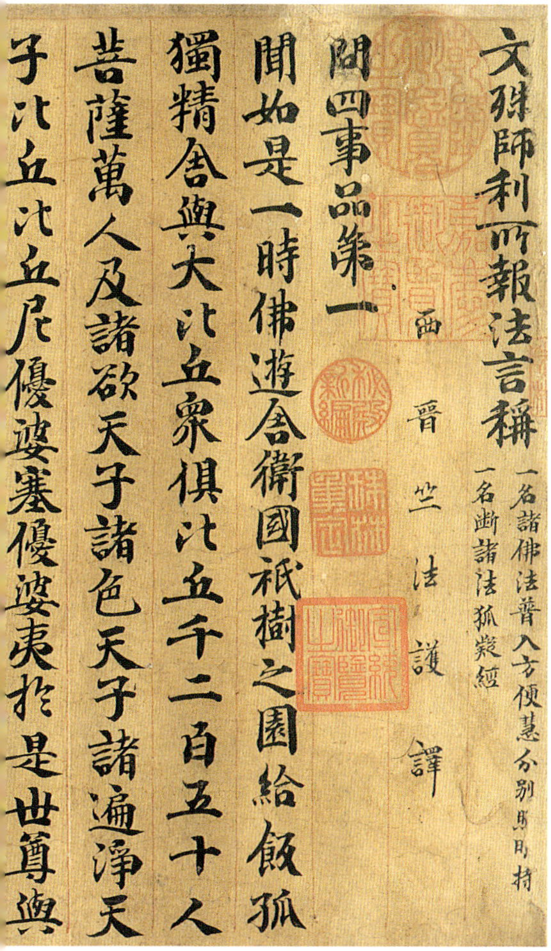
文殊師利所報法言稱 一名諸佛法普入方便慧分別身明持
一名斷諸法狐疑經
西晉竺法護譯
聞四事品第一
聞如是一時佛遊舍衛國祇樹之園給孤
獨精舍與大比丘衆俱比丘千二百五十人
菩薩萬人及諸欲天子諸色天子諸遍淨天
子比丘比丘尼優婆塞優婆夷於是世尊與

150
Buddhist *sūtra* with illustration:
Da bo nie pan jing
(Mahā-parinirvāṇa-sūtra)
Yuan dynasty, about 1301
Album of woodblock prints (Ji-sha edition). 30.2 x 11.2 cm.
Marshall H. Gould Fund. 1984.415

This woodblock print is a frontispiece illustration from the Jisha edition of the Buddhist Tripitaka*, which began to be printed in the Song dynasty (1231) and was completed during the Yuan dynasty (1322).*

The sūtra *is inscribed : "painted by Chen Sheng and printed by Chen Ning." Both names appear on at least six other woodblock-print* sūtra *illustrations, including five from the Jisha edition, published in Suzhou, and one from the* Hexi *edition of the Yuan* Tripitaka *in Uighur script, discovered in Xinjiang province (Chinese Turkestan). These woodblock prints were distributed thousands of miles apart for people who speak different languages and express themselves through different styles. The* Jisha *edition displays strong Nepalese and Tibetan influences typical of the Yuan dynasty, while the Tripitaka in Uigur script is typical of the Chinese orthodox style of the Liao-Jin period.*

With the invasion of the Mongols and the subsequent establishment of the Yuan dynasty, Tibetan Buddhism was introduced to China. The conventions used to depict facial features as well as fleshy body types are indicative of Tibetan influences. Decorative motifs and patterning used on the throne and robes here are also characteristic of Himalayan arts.

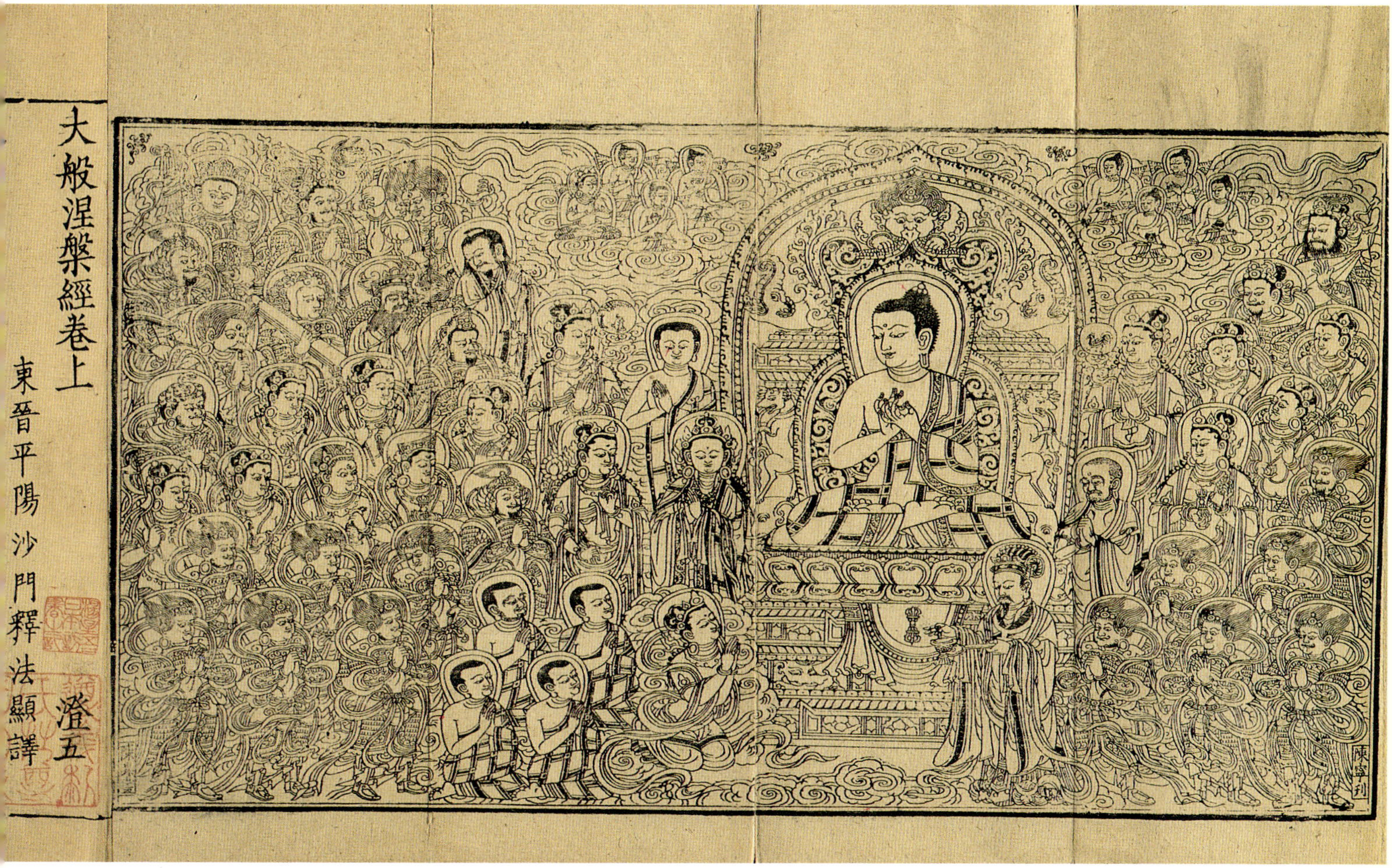

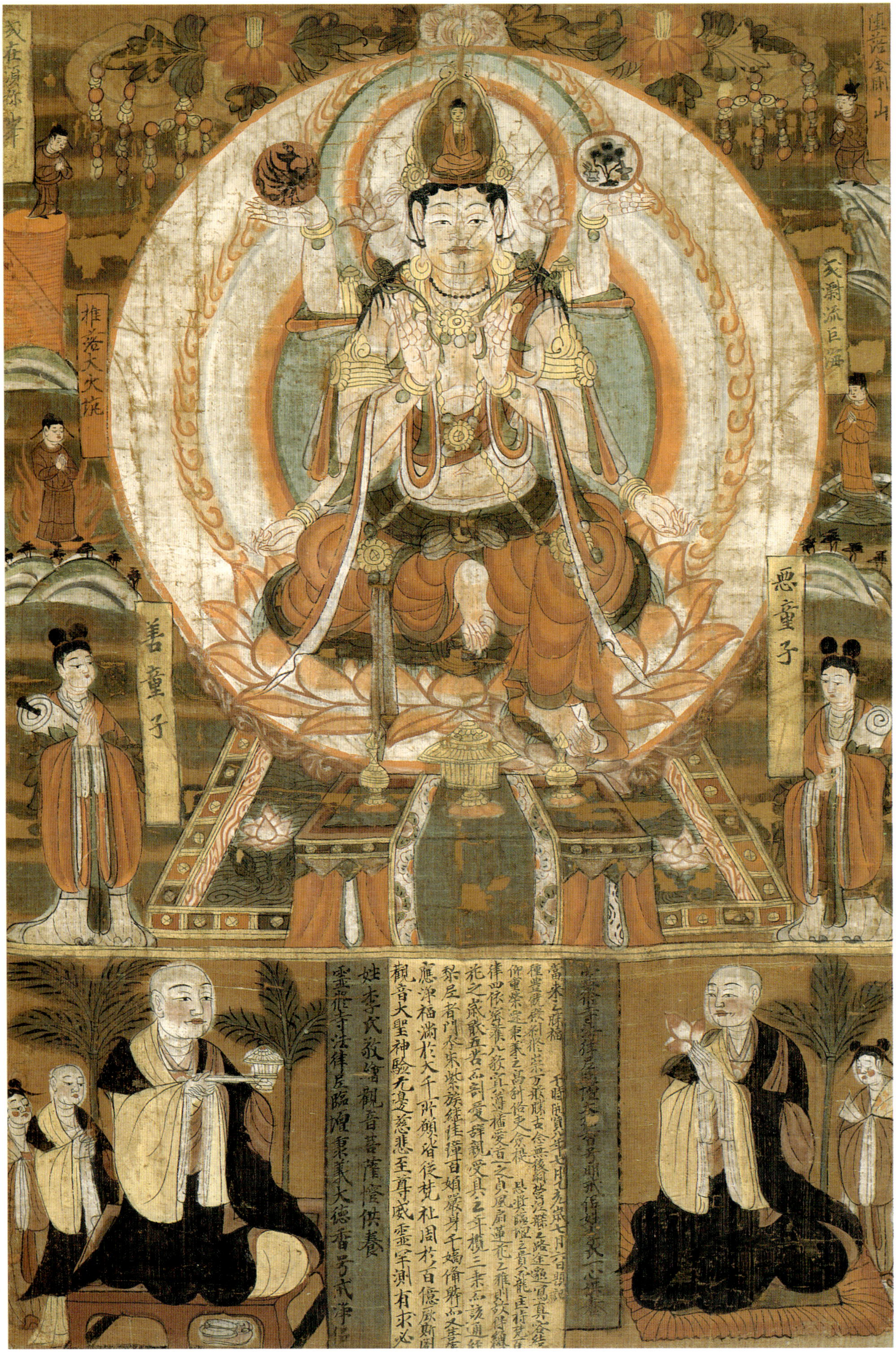
推落大火坑
或漂流巨海
善童子
惡童子
姓李氏敬繪觀音菩薩供養
靈巖寺法律臨壇東義大德香号戒淨
觀音大聖神驗无邊慈悲至尊威靈罕測有求必

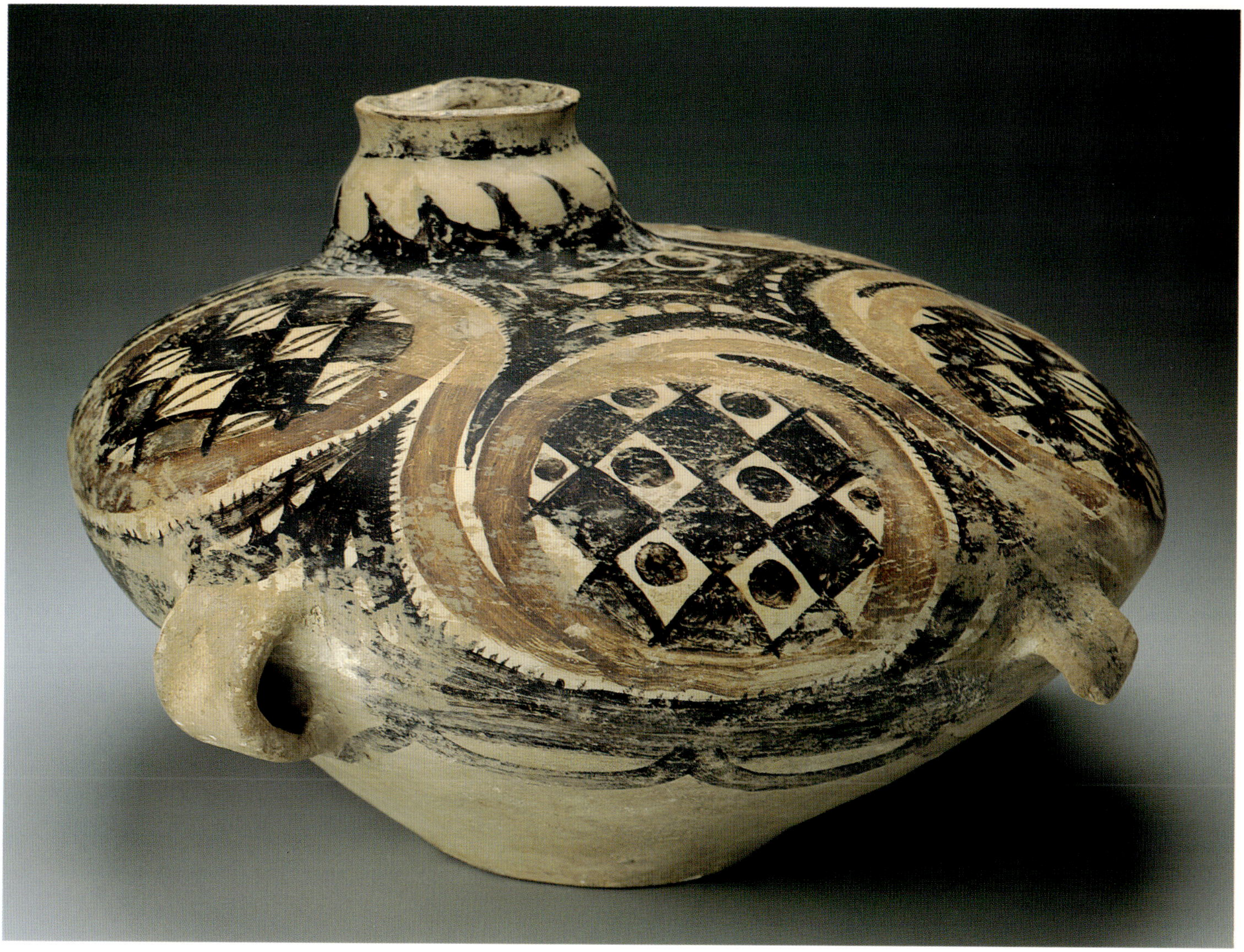

151
Avalokiteśvara Bodhisattva
Northern Song dynasty (from Dunhuang), dated 975
Hanging scroll mounted as panel; ink and colors on silk.
89 x 58.6 cm.
Maria Antoinette Evans Fund. 27.570

This painting of the Bodhisattva Avalokiteśvara (Guanyin) as "the savior from perils" was originally a votive hanging dedicated by the nuns of a Buddhist temple named "Ling Xiu Si." Avalokiteśvara is shown with six arms and seated on a lotus throne that rises from a pond. Of the six arms, the first pair is raised, supporting in each open palm the sun and moon, respectively. The second pair of hands is in the "sign of exposition," raised to the breast, each hand holding a long-stemmed lotus flower. The third pair is held at the sides, each hand forming possibly the "sign of bountifulness." On the crown is a seated figure of Amitābha, the Buddha of Infinite Light.

There are four separate scenes, two on either side of the central figure, illustrating subjects taken from the sūtra Miaofa Lianhuajing. *The scenes depict individuals in various fatal circumstances — about to be pushed off a cliff or engulfed in a pit of fire or a tidal wave. According to the* sūtra, *if an individual in such a dangerous situation concentrates all his attention on the power of Guanyin, he will be saved.*

On either side of the Bodhisattva stands a young person, the one on the proper right labeled "good young boy" and the one on the left "evil young boy," each holding a scroll. The story of these princes, who were brothers, is related in Buddhist scriptures. Briefly, the boys set out together to get possession of the jewel that grants all wishes. The good prince acquires it, but the evil one, after blinding his brother, steals the precious pearl. Upon recovering his sight and saving his brother from punishment at the hands of their father, the good prince proves to be an incarnation of Śākyamuni in a previous life; the evil one was Devadatta.

152
Spouted vessel with handles and lug
Gansu province, Neolithic period, Banshan type, middle of 3rd millennium B.C.
Earthenware with painted decoration over slip. H: 24 cm.
Gift of Mrs. Eugene Bernat and Anonymous Gift in memory of Paul Bernat. 1988.534

The unusual shape of this masterfully potted vessel makes it one of the rarest examples of Neolithic pottery from the Gansu-Qinghai area in western China. The solidity of construction and the unusual whiteness and refinement of the clay suggest that Banshan potters were more familiar with sophisticated firing and purification techniques than those who created the earlier Majia wares or the later Machang wares. The bold geometric designs characteristic of Banshan pottery — fluid, veinlike curves, checkerboard patterns, and the so-called sawtooth motif — accentuate the vessel's beautiful proportions.

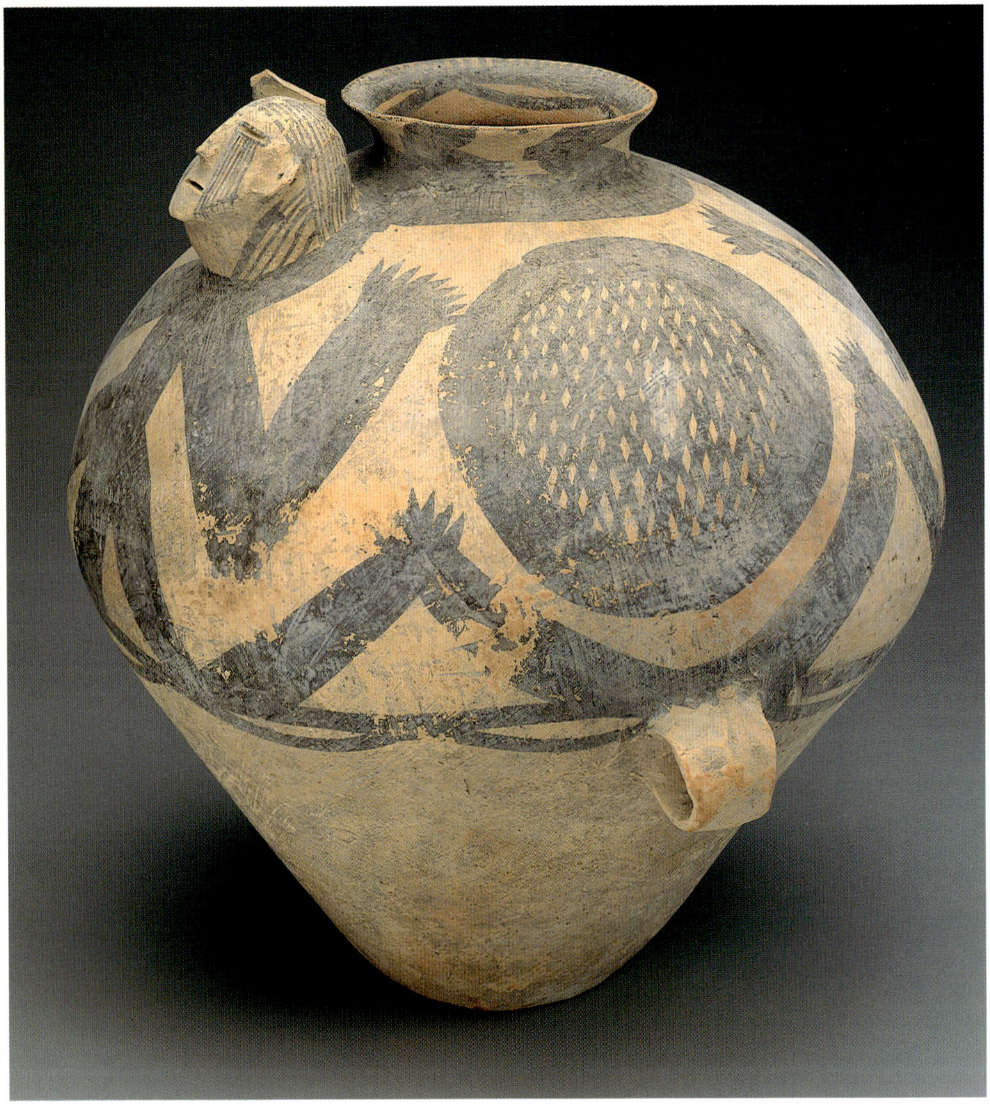

153
Vessel
Gansu province, Neolithic period, Machang type, 3rd millennium B.C.
Earthenware with painted decoration over slip. H: 39.5 cm.
E. Rhodes and Leona B. Carpenter Foundation Grant and Edwin E. Jack Fund. 1988.29

Naturalistically rendered human images seldom appear as decoration on Chinese Neolithic ceramics, most of which bear geometric designs often depicting a stylized body and limbs. For decades scholars have speculated about their meaning and interpreted them variously as a frog, a turtle, a bird, or a creature half-human, half-frog. Given the presence of the sculpted human head on this example, the tattooing of the face, the hair style, and the furlike motif at the elbows suggest that the figure represents a shaman or the chief of a tribe.

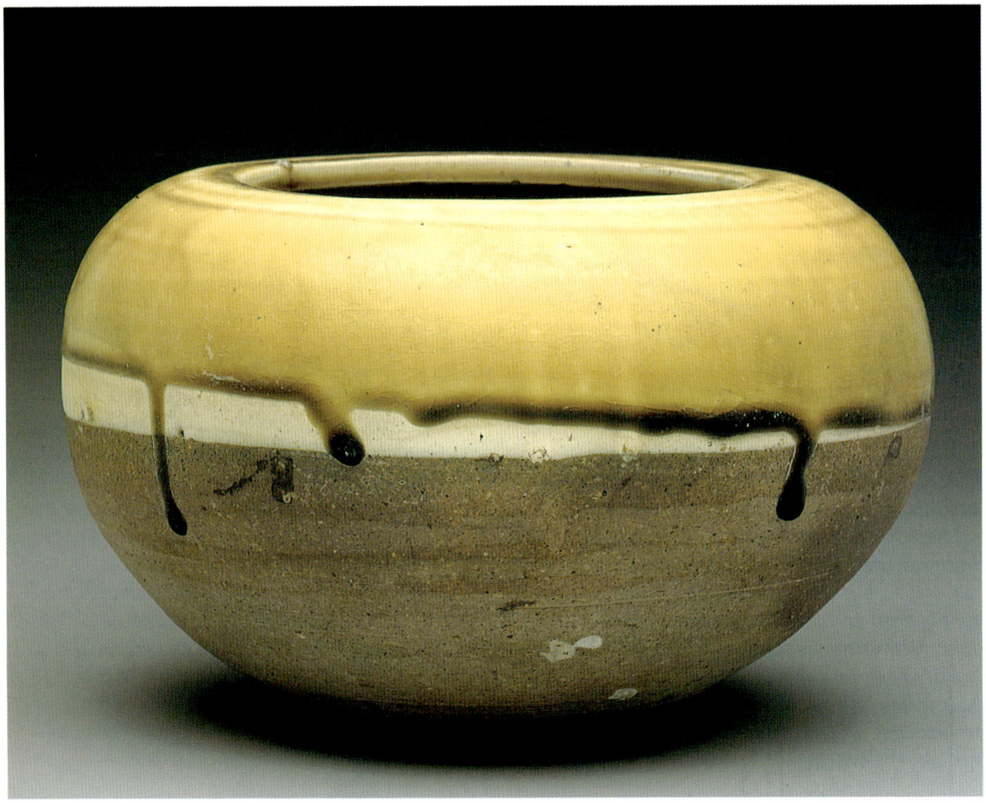

154
Jar
Northern Qi dynasty, late 6th century
Northern stoneware with yellow glaze over white slip. H: 13.5 cm.
Helen S. Coolidge Fund. 1990.120

Characterized by a sense of volume and solidity, this rare early globular jar is a brilliant example of the Northern Qi aesthetic. Its unadorned shape is enhanced by a pale yellowish glaze all but covering a layer of creamy white slip, which contrasts vividly with the bare reddish-brown lower half. While the interior is fully and evenly covered by a coat of celadon glaze, the potter emphasized the fluidity of the glaze on the exterior by applying it in an uneven, spontaneous manner so that it forms drips and does not completely cover the white slip.

This type of vessel would have been used in Buddhist rituals. Its shape probably derives from metalwork imported from Persia, with whom the Northern Qi court had close ties.

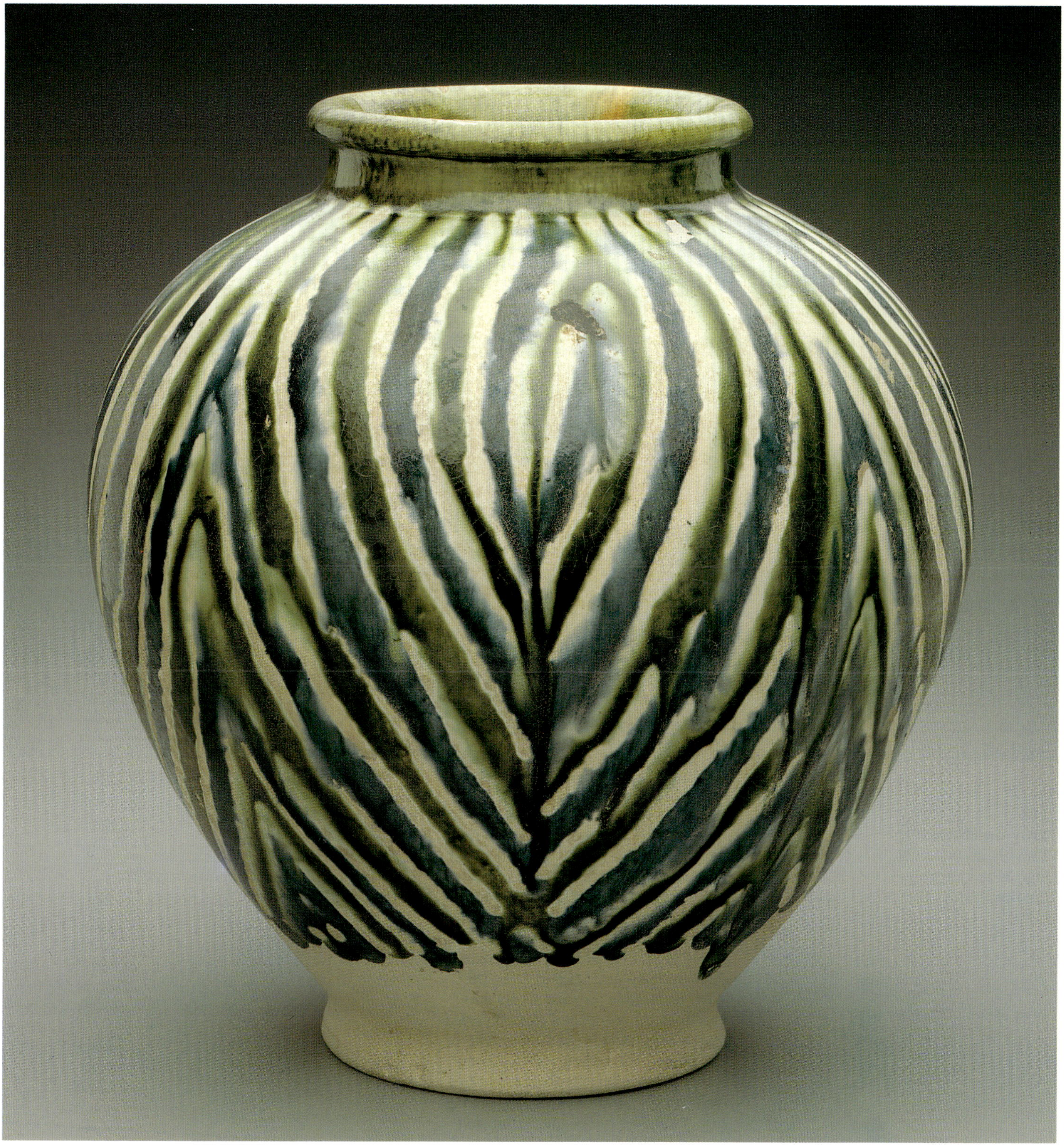

155
Jar
Tang dynasty, first half of 8th century
Glazed earthenware; geometric decoration in cobalt blue and copper green.
H: 28.2 cm.
Charles B. Hoyt Collection. 50.879

The production of glazed earthenwares in China reached its zenith during the first half of the eighth century, the most prosperous period of the Tang dynasty. The fine-textured clay used is white or light buff in color after firing, the color glazes are brilliant and clear, and the potting is strong and sensitive at the same time. Glazing techniques included dripping, painting (brushing), and a wax-resist method for "reserved" patterns. Usually applied over a transparent lead glaze, the color glazes ran into each other and formed drops along the lower edges, creating effects not unlike those of acrylic paints on an unprimed canvas. Indeed, the artistic sensibility that underlay the decorative glazing of Tang earthenwares finds striking parallels in the abstract art of North America in the past three decades.

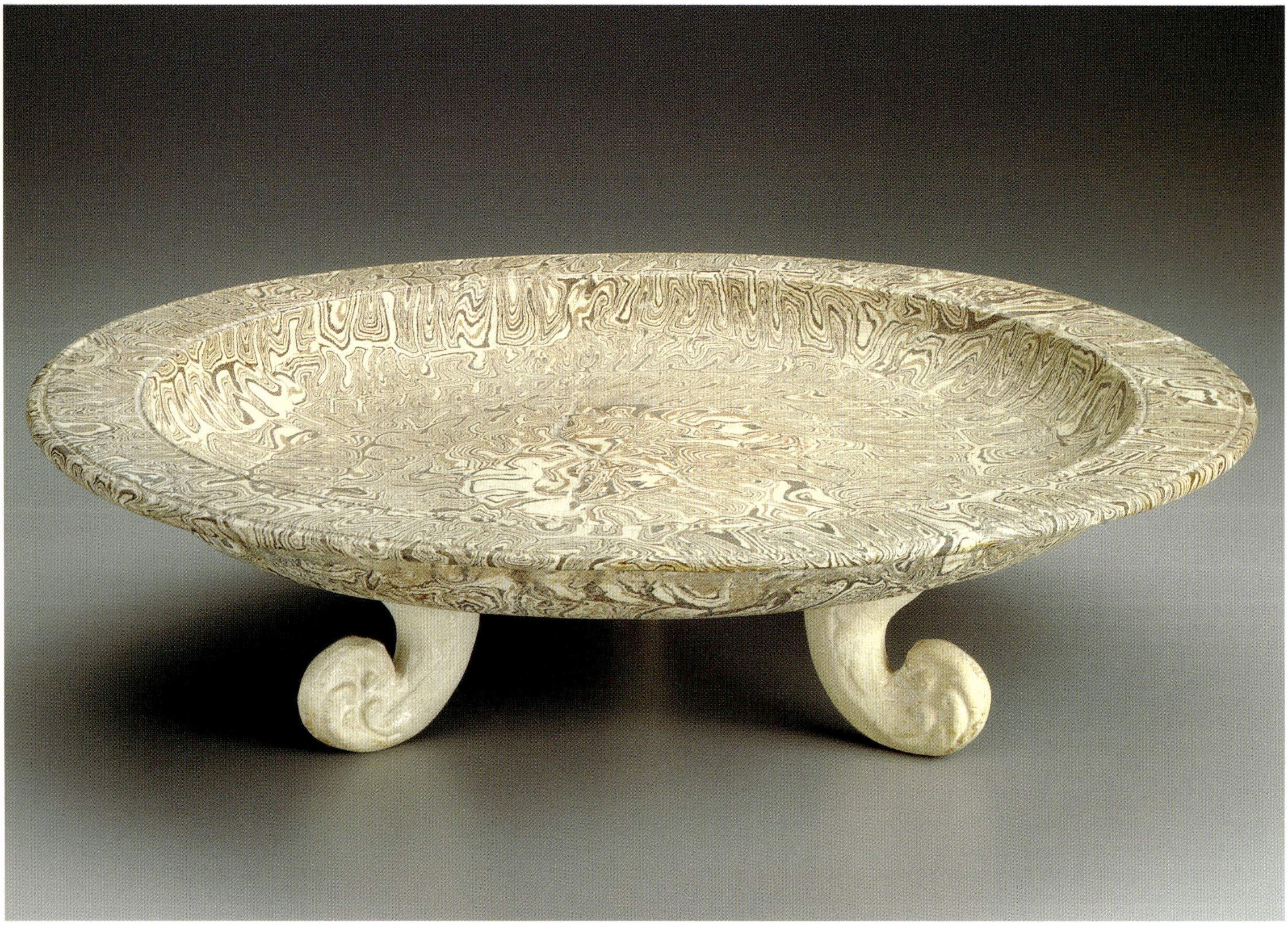

156
Tray on three feet
Tang dynasty, early 8th century
Marbleized earthenware. H: 8.3 cm.
Charles B. Hoyt Collection. 50.1979

Known as jiao tai *in Chinese, marbleized ware appears to have originated in the Tang period. No pre-Tang examples have been discovered, and although Song and later periods continued this potting technique, the Tang dynasty shows the most variety. Even horses of marbleized clay were discovered in the Tang tomb of Princess Yong-tai, buried in A.D. 706.*

The inspiration for these works may have been the marbleized glass imported from western Asia to the Tang capital in the late seventh or early eighth century A.D. Chinese potters probably tried to imitate the effect of such glass by mixing clay of different colors and cutting and reorganizing it in blocks to be reformed for modeling. Close examination reveals the pressed effects of molding. Marbleized ware was once thought to have been shaped by traditional potting techniques, but the pulling and shaping of the clay would have destroyed the distinctive patterns.

Burial accretions covering half the body of this exceptionally large plate were recently cleaned away, revealing it for the first time in its entirety. Made of cut segments of white, rust, and brown clays formed into a spiral, the thick body rounds into short tapering sides; two pressed lines border either edge of the flat extended lip. Three supporting feet are molded of creamy tan clay in a typical Tang scroll design.

157
Jar with handles
Tang dynasty, 9th century
Northern stoneware with tea-dust glaze. H: 13.3 cm.
Anonymous Gift. 1990.107

The finely speckled "tea-dust" (cha hua mo) *glaze on this jar was invented during the Tang dynasty (ninth century); however, the technique was lost soon afterward and was not rediscovered until the Qing dynasty (seventeenth century). Early examples are exceedingly rare, and of the few that exist none rivals the elegantly proportioned ovoid shape and rich glazing of this particular piece. The clay body, visible on the unglazed lower portion, is a highly refined buff-white type.*

This jar was originally part of the famous Eugene Bernat collection in Boston, loaned to the Museum of Fine Arts from 1947 until 1980, when the family sold the collection at auction. Its return to the Museum is a welcome homecoming.

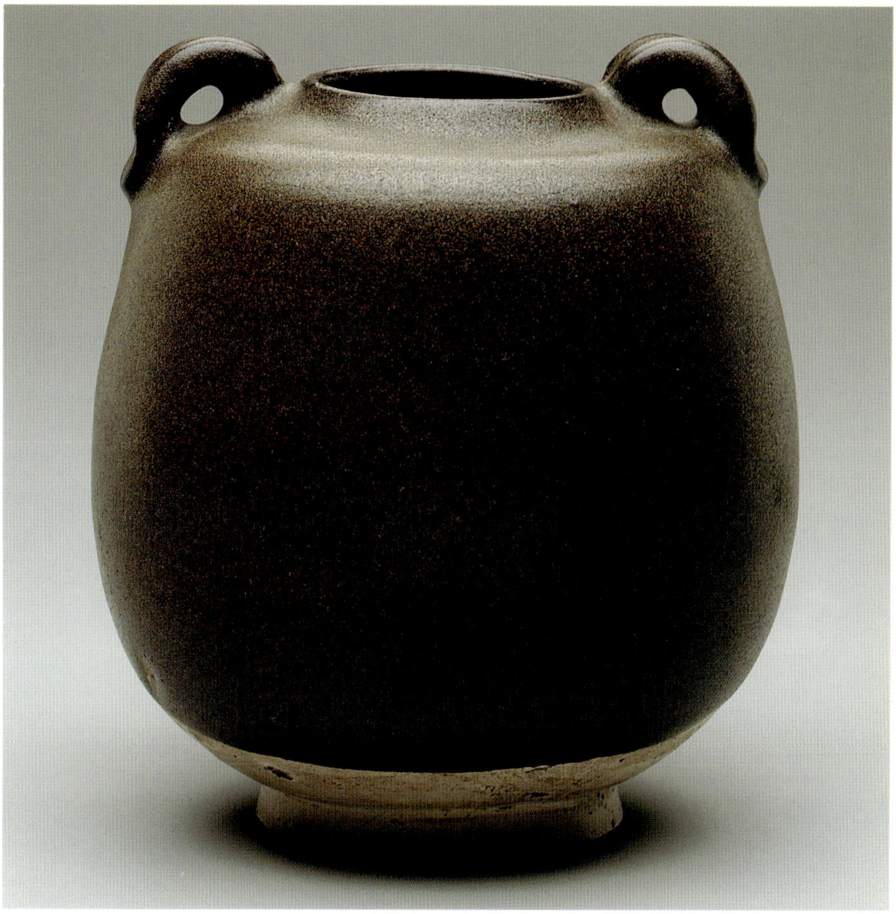

158
Ewer with double spout
Northern Song dynasty, early 11th century
Northern green-glazed stoneware with deep carved floral design.
H: 19.7 cm.
Charles B. Hoyt Collection. 50.2009

This double-spouted ewer is often cited as one of a few known examples of the so-called Dong ware — identified by scholars as an imperial greenware commissioned by the Emperor Huizong (r. 1101-1126) of the Northern Song dynasty. However, no archaeological evidence has been found to substantiate the existence of a Dong kiln. Moreover, the deeply carved and strongly incised decoration of the Boston ewer and related pieces are more akin to the style and aesthetics of early Northern Song greenwares, produced at the Yaozhou kilns in Shaanxi province, than to the late Northern Song taste associated with the Emperor Huizong's court, which was characterized by restrained shapes with lush, sensual glazes and minimal decoration. Further excavations in China are needed to determine the validity of the Dong-ware classification and the position of these ceramics in the Northern greenware tradition.

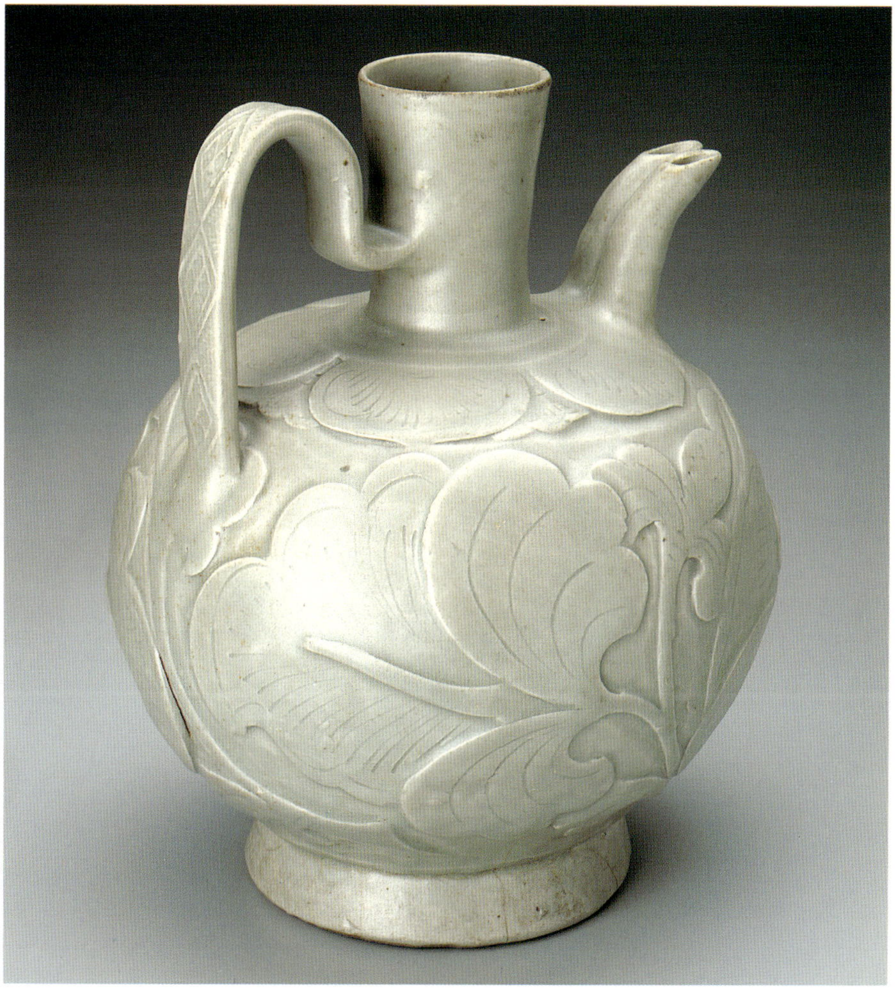

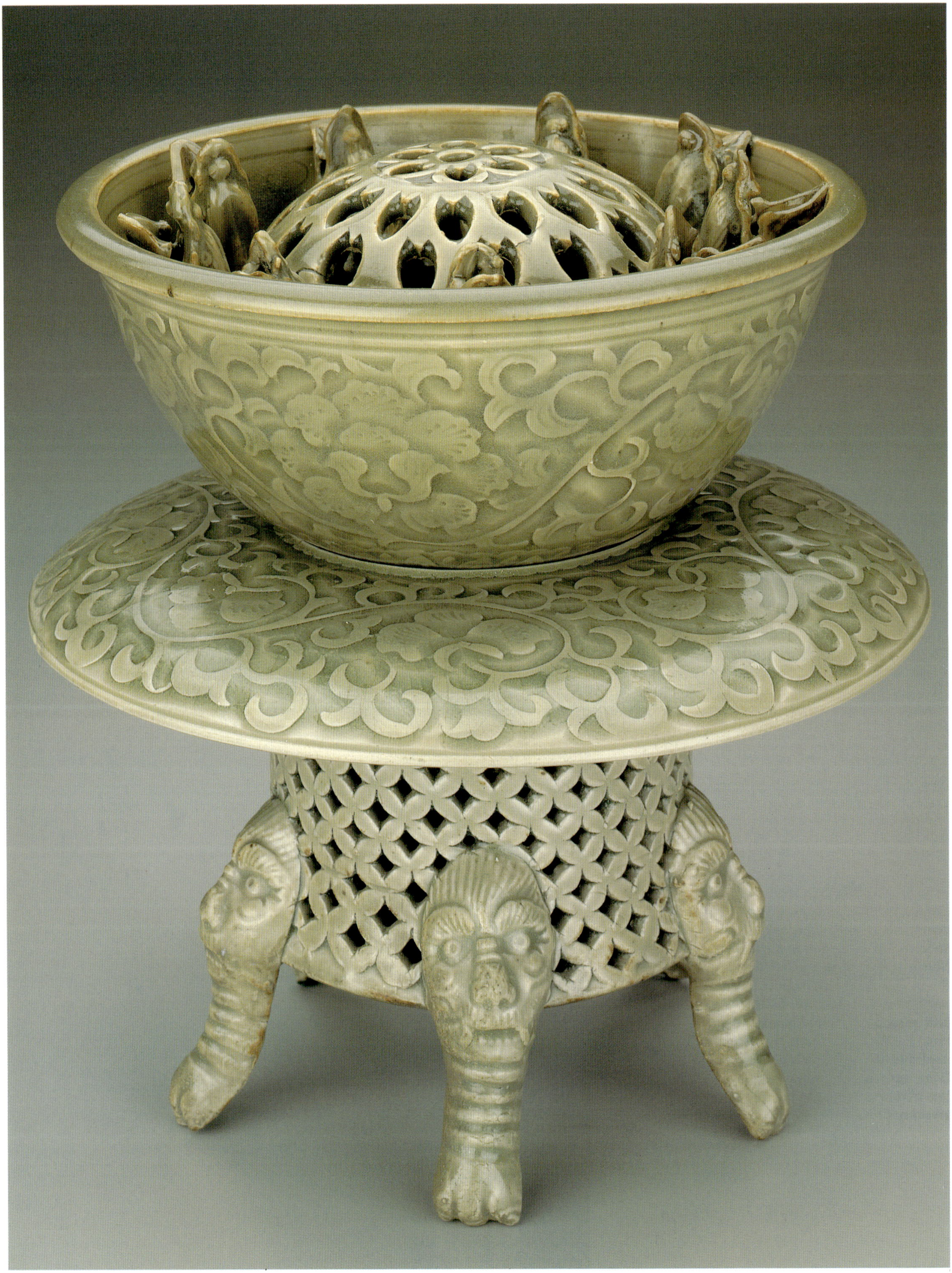

159
Ceremonial bowl and stand
Northern Song dynasty, 11th century
Yaozhou glazed stoneware; carved and incised decoration. H: 21.6 cm.
Charles B. Hoyt Collection. 50.939 and 50.943

The bowl is a unique Yaozhou piece, there being no other known examples of this type. It has deep curving sides and a slightly flaring high foot. The upper portion develops into an everted lip with a rounded edge. Inside is a dome with carved geometric openwork and an incised wave pattern, presumably a suitable habitat for the "King of the Seas" dragons whose heads extend upward with open mouths. The exterior is decorated with carved floral designs and incised blossoms under an olive-green glaze. The base and inside of the foot were glazed brown, leaving only a narrow band of unglazed sandy foot ring to reveal a grayish clay body. Especially impressive is the sharp and precise carving of the openwork on the dome.

The stand has a wide mushroomlike rim flange with a deep cavity in the center surrounded by an openwork body, which is then supported by five monster-headed legs with three-toed paws. The surface of the flange is carved much the same as the exterior of the bowl. It is also glazed olive-green, except for the interior of the cavity and the tips of the feet. Although we cannot be absolutely certain that the bowl and the stand were created as a set, they fit perfectly when joined, forming a unified shape. Some scholars believe that the stand was intended to be used as a base for an incense burner, while the bowl was most likely used for flower arrangements in Buddhist ceremonies.

160
Vase
Northern Song dynasty, 11th century
Cizhou glazed stoneware; carved floral design. H: 42.8 cm.
Charles B. Hoyt Collection. 50.1056

This ovoid vase with a long neck and wide, saucer-shaped mouth is covered with carved decoration of peonies and lotus leaves, partially cut through the white slip to the stained clay body. The technique is typical of wares of the Cizhou type, which were made all over northern China during the Song period. Their exact provenance has not yet been firmly established. The present vase has been described as a product of the Xiuwu kilns at Dangyangyu (Henan province), but recently a similar piece has been published as a product of kilns in Dengfeng.

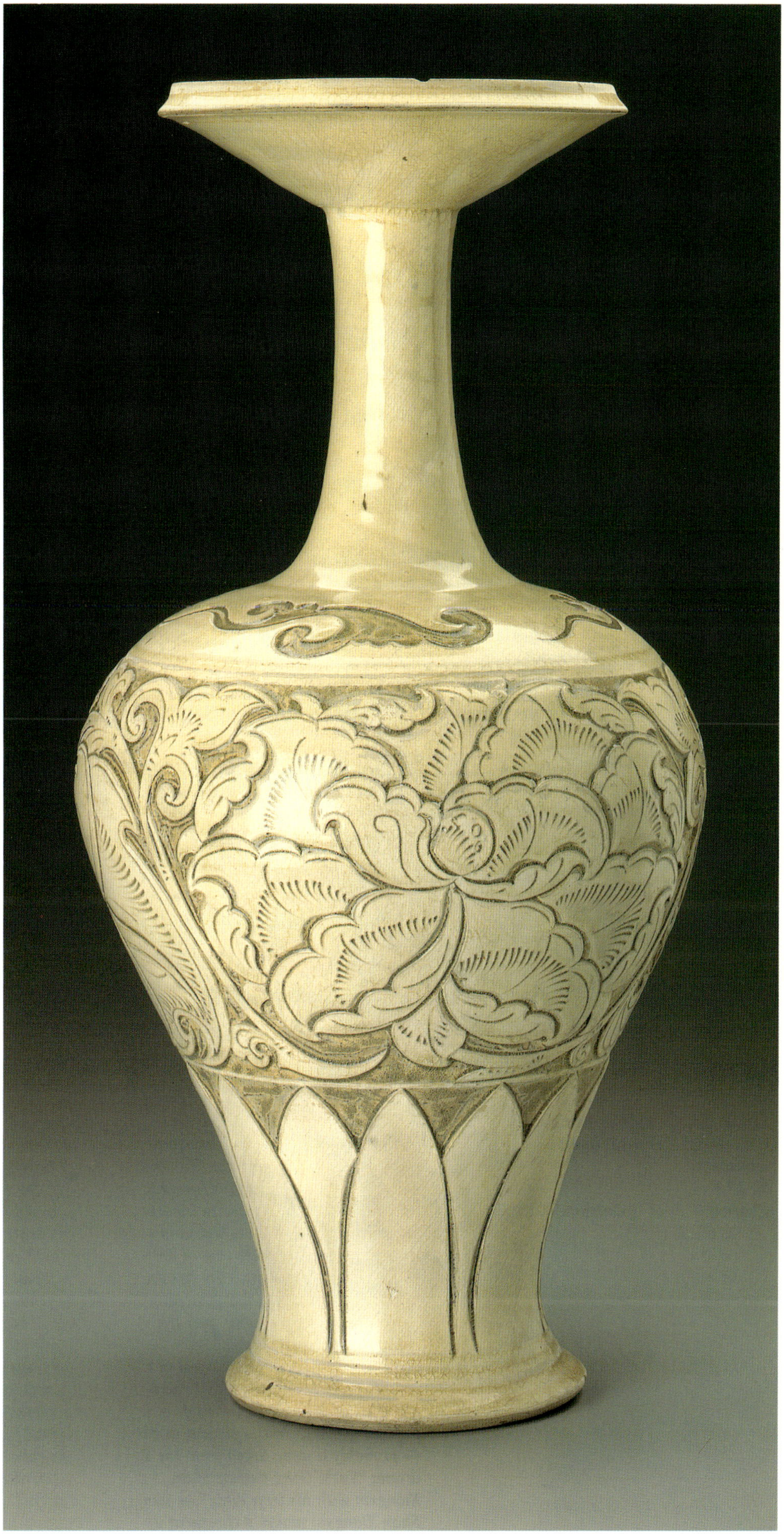

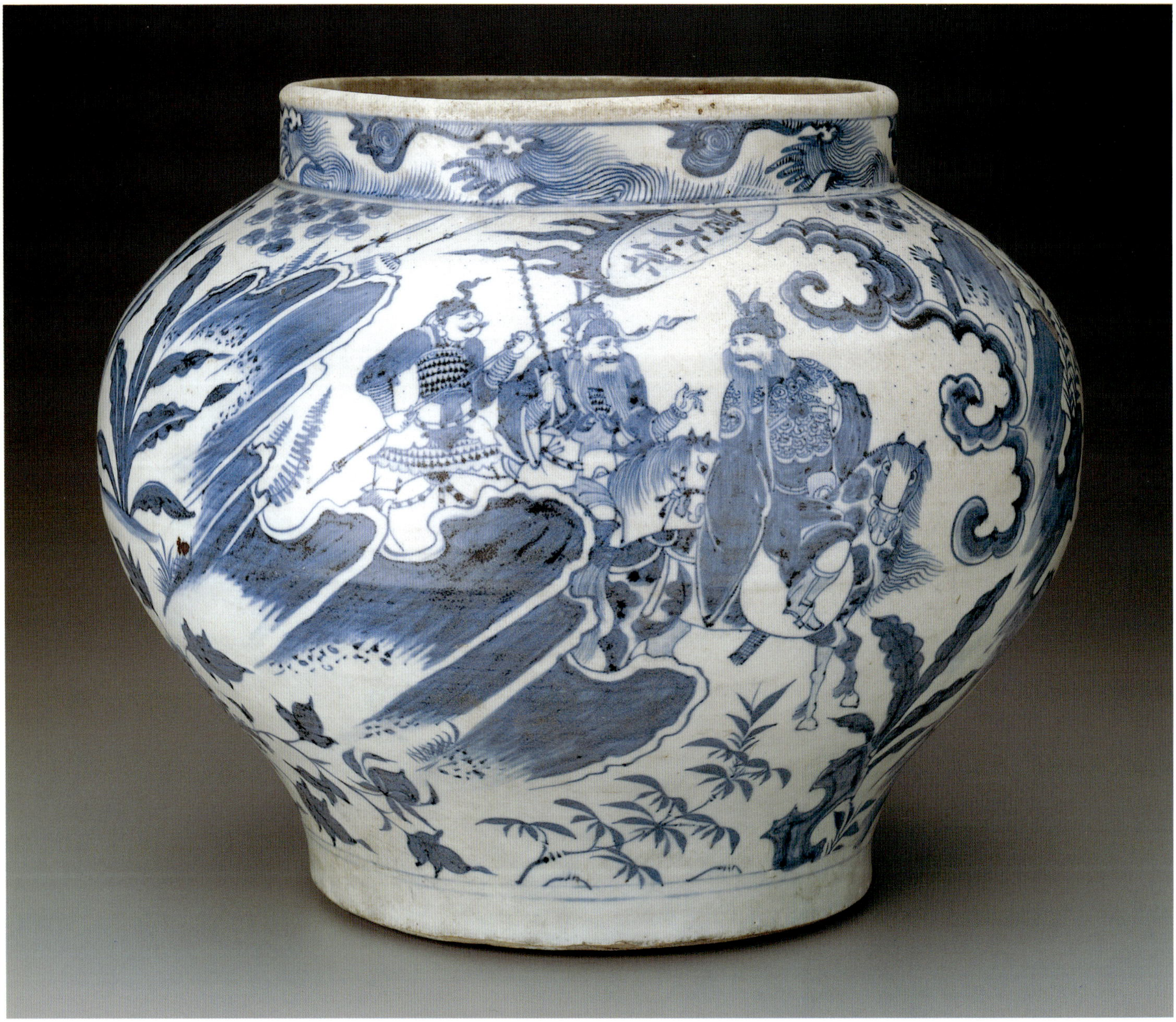

161
Jar
Late Yuan dynasty, 14th century
Jingdezhen porcelain; painted in underglaze blue with figures in a landscape.
H: 27.8 cm.
Charles B. Hoyt Collection. 50.1339

Porcelain decorated in underglaze cobalt blue was produced in the Yuan period mainly for the export market. As there was a sizable Islamic trading community living in the port cities on the southern coast of China and since the Middle East was the biggest market for Chinese trade porcelain, a strong Islamic influence is discernible on these early blue-and-white wares. This is especially true of the pictorial composition, which always consists of traditional Chinese motifs arranged as purely decorative elements over the entire surface of the vessel.

Occasionally, the main subject of the decoration derives from illustrations to historic tales played on the stage of the popular theater. In the present instance — probably a scene taken from the Yuan drama "Yuchi Gong defeats Shan Xiongxin with his Iron Whip" — General Shan Xiongxin makes a charge at a group of figures, one of them identified by a banner as Emperor Taizong, the founder of the Tang dynasty. Yuchi Gong, who, as one of the chief generals in Taizong's army, helped to found the dynasty, rides beside his liege holding his famous weapon, the iron whip.

In a painted or woodblock-printed illustration to the story, the background would consist of a conventional landscape in which spatial elements play an important part in the composition. Here, however, the "landscape" is made up of incongruous components such as bamboo growing beside rocks, peony bushes, and cloud forms, filling up every available space in the background. The robust form of the jar, the brilliance of the cobalt blue, and the vigorous brushwork all contribute to a feeling of exuberance and vitality befitting an artistic expression in its nascent form.

162
Dish
Qing dynasty, Yongzheng period (1723-1735)
Jingdezhen porcelain with overglaze sepia enamel painting and calligraphy. H: 3.3 cm.
Gift of Paul and Helen Bernat. 61.1255

Besides the refined shape and glaze typical of Qing porcelains, this dish is notable for the painting of the sepia figural decoration, far rarer than landscape during the period. It is remarkable to see achieved through firing and glazing techniques what is usually done through the media of paper or silk. Related to seventeenth-century figure painting, the style is, however, not as eccentric as works by the masters Chen Hongshou and Cui Zizhong, although it was probably influenced by them. The story represents the famous Northern Song literati artist Mi Fu (1052-1107), accompanied by a boy servant, demonstrating his appreciation of the beauty in nature by paying respects to a naturally shaped and weathered fantastic Taihu rock. In the upper right corner is a two-line inscription identifying the subject matter. "Da," written in seal script in a double square with overglaze red enamel, is possibly the name of the artist. The entire painting is shaded to show the depths of the rock and the folds of the drapery. Faces and hands are colored with a slightly pinkish overglaze enamel.

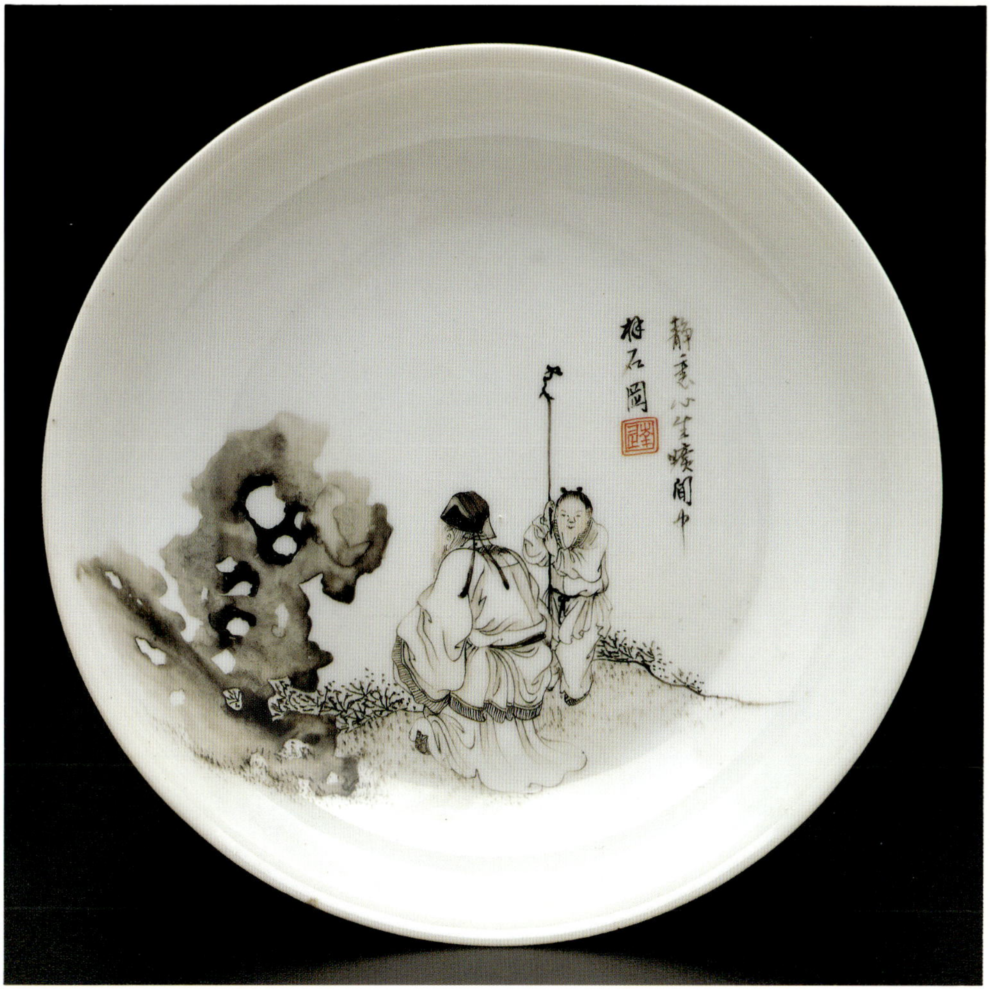

163
Bowl
Qing dynasty, Kangxi period (1662-1722)
Jingdezhen porcelain; enameled floral decoration; four-character mark written in enamel on the base. H: 6.4 cm.
Gift of Paul and Helen Bernat.
1977.760

The thinly potted body and vibrant colors of this elegant bowl represent a high point in the production of wares decorated with overglaze enamels at the imperial kilns in the late Kangxi era. The use of overglaze enamel to decorate porcelain works was one of the principal technological innovations achieved during the reign of the emperor Kangxi (1662-1722). Distinguished by the brilliance of their colors, these overglaze-enameled porcelains reflect the taste of the non-Chinese rulers of the Qing dynasty.
The masterful painting of these flowers is reminiscent of contemporaneous paintings and textiles. Produced at the ceramic center Jingdezhen, the porcelain was likely painted at the emperor's request by a court painter and then refired in a special kiln in the Forbidden City.

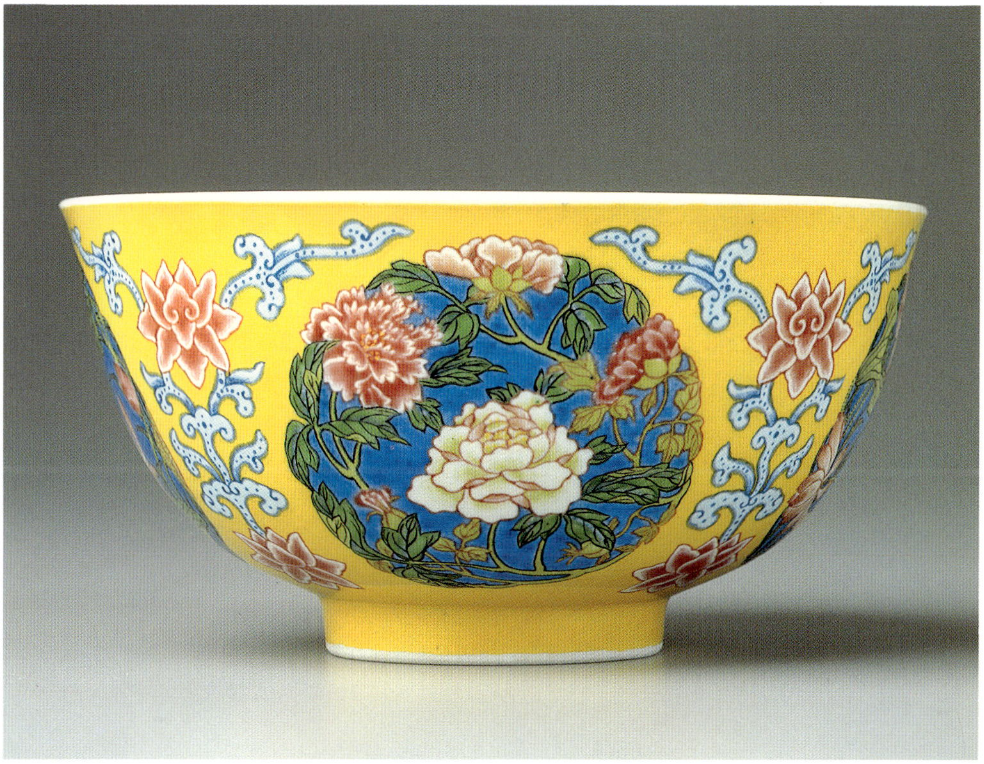

164
Head of a *lohan*
Southern Song dynasty,
11th-12th century
Dry lacquer. H: 30.6 cm.
Charles B. Hoyt Collection. 50.1937

Lohans are enlightened Indian sages, and in Chinese Buddhist art they are represented with facial features that the Chinese believed to be typically Indian. This lohan *is shown with open mouth, as if he were chanting. He has a long nose, elongated earlobes, and a wrinkled forehead. The head is all that is left of a statue made in a technique known in China as early as the sixth century. A dry-lacquer statue is created by forming the basic shape in clay and using it as a foundation for layers of hemp cloth drenched in lacquer, applied over the clay core until the required thickness is obtained. Details are modeled in lacquer paste on the cloth. Once the lacquer has dried, the clay foundation is removed, leaving a hollow lacquer figure that can be transported easily.*

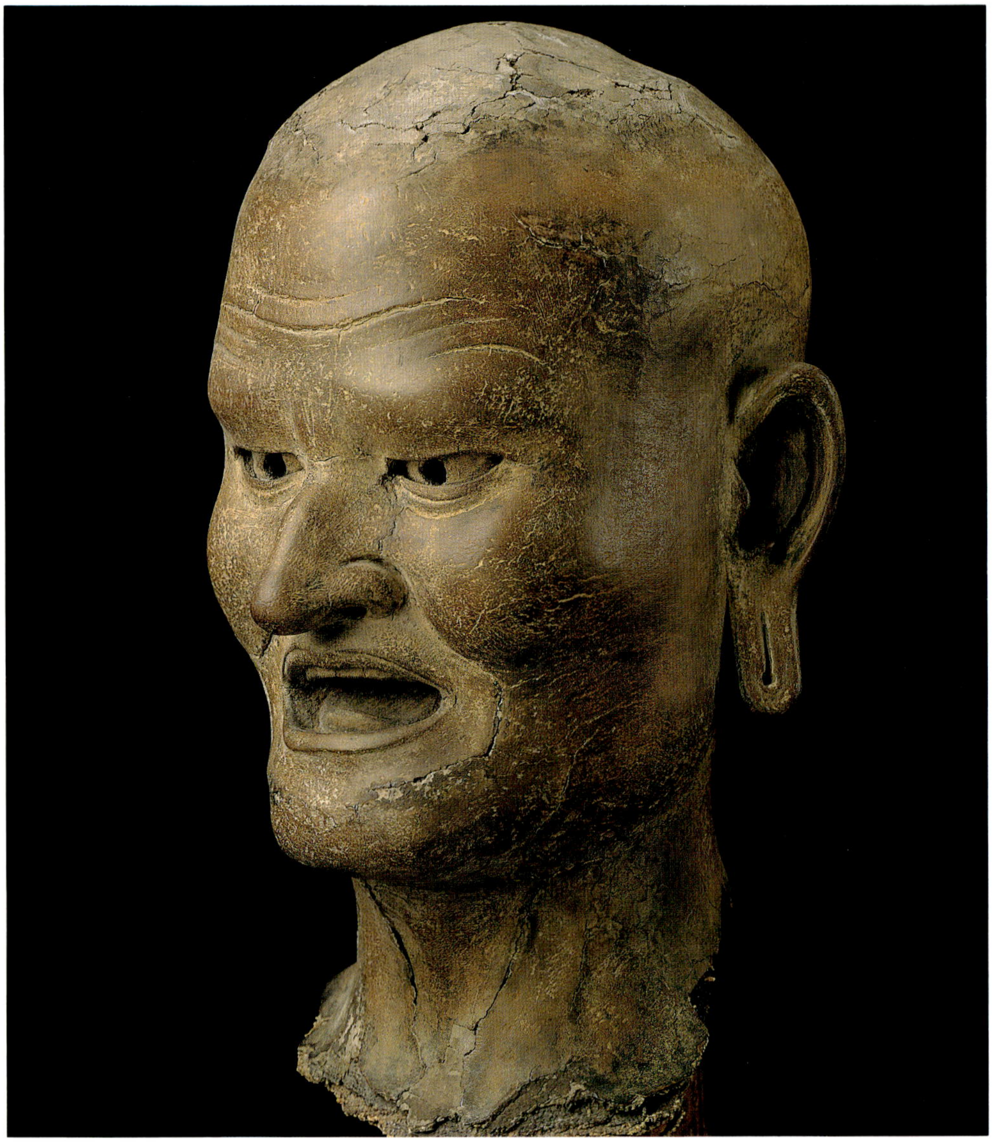

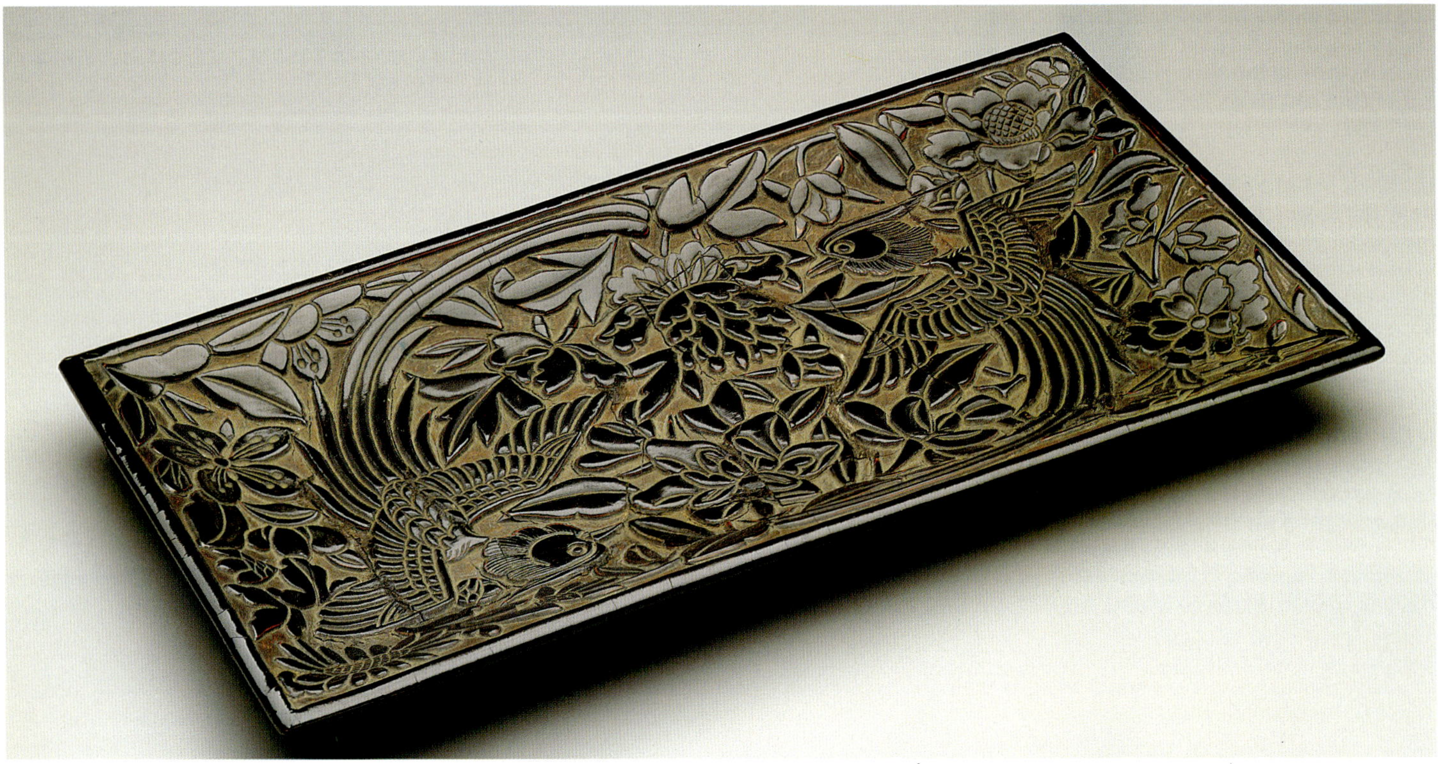

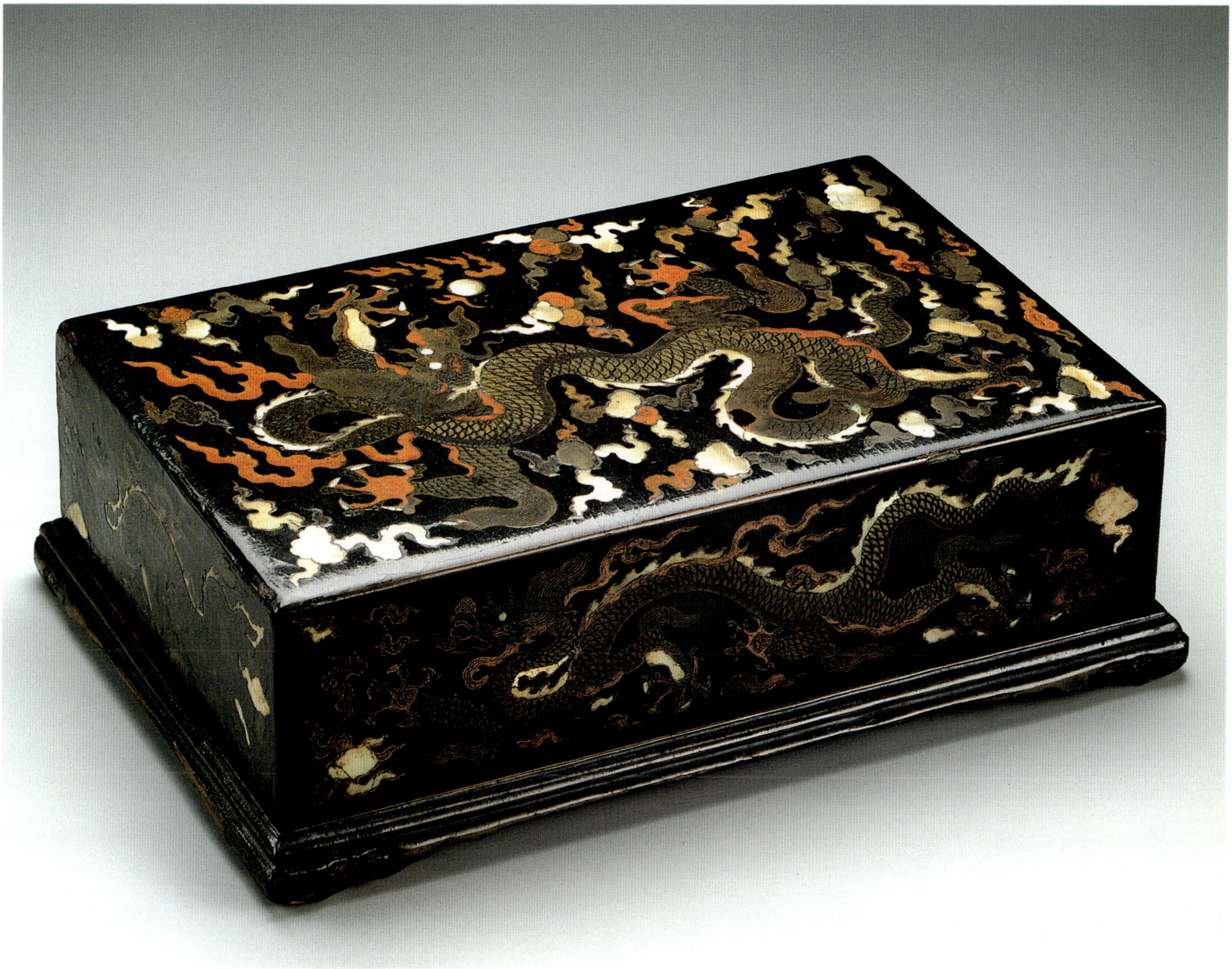

165
Tray with bird and flower design
Southern Song or Yuan dynasty,
13th century
Carved lacquer. L: 23 cm.
Asiatic Curator's Fund. 58.689

Literary evidence indicates that the technique of carving lacquer began in the Song dynasty, but there are very few pieces of carved lacquer extant from this period. Among the best candidates for a Song date in carved lacquer are several objects in the Enkaku-ji in Kamakura, which were brought to the temple by the monk Xu Ziyuan in the year corresponding to 1279 (according to the records of the temple). Several other pieces, including the present example, can be dated to the thirteenth century by comparison with the Enkaku-ji group.

On the back of this tray is the incised inscription jiawu Lu Pu zao *("made by [the] Lu [family] shop in the year* jiawu*"). (It is most likely that the cyclical date of* jiawu *corresponds to the year 1294, but the date of 1234 cannot be ruled out.) Comparable marks appear on two carved lacquer pieces dated to the thirteenth century, one of them conceivably from the same shop as the MFA example. Incised with the mark* Hongfu Qiao Lu Pu zao *("made by the Lu [family] shop of [the district of] Hongfu Qiao"), a rectangular covered box, in the collection of the National Museum in Tokyo, is carved in a similar style. The other piece, a rectangular dish in the Tokugawa Art Museum, has an incised inscription reading:* wushen Ruan Pu zao *("made in the Ruan [family] shop in the year* wushen*") on the base. (In this case, the year wushen probably corresponds to 1268.)*

What distinguishes the thirteenth-century (late Song to early Yuan) group of carved lacquer from the better-known fourteenth-century style is the relatively large area of exposed "ground." Also, individual elements such as the leaves and stems of a floral design that makes up the total composition are relatively small in size and do not overlap.

166
Covered box with inside drawer
Ming dynasty, first half of 15th century
Lacquer on wood with mother-of-pearl inlay and painted design.
11.5 x 36 x 25 cm.
Keith McLeod Fund. 1985.21

Lacquerware with painted decoration has a history of more than two thousand years in China. Apart from very early examples (fifth century or earlier) recovered from archaeological sites few pieces predating the sixteenth century have survived.

This box, which can be ascribed to the first half of the fifteenth century by comparison with a similar example from a tomb (dated 1410) of a royal prince of the Ming dynasty, is the only piece of its kind to have come into a museum collection outside of China. The combined use of polychrome painting and mother-of-pearl inlay in an integrated decorative composition is extremely rare. Even in the late sixteenth century, when these techniques were in common use, they occurred separately.

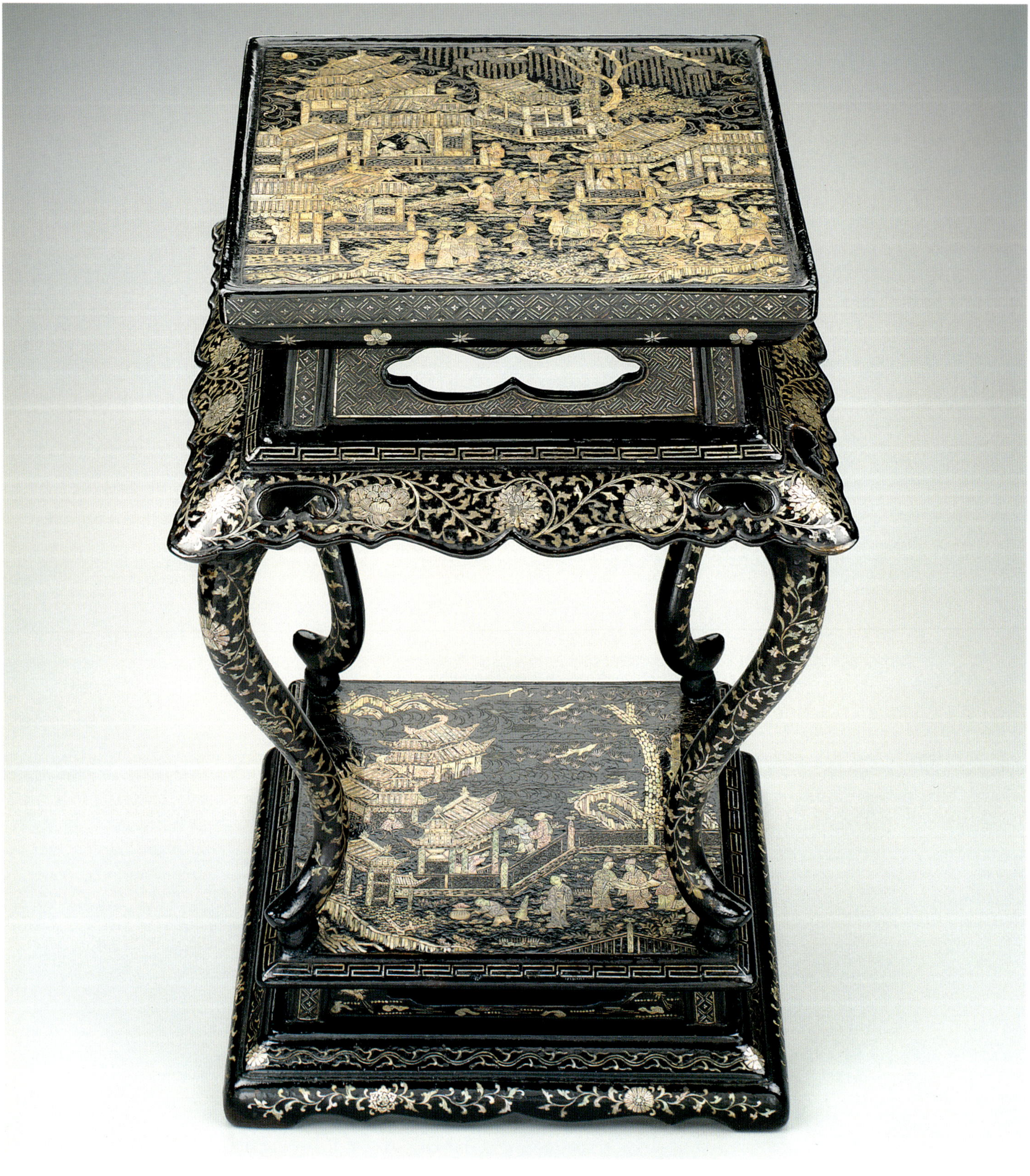

167
Two-tiered stand
Ming dynasty, early 16th century
Hardwood; lacquered and inlaid with mother-of-pearl. H: 45.7 cm.
Anonymous Gift and Charles Bain Hoyt Fund. 1986.513

Chinese lacquer objects inlaid with mother-of-pearl are sometimes termed "pictorial lacquer" because of the elaborate narrative designs with which they are embellished. On this table, innumerable minute pieces of mother-of-pearl have been carefully chosen and shaped to create the elegant flowering scroll and geometric designs that decorate the sides and legs, as well as the two narrative scenes found at the top and the base. Using traditional Ming-dynasty imagery, these scenes portray the family reception of a young scholar who has returned home after obtaining the prestigious jinshi degree (top) and more intimate moments, such as the viewing of a painting in his private garden (base). Both

168
Pendant
Neolithic period, Hongshan culture, 4th millennium B.C.
Nephrite with carved detail of a face.
H: 6 cm.; W: 5.4 cm.
Charles Bain Hoyt Fund. 1988.286

This ornament in the shape of a human mask has a pronounced primitive quality, especially with regard to its facial structure and lineal cutting technique. Judging from its small size and the way the loop hole is drilled on its back, the mask most likely served as the centerpiece of a necklace accompanied by other jade stones and ornaments, perhaps used by the chief of a tribe for either ritual or funeral purposes. The color and texture of this jade piece are similar to examples from the Hongshan culture.

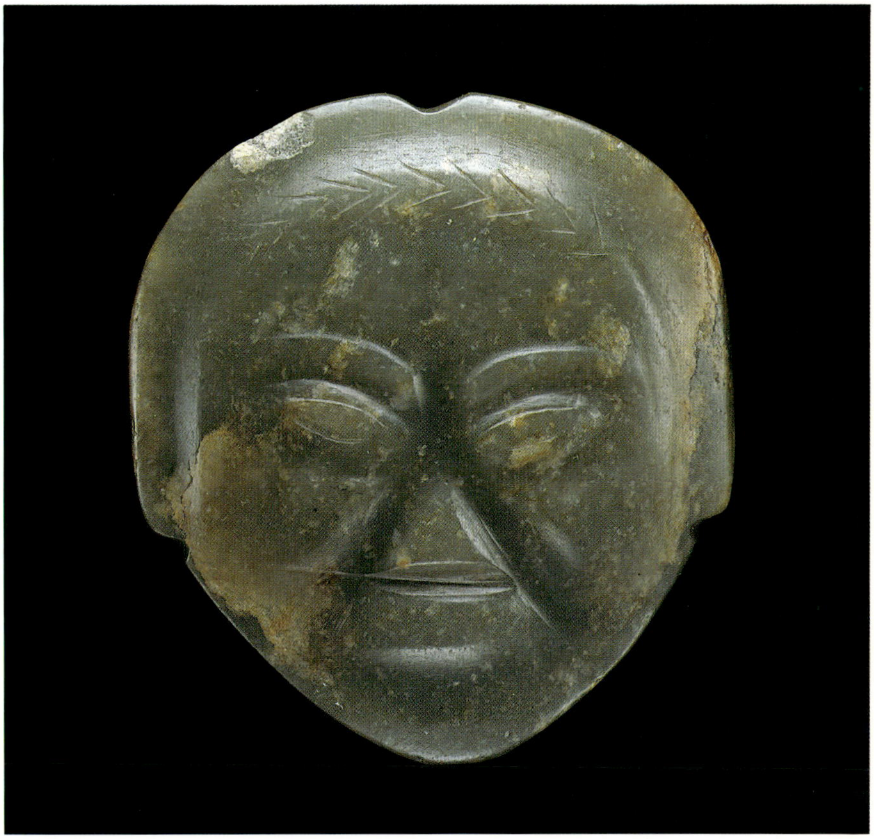

169
Plaque
Neolithic period, Liangzhu culture, early 3rd millennium B.C.
Nephrite jade with engraved figural decoration. H: 5.5 cm.
Charles Bain Hoyt Fund, Asiatic Curator's Fund, and Anonymous Gift.
1990.313

A great variety of jade types have been found at Liangzhu sites, many of them with geometric designs. It is only recently, however, that jade plaques depicting human figures with mythical beasts (shen shou) *have come from a controlled excavation of major tombs in the greater Liangzhu area. Discovering objects of this type on the skulls of skeletons there, Chinese archaeologists have concluded that such jade plaques were used as symbols of power to ornament the headgear or necklaces worn by authoritative figures, possibly shamans.*

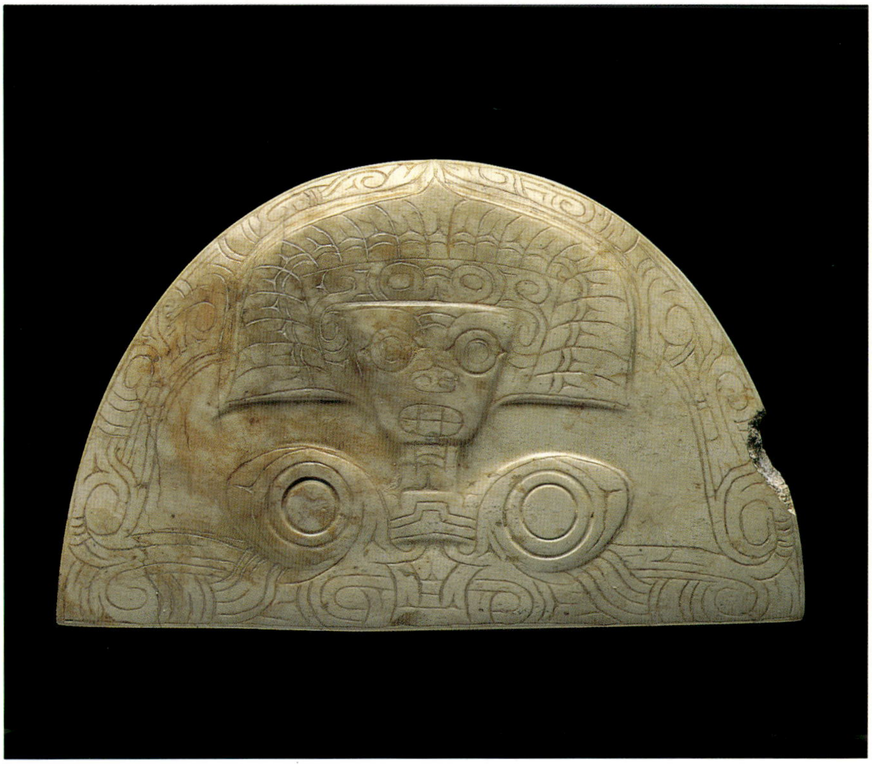

themes are particularly appropriate for this stand, which was most likely used to hold an incense burner or some similar object as part of the furnishings of a scholar's living quarters.

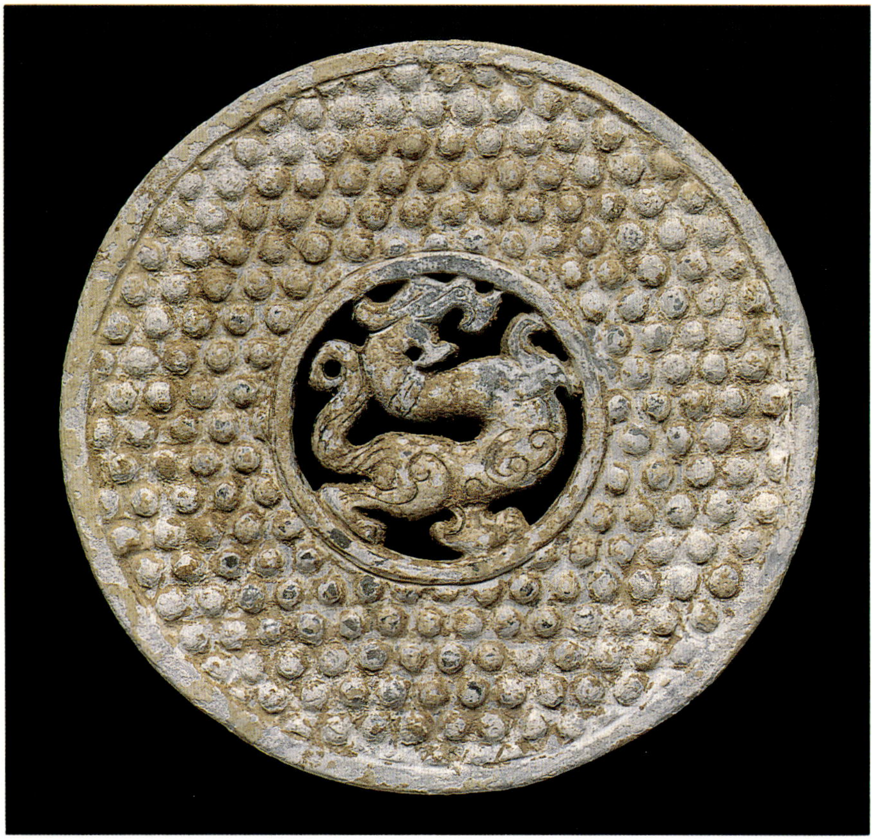

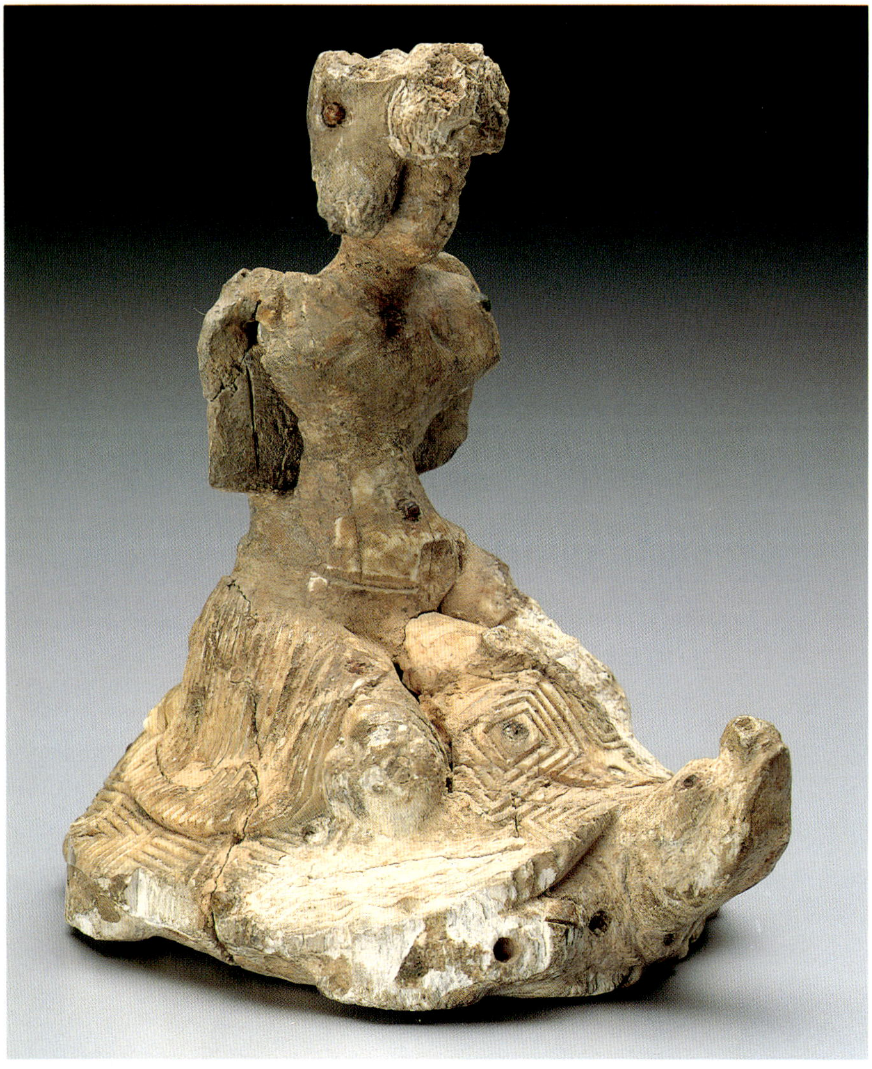

170
Disk *(bi)* with carved openwork design of dragon
Warring States Period, 3rd century B.C.
Nephrite or glass. D: 11.1 cm.
Charles Bain Hoyt Fund and
Anonymous Gift. 1989.102

One of the oldest Chinese ritual motifs is the disk, known in Chinese as bi. *During the Neolithic period jade* bi *were believed to possess magical powers that enabled shamans to communicate with the afterworld. While the ritual significance of* bi *diminished gradually over the centuries, they continued to be placed in tombs as symbols of Heaven. By the late Warring States period (about 300 B.C.), when this object was made, jade* bi *were prized works of art, treasured by noblemen during their life and buried in their tombs at death. Similar pieces have been excavated by Chinese archaeologists from many tombs dating from this time.*

171
Female deity riding a tortoise
Southern Dynasties period,
6th century A.D.
Carved ivory with inlaid stones.
H: 10.8 cm.; L: 10.5 cm.
Charles B. Hoyt Collection. 50.1950

In the large pantheon of Chinese mythology there are several deities with a tortoise as a mount. This ivory statuette represents one in a kneeling/sitting pose, with hairstyle and facial expression typical of the Southern Dynasties period. The details of her face and of the tortoise are carved with sharp precision. Concentric-square and diamond-shaped patterning decorate the carapace of the tortoise, a feature that enhances its archaic appearance. Cinnabar-red pigment is visible here and there, and scattered over the surface are inlaid stones, possibly associated with the constellations.

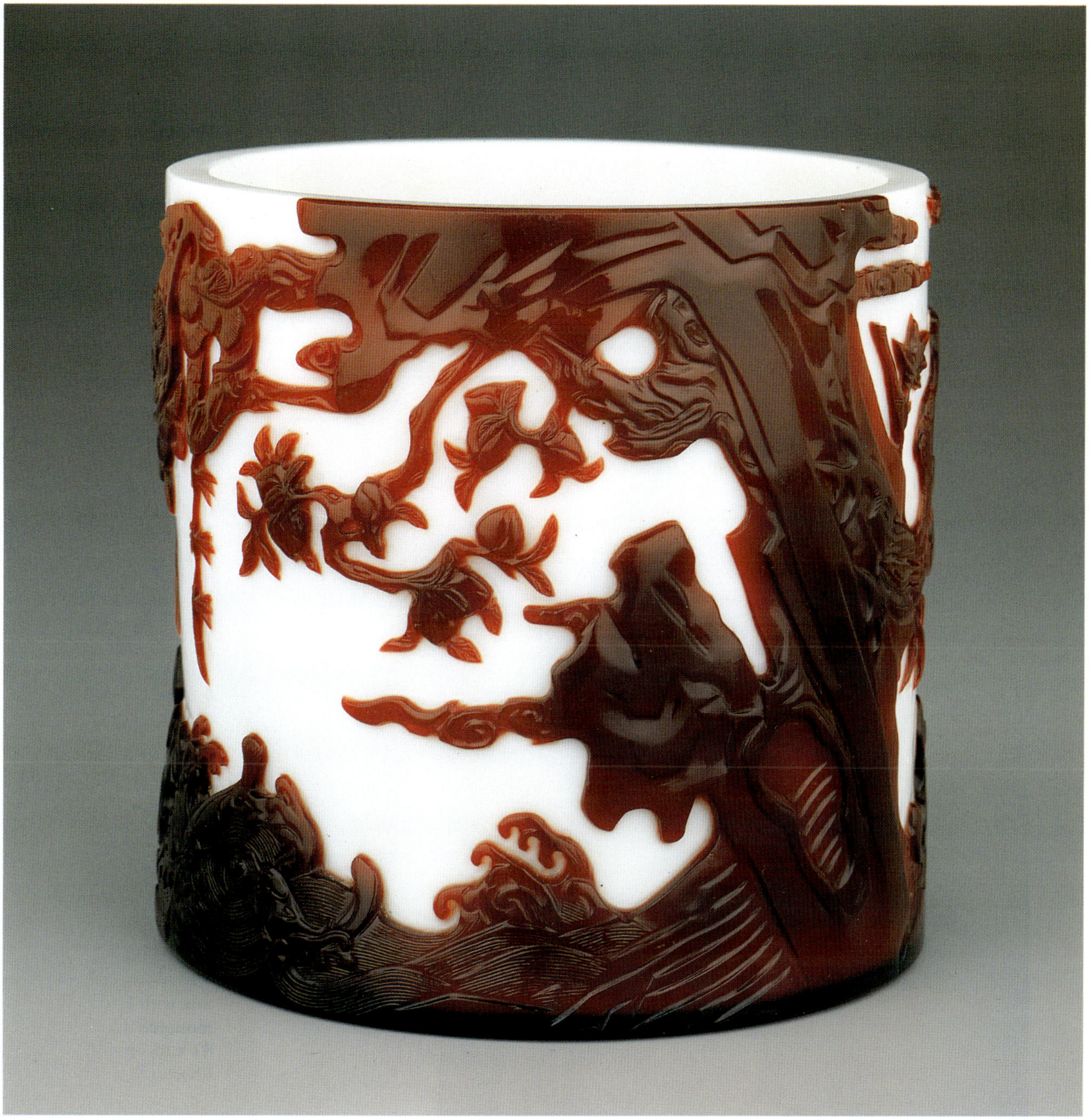

172
Brush holder
Qing dynasty, Yongzheng period (1723-35)
Carved glass with auspicious symbols in red; four-character mark engraved on the base. H: 12 cm.
Gift of Paul and Helen Bernat.
1986.643

Marked "Yongzheng nian zhi" (made during the reign of the Yongzheng emperor), this superb piece exemplifies Qing glassware at its best. The creamy, opaque white body provides a strong background for traditional motifs carved in high relief in translucent crimson glass on its surface. The rare red color is a signal achievement of the Chinese glass industry.

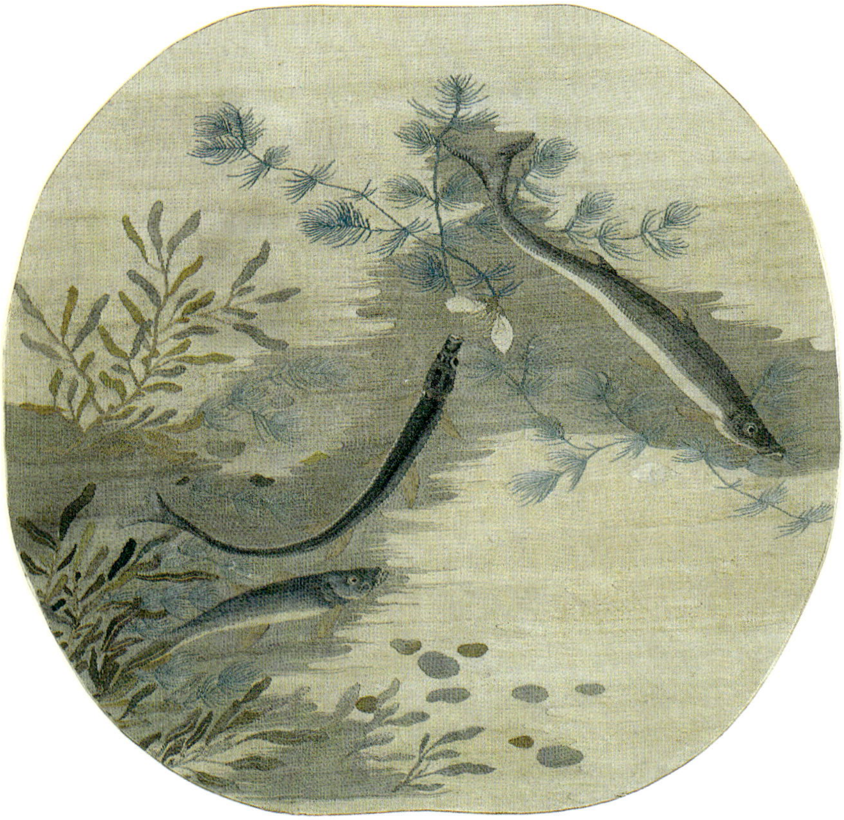

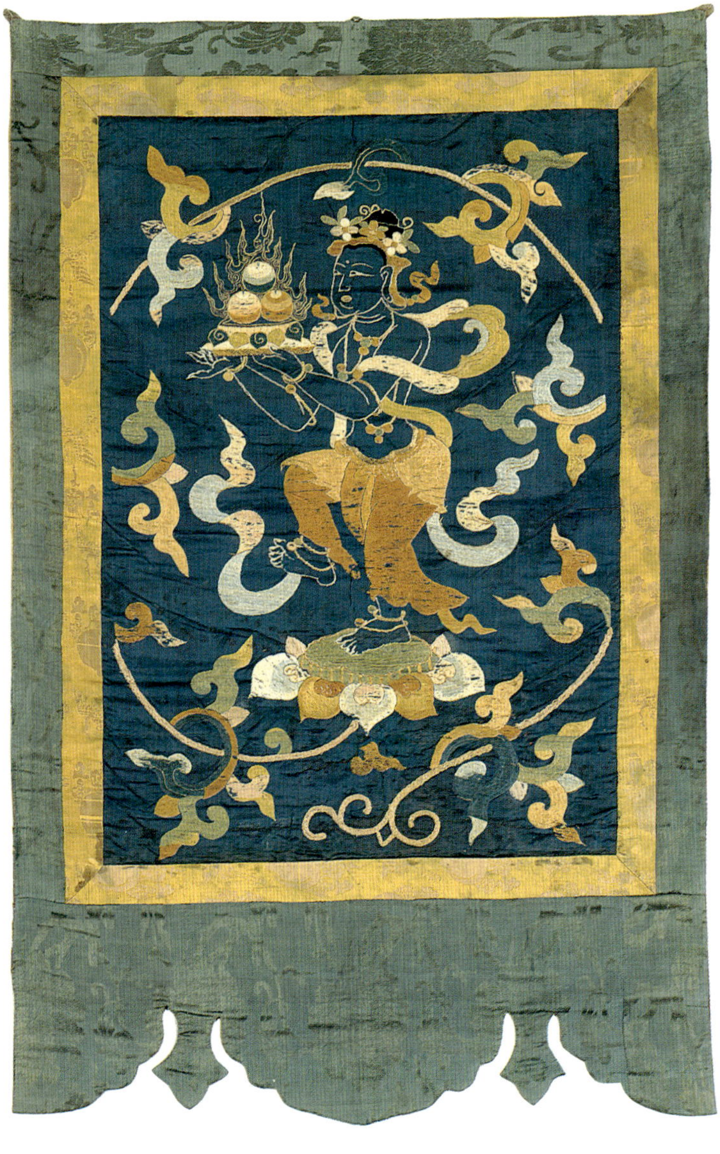

173
Fish
Southern Song dynasty, 13th century
Album leaf; silk tapestry *(kesi)*.
25 x 25 cm.
Chinese and Japanese Special Fund.
17.612

According to Song-dynasty writers, the technique of kesi *(silk tapestry) was introduced into Tang China from Central Asia by the Uighur Turks. The Central Asian origin was confirmed recently when girdles woven in the* kesi *method, dated to the seventh century, were found in Astana, Xinjiang. The technique was enthusiastically taken up in the Southern Song by several artists who became famous for weaving pictorial* kesi *based on contemporary paintings.* Kesi *was also used commonly during the Song period for the protective flap on the back of handscrolls and for covering other small objects.*

Of all kesi *tapestries in Western collections this particular piece, one of a set of five in the collection, is unique in terms of the extremely refined rendering of the pictorial elements. The animated, calligraphic quality of the fish, achieved not by the use of brush and ink but through weaving, shows the relationship between this* kesi *album leaf and Song academic painting . Scholars have debated the dating of the present group, placing it anywhere from the Southern Song dynasty to the Ming dynasty. We believe it dates from the earlier period.*

174
Buddhist Devotee
Ming dynasty, 15th century
Silk with embroidery on satin ground; mounted as a banner.
81 x 55 cm.
Charles Bain Hoyt Fund. 1989.319

This beautifully executed embroidery was created at the Ming court for a lamaist temple, either in the Chinese capital or in Tibet. The figure type is comparable to those seen in Yuan-dynasty drawings of the fourteenth century, but the rest of the composition is closely related to the early Ming style. Particularly innovative is the naturalistic rendering of the devotee imposed upon a background of abstract motifs reminiscent of ceramic designs. Although the color of the embroidery has faded through centuries of wear, its vivid contrasts are still discernible: the artist used delicate, thin lines to outline the body, the face, and the flames of the three pearls, while the floral motifs, the flying scarf, and the lotus blossom are embroidered colorfully and broadly around the figure.

The Himalayas

The collection of Himalayan art consists primarily of Tibetan and Nepalese painting and metal sculpture; other aspects of Himalayan artistic activity are represented with ritual implements, clay votive images, and jewelry. The collection is overwhelmingly Buddhist in orientation, with only a few of the Nepalese works stemming from the context of Hinduism.

The beginning of the Himalayan collection dates to the early years of this century during the curatorship of Okakura Kakuzō. Both curatorial purchases and the generosity of patrons have contributed to the continuous growth of this collection. Foremost among its many benefactors are Denman Waldo Ross, William Sturgis Bigelow, Lucy T. Aldrich, and John Goelet. These donors contributed many masterpieces, including a number of outstanding paintings, some from the famous N̄or school of Tibet. Purchases arranged by Okakura and his successors brought still other works into the collection.

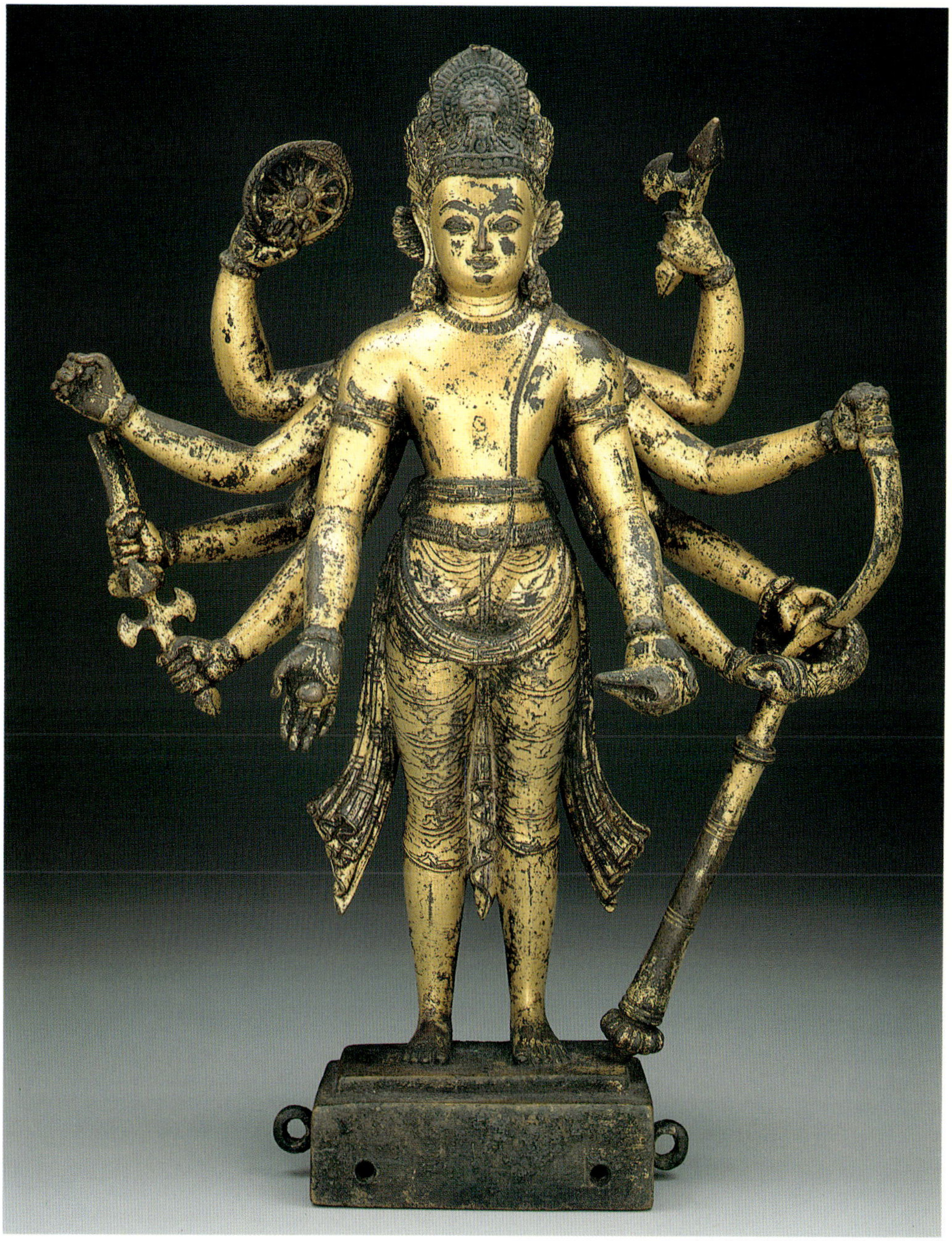

175
Viṣṇu in his Universal Form
(Viśvarūpa Viṣṇu)
Nepal, 9th-10th century
Gilt copper. H: 31.8 cm.
Keith McLeod Fund (from the Nasli and Alice Heeramaneck Collection). 67.5

Both Buddhism and Hinduism influenced the art and culture of India's eastern neighbor Nepal. This statue depicting Viṣṇu, a primary god of the Hindu pantheon, is one of the earliest extant works of Nepalese art. The muscular form, rich modeling, and sculptural ornamentation date it to the ninth or tenth century A.D.

The ten-armed Viṣṇu wears a skirt decorated with a printed design and stands firmly on a rectangular pedestal. His attributes—discus, sword, ax, bow, shield, mace, and conch shell—identify him as an image of Viṣṇu in his universal form.

According to the Bhagavad Gītā, *a celebrated poem composed around the third century B.C., Kṛṣṇa, a manifestation of the god Viṣṇu, serves as the charioteer of the warrior Arjuna during battle. As they race along the battlefield, Kṛṣṇa and Arjuna engage in metaphysical debate until (in the eleventh chapter) Kṛṣṇa reveals himself as Viśvarūpa Viṣṇu in order to increase Arjuna's comprehension of the mysteries of the universe.*

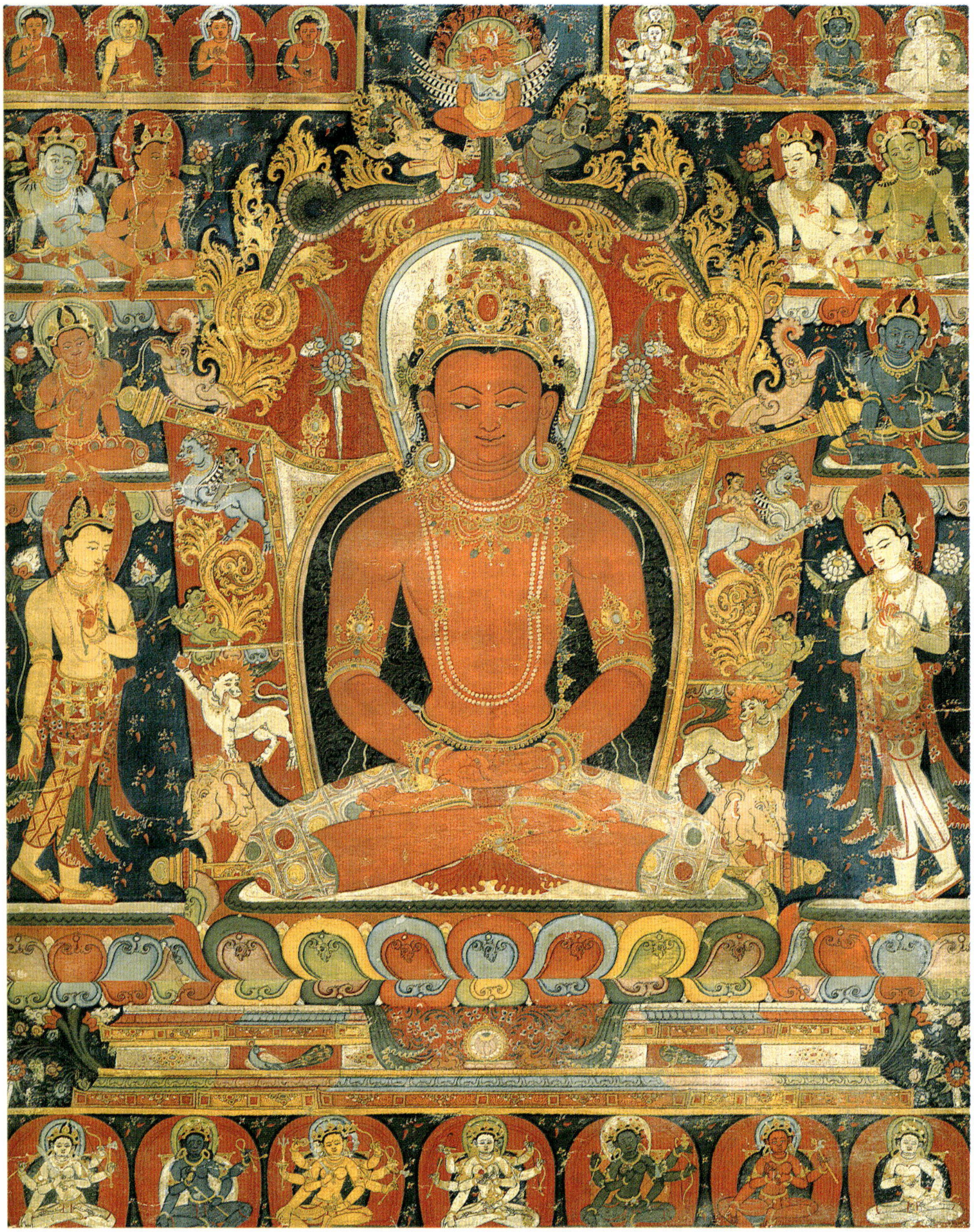

177
Mahākāla and Attendants
Tibet, 16th century
Colors on cotton. 127 x 92 cm.
William Sturgis Bigelow Collection.
12.47

One of the protective deities of Buddhism, venerated by the nomads of Nepal, Tibet, and Mongolia, the three-eyed Mahākāla is depicted in this painting as Lord of the Tent. He is a manifestation of one of the Five Transcendental Buddhas, Akṣobhya, whose blue figure crowns his headdress. Mahākāla stands on a prostrate corpse and is encircled by flames in which appear jackals, crows, dogs, and other denizens of the cemeteries he inhabits.

Attending Mahākāla are four conceptually similar deities who are considered his brothers and sisters. To the right, his sisters are Ekajaṭā, with one knot of hair, and the four-armed Śrī Devī, riding a mule that has an additional eye in its haunch. Śrī Devī is attended by Makaravaktrā, a green monster who has a human head and the body of a mythological makara. *Mahākāla's "brothers" are simultaneously independent deities and additional manifestations of his power. They are the four-armed Caturbhuja Mahākāla, at the upper left, and Vyāghravāhana Mahākāla, on a tiger, at the lower left.*

The rich coloring, lush background, and flaming arches surrounding the five deities point to a sixteenth-century date for this painting.

176
Buddha of Eternal Life (Amitāyus Buddha) and Eight Bodhisattvas
Nepal, 11th century
Colors on cotton. 41.3 x 33 cm.
Gift of John Goelet. 67.818

Seated on an elaborate peacock throne in the center of the painting, the Buddha of Eternal Life is encircled by a halo in which appear natural and mythical beings, including elephants, snakes, lions, flying goats, boys, and, at its peak, the bird Garuḍa.

The eight bodhisattvas *surrounding the central figure are identified by small attributes found in the lotuses they hold. Additional Buddhist deities decorate the top border of the painting, while seven goddesses sit in an arcade in the lower border. The Five Protective Goddesses (Pañcarakṣā) are shown with Uṣṇīsavijayā and White Tārā, suggesting that they are depicted here as individual deities and not as the group of five standard in later iconography. The stylized walk of the standing* bodhisattvas *and the exaggerated posture of the seated* bodhisattvas *parallel similar depictions in illustrated manuscripts datable to the eleventh century.*

This painting and a nearly identical work in the Los Angeles County Museum of Art, depicting the Buddha Ratnasambhava accompanied by eight bohisattvas, *are in all likelihood from a set of five depicting the Five Transcendental Buddhas.*

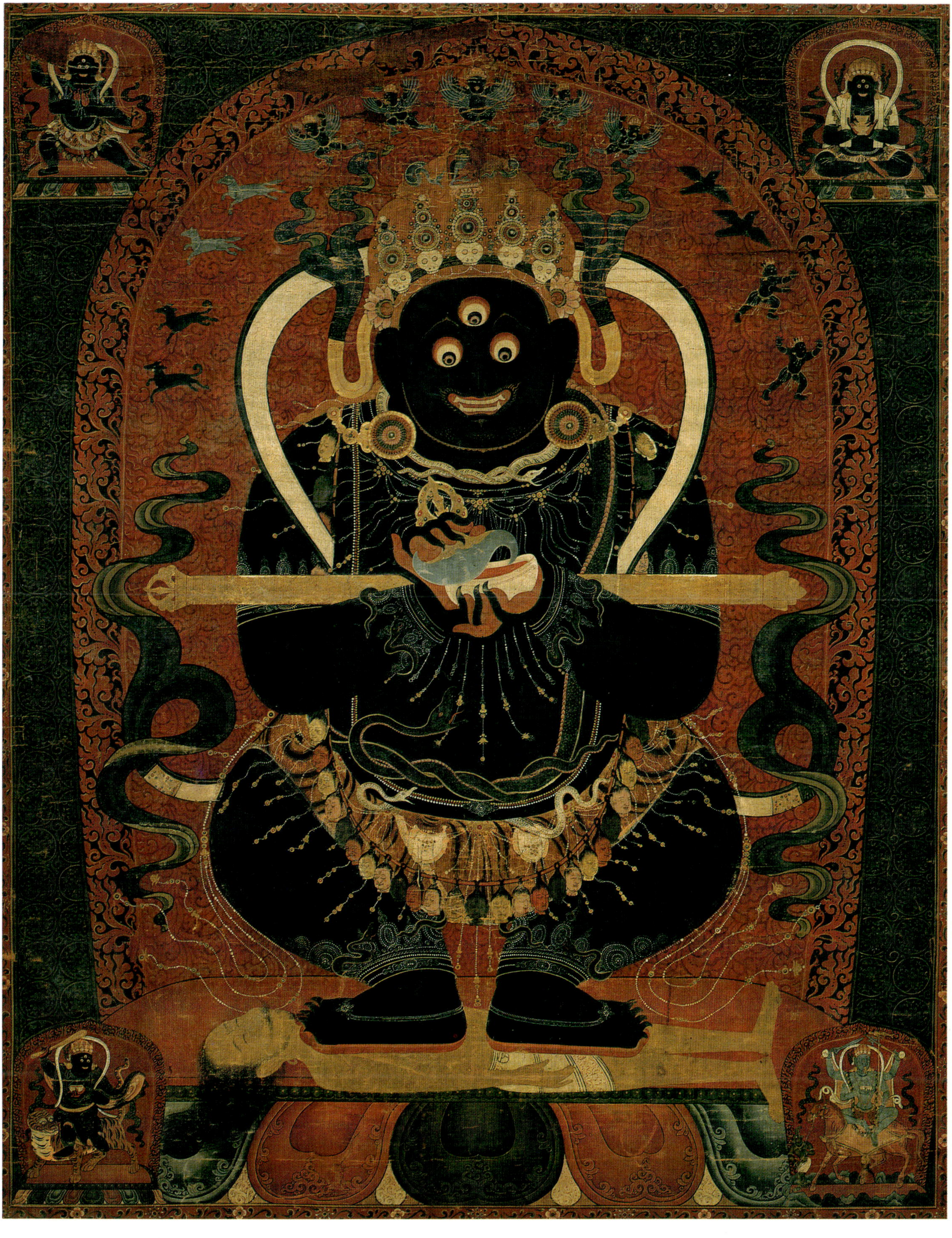

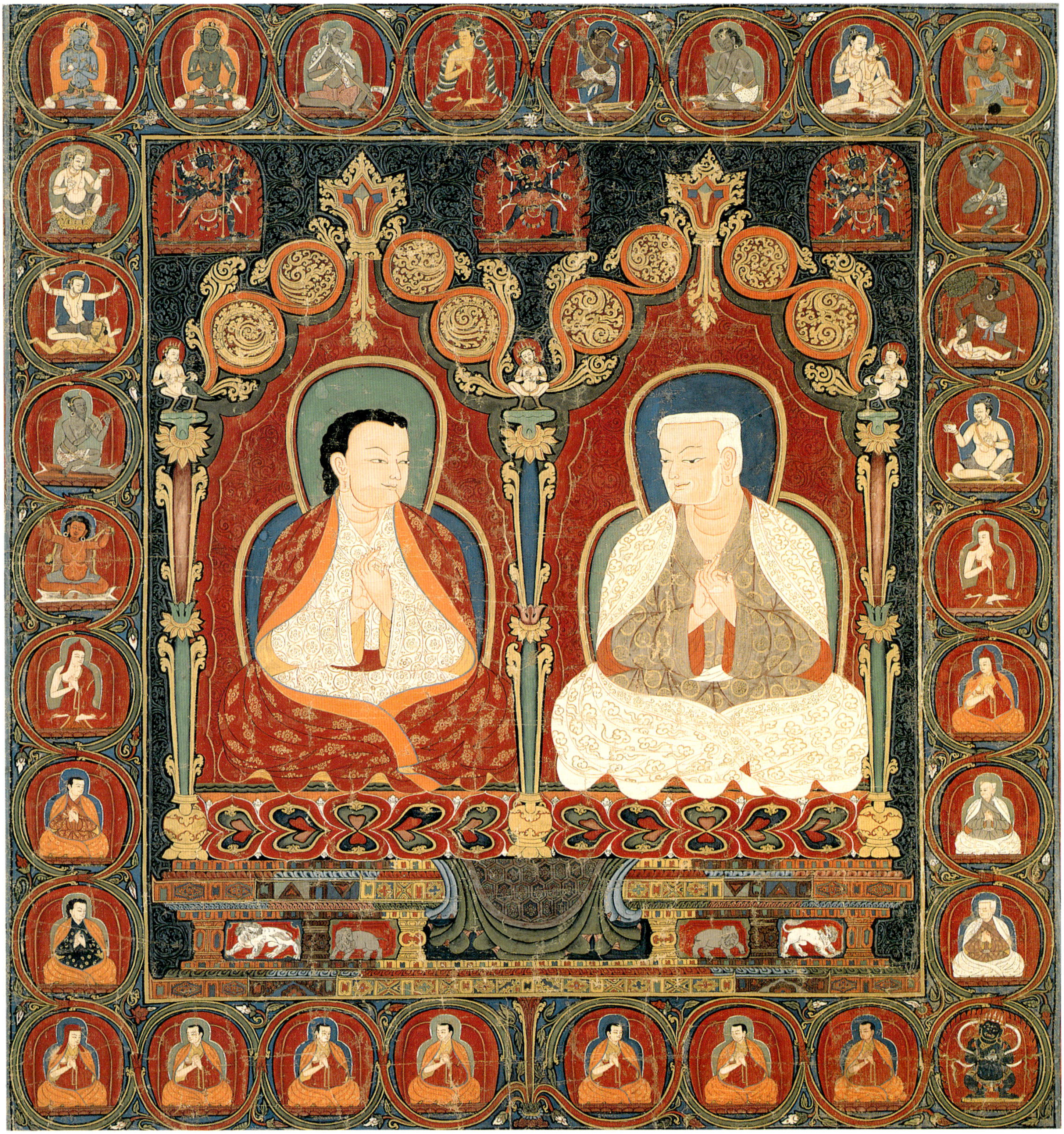

178
Two Śākya-pa Patriarchs
Tibet, 18th century
Colors on cotton. 83 x 77 cm.
Gift of John Goelet. 67.831

The two fully robed lamas are seated on thrones confronting each other, their hands performing the gesture of turning the Wheel of the Law (dharma-cakrapravartanamudrā). *The only figures in the* tangka *not identified by inscriptions, they are obviously teacher and disciple, for one of them is a much older man. rDo-rie-ac'an, or Vajradhara, from whom the Śākya-pas draw their inspiration, is the first figure in the upper row. He is followed by Vajrasattva and several* mahāsiddhas *both along the top and along the sides down to the middle of the* tangka. *The remaining figures along the sides and the bottom row are important lamas of the sect, with one exception: mGon po, or Mahākāla, the ferocious figure in the lower right corner. Immediately above the two monks are three manifestations of bDem chog, or Samvara, in* yab-yum *(mystic union with Nairātmā).*

The early date of this tangka is sug-

gested by a comparison with Nepalese materials of the thirteenth and fourteenth centuries. Against an exuberant background of red and blue scroll design, the figures are articulated with concise sobriety. The māhasiddhas, *in various postures and gestures, enliven the whole composition with their miraculous activities, in contrast to which the monks appear dignified but static. Unity and concord between the different worlds of the divinities and the lamas is emphasized by the interrelationship of the lotus rhizomes, which originate in the parent stem below the center. The colors used are the primary ones, along with a number of different shades of blue and green, and others such as pink, gray, and purple. Gold heightens the effect of the decorative design, especially of the throne and arches.*

179
The Fifth King of Śambhala
Tibet or China, second half of 17th century
Colors on cotton. 80.9 x 43.3 cm.
Denman Waldo Ross Collection.
06.324

This is one of a set of paintings portraying the kings of Śambhala, *a mythical region in Central Asia (in the Tarim basin) where successive generations of pious kings are said to have ruled and to have transmitted from one generation to the next the* Kālacakra, *an esoteric system that formed an essential part of Lamaism. Because of its association with the* Kālacakra, Śambhala *was held in special veneration by the lamaists. (Accounts of this mythical land and of its kings may be found in the* Śambhala Lam Yig.*)*

The colors are bright and strong, similar in their intensity to eighteenth-century paintings known to have been executed in the Tashilunpo monastery. This work, however, was probably done somewhere in eastern Tibet or in China proper.

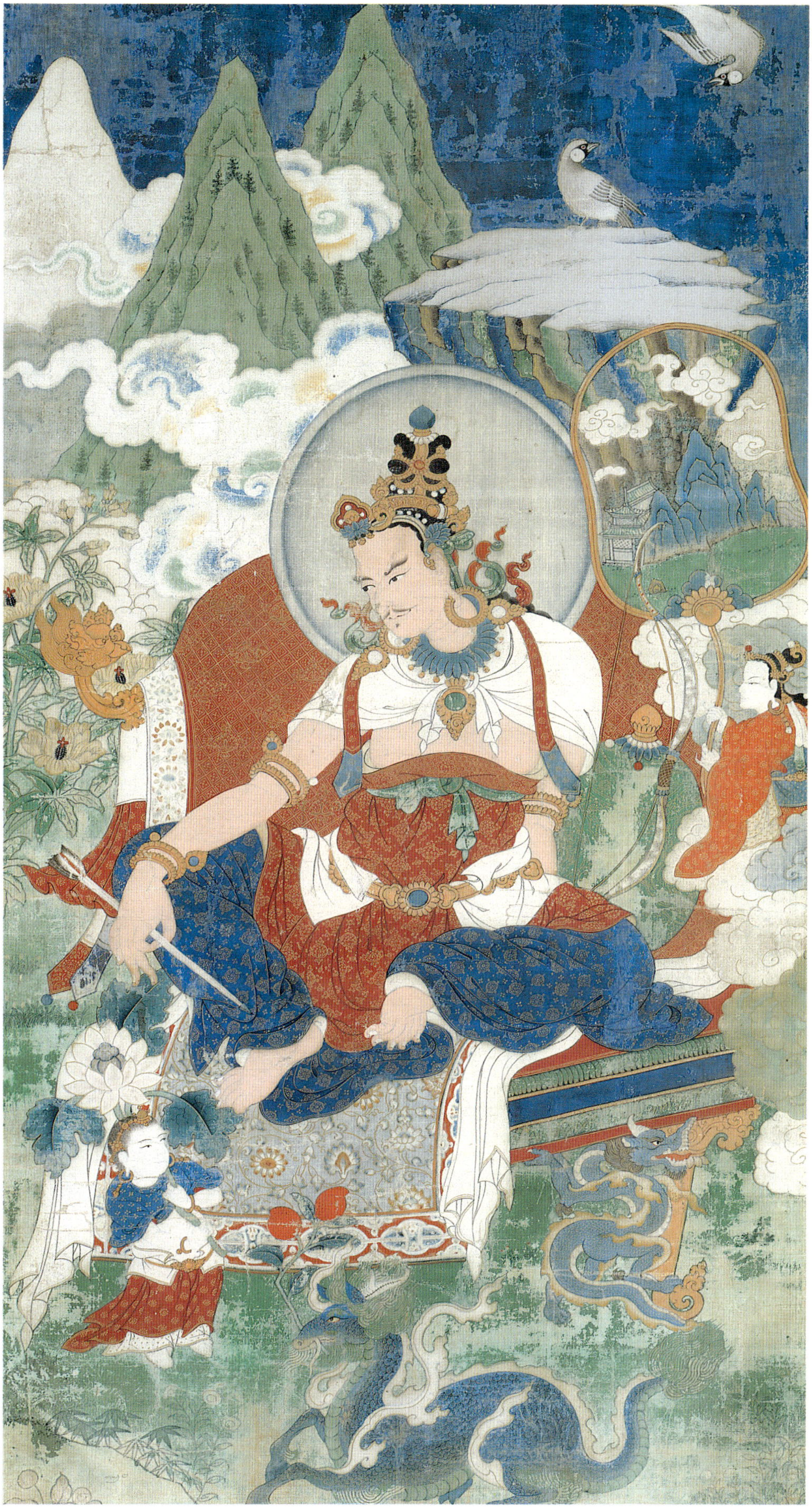

Southeast Asia

The collection of Southeast Asian art owes much of its diversity and quality to the discerning eye and the wide ranging interests of Denman Waldo Ross. As a collector, Dr. Ross went through many phases, each time discovering new art forms, styles, and regions, and donating to the Museum the collections acquired in this process, when his interest shifted to other fields. It is to his fascination with the arts of Cambodia that the Museum owes its fine collection of Khmer art, ranging from the gigantic Angkor stone heads to the elegant bronze *apsaras.*

Ananda Coomaraswamy provided English readers with the first general survey of Indonesian art in his *History of Indian and Indonesian Art* (1927). With Denman Ross he shared his keen perception of the beauty of the arts of the Indonesian archipelago, and their long association resulted in the acquisition of several fine examples of Javanes stone sculpture. A visit to Indonesia by Congressman George Holden Tinkham brought to the Museum the only head of a Buddha for which the provenance from Chandi Sewu (late eighth century) is well established. In more recent years monumental stone sculpture, such as the Bhairava or Mahākāla from eastern Java, and several bronzes and pieces of jewelry have enabled us to show the full chronological range of the Hinduized cultures of that country.

While the arts of Thailand and Burma are much less well represented, the collections contain pieces of sculpture from both countries. Particularly important are a group of Buddhist clay tablets from Burma.

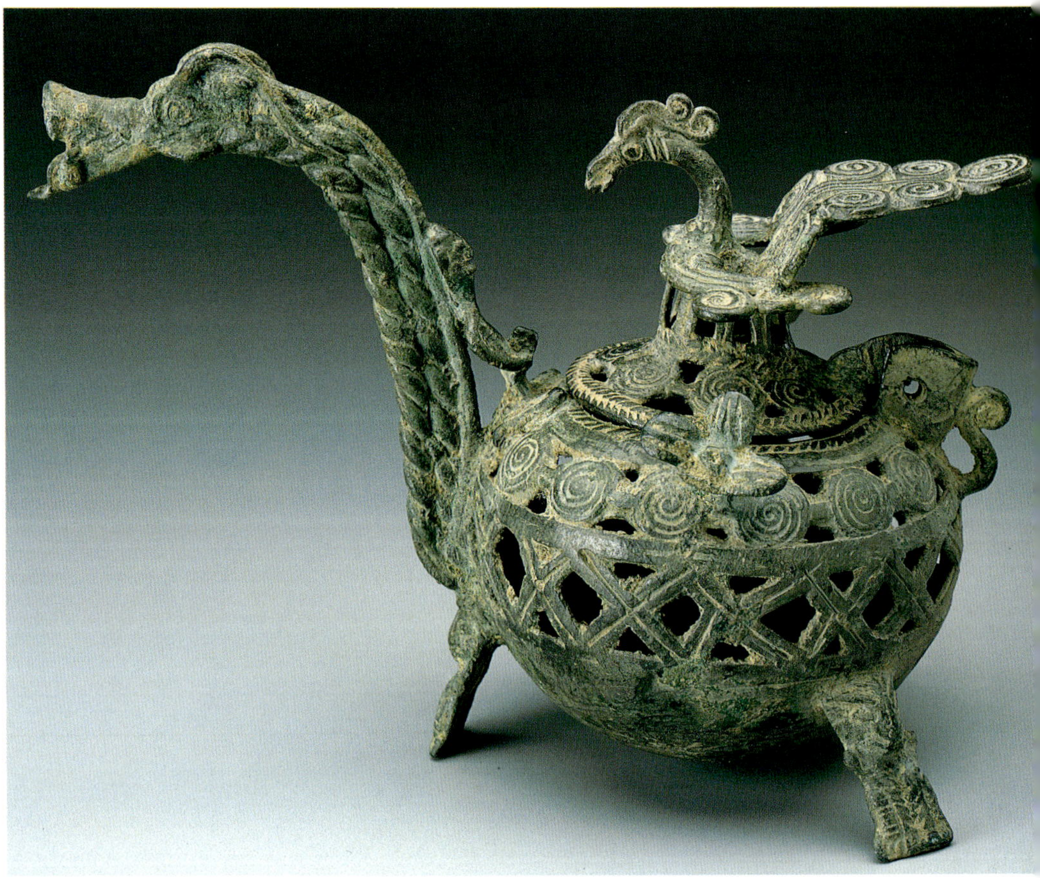

180
Three-legged incense burner with dragon handle and phoenix cover
Vietnam, Dongso'n culture, 3rd century A.D.
Cast bronze with applied decorative motifs of dragon, phoenix, and human figure. H: 13.5 cm.; L: 19.0 cm.
Anonymous Gift. 1991.90

Bronze vessels and implements played a crucial role in ritualistic ceremonies of the ancient societies of southwestern China and northern Vietnam. During China's Eastern Han dynasty (A.D. 25-220) the status of northern Vietnam changed from a colony to an actual province of the empire. It is from the end of this period that the present bronze incense burner dates. The sophisticated treatment of the bronze reflects both the technological and the artistic mastery of the medium that was attained in the region. Although it is a uniquely Vietnamese creation, there was an inevitable sharing of motifs with neighboring cultures. Chinese incense burners with comparable motifs are known; however, the concept behind their function and structure is quite different. They are typically in the form of a mountain, referred to in Chinese as Boshanlu. *Vertically oriented, the burners were intended to sit on a table or stand while burning. This Vietnamese burner, on the other hand, has a horizontal form, its long handle enabling it to be carried — perhaps during a ceremonial procession.*

The globular body of the incense burner is meticulously executed in openwork with three legs, a handle, and a cover that was originally hinged to the body. A dragon's neck and head form the object's handle. In all East Asian countries, the dragon has been viewed traditionally as a Taoist symbol of yang — the masculine force. Perched on the dragon, forming the lid of the incense burner, is a mythical bird, also known as the Vermillion Bird of the South, messenger of the Fire God — an image associated with the kingdom of Yue (Vietnam). Leaning on the back of the dragon's neck, a human figure, the dragon's groom, gazes up at the phoenix, while three human-shaped figures form the legs of the burner. The two flower motifs on either side of the body may relate to the ritual of burning herbal incense in ancient times.

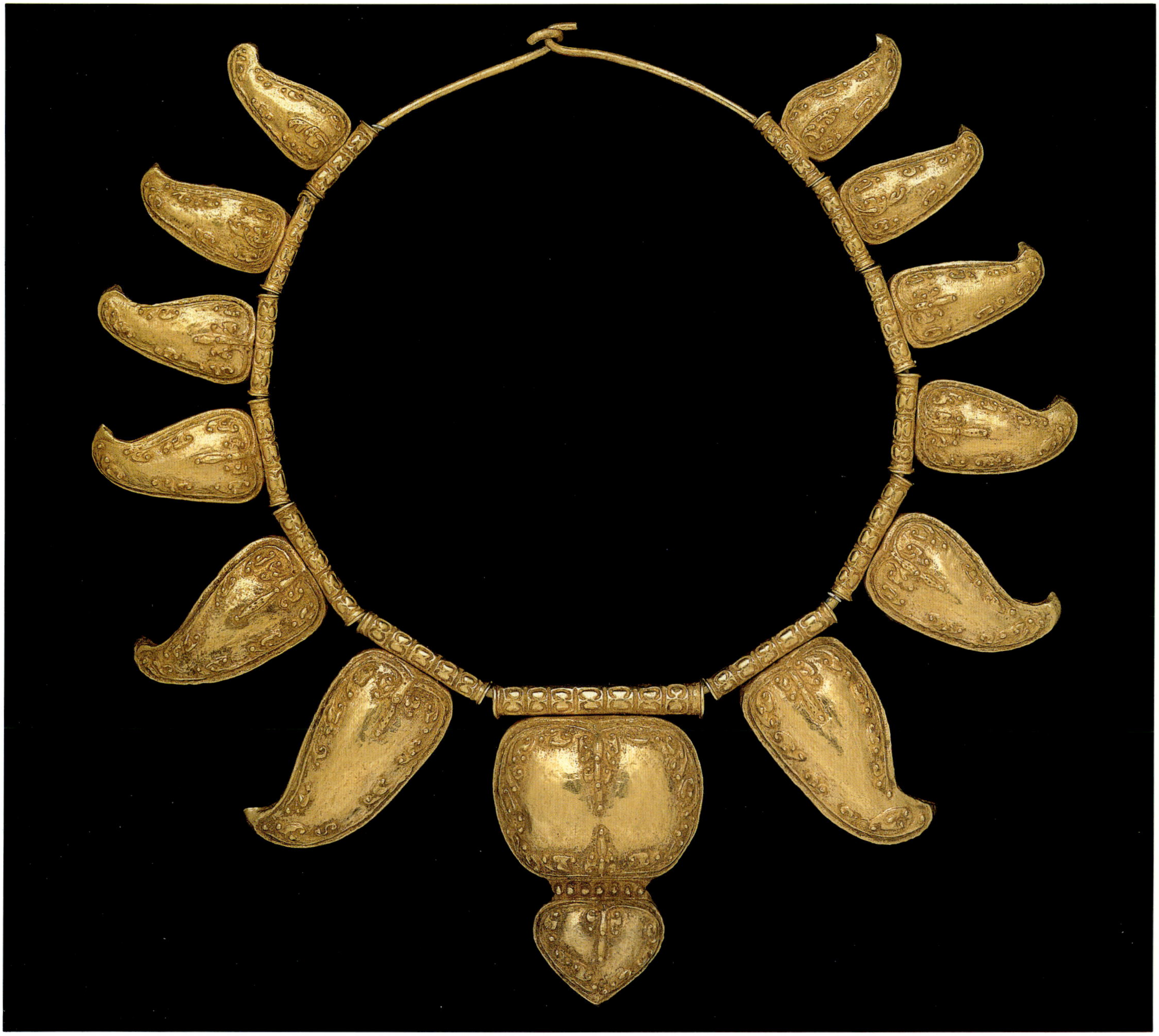

181
Necklace
Java, Indonesia, 9th century
Gold, probably cast and worked from the back. L: 31 cm.
Frederick L. Jack Fund. 1981.44

The necklace consists of twelve leaf- or petal-shaped pendants and a centerpiece in the shape of a stylized tortoise. The pendants are attached to thin tubes through which the necklace is strung. When the necklace was acquired by the Museum, the original string had been lost, and the piece had been restrung with the rounded tips of the petals pointing inward, probably after the example of a necklace in the Mangkunagoro Collection in Solo.

In 1982 the Mpu Tantular Museum in Surabaya acquired a number of gold objects dug up by a farmer in the hamlet of Cogembung near the village of Ponorogo (East Java). Among the items excavated was a thirteen-piece gold necklace. A hollow bell-shaped pendant, which may once have held a crystal or semiprecious stone, is the center around which six pendants in the shape of petals and six in the shape of tortoises have been strung in alternating fashion. The necklace is held together by a string of braided gold wire, complete with its hook and eyelet in what is undoubtedly the original arrangement, leaf-shaped pendants strung turning outward. The discovery of this incontrovertible piece of evidence prompted the Museum to restring its necklace accordingly.

Apart from the improved appearance of the necklace, the new arrangement finds further confirmation in a stone statue from Kediri (National Museum, Jakarta, inv. no. 15a). It represents a four-headed, four-armed deity wearing a necklace of leaf-shaped pendants pointing outward. While these petals are close to floral shapes found in nature, fragments from other areas suggest a connection with the necklaces made of tiger teeth or tiger claws that were worn as a magic charm by boys, by the young Kṛṣṇa, and by such gods and bodhisattvas of youthful appearance as, for instance, Mañjuśrī. In these necklaces the teeth and claws invariably turn outward.

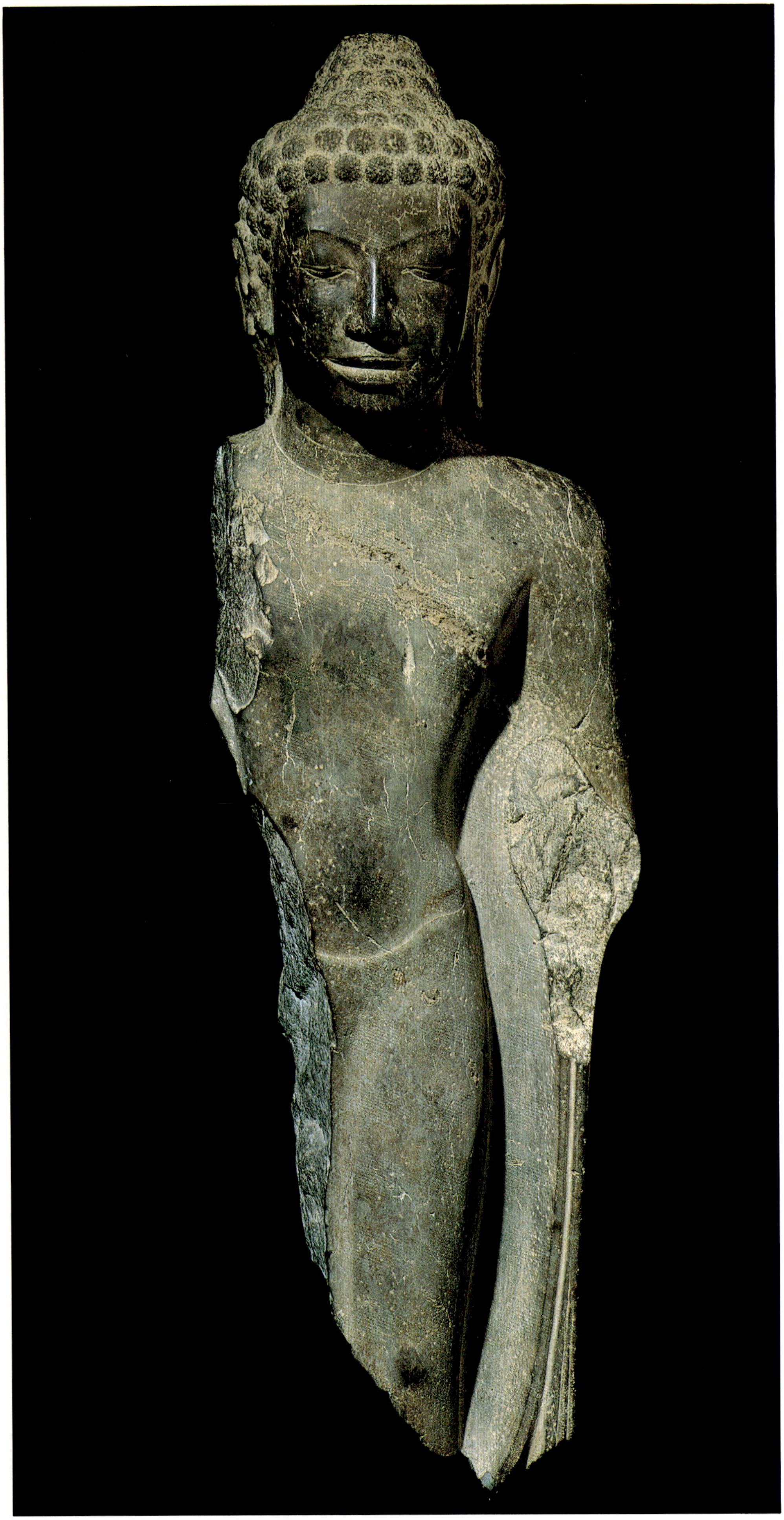

182
Buddha
Thailand, Dvaravati type, about 8th century A.D.
Limestone. H: 86 cm.
Gift of John Adams Thierry in Memory of Adelaide Hamlin Thierry. 1973.694

From the seventh to the eleventh century, lower Burma and Thailand were inhabited by tribes of the Mon people, who had adopted Buddhism and whose culture reflected Indian influences brought first to these regions by merchants and missionaries from the Indian subcontinent. One of the principal Mon kingdoms was that of Dvaravati, the name of which is confirmed by texts on coins, but the extent and duration of which remains unclear. Theravāda Buddhism became the predominant religion of the Dvaravati kingdom; thus, images such as this Buddha Śākyamuni, the founder of Buddhism, dominate the sculpture of the period.

This standing Buddha typifies the art of the Dvaravati kingdom. The broad shoulders, tapering body, and thin drapery of the statue reflect the Gupta style that flourished in India during the fifth and sixth centuries, while the frontality and restraint in the figure distinguish it from its Indian prototypes. The Buddha's broad face, full lips, and stylized eyebrows are characteristic of Mon sculpture and are thought to reflect the physical traits of those tribes.

183
Seated Buddha
Central Java, Indonesia, early 9th century
Gilt bronze. H: 29.8 cm.
Gift of The Honorable Lady Hood, Dona L. Coomaraswamy, William F. Whittemore, The MFA Expedition, The MFA Expedition and the University Museum of Philadelphia, Reginald Jenney, N.M. Heeramaneck, W.O. Comstock, Abdul Farag Shaer, Gift of Dr. Eliza A. Melkon, John Ware Willard Fund, Marshall H. Gould Fund, Maria Antoinette Evans Fund, and Samuel Putnam Avery Fund, by exchange, and Mary S. and Edward J. Holmes Fund.
1988.151

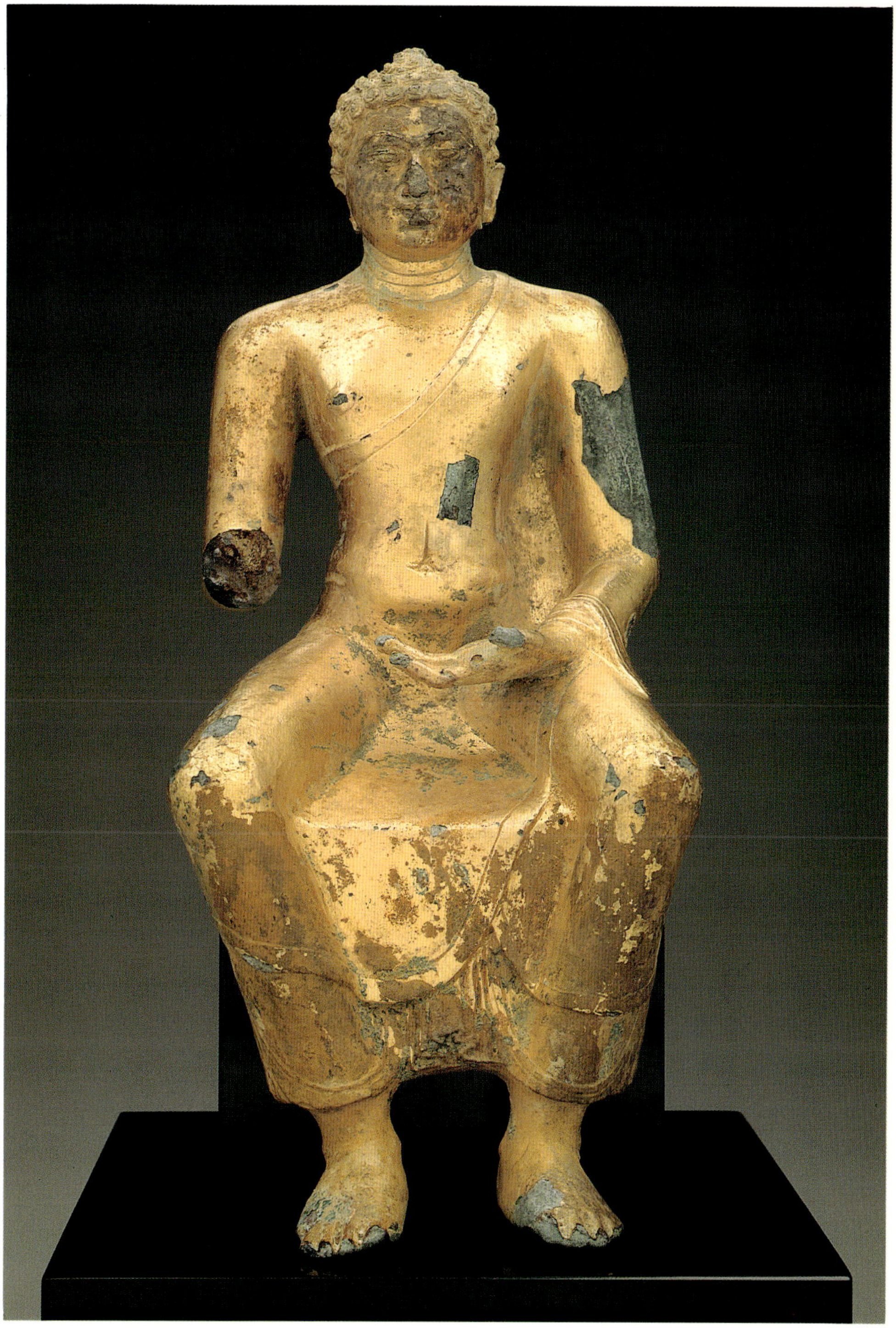

The Buddha is seated in the Western manner, his left wrist resting on his left thigh with the palm, in which the remnants of a mark are discernible, turned upward. The lower right arm and hand, probably raised in the symbolic gesture of exposition, have been lost. A monk's robe that leaves the right shoulder bare is the Buddha's only garment, its double hem crossing the chest as if it were the sacred thread worn by upper-caste Hindus. Across the lower legs and ankles, the hem of the robe and the undergarment are clearly indicated.

Although the claim of a Javanese provenance for this statue cannot be substantiated, its close similarity to a gilt-bronze Buddha of slightly larger size (35.5 cm.) from Sidarejo in the regency of Cilacap argues strongly in favor of the attribution. Both statues are cast of solid bronze to which a coating of gold has been applied. In both cases the way in which part of the gold has flaked off suggested, at first sight, that it had been applied by hammering. However, a closer examination of the Boston statue indicates that the gold was applied by the mercury-amalgam technique, commonly used for gilt statues of this period. Although the hands of the Sidarejo and Boston statues formed different mudrās, *the pose of the figures and the shape of the limbs and head are very similar, as is the treatment of the drapery.*

Of the numerous images of the Buddha in a variety of Indian-derived styles found in Java, Sumatra, Kalimantan, Sulawesi, and Lombok, the Boston and Sidarejo statues belong to a small group that seem to have been inspired primarily by prototypes from South India. The technique of gilding, the drapery of the monk's garb with the pronounced hem across the chest, the tapering shape of the arms, and the mark in the palm of the Buddha's left hand all recall South Indian statuary. Although the hallmark of Nagapattinam Buddha statues — a cranial protuberance surmounted by a flame — is absent on both statues, their close affinity to a gilt-bronze Buddha from Nagapattinam (see acc. nos.1970.3 and 67.4) is evident.

While provenance and exact date remain uncertain, it is clear that statuary of this South Indian type exerted a strong influence in Java. An example is the Buddha from Ampel in which this southern style has been blended harmoniously with ideas and techniques deriving from other centers of bronze casting in India.

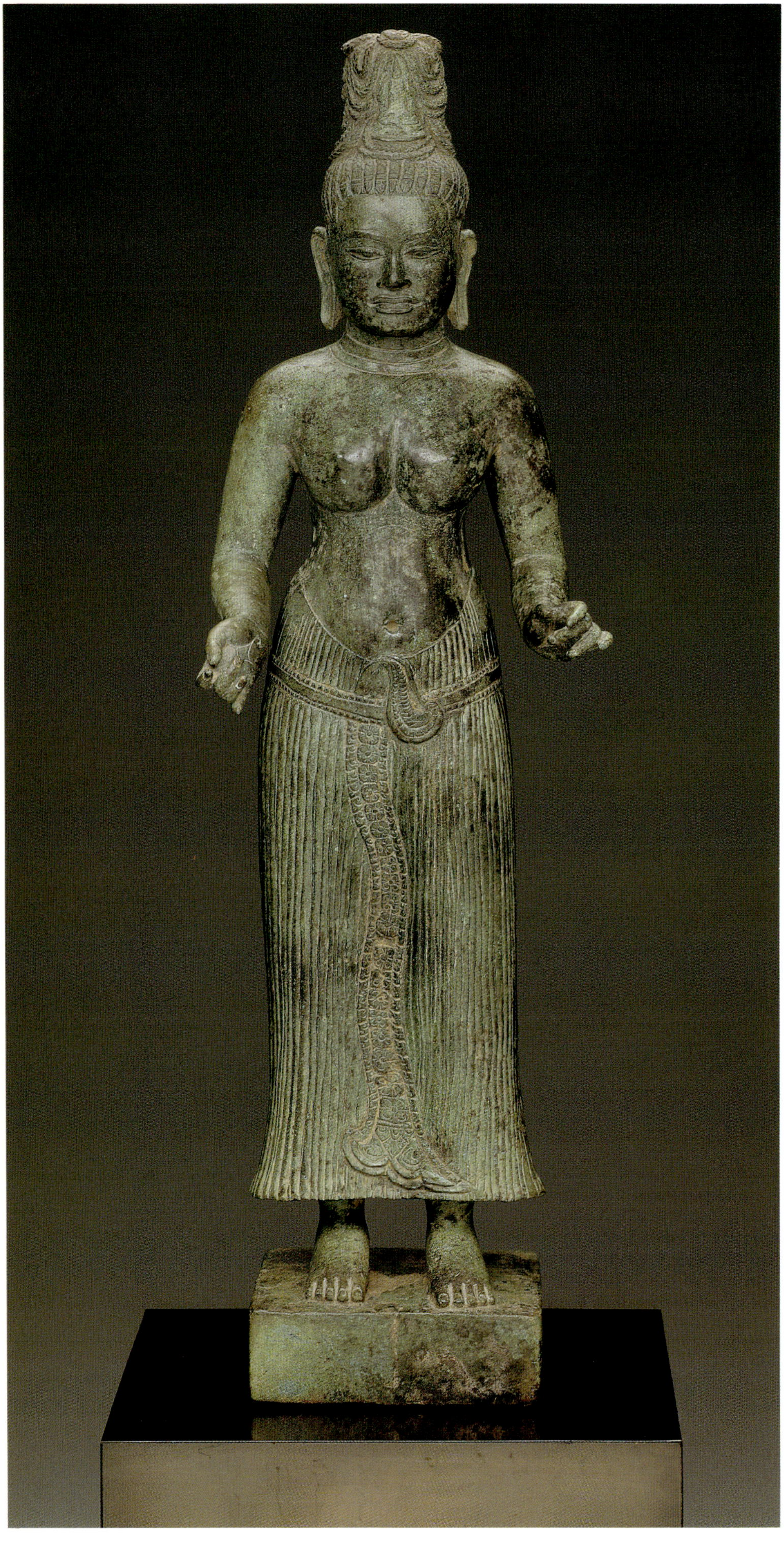

184
Female deity
Cambodia, late 10th century
Bronze. H: 62.7 cm.
University Museum of Philadelphia and MFA Persian Expedition, MFA Expedition, Theodora Wilbour Fund in Memory of Zoe Wilbour, Gift of the John Goelet Foundation, Arthur Mason Knapp Fund, Gift of the Estate of William F. Whittemore, Gift of Ananda K. Coomaraswamy, Gift of the Honorable Lady Hood, Bequest of Dona Luisa Coomaraswamy, Gift of Mrs. Henry Lyman, General Funds, Gift of Abdul Farag Shaer, Anonymous Gift, Gift of Reginald Jenney, Gift of N.M. Heeramaneck, Gift of W.O. Comstock, by exchange and William Francis Warden Fund. 1988.484

Standing upright on a small base, with a sense of movement implied in the subtle sway of her torso, this remarkable bronze figure exudes the earthy elegance associated with the very best of Khmer sculptures. Careful attention to details—elegant hand gestures, slightly upturned edges of the skirt, the wave of the fishtail-fold cloth hanging over the pleated skirt, and the hesitant smile seen at the corners of the lips—reflects an extraordinary level of craftsmanship.

*The iconography of this unadorned image is difficult to determine. A cylindrical hairstyle of semielliptical layered arcs (*jaṭāmukaṭa*) is generally associated with Śaiva figures such as Umā, the consort of Śiva. The presence of a seated figure in the* jaṭāmukaṭa*, on the other hand, suggests that the sculpture may represent the Buddhist goddess of wisdom, Prajñāpāramitā. Gentle hand gestures of blessing (with the right hand) and of holding a flower (with the left) are associated with all female goddesses, Hindu and Buddhist.*

Stylistically, the sculpture dates from the early phase of the Angkor period. The hairstyle of matted locks is very similar to the linear tresses found in Buddhist figures of the pre-Angkor period. First found in the stone sculptures at Bantei Srei (967-1000), the pleated skirt (sarong) with a slight suggestion of folds at the hem, as well as the gentle, sloping curve of the waistline of the skirt, suggest similar dating in the late tenth century. The overall emphasis on visual unity and the combination of soft, rounded planes and gentle, linear patterns place the sculpture at the transitional point of Khmer art.

185
Dancing celestial figure *(apsaras)*
Cambodia, late 11th century
Bronze. H: 39.3 cm.
Gift of Denman Waldo Ross. 22.686

The celestial figure—framed by a flame-like arch that terminates in a nāga head on the right lower end—dances on a fully blossomed lotus flower springing from a branch sprouting two additional buds. One of the buds is half opened and reveals another dancing figure.

This well-preserved fragment of great beauty and elegance may once have been tenoned into an elaborate lamp or incense burner. Dancing celestial figures constitute an appropriate decoration for a lamp suspended from the ceiling, and its flickering light would have enhanced the suggestion of movement so skillfully captivated by the artist.

The Indian tradition of making elaborate votive lamps was further developed in Southeast Asia, especially in Indonesia. Unfortunately, only a few fragments of such fragile bronze objects have survived in Cambodia.

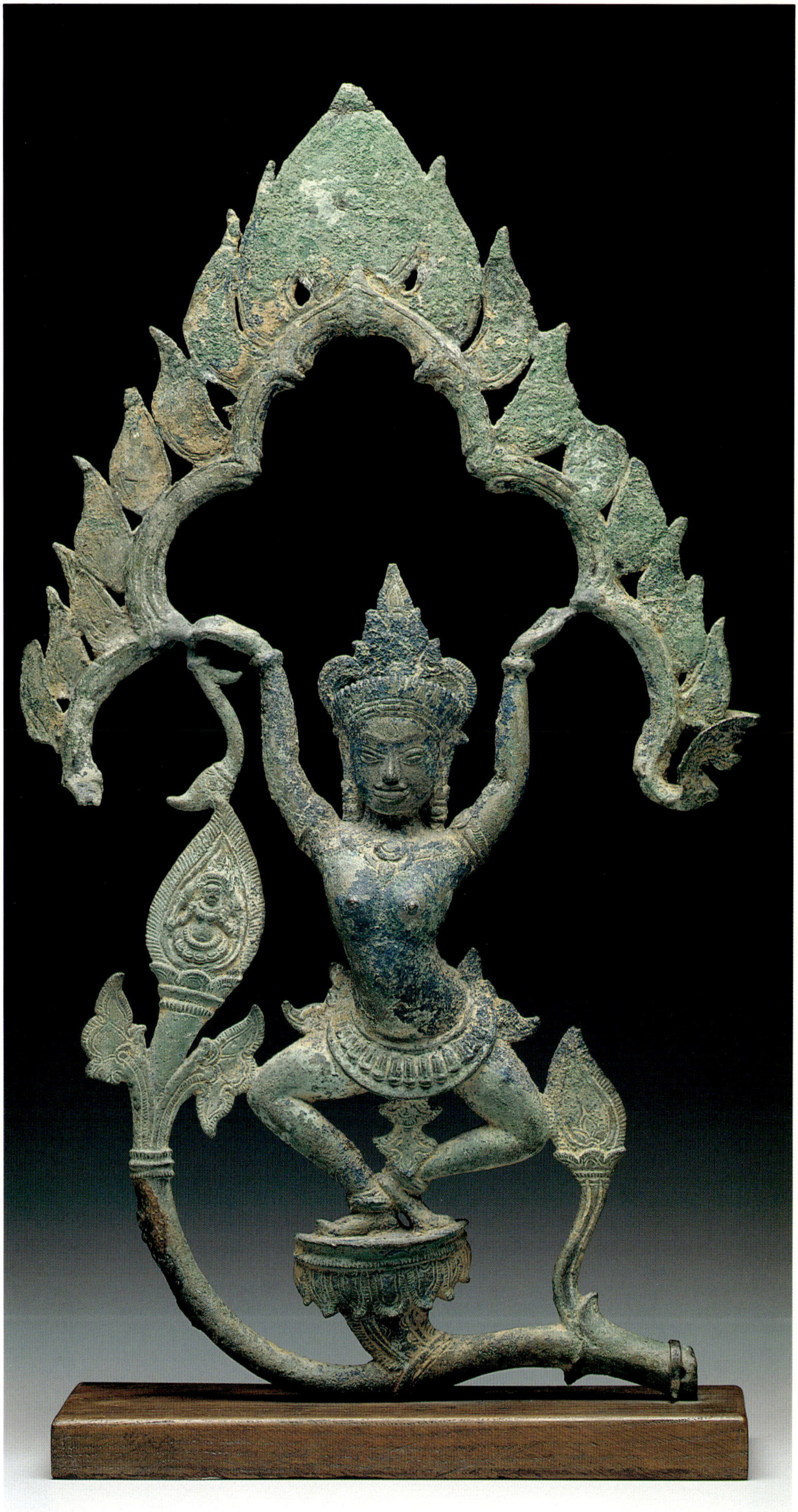

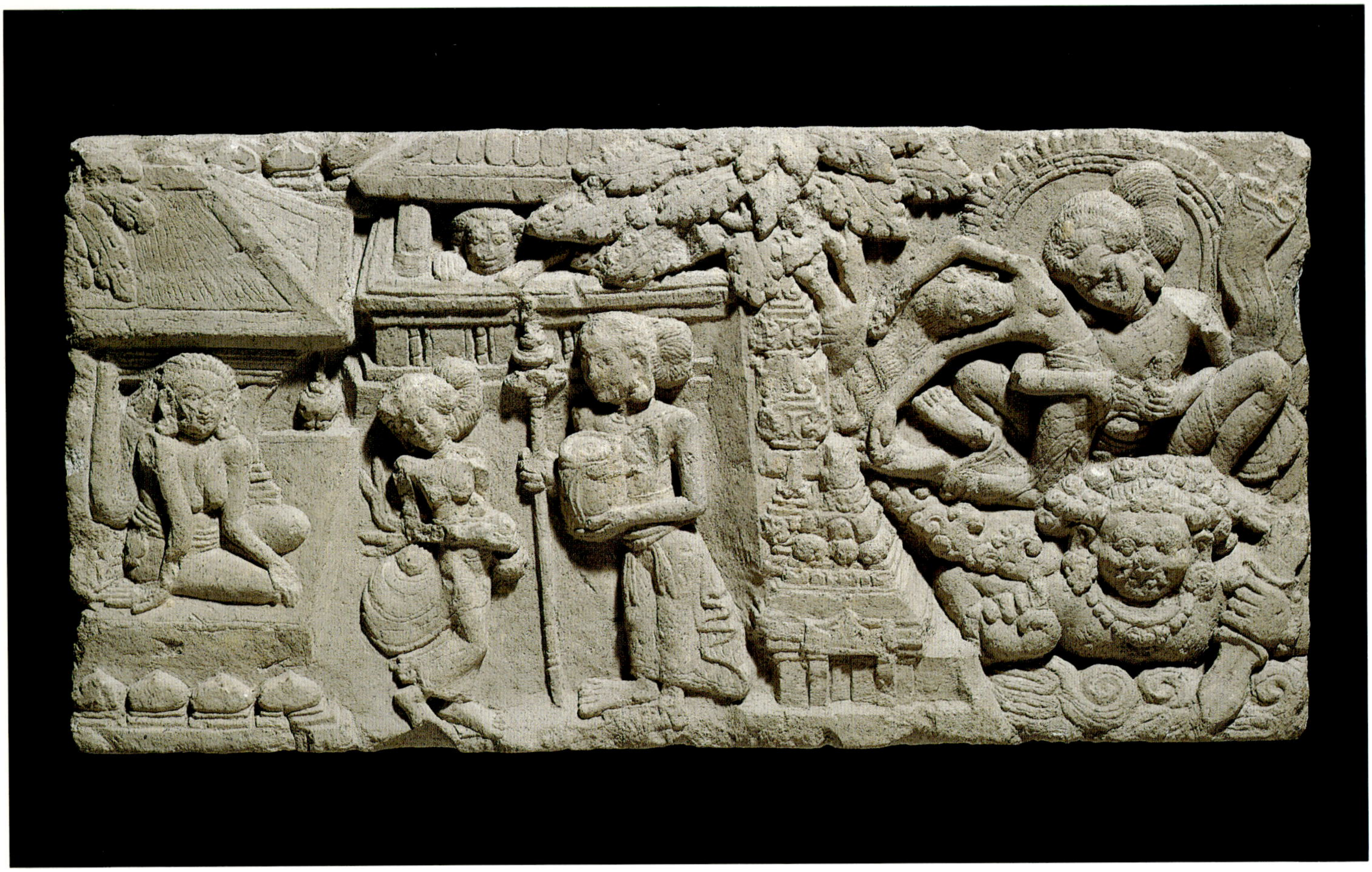

186
Rāvaṇa Abducting Sītā
Java, Indonesia, ca. 11th century
Sandstone. H: 39.3 cm. W: 77.4 cm.
Asiatic Curator's Fund. 67.1005

This relief depicts one of the key dramatic episodes in the Indian epic Rāmāyaṇa: *the abduction of Sītā by Rāvaṇa. After Sītā's husband Rāma and his faithful brother Lakṣmaṇa have been lured away from the hermitage in the forest of Daṇḍaka, in which the three of them are living together in exile, Rāvaṇa gains admission to the hemitage disguised as an itinerant priest. When Sītā turns down his advances, Rāvaṇa reveals his true identity, overpowers the resisting Sītā, and carries her off on his mount, Puṣpaka, to the island kingdom of Laṅkā.*

The relief is divided into two halves by a tree and a row of caṇḍis *seen in a type of bird's-eye perspective not unlike that used by the sculptors of Borobudur. The row of temples, resembling the rock-cut* caṇḍis *of Tampak Siring (in Bali, dated 1079), are part of the enclosure of the hermitage, the walls of which are crowded by decorations in the shape of keben fruit. In the central foreground stands the heroine Sītā, her head demurely turned away from the bogus priest Rāvaṇa, who carries a gourd on a strap and a jingling staff as the attributes of his disguise.*

The identification of the two figures in the buildings of the hermitage is less certain. The seated woman on the left may be Rāvaṇa's sister Sūrpanakhā, whose nose was cut off by Lakṣmaṇa, the cruel act for which Sītā's abduction was the revenge. As many of the protruding parts of the relief have been damaged, it is unclear whether the defacement of woman's nose was accidental or intended by the sculptor. The figure at the back, who seems to be spying on the scene in the foreground, is probably a second representation of Sūrpanakhā, the result of the artist's synoptic method and based upon the passage that is rendered in the old Javanese kakawin *as: "There was a certain demoness, Sūrpanakhā, who was a spy for Rāvaṇa. She wandered through the forest and arrived at the hermitage in the Daṇḍaka Forest" (old Javanese* Rāmāyana, *4:27).*

The right half of the relief depicts the actual abduction. Rāvaṇa has slung his right arm around the waist of his victim, whose posture expresses both her utter despair and the speed with which she is being carried off. She raises her arms in a helpless gesture, her hair trailing behind her in waves. Rāvaṇa is riding Puṣpaka, a demon who raises his right hand and index finger in the threatening tarjani *gesture and who holds a twin-bladed weapon in his left hand. Stylized clouds indicate that Puṣpaka is already airborne.*

Sītā's dress and hairdo, the architectural style of the caṇḍi, *and the* keben *on the wall of the hermitage, as well as the tree separating the preliminary encounter from the abduction, are reminiscent of Jalatunda reliefs. A relief in the National Museum of Jakarta (inv. no. 396a)—identical in size to the Boston relief and probably representing Hanumān's return to Rāma's camp from Laṅkā—was once thought to come from Jalatunda. Its carving is less deep, however, and its theme does not seem to fit into the iconographic program of Jalatunda. It is possible that both reliefs came from a now-vanished temple decorated with* Rāmāyaṇa *reliefs, dating perhaps from the eleventh century, the only known architectural illustration of this epic theme between Prambanan (about 900) and Panataran (fourteenth century).*

187
Architectural fragment with celestial figures *(apsaras)*
From the temple Prasāt Khna Sen Keo, Kompong Thom.
Cambodia, second half of 11th century
Sandstone. H: 120.4 cm.
Denman Waldo Ross Collection.
23.445

Consisting of two blocks of stone, this large sculpture with two celestial figures represents the last phase of the "Baphuon" style and is an important transitional link to the "Angkor Wat" style of the twelfth century. The figure in the front leans to her left as she holds her knotted hair with one hand and a lotus bud in the other. The second figure, much more incomplete, is similarly designed but in a reverse position. Such celestial figures decorated temple walls and enhanced the divine essence of a temple.

In keeping with the tradition of the god-king (Devarāja) *cult, Khmer temples were built by kings for religious worship as well as for their own deification. Prasāt Khna Sen Keo, a temple site at which the Museum fragment once adorned a corner wall, is associated with the reign of the Khmer king Udayādityavarman II, who ruled Cambodia from 1050 to 1066. Named for the most important temple complex of his reign, the Baphuon, sculptures like this are characterized by restrained elegance, gentle smiles, and clothing details such as the carefully articulated pleats, the gentle curve of the skirts, and a drape in front in the form of a fish tail.*

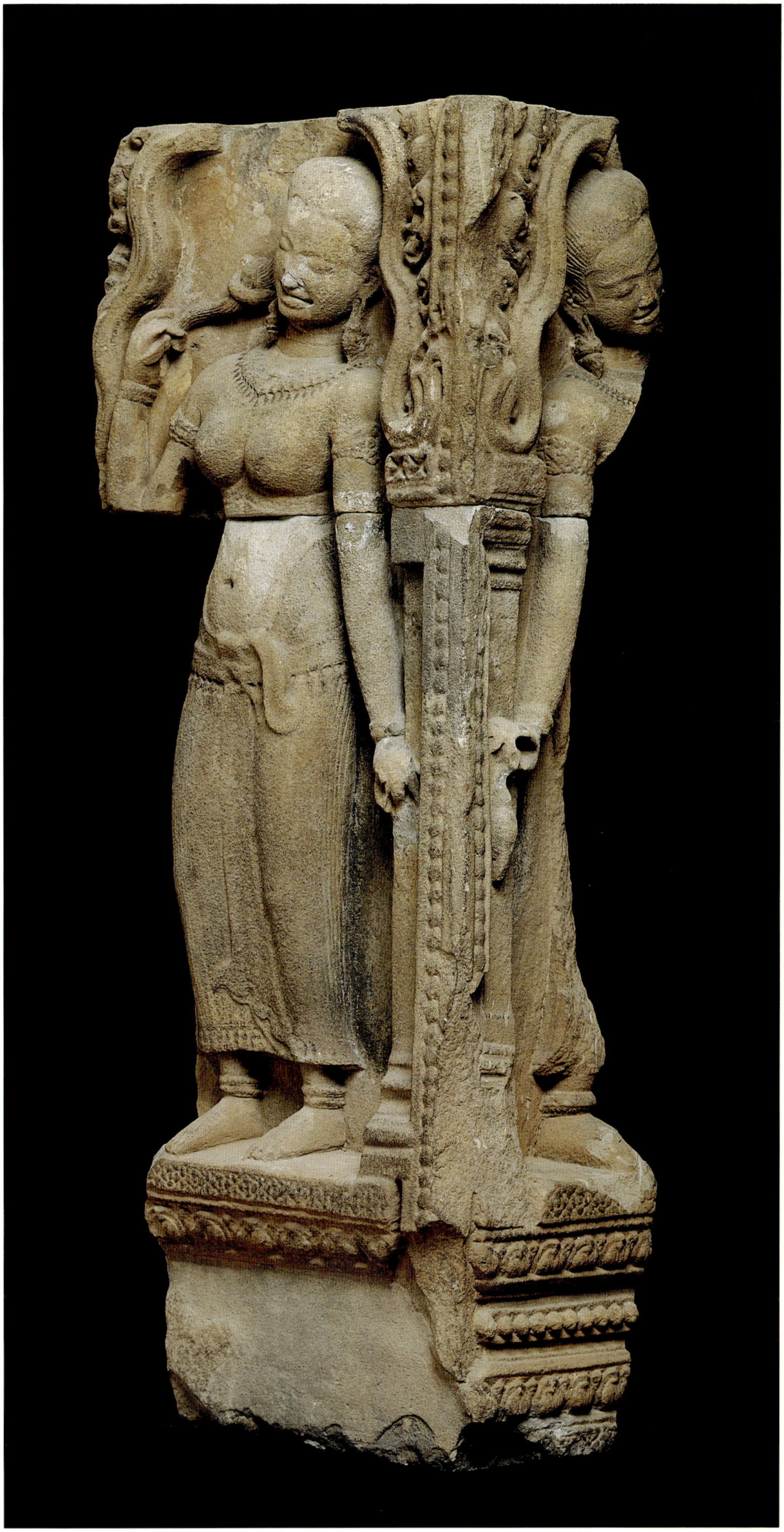

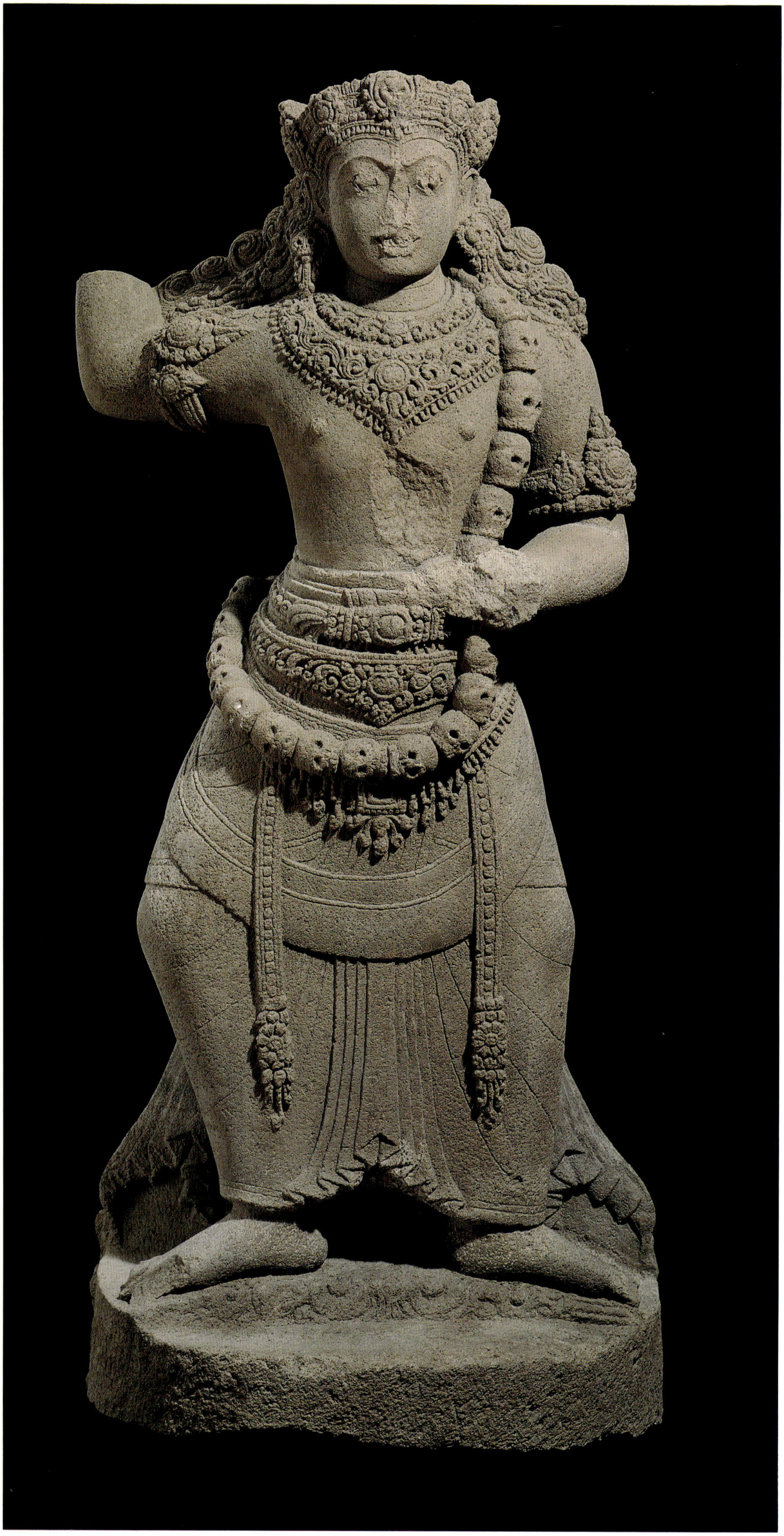

188
Bhairava or Mahākāla
Eastern Java, Indonesia, 14th century
Volcanic stone (andesite). H: 198 cm.
Frederick L. Jack Fund. 1972.951

The slightly bent knees and the legs and feet spread in an aggressive, defiant posture give the deity a pose reminiscent of that of Durgā slaying the demon Mahiṣa. His right forearm with the hand holding a weapon, once tenoned into the raised arm, has been lost. The left hand, which once held a skull cup in front of the chest, has also broken off. The god wears a garland of skulls, and skulls decorate the headdress and the earrings. Repetition of the skull motif is typical for the demonic forms of deities, and the thick, curly hair that cascades over the shoulders is like that of rākṣasas or other demons. Despite the considerable damage inflicted upon the nose and mouth, the fangs that flanked the rows of teeth can still be discerned.

Like the statue of Cāmuṇḍī, dated in accordance with 1292, which was found at Ardimulyo near Singasari (East Java) in 1927, this statue was smashed into several pieces. It remained in this condition for many years and was considered beyond repair when it was acquired in 1972. The research laboratory of the Museum succeeded in reassembling the pieces into a nearly complete statue; only small sections of the back, the base, and the drapery flanking the statue have been filled with new material.

Two-armed demonic figures holding a skull cup in the left hand and a weapon — a trident, club, sword, or chopper — in the right hand usually represent Mahākāla, the Buddhist god of death, or Bhairava, a demonic form of Śiva. These two deities have so many iconographic characteristics in common that it is often difficult to draw clear distinctions between them. In India, as in Indonesia, the identity of statues of these deities cannot always be determined with certainty. This is especially true of statues created during the Majapahit period, when Buddhism and Hinduism became closely intertwined. References in contemporary literature to the cult of Bhairava make an identification as that deity most likely.

189
Demon Mahiṣa
Eastern Java, Indonesia, 14th century
Volcanic stone (andesite). H: 84 cm.
Asiatic Curator's Fund. 1971.625

During the Eastern Javanese period (tenth - fourteenth century) the goddess Durgā was one of the deities most frequently worshiped. She was usually portrayed with eight arms and standing on top of the buffalo Mahiṣa, from whose head (split by her sword) emerges the slain demon.

By far the most illustrious statue of this form of Durgā is the sculpture from Candi Singasari (about 1300) in the Leiden Museum of Ethnology. This monumental sculpture shows the goddess standing defiantly, legs akimbo, on the back of the buffalo, quite different from the more static earlier representations. While the Boston statue represents only a fragment of a Durgā ensemble, it is evident from the size of the demon that the entire group was once considerably larger than the celebrated Singasari statue. In all probability it dates from a slightly later time, perhaps around the middle of the fourteenth century.

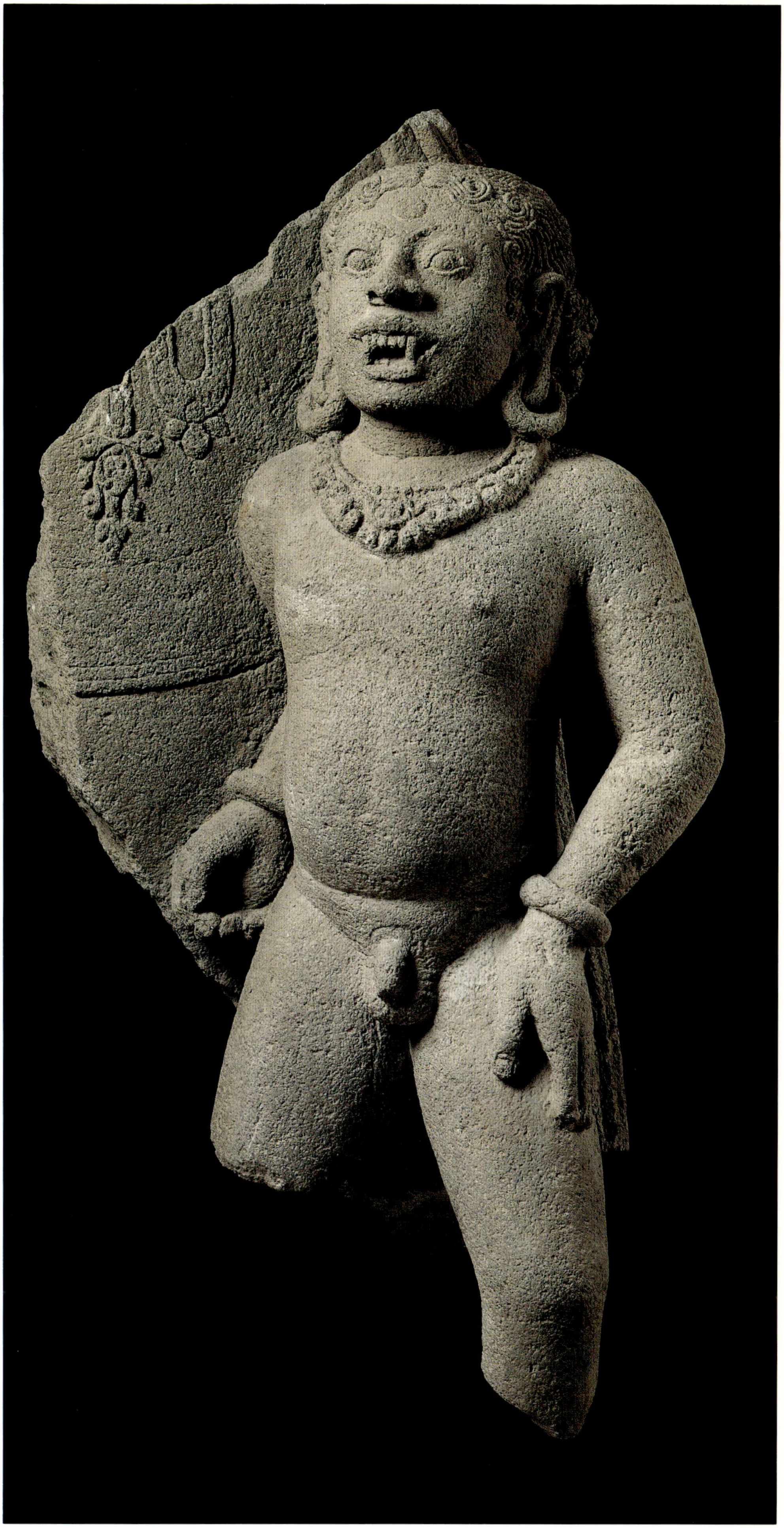

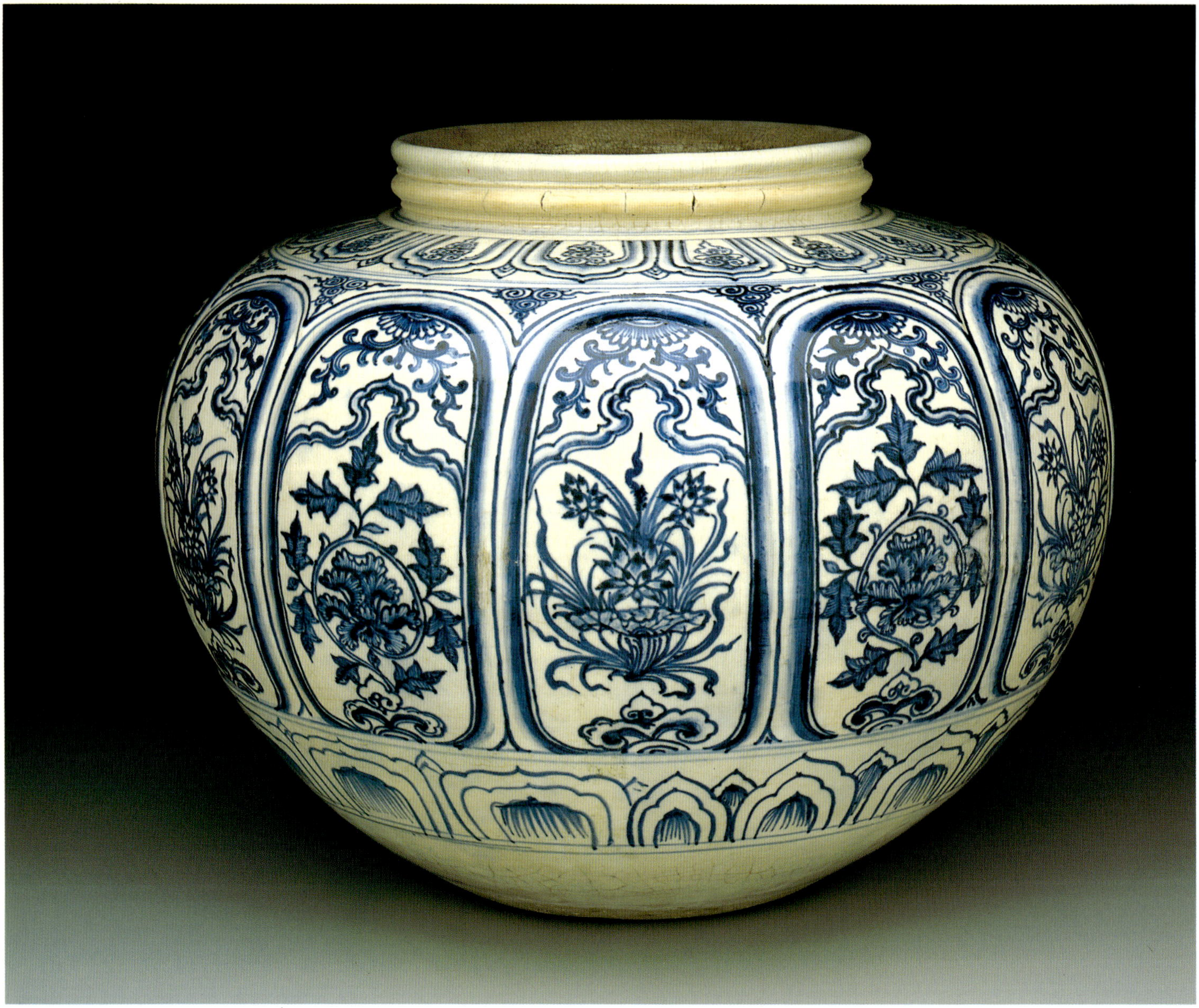

190
Jar
Vietnam, Le dynasty, mid-15th century
High-fired stoneware with underglaze cobalt-blue decoration. H: 26.5 cm.
Charles Bain Hoyt Fund. 1990.315

During the fifteenth and sixteenth centuries, Vietnamese kilns produced blue-and-white ceramics of exceptional quality. The most successful examples, such as this large fifteenth-century jar, were either exported to select clients along Southeast Asian and Middle Eastern trade routes or commissioned exclusively for imperial use. Inspired by Chinese blue-and-white porcelain of the Yuan and Ming periods, this ceramic style rivals, and in some respects surpasses, its Chinese prototype. The Vietnamese achieved a more intense blue color by employing an arsenic- rather than a manganese-based cobalt imported from the Middle East. Vietnamese potters possessed not only technical sophistication but also a highly imaginative decorative style. The motifs on this jar's central panels —(from top to bottom) chrysanthemum, scroll, peony/lotus (in alternating sequence), and "magic fungus" — represent an elaboration of traditional Chinese designs. Unlike Chinese, Japanese, and Korean decorative styles on blue-and-white wares, however, the outlines are of even width, not calligraphic. The lotus and peonies are depicted with shading and hatching and an attention to naturalism unknown in Chinese examples of this period. Such a drawing style parallels closely a Vietnamese blue-and-white bottle in Istanbul's Topkapu Museum collection, which bears an inscribed date of 1450 and gives Nam-sach province (near today's Hanoi) as the place of production. The melon shape and "rolled" mouth rim of this jar are also Vietnamese innovations. Gentle carving and a cobalt-blue wash around each panel's edges lend definition to the design and create a subtle lobed effect on the surface. Such superb Vietnamese works must have posed a strong challenge to the Chinese, who had dominated the Middle Eastern ceramic trade for centuries.

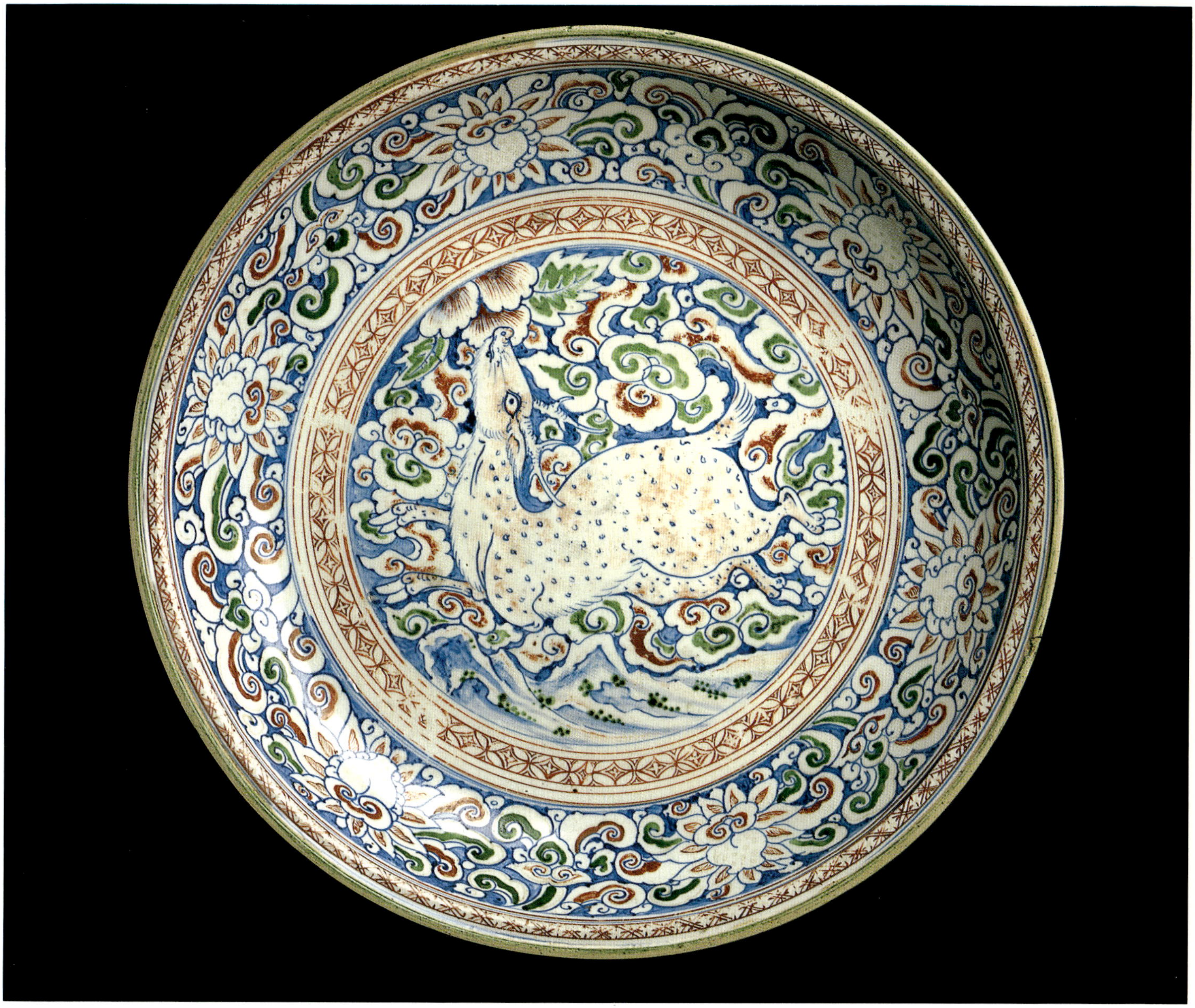

191
Plate
Vietnam, 15th century
Porcelain with underglaze blue, overglaze polychrome enamels, and traces of gold. Diam: 44 cm.
Charles Bain Hoyt Fund. 1985.334

One of the most impressive types of Vietnamese ceramic ware of any period is the polychrome porcelain decorated in both underglaze blue and overglaze enamels. They were produced in the fifteenth century, together with the more common blue-and-white variety, for the active sea trade between the Asiatic mainland and the island states of Southeast Asia. Most of the finest examples of Vietnamese ceramics have been preserved on the islands of Indonesia and the southern Philippines, while little of good quality has survived in Vietnam itself.

The present piece is reputed to have come from a "princely family" from Atjeh, North Sumatra, now living in the Netherlands. It is unique in terms of its large size, the well-executed decorative painting, the unusual motif of the deer with dragonlike antlers in full gallop over dwarfed mountains, and the excellent state of preservation with much of the original gold enameling still intact on the outer wall of the dish. The base is covered with a dark brown colored slip, as is the case with Vietnamese wares of this period.

India

The earliest and one of the most comprehensive in the United States, the Indian collection at the Museum was developed primarily through the collaboration of Ananda K. Coomaraswamy, the first keeper of Indian art and a pioneering scholar in the field, and Denman Waldo Ross, the Museum trustee who was responsible for purchasing Coomaraswamy's personal collection for the Museum and for bringing him to Boston.

The strengths of the Indian collection lie in the vast holdings of paintings and an excellent group of early sculptures. Some of the finest Mughal paintings—*Darbār of Jahāngīr, Dying Ināyat Khān,* and *Birth of a Prince,* to name a few—were purchased in 1914 from the French collector Victor Goloubew and were some of the earliest Indian acquisitions by an American museum. Rajput painting, "discovered" by Dr. Coomaraswamy in the first decade of the twentieth century, was the next major phase of Indian art to be acquired by the Museum. Among some 900 paintings and drawings gathered by Coomaraswamy prior to his appointment at the Museum were some of the best-known works from various Rajput courts and the earliest known paintings from the Punjab Hills. The Museum has acquired additional Rajput paintings and has strengthened its holdings of Rajasthani works over the years, particularly through the generosity of John Goelet.

Unlike the paintings collections, which came in large groups, early Indian sculpture has been acquired gradually, and all phases are well represented. Among the masterpieces are the torso of a fertility goddess (*yaksī*)from the great *stūpa* at Sanchi and ạ fragment of a *yaksī* from the Bharhut *stūpa*. A strong collection of Kusāna dynasty Buddhist sculptures from Gandhara and Mathura, along with a group of relief sculptures from the Amaravati region in South India and some very fine examples of Gupta art, give the visitor a comprehensive view of the development of early Buddhist art in India.

The Museum of Fine Arts is one of the few institutions in North America to possess an extensive collection of terracotta sculptures and archaelogical fragments, ranging from Indus Valley sites to the Gupta period. A large number of these objects came to the Museum as a result of an expedition to Chanhu-daro in the Indus valley, jointly sponsored by the Museum and the University of Pennsylvania.

The Museum's medieval Indian sculpture includes objects from almost all regions of India. Particularly noteworthy are large stone sculptures from the Cola period in South India. Other significant areas of the collection include Indian jewelry and fine ivory sculptures from Kashmir and Orissa.

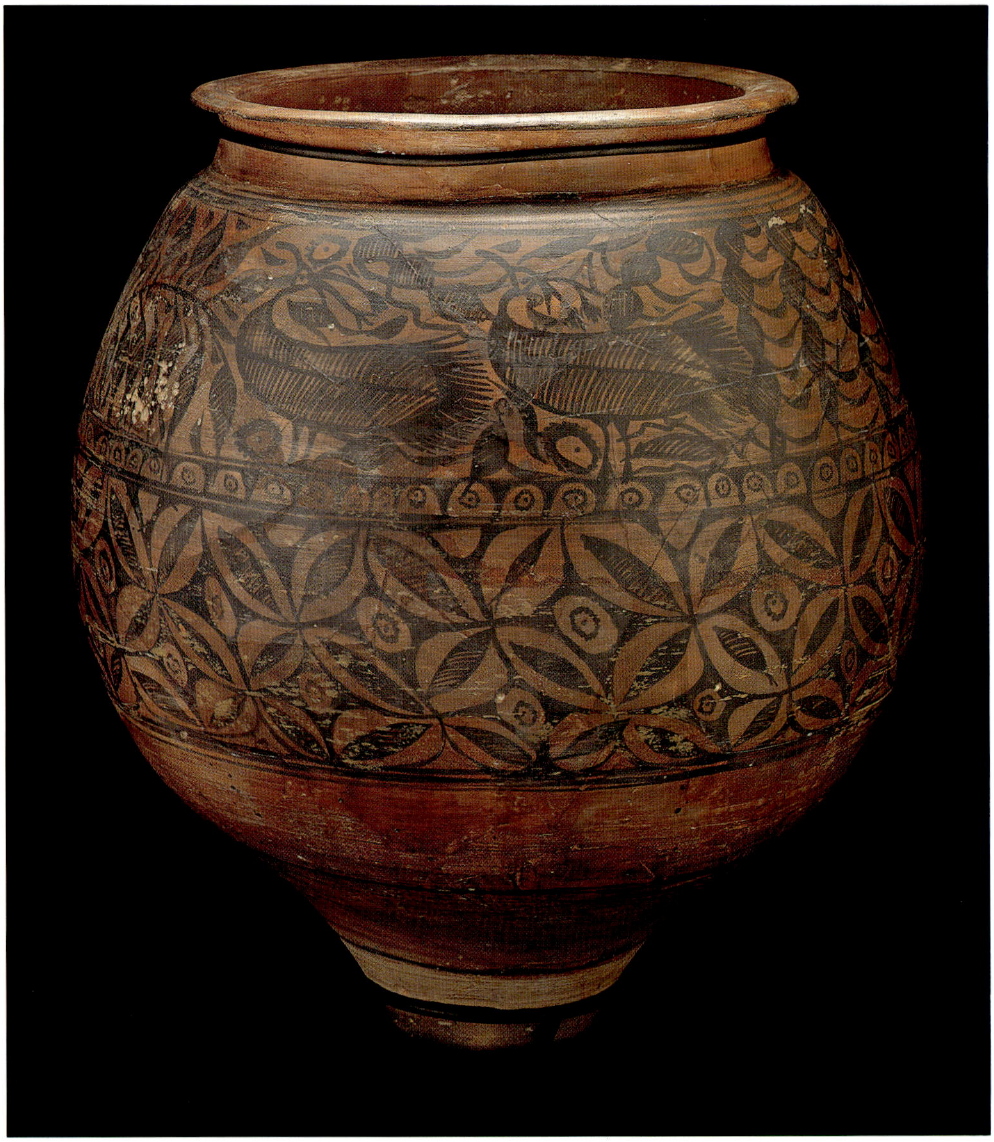

192
Jar
Chanhu Daro, Sindh (Pakistan), Harappa Culture, about 2500 B.C.
Reddish earthenware with painted decoration in black. H: 55.2 cm.
Joint Expedition of the American School of India and Iranian Studies and the Museum of Fine Arts. 36.2977

One of the largest painted jars to survive from the Indus Valley civilization, this elaborately decorated grain jar was excavated at the site of Chanhu Daro. Located near the Indus River and the Khirthar mountains in present-day Pakistan, the ancient city of Chanhu Daro was closely related to other major centers of the Indus valley civilization.

The decoration of plant and floral designs with schematic renditions of peacocks is characteristic of early Indian pottery. The close association of plant forms with peacocks may be of particular significance, for this bird is often associated with earth worship in India.

193
Torso of fertility goddess *(yakṣī)*
Sanchi, central India, 25 B.C. - A.D. 25
Sandstone; from a gateway of the Great Stupa. H: 72 cm.
Denman Waldo Ross Collection.
29.999

Yakṣas *and* yakṣīs *function as local tutelary deities, nature spirits, and guardians. Incorporated fairly early on into the religious vocabulary of Buddhism, these semidivine figures were often placed at the entrances of religious monuments to provide the faith with a more life-affirming viewpoint and make it easier for devotees to embrace the new religion. Tree dryads or tree-dwelling* yakṣīs *such as this one were associated with fertility and were often worshiped by those who desired children. The unabashed sensuality of the figure and the emphasis on the feminine parts affirm the symbolic meaning of the* yakṣī *as a fertility goddess.*

The Museum torso comes from one of the oldest surviving monuments of Buddhism—the Great Stūpa *at Sanchi—and was one of eight large tree dryads that served as bracket figures on the four gateways of the* stūpa. *Like the figures that still survive in situ, this* yakṣī *would have been standing on or near the roots of a tree, her arms holding a branch or a trunk. The foliage of the tree would have framed her from above.*

One of the striking features of this piece is the contrast of forms. While the contours in the front are very rounded and there are subtle curves that move the eye from one plane to another, the back of the yakṣī *is relatively flat with heavily decorated surfaces representing the folds of her transparent garment, a belt, braids of hair, and an elaborate hair decoration. When viewing the figure from the side, it becomes clear that the artist did not intend to create in the round; rather, still bound by the relief-carving traditions of earlier generations, he made the front and back as separate entities. This was perfectly appropriate, since the viewer would have first encountered the* yakṣī *frontally and would not have seen her back until well inside the enclosure of the* stūpa.

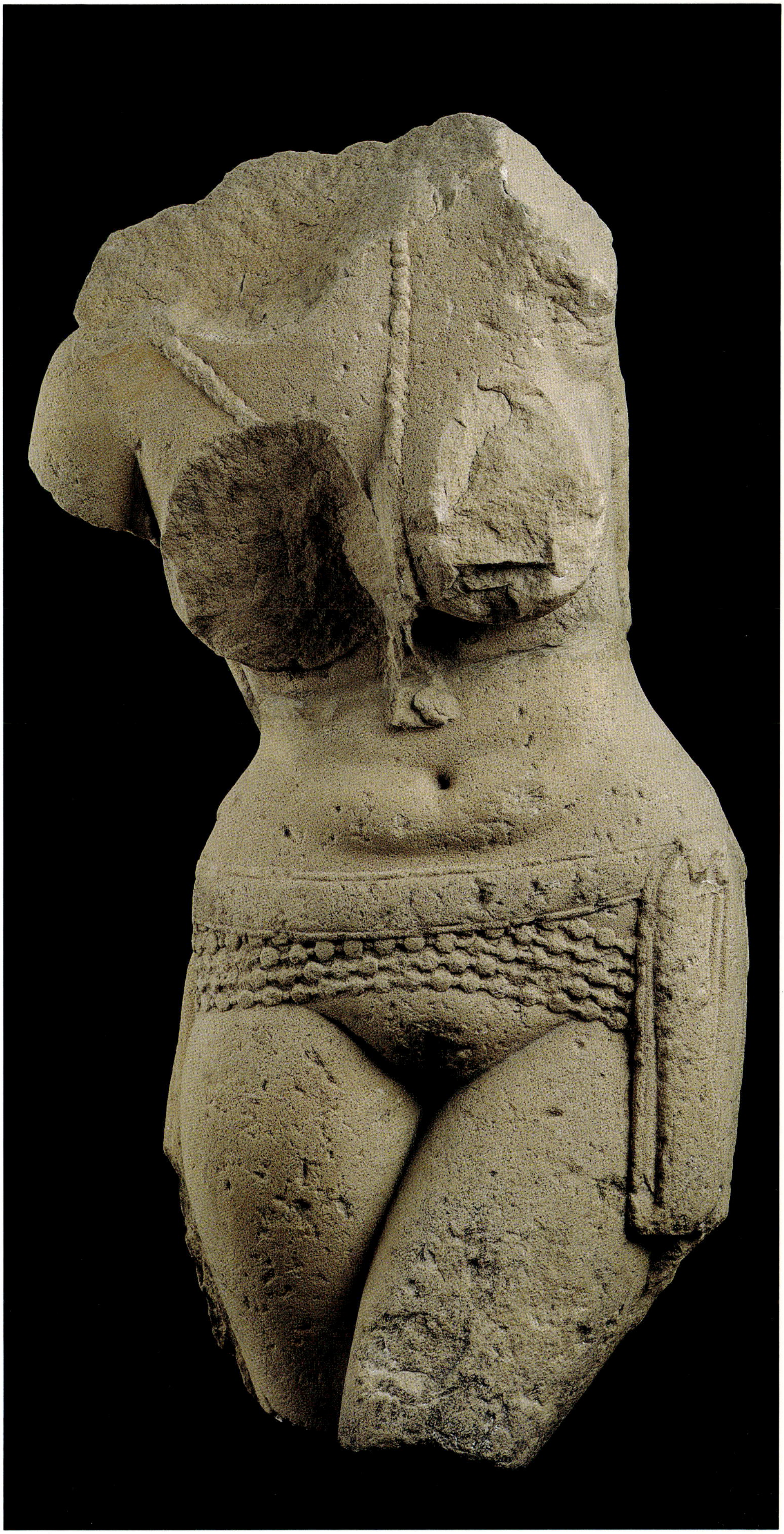

194
Bath of the Buddha in the Nairañjana River
Amaravati region, southern India, about A.D. 50
Schistose marble; slab from an enclosing wall of a stupa.
H: 157.6 cm.
Denman Waldo Ross Collection.
29.151

Located in the ancient Andhra kingdom in southern India, Amaravati was the site of a complex sanctuary centered around one of the largest Buddhist stūpas *in the world. This two-sided relief from the Amaravati region probably once decorated the outer wall of a* stūpa. *The side visible here depicts the sacred bath of the Buddha-to-be just before he sat beneath the Bodhi tree to attain enlightenment. In keeping with early conventions of representing the historical Buddha through symbols rather than in a human form, the presence of the sage is indicated here by footprints in the river. The water is represented by wavy lines engraved in the band and by water creatures:* makaras, *turtles, and fish. Paying homage to the Buddha-to-be are the great serpent king Nāga and his two consorts; above them, four river goddesses with vessels on their heads glide through the sky to witness the auspicious occasion.*

This side of the relief was carved in the early part of the first century A.D. About a hundred years later, when the stūpa *was refurbished, the stone was removed from the wall, turned around, and recarved on the other side with a representation of a* stūpa. *It gives us a fairly accurate idea of the construction and decoration of* stūpas *in southern India.*

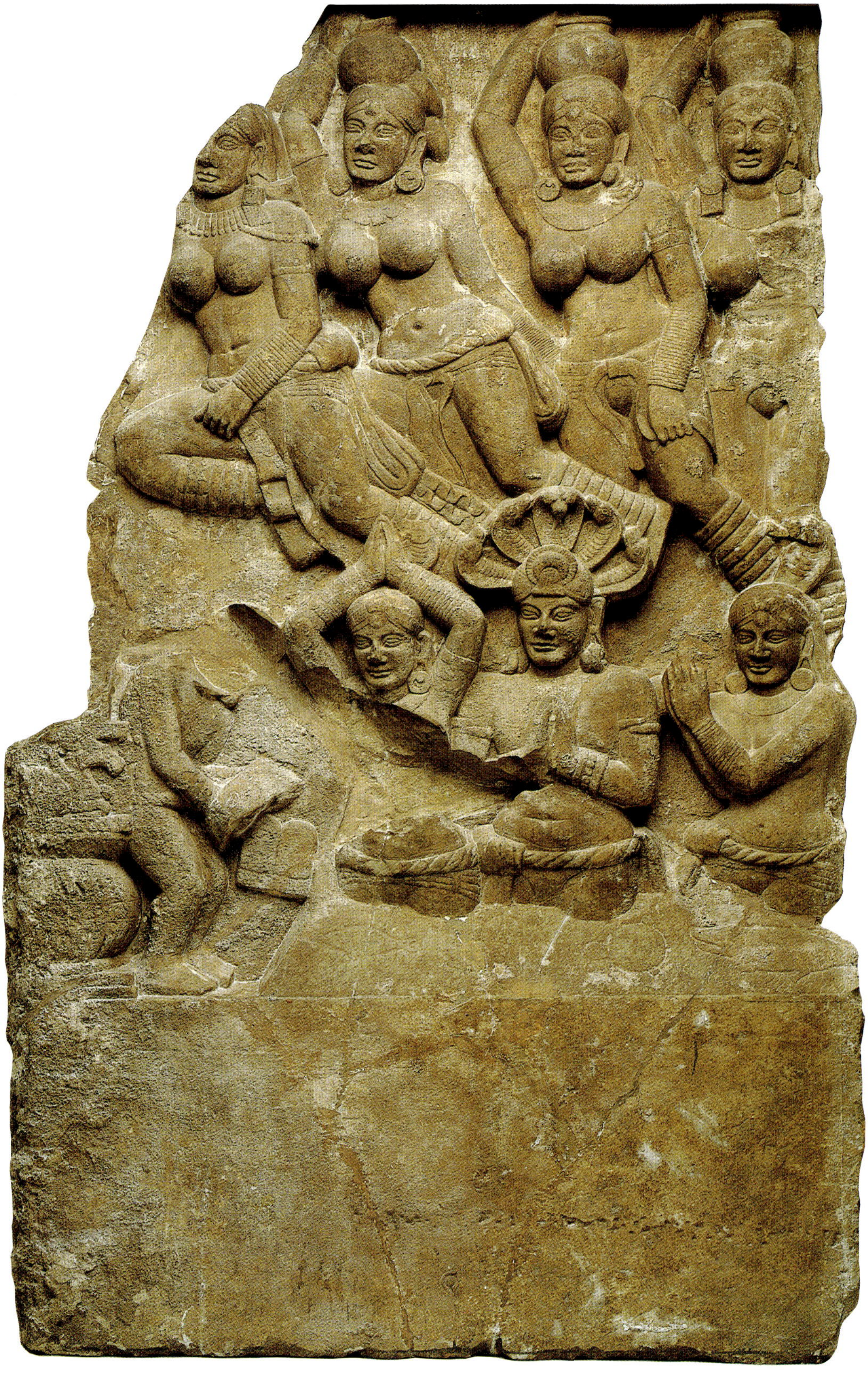

195
River Goddess Gaṅgā
(Gaṅgā Devī)
Besnagar, central India, mid-5th century A.D.
Sandstone. H: 73.5 cm.
Charles Amos Cummings Bequest Fund. 26.26

Images of the river goddesses Gaṅgā and Yamunā were frequently placed at the entrances of Buddhist and Hindu shrines to enhance the religious essence of the monuments and to "purify" the devotee with the symbolic presence of water prior to entering the inner chamber of the gods. This well-known image is probably from the upper right corner of a temple doorway and would have been balanced on the other side with an image of the river goddess Yamunā.

The mount on which Gaṅgā Devī traditionally stands, the makara, *is a mythical aquatic creature combining features of a crocodile, a fish, and an elephant. An auspicious symbol associated with fertility, the* makara *is frequently used as a decorative device as well. Its life-giving force is symbolized here through a semidivine dwarf* (gaṇa) *who extracts pearls from the* makara's *mouth. Another* gaṇa *stands on the* makara's *tail, gazing at the goddess in adoration. The pose of Gaṅgā Devī is similar to that of earlier fertility goddesses with whom she shares traits.*

The delicate balance between the modeled figures in high relief and the deeply undercut background, and between the quietly posed goddess and the energetic makara, *exemplifies a highly developed Indian aesthetic sensibility in the fifth century.*

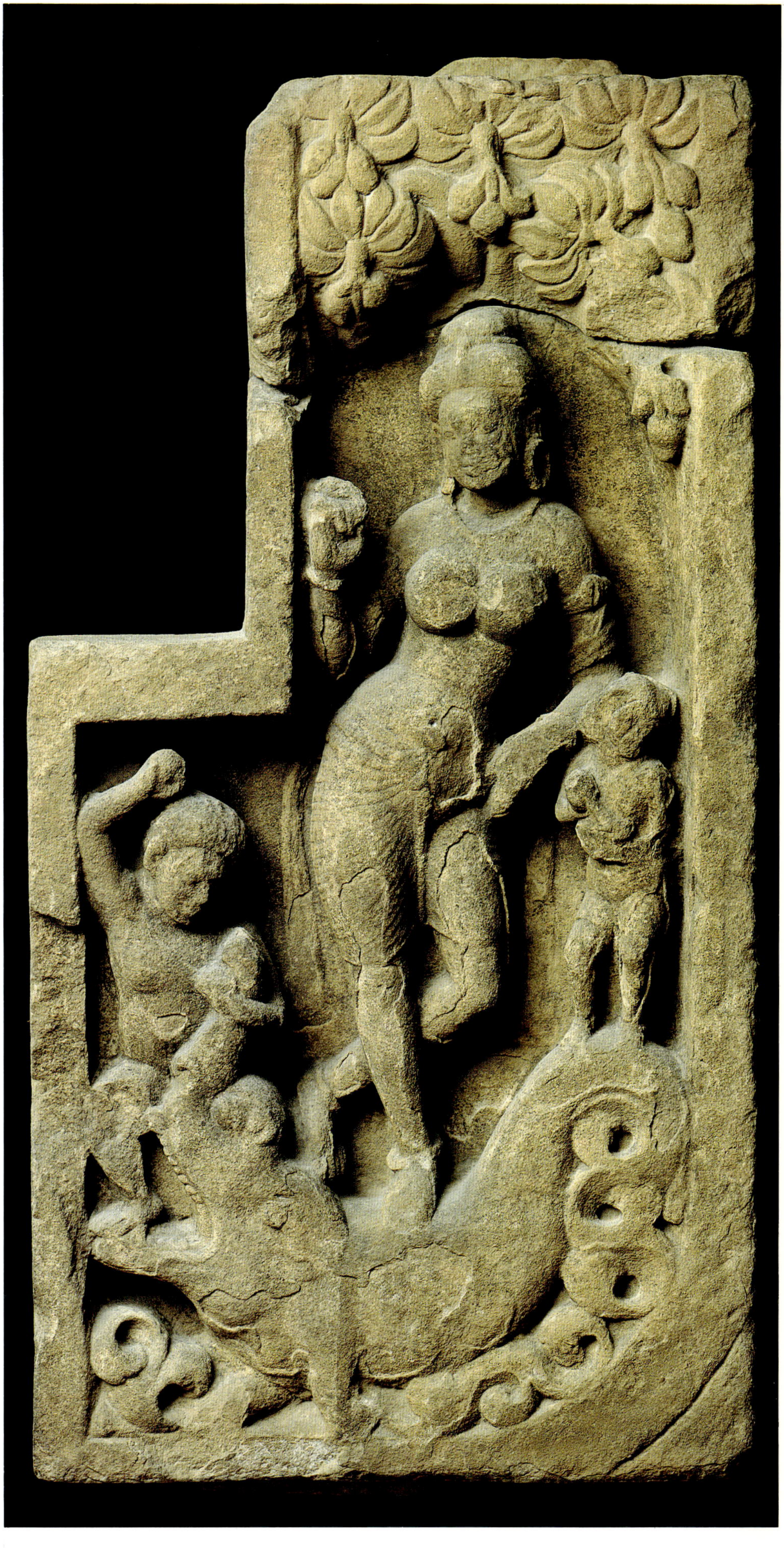

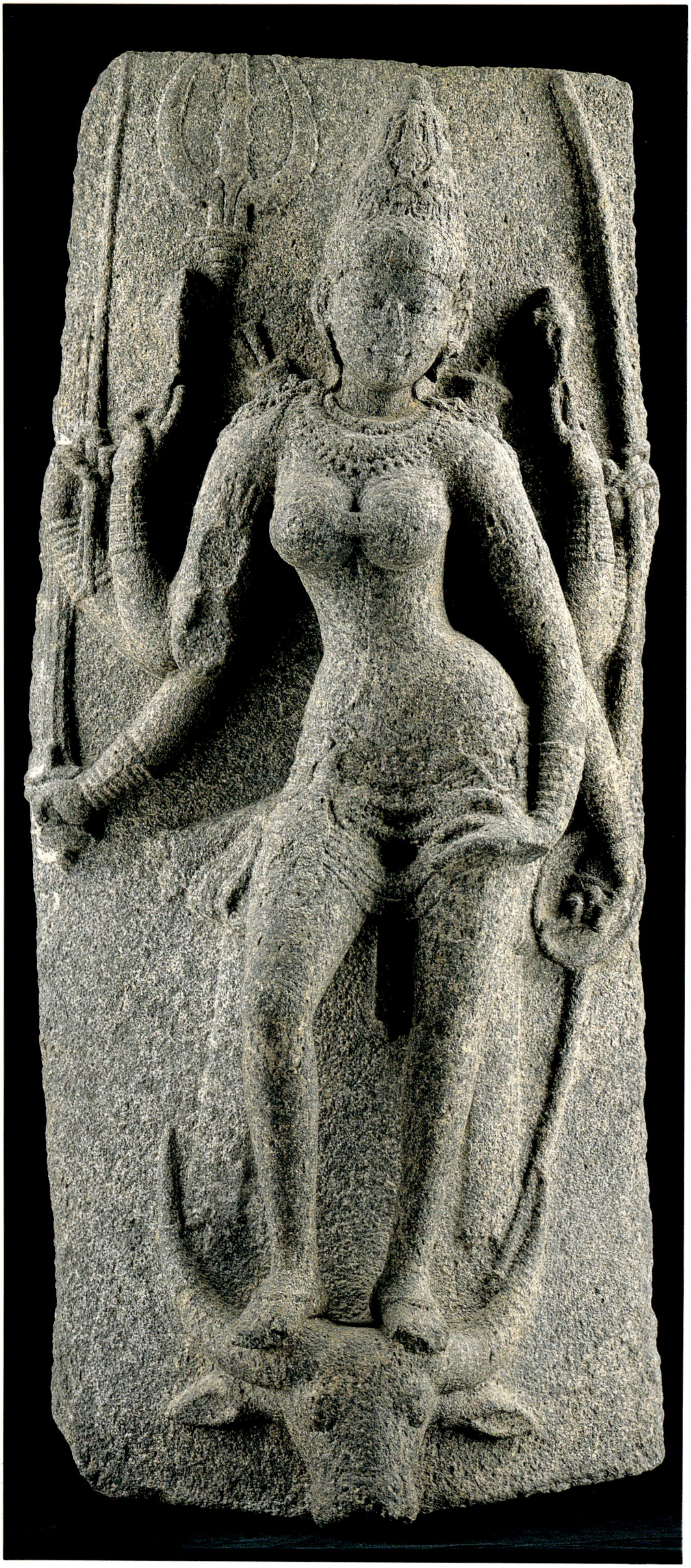

196

Durgā as the Slayer of the Buffalo Demon *(Durgā Mahiṣāsuramardinī)*

Southern India, 8th century A.D.
Granulite. H: 150 cm.
Gift of Denman Waldo Ross. 27.171

Durgā is a terrifying form of the Indian goddess Devī and is usually associated with the Śaiva cult. Seen here in one of her aspects, as a slayer of the buffalo demon Mahiṣa, she stands on the head of her adversary, holding a variety of weapons lent to her by different gods: a trident, a discus and conch, a sword and shield, a dart, and quiver and arrows.

According to various Hindu myths, the half-human and half-buffalo demon was indestructible. Endowed with supernatural powers acquired through austerity, he began creating havoc on earth and threatened to destroy the cosmic order of the universe. All the gods assembled and pleaded with Devī to confront the enemy. Ultimately, with the help of weapons from other gods and her own energy, she was able to slay the demon and restore order to the universe.

This fairly complete image of Durgā Mahiṣāsuramardinī (missing only the lower right hand) would have been placed in a niche on the outside wall of a Śiva temple. On the basis of stylistic analysis and a comparison with other known images from the Pallava and Cōḷa dynasties in South India, the Durgā can be dated to the second half of the eighth century.

197
Seated Buddha
Nagapattinam, southern India, about 9th century A.D.
Gilt bronze with silver inlay. H: 60 cm. (throne back); 39 cm. (figure)
Marshall H. Gould and Keith McLeod Funds. 1970.3; 67.4

Nagapattinam is an important harbor on the east coast of southern India, where the Buddha continued to be venerated long after the Buddhist law had been replaced by Śaiva and Vaiṣṇava cults in other parts of the subcontinent.

The Buddha, who resembles statuary of the northern Indian Gupta type, but whose provenance from southern India is evident from the flame-shaped protuberance on top of his head, is dressed in a simple, thin monk's robe. As if to contrast the spiritual with the phenomenal world, the artist placed the simply dressed figure in front of a throne back decorated with a profusion of animal and floral ornamentation. Above his head a canopy, cast separately and surmounted by stylized branches of a tree, is attached by a tenon to the top of the throne back.

Two attendant figures, one representing Maitreya, the Buddha-to-be, and one Avalokiteśvara, the Bodhisattva of Mercy, were attached originally to the back of the screen. Cast solid like all southern Indian icons, the statue has survived intact, but the thinner, more fragile throne and pedestal have been lost. Although incompletely preserved, the altarpiece represents the highest achievement of southern Indian Buddhist sculpture. Statues of this type, exported to the countries of Southeast Asia, exerted a strong influence on the art styles of the Javanese kingdoms, where the Buddhist art of the Gupta period reached its ultimate perfection on foreign soil in the art of Borobudur and Chandi Sewu.

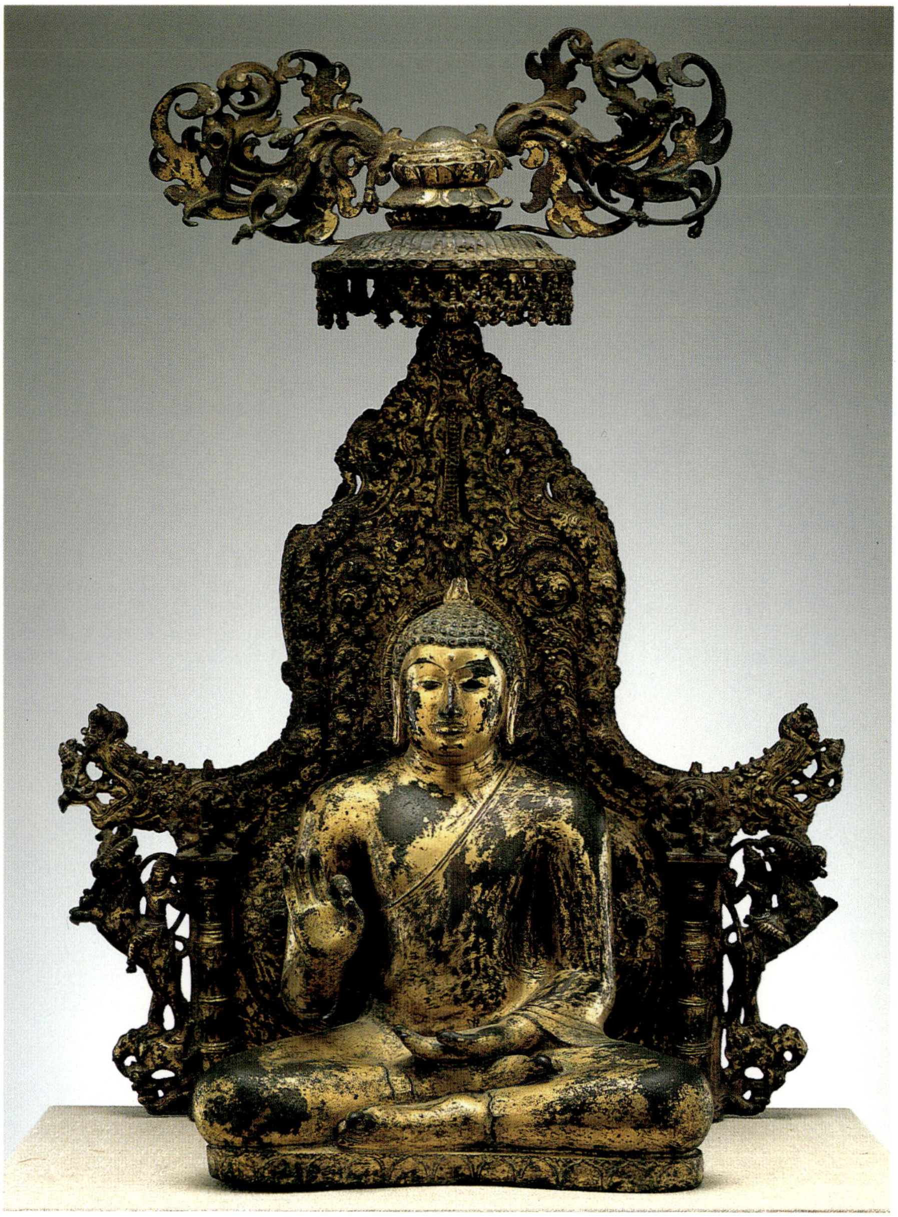

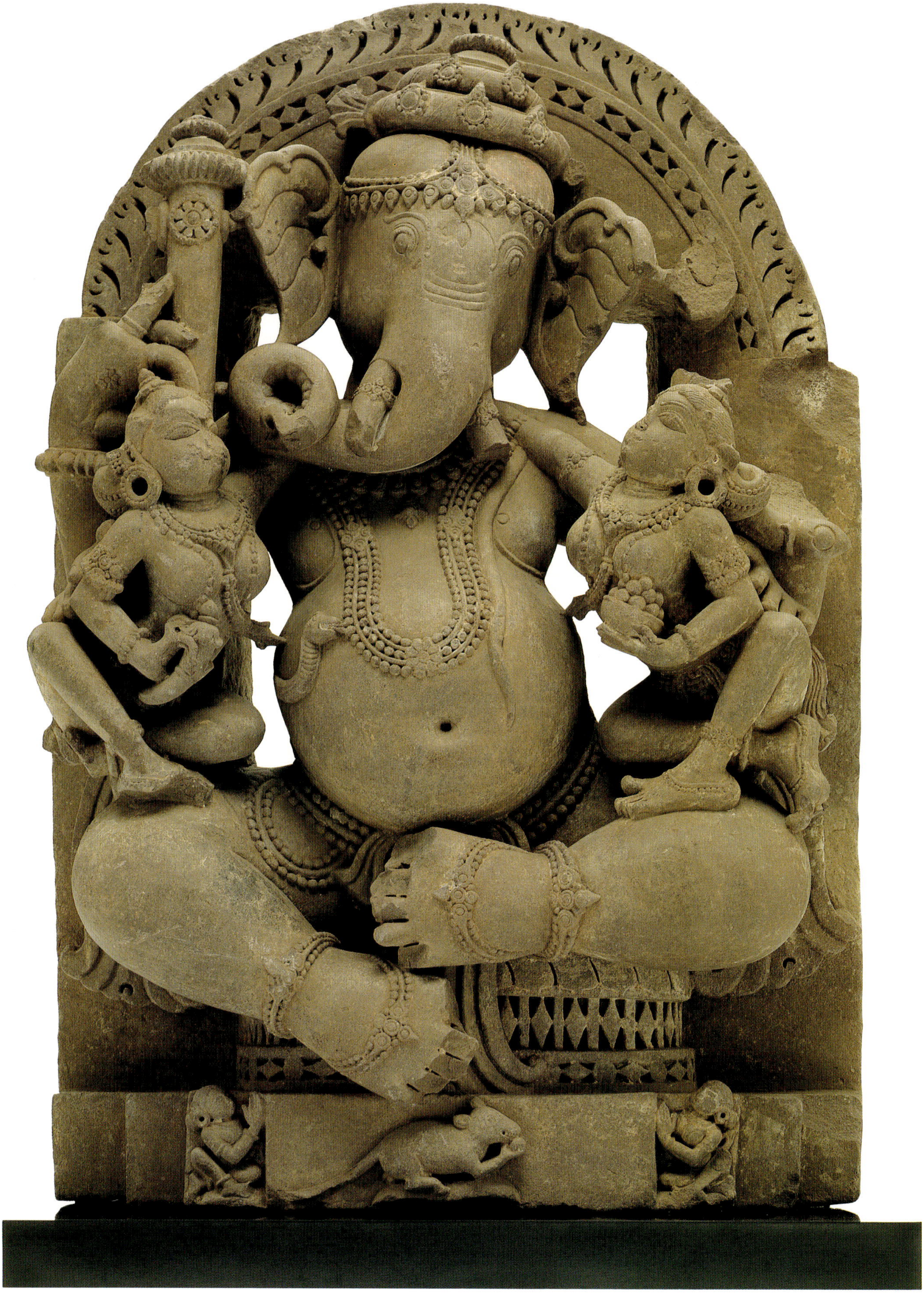

198
Hindu God Gaṇeśa with his Consorts
Madhya Pradesh or Rajasthan, northern India, early 11th century
Cream sandstone. H: 105.2 cm.
John H. and Ernestine A. Payne Fund, Helen S. Coolidge Fund, and Keith McLeod Fund. 1989.312

Seated in the characteristic pose of "royal ease" (lalitāsana), *this rotund Hindu god of good fortune and remover of obstacles, Gaṇeśa, holds his two consorts gently on either side of his lap. The sprightly young women, Riddhi and Siddhi, reach up to the heavy-set god not only with their arms but also with their energetic posture. Although there are references to two consorts of Gaṇeśa in the religious literature, it is unusual to find visual depictions of the god with both of them.*

Temple architecture in northern and central India reached its zenith in the late tenth and early eleventh century, when some of the best-known temples, such as the complex at Khajuraho, were built with elaborate sculptural decoration. The broad faces of the women, the somewhat simplified forms of the jewelry, and the slightly abbreviated style of the leaf decoration at the top suggest western Madhya Pradesh or northeastern Rajasthan as the likely center for the creation of this sculpture. Such large images of Ganesa were often placed in a niche on the left side of a temple platform toward the entrance, where he would be encountered at the beginning of the devotee's ritual clockwise walk around the temple, or in a niche on the center of the temple's south wall.

199
Bodhisattva Avalokiteśvara (Bodhisattva of Compassion)
Bihar, eastern India, mid-tenth century
Gray schist. H: 88.9 cm.
Marshall H. Gould and Frederick L. Jack Funds. 63.418

The Bodhisattva of Compassion, identified by the presence of the seated Buddha in his crown and elaborate jewelry, is seated in the position of "royal ease" (lalitāsana) *on a lotus base. His left foot rests on a lotus plant, while he holds a lotus blossom in his left hand. The combined effect of the lush floral decoration, gently curving forms, and rich ornamentation is one of understated opulence and sensuality befitting this elegant deity. The fleshiness of the torso, the high-relief carving, and the softness of the face of the* bodhisattva *are characteristic of mid- to late-tenth-century stone sculptures at the famous Buddhist monastery at Nalanda in Bihar.*

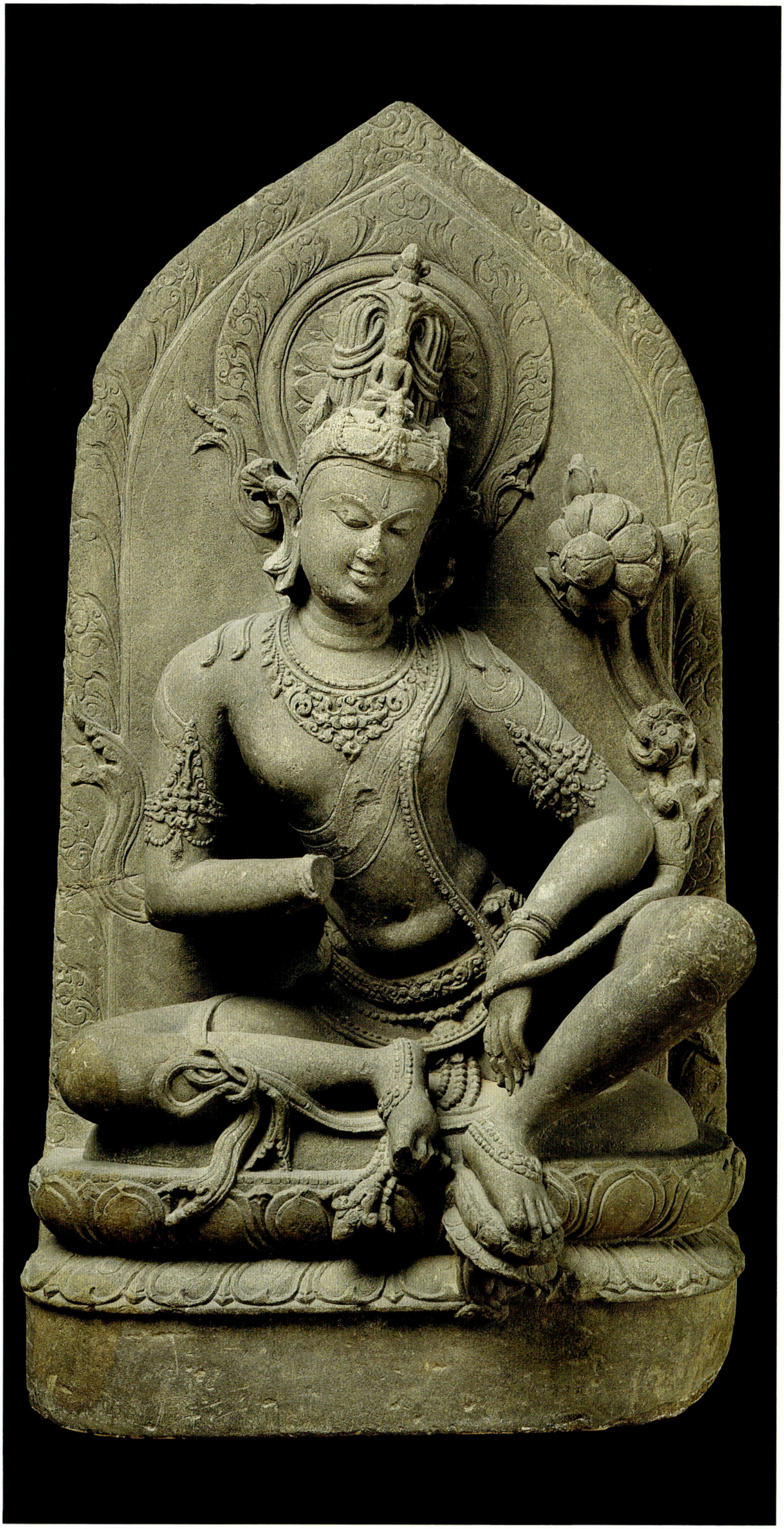

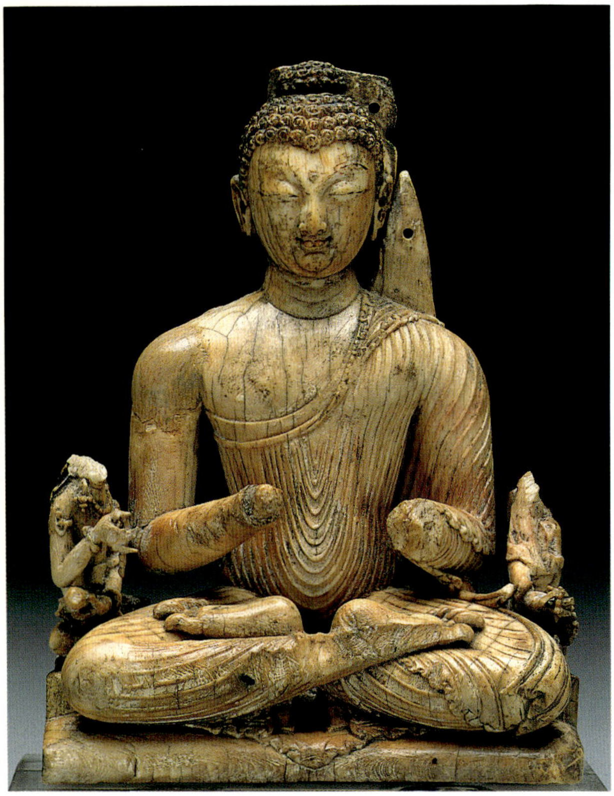

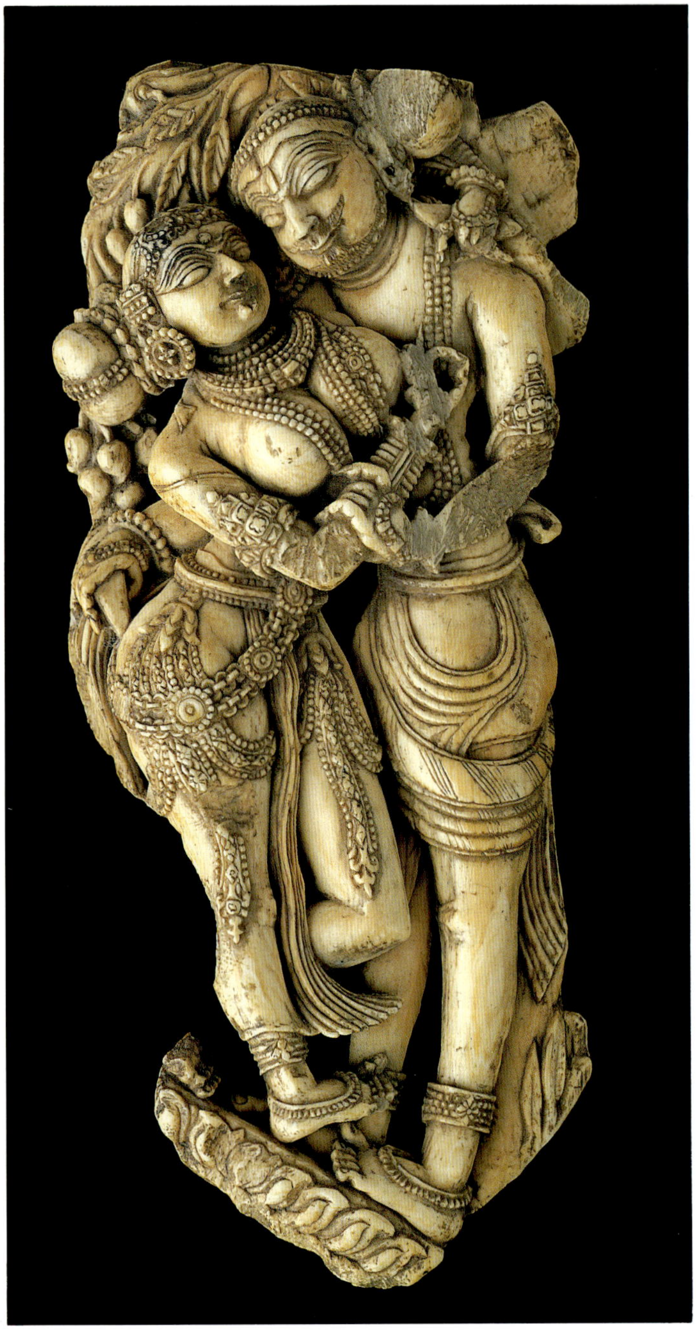

200
Seated Buddha with two attendant bodhisattvas
Kashmir, northern India,
8th century A.D.
Ivory. H: 13.8 cm.
Charles B. Hoyt, Marshall H. Gould, and John Ware Willard Funds. 63.1495

The Buddha is seated in the lotus position (padmāsana) *and wears a simple robe draped over his left shoulder. On either side are seated bodhisattvas who cannot be identified specifically because of their damaged condition. Soon after this piece came to the Museum, without its head, scholars demonstrated convincingly that the Cleveland Museum of Art had the missing portion. Through an exchange, the Museum of Fine Arts was able to acquire the head and join the two parts.*

Religious sculptures in ivory are not common in India, where Hindus considered ivory slightly impure because of its animal source and used it typically for secular objects. Buddhists, on the other hand, were inclined to use ivory for religious sculpture. This delicately carved image belongs to a group of seated and standing Buddhas in ivory, all of which are from Kashmir and are usually dated to the eighth century. Most of them are similar in style and iconography and point to an active ivory-carving center in Kashmir. In both ivory and bronze, Kashmiri artists borrowed the Gandharan linear garment patterns and meditative countenance, as well as the supple and sensual delineation of the human figure characteristic of the main Gupta centers in the Ganges River valley. The MFA Buddha reflects a sophisticated amalgamation of these divergent styles.

201
Lovers *(Mithuna)*
Orissa, eastern India, 13th century
Ivory. H: 15.9 cm.
Keith McLeod Fund and Seth K. Sweetser Fund, by exchange. 1987.622

Standing on a lotus pedestal and flanked by a fruit-bearing mango tree, the royal couple is seen in an intimate moment. The voluptuous female embraces her partner while she raises her right hand, partially broken, in a dance gesture denoting explication. Body positions and drapery emphasize movement and gentle eroticism. The balanced interplay of precise, detailed jewelry with softly rounded flesh reflects the eastern Indian origin of the sculpture. The facial features—broad faces, pointed chins, and bulging eyes—also suggest the Orissan provenance. Stylistically, the figures are very close to the erotic stone sculptures on the Sun temple at Konarak, built by King Narasiṅha in the thirteenth century. This work is thus one of the earliest Orissan ivories known.

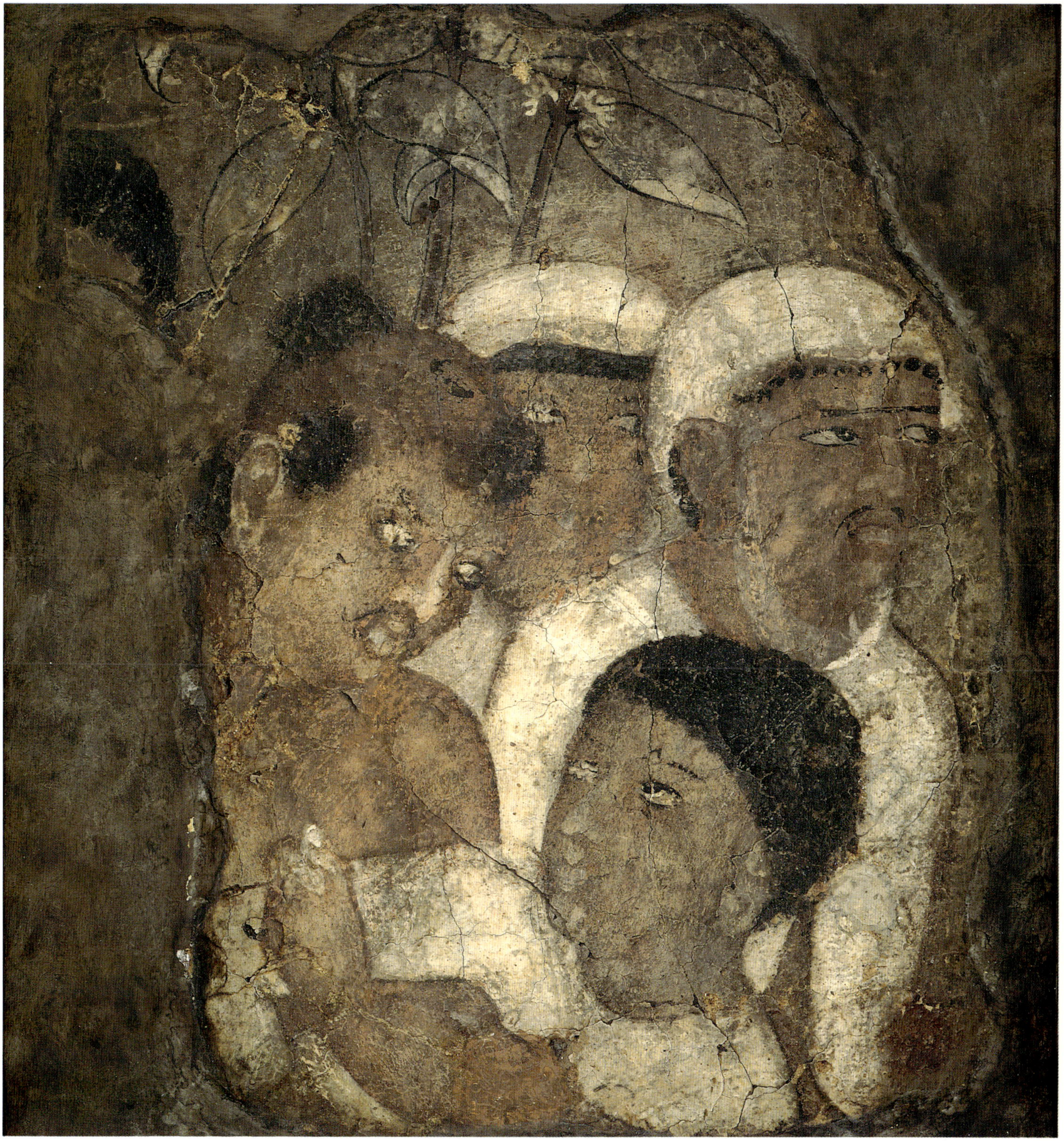

202
Fragment from *The Conversion of Nanda*
Cave 16 at Ajanta, Deccan, late 5th century A.D.
Watercolor on a layer of plaster and stucco, from a wall painting in a rock-cut cave. 38 x 26 cm.
Clara Bertram Kimball Fund. 21.1286

This fragile fragment from the famous Buddhist cave site of Ajanta is the sole section of its wall painting to exist apart from the site. It was removed in the early nineteenth century.

The painting, consisting of four figures and a section of a tree, is from the famous narrative of the conversion of Buddha's half-brother Nanda to Buddhism and his initiation into monkhood. Two male figures in the dramatic interlocking position in the foreground of the Boston panel can be identified as the bare-chested barber who comes to cut Nanda's hair in preparation for his new life as a monk and an attendant who tries to restrain the barber.

The animated expression of the figures, their carefully modeled and differentiated physiognomy, bear vivid testimony to the rich tradition of wall painting in early Indian art.

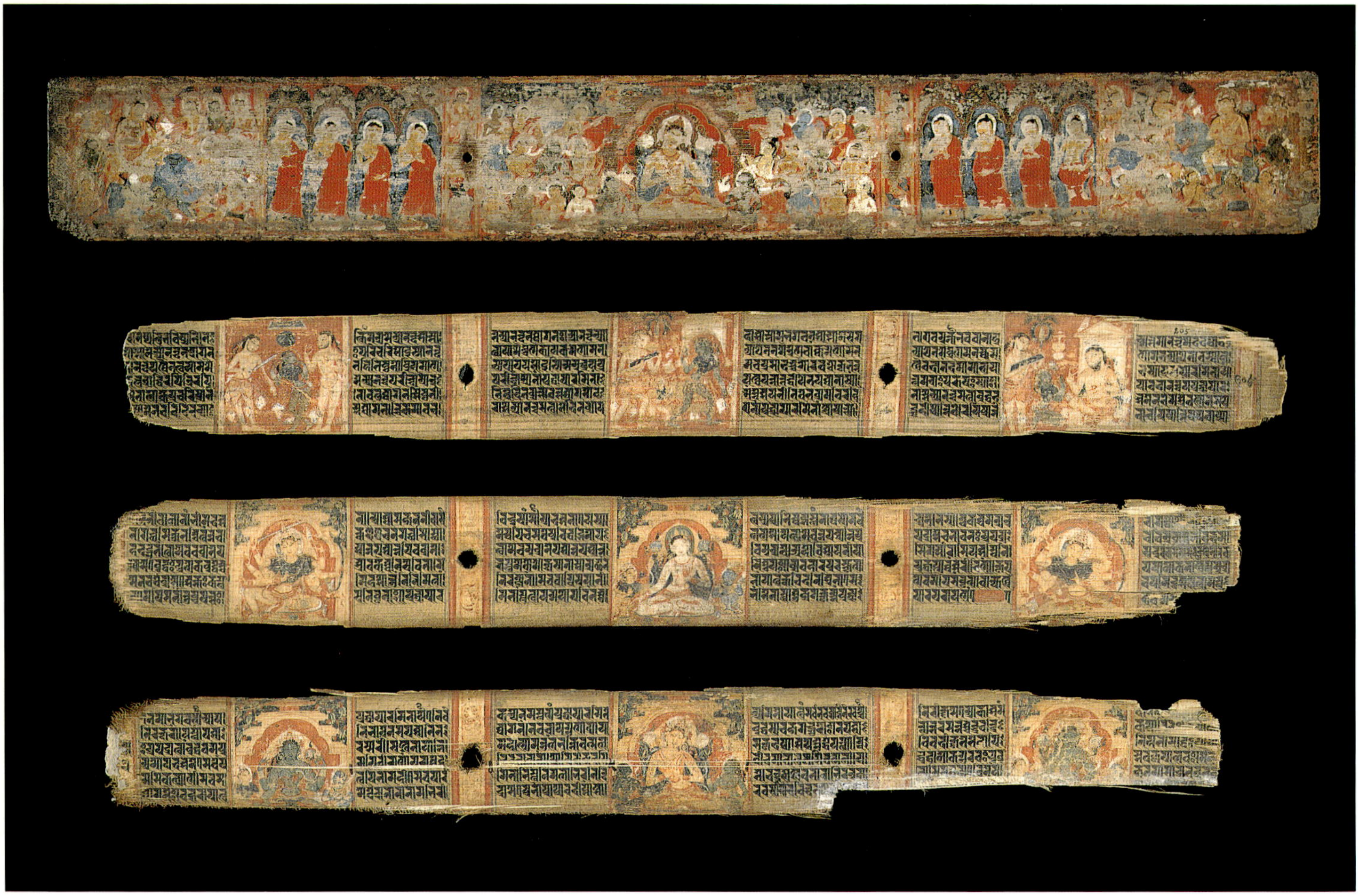

203
Illustrated manuscript of *Aṣṭasahasrika Prajñāpāramitā*
Bengal, eastern India, dated 1134
Opaque watercolor on palm leaf; opaque watercolor on wood.
Page 1: 51.9 x 6 cm. Page 2: 53.7 x 6 cm. Page 3: 52.3 x 6 cm.
Wooden cover: 58 x 7.5 cm.
Purchased from Dr. Ananda Coomaraswamy. 20.589

One of the last strongholds of Buddhism in India was the region under Pāla kings in the eleventh and twelfth centuries in eastern India. This dated manuscript of one of the most fundamental works of the complex Mahāyāna branch ("Greater Vehicle") of Buddhism consists of 206 palm-leaf pages with original painted wood covers. Six of the pages have depictions of the Buddhist goddess Tārā, the protective god Dharmapāla, and an illustration of one of the Buddhist jātaka *tales. The painted wood covers show various bodhisattvas as well as some of the major events from the life of the historical Buddha.*

Despite its frail condition, the elegant script, rich color scheme and accomplished draftsmanship of the manuscript point to a fairly high level of patronage.

204
Scenes from an illustrated manuscript of *Hamza-nāma*
Mughal school, northern India, about 1562-1577
Watercolor on paper backed by cloth.
68.5 x 52 cm.
Horace G. Tucker Memorial and Seth Augustus Fowle Funds. 24.129

Dastān-i Amīr Hamza *(or* Hamza-nāma) *is a combination of historical and mythical adventures associated with Amīr Hamza, an uncle of the prophet Muhammad. Seeking to spread Islam all over the world, Amīr Hamza traveled through foreign lands, including Sri Lanka, Egypt, and the Caucasus.*

According to the partially legible inscription on the front and the text on the back, this painting illustrates the finding of Alexander by one of the legendary kings of Iran; it is from the second part of the story of Hamza, which deals with his struggles against the Zoroastrians and other nonbelievers of Islam. In this context, Alexander is seen as a hero who exalts the virtues of Islam. The Hamza-nāma *was a favorite of the Mughal emperor Akbar, who often relaxed while listening to the tales. In fact, it is recorded that Akbar liked to recite them himself in the palace harem.*

The illustrated manuscript of Hamza-nama *was one of the earliest and most monumental projects of Mughal painters under the patronage of Akbar. It consisted originally of 1,400 illustrations and was organized in fourteen volumes. Of these, approximately 150 pages have survived in various public and private collections throughout the world. According to contemporary historical sources, the project was supervised initially by the aging Iranian master painter Mīr Sayyid 'Alī and then was taken over by 'Abd al-Ṣamad, another accomplished painter from the Safavid court of Iran. Recent scholarship has shown convincingly that the entire illustrated manuscript was executed between 1562 and 1577.*

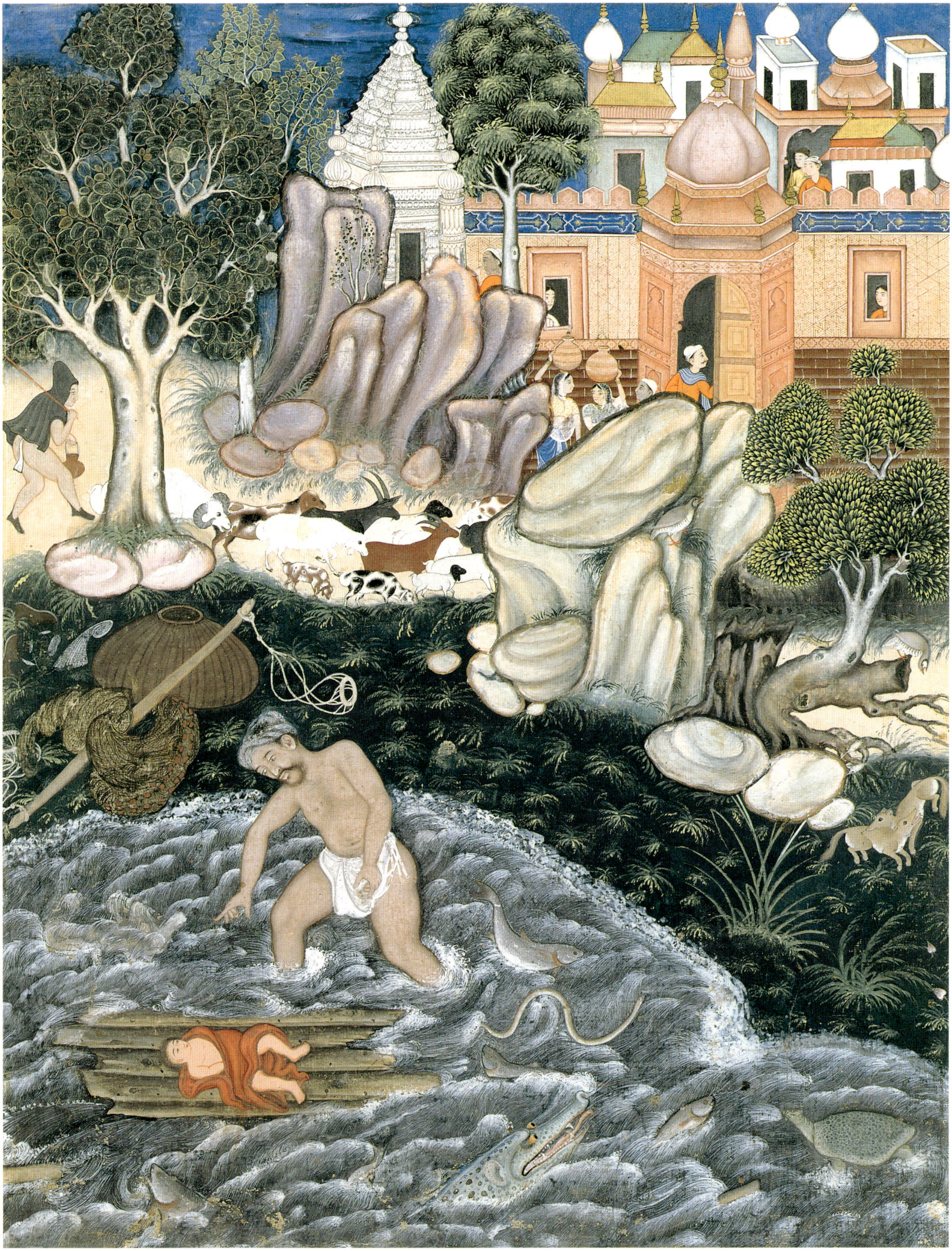

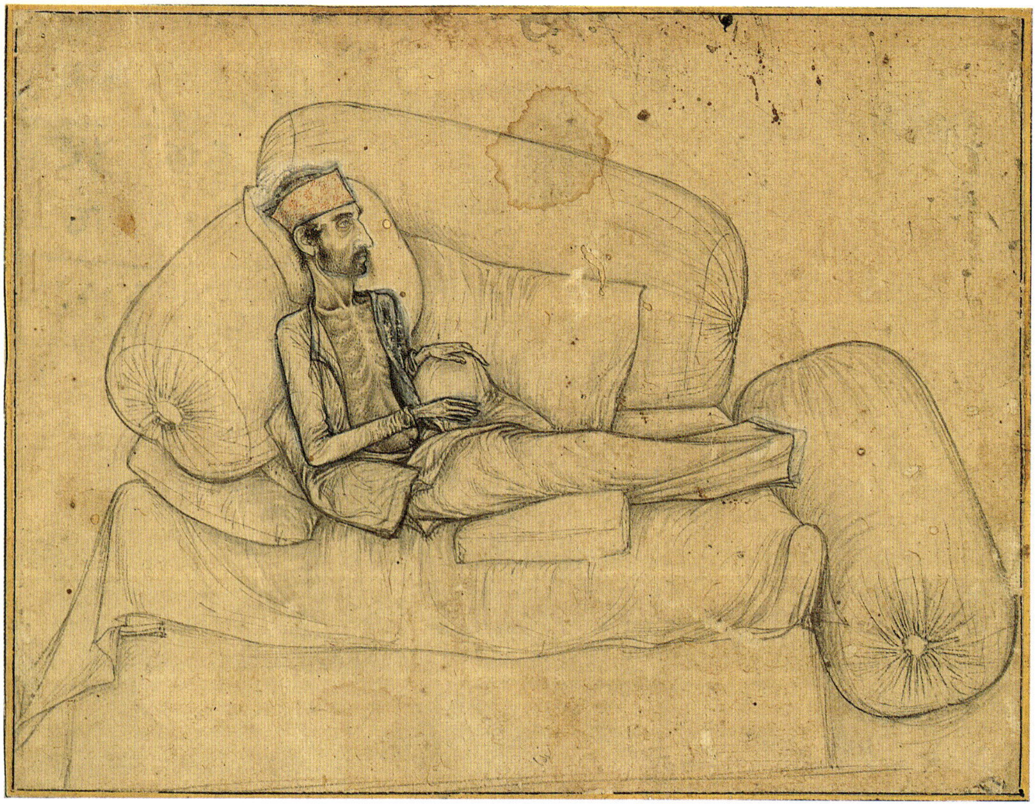

205
The Dying 'Ināyat Khān
Mughal school, northern India, about 1618-1619
Ink and watercolor on paper.
9.5 x 13.3 cm.
Francis Bartlett Donation of 1912 and Picture Fund. 14.679

'Ināyat Khān was one of the intimate attendants of the Mughal emperor Jahāngīr. The occasion of this drawing is described in Jahāngīr's memoirs (Tūzuk-i Jahāngīrī) *during the thirteenth year (1618-1619) of his reign.*

On this day news came of the death of 'Ināyat Khān...As he was addicted to opium and when he had the chance, to drinking as well, by degrees he became maddened with wine. As he was weakly built, he took more than he could digest, and was attacked by the disease of diarrhea, and in this weak state he two or three times fainted. At last he became dropsical, and exceedingly low and weak. Some days before this he had petitioned that he might go to Agra. I ordered him to come into my presence and obtain leave. They put him into a palanquin and brought him. He appeared so low and weak that I was astonished. He was skin drawn over bones, or rather, his bones too had dissolved. Though painters have striven much in drawing an emaciated face, I have never seen anything like this, nor even approaching to it. Good God, can a son of man come to such a shape and fashion? As it was a very extraordinary case, I directed painters to take his portrait...Next day he traveled the road of non-existence.
(from Tūzuk-i-Jahāngīrī *[trans. A. Rogers and H. Beveridge], London, 1909-1914, vol. 2, p. 43)*

This drawing is a perfect example of Jahāngīr's passionate interest in recording images of exotic and unusual nature, ranging from imported animals to a dying servant. It also shows his close relationship with court painters, who were always present by his side, whether in a court assembly or a hunt. The lifelike drawing, a preparatory study for a finished painting now in the Bodleian Library in Oxford, has more immediacy than its painted counterpart.

206
Darbār of Jahāngīr
Mughal school, northern India, about 1620
Watercolor on paper; from a Jahāngīrnāma manuscript. 34.5 x 19.5 cm.
Francis Bartlett Donation of 1912 and Picture Fund. 14.654

The official audience of an emperor was one of the most spectacular types of event at the Mughal court. It was at such a meeting, known as the darbār, *that the business of the court was carried out. Here, Jahāngīr is seen in* darbār *in the audience hall at Agra. Closest to him is his four-year-old grandson Shah Shujā' whose father, prince Khurram (Shāh Jahān), stands to the left of the emperor. His second son, Parwiz, is seen in the center, saluting his father. It is likely that this painting illustrates the* darbār *of 1619 between the months of March and October, when Shāh Jahām had gained status as the heir-apparent while Parwiz was effectively demoted.*

The courtiers, nearly all identified through inscriptions on their hats and collars, are either at attention or saluting the emperor. The presence of the Jesuit priest in the lower left corner of the picture, as well as the Virgin Mary and flying cherubs in the canopy above the emperor, are vivid testimony to Jahāngīr's eclectic taste in exotic religions, especially Christianity.

Since Jahāngīr was interested in an accurate portrayal of events, objects, and people, he encouraged his artists to be present at the darbār *to make sketches of the scene and carry out the finished paintings later. The intricate composition of this painting was achieved by tracing and arranging preexisting portraits of nobles— a fact that accounts for the discrepancy in the size of individual figures and the somewhat dense spatial arrangement of the picture.*

This illustration, which must have been painted for the largest and finest history of Jahāngīr's reign, has been attributed recently to Manōhar. A leading painter at the court of Jahāngīr, Manōhar was noted for his extraordinary draftsmanship and delicately modeled formal portraits.

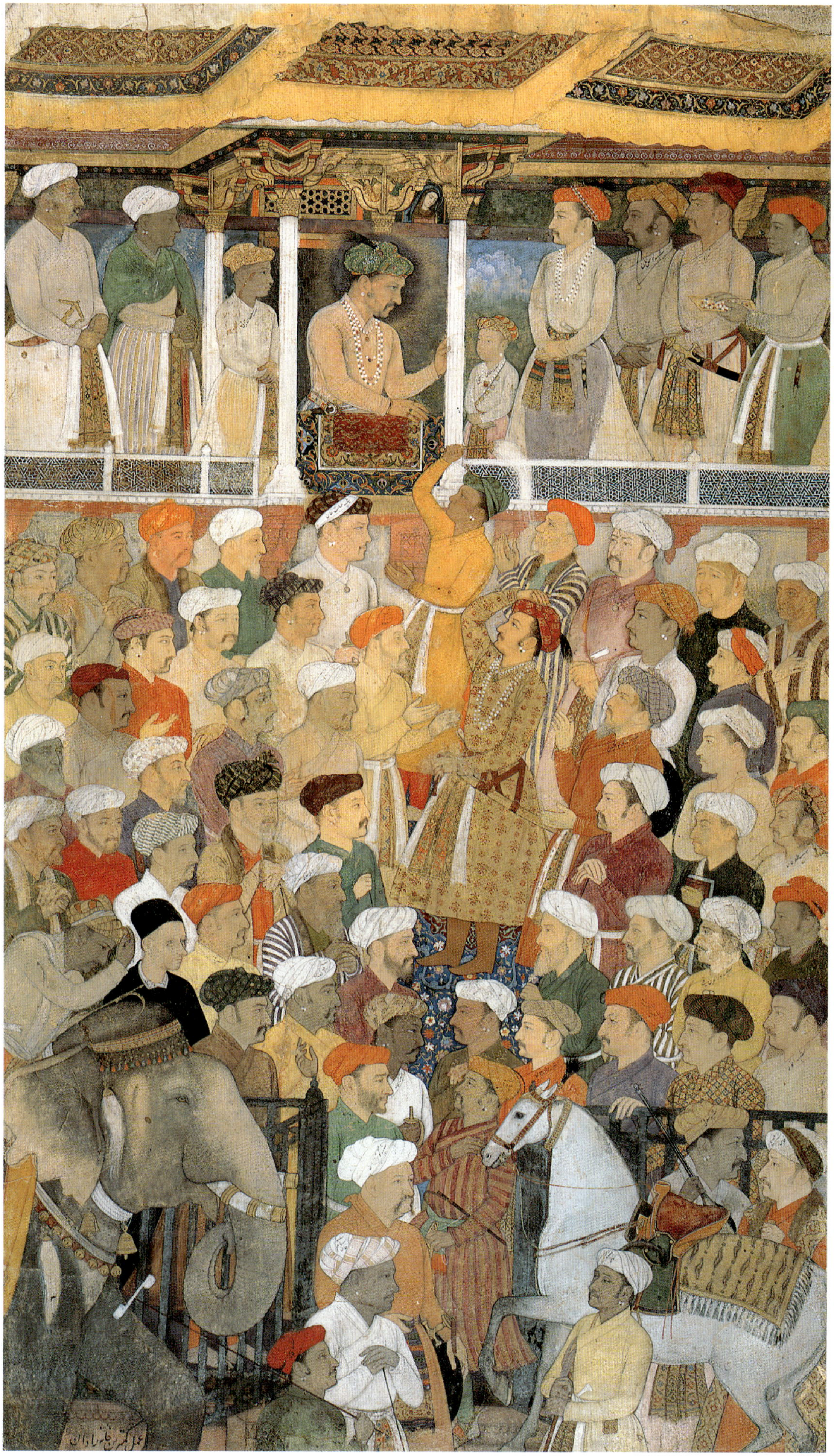

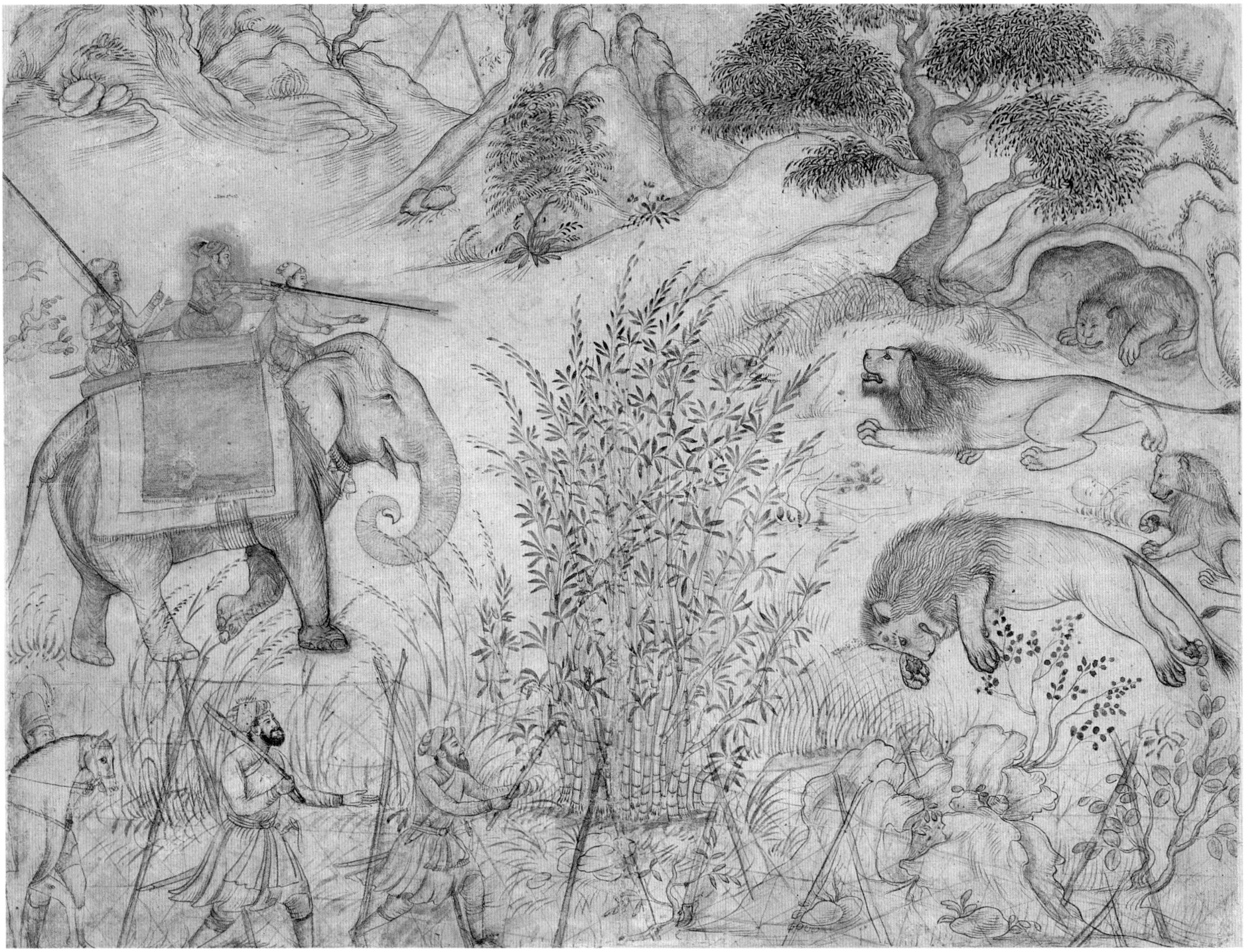

207
A Royal Lion Hunt
Mughal school, northern India, about 1640-50
Ink, light color and gold on paper
28 x 36 cm.
Keith McLeod Fund. 1989.244

The violent theme of a lion hunt is brought to an almost domesticated setting of gracefully arching trees, gently billowing bamboo, and softly modulated hills. Two lions charge toward the hunting prince and his entourage, a third has already been shot, and another cowers in its lair. Remnants of the lion's human prey lie scattered at their feet. In keeping with the Mongol fashion of hunting, the shooting takes place in a confined space. Animals are driven into a fenced enclosure by beaters and noisemakers, as seen at the lower left. This method insured members of the royal family a kill, allowing them to appear always courageous and successful. According to contemporary accounts, lion hunting was considered not only the most perilous sport but also exclusively a royal prerogative.

That the hunter is a member of the Mughal imperial family is clear from the presence of a plume in his headdress and pearl ornaments. The discoloration around him and his reworked face indicate the characteristic Indian practice of giving a proper formal appearance to royal figures even in unfinished sketches. On the basis of comparisons with other known portraits, it is possible to identify the prince as Dārā Shikoh, Shāh Jahān's favorite son, declared as heir-apparent but never to reach the throne.

This large sketch of a royal hunt is quite different in its horizontal format from the pages of the imperial illustrated manuscript of the Pādshāhnāma (the history of the reign of Shāh Jahān), now in the Windsor Castle collection. However, the drawing's overall composition bears some resemblance to one of the five hunt scenes in that manuscript and it may have been intended as a study for the lion hunt painting in the Pādshāhnāma.

208
Lady at her Toilette
Basohli, Punjab Hills, northern India, 1690-1700
Watercolor on paper. 22.4 x 11.9 cm.
Ross-Coomaraswamy Collection.
17.2798

Women engaged in a variety of leisurely activities was a favorite theme of Rajput painters and their patrons. This striking image of a woman wringing the water from her black hair would have suggested multiple levels of meaning to a knowledgeable viewer. On the one hand, it is part of a tradition of genre paintings of harem scenes. On the other hand, in Indian literature, a woman at her toilette is often identified with a heroine getting dressed in anticipation of her lover's arrival, the single bird on the cypress tree echoing her sentiments. In Rādhā-Kṛṣṇa texts with religious and erotic overtones, such an image would also represent Kṛṣṇa's first glimpse of Rādhā in an intimate setting. Origins of the depictions of toilette scenes in Indian art can be traced back to the early centuries of the Christian era, when female fertility goddesses were represented in similar poses on the railings of religious monuments.

The small kingdom of Basohli produced a style that combines the bright contrasting colors and persistent two-dimensionality of earlier Rajasthani painting and the Mughal predilection for meticulous detail and refined line.

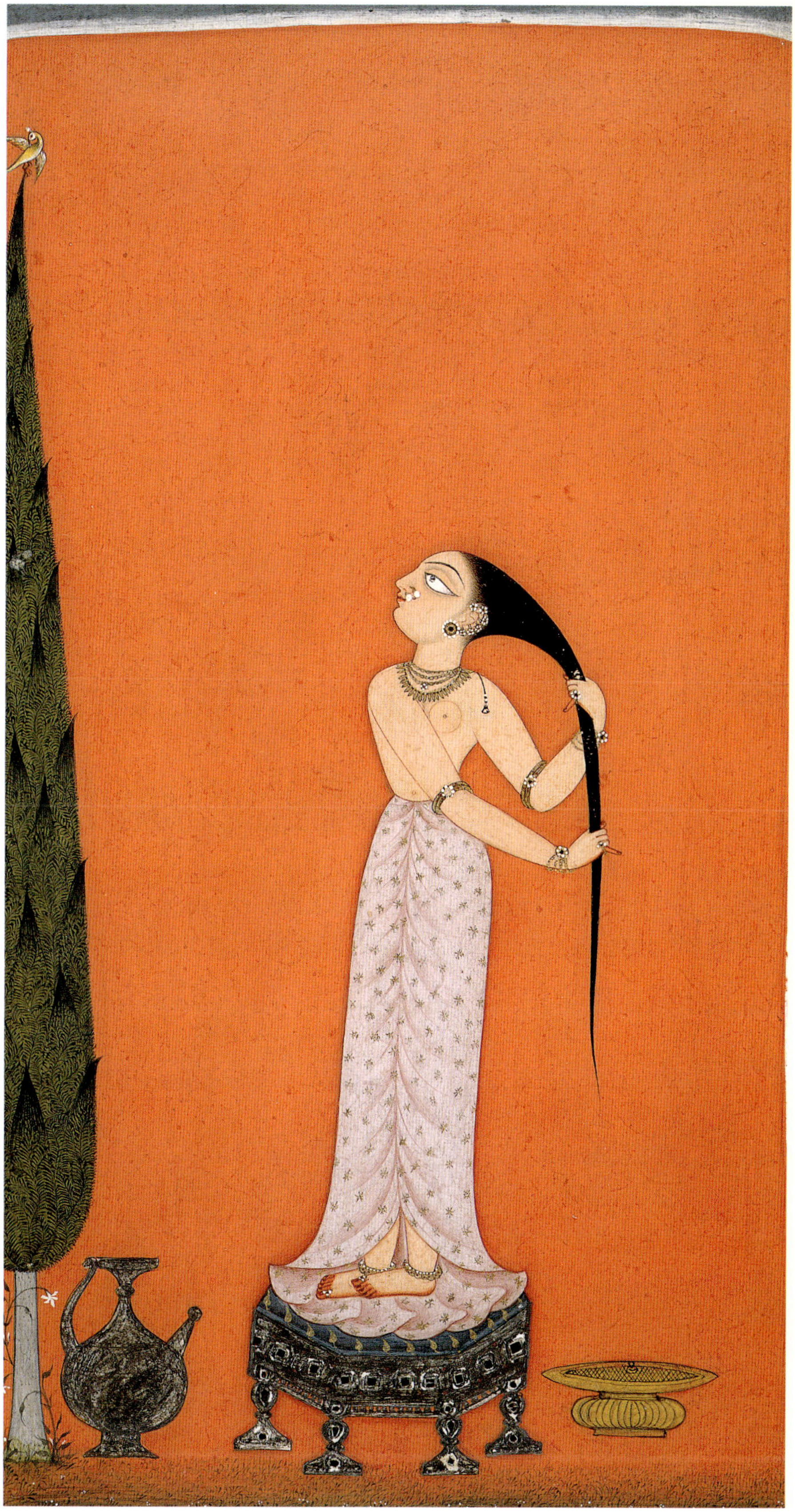

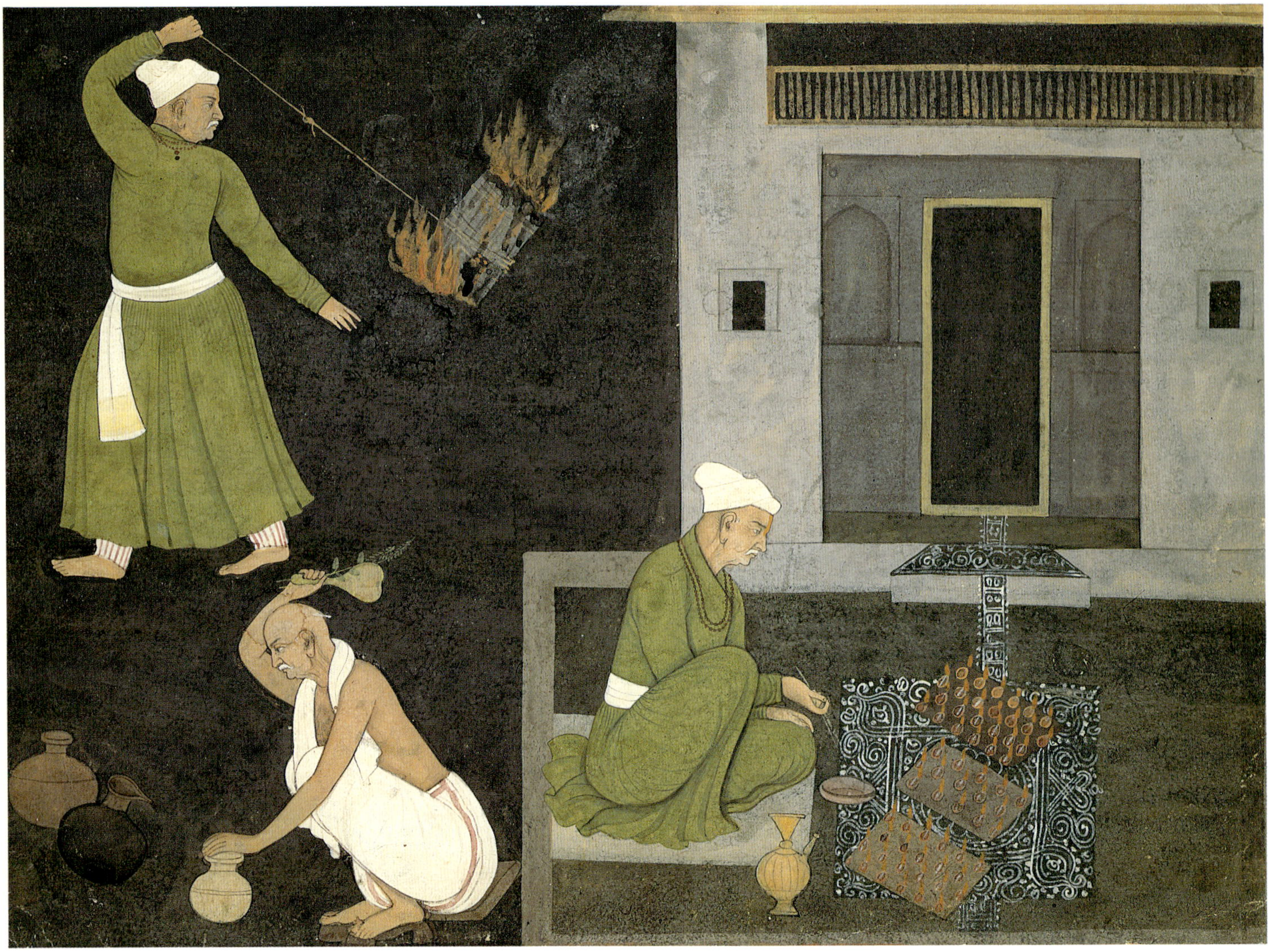

209
Attributed to Nainsukh
New Year Rituals
Punjab Hills, Jasrota, northern India, 1760-1770
Opaque watercolor on paper.
35.5 x 45.7 cm.
Ross-Coomaraswamy Collection.
17.2622

This highly unusual image, offering a vivid glimpse of the personal rituals of a priest in commemoration of the new year, shows three activities at the same time, in the characteristic Punjab Hills format of simultaneous narration. The priest washes and breaks old pots, burns a bundle of old clothes, and lights the small earthen lamps placed on floral and geometric designs (alpana) *painted with wet sand. As the couplet on the reverse suggests, these rituals and the sacred bath are appropriate for the night before the Indian Festival of Lights (Dīwālī). The Sanskrit verse also states that the devotee who bathes in this manner and lights the lamps can escape eternal damnation.*

The uniqueness of the painting lies in the extraordinary individualization of the priest's face. It was probably painted by Nainsukh, best known for his portraits of Raja Balwant Singh. The cleric, seen in at least two other paintings accompanying Balwant Singh, is likely to be Pandit Hari Saran, who was a family priest of the kings of Jasrota.

210

Musical Mode Todī (Todī Rāgiṇī)

Bundi, Rajasthan, western India, about 1720

Watercolor on paper; from a set of Rāgamālā paintings.

18.2 x 12.1 cm.

Gift of John Goelet. 67.797

Along with Kṛṣṇa themes and secular subjects, musical melodies known as rāgamālās *(garlands of* rāgas*) were some of the most popular themes to be depicted by the painters at the Hindu courts in Rajasthan and in the Punjab Hills.*

Rāgamālā *paintings illustrate poems that describe or evoke the mood of Indian* rāgas. *Most of the* rāgas, *loosely translated as "musical modes," are described in terms of human emotions. In general, the sets comprise thirty to forty-two paintings classified into "families," each consisting of a male melody (a* rāga*), five or six female melodies (*rāgiṇīs*), and occasionally "sons of* rāgas" (rāgaputras).

Todī Rāgiṇī, *as seen here, is usually identified as a lone woman wandering through the forest with her lute, attracting deer along the way. She is associated with the archetypal heroine longing to meet her lover. The verse accompanying the* rāgiṇī *is absent in the image, but the cursory inscription identifies it as "*Todī, Rāgiṇī *of Bhairu; to be sung in the day."*

This painting — with its rich, subtle gradations of delicate green, blue, and purple strokes to suggest the texture of the trees as well as the ground — is from a large set of rāgamālā *paintings from the court of Bundi, one of the centers of Rajput painting. Based on earlier models, this example represents one of the most opulent sets of* rāgamālā *painting from Rajasthan.*

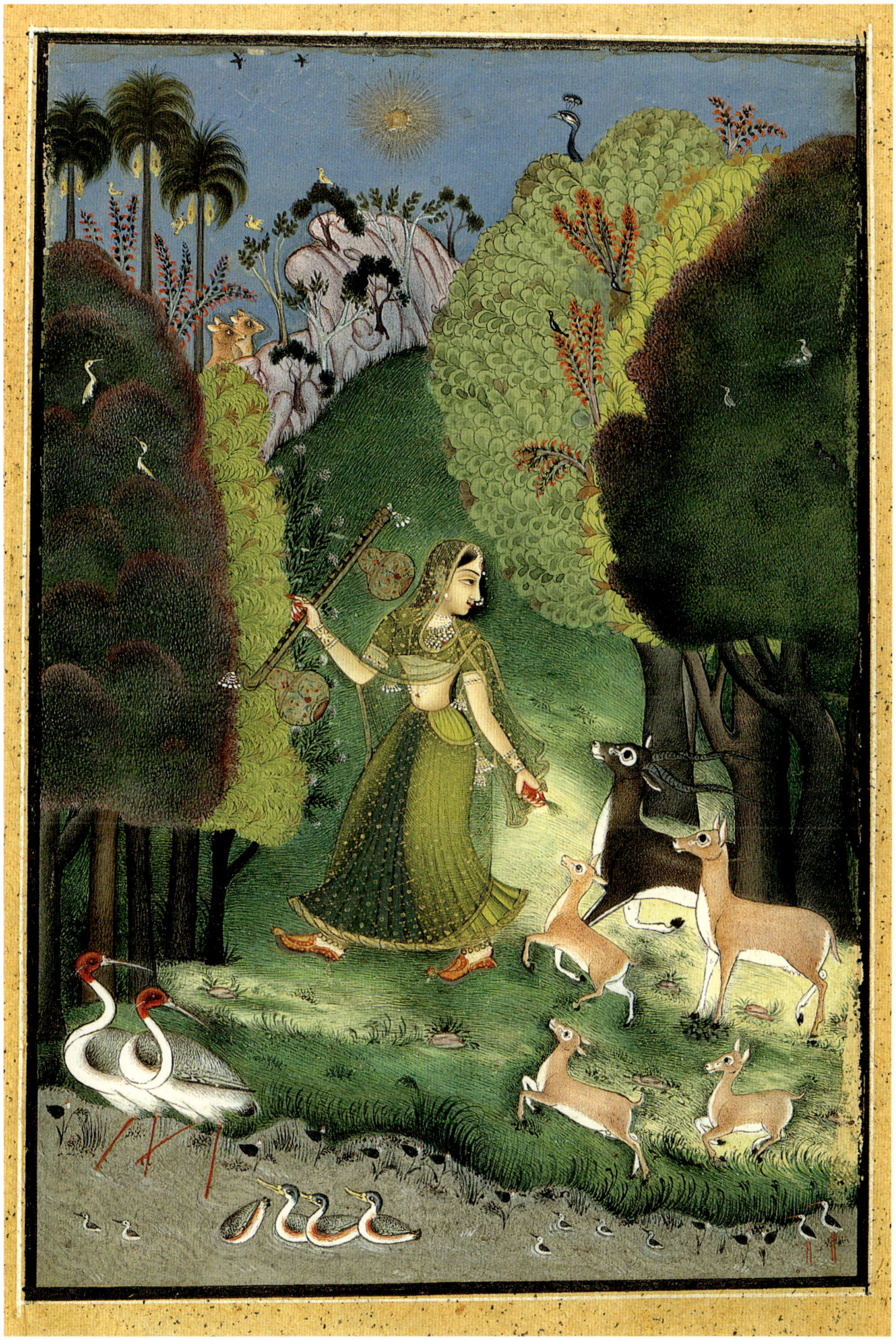

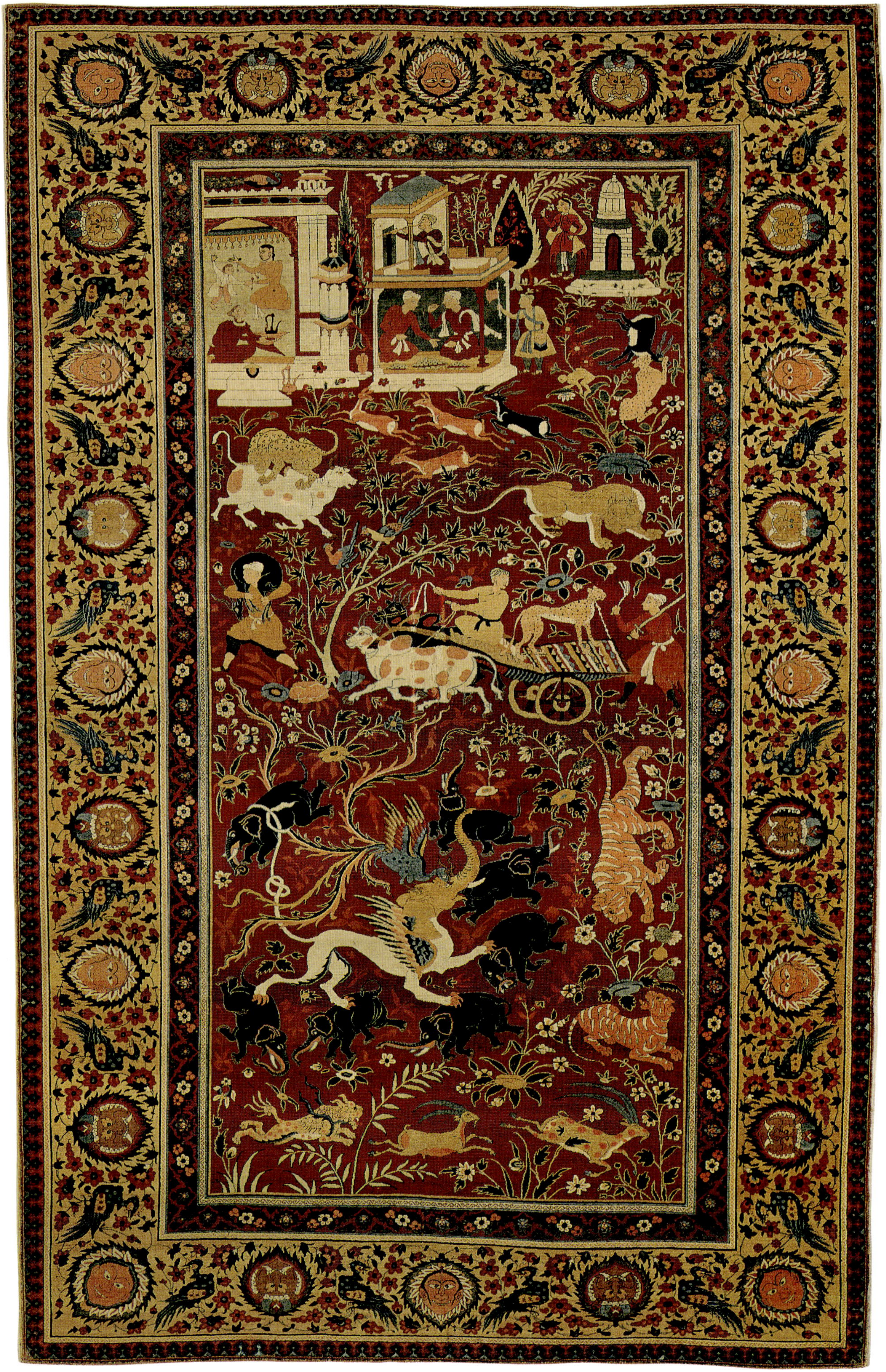

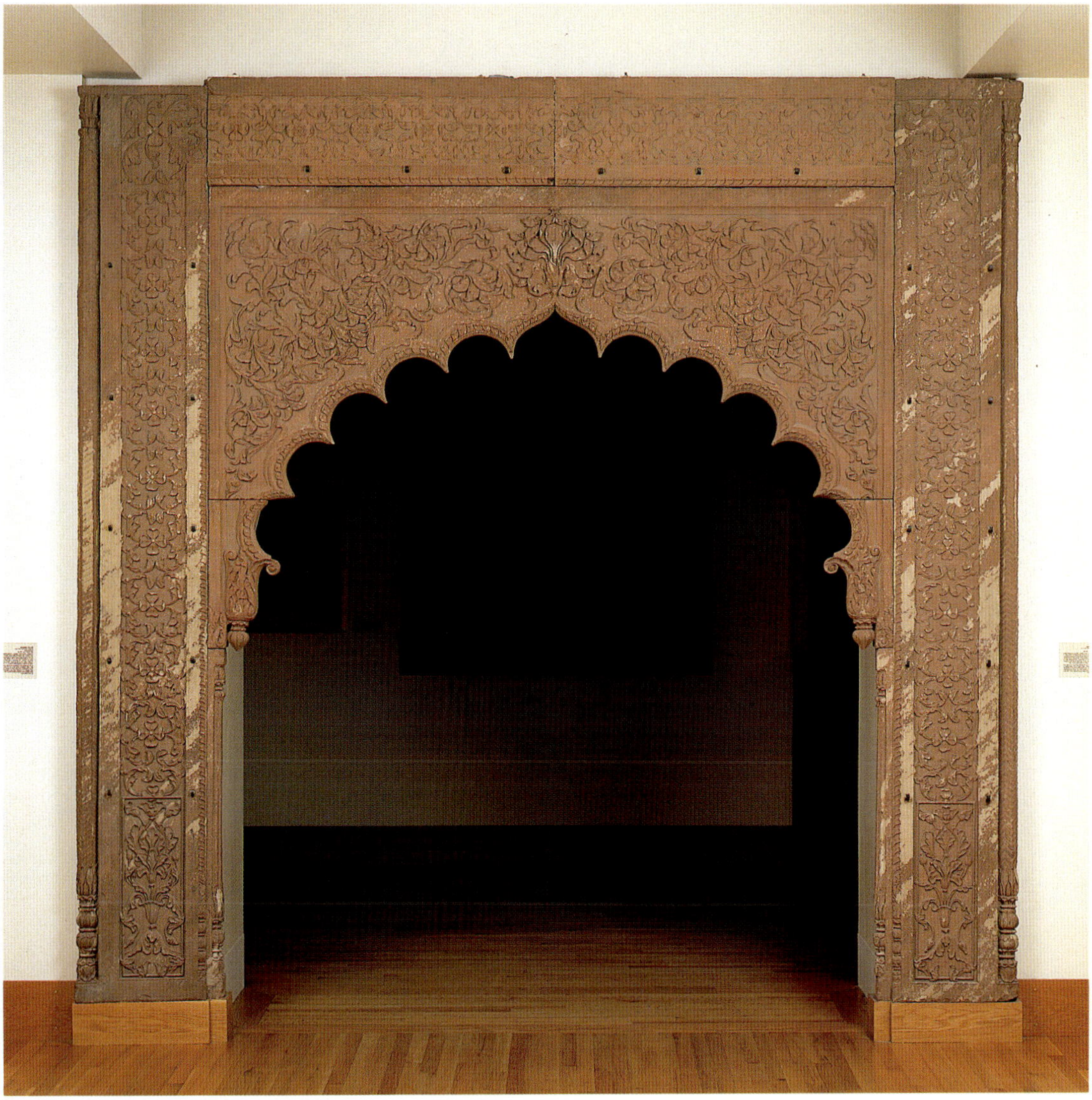

211
Carpet
Mughal, northern India, late 16th-early 17th century
Knotted wool pile (senna knot); cotton warp and weft.
243 x 154 cm.
Gift of Mrs. Frederick L. Ames in the Name of Frederick L. Ames. 93.1480

Carpet weaving is not native to India, and it is not known precisely when this art was first introduced on the subcontinent. The earliest documentary references to the production of carpets in India occur in the latter half of the sixteenth century during the rule of the Mughal emperor Akbar. According to his official biographer, Abū'l Faẓl, carpet weaving was a flourishing trade in the late sixteenth century and a number of weavers from Iran and Afghanistan had settled in India by this time.

Mughal carpets use floral patterns and symmetrical designs like the Iranian. At times, however, they can reflect Mughal court painting and show naturalistically rendered humans, plants, and animals.

A variety of scenes — including activities of daily life in the upper section, a hunt in the middle section, and a mythical animal with other realistic and fantastic creatures in the lower part — make up the field of this carpet.

This was the first important carpet to come to the Museum. The famous architect H.H. Richardson selected it for a new house he had designed for Mr. and Mrs. Frederick Ames, who later donated it.

212
Gateway
Mughal, Delhi area, 1677
Red sandstone carved with floral decoration. 305 x 305 cm.
Keith McLeod Fund. 1983.386

The intricately carved floral designs, chevron-patterned pillars and pilasters, and elegantly delineated leaf forms of this monumental sandstone gateway are characteristic of late-seventeenth-century Mughal architecture. A stone slab inscribed with a Muslim date corresponding to 1677, found accompanying this gateway, dates the piece firmly to the reign of Aurangzeb, whose father Shāh Jahān conceived the Taj Mahal as a mausoleum for his consort, the empress Mumtāz Mahal. The Museum gateway shares certain decorative motifs with that Mughal masterpiece, built of marble about twenty-five years earlier. However, the relative thinness of the gateway's central panel and the horizontal slab above it indicates that the unknown building to which it was attached as a facade was constructed of brick and rubble and faced with stucco and carved stones.

Although Mughal successors continued to reign until 1857, this formidable empire had begun to show signs of weakness by the time of Aurangzeb's ascent to the throne. By the mid-eighteenth century both Delhi and Agra were under constant attack by invaders such as the neighboring Jāt kings of Bharatpur. The latter group took parts of Mughal buildings for their own palaces. It is thus possible that this piece came to the West by way of Bharatpur.

Islam

The Museum has a comprehensive collection of objects from the Islamic countries including Iran, Iraq, Egypt, Turkey, and a number of smaller countries in the Far East. The core of the collection is a large number of paintings, ranging from early scientific manuscripts to the courtly paintings of the Safavid dynasty in Iran, which came to the Museum in 1914 from the French collector Victor Goloubew. There are also unusually fine examples of Islamic metalwork, including dated candlesticks from Seljuk Iran and Mamluk Egypt.

The Museum is fortunate in having one of the most extensive collections of Islamic ceramics in the United States. Notable groups are wares from Rayy in Iran and Iznik wares from Turkey. The Rayy material is particularly important from an archaeological perspective, since a large number of objects were excavated, the expeditions sponsored jointly by the University of Pennsylvania and the Museum.

Other important areas include superb calligraphy pages and book bindings, as well as a small but comprehensive collection of early glass.

213
Candlestick
Egypt, Mamluk period, 1342
Hammered brass inlaid with silver and gold. H: 35.6 cm.
Ellen Frances Mason Fund. 34.168

During the late thirteenth and first half of the fourteenth century, Mamluk metalworkers were noted for their skill in the use of inlay, and the products of their workshops were highly prized in both the Islamic and the European world. Mamluk sultāns, administrators, and literati *were constant patrons of the metalworkers, commissioning objects for imperial, ceremonial, and personal use.*

The thuluth *scripts that decorate the main areas have been read only partially, but there is enough known to tell us that the candlestick was originally made for the son of Sultān Muhammad ibn Qala'un, when he came to power in 1342. He reigned only a few months and was succeeded by a brother. With the change in rulers, the candlestick was reinlaid with the name of the new sultan.*

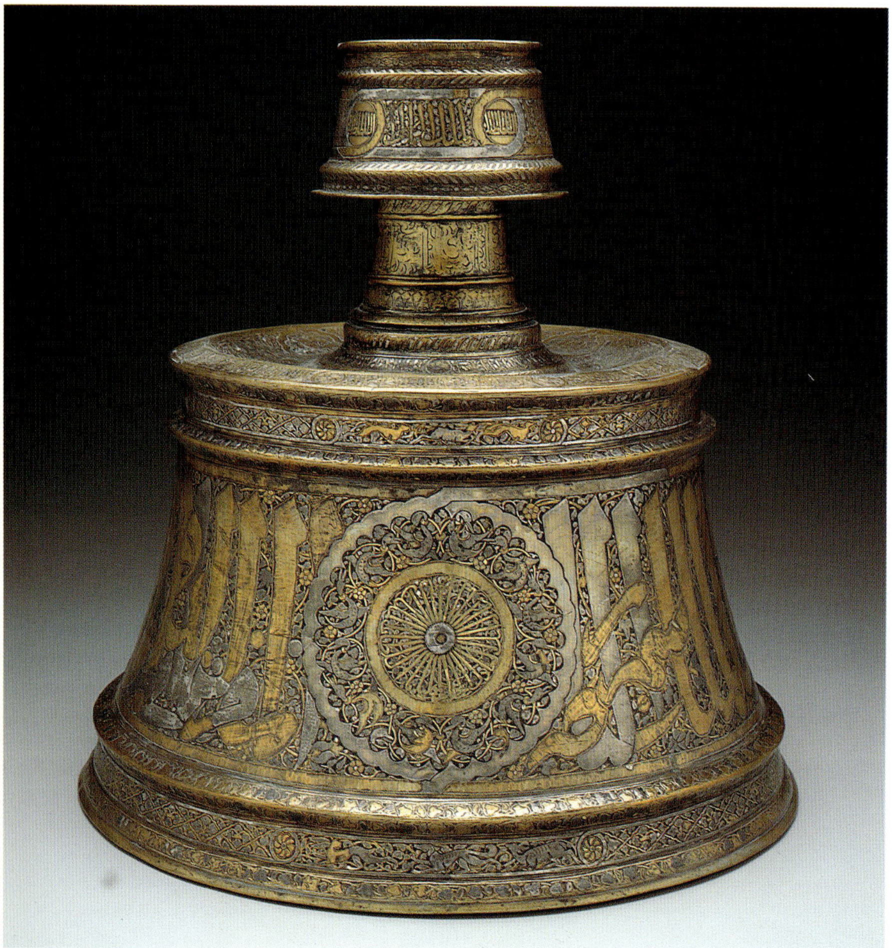

The animals prancing in horizontal bands along the base and the rim of the body of the candlestick derive from ornamental traditions of the Mosul school of metalwork, which flourished in Iraq in the thirteenth century. As a result of the Mongol conquest of Iraq and Iran in the latter part of that century, many Mosul metalworkers fled to the relative safety of the Mamluk capital in Cairo, carrying with them their predilection for figural ornament.

214
Alexander Fights the Habāsh Monster
From a manuscript of the *Shāh-nāma*
Iran, Mongol period, 1330-1340
Gouache on paper. 59 x 39.6 cm.
Denman Waldo Ross Collection. 30.105

From the time Alexander successfully defeated the Iranian king Darius in 331 B.C., he became an important part of Iranian legends. In fact, when the poet Firdausi finished the Shāh-nāma *in 1010, Alexander, known in Iran as "Iskandar," was thought of as a great hero. Describing him as "an agent of God sent to punish the impure people..." and a messenger of the prophet Muhammad, Firdausi utilized various sources— Greek, Syrian, and Iranian— to develop his own version of the adventures of Alexander.*

Produced during the Mongol period in Iran, this manuscript has come to be called the Demotte Shāh-nāma *after the name of the dealer who separated and sold its folios one by one. Traditionally, the painting is identified as the Battle of Alexander with a Dragon, an encounter that takes place in the following section of the text. However, the specific description of the beast of Habāsh "...with a dusky horn on its head" fits the monster in the painting, which has recently been reidentified.*

Early-fourteenth-century miniatures show a greatly developed color range, evident here when compared with others of earlier periods. Despite the strong influence of Chinese landscapes seen in the striated mountains, present-day scholors have concluded in general that the work is a highly original artistic creation, especially in the way the figures are drawn and in the treatment of space.

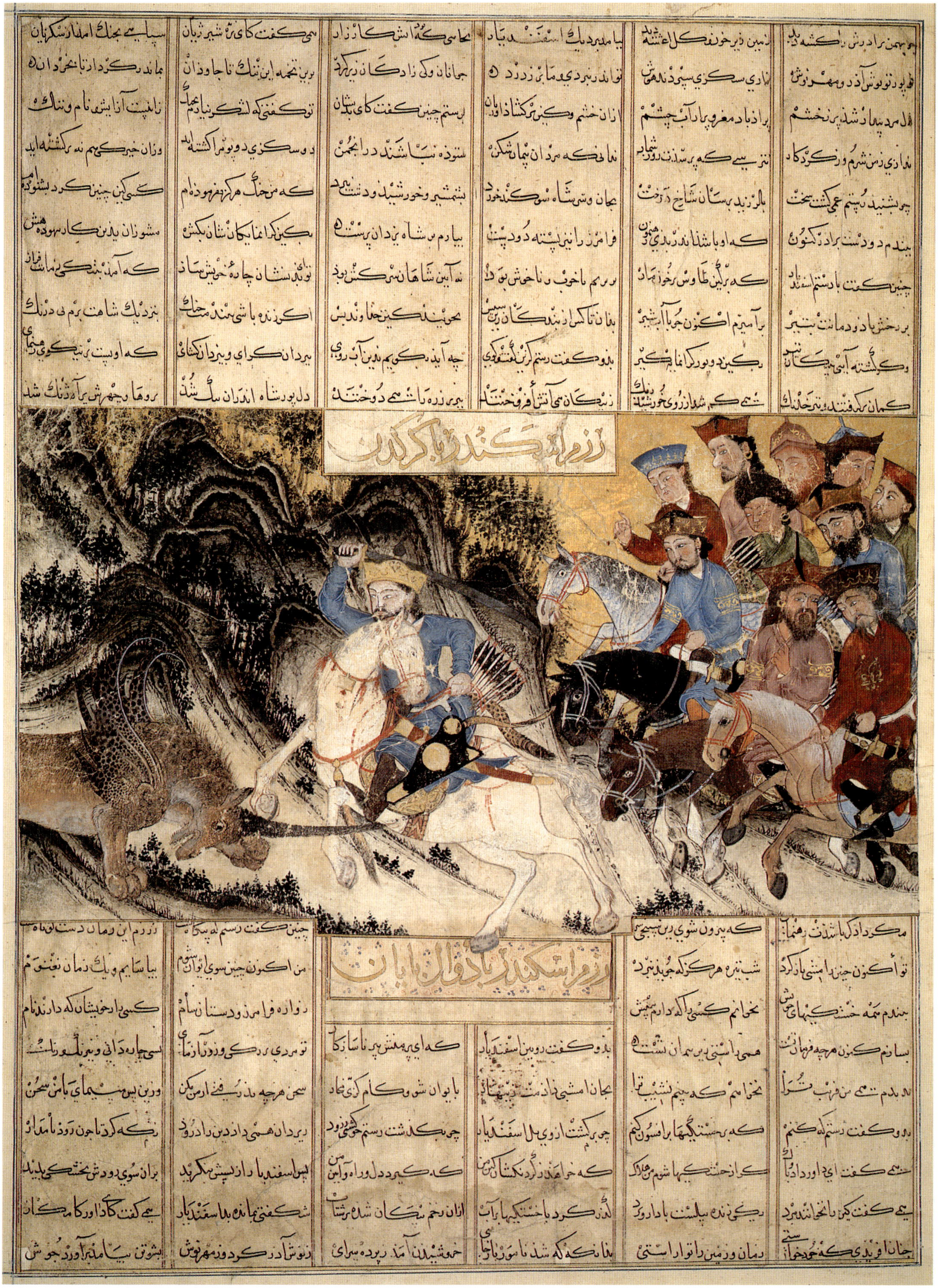
رزم اسکندر با کرگدن
رزم اسکندر با دوال پایان

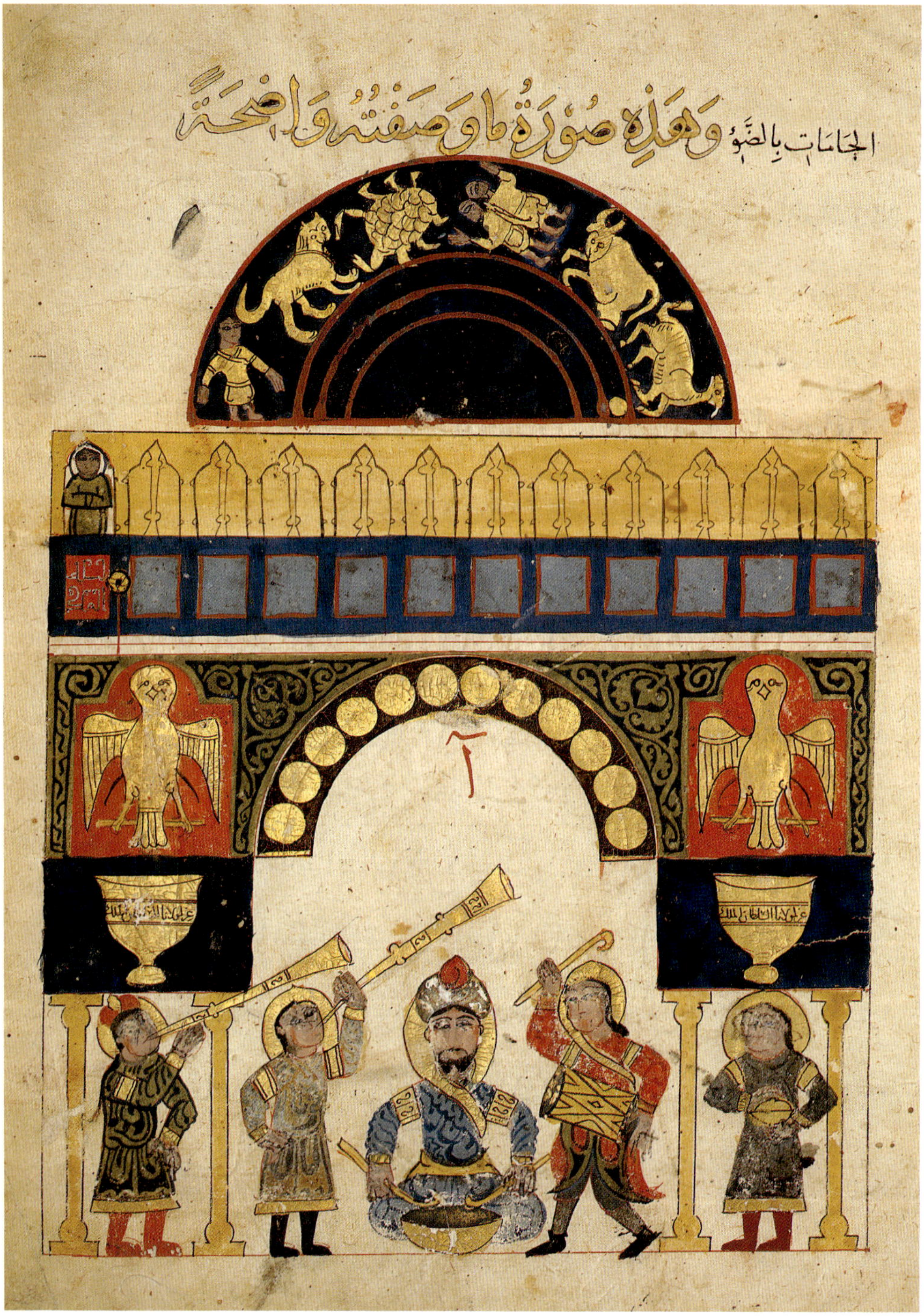

215
Water clock
From an illustrated manuscript of the "Automata"
Egypt, 1354
Watercolor on paper. 39.5 x 27.5 cm.
Francis Bartlett Donation of 1912 and Picture Fund. 14.533

The Book of Knowledge of Ingenious Mechanical Devices, *commonly called the "Automata" (in Arabic: Kitāb fī Ma'rifat al-Hiyāl al-Handasīya), written in 1206 by Bādī al-Zamān ibn al-Razzāz al-Jazarī, was devoted to the construction of over 100 mechanical devices grouped in six categories. The first category, from which the present painting is taken, lists ten different clocks run by water or by heat.*

The first and one of the most elaborate examples described in the text, this clock is constructed with the facade of a house and operated with a hydraulic system hidden behind the facade. To tell the hour, the birds in the two niches drop balls from their beaks into the vases, ringing cymbals that are hung inside. At the same time, the windows in the upper part open and a figure emerges; the panels behind him then turn over and change color. At six, nine, and twelve o'clock the musicians in front of the house play their musical instruments. The zodiac disk in the upper section revolves, and the sun and the moon in the semicircle just below show the actual positions and state of the sun and moon in relation to the zodiac for each day.

This page is from a manuscript of the "Automata" that, according to the colophon page, was completed in February-March of 1354 by Muhammad ibn Ahmed al-Izmīrī for the treasury of a son of the Arab officials who served the Mamluk sultān al-Malik al-Nāṣr Ḥasan in the fourteenth century. The bulk of the manuscript is in the Süleymaniye Library, Aya Sofya, Istanbul; among several paintings that are dispersed, six are owned by the Museum.

216
Final page from a manuscript of the *Shāh-nāma*
Iran and Turkey, 1562-1583
Watercolor and gold on paper.
47.5 x 33 cm.
Francis Bartlett Donation of 1912 and Picture Fund. 14.692

One of the most luxuriant examples of Islamic calligraphy, this page was originally the last folio of a large copy of Firdausi's Shāh-nāma. *(It contained approximately 570 folios, of which seven pages are known today; three are in the Museum's collection.) Written in small fine* nasta'liq, *the final text of the* Shāh-nāma *occupies only the central rectangle and is surrounded by sumptuously decorated margins with ten lines of commentary in a* naskhi *script. Although the juxtaposition of different scripts on the same page is not unusual, the balance and harmony of the writing with the striking arrangement of colors and shapes is highly original.*

The main text of this Shāh-nāma *was copied by Muḥammad al-Qiwam, a well-known calligrapher, in his hometown of Shiraz in Iran. According to the colophon, he began writing after 970 A.H. (A.D. 1562), but the illustrations on the verso were created after it ended up in the hands of the Ottoman rulers, presumably as a gift from an Iranian Safavid official. The entire project, with added commentaries by another calligrapher-illuminator, Muḥammad Tāj al-Dīn Ḥaydar, was completed in 991 A.H. (1583), after the original scribe had died. This splendid page and the accompanying double-page illustration of a triumphant procession (also in the Museum's collection: acc. no. 14.691) are some of the most opulent Turkish paintings executed in the manner of sixteenth-century painting from Shiraz.*

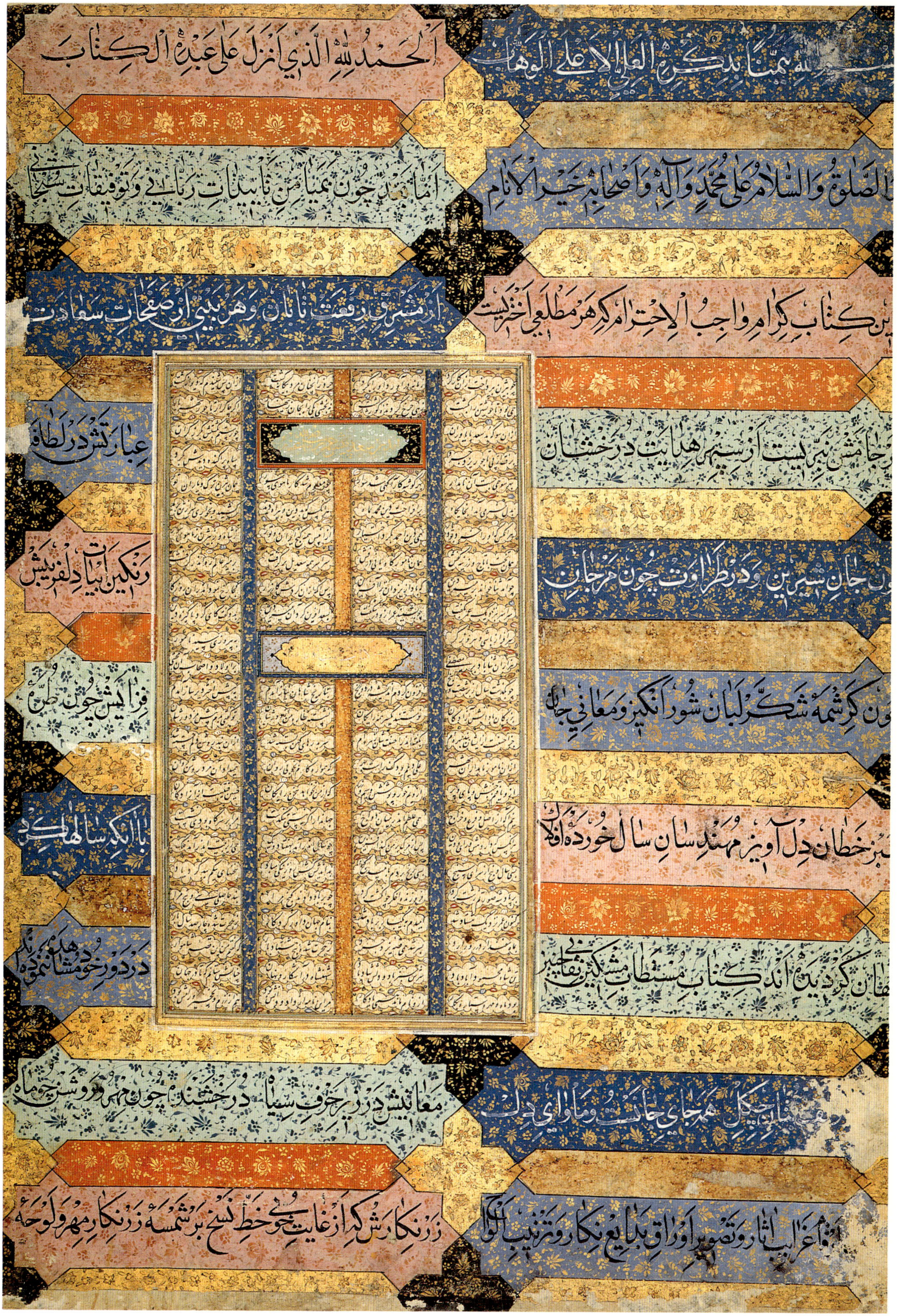
الحمد لله الذي انزل علی عبده الکتاب

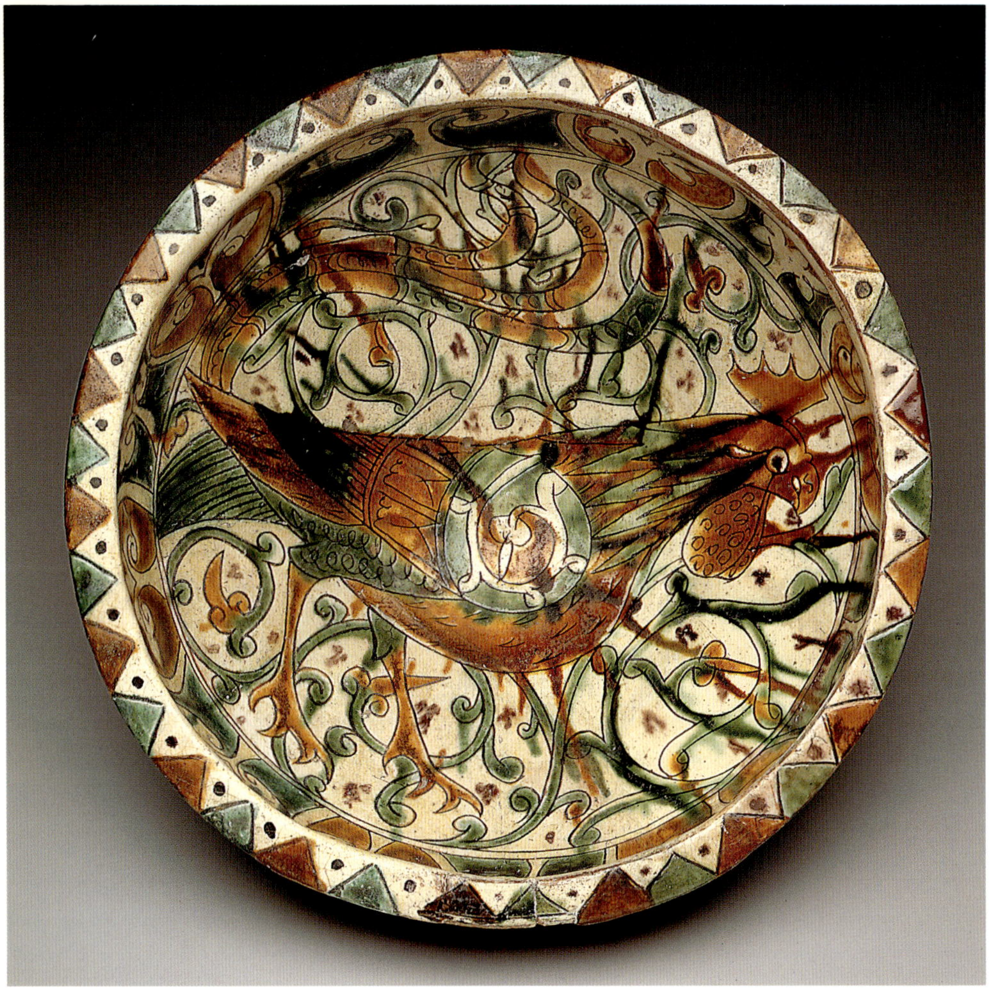

217
Bowl
Iran, Akhand, Seljuk dynasty, 12th-13th century
Earthenware; design incised through slip and filled with colored glazes.
H: 13 cm.
Holmes Collection. 58.93

The polychrome lead glaze of this bowl was clearly inspired by the Chinese sancai wares of the Tang period that were exported to the Islamic world. Several factors — the execution of the large bird on the interior — along with the size and shape of the bowl, attest to its being purely an Islamic creation.

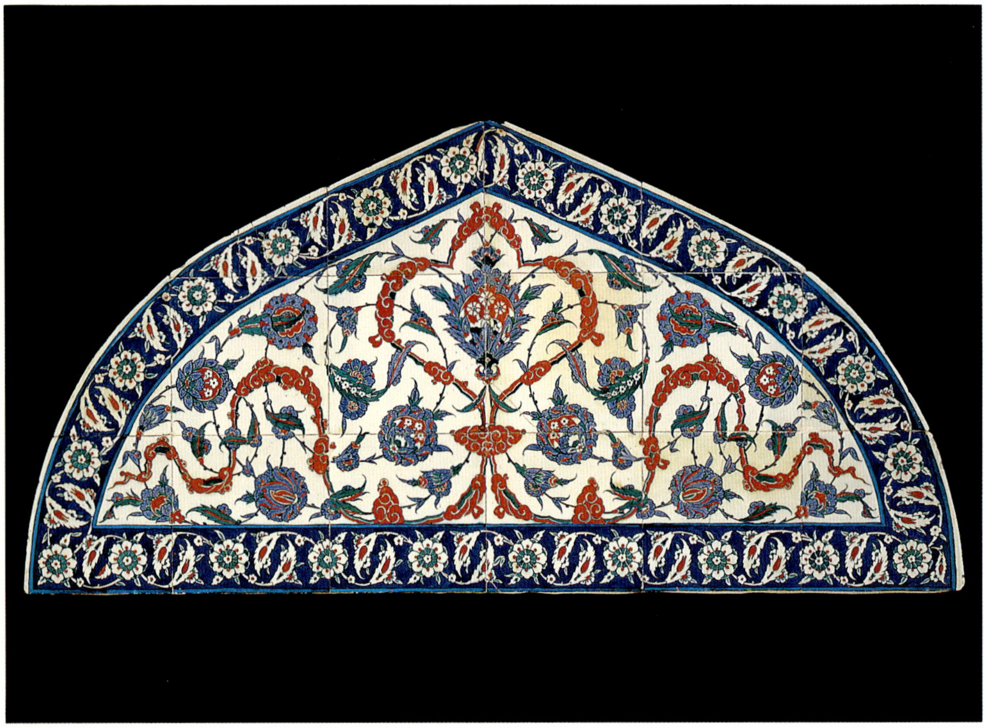

218
Tile panel
Turkey, Ottoman period, late 16th century
Composite body; underglaze painted.
H: 141.5 cm.
Bequest of Mrs. Martin Brimmer. 06.2437

Toward the end of fifteenth century, the Ottoman court at Istanbul began to patronize the kilns in the neighboring town of Iznik. These kilns prospered throughout the sixteenth and seventeenth centuries, providing ceramics to much of the vast Ottoman empire and to many European courts.

The early pottery of Iznik was strongly influenced by the blue-and-white pottery of China. By the mid-sixteenth century, however, local motifs and techniques flourished once again. The floral motifs and expanded palette of this panel are characteristic of the mid- to late-sixteenth-century traditions of the Iznik kilns. The bright red pigment used here, frequently called "madder" red or Armenian bole, was used in Iznik only after 1550.

After the middle of the sixteenth century, the majority of the ceramics produced at Iznik were tiles designed for the decoration of buildings. This example and identical ones in four European museum collections are thought to have decorated areas over the doors and windows of a mosque built in Istanbul in l574 by the Turkish admiral Piyale Pasha.

Map

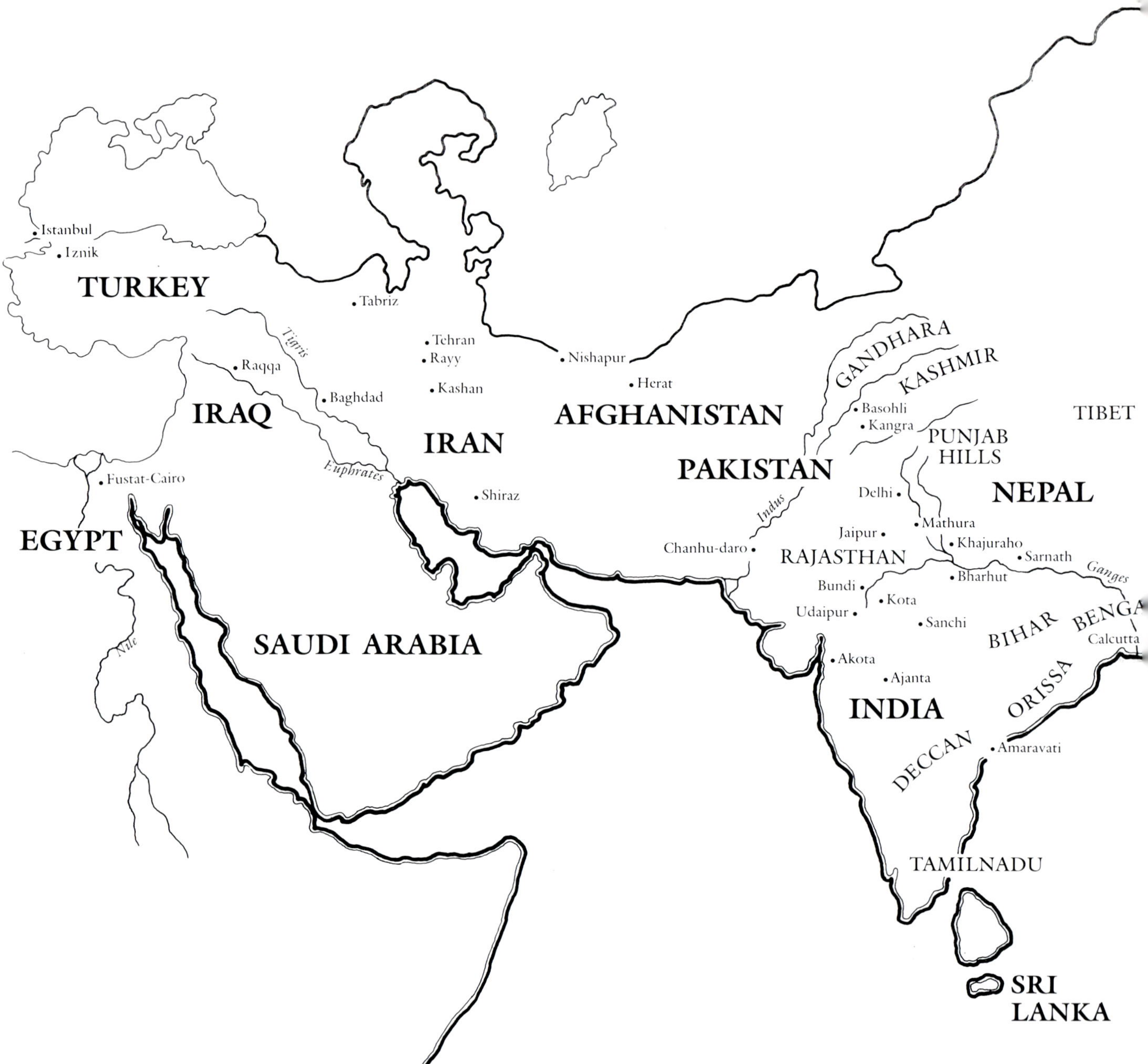
Istanbul
Iznik
TURKEY
Tabriz
Tigris
Raqqa
Baghdad
IRAQ
Tehran
Rayy
Kashan
IRAN
Nishapur
Herat
AFGHANISTAN
Euphrates
Shiraz
Fustat-Cairo
EGYPT
Nile
SAUDI ARABIA
GANDHARA
KASHMIR
Basohli
Kangra
PUNJAB HILLS
TIBET
PAKISTAN
NEPAL
Indus
Delhi
Mathura
Jaipur
Chanhu-daro
Khajuraho
RAJASTHAN
Sarnath
Ganges
Bharhut
Bundi
Kota
Udaipur
Sanchi
BIHAR
Calcutta
Akota
Ajanta
INDIA
ORISSA
DECCAN
Amaravati
TAMILNADU
SRI LANKA

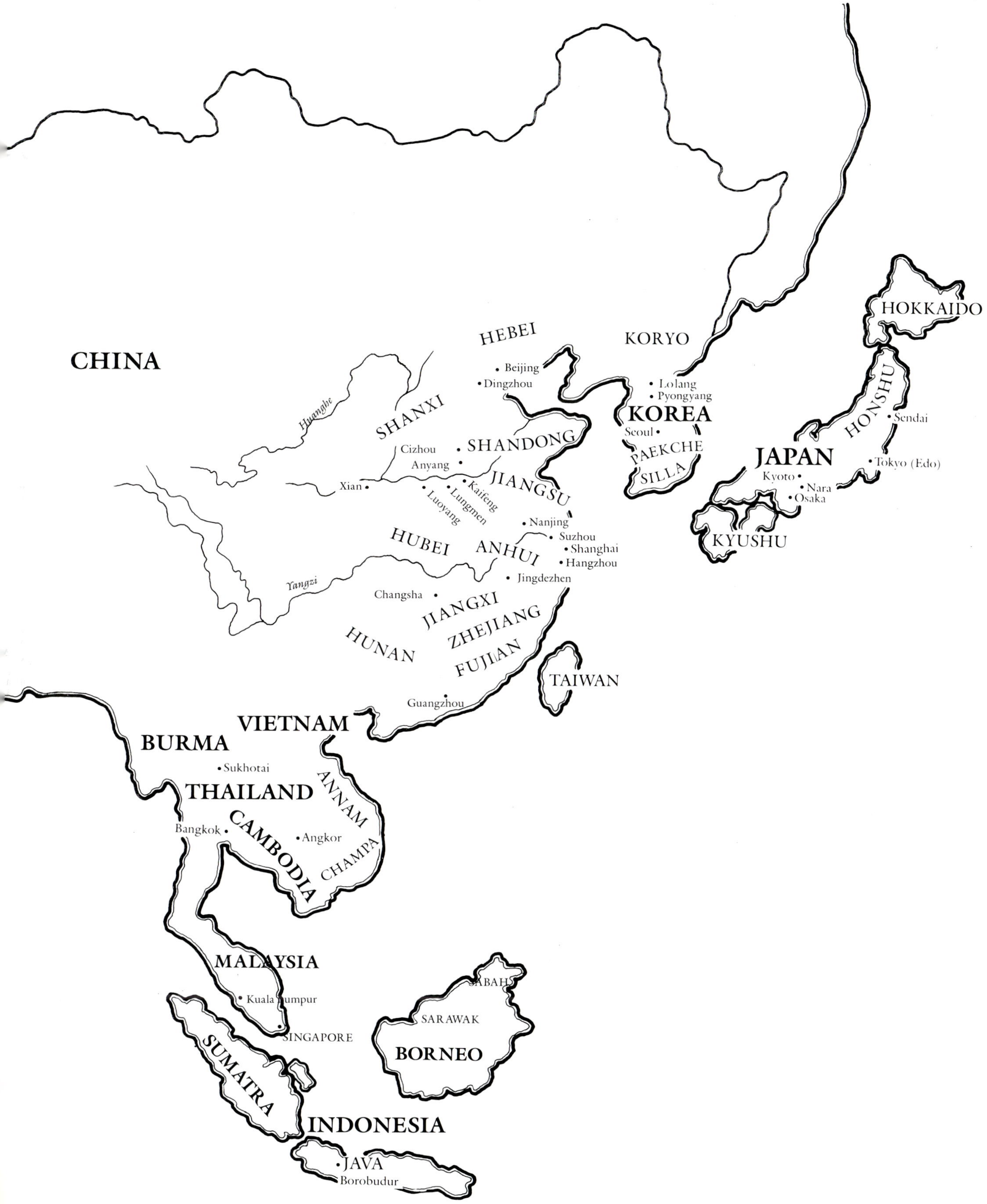

CHINA
HEBEI
KORYO
HOKKAIDO
Beijing
Dingzhou
Lolang
Pyongyang
KOREA
Huanghe
SHANXI
HONSHU
Sendai
Seoul
PAEKCHE
SILLA
JAPAN
Tokyo (Edo)
Cizhou
Anyang
SHANDONG
JIANGSU
Kyoto
Nara
Osaka
Xian
Kaifeng
Lungmen
Luoyang
Nanjing
Suzhou
Shanghai
Hangzhou
KYUSHU
HUBEI
ANHUI
Yangzi
Jingdezhen
Changsha
JIANGXI
ZHEJIANG
HUNAN
FUJIAN
TAIWAN
Guangzhou
VIETNAM
BURMA
Sukhotai
THAILAND
ANNAM
Bangkok
CAMBODIA
Angkor
CHAMPA
MALAYSIA
SABAH
Kuala Lumpur
SARAWAK
SINGAPORE
SUMATRA
BORNEO
INDONESIA
JAVA
Borobudur